Empowering Women

Pitt Latin American Studies

Billie R. DeWalt, *General Editor*
Reid Andrews, Catherine Conaghan, and
Jorge I. Domínguez, *Associate Editors*

Empowering Women

Land and Property Rights in Latin America

Carmen Diana Deere and Magdalena León

UNIVERSITY OF PITTSBURGH PRESS

To our parents,

Carmen García Deere and Don U. Deere

and the memory of

Lola Gómez de León and Juan Francisco León

Published by the University of Pittsburgh Press, Pittsburgh, Pa. 15261

Copyright © 2001, University of Pittsburgh Press

All rights reserved

Manufactured in the United States of America

Printed on acid-free paper

10 9 8 7 6 5 4 3 2 1

Library of Congress Cataloging-in-Publication Data

Deere, Carmen Diana.

    Empowering women: land and property rights in Latin America / Carmen Diana Deere and Magdalena Leâon.

      p. cm. — (Pitt Latin American series)

Includes bibliographical references and index.

    ISBN 0-8229-4161-9 (cloth : alk. paper) — ISBN 0-8229-5767-1 (pbk. : alk paper)

    1. Real property—Latin America. 2. Sex discrimination against women—Latin America. 3. Equality before the law—Latin America. I. Leâon de Leal, Magdalena. II. Title. III. Series.

    KG173 .D44 2001

    346.804'32--dc21

                                        2001002752

Contents

List of Tables   vii

List of Abbreviations and Acronyms   ix

Preface   xxi

one The Importance of Gender and Property   1
Women's Well-Being and the Family 11 / *Equality between*
Women and Men 17 / *The Empowerment of Women* 23

two Gender, Property Rights, and Citizenship   32
Comparative and Historical Perspectives on Women's Property
Rights 33 / *Civil Code Reform, Suffrage, and the Women's*
Movement 41 / *Marital Regimes and the Recognition of*
Consensual Unions 50 / *Inheritance Rights* 56

three Gender Exclusionary Agrarian Reform   62
Comparative Aspects of the Reform 65 / *The Pioneers: Mexico,*
Bolivia, and Cuba 68 / *The Alliance for Progress Agrarian*
Reforms 79 / *More Radical Reforms of the 1970s: Peru and*
Chile 90 / *Land Reform and Civil War: The 1980s in Central*
America 95 / *The Exclusion of Women* 99

four Building Blocks toward Gender-Progressive Change   107
Property and Land Rights in the International Arena 114 /
The Commitment to Equality by Latin America States 120 / *The*
Organization of Rural Women 127

five Engendering the Neo-Liberal Counter-Reforms   137

Chile: The Neo-Liberal Pioneer 141 / Neo-Liberal Agrarian Codes of the 1980s and 1990s: Peru, Mexico, Honduras, and Ecuador 145 / Special Cases: Neo-Liberalism and the Peace Processes in Central America 160 / Special Cases: The Market and Social Justice in Colombia, Bolivia, and Brazil 171

six The Struggle for Women's Land Rights and Increased Ownership of Land   184

Joint Allocation and Titling 187 / A Parcel of One's Own: The Peace Accords in El Salvador 210 / The Peace Accords and the Process of Empowerment among Guatemalan Women Refugees 216

seven In Defense of Community: Struggles over Individual and Collective Land Rights   228

Feminist and Cultural-Relativist Critiques of Universal Human Rights 230 / Indigenous Rights in the International Arena 232 / The Defense of Community under Neo-Liberalism: Ecuador and Bolivia 236 / Organized Indigenous Women, Defense of Collective Land, and Traditional Customs and Practices 247 / Reconciling Culturalist and Feminist Perspectives 258

eight Inheritance of Land in Practice   264

The Mixed Evidence on Bilateral Inheritance in the Andes 266 / Strong Male Preference in Land Rights: Mexico, Chile, and Brazil 273 / Who Will Control the Family Farm? Inheritance of Land by Wives 281

nine Women Property Owners: Land Titling, Inheritance, and the Market   292

Gender Outcomes of Land Titling Projects 294 / Women's Acquisition of Land: Inheritance versus the Market 312 / Will the Land Market be Gender Neutral? 318

ten Land and Property in a Feminist Agenda   330

Appendix   353

Notes   363

References   423

Index   479

List of Tables

Text Tables

2.1   Enhancing Married Women's Property Rights, Selected Latin American Countries

2.2   Attainment of Female Suffrage in Latin America

2.3   Marital Regimes in Twelve Latin American Countries

2.4   Status of Consensual Unions in Twelve Latin American Countries

2.5   Inheritance Rules for Deceased Spouse's Estate under Default Marital Regime, Twelve Latin American Countries, 1990s

3.1   Adjudication of Land to Women, 1956–1994, Bolivia

3.2   Percentage of Female Beneficiaries in Thirteen Latin American Agrarian Reform and Colonization Programs

3.3   Beneficiary Criteria of the Agrarian Reforms

4.1   Steps toward Gender Equality in Latin America

5.1   Institutional Change under Neo-Liberalism

6.1   Changes in Agrarian Codes with Respect to Gender, Twelve Countries

6.2   Beneficiaries of Law 160, Adjudications during 1995–1998, Colombia

6.3   Land Allocations by Sex, 1986–1992, Costa Rica

6.4   Adjudication and Titling by Sex, 1992–2000, Nicaragua

7.1   Ratification of ILO Convention No. 169 and Indigenous Population in Latin America, early 1990s

7.2   Collective Land Rights in New Constitutions and Agrarian Codes

8.1   Inheritance of Land in Chitapampa, Department of Cuzco, Peru

8.2   Factors Influencing the Possibility of Wives Retaining Controlling Ownership of Family Farms

8.3   Registered Heirs of *Ejidatarios,* 1993–1995, Mexico

9.1   Titles Registered by Sex, Non-Reformed Sector, 1995–2000, Honduras

9.2   Titling of Public Lands by Sex, 1996–1997 and 1999, Colombia

9.3   Titling in the *Ejido* Sector by Form of Holding and Sex, 1993–1998, Mexico

9.4   Land Titles Issued by PRONADER by Sex and Marital Status, 1992–1996, Ecuador

9.5   Land Titling of Plots and Farms by Sex, 1993–1996, Chile

9.6   Ownership of Land by Sex, Regional Comparisons, Ecuador and Brazil

9.7   Form of Land Acquisition by Sex, Peru

9.8   Form of Acquisition of Plots and Farms by Sex, Chile

9.9   Form of Land Acquisition by Owners by Sex, Nicaragua

9.10 Source of Land Acquired by *Ejidatarias,* Mexico

9.11 Differences by Sex in the Amount of Land Owned, 1990s

9.12 Characteristics of Male and Female Farmers, 1994, Peru

10.1 Proportion of Beneficiaries by Sex and Form of Title in Land Allocation and Titling Programs in Latin America, 1990s

Appendix Tables

1   Form of Acquisition of Land for Agrarian Reform and Colonization, Thirteen Latin American Countries

2   Form of Distribution to Beneficiaries of Agrarian Reform and Colonization Programs, Thirteen Countries

3   National Offices on Women and Gender Affairs, Twelve Countries

4   Rural Women's Offices and Secretariats in Mixed Peasant Organizations, Twelve Countries

5   National Rural Women's Organizations, Twelve Countries

6   Comparative Sectoral Data, Latin America, mid-1990s

List of Abbreviations and Acronyms

ACNUR   Alto Comisionado de las Naciones Unidas para los Refugiados (Guatemala), UN High Commission for Refugees

ACPD   Asamblea Constitutiva de las Poblaciones Desarraigadas (Guatemala), Constitutive Assembly of the Displaced Population

ADC   Alianza Democrática Campesina (El Salvador), Democratic Peasant Alliance

ADP   Acciones para el Desarrollo y Población (Honduras), Actions for Population and Development

AMNLAE   Asociación de Mujeres Nicaragüenses "Luisa Amanda Espinoza" (Nicaragua), "Luisa Amanda Espinoza" Association of Nicaraguan Women

AMS   Asociación de Mujeres de El Salvador, Women's Association of El Salvador

AMTRS   Articulação de Mulheres Trabalhadoras Rurais do Sul (Brazil), Articulation of Rural Women Workers of the South

ANAP   Asociación Nacional de Agricultores Pequeños (Cuba), National Association of Small Farmers

ANIPA   Asamblea Nacional Indígena por la Autonomía (Mexico), National Indigenous Assembly for Autonomy

ANMTR   Articulação Nacional de Mulheres Trabalhadoras Rurais (Brazil), National Articulation of Rural Women Workers

ANMUCIC Asociación Nacional de Mujeres Campesinas e Indígenas de Colombia, National Association of Peasant and Indigenous Women of Colombia

ANUC Asociación Nacional de Usuarios Campesinos (Colombia), National Association of Peasant Beneficiaries

ARDIGUA Asociación de Refugiados Dispersos de Guatemala, Association of Dispersed Refugees of Guatemala

ASC Asamblea de la Sociedad Civil (Guatemala), Assembly of Civil Society

ATC Asociación de Trabajadores del Campo (Nicaragua), Association of Rural Workers

AVANCSO Asociación para el Avance de las Ciencias Sociales (Guatemala), Association for the Advancement of the Social Sciences

BANDESA Banco Nacional de Desarrollo Agrícola (Honduras), National Agricultural Development Bank

BANRURAL Banco Nacional Rural (Guatemala), National Rural Bank

BID Banco Interamericano de Desarrollo (Washington, D.C.), Inter-American Development Bank (IADB)

CAN Comisión Agraria Nacional (Bolivia), National Agrarian Commission

CAP Consejo Agrario Permanente (Mexico), Permanent Agrarian Council

CAS Cooperativas Agrarias Sandinistas (Nicaragua), Sandinista Agrarian Cooperatives

CCPP Comisiones Permanentes de Representantes de Refugiados en México (Guatemala), Permanent Commissions of Refugee Representatives in Mexico

CCS Cooperativa de Crédito y Servicio (Cuba, Nicaragua), Credit and Service Cooperative

CDT Centro de Desarrollo Tecnológico (El Salvador), Center for Technological Development

CEAR Comisión Especial para Atención a los Refugiados (Guatemala), Special Commission for the Repatriated, Refugee and Displaced Population

CEB   Comunidade eclesiais de base (Brazil), Christian base community (CBC)

CEDAW   Commission for the Elimination of All Forms of Discrimination against Women (UN)

CEDEM   Centro de Estudios de la Mujer (Chile), Center for the Study of Women

CEDLA   Centro de Estudios del Desarrollo Laboral y Agrario (Bolivia), Center for the Study of Labor and Agrarian Development

CEDLA   Centro de Estudios y Documentación Latinoamericano (The Netherlands), Center for Latin American Research and Documentation

CEFEMINA   Centro Feminista de Información y Acción (Costa Rica), Feminist Center for Information and Action

CEIMME   Centro de Estudios e Investigación sobre el Maltrato de la Mujer Ecuatoriana (Ecuador), Center for Research on Battered Women

CEMA   Centro de Madres (Chile), Mother's Center

CEMH   Centro de Estudios de la Mujer Hondureña (Honduras), Center for the Study of the Honduran Woman

CENTA   Centro Nacional de Tecnología Agropecuaria y Forestal (El Salvador), National Center of Agricultural and Forestry Technology

CEPAL   Comisión Económica para América Latina (UN), Economic Commission for Latin America

CEPAM   Centro Ecuatoriano para la Promoción y la Acción de la Mujer (Ecuador), Ecuadorian Center for Women's Promotion and Action

CEPES   Centro Peruano de Estudios Sociales (Peru), Peruvian Center for Social Studies

CEPLAES   Centro de Planificación y Estudios Sociales (Ecuador), Center for Planning and Social Studies

CERA   Centro de Reforma Agraria (Chile), Center for Agrarian Reform

CERJ   Consejo de Comunidades Étnicas "Runujel Junam" (Guatemala), Council of Ethnic Communities "Runujel Junam"

CESADE   Centro de Estudios y Acción para el Desarrollo (Nicaragua), Center of Studies and Action for Development

CIDEM   Centro de Información y Desarrollo de la Mujer (Bolivia), Center of Information and Development of Women

CIDES   Centro sobre Derecho y Sociedad (Ecuador), Center on Rights and Society

CIDOB   Confederación Indígena del Oriente, Chaco, y Amazonia (Bolivia), Indigenous Confederation of Oriente, Chaco, and Amazonia

CIERA   Centro de Investigación y Estudios de la Reforma Agraria (Nicaragua), Center for the Research and Study of the Agrarian Reform

CIPDER   Consorcio Interinstitucional para el Desarrollo Regional (Peru), Inter-institutional Consortium for Regional Development

CIPRES   Centro para la Investigación y la Promoción del Desarrollo Rural y Social (Nicaragua), Center for Research and Promotion of Rural and Social Development

CIT   Confederación Internacional del Trabajo, International Labor Confederation

CMC   Central de Mujeres Campesinas (El Salvador), Peasant Women's Union

CMF   Centro Nacional de Desarrollo de la Mujer y la Familia (Costa Rica), National Center for the Development of Women and the Family

CMYDR   Comisión Mujer y Desarrollo Rural (Nicaragua), Woman and Rural Development Commission

CNC   Comisión Nacional Campesina (Chile), National Peasant Commission

CNC   Confederación Nacional Campesina (Mexico), National Peasant Confederation

CNDM	Conselho Nacional dos Direitos da Mulher (Brazil), National Council on Women's Rights
CNRA	Consejo Nacional de Reforma Agraria (Bolivia), National Council of Agrarian Reform
CODIMCA	Consejo para el Desarrollo Integral de la Mujer Campesina (Honduras), Council for the Integrated Development of Peasant Women
CONADEA	Consejo Nacional de Desarrollo Agrícola (Guatemala), National Council of Agricultural Development
CONAIE	Confederación de Nacionalidades Indígenas del Ecuador, Confederation of Indigenous Nationalities of Ecuador
CONAMPRU	Coordinadora Nacional de Pequeños y Medianos Productores (Guatemala), National Coordination of Small and Medium Producers
CONAMU	Consejo Nacional de las Mujeres (Ecuador), National Women's Council
CONAVIGUA	Coordinadora Nacional de Viudas de Guatemala, National Coordination of Widows of Guatemala
CONDEG	Consejo Nacional de Desplazados de Guatemala, National Council of the Displaced Population of Guatemala
CONFENIAE	Confederación de Nacionalidades Indígenas de la Amazonia Ecuatoriana (Ecuador), Confederation of Indigenous Nationalities of the Ecuadorian Amazon
CONIC	Coordinadora Nacional Indígena y Campesina de Guatemala, National Indigenous and Peasant Coordinator of Guatemala
CONMIE	Consejo Nacional de Mujeres Indígenas del Ecuador, National Council of Indigenous Women of Ecuador
CONTAG	Confederação Nacional dos Trabalhadores na Agricultura (Brazil), National Confederation of Agricultural Workers
CONTIERRA	Dependencia Presidencial para la Resolución de Conflictos (Guatemala), Presidential Office for Conflict Resolution
COPMAGUA	Coordinadora de Organizaciones del Pueblo Maya de Guatemala, Coordinator of Organizations of the Mayan People of Guatemala

CORA   Corporación de Reforma Agraria (Chile), Agrarian Reform Corporation

CPR   Comunidades de Población en Resistencia (Guatemala), Communities of Population in Resistence

CPT   Comissão Pastoral da Terra (Brazil), Pastoral Land Commission

CSUTCB   Confederación Sindical Única de Trabajadores Campesinos de Bolivia, Confederation of Peasant Workers of Bolivia

CTEAR   Comisión Técnica de Reasentados (Guatemala), Technical Commission of the Resettled

CUT   Central Única dos Trabalhadores (Brazil), Central Workers' Union

CVP   Centro Vecinal de Productores (El Salvador), Neighborhood Producer Center

DAWN   Development Alternatives for a New Era (an international network of Third World women)

DINAMU   Dirección Nacional de la Mujer (Ecuador), National Directorate of Women

DNP   Departamento Nacional de Planificación (Colombia), National Department of Planning

DRI   Programa de Desarrollo Rural Integrado (Colombia), Integrated Rural Development Program

ECUARUNARI   Ecuador Runacunapac Riccharicmui, Gente del Ecuador, Levántase, People of Ecuador Awake

ENLAC   Encuentro Latinoamericano y del Caribe de la Mujer Trabajadora Rural, Latin American and Caribbean Meeting of Rural Women Workers

EZLN   Ejército Zapatista de Liberación Nacional (Mexico), Zapatista National Liberation Army

FAMDEGUA   Asociación de Familiares de Detenidos-Desaparecidos de Guatemala, Association of Relatives of the Detained-Disappeared of Guatemala

FAO   Food and Agricultural Organization (UN)

FARC   Fuerzas Armadas Revolucionarias de Colombia, Revolutionary Armed Forces of Colombia

FEMUC   Federación de Mujeres Campesinas (Honduras), Federation of Peasant Women

FEMUPROCAN   Federación de Mujeres Productoras de Nicaragua, Federation of Women Producers of Nicaragua

FEPP   Fondo Ecuatoriano Populorum Progresso (Ecuador), Ecuadorian Fund Populorum Progresso

FIDEG   Fundación Internacional para el Desafío Económico Global (Nicaragua), International Foundation for the Global Economic Challenge

FINATA   Financiera Nacional de Tierras Agrícolas (El Salvador), National Bank for Agricultural Land

FLACSO   Facultad Latinoamericana de Ciencias Sociales, Latin American Faculty of Social Sciences

FMC   Federación de Mujeres Cubanas (Cuba), Federation of Cuban Women

FMLN   Frente Farabundo Martí de la Liberación Nacional (El Salvador), Farabundo Martí Front for National Liberation

FOIN   Federación de Organizaciones Indígenas (Ecuador), Federation of Indigenous Organizations

FONAPAZ   Fondo para la Paz (Guatemala), Fund for Peace

FONATIERRA   Fondo Nacional de Tierras (Guatemala), National Land Fund

FONTIERRA   Fondo de Tierras Acuerdo de Paz (Guatemala), Peace Agreement Land Fund

FOREAP   Fondo para la Reinserción Laboral y Productiva de la Población Repatriada (Guatemala), Fund for Labor and Productive Reintegration of the Repatriated Population

FPL   Fuerzas Populares de Liberación (El Salvador), Popular Liberation Forces

FSLN   Frente Sandinista de Liberación Nacional (Nicaragua), Sandinista National Liberation Front

FUNDACEN Fundación del Centavo (Guatemala), Penny Foundation

FUSADES Fundación Salvadoreña para el Desarrollo Económico y Social, Salvadoran Foundation for Economic and Social Development

GAM Grupo de Apoyo Mutuo (Guatemala), Mutual Support Group

GIMTRAP Grupo Interdisciplinario sobre Mujer, Trabajo y Pobreza (Mexico), Interdisciplinary Group on Women, Work and Poverty

GOES Gobierno de El Salvador, Government of El Salvador

GTZ Cooperación Técnica de la República Federal de Alemania (Germany) German Technical Cooperation

GYTT Generación y Transferencia de Tecnología (El Salvador), Technology Generation and Transfer

IACW Inter-American Commission of Women (Washington, D.C.)

IADB Inter-American Development Bank (Washington, D.C.)

IAFFE International Association for Feminist Economics

IDA Instituto de Desarrollo Agropecuario (Costa Rica), Institute for Agricultural Development

IDEA Instituto de Estrategias Agropecuarias (Ecuador), Institute for Agricultural Strategies

IERAC Instituto Ecuatoriano de Reforma Agraria y Colonización (Ecuador), Ecuadorian Institute of Agrarian Reform and Colonization

IFAD International Fund for Agricultural Development (Rome)

IFI International financial institutions

IICA Instituto Interamericano de Cooperación para la Agricultura (San José), Interamerican Institute of Agricultural Cooperation

ILO International Labor Organization (UN)

IMU Instituto de Investigación, Capacitación y Desarrollo de la Mujer (El Salvador), Institute for Research, Training and Development of Women

INA   Instituto Nacional Agrario (Honduras), National Agrarian Institute

INACOP   Instituto Nacional de Cooperativas (Guatemala), National Institute of Cooperatives

INC   Instituto Nacional de Colonización (Bolivia), National Institute of Colonization

INCORA   Instituto Colombiano de Reforma Agraria (Colombia), Colombian Institute of Agrarian Reform

INCRA   Instituto Nacional de Colonização e Reforma Agraria (Brazil), National Institute of Colonization and Agrarian Reform

INDA   Instituto Nacional de Desarrollo Agrario (Ecuador), National Institute of Agrarian Development

INDAP   Instituto de Desarrollo Agropecuario (Chile), Institute of Agricultural Development

INESC   Instituto de Estudos Socio-Econômicos (Brazil), Institute for Socioeconomic Studies

INIM   Instituto Nicaragüense de la Mujer (Nicaragua), Nicaraguan Institute for Women

INRA   Instituto Nacional de la Reforma Agraria (Bolivia), National Institute for Agrarian Reform

INRA   Instituto Nicaragüense de la Reforma Agraria (Nicaragua), Nicaraguan Institute for Agrarian Reform

INTA   Instituto de Transformación Agraria (Guatemala), Institute of Agrarian Transformation

ISDEMU   Instituto Salvadoreño de la Mujer (El Salvador), Salvadoran Women's Institute

ISTA   Instituto Salvadoreño de Transformación Agraria (El Salvador), Salvadoran Institute for Agrarian Transformation

ITCO   Instituto de Tierras y Colonización (Costa Rica), Land and Colonization Institute

MAG   Ministerio de Agricultura (El Salvador), Ministry of Agriculture

MAGA	Ministerio de Agricultura y Ganadería (Guatemala), Ministry of Agriculture and Livestock
MAM	Movimiento de Mujeres "Melida Amaya Montés" (El Salvador), "Melida Amaya Montés" Women's Movement
MINUGUA	Misión de Naciones Unidas en Guatemala, UN Mission in Guatemala
MIRAD	Ministerio de Reforma Agraria y Desarrollo Rural (Brazil), Ministry of Agrarian Reform and Rural Development
MMTR	Movimento de Mulheres Trabalhadoras Rurais (Brazil), Rural Women Worker's Movement
MMTR-NE	Movimento de Mulheres Trabalhadoras Rurais, Nordeste (Brazil), Rural Women Worker's Movement, Northeast
MNR	Movimiento Nacional Revolucionario (Bolivia), National Revolutionary Movement
MST	Movimento dos Trabalhadores Rurais Sem Terra (Brazil), Landless Rural Workers' Movement
ONAM	Oficina Nacional de la Mujer (Guatemala), National Women's Office
ONUSAL	Organización de las Naciones Unidas en El Salvador, United Nations Organization in El Salvador
OPIP	Organización de Pueblos Indígenas (Ecuador), Organization of Indigenous People
PERA	Proyecto de Evaluación de la Reforma Agraria (El Salvador), Evaluation of the Agrarian Reform Project
PETT	Proyecto Especial de Titulación y Catastro Rural (Peru), Special Titling and Rural Land Registry Project
PIEM	Programa de Estudios de Género (El Colegio de México), Gender Studies Program
PIOMH	Plan para la Igualdad de Oportunidades entre Mujeres y Hombres (Costa Rica), Plan for Equal Opportunities between Women and Men
PNCTR	Programa Nacional de Catastro, Titulación y Regularización del Propiedad (Nicaragua), National Program of Land Registry, Titling, and Regularization of Property

PNM   Política Nacional de la Mujer (El Salvador), National Women's Policy

PNRA-NR   Programa Nacional de Reforma Agraria—Nova República (Brazil), National Program of Agrarian Reform—New Republic

PRI   Partido Revolucionario Institucional (Mexico), Institutional Revolutionary Party

PROCEDE   Programa de Certificación de Derechos Ejidales y Titulación de Solares Urbanos (Mexico), Program of Certification of Ejido Rights and Titling of Urban Plots

PROMUDER   Programa de Acción para la Participación de la Mujer Campesina (Mexico), Program of Action for the Participation of Peasant Women

PRONADER   Progama Nacional de Desarrollo Rural (Ecuador), National Program of Rural Development

PROTIERRA   Comisión Institucional para el Desarrollo y Fortalecimiento de la Propiedad de la Tierra (Guatemala), Institutional Commission for the Development and Strengthening of Landed Property

PT   Partido dos Trabalhadores (Brazil), Workers' Party

PTMT   Programa de Titulación Masiva de Tierras (Honduras), Program of Massive Land Titling

PTT   Programa de Titulación de Tierras para Pequeños Productores (Honduras), Land Titling Program for Small Producers

PTT   Programa de Transferencia de Tierras (El Salvador), Land Transfer Program

REDNAMURH   Red Nacional de Mujeres Rurales de Honduras, National Network of Rural Women of Honduras

RN   Resistencia Nacional (El Salvador), National Resistance

SAIS   Sociedades Agrícolas de Interés Social (Peru), Agrarian Societies of Social Interest

SERNAM   Servicio Nacional de la Mujer (Chile), National Women's Service

SIGN   Sistema de Información Geográfica Nacional (Guatemala), National Geographic Information System

SSRC   Social Science Research Council (New York)

TIERRA   Taller de Iniciativas en Estudios Rurales y Reforma Agraria (Bolivia), Working Group for Rural Studies and Agrarian Reform Initiatives

TPIS   Títulos de Participación Individual (Honduras), Titles of Individual Participation

UAIM   Unidad Agrícola Industrial de la Mujer Campesina (Mexico), Peasant Women's Agro-industrial Unit

UCA   Universidad Centroamericana (Nicaragua), Central American University

UNAG   Unión Nacional de Agricultores y Ganaderos (Nicaragua), National Union of Agriculturalists and Cattlemen

UNC   Unión Nacional Campesina (Honduras), National Peasant Union

UNO   Unión Nacional Opositora (Nicaragua), Union of National Opposition

UP   Unidad Popular (Chile), Popular Unity

URNG   Unión Revolucionaria Nacional Guatemalteca (Guatemala), National Guatemalan Revolutionary Union

USAID   United States Agency for International Development

Preface

THIS BOOK WAS largely motivated by a challenge posed to us by Bina Agarwal, when she was organizing a panel on gender and land rights for IAFFE (the International Association for Feminist Economics) for the NGO (non-governmental organization) forum at the United Nations Fourth World Conference on Women in Beijing in late August 1995. The thought of writing an overview paper on Latin America on this issue initially seemed daunting, but Deere agreed to survey the available literature. Unable to attend the Beijing conference, she asked her long-time collaborator, León, a member of the official Colombian delegation, to present the paper at the IAFFE panel. This experience convinced us to pursue this collaborative project. Relatively little research had been carried out on gender and land rights in Latin America since our initial research on this topic in the 1970s and 1980s, and virtually no attention had yet been given to the gendered implications of the neo-liberal counter-reform in agriculture. At Beijing León had also been struck by how issues of property received less attention in the NGO forum than such other critical feminist issues as representation, diversity, citizenship, and empowerment. Moreover, in the official debates over the Platform for Action, different views of equality versus equity in inheritance rights almost ended up aborting the entire consensus of the Beijing platform.

Our next step was to investigate the Colombian case and engage our "social capital," sending out faxes and e-mails to colleagues in the feminist movement throughout the region for assistance in locating materials. Our country case studies of women and land rights gradually expanded from the four initially reviewed for the Beijing conference paper (Chile,

Mexico, Nicaragua, and Peru) to eight (adding Colombia, Costa Rica, El Salvador, and Honduras). By then we were convinced that our subject matter merited a book-length treatment, but that would require fieldwork in each country, and we were constrained by both time—each of us held a full-time university appointment—and costs.

A coincidence of circumstances took us both to Mexico City in January 1997, and we asked María Luisa Tarres of the Colegio de México to organize a seminar on our behalf to present the preliminary, comparative results of our research. This seminar was instrumental in the development of the research methodology for the country case studies that followed. During this trip we also met with Michael Conroy, then the rural development officer in the Ford Foundation's regional office for Mexico and Central America, and with his encouragement we developed a successful funding proposal to carry out further research in twelve countries. (Added to the study at this point were Bolivia, Brazil, Ecuador, and Guatemala.) This grant was jointly funded by the Ford Foundation's regional offices for Mexico and the Caribbean, the Andes, and Brazil, and the foundation will also fund the translation and publication of this book in Spanish and Portuguese. In addition to Conroy, we are indebted to Alexander Wilde and Gabriel López of the Ford Foundation for their enthusiasm and support for this project.

We initiated the second phase of the project in July 1997 with a research visit to the Andean region.[1] The methodology of our country case studies followed and improved upon the model with which we had experimented in Mexico City. During July and August 1997 we held a one-day seminar on gender and land rights in each Andean country. The participants included researchers on agrarian and rural women's issues; feminist activists; government functionaries from the national women's offices, ministry of agriculture, and other ministries; and leaders of the rural women's and peasant movements. The usual format consisted of a half-day session during which we presented our preliminary comparative analysis, and another half-day session on women's land rights in the particular country. In most countries the seminars were hosted by a feminist NGO. We are very grateful for the collaboration of the following organizations and individuals, who also arranged many of our interviews: the Red Mujer Rural of the Centro de la Mujer Peruana "Flora Tristán" in Lima, Peru, and Blanca Fernández, the coordinator of the network; CEDLA (Centro de Estudios de Desarrollo Laboral y Agrario), CIDEM (Centro de Información y Desarrollo de la Mujer), and the consultancy group "rym, a.c." in La Paz, Bolivia, and particularly Sonia Montaño and Jimena Rojas of the latter group; CEDEM (Centro de Estudios de la Mujer) in Santiago, Chile, and its director, Ximena Valdés; CEPAM (Centro Ecuatoriano para la Promoción y Acción de la Mujer) in Quito, Ecuador, and its director, María Mercedes Placensia; and the Fondo de Documentación "Mujer y Género" of the National University of Colombia, in Bogotá.

In Central America we coordinated the country research visits through the Fundación Arias para el Progreso Humano, since researchers there had just completed a region-wide study of women and land rights and during 1997–98 were engaged in a project to strengthen rural women's organizations in the region. We are grateful to Lara Blanco and Ana Elena Badilla for their collaboration. The country seminars were held during January 1998 and were co-hosted by the Fundación Guatemala in Guatemala City, Guatemala; IMU (Instituto por la Investigación, Capacitación, y Desarrollo de la Mujer) in San Salvador, El Salvador; REDNAMURH (Red de Mujeres Rurales de Honduras) in Tegucigalpa, Honduras; CIPRES (Centro para la Investigación y la Promoción del Desarrollo Rural y Social), and CESADE (Centro de Estudios y Acción para el Desarrollo) in Managua, Nicaragua. We are particularly grateful to Blanca Mendoza de Sánchez, Deysi Cheyne, Leoncia Solorzano, and Melba Reyes, who arranged the seminars and many of our interviews in each country. María Emma Prada, president of ANMUCIC (Asociación Nacional de Mujeres Campesinas e Indígenas de Colombia), and Lara Blanco also participated in these seminars, and we very much appreciated their insights. Our three-week visit to Brazil during June 1998 included Recife, Rio de Janeiro, Brasilia, and São Paolo. In Recife SOS Corpo hosted a one-day workshop with rural women leaders of the state of Pernambuco, for which we are grateful to Silvia Camuco and Ana Paola Portela. In Brasilia INESC (Instituto de Estudios Socio-econômicos) hosted a one-day seminar, and we appreciate the efforts of Edelcio Vigna de Oliveira on our behalf, including arranging visits to field sites.

The solidarity and generosity of a great number of other feminist researchers were absolutely essential to the productiveness of these research visits. At the risk of omission, we particularly wish to thank Mercedes Barquet, Carlota Botey, Margarita Flores, Marta Lamas, María Consuelo Mejía, and Beatriz Schmukler in Mexico; Maruja Barrig and Virginia Guzmán in Peru; Gloria Ardaya, Isabel Lavadenz, and Ana Quiroga in Bolivia; Pilar Campaña, Mari Sol Lago, and Teresa Valdéz in Chile; Pilar Vidal in Colombia; Susana Balerazo, Elizabeth García, Gioconda Páez,

Mercedes Prieto, and Rocío Rocero in Ecuador; Clara Arenas, Ana Leticia Herrera, and Alicia Martínez in Guatemala; Sara Elisa Rosales in Honduras; Paola Pérez Alemán, Patricia Hernández, and Malena de Montis in Nicaragua; Fabiola Campillo, Ana Carcedo, Jorge Dandler, Ana Isabel García, and Monserrat Sagot in Costa Rica; and Leila Linhares Barsted, Paola Capellini, Maria José Carneiro, Heleithe Saffioti, and Cheywa Spindel in Brazil.

Many other feminists, scholars, lawyers, and government officials gave very generously of their time and shared their experiences and published and unpublished research with us. We wish to thank the Ministry of National Property in Chile and the Agrarian Information Office of the Ministry of Agriculture in Peru for making available to us several unpublished data sets. All told, we conducted well over 200 interviews for this study, and over 360 participants attended the thirteen workshops and seminars. Many of the people mentioned above, including the coordinators of the seminars and a number of experts on family law, continued to collaborate with us until the completion of this book.

This phase of the project concluded with the preparation of twelve country case studies that served as the raw material for the comparative analysis of the book. Since we were eager to disseminate our research findings in the respective countries, we translated and published eight of these as working papers or articles.[2] We began the third phase, the comparative analysis, in July 1998 thanks to a grant from the Rockefeller Foundation for a month-long residency at their Bellagio Research and Study Center in Italy. Much of the writing took place in St. Augustine, Florida, and we are indebted to Don and Carmen G. Deere for the use of their condominium and for their unwavering support, and to Francisco Leal for his cheerful company during some of these research periods and for his understanding when he was left at home.

Support for this stage of the project was also secured by León from COLCIENCAS, the national research foundation of Colombia. Excellent research assistance at different stages was provided by Jenny Newton, Olgita Vásquez, and Lya Yaneth Fuentes in Bogotá, and by Karen Graubart, Pável Isa, and Maliha Safri in Amherst. Peter Stern, Latin American bibliographer at the University of Massachusetts, was most helpful in locating some of the primary materials utilized in this study. We are also grateful for the assistance of Patricia Molina in the transcription of the interviews; Angela García in the translation of the working papers; and Rosita de Rojas of the Fundación Amigos del IEPRI (Instituto de Estudios

Políticos y Relaciones Internacionales) for administration of the Ford Foundation grant. We must also recognize the support that we have received from our respective institutions: the Program in Gender and Women's Studies, the Department of Social Work, and the Faculty of Humanities and Social Sciences at the National University of Colombia, Bogotá; and the Department of Economics and the Center for Latin American, Caribbean, and Latino Studies at the University of Massachusetts, Amherst.

Over the last five years we have had the opportunity to present various versions of our work-in-progress at a large number of conferences, workshops, and seminars, too many to detail. We are grateful to the organizers and participants for their helpful comments and criticisms. A number of colleagues read draft versions of different chapters of this book, and we are most indebted for their feedback: Bina Agarwal, Silvia Arrom, Elsa Chaney, Jacquelyn Chase, María Cuvi, Billie DeWalt, Karen Graubart, Carol Heim, Dony Meertens, Patricia Prieto, Verena Stolke, Ann Varley, and María Ema Wills. We also appreciate the suggestions and comments of two anonymous reviewers of the manuscript, as well as the excellent editorial assistance of Cynthia Miller at the University of Pittsburgh Press and the fine copyediting by Elizabeth Johns. Finally, we wish to thank each other. A multi-disciplinary research project of this magnitude and complexity would simply not have been possible except as a collaborative venture. Moreover, we challenged each other intellectually and professionally and managed to deepen a twenty-five-year friendship.

one

The Importance of Gender and Property

> *To be a woman is to have children . . . to not have access to a parcel of one's own . . . to do the housework and the field work. . . . Why is it a scandal whenever a baby girl is born?[1]*

> *Land for women has to do with survival; for men it has to do with power . . . the men will be the first ones to oppose our participation in land tenancy.[2]*

THIS BOOK IS ABOUT the disjuncture in Latin America between men's and women's formal equality before the law and the achievement of real equality between them, an issue particularly well illuminated by the gap between women's property rights and their actual ownership of property. Until the early twentieth century, a major factor limiting women's ownership of property was the restricted nature of married women's property rights. The struggle to expand these was one of the main achievements of the first wave of feminism in Latin America, and it was intimately linked with the struggle to secure other civil and political rights for women. Because of the contentious nature of these measures, in most Latin American countries women achieved greater property rights and suffrage only in a piecemeal fashion during the first half of this century.

The next watershed, a product of the second wave of international feminism, was the 1979 UN Convention on the Elimination of All Forms of Discrimination against Women (UN 1982). Most Latin American states that had not already done so subsequently revised their constitutions to guarantee explicit equality between men and women before the law and reformed their civil codes to establish the dual-headed household, where both men and women represent the family and share responsibility for the administration of its common property. Nonetheless, the attainment of formal equality of property rights has not resulted in anything like real equality in the distribution of assets between men and women.[3] This disjuncture is probably at its greatest in terms of rural women's property rights and their ownership and control of land.

Unfortunately, few studies have been carried out on the distribution of assets by gender. An oft-cited estimate is that women constitute one-half of the world's population, one-third of the official labor force, do two-thirds of the work, but earn only one-tenth of the world's income and own only one percent of the world's property (UN 1980: 8). Data on the distribution of asset ownership is notoriously difficult to come by, but even if this estimate—produced for the Second UN World Conference on Women in Copenhagen in 1980—is only a very rough approximation, it is intended to put into stark relief the glaring inequality between men and women with respect to command over resources. Data on the distribution of land ownership by sex is equally difficult to generate. Notwithstanding several decades of "women in development" efforts, most Latin American agricultural censuses still fail to report the gender of their nation's farmers.[4] Moreover, the censuses as well as most household surveys rarely inquire about farm ownership by sex, highlighting the general lack of attention to this issue until recently. As we will demonstrate, rural women in Latin America are less likely to own land than men; and when they do so, they own less land than men, motivating one of the central questions of this study: Why is the distribution of land ownership between men and women in Latin America so unequal?

We argue that gender inequality in land ownership in Latin America is attributable to the family, community, the state, and the market. The principal means through which ownership of land is acquired include inheritance, adjudication by the state, and purchase in the market. We show that gender inequality in land ownership is due to male preference in inheritance, male privilege in marriage, male bias in state programs of land distribution, and gender inequality in the land market, where women are less likely to be buyers than men. In many regions of Latin America, land is owned or held collectively by indigenous and/or peasant communities, with the internal distribution of land governed by traditional customs and practices. We show that gender inequality also permeates these practices, with land rights primarily vested in male household heads.

Following Bina Agarwal (1994a: 19), who pioneered the study of gender and land rights, we define land rights as the "ownership or . . . usufruct (that is, rights of use) associated with different degrees of freedom to lease out, mortgage, bequeath or sell" land. Land rights must be distinguished from the more general and loosely used term "access" to land. Whereas rights are "claims that are legally and socially recognized and enforceable by an external legitimized authority," such as the community or state, access to land includes not only land rights but also informal means of obtaining land, such as by borrowing it for a cropping season from a relative or neighbor (ibid.).[5] Land rights, as opposed to land access, thus imply a measure of security tied to an enforceable claim.[6]

This book investigates how, until recently, women have been excluded from land rights, and it explores the struggles that have led to their attaining them. The mechanisms excluding women from land rights have been legal, cultural, structural, and institutional. They are interrelated and have as their basis patriarchal ideologies embedded in constructions of masculinity and femininity and the "proper" gender division of labor between and within public and private spheres. One of the main mechanisms excluding women from land rights has been that these are often ceded by communities and the state only to household heads, the great majority of whom are male. In the Latin American agrarian reforms, for example, it was assumed that by benefiting male household heads, all household members would benefit as well. This practice was supported by civil codes under which the husband represented the family in all external matters and was the administrator of the common property of the household. This practice was also supported by a gendered division of labor in which men were socially recognized as agriculturalists and women were regarded only as "helpers," or secondary family workers, irrespective of the amount of time they dedicated to agricultural activities. Further, an objective of the agrarian reforms was to change the structure of land tenancy in favor of the creation of family farms. In this context it was inconceivable to reform planners—as well as to the leadership of the peasant organizations who led the struggle for agrarian reform in Latin America—that women might want either joint or independent rights in land.

A number of conditions had to change before the question of women's land rights could begin to be addressed. Of singular importance was the rise of the second wave of feminism internationally and the growth and consolidation of national and local women's movements in Latin America. Since the 1970s the series of United Nations World Conferences on Women, which began with the UN Decade on Women in 1975, focused attention on ending discrimination against women, achieving equality between men and women, and incorporating women and gender concerns into national development plans.[7] In addition to securing and expanding married women's property rights, another thrust has been to establish rural women's land rights, specifically by including them in state programs of land reform, colonization, and titling, and by guaranteeing their inheritance rights.

The rise and consolidation of the women's movement throughout the region coincided with the rise to dominance of the neo-liberal model of development in Latin America in the 1980s, motivating two of the other questions of this study: What has happened in terms of rural women's land rights and ownership of land under neo-liberalism? And what difference has the contemporary women's movement made with respect to women's property and land rights? Most of the early literature on gender and neo-liberalism focused on the impact of the debt crisis and structural adjustment policies on women, as well it should, given the role of these policies in producing the "Lost Decade" in Latin America, a period during which growth rates tumbled and poverty rates skyrocketed in most countries in the region.[8] Besides a transfer of surplus from the Third World to the advanced capitalist countries, and from workers to capital, structural adjustment policies brought about a shift in the costs of reproduction of labor from the state to households, and within households, from men to women.[9]

The economic crisis, nonetheless, had a number of unintended consequences. For example, it contributed to the expansion of the women's movement beyond its original social base in the middle class to include a popular women's movement. The latter was largely a product of poor women's survival strategies and collective action, supported by a growing network of nongovernmental organizations (NGOs). It led to growing awareness within policy circles that public policy was not gender neutral —that is, policies that were apparently gender blind were, more often than not, gender biased.[10] And the crisis led to a dialogue between the women's movement (which up to that time had been quite anti-state in its positions) and the state regarding the vulnerability of women as a social category, which then legitimized state action.

By the end of that decade, the state-oriented model of development associated with import-substitution industrialization had been largely discredited in favor of a renewed focus on export-oriented growth, liberalization of the economy, and a reduced role of the state in the economy. The sectoral and gender consequences of this shift were reflected in the growth in the literature on women in the free trade or export processing zones, women in the informal sector, and the feminization of agricultural labor.[11] As Latin America struggled to compete under new terms in international markets in the 1990s, this sectoral restructuring would become known by the process that was orchestrating it: economic globalization.

Globalization required a second round of economic reforms in Latin America to deepen the reliance on market mechanisms, internally as well as externally.[12] With respect to the agricultural sector, these policies are often referred to as "modernizing agriculture" but may be characterized more accurately by their intent of "getting prices and institutions 'right'" (Carter and Barham 1996: 1142). Under the neo-liberal agrarian legislation of the 1990s, the agrarian reforms of past decades were brought to a formal end or undone by the parcelization of production cooperatives and collectively held land and by the withdrawal of the state from the provision of services, such as credit and technical assistance, a process we refer to as "counter-reform." In addition, the preconditions for the invigoration of land markets were laid in place through land titling projects and programs to modernize registration and cadastral systems. These changes raise the question of what has happened in terms of rural women's land rights as the state withdraws from the process of land redistribution.

Our previous research showed that rural women fared quite poorly in the agrarian reforms of the past.[13] With the withdrawal of the state from land redistribution, would rural women be in any better position to benefit from new opportunities to acquire land through the market? And would the land market be gender neutral or as gender biased as state programs of land distribution in the reform period? The new factor here was the women's movement and its potential impact on the neo-liberal agrarian legislation that in the early 1990s was defining the new rules of the game.[14]

The rise and consolidation of the women's movement in Latin America coincided not only with the rise to dominance of the neo-liberal paradigm in the region but also with the struggle for democratization and the subsequent transition to democracy in areas such as Brazil and the Southern Cone.[15] Moreover, the women's movement was supported by and gave impetus to the development and expansion of national women's offices within Latin American states, offices committed to promoting the rights of women. State support for these offices and attention to gender issues was also a product of the growing international consensus around these goals, particularly after the 1979 UN Convention on ending discrimination against women went into effect. The development of national women's movements was also supported by the expanded activities of nongovernmental organizations (NGOs), which were, in turn, related to the shrinkage of the state and moves to enhance the status of civil society in the 1990s. The consolidation of feminist and research-and-action-oriented NGOs greatly contributed to the growth of the women's movement at the local level, and many of these focused their attention on rural women and their aspiring organizations in this period. These factors motivate a question about the extent to which the consolidation of the women's movement has influenced neo-liberal policies. Specifically, to what extent is neo-liberal agrarian legislation more gender-progressive than the agrarian legislation of the past? Following Agarwal (1994a: 9), we define gender-progressive as "those laws, practices, policies, etc. which reduce or eliminate the inequities (economic, social or political) that women face in relation to men." Further, has gender-progressive agrarian legislation increased women's ownership of land?

The women's movement was not the only new social actor of the 1980s and 1990s.[16] In a number of Latin American countries, the indigenous movement erupted on the national scene with the events leading up to 1992, the quincentennial of the European discovery of the Americas, which generated the 500 Years of Resistance Campaign. Among the main demands of indigenous organizations was recognition of the territories to which they have traditionally had access, guarantees of collective property rights, and autonomy with respect to the exercise of traditional customs and practices. Their intervention into the debates regarding the adoption of neo-liberal agrarian legislation prevented neo-liberal advocates in most countries from dismissing collective property rights altogether. The agenda of the indigenous movement also raised the issue for feminists of whether collective rights might be an obstacle to achieving women's individual rights. Another major concern of this study thus became the apparent tension between respecting the collective land rights of communities and guaranteeing the individual rights of women, if land continued to be distributed according to traditional customs and practices that discriminate against women. In addition, was there any way that gender equity could be pursued if women did not directly participate in the decisions governing how collective land was distributed to households and to the individuals within them?

Agarwal (1994a: 19) defines effective rights in land as including legal rights as well as the social recognition of these rights and the effective control over land, an important distinction in Latin America. For example, within the collective landholding system in Mexico known as the *ejido,* the state (between 1971 and 1992) guaranteed land rights to all adults above a certain age, irrespective of sex. However, effective land rights were tied to membership within the *ejido* and only one person per household, generally the male household head, could be an *ejido* member. Thus, while men and women may have been equal before the law, in that either could potentially obtain land rights, in practice the rules of *ejido* membership excluded married women from effective land rights. Moreover, when new national legislation in 1992 permitted *ejidos* to be legally parcelized and converted to individual private property, the majority of women were excluded from participating in this crucially important decision regarding the future of their communities.

Inheritance rights offer another pertinent example. All Latin American civil codes provide, when a person dies intestate, for equal inheritance among all children irrespective of sex. However, in many regions women are not considered to work in agriculture so that it is not considered socially legitimate for them to inherit land. Thus, in those cases where a formal division of the property takes place, women are expected to renounce their inheritance share of land or, at best, to sell this share to a brother. Moreover, even where women's work in agriculture is socially recognized, in practice the rules of residence may effectively hinder women's inheritance of land.

Effective control over land includes control over the decisions about how land is to be utilized and control of the benefits it produces. Thus it includes control over such decisions as whether land is to be farmed directly or let out under a tenancy agreement, what is to be produced and how, and on the disposition of the products produced or of the income generated from its rental (Agarwal 1994a: 19). Thus, while a woman may inherit and own land in her own name in Latin America, she may not effectively control it if, for instance, her inheritance is incorporated into the family patrimony managed by the male household head.

In her path-breaking book *A Field of One's Own,* Agarwal (1994a: 3) defines independent land rights for women as those "that are formally untied to male ownership or control"; that is, independent land rights exclude joint titles with men. Her reasoning:

> Independent rights would be preferable to joint titles with husbands for several reasons: one, with joint titles it could prove difficult for women to gain control over their share in case of marital breakup.

Two, women would also be less in a position to escape from a situation of marital conflict or violence. . . . Three, wives may have different land-use priorities from husbands which they would be in a better position to act upon with independent land rights. Four, women with independent land rights would be better placed to control the produce. Five, with joint titles the question of how the land would subsequently be inherited could prove a contentious one. This is not to deny that having joint titles with husbands would be better for women than having no land rights at all; but many of the advantages of having land would not accrue to women by joint titles alone. (Agarwal 1994a: 20)

We argue that joint titling of land and other assets such as housing is a crucially important mechanism of inclusion of women in the ownership of property. In Latin America the achievement of joint titling represents the culmination of a century-long struggle to secure women's property rights within marriage and consensual unions and to establish joint management of the common property of the household. Nonetheless, the dual-headed household represents a formal mechanism of inclusion. What might contribute toward real equality in practice—that is, a more equitable distribution of household assets between men and women—is precisely joint titling.[17]

This is not to take issue with Agarwal's proposition that independent land rights for women are preferable to land rights shared with men. In Latin America, as in South Asia, independent land rights (as illustrated in the case of the inheritance of land, which is almost always on an individual basis) are associated with an increase in women's bargaining power within the household and community and with female economic autonomy, factors that contribute to women's empowerment and enhance their well-being and that of their children. Rather, given the prevalence of family farming in Latin America, and the current conjuncture—when the most important state initiative in agriculture consists of land-titling programs —joint titling of land to couples will potentially benefit more rural women than any other measure.

In Latin America the discussion of independent land rights for women has been largely limited to the case of female household heads. A particularly important mechanism of inclusion of women has been the priority that a few land-reform and land-titling programs have given in recent years to female heads of household. These can be viewed as a form of affirmative action in that they represent an attempt to redress the discrimination in land rights to which women have been subject in the past.

There have also been a few experiments in giving certain other categories of women priority land rights as a social group, but these attempts have been poorly understood or highly contested.

The discussion of property rights and the mechanisms of inclusion of women in the ownership of assets is potentially as important to urban as to rural women, as seen in recent struggles for access to decent housing and for women's ownership rights in a number of countries. As part of the urban housing movement, women are participating in land takeovers and assuming responsibility for legalizing their claims; they are also contributing their savings as well as their labor to self-help housing schemes (Valenzuela 1997; Sagot 1997; González and Durán 1992; Sevilla 1992; Varley 1994). All too often, as happens to rural women with land, at the moment of titling these properties, officials give preference to male household heads, titling the home only in the name of the husband. This makes women particularly vulnerable. In the event they are abandoned, separated, or widowed, they may not have any legal claim to the property (AVP et al. 1995: 10; Meertens 1986: 44; Molina, Sagot, and Carcedo 1992; Varley 1996; Barrig 1988: 155; Moser 1987: 199).

Nonetheless, the women's movement in Latin America in recent years has given lower priority to the defense of property rights relative to such issues as reproductive rights or ending domestic violence against women. This is partly because the theoretical energy of feminists in Latin America as well as internationally has centered on what Nancy Fraser (1997: 2) has called issues of recognition rather than redistribution. Primary attention has focused on women's gender identity and the struggle for recognition of the differences between men and women, coupled with the understanding that the category "women" is marked by fundamental differences of class, race, ethnicity, nationality, sexual preference, and so on. The rise of identity politics more broadly in the postsocialist neo-liberal era in both North and South has shifted, in Fraser's terms, the "political imaginary of justice" away from issues of class, political economy, and redistribution to the cultural realm. Our intention in this book is to bring "the material" back in and to show its interconnection with issues of recognition. We argue that the relationship between gender and property has been insufficiently explored and that attention to issues of redistribution, particularly of property, is fundamental for transforming gender relations and ending women's subordination to men.

Until the publication of Bina Agarwal's (1994a) book, the relation between gender and property had been understudied and undertheorized.

The primary point of reference had been Engels's classic text, *The Origin of the Family, Private Property, and the State* (1884/1972), which has had enduring influence upon socialist feminists. The kernel of Engels's theory was that the subordination of women was associated with the rise of male-owned private property and the patriarchal family alongside that of class-divided society, which led in turn to the development of the modern state.[18] In brief, the transformation of women from equal, productive members of society to subordinate and dependent wives was associated with the transition from production for use and communal ownership of property to production for exchange and individual male ownership of private property in a class-divided society.

Engels's theory has been the subject of much criticism and debate, particularly with regard to the origins of women's subordination.[19] Our main concern is with Engels's proposition regarding gender and property relations under capitalism. He argued that

> gender relations would be hierarchical among the property-owning families of the bourgeoisie where women did not go out to work and were economically dependent on men, and egalitarian in propertyless proletarian families where women were in the labour force. The ultimate restoration of women to their rightful status, in his view, required the total abolition of private property (i.e., a move to socialism), the socialization of housework and childcare, and the full participation of women in the labor force. (Agarwal 1994a: 12)

That gender relations among propertyless proletarian households could hardly be characterized as egalitarian was amply documented by feminists from almost the time that Engels's manuscript was published. But this did not diminish the appeal of his prescription for the emancipation of women: their full-scale entry into the labor force accompanied by the socialization of housework and childcare in the transition to socialism.[20] Agarwal rightly praises Engels for his "emphasis on women's economic dependency as a critical constituent of the material bases of gender oppression" (1994a: 13). Nonetheless, she argues that by advocating the abolition of private property, Engels bypassed the question of women's property rights altogether. He failed to consider the impact on gender relations in propertied households if women, too, owned property and did not consider other alternatives, besides their joining the labor force, that would change women's status of economic dependence. As Agarwal demonstrates, independent property rights for women—particularly when accompanied by effective control over property—can be equally successful, if not more so, in promoting women's economic autonomy and bargaining power.

Engels's failure—not considering alternatives to wage labor as a means to change women's economic position—has been mirrored in feminist research on Latin America. In the 1970s and early 1980s the driving issues in the new field of women and development concerned the gendered division of labor, making women's work visible, and the implications of women's growing presence in the labor force. Whether women's labor force participation automatically led to an improvement in their status was widely debated,[21] but little attention was given to women's property rights as an alternative means of enhancing women's position and challenging existing gender relations. And while the economic crisis kept empirical research focused on economic issues, the theoretical energy of the feminist movement in the 1990s increasingly turned to questions of identity, difference, representation, and political participation, with less attention to the material realm. Moreover, while there was considerable theoretical interest in questions of autonomy and empowerment, few connections were made to the factors that might promote these, such as an increase in women's bargaining power as a result of enhanced property rights or ownership of assets.

In *A Field of One's Own,* Agarwal (1994a) argues for the importance of gender and land rights in terms of women's welfare, efficiency, equality, and empowerment. We draw upon and expand these below in terms of women's well-being, equality, and empowerment.

Women's Well-Being and the Family

The basis of Agarwal's welfare argument regarding gender, property, and land rights is that—given intra-household gender inequalities in the distribution of benefits, the differences in how men and women spend their incomes, and the positive links between children's nutritional status and income controlled by mothers—"the risk of poverty and the physical well-being of a woman and her children could depend significantly on whether or not she has *direct* access to income and productive assets such as land, and not just access *mediated* through her husband or other male family members" (Agarwal 1994a: 31).

To illustrate the general case that a woman's economic condition is not necessarily the same as that of her family or household, and to understand the importance of a woman's ownership of assets to her well-being, consider the case of a hypothetical adult single woman living alone. For simplicity, let us assume that she has no family or other ties upon which she may draw for support. Under these conditions, the assets she owns and controls largely determine her income-generating possibilities (particularly whether she will need to engage in wage labor) as well as her ability to deal with adversity.[22] Ownership of real estate would place this woman in a privileged position, for she could generate income by renting her home, taking in boarders, or using her house for income-generating activities. Ownership of durable goods might also provide the means of production for a series of possible income-producing activities (such as preparing foodstuffs for sale or becoming a seamstress). Moreover, any of these assets may serve as collateral for the credit she needs to invest in any of these ventures, making her more productive. Access to savings plays an important role in being able to postpone the decision to enter the labor market, to weather unemployment and underemployment, and perhaps to invest in additional productive assets. Finally, the possibility of selling an asset is another important form of security. What we want to highlight is that ownership of assets, even for a poor woman, expands the range of income-generating activities in which she may engage, increasing her options and available strategies.

Among these options and strategies is the decision whether to marry. Holding other, non-economic factors constant (such as falling in love, wanting to form a family, familial pressure to marry), this decision is influenced by the assets that each partner brings to the union and the terms of that union. Once married, the options of this woman are conditioned by the legal rights of married women and by the marital regime governing the union. Marital regimes in Latin America vary according the disposition of property brought into and acquired during the marriage and thus define the property rights of married men and women. For simplicity, assume that there is only one legal marital regime, that of full common property (known as *comunidad absoluta* or *comunidad de bienes*), in which all property acquired before or during the marriage by either spouse is pooled, along with all the income generated during the marriage. Until recent decades in many countries, the common property of the household was controlled by the husband; this included the property that a woman brought into marriage as well as her own earnings. A married woman could not legally enter into contracts, run a business, or engage in wage labor without her husband's consent. By establishing the property rights of married women, we refer to those revisions of the civil codes that allowed married women at least to control their own individual assets and earnings. The reforms that established wives and husbands as joint administrators of common property are even more recent, and have yet to be attained in several countries in the region.

Before these reforms, the economic autonomy of married women was extremely limited. Without economic assets under their direct command, married women were extremely vulnerable, for their well-being (and that of their children) largely depended on their husbands' skills in managing the income and assets of the family, as well as their good faith. In the case of separation, divorce, or widowhood, nonetheless, women in Latin America found some protection from the state. Under the common-property regime, women were entitled to half the common property if the union was dissolved, irrespective of their own contribution. While this system gave women a certain degree of bargaining power during marriage, whether there was any common property left to distribute was still largely dependent upon their husbands' sound management of household income and assets and their good faith.

In the past, it was primarily through inheritance that men's and women's endowments were initially established, influencing their marriage options, bargaining position in marriage, and the range of their income-generating opportunities.[23] If inheritance had followed the legal norm of equal inheritance among all children, irrespective of gender, the distribution of assets in Latin America today would be relatively equal between the sexes, a situation that is hardly the case. Social norms governing the transmission of productive assets—that is, the social construction of masculinity and femininity such that men are defined as the producers and primary income earners and women as dependent housewives—have generated considerable gender inequality in the ownership of assets. In addition, while under the common-property regime a widow automatically receives half of the common property of the household upon her husband's death, she does not automatically inherit from her husband's share of the estate. Thus, for example, if a husband willed all his assets to his children, a widow would not necessarily remain in control of the family home, farm, or business.

The full common-property marital regime as described above could be viewed as an attempt by the state to legislate income pooling and asset sharing among household members under the purview of the household head, who is charged with its administration for the presumed benefit of all its members. This case parallels the assumptions of neo-classical economics regarding households—specifically, that the male head of household acts as a benevolent dictator, basing his decisions on the desire to maximize the welfare and well-being of all household members. Recent advances in feminist economic theory (Folbre 1986a, 1986b; Kabeer 1994; Agarwal 1994a) have challenged the view that households are governed by altruism rather than by self-interest. Moreover, a considerable amount of empirical evidence has been amassed cross-culturally demonstrating that (1) not all income generated by household members is necessarily pooled; (2) men and women spend their income in different ways; and (3) pooled income does not necessarily result in shared consumption or equal consumption shares for all household members. It has been found that the income controlled by women is more likely to contribute to household food security and child welfare than income controlled by men (ibid.; Moser 1989; Quisumbing et al. 1995; Quisumbing and Maluccio 1999).

In the Latin American case, there is a growing body of evidence showing that women are more likely to pool any income they earn individually for the family's benefit. Men are more likely to spend part of their income for their own individual wants (particularly liquor and tobacco), contributing only a portion of their earnings to the household fund (Bourque and Warren 1981: 107; Benería and Roldán 1987: 114–19; Deere 1990: 287–89; Brunt 1992: 91–92).[24] The distribution of male income between discretionary consumption and household expenses is rarely a household decision (although it is commonly a source of tension and conflict), often being made unilaterally by the husband (ibid.).

Intra-household gender inequality in the sharing of benefits is apparent in a number of ways. For example, on peasant family farms in the Andes men generally control the fruits of the collective labor of all household members: "Prevailing norms supported an unequal distribution of benefits among family members, with women and children, in particular, having little recourse even when his decision meant their material deprivation" (Reinhardt 1988: 55). Similarly, in northern Peru, "Among poor peasant households, female economic autonomy was a necessary condition to guarantee shared consumption of the family labor product. Poor peasant men could walk away from a sale on market day right into a bar and drink away a month's worth of family labor. It was not unusual to see a woman desperately trying to pull her husband out of a *chichería* [canteen] for exactly this reason" (Deere 1990: 287).

With respect to the distribution of food, it is commonly observed that men are served first and given the largest helpings and the choicest morsels, including the majority of the protein (Reinhardt 1988: 215; Bourque and Warren 1981: 121), biasing the intra-household distribution of nutrients against women and young children, as in highland Guatemala (Katz 2000). A survey of household nutritional practices in Ecuador found that in over one-third of the households fathers received a larger portion of food than other household members, and in one-quarter they received extra meat and rice when these were available. Another study noted that the rationale for giving preference to men in the allocation of foodstuffs was not the greater physical energy they expended (since women also play an active role in agricultural work) but rather that the father's role as principal breadwinner entitled him to certain privileges (Luzuriaga 1982: 34).

Detailed studies of the spending patterns of men and women in the region indicate that income controlled by women is more likely to improve household and children's nutrition (Engle 1995: 155, 172–74). A study of urban households in Brazil showed that, relative to men, women's control of income was associated with increased protein intake, positive weight-for-height ratios, and increased child survival (Thomas 1990: 646–67). A study in rural Guatemala found that the biggest improvement in food and nutritional outcomes was linked to women's income-earning opportunities (Katz 2000). If women are more likely than men to spend a larger share of their income on items that are related to children, such as food, then it is not surprising that some studies have found female household headship to be associated with improved child welfare (Desai and Ahmad 1998: 232). As the UN's 1997 *Human Development Report* concluded, "Gender equality needs to be part of each country's strategy for eradicating poverty, both as an end and as a means to eradicating other forms of human poverty. This means . . . empowering women by ensuring equal rights and access to land, credit and job opportunities" (UNDP 1997: 7).

Another factor that must be taken into account in the discussion of women's well-being is the role of independent assets in reducing women's vulnerability in old age. Given the low coverage of social security programs (particularly in the rural sector), the trend toward privatization of these programs under neo-liberalism, the lengthening of life expectancy in the region, and its gender gap,[25] care of the elderly is becoming as urgent an issue in Latin America as in the advanced countries. This issue has not been addressed in recent reforms of the civil codes, and in most countries inheritance rights favor children over widows, making widows particularly vulnerable.

Bina Agarwal (1994a) makes a strong case for the special role of land as a productive asset in rural societies, particularly those characterized by limited non-farm opportunities. In Latin America, as in South Asia, land has played a special role as a productive resource, means of livelihood and of accumulating wealth, and source of status and political power. Until recent decades, the unequal distribution of land in Latin America was probably the most important single factor in explaining the extremely unequal distribution of wealth and income in the region, which was *the* most unequal among regions of the world (IADB 1997: 41). Agarwal (1994a: 31) argues that in South Asia land serves as one of the best forms of security against poverty. In Latin America the evidence supporting this point is mixed.[26] Nonetheless, while access to land may not keep a household above the poverty level, it may still serve as an important form of food security by allowing households—and specifically the women within them, if they have independent land rights—to meet at least a portion of their basic needs and keep from falling into extreme poverty or destitution. Agarwal also points to the many indirect advantages of owning land, one of the most important being, in the Latin American case, that it allows the pursuit of a more diversified livelihood system.

The thrust of Agarwal's (1994a: 34) efficiency argument is that the ownership and control of land increases women's productive possibilities and the likelihood that they will have access to credit, technical assistance, and greater information. Secure ownership of land increases women's efficiency in that it directly increases both their capacity and incentive to invest, leading to higher productivity and production levels. Higher levels of production should lead to higher levels of income, which if also controlled by women should lead to higher levels of consumption and well-being for women and their children. Secure ownership of land can also improve natural resource management in terms of efficiency and environmental sustainability (ibid.: 37; Meinzen-Dick et al., 1997). Moreover, a woman's direct control of land, to the extent that it results in higher levels of investment in her own or her children's health and education, also results in greater labor productivity, or human capital accumulation.

The efficiency argument for women's access to and control of land focuses not only on women's well-being but on that of society in general through the increased production that women agriculturalists will generate. As Agnes Quisumbing et al. (1995: 7) argue, "Barriers to women's productivity and the use of their experience and knowledge may impose a large opportunity cost to society in terms of foregone output and incomes, the magnitude of which is only now being realized." Perhaps because of this reason, it is the argument that tends to be highlighted by women-in-development advocates, particularly in the context of structural adjustment policies. We call this the "productionist" argument to distinguish it from arguments that focus on why women's ownership and control of land is critical whether or not women work the land directly themselves, or what we term the "equality and empowerment" arguments.

Equality between Women and Men

Agarwal's third argument is framed in terms of achieving equality between men and women. Our objective is to clarify the various ways in which the concept of equality has been utilized, to review the various means that have been posited to achieve real (as opposed to formal) equality, and to explore the relationship between equality and equity. Equality is a normative and historically constructed concept that is subject to differing interpretations and meanings (Jiménez 1995: 12). Feminist philosophers distinguish between the horizontal and vertical relations implicit in the concept. "Equality between" is a relation of reciprocal similarity in that it is established horizontally, between individuals at the same level. In contrast, "equality to" is unidirectional and implies hierarchies and dependencies, or vertical relations. The concern of feminists is that, in the struggle for sexual equality, women will be pressed to conform to a paradigm of "humanity" defined in masculine terms. This point was at the crux of the "equality versus difference" debate that dominated feminist theoretical concerns in the 1970s and early 1980s.[27]

In brief, "equality" and "difference" feminists had conflicting views of gender differences and the causes of gender injustice and, hence, opposing views of gender equity (Fraser 1997: 177). For "equality" feminists gender differences have been used historically to rationalize women's subordination, and thus to stress these was to reinforce women's domestic role and marginalization. In contrast, for "difference" or "cultural" feminists gender differences were the foundation of women's identity, and androcentrism was the main problem.[28] Whereas for the latter, gender equity had to be built around the recognition and revaluation of femininity, for the former it involved minimizing gender differences and establishing equal participation and distribution of valued goods.

In Fraser's reading, this debate was never really settled. While each side had convincing criticisms, neither had a fully defensible position. A solution would have been to integrate social and cultural demands, so that social inequality and cultural androcentrism were attacked simultaneously (Fraser 1997: 177–78). But before this could happen, the focus on gender differences gave way in the mid-1980s to that on "differences among women." This debate had several axes: in the North it was spearheaded by lesbians and feminists of color who challenged the white, middle-class, heterosexual origins and perspectives of second-wave feminism; in the South, it was led by feminists who challenged Western conceptions of a universal feminine identity as well as the presumed unity of interests between women of North and South, an assumption made problematic by imperialism and class injustices. As the differences among and between women due to class, race, ethnicity, nationality, sexual preference, and so on began to be taken into account, both theoretically and politically, the feminist movement was poised to begin integrating cultural and social demands around "multiple intersecting differences." Fraser (ibid.: 180–81) argues that this did not happen; rather, the politics of recognition were disassociated from the politics of redistribution, and, at least in the North, the former eclipsed the latter.[29] This schism has been less evident in Latin America, where the social movements of the 1990s (the indigenous and women's movements, in particular) could not afford to neglect issues of maldistribution and the pressing demand for social equality. But it has served to orient priorities so that in the case of the women's movement, these have focused on issues of recognition (e.g., reproductive rights and violence against women) rather than economic redistribution.

In response to the "equality versus difference" debate, since the 1980s feminists have placed great stress on the difference between "equality to" and "equality between," emphasizing that the latter is the goal. What equality between requires, among other factors, is the capacity to choose and decide between alternatives, or equality between individuals with the *same* capacity to exercise power and authority (Santa Cruz 1992: 147). A precondition of equality between is hence a process of empowerment, a concept discussed in the next section. What we want to stress here is that equality between requires much more than just formal equality as defined in liberal political theory.

Another main concern of feminists has been the distinction between formal and real equality. Whereas formal equality refers to equality of rights, real equality refers to equality of outcomes.[30] Equality of rights encompasses "all of the fundamental rights enumerated in a constitution, such as civil and political rights." These are abstract, general rights in contrast to equality before the law, which is "a specific form, historically determined of equality of rights" (Bobbio 1993: 75–76). Equality of all citizens before the law, to the extent that it implies the abolition of all privilege, includes the principle of non-discrimination. As equality and political rights have been extended to new groups, this principle has evolved to include differences of sex, ethnicity, religion, and sexual orientation. Non-discrimination might be considered the first step in achieving real as opposed to formal equality between men and women. A second step is equality of opportunities.

In the liberal conception of equality of opportunities, social, economic, political, and cultural conditions must be restructured to allow individuals equal access to education, health care, employment, and other important social goods. In its narrowest form, as argued by conservatives, the goal is to end the obstacles to equality of opportunity that arise from explicit or implicit discrimination based on sex. Once opportunities are created, it is up to individuals to use them; in this view, the unequal utilization of opportunities is what accounts for unequal outcomes. This position has been criticized by feminists who argue that men and women do not share the same point of departure (Astelarra 1995: 31–33).[31] As long as existing gender roles persist and the gender division of labor remains unchanged, men and women will not have the same equality of opportunities.

The principle of affirmative action (a third step toward achieving real equality) emerged as a response to these criticisms. Affirmative action, also known as positive action or pro-active measures,[32] can be defined as a strategy to establish equality of opportunities "through a series of temporary measures that allow for the correction of discrimination which results from practices or social systems" (Osborne 1995: 301). Affirmative action recognizes that formal equality before the law and the liberal principle of equality of opportunity are insufficient for disadvantaged groups to achieve equality of outcomes. In order to "level the playing field" in terms of equality of opportunity, affirmative action policies include measures, for example, to increase the proportion of girls who graduate from high school or college and who have the appropriate skills, and to change the socialization of girls so that they become willing to acquire non-traditional skills and compete for non-traditional jobs.

Affirmative action measures in the workplace may include hiring a certain proportion of women applicants, even if they do not have the necessary skills for the job, with these to be provided by the employer. These are more radical measures since they often require what is known as positive or "reverse discrimination," including the hiring of less qualified women over more qualified men. Another strategy employed to achieve equality of outcomes is the use of quotas, where a certain share of jobs or other benefits (such as housing or land) is set aside for a given group. The main argument in favor of such policies is that, given the history of male privilege, until the underlying gender relations and social institutions can be changed, temporary measures are justified to move toward real as opposed to formal equality of opportunity.[33] That is, positive discrimination is justified on grounds of gender equity.

In terms of property rights, an example of the pursuit of formal equality before the law is the effort to establish the same property rights for men and women within marriage—that is, where both administer the common property of the union. But to establish real equality with respect to the outcome of equal property rights, that is, to change the distribution of asset ownership, requires a number of additional steps. A first step is the application of the principle of non-discrimination, for example, when men and women apply for the adjudication of a land parcel or a housing subsidy. To achieve equality of outcomes, a second step—affirmative action—is often necessary since men and women are socialized differently. In self-help housing programs, for example, applicants usually must be willing to contribute their own labor. Given gender socialization, women are less likely than men to have the necessary skills to work in construction. Thus establishing equality of opportunities would require the provision of training so that women could acquire the necessary skills to participate in such programs.[34] A third step—positive discrimination—recognizes that women have often been discriminated against in terms of access to housing in the past. Also, female heads of household might have a more difficult time contributing labor for a self-help project since they are responsible for their family's sustenance as well as for domestic labor. Programs designed to achieve real equality, or equality of outcomes, would prioritize female household heads, notwithstanding the fact that by traditional criteria they might be judged less qualified than male applicants. Prioritizing female household heads in this case would increase women's ownership of real estate and thus translate a principle of formal equality before the law—property rights—into a concrete measure to achieve real gender equality via the redistribution of assets. The justification for doing so would be the pursuit of gender equity.

Equity refers to fairness, or what is considered to be just according to the dominant values of a society. One problem in defining gender equity is that most theories of justice do not take into account gender roles and, specifically, the family. According to Susan Okin (1989: 8–9), "In the past, political theorists often used to distinguish clearly between 'private' domestic life and the 'public' life of politics and the marketplace, claiming explicitly that the two spheres operated in accordance with different principles." While contemporary political theories give the appearance of being inclusive of women,[35] Okin argues that they continue the same "separate spheres" tradition "by ignoring the family, its division of labor, and the related economic dependency and restricted opportunities of most women." The family may be ignored completely, with the subject of analysis being the "individual," who is assumed to be the male head of a traditional, patriarchal household. In this approach, the application of principles of justice to relations between men and women or within the household are ruled out from the start. Or, as in "the most influential of all twentieth-century theories of justice, that of John Rawls, family life is not only assumed, but is assumed to be just—and yet the prevalent gendered division of labor within the family is neglected, along with the associated distribution of power, responsibility, and privilege" (ibid.).

Okin, in *Justice, Gender and the Family*, argues that any satisfactory theory of justice must include women and address gender relations; that the principle of equality of opportunity is seriously undermined by the current gender injustices found in most societies; and that the family must be just if we are to have a just society. In her analysis "the family is the linchpin of gender, reproducing it from one generation to the next," and the traditional division of labor within the family is not just, either to women or to children. Moreover, "a just future would be one without gender" (ibid.: 170–71).

In the aftermath of the "equality versus difference" debate, there is consensus among feminists that gender relations must be transformed if gender equity and real equality between men and women are to be achieved. The challenge is how to develop a workable conception of gender equity to map progress toward that goal or to set standards to evaluate alternative propositions. Fraser (1997: 45) argues that we must break with the assumption that gender equity can be identified with any single value or norm; rather, the task is to develop a complex conception that encompasses a plurality of distinct normative principles. In *Justice Interruptus* she develops such a concept of gender equity, based on seven distinct yet interdependent normative principles, to evaluate alternative visions of a postindustrial welfare state.[36] One of her contributions in doing so is to illustrate how such a complex conception of gender equity must necessarily include elements of recognition and redistribution, of culture and the economy.

Latin American feminists are increasingly cognizant of this challenge —of the need to build a concept of gender equity around a plurality of normative principles as a framework for action (Valdés 2000). This task has a certain urgency since the language of gender equity is gaining increased currency in international and national public policy circles, where it is often stripped of its transformative potential. But there is also growing recognition that public policies once considered to be gender neutral were, in fact, gender biased. In the words of the Secretary General of the UN Economic Commission for Latin America and the Caribbean (ECLAC or CEPAL, as it is known by its Spanish acronym), understanding "the differential impact of public policy on men and women has meant that any serious analysis of economic and social policy today must include a gender perspective, that is, a preoccupation with gender equity" (Ocampo 1998: 311). Among the key elements recognized by CEPAL researchers as obstacles to achieving gender equity are (1) the gendered division of labor governing production and reproduction; (2) women's exclusion from decision making and the exercise of power; and (3) women's unequal access to resources (CEPAL 1993a: 19). It is worth mentioning that this report, which is almost visionary in its analysis of how citizenship must be reconceptualized and domestic relations transformed to achieve gender equity, gives little specific attention to gender and property rights and to how equality between men and women is to be achieved in terms of the ownership of assets. That is, the tough issues of redistribution take a back seat to those of recognition.

Similarly, during the 1990s a growing number of Latin American states adopted national plans to achieve equality of opportunities for women. Most of these consist of a combination of general and specific objectives to be accomplished through state action in some specified time period (Martínez and Soto 1996: 20). They usually incorporate various forms of the affirmative action strategies discussed above, and recognize that women's lack of access to resources constitutes one of the main forms of inequality between the sexes. At the same time, these plans often refrain from recommending concrete forms of positive discrimination that would increase women's access to property. Thus, while considerable gains have been made in strengthening women's property rights in pursuit of formal gender equality, there have been few concrete advances in remedying inequality in terms of men's and women's ownership of assets—that is, in terms of redistribution. If ownership of property is critical for women's well-being as well as for establishing equality between men and women, inattention to gender and the distribution of assets remains one of the largest deficiencies in public policy.

The Empowerment of Women

Achieving equality between men and women requires a transformation in women's access to both property and power, which itself depends on a process of empowerment of women. At the same time, the empowerment of women is transformative of gender relations and is thus a pre-condition for achieving equality between men and women.[37] For feminists empowerment implies "the radical alteration of the processes and structures which reproduce women's subordinate position as a gender" (Young 1993: 158). But the term "cmpowerment" has been used in a multitude of ways, and not always in an emancipatory sense. In the development field it is sometimes used as a synonym for people's participation or integration into planning and development and confused with welfare or poverty reduction (Batliwala 1997: 187; Kabeer 1997: 120). But implicit in the different uses of the word is the notion of people acquiring control over their own lives and defining their own agendas; it is usually associated with the interests of those dispossessed of power and assumed to be an expression of desired change without specifying what that change implies.

In discussions over the appearance of the concept of empowerment within the women's movement, the most cited text is Gita Sen and Caren Grown's (1985) *Development, Crises and Alternative Visions*, a manuscript drawn up by a collective of feminist academic researchers and activists for the Third UN World Conference on Women in Nairobi in 1985. In this document the concept of empowerment appears as a strategy championed by Third World women to change their own lives at the same time that it generates a process of social transformation, the ultimate objective of the women's movement. Empowerment is seen as the basis for generating alternative visions by women as well as the process through which these visions will become realities as social relations are changed. Among the preconditions for the empowerment of women are democratic and participatory spaces as well as the organization of women.

The term "empowerment" calls attention to the word "power" and the concept of power as a social relation. Power conditions the experience of women in a double sense: "it is a source of her oppression when it is abused and a source of emancipation in its use" (Radtke and Stam 1994, in Rowlands 1997: 21). Relations of power can mean domination, but they can also be a mechanism for resisting or gaining control over existing sources of power. In order to further the development of the concept of empowerment, Jo Rowlands (1997: 218–23) differentiates four types of power: *power over, power for, power with,* and *power within.* "Power over" represents a zero sum game; an increase in the power of one means a loss of power by another. In contrast, the other three forms— power to, power with, power within—are all positive and additive: An increase in the power of one increases the total power available or the power of all.

Because it was assumed that the only form of power was power over, Latin American feminists long ignored the discussion of power; women in society were understood as victims, lacking in power. One of the first open discussions of the myths guiding the political practices of the movement took place at the Fourth Latin American Feminist Meeting in Taxco, Mexico, in 1987. There it was concluded that the number one myth, and one that had been an obstacle to effective action, was that "as feminists we are not interested in power."[38] Attention was called to the need to recognize the exercise of power in the activities of the movement and to see power as a resource for transformation. According to Marta Lamas (1998: 105), the recognition of this myth allowed "criticism of the denying and victimized way we feminists handle power" and the denunciation of the "idealization of our activism."[39] In the process of recognizing "power over," the possibility of resistance, or of manipulating power in one's favor, becomes apparent, reducing the association of power with victimization.

The Taxco meeting initiated a process in the Latin American women's movement that has allowed constructive thinking about the other forms of power, as well as recognition of the positive and additive qualities of "power to," "power with," and "power from within." "Power to" serves to catalyze change when one person or a group leader galvanizes the enthusiasm and action of others. It is a generative or productive power, a creative or facilitating power that opens up possibilities and actions without domination—that is, without the use of "power over." "Power to" is related to "power with" in that it allows power to be shared. It is apparent when a group generates a collective solution to a common problem, allowing all potentialities to be expressed in the construction of a group agenda that is also assumed individually. It serves to confirm that the group can be superior to the sum of its individual parts. Another form of positive and additive power is "power from within" or internal power. It has to do with generating strength from within oneself and is related to self-esteem. "Power from within" is apparent when someone is able to resist the power of others by rejecting undesired demands. It also includes the recognition, which one gains from experience, of how women's subordination is maintained and reproduced.

The empowerment of women challenges patriarchal familial relations, for it may lead to the disempowerment of men and certainly to the loss of the privileged position they have held under patriarchy. For empowerment occurs when a change has taken place in men's traditional domination of women, whether with respect to control of their life options, assets, opinions, or sexuality. It is apparent when unilateral decision making is no longer the norm within the family. But from another point of view, the empowerment of women liberates and empowers men in both the material and psychological realms. For example, women begin sharing in formerly male responsibilities, such as breadwinning. And when men are liberated from gender stereotypes, new emotional experiences become possible for them (Olavarria 2000: 11–12). Hence, the empowerment of women implies changes not only in their own experiences but also in those of their partners and family.

Since women's subordination seems natural within patriarchal ideology, it is difficult for change to erupt spontaneously from the condition of subordination. Empowerment must be induced by first creating consciousness of gender discrimination.[40] This requires women to change their negative self-perceptions as well as their beliefs regarding their rights and capabilities. To facilitate the conditions that encourage such changes is the role of external agents. But is it possible for one person to empower another? Is this notion at odds with the very concept of empowerment? These are not easy questions to answer. Experience has demonstrated that empowerment takes place in different scenarios: Stromquist (1997: 79–82) talks of phases; Wieringa (1997: 159) of spheres or parts of a matrix; and Rowlands (1997: 222–30) of dimensions. There are no magic formulas or infallible designs, no single recipe or prescriptive model.[41] Empowerment is not a linear process with a well-defined beginning and ending that is the same for all women. Empowerment is shaped for each individual or group by their lives, context, and history, as well as according to the location of subordination in the personal, familiar, communal, and higher levels.

One of the other major currents in the development of the concept of empowerment has come from feminist economists focusing on economic autonomy and how it is related to and constitutive of the relative bargaining positions of men and women within the household, community, and society. The bargaining-power approach was largely inspired by feminist critiques of the neo-classical model of the unitary family. In this model the household was treated as an undifferentiated unit of consumption and production where resources and incomes were pooled. It was assumed that household resources were allocated by an altruistic male household head who represented the household's tastes and preferences and sought to maximize household utility (Agarwal 1997: 4–5). Nancy Folbre (1986a and 1986b) was one of the first to question the contradictory nature of these assumptions, pointing out that since the time of Adam Smith, rational economic actors have been assumed to maximize their own self-interest. Why, then, was altruism posited to govern behavior within the family? Moreover, this story did not fit very well with the facts, for a growing body of evidence suggested that household relations were permeated by economic inequality. In response to the question of whether the household was governed by altruism or self-interest, economists began to develop alternative approaches to the study of intra-household interactions, in large measure inspired by game theory.[42]

In Agarwal's (1994a: 54–71) approach, households are conceptualized "as a complex matrix of relationships in which there is ongoing (often implicit) negotiation, subject to the constraints set by gender, age, type of relationship (kinship association)" and what is socially permissible to be bargained about. Following Sen (1980; 1990), household relations are posited to be characterized by elements of both cooperation and conflict: "The members of a household cooperate in so far as cooperative arrangements make each of them better off than noncooperation" (Agarwal 1994a: 54). One can envision a multitude of activities in which household members gain through cooperation—for example, by pooling resources and labor to prepare only one large meal a day. However, many different outcomes are possible in just this one cooperative activity—in terms of who does what, who gets what, and how each member is treated in the process. On one hand, all of these outcomes of cooperation may be more beneficial to the participants than the alternative of noncooperation (where the outcome is that no large meal is prepared). On the other hand, among the set of cooperative outcomes some are more favorable to each participant than others. The possibility of one person's gain being another person's loss highlights the conflict that may underlie cooperation. What determines which outcome prevails?

Which outcome will emerge depends on the relative bargaining power of the household members. A member's bargaining power would be defined by a range of factors, in particular the strength of the person's fall-back position (the outside options which determine how well-off he or she would be if cooperation ceased), and the degree to which his/her claim is seen as socially and legally legitimate. The person who has a stronger fall-back position (better outside options), and/or whose claim enjoys greater legitimacy, would emerge with a more favourable outcome, although both parties would be better-off than if they did not cooperate. (ibid.: 54–55)

According to Agarwal (1994a: 62), the most important elements of a person's fall-back position in a rural household include: (1) ownership and control of property, particularly land; (2) access to employment or other means of income generation; (3) access to communal resources (such as forests and grazing pastures); (4) access to traditional external social support systems (within the community or extended family); and (5) access to state support or that of NGOs. All five factors influence a person's ability to meet subsistence needs outside the household: "The premise here is that the greater a person's ability to physically survive outside the family, the greater would be her/his bargaining power" in relation to resource sharing within it (ibid.: 63).

Agarwal (1994a: 64–65) argues that under present-day conditions in South Asia, private rights in land hold a privileged position.[43] She goes on to argue that "effective independent rights in private land could strengthen rural women's fall-back position in ways that employment alone may not." This is not to argue against measures to enhance women's employment opportunities. Rather, "land ownership provides more than employment can, including a stronger base for social and political participation, and so for challenging gender inequality on several other fronts." This proposition seems particularly apt in the Latin American case, given the low wages and seasonal and part-time nature of female agricultural wage employment, even in regions that have favored female employment as a result of the development of non-traditional export crops.

As Agarwal (1994a: 66–67) demonstrates, bargaining may take place not only over the distribution of subsistence resources within the household but also over the endowments that constitute and contribute to each household member's fall-back position. Consider the case of women's ownership of land. Whether or not women bring land into a newly formed household largely depends on inheritance rights and practices. In Latin

America, in contrast to South Asia, the legal framework favors bilateral inheritance, with all children, irrespective of sex, entitled to equal shares of their parents' estate. Among the factors influencing whether a daughter is able to successfully claim an inheritance share, as in South Asia, are the following: (1) women's literacy; (2) the daughter's knowledge of her legal rights; (3) the social legitimacy of her claim within the community; (4) her access to the legal machinery to enforce a claim; and (5) her access to resources for survival outside the support systems provided by potential contending claimants, such as brothers (ibid.: 66). These factors are, in turn, influenced by a series of other economic and non-economic factors and are, at times, interdependent. Women's attainment of literacy, for example, depends on the availability of schooling and the propensity of parents to invest in the education of girls. A woman's use of the legal machinery to press land claims is largely influenced by the social legitimacy of her claim (how common and acceptable it is for women to inherit land), the costs of pressing a claim (direct monetary costs and time), and her degree of economic and emotional dependence on the kinfolk who might contest the claim. As Agarwal (ibid.: 67) argues, "individual women's struggles to acquire a share in family land would require interlinked struggles outside the household arena as well, such as struggles to legitimize women's need for independent rights in land and to mobilize economic, social, and political support for the cause." The point here is that "gender differences in intra-household bargaining power are thus linked with the person's extra-household bargaining power with the community and the State" (ibid.).

Women's ownership of land, and of assets in general, enhances their bargaining power not only within the household but also, potentially, within the community and wider society. In another contribution, Agarwal (1997: 14–22) provides a provocative discussion of social norms: of how these set limits on what can be bargained about, how they determine bargaining power, and how they affect the way bargaining is conducted. She also demonstrates how social norms constitute a factor to be bargained over—that is, they themselves can be subject to negotiation and change. This analysis is an important building block as we begin to conceptualize how gender relations are constituted, maintained, and reproduced over time, both within and outside the household, and how they can be altered.

To date little systematic research has been carried out in Latin America linking women's ownership of assets to their bargaining power within the household and community, although case studies and anecdotal evidence support this proposition. There is good evidence on how peasant women's inheritance prospects condition their marriage possibilities and relations within the marriage. In the northern Peruvian highlands, for example, daughters who stood to inherit land were more likely to marry and settle in the region than daughters of the poor peasant strata, whose main options lay in permanent migration. The former were also more likely to form households that reside uxorilocally (with or near the wife's parents), another factor associated with women's greater bargaining position within the household (Deere 1990: 141, 288). In the Yungas region, north of La Paz, Bolivia, bilateral inheritance of land has also supported uxorilocal residence, since young couples usually reside near the parents who have the most land. In the 1990s, approximately one-third of the households resided with or near a woman's family. Alison Spedding (1997: 325–26) notes that the spouse who resides away from their community of origin has less bargaining power in marital disputes than the spouse who is living among family members.

In the northern Peruvian highlands women landowners play a greater role in farm management, have a greater say in intra-household labor and income allocation, and play a decisive role in decisions regarding their children's future—such as which child will finish school, learn a trade, or migrate permanently from the region (Deere 1990: 288, 309–10). Similarly, the association between inheritance and ownership of land, women's participation in household and farm decision making, and their stronger bargaining position in household affairs has been noted in Ecuador and southern Brazil (Hamilton 1998; Stephen 1997: 212).

In the northern Peruvian highlands, women's lack of access to land has also been associated with domestic violence. As Ana de la Torre (1995: 15) found, "In family life, the main problem reported by women which generates violence against them is related to scarce resources, particularly in terms of the lands which they brought into marriage. . . . 'If I didn't bring much, or very little, then I can't ask for much, much less have an influence on economic decisions in the family without creating conflicts.'" There is also considerable evidence that landed peasant women have been able to use their superior fall-back position, terminating unhappy marriages when a husband's behavior became too abusive. In this region, considerable marriage instability could be observed in the mid-1970s among all groups of peasant women, but women landowners were in much a stronger position to use "the threat-point" and evict a spouse than women who had no land or home of their own. Moreover, landed women were also quick to remarry, often marrying men much younger than themselves, with their ownership of land serving as an element of attraction (Deere 1990: 128–29, 141, 309, 313).

Sarah Bradshaw (1995b: 121) also notes how in rural Honduras land plays a critical role in conditioning the ability of women to separate from an unhappy marriage. Land ownership by women also enhances their security in old age by increasing their bargaining power over grown children. Ester Roquas's (1995) Honduran case study documents in detail the crucial role that ownership of land plays for widows. While elderly women will often rent their land, with rental income being one of their main sources of income, it also is not uncommon for them to work part of the land themselves with the help of wage labor, such as a parcel planted with coffee trees. Most importantly for widows living alone, their ownership of land considerably enhances their bargaining power in relations with their grown children, who are more likely to keep assisting their mother— through the provision of labor or cash—while she keeps control of her own landholdings.[44]

These examples demonstrate some of the ways in which rural women's ownership of land strengthens their fall-back position and hence their bargaining position within the household and family, leading to potentially more favorable outcomes for them. They also illustrate the more general point that ownership of assets is related to women's ability to act autonomously and to voice their own interests in negotiations affecting their own lives and those of their children. Not surprisingly, women's ownership of land can also be a cause of tension and domestic conflict, for it challenges relations of power: "The fact that women are owners of property is resented by their partners, and is not well viewed publicly, particularly when they are wealthier than men, for this goes against the view that men are the breadwinners and providers. The immediate association is one that links property to domination and authority; thus, when both members of a couple are owners it requires new gender arrangements and obliges them to negotiate" (Castañeda 2000: 10). In other words, command over property strengthens women's bargaining power in the terms introduced earlier, both "power over" and "power with." If increased bargaining power enhances the power to command the compliance of others or to control their actions, we are talking about "power over"; to the extent that increased bargaining power results in the ability to negotiate as equals, based on a position of strength, we are talking about "power with," which is the goal of feminist processes of empowerment.

This analysis of women's ownership of land, and of assets in general, is important at two levels. It is important for what it reveals in terms of the constituent elements of economic empowerment and also about the transformative potential of women's struggle for asset ownership. As Agarwal (1994a: 44–45) argues:

> It is not just an increase in women's command over economic resources, but also the *process* by which that increase occurs that has a critical bearing on gender relations. Land rights are not a "given" and will not be "provided" to most South Asian women without contestation. Acquiring those rights . . . will require simultaneous struggles against many different facets of gender inequalities embedded in social norms and practices. . . . It will require shifts in power balances in women's favour in several different arenas: within the household, in the community and market, and at different tiers of the State apparatus. Even to organize collectively often requires challenging existing norms. . . . it is precisely the complex and wide-ranging nature of these obstacles that gives the struggle to overcome them a transformative potential; and this is also why a successful struggle by women for land is likely to have more far-reaching implications for gender relations in South Asia than possibly any other single factor.

One of the main reasons that we embarked on this research was to join and contribute to the ongoing process of contestation over land rights in which rural women in Latin America are currently engaged. We undertook this task with a certain urgency because the late 1990s and early years of the new millennium may constitute the defining moment for rural women's ownership of land, given the fact that most Latin American governments are currently pursuing relatively large-scale land-titling projects among smallholders. Once those land titles are issued and registered, it will be much more difficult to contest ownership of land within the household and community. Thus, rather than demonstrating how women's ownership and control over land results in women's greater bargaining power— an issue that requires much further empirical research—our primary focus is on documenting what rural women have already gained or achieved with respect to land rights and ownership of land as well as the process through which they have successfully done so in different contexts. Our aim is that the information and analysis contained in this book will contribute to the ongoing process of empowerment of rural women.

two

Gender, Property Rights, and Citizenship

Potestad marital *is the sum of rights that the law gives to the husband over the person and property of his wife.*[1]

NOTWITHSTANDING DIFFERENT LEGAL TRADITIONS, in the early
nineteenth century married women in Latin America shared a similar status to their counterparts in the United States, England, and most of continental Europe: they were subject to the authority of their husbands in
almost all of their affairs. Nonetheless, married women in colonial Latin
America had greater bargaining power within marriage than did their
counterparts in the United States and England. Under the Iberian codified
tradition, in contrast to British common law, married women could own,
inherit, and will property; moreover, inheritance norms favored gender-
equitable distribution of property. A married woman's fall-back position
in Latin America was thus much stronger for, in case of separation or
widowhood, women were entitled to the property they brought into the
marriage as well as one-half the common property, possibilities denied
under common law.

Over the course of the nineteenth century, these patterns were reversed:
married women in the United States and England gained greater disposi-

tion over their own property and incomes while the property rights of their counterparts in Latin America failed to improve much with independence. The reform of Latin American civil codes during the last quarter of the nineteenth and first half of the twentieth century was highly contested, but country by country and in a piecemeal fashion married women attained a full legal personality and stronger property rights. Latin American women lagged behind their northern counterparts not only in attaining these but also in acquiring citizenship, with women not being granted the vote in most countries until the 1940s and 1950s.

It should be borne in mind that, until recent decades, any discussion of the property rights of married women excluded a large share of the adult, nonwhite female population. Women in consensual unions were legally single,[2] so that they were free of most of the restrictions applicable to married women. However, they did not enjoy any legal protection in terms of property rights within the union, nor did their children in terms of inheritance rights. Class, race, and ethnicity were strongly correlated with the incidence of marriage versus living in a consensual union, with the latter principally characterizing the popular sectors.[3] Two other reforms critical to improving women's bargaining power within marriage—besides the legal recognition of consensual unions—would also have to await the second wave of feminism in Latin America: the establishment of the dual-headed household—where husband and wife share responsibility for household representation and the management of property—and civil divorce.

Comparative and Historical Perspectives on Property Rights

The legal heritage of the Spanish American republics was based on Hispanic law as codified in the Iberian province of Castile from the thirteenth century on.[4] According to legal scholar José María Ots y Capdequi (1969: 51), transposed to the New World "the basis of personal relations between spouses within marriage was the subordination of women to the authority of their husbands." For Silvia Arrom (1985a: 56–62), the historian who has given most detailed attention to women's legal position under Spanish law, the legal inequality of women in Hispanic America was due to a combination of restriction and protection. Because of their sex, all women were presumed to be incapable of certain activities, such as those involving leadership or governance.[5] Arrom holds that while women were generally considered to be less judicious than men, this was not always due to their presumed mental inferiority but rather because such activities were considered to be unbecoming to women. That is, inequities were justified on the grounds of propriety and tradition. Arrom argues that Hispanic law did acknowledge women's mental capacities in that single women, whether widows or emancipated daughters, had the right to conduct their own legal affairs.[6] Wives also maintained an independent juridical personality, although to conduct most activities they required their husbands' consent. Dating back to the Siete Partidas of the thirteenth century, women enjoyed the "privilege" of protection because they were considered to be weaker than men in body, mind, and character (ibid.: 56). In return for a husband's protection and economic support, a wife owed him obedience and was subject to his authority in almost every aspect of her life.

In Spanish America this protection took a number of forms with respect to property rights.[7] A father of sufficient economic means was required to endow his daughters at the time of their marriage. The dowry was designed to help provision a new couple in addition to being a form of financial security for the bride in case she was widowed or separated. It was considered the property of the wife although it was managed by her husband. The dowry could not be used as collateral, and if a husband went bankrupt, it was exempt from foreclosure. Moreover, if a husband mismanaged the dowry, it could be removed from his control and, in case of separation, management of the dowry reverted to the wife. At marriage husbands could also endow their wives with a gift of property known as the *arras*.[8] This too was managed by the husband, but it too could not be used as collateral nor foreclosed in the case of bankruptcy.

The marital regime—known today as the "participation in profits regime" (*gananciales*)—was built around the notion of a conjugal society composed of three types of properties: those belonging to the husband, those belonging to the wife, and the common property of the couple, which belonged equally to them both. The latter included any property acquired during marriage from the salary or earnings of either spouse; rents from real estate; and the rent, income, or profits generated by their separate funds. Specifically excluded from common property was any property that each spouse brought into marriage or acquired through inheritance or donation after marriage. Common property was managed by the husband, and he could dispose of it (including his wife's earnings) without her consent. But the system was quite favorable to widows. Should the husband die, half of the common property was automatically retained by the widow, irrespective of how much each had brought to the marriage or who had worked to produce it. Another characteristic of property rights under the Spanish colonial regime was its flexibility. Under what are known as *capitulaciones matrimoniales,* the couple could contract at the time of marriage to exclude any specific property from the participation-in-profits regime, or all property, forming what would become known as the "separation-of-property" marital regime. Alternatively, through *capitulaciones,* a couple could establish an "absolute community of property," or full common-property regime, whereby all individual property brought into or inherited during marriage was treated as the common property of both spouses (Ots y Capdequi 1969: 56).

With respect to inheritance, married women had the right to make out their own will, bequeathing their own property as well as their half of the common property. Persons could only freely will one-fifth of their estate if they had living children. Four-fifths of the estate went automatically to the children, in equal shares irrespective of sex.[9] A wife had the right to accept and manage an unencumbered inheritance; she needed a husband's permission to renounce an inheritance or to accept one that was encumbered (since this might be financially prejudicial to her). Any earnings from these inheritances, however, formed part of the common property.

Besides inheritances, the other property that a married woman owned and managed consisted of her personal belongings, such as the jewelry and clothes she brought into marriage. These were known as *bienes parafernales.* In sum, a husband controlled most but not all of a wife's property. He was also her legal representative and could act in her name without her permission. While a wife could enter into contracts or initiate a suit in court, she needed her husband's permission in order to act on her own behalf. However, a wife could file suit against her husband in order to separate from him and recover her property (including half of the common property) and punish him for mistreating her (Arrom 1985a: 67). Married women, particularly those of means, thus had a relatively strong fall-back position.

The extent to which married women were legally incapable under Spanish law, accorded the same status as minors or the demented, is a point of contention in the literature. According to María Gabriela Leret de Matheus (1975: 55), in one of the few books on the comparative legal status of women in Latin America, the incompetence of married women was established in the Leyes de Toro, which laid out precisely what women could and could not do without the permission of their husbands. She cites favorably the text by legal scholars Ambrosio Colin and Henry Capitant stating that "the incapacity of married women in Latin American legislation appears as a bastard institution, born of two different tendencies: the old trunk of *potestad marital,* which forms its base, with a new idea of protection" of women (ibid.: 55). *Potestad marital,* with its roots in Roman law, has been defined as "the sum of rights that the law gives to the husband over the person and property of his wife."[10]

Arrom (1985a: 73) stresses the protective aspects of Hispanic law but argues that the status of women was different from that of minors. For example, wives could have some property removed from the control of their husbands if they mismanaged it, but minors could not do the same. Neither did minors have separate funds (the *bienes parafernales*), nor could they write a will. Legal scholar Beatriz Bernal de Bugeda (1975: 26–27) emphasizes how the basic principle of Spanish law with respect to matrimony was the total submission of wives to their husbands' authority. While this placed limitations on women's legal competence, she argues that this was mediated by a series of regulations that, in effect, recognized her mental capacity. For example, a husband could give his wife a general license to undertake almost all legal actions without his explicit consent; and if she acted without his permission, her actions could be legally recognized by him after the fact. In sum, the incapacity of married women was a *relative* incapacity.

The position of married women in colonial Brazil was similar in most respects to that of their counterparts in colonial Spanish America. The main difference was in terms of the default regime governing marriage, which was that of full common property (*comunhão universal*). Also, the rules of inheritance were slightly different, with testamentary freedom limited to one-third of a person's estate (Nazzari 1995; Lewin 1992).

In comparison, under British common law (the body of legal doctrine resulting from court decisions since medieval times), married women were viewed as an extension of their husbands. Writing in 1769, William Blackstone, a leading expert on British common law, described the situation as follows: "By marriage, the husband and the wife are one person in the law . . . the very being and legal existence of the woman is suspended during the marriage, or at least is incorporated into that of her husband under whose wing [and] protection she performs everything" (in Nicholas et al. 1986: 27).

In the United States, the British common law tradition formed the basis of the "merger of identities" doctrine that governed family affairs in most states until the last quarter of the nineteenth century (Nicholas et al. 1986: 27–28). This meant that upon marriage the wife became a legal "non-person." With respect to property, wives lost the right to manage any real estate they brought into marriage. Husbands gained not only managerial rights but also complete ownership of any other kind of property that had belonged to the wife. Married women could not make out a will; thus upon a wife's death a husband automatically acquired ownership of her real estate. They also could not inherit property in their own names, and hence a wife's inheritance became her husband's property. Married women could not sue or be sued but rather had to rely upon their husbands, who became the legal owner of any damage awards won by her suit. Moreover, any wages earned by a married woman belonged to her husband. In case of separation or divorce, wives were not automatically entitled to a share of the property acquired during marriage nor to the gains derived from any property they had brought into marriage.[11]

It was this latter point, in particular, that made the position of married women so much more onerous in the early nineteenth-century United States, as compared to Latin America, for a married woman in the United States had very little bargaining power over an abusive husband.[12] While ecclesiastic divorce was rare in Spanish America, the threat of divorce—with the possibility that a wife could gain control over her half of the common property in addition to her dowry—was often sufficient to alter a husband's behavior (Arrom 1985a: 80). Arrom argues that, in general, the protective features of Hispanic law with respect to a married woman's property gave women some power in marriage. Asunción Lavrin and Edith Couturier (1979: 303) also argue that the system of partible and bilateral inheritance—with sons and daughters inheriting equal shares from both parents—provided married women with a means to exert their will and choice, a source of bargaining power not available to women in England and the United States in this period. But on one point Luso-Hispanic law and the English common law tradition coincided, severely weakening the bargaining position of women: the husband was the sole responsible parent of any children born of marriage and, unless he was the guilty party, he automatically obtained custody of children above a certain age in case of separation.[13] But the fact that in Hispanic America women maintained an independent juridical personality, so that they could own property and bequeath it, also meant that mothers had greater bargaining power over their children and their futures.

In the United States and Great Britain, the organized campaign for married women's property rights, suffrage, and equal citizenship began in the mid-nineteenth century and gained strength with the Married Women's Property Acts in the last quarter of that century. In the United States, the Married Women's Property Acts were passed state by state and on a step-by-step basis beginning in mid-century until the early twentieth century.[14] New York in 1848 was among the first states to recognize the property rights of married women in the following terms: "The real and personal property, and the rents, issues and profits thereof of any female now married shall not be subject to the disposal of her husband, but shall be her sole and separate property as if she were a single female" (in Nicholas et al. 1986: 32). As a result of the Married Women's Property Acts, by the early twentieth century married women in most states could own and dispose of their own property, leave wills, retain and spend their own wages, manage their own businesses, and sue and be sued (ibid.: 28). In England the process began in 1870 with a law that allowed married women to dispose of their own wages and independent earnings.[15] The Married Women's Property Act of 1882 gave married women further economic autonomy by allowing them to enter into contracts, join suits, and leave wills (Claro Solar 1978, vol. 1, t. 2: 78; Whittick 1979: 24).

Those who wrote the post-independence constitutions of Latin America assumed that women had a nationality but not a citizenship defined by the exercise of political rights (Lavrin 1994: 105). Most of these constitutions were inspired by the democratic ideals contained in the constitutions of the United States and France, which proclaimed all citizens to be equal under the law. As in those countries in this period, citizenship, nonetheless, was implicitly defined as a male domain. The language of citizenship proved a difficulty for nineteenth-century Latin American legislators, for even though the word "citizen" in Spanish (*ciudadano*) is grammatically masculine, it does not explicitly exclude women.[16] The case of Costa Rica is illustrative. Due to internal political unrest, between 1821 and 1949 this country had eighteen different constitutions.[17] In the constitution of 1824 voting citizens were defined "as all inhabitants, native born or naturalized, who were eighteen years of age, had an honest job or profession, and could exercise their rights (i.e., were not mentally incompetent or criminals)" (Sharratt 1997: 63). The constitution of 1841 was more restrictive, adding a property requirement, but women were not explicitly denied the vote until 1848. In that constitution "women were *explicitly* excluded from voting when a *citizen* was defined as a male, age twenty-one or over" (ibid.: 64). The word "male" was dropped from the 1859 constitution, and this definition of citizenship prevailed in the constitutions of 1869 and 1871, with the main requirements for voting being the ownership of property or gainful

employment and literacy. As Sara Sharratt argues, "Only patriarchal interpretation decided that women were excluded from the above definition"
(ibid.). Perhaps to clarify matters, the 1917 constitution once again specifically excluded women. Paradoxically, all constitutions since 1825 have
stated that "all Costa Ricans are equal under the law" (ibid.).[18]

It was a number of years after independence before Latin American
legislators turned their attention to sorting through the morass of colonial laws governing civil affairs. Particularly appealing was the relative
simplicity of the Napoleonic Code of 1804, inspired by the individualism
and egalitarianism of the French Revolution. But while the basic pillar of
the Napoleonic Code was that all were equal before the law, this equality
did not extend to married men and women. According to Article 213 of
this code, "The husband owes his wife protection; the wife obedience to
her husband" (Mazeaud and Mazeaud 1976: 7). Various authors link the
relative legal incapacity of married women in the civil codes adopted in
Latin America in the nineteenth century to the Napoleonic Code, and argue
that it was because of this code that the concepts of *potestad marital* and
patria potestad were retained in the codes of the new republics (FAO 1992:
15, 22).[19] According to Leret (1975: 59), "That French code consecrates the
highest conception of the condition of man, and at the same time maintains that odious, traditional conception of women's subordination and
tutelage in society. She can do anything with the husband's consent. She can
do nothing without the husband's permission. And due to that Corsican
soldier many Latin American women are still subject to *potestad marital*."

While Article 213 of the Napoleonic Code would subsequently be
copied verbatim into a number of the Latin American civil codes,[20] most
of the nineteenth-century Latin American civil codes closely followed Spanish colonial legal tradition with respect to personal and family law. Among
the common features of the civil codes adopted by most Latin American
countries in the nineteenth century were the following: (1) limited female
legal capacity under *potestad marital;* (2) male representation of the household; (3) administration by the husband of the common property of the
conjugal society and of the property brought into marriage by the wife;
(4) the right of the husband to restrict his wife's employment outside the
home and to control her earnings; (5) the right of the husband to determine the residency of the couple; (6) the requirement that wives pledge
obedience and fidelity to their husbands; and (7) the authority of the father
over children and their property (*patria potestad*) (FAO 1992; Valencia Zea
and Ortiz Monsalve 1995; Lavrin 1995: 194–97).

Nineteenth-century civil codes regulated the contractual aspects of marriage but deferred to canon law in terms of the consecration of marriage. One of the main issues in the stormy relationship between church and state throughout the nineteenth century was the establishment of civil marriage. Lavrin (1995: 193) argues that before the juridical personality of women within the family could change, church-state relations first had to change.[21] This process was initiated in Mexico with the anticleric reform of 1859 (Arrom 1985b: 305), in the Southern Cone in the years 1884–89, and in Central America with the liberal revolutions of this same period.[22]

During the second half of the nineteenth century there were two main departures from Spanish colonial law with respect to property rights, one expanding the choice of property regimes from which couples could choose upon marriage, and the other regarding inheritance rights. These latter changes are analyzed in a subsequent section. Mexico in its 1870 civil code was the pioneer in the region in introducing a choice in marital regimes.[23] Besides the colonial default regime of *gananciales,* couples could choose at the time of marriage to maintain separate ownership and administration of their property, including any property they acquired during marriage and the fruits of this property (Arrom 1985b: 312).

This option represented an enhancement of women's property rights because married women, for the first time, had the formal option of choosing to control their own income directly. But, as Arrom points out, whether it served to improve women's position very much depended on their class position and the relative value of their assets and income as compared to those of their husbands. It surely was an advance for working women who under this option would no longer have to turn over control of their wages or other income to them. Whether it benefited a woman of property depended on the relative value of her own and her husband's individual estates, their relative income-generating possibilities, and his skill at managing their individual and joint estates. For women with inherited capital and business acumen, the separation-of-property regime might prove very attractive. As Arrom argues, in the case of women who neither owned property nor earned wages or other income this option could mean a loss of economic protection for, if separated or widowed, they would no longer be entitled to half of the common property generated through the husband's earnings during the marriage. Perhaps cognizant of the uneven effects of this option on different groups of women, the authors of the 1870 code retained the *gananciales* regime as the default option, that is, as the regime governing marriage unless otherwise specified.[24]

The introduction of the separation-of-property regime in Mexico expanded the range of personal choice available to husbands and wives. Nonetheless, this reform was discriminatory in that a wife still required her husband's consent to alienate or donate her property whereas a similar restriction did not apply to the husband's management of his separate property (Arrom 1985b: 313). Another reform to the rules governing the *gananciales* marital regime did increase the bargaining power of wives within marriage. The 1870 code specified for the first time that "Dominion and possession of common property is to reside with both spouses," meaning that a wife's consent was required to sell or mortgage real estate pertaining to the common fund; similarly, her consent was required either to accept or reject a common inheritance (Arrom 1980: 504). While this was a definite enhancement of women's property rights, it was only applicable to real estate, and the husband could sell or mortgage other property without the consent of his wife. Overall, then, as Arrom concludes, this reform hardly eradicated but did help mitigate the disparity in women's and men's property rights in marriage.[25]

Civil Code Reform, Suffrage, and the Women's Movement

The first wave of the women's movement, which emerged in Latin America at the end of the nineteenth and in the early decades of the twentieth century, necessarily had a broad agenda, one that included demands for female suffrage, enhancement of the legal capacity of married women, and attainment of their full property rights. This struggle was highly contested and spanned most of the century. Women gained the vote in Latin America much later than their counterparts in New Zealand (1893), Europe (beginning in 1910), and the United States (1920) (Daley and Nolan 1994: 349–50), and in some cases decades after the establishment of universal male suffrage in the region.[26] In some cases, following the pattern in the United States and England, married women gained broader property rights many decades before women were granted the vote. In other cases, the attainment of suffrage went hand in hand with married women securing full property rights, and sometimes suffrage preceded civil code reform. The particular sequence of events largely reflected country-specific factors.[27]

The reform of property rights that began in Mexico spread throughout Central America in concert with the liberal revolutions in that region. In Table 2.1 we attempt to distinguish between married women's achievement of fuller legal capacity and their right to administer their own property because achieving a juridical personality to be a witness, appear in court, sue, and be sued—without their husbands' permission—did not always go in tandem with married women achieving the right to administer their own property. The latter was usually accomplished by the adoption in civil codes of the separation-of-property marital regime option (as in Mexico) or by special legislation for married working women. The process of ridding civil codes of all vestiges of *potestad marital* was slow and piecemeal; not all aspects of a husband's rights over the person and property of his wife were eradicated at once.

In 1887 Costa Rica's new civil code recognized married women's legal capacity and established the separation-of-property regime as the *default* regime governing marriage, being the first Latin American country to do so (Claro Solar 1978, vol. 1, t. 2: 78). Unless otherwise specified at the time of marriage (through *capitulaciones*), married women retained ownership and control over any property they acquired prior to or during marriage and the earnings these generated; they were also permitted to enter into contracts and join in suits without their husbands' consent (Articles 76 and 78 in Costa Rica 1887). But this enhancement came at a cost, since wives no longer had any automatic claim on the income or profits generated by their husbands during marriage unless they specifically contracted to pool certain income to create common property. While this reform abolished certain aspects of *potestad marital,* it maintained others regarding the husband's rights over the person of his wife. For example, a wife must obey her husband and live with him and follow him should he change residence; in return, the husband owed the wife protection and was responsible for the family's maintenance (Articles 73 and 74).

The civil code reforms at the turn of the century in neighboring El Salvador, Nicaragua, and Honduras also recognized married women's legal capacity and fuller property rights, adopting the separation-of-property regime as the default option. The commission that drafted El Salvador's 1902 civil code gave eloquent reasons for abolishing *potestad marital:* "With the pretext of protecting the married woman and taking care of her interests, civil law deprives her of the administration and enjoyment of her property, inhibits her from disposing of what is hers, and submits her to the *potestad* or tutelage of her husband, without whose intervention or authorization she cannot contract or join a suit. . . . That such a regime is inconsistent with the principles of natural rights is a point of which the Commission has no doubt" (El Salvador 1959: 17–18). Nonetheless, the

TABLE 2.1. Enhancing Married Women's Property Rights,
Selected Latin American Countries

	Civil Code Reformed	Legal Capacity of Married Women	Administration of Own Property	Gender Equality in Household Representation and Management
Argentina	1869	1968	1926	No
Bolivia	1830	1972	1972	1972
Brazil	1916	1962	1962	1988
Chile	1855	1979	1925	No
Colombia	1873	1932	1932	1974
Costa Rica	1841	1887	1887	1973
Cuba	1889	1917	1917	1975
Ecuador	1860	1970	1949	1989
El Salvador	1859	1902	1902	1994
Guatemala	1877	1963	1986	1998
Honduras	1898	1906	1906	No
Mexico	1866	1917	1870	1928
Nicaragua	1867	1904	1904	No
Peru	1852	1984	1936	1984
Uruguay	1868	1946	1946	1946
Venezuela	1847	1942	1942	1992

Sources: Valdés and Gomáriz (1995: 140–43); Leret (1975: 71–95); Lavrin (1995: chap. 6); Zimmerman (1954); Claro Solar (1978, vols. 1, 2); Galán (1998); and authors' interviews. Also see, for Bolivia, Iñíguiz de Salinas and Pérez (1997); for Brazil, Barsted and Garcez (1999); for Chile, Chile (1995); for Cuba, Stoner (1991) and Figueras (1945); for Colombia, Valencia Zea and Ortiz Monsalve (1997: 75–92; 1995: 173–75); for Ecuador, García (1992); for Honduras, Honduras (1997b); for Guatemala, Diario de Centro América 260, no. 56 (1998): 2; for Mexico, Arrom (1985b), Carreras Maldonado and Montero Duhalt (1975), and Morineau (1975: 43); for Nicaragua, Nicaragua (1997a); and for Peru, Comisión de la Mujer (1997).

Note: The dates of the civil codes and their reforms are sometimes reported differently in the various sources, depending on whether they refer to the year of approval or when they went into effect. We report the earlier year.

civil code reform kept Article 182, which stated that "the husband owes protection to the woman, and the woman obedience to her husband." Moreover, *patria potestad* was maintained and thus the unequal position of parents with respect to their rights over their children. The new liberal codes in Nicaragua and Honduras also explicitly maintained that households were to be represented by the husband (Nicaragua 1997a; Honduras 1997).

After the Mexican revolution, the Carranza government's 1917 Law of Domestic Relations corrected some of the more glaring injustices faced by married women in the 1870 and 1884 civil codes. Married women acquired a full legal personality to administer their own property, draw up contracts, and take part in suits, being able to do so without their husbands' permission. This law also got rid of the clause whereby husbands owed their wives protection and wives obedience to their husbands. Nonetheless, women could only work outside the home with permission of their husbands. Other advances for women included the establishment of civil divorce and shared *patria potestad* (Carreras and Montero 1975: 72–80). The 1928 civil code went a step further, establishing complete juridical equality between men and women, and specifically gender equality in household representation and administration.[28] Nonetheless, this code still sanctioned the gendered division of labor whereby wives were explicitly charged with the direction of domestic work. Moreover, married women could work outside the home only if it did not impinge on their morality or interfere with their direction of the domestic work (Leret 1975: 88).

In Argentina, the most industrialized country in early twentieth-century Latin America, the move to reform its 1869 civil code was led by socialist feminists[29] supported by the growing number of women acquiring secondary and higher education and entering the labor force. Nonetheless, it took repeated attempts between 1918 and 1926 before reform measures were finally approved by the congress in that latter year (Little 1978: 243; Lavrin 1995: 209–11). While *potestad marital* was not formally suppressed, the 1926 code did lay out a series of activities that married women could undertake without permission from their husbands: administering and disposing of their own property;[30] accepting an inheritance; acting in suits; having a profession or a job and administering the earnings from such an activity; and joining civil, commercial, or cooperative associations (Leret 1975: 71–72). The reform fell short of feminist demands—the husband was still the administrator of the conjugal society, for example, and he continued to exercise *patria potestad* over the children—but it was considered a considerable improvement in the status of married women.

One of the reasons why the struggle for women's full citizenship in Latin America may have lagged behind that of the United States and Europe[31] was that within *potestad marital* there was actually considerable more flexibility with respect to property rights than in the northern common-law regimes and within marriage women had a stronger bargaining position. The potentially stronger position of elite Latin American women with respect to property rights provides one important explanation of why the struggle for women's full citizenship in Latin America would have to await the growth of a middle class, a process that accompanied the development of import-substitution industrialization. According to Francesca Miller (1991: 71), "Whereas many of the early proponents of women's rights in Latin America were upper-class women . . . it was female school teachers who formed the nucleus of the first women's groups to articulate what may be defined as a feminist critique of society, that is to protest against the pervasive inequality of the sexes in legal status, access to education and political and economic power." Besides the differing class structure, another factor limiting the growth of a reform movement in Latin America, and shaping its heterogeneity, was the high level of illiteracy among women through the 1950s.[32]

One factor fueling the demand for reform of property rights was the growing participation of women in the labor force, and the need in some countries to encourage such to support the industrialization effort (Velásquez Toro 1995: 191). Among the most egregious limitations faced by married women workers was the right of husbands to control their wages. As Lavrin (1995: 197) argues, the growing number of economically independent women—from both the working and middle class—"created new legal circumstances" not foreseen in the codes, encouraging review and revisions of the existing legislation.

A factor giving legitimacy to the growing demand for women's legal equality in the 1920s was a number of international conferences that brought together women as well as reform-minded men from throughout the Americas. The first International Feminine Congress in Latin America was held in Buenos Aires in 1910. Convened by the University Women of Argentina, it was attended by over two hundred women from Argentina, Uruguay, Paraguay, Chile, and Peru (Miller 1991: 73). The first efforts to create a regional organization of women in support of women's rights date from 1916. Women had been excluded as participants in the Second Pan-American Scientific Congress held in Washington, D.C., and the women in attendance held a parallel congress that voted to organize a Pan American Union of Women. National committees were subsequently organized throughout the hemisphere, and in 1922 these convoked the first Pan American Congress of Women in Baltimore. Most of the leadership of the Latin American women's movement was there, and they took the lead in the formation of the Pan American Association for the Advancement of Women. Carrie Chapman Catt, who led the struggle for women's suffrage in the United States, was elected its first president and Brazilian feminist Bertha Lutz became vice president. The main goals of the association were the attainment of women's suffrage and fuller property rights, and following the conference national umbrella groups were formed in most countries (ibid.: 83–87).

In Brazil Lutz subsequently established the Brazilian Federation for the Advancement of Women (Federação Brasileira pelo Progresso Feminino), an organization that was national in scope, in contrast to previous women's organizations. Chapman Catt began her South American tour at its inaugural conference in late 1922, events that generated momentum toward the attainment of women's suffrage in that country a decade later (Miller 1991: 83–87). One of the foremost tasks of the newly formed Pan American Association, according to Chapman Catt, was to expand women's property rights. Particularly egregious in her opinion was the fact that the property of married women passed to the control of their husbands and that husbands could claim their wives' wages (Hahner 1980: 82). According to Chapman Catt, "The vote is far less important to [South American] women than individual liberation from code and custom." This she explained by noting that "elections were almost meaningless" given the frequency of revolutions and prevalence of authoritarian governments (ibid.: 84).

Although few countries had a history of effective male suffrage, given the region's legacy of caudillo (strongman) rule, there are several other reasons why many Latin American feminist leaders initially gave less attention to suffrage than to the struggle for women's civil rights. Feminists were divided on the value of the vote, some disdaining to participate in what they considered a corrupt, masculine realm and others fearing that the female vote would be unduly influenced by the Catholic Church and supportive of the status quo rather than of the cause of feminism and reform. Others, however, championed the vote as a means to promote legislation enhancing women's property rights (Miller 1991: 86). During the 1920s, there was growing consensus in favor of the importance of women's suffrage, inspired partly by its attainment in the United States and partly by the growing legitimacy of the demand for women's civil and political equality in the hemisphere.

The Inter-American Commission of Women (IACW) was established as an official body at the Sixth Pan American Conference of the Pan American Union in 1928 in Havana. The first governmental organization to work for the rights of women, it held its initial hemispheric conference in 1930.[33] It was in this period that women first gained the vote in Ecuador, Brazil, Uruguay, and Cuba (see Table 2.2). Whereas in Ecuador women

TABLE 2.2. Attainment of Female Suffrage in Latin America

Pioneers:	Ecuador	1929/46
	Brazil	1932
	Uruguay	1932
	Cuba	1934
World War II period:	El Salvador	1939/50
	Dominican Republic	1942
	Guatemala	1945
	Panama	1945/46
	Costa Rica	1945/49
Post–World War II:	Argentina	1947
	Venezuela	1947
	Chile	1948/49
	Bolivia	1952
	Mexico	1953
	Colombia	1954
	Honduras	1955
	Nicaragua	1955
	Peru	1955
	Paraguay	1961

Sources: Miller (1991: 96); Chaney (1979: 69); Lavrin (1994: 184); and Valdés and Gomáriz (1995: 139).

Note: Where two years are noted, initial suffrage was limited or conditioned, or the legislation did not take effect until the latter year.

were granted the vote by a conservative regime hoping to expand its base of support, in these other countries suffrage was the result of years of struggle by the women's movement (Miller 1991: 96–97).

Among the factors that delayed women's suffrage in other countries was the competition between liberals and conservatives. While liberals generally supported social and economic reforms, including those improving women's legal status and property rights, they were wary of women's ties to the Catholic Church and afraid that women would overwhelmingly vote conservative (Valdés and Gomáriz 1995: 159–60). As Table 2.2 shows, only a few other countries granted women the vote prior to the end of World War II.[34] Most did so in the postwar period, when international opinion strongly favored women's suffrage.[35] The last country in Latin America to grant women the vote was Paraguay in 1961, a country then still characterized by caudillo rule.

The reform of Latin American civil codes began with married women attaining an enhanced legal capacity and the right to manage their own property and income, although these measures were often partial and incomplete. Moreover, in some countries—such as Brazil, Uruguay, Ecuador, Guatemala, and Bolivia—women gained suffrage before married women gained control over their economic affairs. Further, in most countries, even after these reforms, husbands continued to represent the household legally and to be charged with administering its affairs. In Colombia, for example, the 1932 civil code recognized the legal capacity of married women and established that they could manage and dispose of their own property. The reform, however, maintained Article 177 regarding *potestad marital,* or the rights a husband had over the person of his wife, although not her property. It was not until 1954 that female suffrage was attained. Gender equality in household representation and administration was not established until 1974. Until that year the husband was still charged with determining the couple's residency and had exclusive *patria potestad* over the children, and wives still had to pledge obedience as well as fidelity to their husbands (Valencia Zea and Ortiz Monsalve 1995, 1997).

In Brazil almost three decades passed after women obtained the vote before married women gained full legal capacity and enhanced property rights. Although the 1962 Civil Statute of Married Women maintained the male headship of the family, the statute "recognized the woman as the 'collaborator of the husband' in the management of the household" and granted her "innumerable rights independent of the husband's permission," such as to exercise a profession (Barsted and Garcez 1999: 22). In addition, this law created the special category of "reserved assets" (*bem reservado*) of married women, which were assets purchased by her from her own income. Married women were not required to share these assets with their spouses and were authorized to manage these independently. This was a major departure from the 1916 Civil Code, which had established the option of the separation-of-property regime, but had required that a married woman's assets be administered by her husband. It was not until the 1988 constitution that gender equality in household representation and management was established (ibid.).

Ecuador, which was also one of the pioneers in the region with respect to women's suffrage, did not abolish *potestad marital* until its 1970 reform of the civil code. While married women finally became legally capable, that infamous article of the Napoleonic code was retained: "a husband owes his wife protection and the woman obedience to the husband"

(Leret 1975: 73). Moreover, husbands continued to be the legal administrators of the property of the marital society, a situation that continued until the 1989 reform of the civil code. And although the 1989 reform established gender equality in household representation and administration, shared duties had to be declared at the time of marriage; otherwise, the default clause is still that a husband represents the family.[36]

The Guatemalan case also illustrates the contradictory nature of some of these civil codes well into the late twentieth century. In keeping with the 1985 constitutional reform that established equal rights between men and women, Article 78 of the 1986 civil code established the equality of rights and obligations of both spouses in marriage. Nonetheless, Article 109 maintained the husband as the sole representative of the household, although within it both spouses were to share authority over children and the domestic economy, including the choice of residency. Thus what was maintained as the essence of legal patriarchy was male household headship. This was supported by the gendered roles specified in Article 110, whereby "the husband owes the wife protection and assistance," and "the wife has the particular right and obligation to care for the younger children and direct the domestic work." The husband could also prohibit his wife's employment outside the home (Guatemala 1986: 72). These anomalies were not corrected until 1998, after a protracted struggle led by Guatemala's national women's office (ONAM 1997a, 1997b).

In Argentina, Chile, Nicaragua, and Honduras the husband still represents the household and is the sole administrator of the conjugal society under the default marital regime. This continues as the main form of legal discrimination against married women even though these countries are signatories to the 1979 UN Convention to End All Forms of Discrimination against Women, a convention that explicitly guarantees men and women equal rights before the law. This last vestige of legal patriarchy upholds the husband as the head of household for a number of reasons. While the changing economic circumstances of the twentieth century (industrialization, the growing dominance of capitalist class relations, and the increase in women's formal labor force participation) required that women exercise their full legal capacity, the primary fear of reformers and conservatives alike was of the challenge that equality posed to the stability of the family as the basic unit of society, a fear loudly voiced by the Catholic Church. It was inconceivable to many that a household could have two heads. As Lavrin (1995: 196) suggests, the obedience of wife to husband was seen as a "pragmatic solution to assigning the guiding role in a society of two persons implicitly assumed to be equal." But while it may have seemed pragmatic, it served to reproduce women's subordination to men.

The other practice that was slow to be adopted and highly contested— but necessary to enhancing women's bargaining position within marriage —was civil divorce, largely due to the opposition of the Catholic Church. Divorce has been one of the thorniest issues in church-state relations during this century, only having been legally recognized in Argentina in 1954, Colombia in 1976,[37] and Brazil in 1977.[38] Civil divorce is now possible in all Latin American countries with the exception of Chile (Valdés and Gomáriz 1995: 144), critically enhancing women's bargaining position within marriage.

Marital Regimes and the Recognition of Consensual Unions

Latin America today is characterized by three property regimes governing marriage, as shown in Table 2.3, with some minor variations: the full common-property regime; the participation-in-profits regime; and the complete separation-of-property regime.[39] The full common-property regime (*comunidad absoluta* or *diferida* or, in Brazil, *comunhão universal*) is based on the pooling of all property brought into or acquired during marriage. All profits or rents generated from such property are also pooled, as are the wages, salaries, or other income earned by either spouse. In the case of separation or divorce, all property and income is divided in equal shares between the spouses; in case of the death of one of them, his or her estate also consists of one-half of the common property, with the other half remaining with the surviving spouse.

The participation-in-profits regime (*sociedad conjugal, participación en los bienes gananciales, comunidad de gananciales,* or, in Brazil, *comunhão parcial*) is based on the separate recognition of the individual private property brought into or acquired during marriage, including in the latter any inheritances, donations, or concessions received by each spouse. However, any profits, rents, or other income derived from such property during the marriage (the *gananciales*) is considered to be common property. In addition, any property acquired during the marriage from wages, salaries, or other income also forms part of the couple's common property. In case of separation or divorce, half of the common property thus gener-

TABLE 2.3. Marital Regimes in Twelve Latin American Countries

Country/Year	Full Common Property	Participation in Profits	Separation of Property
Bolivia (1988)	—	Yes *	Yes
Brazil (1988)	Yes	Yes *	Yes
Chile (1994)	—	Yes *	Yes
Colombia (1996)	Yes	Yes *	Yes
Costa Rica (1978)	Yes	Yes	Yes *
Ecuador (1989)	—	Yes *	—
El Salvador (1994)	Yes *	Yes	Yes
Guatemala (1964)	Yes	Yes *	Yes
Honduras (1984)	Yes	Yes	Yes *
Mexico (1974)	—	Yes*	Yes
Nicaragua (1959)	Yes	—	Yes *
Peru (1984)	—	Yes *	Yes

Sources: Authors' interviews cited in text, FAO (1992), and, by country: for Bolivia, Bolivia (1990, 1991) and Iñíguez de Salinas and Pérez (1997); for Brazil, CFEMEA (1996) and Barsted (1996); for Chile, Claro Solar (1978, vol. 2) and Chile (1995: 29); for Colombia, Monroy (1979; 1996: 351), Valenzia Zea and Ortiz Monsalve (1995, 1997), and Valencia Zea (1978, 1992); for Costa Rica, Costa Rica (1985) and Badilla and Blanco (1996); for Ecuador, Carrión (1991); El Salvador, Ministerio de Justicia (1993) and CEMUJER (1994a, 1994b, 1994c); for Guatemala, Guatemala (1986); for Honduras, Honduras (1997a) and CDM (n.d.); for Mexico, Lexadin (1996); for Nicaragua, Centro de Derechos Constitucionales (1996a and 1996b) and Nicaragua (1997a); for Peru, Macassi León (1996a) and Eto Cruz (1989).

Note: Year refers to the last year the civil or family code was revised.

* Refers to the default regime.

ated is retained by each of the spouses; similarly, when one spouse dies, his or her estate is made up of half of the common property. Whatever the cause for dissolution of this regime, the individual property brought into marriage or acquired through inheritance is maintained by the spouse who was the original owner. Under the separation-of-property regime, each individual maintains ownership and administration of the property they brought into marriage, as well as that acquired during marriage through inheritance, donation, or concessions and the profits generated from such, and any property acquired during marriage with their own income. If the union is terminated, each spouse retains their own individual property and the gains or profit from these.

While for analytical purposes we have tried to distinguish between countries according to the regimes they offer and their default regime, in several cases this is difficult to do. In the case of Mexico, for example, couples have great flexibility in designing their own regime through *capitulaciones*.[40] The default regime most closely resembles that of participation in profits since if the union is dissolved each spouse retains their own individual property, specifically any property received as an inheritance or gift. The distribution of the profits generated by this separate property (i.e., whether they are pooled and divided in half or retained by the owner of the property that generated them) nonetheless depends on what the couple specifies at the time of marriage; if no *capitulaciones* are made, it is assumed that they are common property.[41]

Most Latin American countries in recent years have adopted gender-equitable norms that establish that the household may be represented either jointly, by the husband and wife, or by either of the spouses, and that common property (in either the full common-property or in the participation-of-profits regime) may be jointly administered. Sometimes, however, the administrator must be specified at the time of marriage, as in the case of Ecuador; if a couple fails to specify the administrator explicitly, the husband is assumed to be the administrator. The exceptions, among our twelve case studies, with respect to provisions for the joint administration of common property are Chile, Honduras, and Nicaragua. By our definition of marital regimes, Chile is characterized by two variants of the participation-in-profits regime. First is what in Chile is termed the *sociedad conjugal,* in which real estate remains the individual property of the spouse who brought it into marriage, with only the profits from such being shared as common property. This variant, which is the default option, is still administered by the husband. The second variant, the *régimen de participación en las gananciales,* is similar to the above except that each partner manages their own individual property, although profits are pooled and divided equally if the regime is dissolved.[42]

As Table 2.3 shows, most of the countries studied here have at least two marital regimes from which couples may choose; six of the twelve countries formally offer all three variants. If no particular regime is chosen at the time of marriage, the default option pertains, and in eight countries (Bolivia, Brazil, Chile, Colombia, Ecuador, Guatemala, Mexico, and Peru) it is the participation-in-profits regime; in one (El Salvador),[43] full common property is followed; and in three (Costa Rica, Honduras, and Nicaragua), the separation-of-property regime prevails.

In most countries at the time of marriage, one can make *capitulaciones,* or written, legal declarations specifying property rights over specific assets. Such declarations are always required in the separation-of-property and sometimes in the participation-in-profits regimes in order to establish clearly which property belongs to each spouse. In countries where the default option is the complete separation of property, through *capitulaciones* a couple may provide for some property to be governed as common property. In most countries couples can change regimes or make *capitulaciones* anytime during the marriage, introducing considerable flexibility into the marital contract.

A particular problem that arises under the separation-of-property regime (and may also occur under the participation-in-profits regime) is that a husband may purchase property with household funds (generated by all or some of the members) but register such property, such as a land title, only in his own name. In the event of separation or divorce, the wife has little recourse in terms of claiming co-ownership if her name does not appear on the title. Moreover, if the wife's name is not on the title, the husband may sell or mortgage this land without her consent. In order to protect wives, some countries have required each spouse's consent (sometimes termed the "double signature") to sell or mortgage any major piece of common property (but usually only real estate, an *inmueble*). This is the case in Chile, a country that has not yet adopted norms of gender equality in the administration of household property. Honduras, where the husband also administers the common property of the marriage, does not have provisions for the double signature. In Bolivia, the civil code specifies that if an item of common property is sold without the consent of one spouse, the other may annul the sale with respect to her or his half of the property (Iñíguez de Salinas and Pérez 1997: 56).[44]

Another provision that has been adopted in almost all of the Latin American civil codes provides for the protection of "family patrimony," the latter defined as the family home or primary residence, although in some cases it also applies to land under a certain size limitation. This family patrimony must usually be officially declared as such before a judge, in which case the property may not be sold, mortgaged, or subject to foreclosure while there is a child residing at home under the legal age of emancipation, or until the union is dissolved. In practice, since the declaration of family patrimony requires legal registration—which is often costly and time consuming—few families actually exercise this right (FAO 1992: 36–37). Moreover, few women, particularly rural women, are aware of this potential protection from dispossession in case of their abandonment or separation.

A few countries have made special provisions in their civil codes regarding agricultural land. In Peru if the marital society breaks up due to the death or permanent absence of the spouse, the remaining spouse is to get preferential adjudication of the home and of the "agricultural establishment."[45] Bolivia is the only country whose civil code specifies that property acquired through concession or adjudication by the state should form part of the common property of the couple, a provision potentially covering land distributed through the agrarian reform.[46]

It is difficult to assert which marital regime is the most favorable to women since different countries have differing provisions to safeguard the interests of wives. Moreover, laws often differ from customary practice. Nonetheless, the extent of gender bias in the legal marital regime is influenced by two crucial factors: the relative amount or value of the property that men and women bring into marriage, and the probability that men and women will earn significantly different levels of income during the marriage. If we assume that, due to discriminatory inheritance practices, men will be more likely than women to bring a larger patrimony into the marriage (or inherit such during the marriage) and also to have greater income-generating capabilities over their lifetimes (because of gender inequities in the division of labor and in employment opportunities, relative wages, and access to capital), then it is apparent that the full common-property regime is most favorable for women. It could also be argued that the common-property regime is the most equitable in that it provides implicit economic recognition of the gendered division of labor by which women are largely responsible for domestic labor and child rearing. To a certain extent, the participation-in-profits regime does this as well. However, should the union be dissolved, the common-property regime is much more favorable than the latter for, given our assumptions, the former would result in a transfer of assets from the husband to the wife for services rendered. By this same set of assumptions, which are particularly relevant to the case of rural women, the least favorable marital regime for women would be that of complete separation of property.

By the above criteria, women are in the most favorable situation today in El Salvador, where full common property is the default option in marriage. They are potentially at the greatest disadvantage in those countries where the separation-of-property regime governs as the default option: Costa Rica, Honduras, and Nicaragua. But it is important to keep in mind that there is often a disjuncture between the legal framework and customary practice. This disjuncture is observed in a number of ways, reflecting the heritage of *potestad marital*. In the case of Ecuador, for example, while any property acquired by a couple automatically forms part of common property, in practice land titled under the name of the husband, even though acquired while the couple was married, is his to dispose of. The double signature required for the sale of durable property is rarely enforced in rural areas if the name of both spouses is not registered on the land title (E. García 1992). Cases are cited where a woman has lost her land because her husband has defaulted on a loan taken out without her consent (Jordan 1996: 62). As an indigenous woman leader reported, "The father gives [her] land and then they marry and the husband sells it. . . . This is against the law, but women are not aware of their rights."[47] In Guatemala the sale of property under the common-property or participation-in-profits regimes requires the formal authorization of both spouses. But until recently the administration of family property was the husband's prerogative, so that even now "the husband is owner and master of all the property . . . he can mortgage, sell or rent it."[48] These examples illustrate the distance that often exists between legal norms and customary practice, and they attest to why joint titling of land and other real estate—that is, the requirement that property be registered in the names of both spouses—is of crucial importance to the economic security of women.

In recent years attention has focused on the fact that at the moment of separation or divorce, women are very dependent on their husbands' goodwill. Among the myriad ways in which husbands have been accused of hiding or reducing common assets in Colombia, for example, are the temporary sale of property to third parties, the constitution of false business corporations, and the creation of fictive debts. Thus lawyers advise that any property acquired during marriage be jointly titled: "This is a form of reciprocal control."[49]

Another major change in women's status in recent decades has been the legal recognition granted to couples in consensual unions, as Table 2.4 shows. This reform has been very important since in a number of countries a relatively high proportion of couples are not formally married;[50] consensual unions are often the norm in rural areas of the Andes and Central America.[51] Official recognition of consensual unions means that such couples have most of the same rights and responsibilities as married couples, which is particularly important with respect to the management and inheritance of property, and thus land. Specifically, recognition means that the rules of the default marital regime apply to these unions.[52] In countries where the full common-property or *gananciales* regimes are enforced, these can bring considerable benefits to women if the earning power or property ownership among the partners is highly unequal, for if the couple breaks up, the common property of the union is recognized and divided in half. When consensual unions were initially recognized, not all countries gave these the same inheritance rights as marriages, as shown in Table 2.4.

Most countries place some requirements on consensual unions in order for these to be granted the same privileges as formal marriages. Generally, couples must prove that they have formed a stable relationship of two to five years' duration and have had children together. In addition, the partners must prove that they do not have any impediments to marriage—that is, that they are not married to and separated from someone else.[53] Usually, the couple must officially register their union in the presence of witnesses before a judge or notary public for it to receive the benefits of marriage.[54] Such procedures can be costly and time consuming, discouraging many rural couples from doing so.

Inheritance Rights

Under Spanish colonial law spouses generally did not inherit from one another. While the common property of the couple was divided into equal shares upon dissolution of the union (whether due to separation or death), the legitimate heirs of each spouse (entitled by law to four-fifths of the estate) were the legitimate children of either sex. Only in the absence of children (or descendants) and other legitimate heirs such as parents (or ascendants), did the widow or widower inherit the deceased spouse's estate. Since spouses did not normally inherit from each other, this meant that if the individually owned property of husband and wife differed significantly in value, children might end up in a much more favorable economic position than the surviving spouse, for only children inherited from the deceased parent. Judges, nonetheless, had considerable flexibility to ensure that a widow or widower not be left destitute.[55]

Chilean legislators sought to codify this latter practice by making provisions for what would become known as the *porción conjugal,* or marital portion, in their 1855 civil code. A share of the estates of deceased persons was automatically set aside for surviving spouses who were in economic need even if the deceased had willed otherwise.[56] This was a new imposition on the traditional limitations on testamentary freedom, one coming at the expense of the potential size of children's inheritance. The marital portion was also applicable in the case the deceased died intestate;

TABLE 2.4. Status of Consensual Unions in Twelve Latin American Countries

	Year Consensual Unions Recognized	Year Same Inheritance Rights as Marriage	Consensual Unions as Percentage of Couples
Bolivia	1938	1938	—
Brazil	1988	1994	—
Chile	No	No	4.8
Colombia	1990	1990	19.2
Costa Rica	1990	1995	14.0
Ecuador	1982	1998	25.6
El Salvador	1994	1994	—
Guatemala	1964	1964	—
Honduras	1984	1984	54.0
Mexico	1974	1928	—
Nicaragua	1987	1987	38.3
Peru	1984	No	28.5

Sources: Year consensual unions recognized and same rights: Authors' interviews and sources cited in Table 2.3. Consensual unions as a percentage of adults living in couples: Valdés and Gomáriz (1995: 54), which in turn is drawn from the country population censuses undertaken in the 1980s.

the other innovation here was that spouses were added (as were "natural" children) to the list of potential heirs, but in the second order of succession.[57] According to the advocates of the 1855 civil code, "We have sought to conciliate the right to property with the obligation to provide for the well-being of those to whom we have given life or whom we have received."[58]

Another change introduced in the 1855 Chilean code, as in other codes following the Chilean model,[59] was that the requirement was dropped whereby parents of means endowed daughters with a dowry. The dowry requirement was also dropped from the 1870 Mexican code, a change mirroring social practice at the time (Arrom 1985b: 315).[60] Of potentially greater consequence for daughters, and an abrupt departure from colonial practice, was the introduction of testamentary freedom in the 1884 Mexican code. Testamentary freedom increased the bargaining power and authority of parents over children since the latter could be dispossessed of any inheritance at all if they displeased their parents.[61] The losers were clearly the children but particularly daughters; this change increased their economic vulnerability, they being less likely to have careers or the same income-generating capabilities as their brothers.[62] Moreover, testamentary freedom introduced a new possibility for increasing gender inequality in the ownership of property since parents could now legally favor sons over daughters in inheritance, potentially undermining an important source of women's bargaining power within marriage.

But full testamentary freedom could also improve the position of some women, particularly widows, since husbands could now will them their entire estate. This reform thus opened up the possibility for widows to retain majority control of family land and businesses and to exert considerably greater bargaining power over their children, thus assuring them of much greater security in old age than had previously been the case. But enhancing women's ownership and control of property in this manner was totally dependent on their husbands' goodwill. This reform thus had potentially contradictory effects on different groups of women, depending on their class and familial (mothers versus daughters) position.

It would be a mistake, in our view, to conclude that the liberal reform of inheritance rights in Mexico, combined with the earlier broadening in marital-regime options, represented an "assault on the privileges of women" comparable to the liberal assault on the land and property rights of indigenous communities and the church, as Elizabeth Dore argues (2000a: 6).[63] Rather, these reforms were contradictory, potentially enhancing and undermining the property rights of different groups of women. Testamentary freedom probably did open the way for greater inequality in property ownership by sex and, due to gender roles, may also have enhanced differences in the composition of inheritance, with sons favored by the inheritance of land. However, if a parent died intestate children continued to inherit in equal shares. Moreover, testamentary freedom did not spread all over the continent; rather, over the next half century reforms of inheritance rights followed two distinct patterns, one favoring it and the other restricting it in order to provide greater security to widows.

In terms of the rules governing wills, as Table 2.5 shows, in four of the twelve countries here examined—Costa Rica, El Salvador, Guatemala, and Mexico—the husband[64] may freely will his estate to whomever he pleases.[65] The majority of countries continue to limit testamentary freedom. Six of the twelve countries studied here protect children from being disinherited. In these countries as long as there are living children (or descendants), a person may only will freely from one-fifth (Bolivia) to one-half (Brazil) of their estate.[66] Brazil and Ecuador include parents along with children among those who may not be excluded from a will. More varied is the degree and kind of protection offered wives.

TABLE 2.5. Inheritance Rules for Deceased Spouse's Estate under Default Marital Regime, Twelve Latin American Countries, 1990s

	Wills	*Intestate*
Country	*Share Free to Will*	*Rank Ordering*
Bolivia	⅕ if living children and spouse	#1 children, spouse, and parents
Brazil	½ if living children or parents	#1 children, spouse (¼) #2 spouse and parents if no living children
Chile	¼ if living children, marital share	#1 children, marital share #2 spouse (¼) and parents if no living children
Colombia	¼ if living children, marital share	#1 children, marital share #2 spouse (¼) and parents if no living children
Costa Rica	all	#1 children, parents, and marital share
Ecuador	¼ if living children and parents, marital share	#1 children, marital share #2 spouse and parents if no living children
El Salvador	all	#1 children, spouse, and parents
Guatemala	all	#1 children, marital share #2 spouse and parents if no living children
Honduras	¾, marital share	#1 children, marital share #2 spouse and parents if no living children
Mexico	all	#1 children, marital share #2 spouse and parents if no living children
Nicaragua	¾, marital share	#1 children, marital share #2 spouse (¼) and parents if no living children
Peru	⅓ if living children or spouse	#1 children, spouse, and parents

Source: Authors' interviews and by country: for Bolivia, Bolivia (1991); for Brazil, CFEMEA (1996) and Lexadin (1998); for Chile, Tomasello (1989); for Colombia, Valenzia Zea (1992) and Código Civil (1996); for Costa Rica, Costa Rica (1985); for Ecuador, Carrión (1991) and Larrea (1996); for El Salvador, Mendoza Orantes (1994) and Ministerio de Justicia (1993); for Guatemala, Guatemala (1986); for Honduras, Honduras (1997b); for Mexico, Lexadin (1996); for Nicaragua, Nicaragua (1997a); for Peru, Peru (1984a).

Note: In the rank ordering, all those listed as in the first order of inheritance (#1) automatically inherit equal shares of the deceased's estate. The exception are countries that place an absolute limit on the spouse's share or where such is determined according to the rules of the marital share. The second order of inheritance (#2) applies in the case that the deceased left no living children.

The civil codes most favorable to widows are those of Bolivia and Peru, for testamentary freedom is restricted in their and their children's favor, irrespective of the size of the spouses' patrimony. In Bolivia four-fifths of the estate must be set aside for the spouse and children, and in Peru two-thirds must be.[67] In the other countries with provisions protecting spouses (Chile, Colombia, Ecuador, Honduras, and Nicaragua), whether the widow is guaranteed a share of her husband's estate if he has willed otherwise depends on her economic need and the relative economic position of husband and wife. Honduras and Nicaragua differ from the three Andean countries in providing near-testamentary freedom (at least three-fourths of an estate can be freely willed), with the only restriction on wills being the *porción conjugal*. These provisions thus represent a combination of the liberal tradition of testamentary freedom with a concern to protect widows.

In most cases the state provides more protection to children and spouses with respect to inheritance when the deceased dies intestate. As Table 2.5 shows, in all countries, all legitimate children, irrespective of sex, are the first beneficiaries of the estate of either of their parents and they inherit equal shares.[68] In only three countries—Bolivia, El Salvador, and Peru—do wives have the same inheritance rights as children, in all three cases with the inheritance also to be shared with the deceased's parents. In all of the other countries the wife is entitled to a marital share of the deceased's estate. In Ecuador, Colombia, Honduras, and Nicaragua this marital share depends on economic need—whether the widow "lacks what is necessary for her reasonable subsistence," as determined by a judge.[69] The actual amount of this share is based on the relative value of the husband's and wife's estate subject to other restrictions; usually, it does not exceed one-fourth of the husband's estate.[70] If a widow does not qualify for the *porción conjugal,* she does not inherit from her husband unless there are no living children, in which case she must share his estate with his parents. In Chile, Colombia, and Nicaragua the widow's share in the second order of succession is limited to one-quarter of her husband's estate.

In Brazil and Guatemala whether and how much a widow inherits from her husband depends on the marital regime. In Brazil under either the default marital regime of *comunhão parcial* or the separation-of-profits regime, a widow has usufruct rights to one-quarter of her husband's estate if there are living children or to one-half of it if there are none. While these provisions appear quite favorable, the widow is not endowed with ownership rights over this property; moreover, she automatically loses this privilege if she remarries (Article 1611 in Lexadin 1998). Under the full common-property regime, a wife does not inherit from her husband at all unless there are no living children or parents (CFEMEA 1996: 63), a norm inherited from Portuguese colonial rule (Lewin 1992: 359). The widow, nonetheless, is guaranteed the usufruct of the family home as long as she does not remarry. Similarly, in Guatemala under the full common-property regime wives inherit from their spouses only if there are no living children. Under the participation-of-profits regime (which is the default regime), the widow is entitled to a marital share (depending on the relative size of the patrimony of each spouse) that may not exceed a child's inheritance share. Under the separation-of-profits regime, she inherits a share equal to that of each of the children (Guatemala 1986).

In terms of the inheritance rights of consensual unions, in some countries the initial reform of the civil code recognizing them either was not explicit with respect to inheritance rights or required further implementing legislation.[71] Thus, as Table 2.4 shows, although in Brazil consensual unions were recognized in 1988, it was not until 1994 that they were granted the same inheritance rights as marriages. Similarly, in Costa Rica these were accorded official status in 1990, but it was not until 1995 that consensual unions were granted similar inheritance rights. In Peru, where consensual unions have been recognized since 1979, partners still do not inherit from each other unless such is specified in a will. Children from consensual unions, however, have the same rights as children born of marriage. Chile is the only Latin American country where consensual unions are not recognized at all, for any purpose.

In the period of agrarian reform in Latin America a number of countries had agrarian codes that regulated inheritance of land distributed through the agrarian reform independently of the civil code. In most cases, these provisions were more favorable to widows and surviving partners than were the civil codes of the time. The primary concern expressed in the civil codes is that widows not be left destitute, and that their patrimony not be less than that which one of the children might inherit. This is expressed most strongly in terms of the rules of succession governing those who die intestate, where every country makes some provision for widows. This concern for the well-being of widows did not extend to impinge upon testamentary freedom in those countries most influenced by nineteenth-century liberalism. Nor did it extend to the possibility of widows maintaining control of the family farm or business—that is, providing for their own economic autonomy.

three

Gender Exclusionary Agrarian Reform

> *The men's organizations in order to get land take their women and children along, but once they acquire land, we women are left with nothing.*[1]

IN 1961 PRESIDENT John F. Kennedy announced a new partnership between the United States and Latin America, the Alliance for Progress, to be based on increased U.S. financial and technical assistance to the region and the commitment by Latin American states to fundamental socioeconomic reforms. In the Declaration to the Peoples of America of the Charter of Punta del Este, the signatory countries agreed

> To encourage, in accordance with the characteristics of each country, programs of comprehensive agrarian reform, leading to the effective transformation, where required, of unjust structures and systems of land tenure and use; with a view to replacing latifundia and dwarf holdings by an equitable system of property so that, supplemented by timely and adequate credit, technical assistance and improved marketing arrangements, the land will become for the *man* who works it the basis of *his* economic stability, the foundation of *his* increasing

welfare and the guarantee of *his* freedom and dignity. (OAS 1961: 3; our emphasis)

It is doubtful that the founding fathers of the Alliance for Progress meant to exclude women this explicitly from the advantages of the reforms, although the beneficiaries were always referred to in masculine terms. But most of the agrarian reforms initiated in this and earlier periods did in fact exclude women as direct beneficiaries. The reforms were meant to assist peasant families residing on large estates who worked under precapitalist forms of tenancy—those who provided labor services to landlords in return for usufruct rights to a plot of land and/or sharecroppers and *arrendatarios* (arrendires, renters)—in addition to landless households and those with insufficient land. It was assumed that peasant households were represented by a male head and that by benefiting household heads, all household members would benefit as well. This assumption corresponded to the provisions of most Latin American civil codes of the time. When the Alliance for Progress was promulgated, husbands were charged with the administration of the common property of the household and its representation in external affairs in all but one (Mexico) of the nineteen Latin American republics. Moreover, in several countries married women had still not acquired full legal capacity or the right to administer their own assets.

The Latin American agrarian reforms of the twentieth century were carried out under varying circumstances and contexts.[2] The first reform, that of Mexico in 1917, coincided with the Bolshevik revolution. Subsequent reforms took place in the context of the Cold War and were viewed through that prism by the United States. Although the United States supported agrarian reforms in Japan (1945), Taiwan (1947), and in Korea, Vietnam, and the Philippines (in the 1950s)—either to guarantee peace and stability or legitimize friendly governments (Montgomery 1984: 116–19) —the determining factor in U.S. support for agrarian reform in the Western hemisphere was the extent to which they affected North American property (Dorner 1992: 7). The United States thus stymied the Guatemalan reform of 1952, which threatened the interests of the United Fruit Company, and abetted the overthrow of the democratically elected government of Jacobo Arbenz the next year, while it supported the agrarian reform resulting from Bolivia's social revolution of 1952. Recognition of the political potency of the land issue, however, was insufficient to prevent U.S. antagonism toward the 1959 agrarian reform in Cuba, where North American interests dominated the large sugar sector. After 1959, nonetheless, the

United States supported agrarian reform to prevent more revolutions in the hemisphere.

Powerful economic arguments were advanced to justify agrarian reform in this period (Dorner and Kanel 1971). Population growth rates were high in the region while land, concentrated in large estates or latifundia, was underutilized and used inefficiently. Distributing land to the landless and underemployed was expected to result in land being used more intensively, leading to increased agricultural growth rates and higher rural incomes. Moreover, precapitalist class relations on haciendas began to be viewed as anachronistic for they resulted in the appropriation of rents by a landlord class more interested in conspicuous consumption than in saving and investment. In addition, the latifundio-*minifundio* (small farm) structure of land tenancy came to be regarded as a fetter on industrial development. Since the 1950s most Latin American countries had been pursuing import-substitution industrialization, which, to be viable, required expanding internal markets. Agrarian reform was expected to provide not only an expanded supply of foodstuffs to urban centers, and thus a way to maintain low real wages, but also, through the higher incomes land-owning peasants would generate, a larger market for the industrialization effort. Agrarian reform thus was seen as the ideal vehicle to promote higher rates of economic growth as well as equity, social justice, and more stable governments.

Seventeen Latin American countries subsequently initiated Alliance for Progress agrarian reforms and created agrarian reform and colonization agencies or institutes.[3] But in most countries efforts at reform in the 1960s were minimal, with land-distribution efforts primarily focused on the colonization of public land on the agricultural frontier.[4] The landlord class was still too powerful and agricultural exports too important to bring about a significant redistribution of landed property. The scope of the agrarian reform was largely to depend on the organized efforts of the peasantry and the potential threat they represented (Thiesenhusen 1995; Kay 1998).

The Alliance for Progress agrarian reforms that ended up having the broadest impact took place in Peru and Chile, but under very different regimes than had initiated them, a progressive military government (led by General Velasco Alvarado) in the former and an elected socialist president (Salvador Allende) in the latter country. Similarly, the relatively broad-based reforms instituted in Central America in the 1980s required a different context than the Alliance for Progress: the Sandinista revolution and Salvadoran civil war. As Peter Dorner (1992: 7) notes, "Beginning with Cuba, a major dilemma has been that any Latin American government radical enough to carry through a redistributionary land reform inevitably came into conflict with the ideological stance of the U.S. government." And thus Chile's agrarian reform was partly undone following the U.S.-supported military coup that deposed President Salvador Allende in 1973, and the Nicaraguan reform was partly reversed after the Sandinista electoral defeat in 1990, a defeat encouraged by the U.S.-supported contra war in that country.

Comparative Aspects of the Reforms

The Latin American agrarian reforms may be differentiated not only according to the contexts in which they took place but also by their content and manner of implementation. In terms of how land was acquired for redistribution, with the exception of Costa Rica, agrarian reform legislation provided for land to be expropriated for purposes of social justice or when it was in the national interest (see Appendix: Table 1). Expropriation was to be accompanied by compensation to owners. Beginning with the 1952 Guatemalan agrarian reform, expropriated land was to be compensated with a combination of cash and agrarian reform bonds (usually maturing in twenty to thirty years), with the land valued at the declared value for tax purposes, a formula replicated in the Alliance for Progress agrarian reforms.[5] In addition, all of these laws provided for landlords to keep a portion of their estates (usually the portion they worked directly or that was below a certain maximum size) as a reserve that was not subject to expropriation.

It is a point of contention whether landlords were ever actually compensated for the expropriated land. In both Mexico and Bolivia, land was expropriated without compensation if it had originally been indigenous community land that had been turned into the private property of the haciendas. Further, when Mexican landowners did receive compensation, it was with government bonds and at a rate below the market value of the estates; however, they usually were allowed to retain the hacienda core as a reserve. In Bolivia, notwithstanding the provisions of the law, large landowners were not compensated for their land or guaranteed a reserve, largely due to landlord opposition to and sabotage of reform efforts that undermined the validity of their claims. In Guatemala the Arbenz government offered to pay the United Fruit Company for the land it had expropriated, but was rebuffed. In Cuba landowners were initially able to keep 401 hectares of their estates as a reserve. It was only after the second agrarian reform law was issued in 1963, when the maximum farm size was reduced to 67 hectares, that many large farms were expropriated in their entirety, often for having been abandoned by their owners. The promised agrarian reform bonds were never issued and became a moot question after most large landowners left the country.

In the reforms of the Alliance for Progress period, landlord resistance to expropriation and over the terms of compensation and reserve land was a major factor in their slow implementation. Often landlord coalitions were successful in blocking expropriation measures altogether. But where expropriations took place, landlords typically received some form of compensation, if not one altogether to their liking. The exception was the short-lived agrarian reform of the Popular Unity government in Chile (1970–73), where peasant militancy was largely responsible for the rapid pace of this reform and for the low priority placed on compensation procedures. In only one case was there outright confiscation of land, the Sandinista agrarian reform in Nicaragua. In 1979 the property owned by the Somoza family and its close associates was expropriated without compensation, a move justified at the time by the large amount of land that had legally and illegally become concentrated in their hands.

The majority of reform programs provided for public or state lands also to be redistributed for agrarian reform purposes. Through the 1970s most Latin American countries still had ample agrarian frontiers, although these largely consisted of fragile terrains in the semitropical or tropical lowlands, such as the Amazon basin in South America or the Atlantic coast of Central America. In many countries the availability of unclaimed land on this frontier facilitated a process whereby agrarian reform efforts largely became colonization schemes, intended to satisfy land hunger while protecting the interests of the landlord class. This was particularly the case in Brazil, Colombia, Costa Rica, Ecuador, and Honduras.

For various reasons, in some countries the state also owned a good number of large estates, and these were among the first to be redistributed.[6] In addition, estates that had fallen to the state through defaults on mortgages to state banks or the nonpayment of taxes formed a relatively conflict-free resource for land-distribution efforts. Chile, Colombia, Costa Rica, and Guatemala also made provisions in their reform legislation for the state to purchase private lands that were voluntarily offered to it for sale. It is impossible to reconstruct with any degree of accuracy the relative composition (private versus public) of the lands that were made available for redistribution through the reforms. But with the exception of the pioneering reforms, and those of Chile, Peru, Nicaragua, and El Salvador, the primary lands made available for redistribution were public lands on the agrarian frontier.

Turning to the form of land distribution, the agrarian reform laws largely envisioned a "land to the tiller" process whereby former tenants would become the owners of the land they cultivated. While the goal was to create a class of family farmers, the actual process of implementation often resulted in land being assigned collectively to groups of peasant farmers or wage workers, rather than as individually held private property (see Appendix: Table 2). In some cases such collective allocations took place only for expediency, for they were far easier to implement than individual land allotments; in these cases the land was usually farmed individually by peasant households. By the 1970s, however, a definite preference emerged for group farming activities of various kinds.

Collective allocations were a response to a number of other factors (Kay 1998). Governments that expropriated modern, capitalist enterprises (such as in Mexico under Cárdenas, and in Cuba, Peru, Chile, Nicaragua, and El Salvador) were not keen to break these up, given the economies of scale that their infrastructure and degree of mechanization provided. Converting these enterprises into production cooperatives, which would be collectively owned and managed by their workers, seemed a much more attractive solution. In Cuba the initial experiment with production cooperatives was short lived, and by 1962 the large estates were formally converted to state farms. The only other country to favor state farms over production cooperatives was Nicaragua, where more land was to remain under state farms than was assigned to production cooperatives. Another factor favoring collective forms of allocation was that in some cases it was evident that the subdivision of estates would not provide viable family farms for all those who qualified as agrarian reform beneficiaries. In addition, the radicalization of peasant groups, such as in Peru and in Chile under Allende, sometimes led to demands that not just permanent but also seasonal workers be deemed beneficiaries of the reform. Associative enterprises with the potential for diversification of income-generating activities were considered the most feasible means of accommodating the large number of claimants to beneficiary status. Also, planners were usually aware that agrarian reform meant more than just land transfers. If agricultural productivity was to increase, enhanced state services would be required in the form of credit, technical assistance, infrastructure investment, and the like. It was more feasible to direct such services to peasant groups and production cooperatives than to a large number of individual farmers.

A final consideration was the issue of the agrarian debt. While in a few of the reforms beneficiaries received their land free of charge (such as in Mexico, Bolivia, and Cuba, and in the first phase of the Ecuadorian reform), in the majority of countries agrarian reform beneficiaries were expected to purchase the land, although generally on quite favorable terms (Appendix: Table 2). The collective allocation of land to peasant groups, with at least some land to be dedicated to group farming for the purpose of generating a marketable surplus for debt repayment, thus often emerged as the most practical solution. In practice, few countries (with the exception of Chile) have been able to collect fully on this debt and in most it has been partly or entirely forgiven.

As a result of all of these factors, the reformed sector that emerged was quite heterogeneous. The agrarian reforms of some countries (such as Colombia, Ecuador, Guatemala, and Honduras) passed through various phases, alternating between favoring individual and then collective farming. In other countries (such as Peru, Nicaragua, and El Salvador) the agrarian reform from the beginning featured a mix of organizational forms, in response to heterogeneous local conditions. Since our primary interest is to examine the gendered impact of these reforms, it is beyond the scope of this chapter to provide a comprehensive evaluation of agrarian reform efforts in Latin America. It should be noted, nonetheless, that it is difficult to compare in rigorous terms the scope of these reforms since the available data for each country are often so inconsistent.[7]

The Pioneers: Mexico, Bolivia, and Cuba

There is general agreement that the first three reforms of the twentieth century—those of Mexico, Bolivia, and Cuba—were the most far reaching, for they were all the product of social revolutions. The Mexican agrarian reform was a product of the revolution of 1910–17, which resulted in almost half of Mexican national territory eventually passing to some 29,659 *ejidos* and indigenous communities.[8] Between 1915 and 1992, an estimated 3.5 million households benefited (Botey 2000: 119).[9] Not much land redistribution took place, however, until the regime of Lázaro Cárdenas

(1934–40), who distributed 17.9 million hectares to 814,537 beneficiary households, more land than all previous administrations combined (Otero 1989: 284). The other major period of land redistribution was during the 1960s, when 33 million hectares were distributed, but by then little of the land available for redistribution was considered arable land (Thiesenhusen 1995: 43).

The second agrarian reform of any lasting consequence was a product of the Bolivian national revolution of 1952, an anti-oligarchic revolution led by the National Revolutionary Movement (MNR, Movimiento Nacional Revolucionario). The Bolivian agrarian reform is usually considered to have been even broader in scope than that of Mexico, resulting in the redistribution of approximately four-fifths of the land in farms at that time and benefiting three-quarters of agricultural households (Kay 1998: 11–12; Thiesenhusen 1989: Table 1).[10] The Cuban agrarian reform, promulgated by Fidel Castro and his July 26th Movement in 1959, brought approximately 70 percent of the nation's farmland into the state sector (Trinchet 1984: 22–23).[11] In addition to creating a huge state-farm sector, the Cuban agrarian reform also created a large landed peasantry by granting every tenant and squatter the right to claim the land they worked; the number of small property owners in rural Cuba more than tripled.[12]

The landholdings expropriated by the Mexican state were ceded as collective property to *ejidos* in perpetuity. The basic principles governing *ejido* and indigenous community land were as follows: the land was generally redistributed to individual families,[13] who could only transmit the usufruct rights to other family members through inheritance (*intransmisibilidad*); land rights could not be sold to non-*ejido* members (*inalienabilidad*), rented to outsiders (*imprescriptibilidad*), or be used as collateral (*inembargabilidad*). The rules established that usufruct parcels within the *ejidos* would constitute family patrimony (Baitenmann 1997: 296).

The initial 1920 *ejido* law, implementing Article 27 of the 1917 constitution, provided for land to be distributed to household heads without mentioning the gender of the beneficiary (Arizpe and Botey 1987: 70). A subsequent 1921 regulation refers to gender for the first time, explicitly including single or widowed women with dependents among potential household heads. According to Helga Baitenmann (1997: 297), it was the 1922 agrarian regulatory law that introduced discrimination against women. It broadened the categories of beneficiaries of land rights to include single men over the age of eighteen. It was discriminatory because men could obtain land rights independent of whether they supported a family whereas women could not (ibid.: 308).[14] In addition, widows sometimes lost their access to parcels when their sons became of working age, making women's land rights temporary whereas those of men were permanent (ibid.: 309). Moreover, the 1934 agrarian code decreed that if an *ejidataria* subsequently married an *ejidatario*, she automatically lost her land rights, with her land reverting to the *ejido* governing board (ibid.: 319).

Subsequent regulations, nonetheless, strengthened women's land rights. In an exception to the norm governing the *ejidos* which stipulated that *ejidatarios* could lose their usufruct parcels if they did not work their land directly for two consecutive years, the 1940 agrarian code allowed *ejidatarias* to rent, sharecrop, or hire wage workers if they had small children and had to attend to domestic chores (Baitenmann 1997: 323). Moreover, the 1943 agrarian code (which continued in effect until 1971) provided that if an *ejidatario* did not work his land for two consecutive years, the land parcel would revert to the family, rather than to the *ejido* commission for redistribution, thus protecting wives from being dispossessed of land (ibid.: 326). Women's inheritance rights on the *ejidos* were also strengthened over time. The initial regulations on inheritance had given *ejidatarios* considerable leeway in specifying their heirs. The 1934 agrarian code established a clear order of succession in case an *ejidatario* died intestate, giving preference to the spouse, followed by the children and then persons of either sex who resided with the family (ibid.: 324). Nonetheless, since the great majority of adult rural women were not formally married, the agrarian code was not as favorable to women as the civil code of 1928. That code had recognized the inheritance rights of women in consensual unions (Carreras and Montero 1975: 120). The 1940 agrarian code recognized this discrepancy in the agrarian legislation and established the following order of succession to land rights on the *ejidos:* the legitimate spouse; the concubine with whom the *ejidatario* had children; the concubine with whom he had lived during the last six months of his life; and then the children (Baitenmann 1997: 326).

From the 1930s on, feminist organizations in Mexico, in the context of the general struggle for women's suffrage, began to demand equal land rights for rural women (Miller 1991: 111). One of the demands of the Unitary Front for Women's Rights (Frente Único Pro Derechos de la Mujer) —an organization that at its peak encompassed some eight hundred women's organizations with approximately fifty thousand members—was that agrarian law be reformed so that women would receive equitable consideration in the distribution of land. Equal land rights was also one of the main demands resulting from the First Congress of Women Workers and Peasants in 1931 (Baitenmann 1997: 321). While agrarian legislation became more favorable to married women and women in consensual unions in the 1930s and 1940s, it was not until 1971 that Mexico established formal equality of land rights between men and women, becoming the first Latin American country to do so.

The Federal Agrarian Reform Law of 1971 established that future beneficiaries were to be "Mexican by birth, male or female over sixteen years of age or of any age if with dependents" (Article 200). Moreover, female *ejido* members were to have rights equal to those of male members (Article 45).[15] Now women no longer lost their *ejidataria* status upon marriage (Article 78); rather, they could establish a separation-of-property marital regime, maintaining their land rights in the *ejido* (Botey 1997: 146–54; Esparza et al. 1996: 24–27). Inheritance provisions continued to protect spouses and partners. In the event an *ejidatario* died intestate, the default clause provided for land rights to pass first to the wife or partner with whom he had children; then to one of his children; then to his partner of the last two years; and finally, in the absence of any of these, to any other person who depended economically on him (Article 82). Moreover, in contrast to the civil code that provided for full testamentary freedom, land rights on the *ejido* could be willed only to the wife or one of the children or, in their absence, to his partner if she was economically dependent on him (Articles 81, 83). In addition, the legal heir was responsible for food provisioning to the children of the deceased *ejidatario* who were under the age of sixteen and to the widow until her death or remarriage (Ochoa Pérez 1998).

The 1971 law also made some specific provisions for the wives and daughters of male *ejido* members. It required *ejidos* to create agro-industrial units for women (UAIM, Unidad Agrícola Industrial de la Mujer), which provided collective access to a parcel of land for special agricultural or agro-industrial projects. This parcel was to be equivalent in size to the average amount of land held by any one *ejidatario;* the UAIM was also given one collective vote in *ejido* meetings. There is general consensus that the UAIMs did not prove to be a very efficacious means of promoting women's role in production or in decision making in *ejido* structures; in addition, they came into being on only 8.6 percent of all *ejidos* (Zapata, Mercado, and López 1994: 189; J. Aranda 1991: 124–32; J. Aranda 1993: 205–12).

Lourdes Arizpe and Carlota Botey (1987: 71) argue that, despite the egalitarian provisions of the 1971 law, women's land rights continued to be limited by discriminatory cultural practices. Although the new law potentially expanded *ejido* membership beyond household heads, internal *ejido* regulations continued to restrict *ejidatario* status to only one member per household, the household head, who was generally male if a man resided in the household. Moreover, by the mid-1970s very little land was being redistributed through the reform (Fox 1994: 244), resulting in few new *ejido* memberships being created. In 1984 female *ejido* members represented approximately 15 percent of the total number of *ejidatarios* (Arizpe and Botey 1987: 71), up from the 1.3 percent of *ejido* members enumerated in 1970 (Valenzuela and Robles 1996: 37). This 15 percent figure roughly corresponds to the number of rural female household heads enumerated in the 1990 census (14.3 percent).[16] According to Arizpe and Botey, the majority of *ejidatarias* were elderly widows who inherited the usufruct rights of their husbands, a proposition supported by case studies throughout Mexico. Few women have succeeded in being granted *ejidatario* status by petitioning for land when it was reapportioned on an *ejido* or when new lands were acquired, although they are legally eligible to do so. Thus one of the recurring demands of organized rural women is that they be given land plots on the *ejido* regardless of their marital status (Stephen 1998: 153).

Arizpe and Botey (1987) also argue that few *ejidatarias* work their parcels themselves, for actual control of the parcels is often in the hands of male family members. The case study evidence is mixed in this regard. Brunt (1992: 183), for example, describes the case of several widows who after they remarried continued to manage their own farms. She also analyzes in detail the greater difficulties that female farm managers face compared to men—for example, in being taken seriously by extension agents or in commanding the respect of wage workers—factors that encourage *ejidatarias* to rent their land or sharecrop it with a relative rather than managing it themselves. Sarah Hamilton (2000a) found considerable variation in whether widows managed agricultural production in the four *ejidos* she studied in different parts of Mexico, although in most cases land was worked by their children or was rented out.

Nonetheless, it is important to keep in mind that even if *ejidatarias* do not manage or work the land themselves, they retain the legal right to attend *ejido* meetings and to vote in the proceedings, a right the wives and partners of male *ejido* members do not have, and this can be a source of empowerment for some women. But the management of agriculture as well as local politics are considered to be men's business:

It is considered natural, a given, that men should be in charge. Women owning land rights oppose this social order, not explicitly, but just by being *ejidatarias*. The men neutralize this by treating women as second rate *ejidatarios*. This becomes very clear in the *ejido* meeting. Their opinions are not asked for, they hardly ever occupy formal positions on the *ejido* board, they are treated as exceptions, exceptions to the rules that should apply to both. For example, if they do not attend *ejido* meetings, this is not regarded as "against the rule," though it is for men. (Brunt 1992: 82)

Billie DeWalt and Martha Rees (1994: 19), in their review of anthropological studies of *ejidos,* note that whether or not they are *ejidatarias,* "women rarely have much influence or participation in the affairs of the *ejido.*" They attribute women's minimal role in decision making to the fact that agriculture is still a male-dominated occupation. But as the share of *ejidatarias* has increased over time, so has their participation within the *ejido* governing structure. A 1998 census of the *ejido* leadership found that 20 percent of the *ejidos* nationally had elected a woman to a leadership position on either the *ejido* governing board (Comisariado Ejidal) or another board or council. Nonetheless, women constituted only 5.2 percent of the persons in leadership positions although they made up 17.6 percent of the *ejidatarios* (Robles et al. 2000: 91, 93). Significant for our argument regarding the relationship between land rights and empowerment is that women's participation in *ejido* leadership is highly correlated with the proportion of women members in an *ejido* (ibid.; Katz 1999b: 9).

The first agrarian reform of this century, born in a revolution in which women were active participants (C. Ramos 1993), thus established a mixed precedent for women's land rights. The land rights of female household heads were formally recognized, but single women were discriminated against compared with single men. Nonetheless, in 1971 Mexico became the first Latin American country to guarantee men and women an equal chance of being an agrarian reform beneficiary. The problem was that by the 1970s little new land was being redistributed; moreover, cultural constructions of gender and the proper division of labor worked against recognition of women's land rights. That women ended up being 15 percent of the *ejidatarios* by the mid-1980s is largely due to favorable inheritance provisions that protected the land rights of widows irrespective of marital status, and it is also due to the struggle of individual rural women to have their land rights recognized.

Bolivia's 1953 agrarian reform law provided for the expropriation of all estates worked under precapitalist forms of tenancy as well as of latifundia consisting of unused or underused farmland. Among the beneficiaries were to be "all Bolivians over 18 years of age, *without distinction of sex*, who dedicate or want to dedicate themselves to agricultural tasks."[17] This law initially appears to be even more advanced than the Mexican law of the time in terms of women's land rights; however, a subsequent article of the law, referring to former tenants on the estates, restricts beneficiaries to peasants who are eighteen years of age if single, or fourteen if married, and to *widows with small children*. Thus, what initially appears to be gender-neutral legislation is undermined by the restriction of beneficiary status, only in the case of women, to those who are widowed mothers. María Fernanda Sostres and Yara Carafa (1992: 63) argue, further, that while Article 78 specifically referred only to former tenants on estates, in practice women were subject to this exclusionary logic in most land-reform adjudications.

The practice of favoring male household heads as beneficiaries was reinforced by other provisions of the legislation, such as one stipulating that each household could be allocated only one agricultural parcel (Article 83) and that beneficiaries had to be recognized agriculturalists (Article 82). The pattern of male privilege was reinforced by the sociopolitical structure that emerged in rural communities in the post-agrarian-reform period. The peasant syndicates organized by the MNR government assumed the functions of communal governance, and only male household heads participated in these structures, in effect consolidating a gendered monopoly over community decision making (Sostres and Carafa 1992: 64).

While the 1953 agrarian reform eradicated the hacienda system in the highlands, it did not resolve the problem of land hunger altogether. In the late 1960s and early 1970s, the state increasingly turned its attention to the development of the agricultural frontier, facilitating colonization, both planned and unplanned, in the humid valleys and lowlands in the northeastern Andean piedmont. Dramatic changes took place in the eastern and Amazonian region of the country during the 1970s. Under the government of General Hugo Banzer, the National Colonization Institute (INC, Instituto Nacional de Colonización) gave away an estimated 12 million hectares of land in large tracts during this decade, mainly to pay off political debts, creating what are termed the "new latifundia" (Urioste 1992: 113). This region became the boom region of Bolivia as sugar cane, cotton, and then soya production rapidly expanded, drawing thousands of temporary workers from the highlands. Even though Bolivia had carried out a thorough agrarian reform in the highlands, the reconcentration of land in the east in subsequent decades resulted in a highly skewed distribution of land by the mid-1980s.[18]

Given the legal and cultural restrictions on women becoming beneficiaries, it is somewhat surprising that women were found to be 17.2 percent of the beneficiaries of agrarian reform and colonization efforts between 1956 and 1994.[19] This figure compares quite favorably with data on female beneficiaries in subsequent Latin American agrarian reforms. Nonetheless, it is important to point out that in the early 1990s rural female household heads constituted 22.3 percent of the total (Bolivia 1993: 154), suggesting that rural women were probably underrepresented as beneficiaries if the intention of the reform was to benefit household heads. The relatively large share of female beneficiaries leads to the speculation that if a family had two parcels of land in its possession, the second parcel may have been registered in the name of the wife at the urging of her spouse, in order to circumvent the provision that each household could be allotted only one parcel.[20] Delving further, as Table 3.1 shows, the greatest number of women benefited during the decade of the 1970s, during the Banzer dictatorship, and they were primarily located in the northern and eastern regions of the country, in the Beni and Santa Cruz. The sizeable share of female beneficiaries in these departments lends weight to the hypothesis that during the Banzer dictatorship women were titled land in order to hide the degree of land concentration taking place. If such was the case, then it was probably women of the middle and upper classes who benefited by having land registered in their names. There were relatively few female beneficiaries from the traditional indigenous departments of La Paz, Oruro, Chuquisaca, Cochabamba, and Potosí. The high percentage of female beneficiaries in Tarija probably corresponds to the relatively high proportion of female-headed households in this department. This is an area of relatively poor lands and particularly high male out-migration to the eastern region of the country.[21] The sizeable share of female beneficiaries during the early 1990s may be a statistical fluke, or it may reflect the high level of corruption that also characterized the 1991–92 period, which may also have resulted in families being titled multiple holdings.[22]

The Bolivian agrarian reform thus had contradictory effects for women. The vast majority of indigenous women in the highland departments were excluded from the reform as direct beneficiaries primarily because they were not household heads nor considered to be agriculturalists. A substantial share of the female beneficiaries of this reform were proba-

TABLE 3.1.   Adjudication of Land to Women, 1956–1994, Bolivia

Period	(%)	Department	(%)
1956–1960	(1.2)	Beni	(46.9)
1961–1970	(12.6)	Chuquisaca	(4.1)
1971–1980	(37.5)	Cochabamba	(3.6)
1981–1990	(18.0)	La Paz	(6.4)
1991–1994	(30.2)	Oruro	(2.1)
Missing data	(0.5)	Pando	(1.2)
		Potosí	(5.7)
		Santa Cruz	(15.6)
		Tarija	(14.4)
Total	(100)		(100)
n = 2,937		n = 2,937	

Source: Isabel Lavadenz, director of INRA, 7 August 1997.

Note: Data for this table are based on the sub-sample of women drawn from a random sample of 17,099 out of a total of 49,684 individual land application forms (*expedientes*).

bly nonindigenous women who were allocated lands on the agricultural frontier as a result of government corruption.

The Cuban agrarian reform law of 1959 was intended to be gender neutral. The beneficiaries were to include the tenants on sugar cane estates and other *arrendatarios,* sharecroppers, and squatters (Article 21, in INRA 1960). Also given priority were landless peasants living near an expropriated estate and the agricultural wage workers who worked and lived on these, in addition to those who demonstrated agricultural expertise (Article 22). The law also prioritized combatants in the armed struggle against the Batista government, victims of the war or repression, and the dependent family members of those who died in the revolutionary struggle (Article 23). According to this latter article, "in all cases priority was to be given to household heads." Thus the "land to the tiller" phase of Cuba's agrarian reform primarily benefited male household heads.

It is sometimes asserted that there were numerous female household heads among the beneficiaries because the very first land title Fidel Castro handed out in 1959 went to a woman.[23] But it is probable that women represented less than 5 percent of those titled land.[24] It was also men who ended up representing the household within the peasant organization ANAP (Asociación Nacional de Agricultores Pequeños), which was charged with developing credit and service cooperatives among private producers. Nonetheless, it made a significant difference in the lives of those female household heads who were beneficiaries, improving their fall-back position, as suggested by the following story of a woman who had been abandoned by her husband: "When the agrarian reform came they gave the title to my mother. Soon after my father returned and pressured her to give him the title to the land. My mother rebuffed his overtures and decided to remain separated. She was helped [in the agricultural tasks] by my brothers and the peasants belonging to the [ANAP] base. . . . She cultivated her tobacco field quite successfully and always participated in the meetings of the base" (Pérez and Echevarría 1998: 13).

The development several years later of an explicit state policy favoring the incorporation of rural women into the agrarian reform process was the result of both ideological and economic considerations. As the Cuban revolution developed its socialist character, the issue of equality, not just between social classes but between men and women, had to be addressed. Drawing on the Marxist classics, the Cubans accepted the theoretical premise that women's equality with men required their incorporation into the labor force. The participation of women in productive labor was seen not only as a necessary step for women's own social development but also for the transformation of the social relations of Cuban society (Castro 1981; PCC 1976). This theoretical position was complemented in the late 1960s by the economic imperative of increasing rural women's participation in agricultural production[25] because of the growing labor shortage in this sector, which resulted from the policy of rapidly expanding sugar cane production.

In 1966 ANAP and the Cuban Women's Federation (FMC, Federación de Mujeres Cubanas) joined forces to promote what became known as the FMC-ANAP brigades of rural women. Initially consisting of volunteer labor, the brigades provided the opportunity for thousands of rural women to participate in social production for the first time (Bengelsdorf and Hageman 1977).[26] The FMC and ANAP also promoted the inclusion of women as permanent workers on the state farms and as members of the credit and service cooperatives (CCS, cooperativas de crédito y servicio) formed by private producers. In the 1970s ANAP changed the criterion for cooperative membership from one based on household headship to one that included all adults within farm households.[27] The FMC-ANAP brigades that had been organized within each CCS to recruit women for temporary agricultural work began to focus on creating the support structure to increase women's participation in the family farming operation and in cooperative decision making (FMC 1975). By the mid-1970s, ANAP had one of the highest proportions, 16 percent, of women in local leadership positions of all the Cuban mass organizations (PCC 1976: 30).

This method of organizing rural women came to fruition when the formation of production cooperatives was promoted in the late 1970s and early 1980s. Following the First Congress of the Cuban Communist Party in 1975, the development of production cooperatives (based on peasants pooling their land and other means of production) became a goal of Cuban policy makers. Recognizing that the peasant sector was not about to disappear and eager to promote the modernization of agriculture, they offered a number of incentives to promote voluntary collectivization. Among them were several aimed at eliciting the support of rural women.

Throughout the 1970s Cuba's housing policy had favored state farm workers by the development of hundreds of new agricultural communities at work centers. These communities featured modern housing with running water, sanitation systems, and electricity, and they offered health centers, day care centers, schools, communal eating facilities, and stores provisioned with basic necessities. In order to foster collectivization, the state now offered the resources to build these communities in locales where production cooperatives were formed. Interviews with peasant women in 1980 revealed that they considered these new communities to offer them substantial benefits, alleviating the burden of domestic work and increasing the standard of living of their families. Another factor of interest to women, one that often led them to be the key actor in a household's decision to collectivize, was the policy of assuring all adult family members membership and work in the new production cooperatives. For many women the production cooperatives offered the possibility of full-time employment for the first time and of economic independence from husbands and fathers. Also, peasants who joined the cooperatives were eligible for social security benefits for the first time, including paid maternity leave and retirement benefits (the latter at age fifty-five for women and sixty for men).

The positive response of rural women to collectivization is evident in the fact that in 1979, when only 725 production cooperatives had been organized nationally, women represented 34.7 percent of the 14,696 members. In contrast, in that year women represented only 6.9 percent of the members of the CCS and other peasant associations, and only 5.5 percent of the members with individual land titles (Stubbs and Alvarez 1987: Table 8.1).[28] The visibility of women in the cooperative sector far outstripped that in the state sector. According to the 1981 census, women represented 14 percent of the permanent workforce on state farms and they held only 6 percent of the professional positions (ibid.: 143). The number of production cooperatives subsequently expanded to over 1,400 by 1983; women then represented 27.7 percent of the 82,515 members. In the mid-1980s the percentage of women members continued to decline, as many older women took advantage of the favorable retirement benefits offered cooperative members. The participation of women in cooperative leadership positions steadily increased, however, reaching 12 percent in 1985 (Stubbs and Alvarez 1987).[29]

While the Cuban agrarian reform may have been intended to be gender blind, the policy of adjudicating land to household heads was gender biased, and it limited the participation of women within the peasant mass organization. It took a concerted effort later by the state and the peasant and women's mass organizations to increase women's participation in agriculture and in the cooperative sector. Among the more important lessons of the Cuban experience from a gender perspective is the importance of making cooperative membership (whether in credit and service or production cooperatives) open to all adult family members and the need for attention to women's domestic responsibilities, particularly the provision of child care services, so that women can take advantage of these opportunities.

The Alliance for Progress Agrarian Reforms

Of the agrarian reform and colonization efforts initiated in the Alliance for Progress period, all those examined here—Costa Rica, Guatemala, Ecuador, Honduras, Colombia, and Brazil—were unsuccessful through the 1980s in benefiting a significant number of women. The Costa Rican case also epitomizes in many ways the dilemma of democratic governments in Latin America with respect to the Alliance for Progress. The conditionality imposed by U.S. development assistance required them to address the demand for land being articulated by a restless peasantry. At the same time, the specter of the Cuban revolution made the landlord class all the more determined to protect private property. The result in Costa Rica was the promulgation of Land and Colonization Law No. 2825 of 1961, which did not even mention the term "agrarian reform" and did not provide for land to be expropriated in the social interest (Barahona 1980: 259). The main task of the newly created Land and Colonization Institute (ITCO, Instituto de Tierras y Colonización) became that of resolving land conflicts through colonization programs on public land, the titling of squatters, and the purchase and subdivision of private farms offered to it for sale.

The beneficiaries of ITCO's programs were to be arrendires, sharecroppers, *colonos* (tenant farmers who provided labor services), squatters, and wage workers (all denoted in the masculine noun form), with preference to be given to "parents who have more than one child" (Article 63, in Escoto León 1965: 11). The only provision that explicitly mentions women is one dealing with the possible abandonment of the land plot and family by the beneficiary, in which case the parcel was to be assigned to the *wife* (Article 68), making explicit the assumption that beneficiaries were to be male household heads.[30] The discrimination against women was also expressed in the point system utilized by the agrarian reform institute to select potential beneficiaries. The system favored household heads with farming experience and the greatest number of dependents, and until 1988 male household heads received more points than did female heads (Guzmán 1991: 208; Madden 1992: 54; Blanco 1997).

Given these criteria, it is somewhat surprising that the proportion of women among the beneficiaries was as high it was, a reported 11.8 percent as of 1988 (Brenes and Antezana 1996: 2).[31] This figure was only slightly less than the share of rural female-headed households in the mid-1980s, 12.9 percent (Costa Rica 1984: Table 6). This reform has also been quite limited in scope, encompassing less than 5 percent of rural households (Madden 1992: 43). One of the reasons it was so limited was that the farms acquired were purchased at market rates, quickly using up the scarce resources budgeted for land acquisition and redistribution.

Guatemala's military regime was also forced by the Alliance for Progress to accept some minimal moves toward land distribution. In 1962 it promulgated the Law of Agrarian Transformation and the next year the Institute of Agrarian Transformation, INTA (Instituto de Transformación Agraria), was created with the mandate to promote colonization and redistribute the remaining national farms.[32] This law defined the land parcels to be distributed as agrarian family patrimony (*patrimonio agrario familiar*); however, their actual allocation and titling was in the name of one person, the household head (Article 73, in Escoto León 1965: 36). Favored as beneficiaries were those with large families and those with agricultural experience. Illustrating how it was assumed that men were to be the primary beneficiaries, the law also specified that such land could not be sold without the written permission of the *wife* or companion (Article 79; our emphasis). Continuing with the practice established in the ill-fated 1952 agrarian reform, the 1962 law also specified that upon the death of the beneficiary, the land title would go to the *wife* or partner and his descendants; the heirs would determine who would manage the family patrimony, subject to INTA's approval (Articles 93 and 94). Since women generally are not considered to be agriculturalists, this placed widows at a disadvantage in being ceded lands if they had a son of working age (Fund. Arias–Tierra Viva 1993: 73–74).

Data on the beneficiaries of agrarian reform and colonization were not compiled by gender until 1996. An analysis of successful land applications revealed that of 116,209 distributions made between 1954 and 1996, only 8 percent represented allocations to women (Rivas and Bautista 1996: 6).[33] In the 1981 census, rural female-headed households constituted 11.2 percent of the total, a figure that increased to 14.9 percent in the 1994 census (Guatemala 1981: 424–26; Guatemala 1996: 27), suggesting that female-headed households were under-represented among agrarian reform beneficiaries. With respect to the form of land allocation to women, the great majority, 59 percent, received urban lots, followed by 19 percent who gained membership in collectively owned farms. Only 15 percent of the women received individual land parcels, with the remainder receiving land in a mixed form (*patrimonios familiares mixtos*) (INTA 1996: graphic 2). The data suggest that women have not been treated seriously as farmers; those female household heads who have been successful in obtaining land have been primarily able to do so in order to construct their home and perhaps maintain a garden plot.[34]

The Fundación Arias–Tierra Viva (1993: 126) report makes an insightful point with respect to the INTA policy since the 1980s of only allocating land collectively. It notes that the majority of requests for land come from organized peasant groups; and although these are often mixed-sex groups, in practice women have little effective participation within them. In effect, the organized groups act as a filter, biasing women's participation in state programs of land distribution. This study also notes how lack of state support in terms of credit and technical assistance has acted as an obstacle to female beneficiaries remaining on the agrarian reform settlements, the *asentamientos*. Their desertion rate has been quite high, further prejudicing agrarian reform officials from including additional women among the beneficiaries (ibid.: 127). Not surprisingly, the impression of some peasant women leaders is that women do not have land rights: "INTA does not allow women. They ask a women if she has a husband and if she doesn't, they don't give her land."[35]

Although Honduras created a National Agrarian Institute (INA, Instituto Nacional Agrario) and enacted an agrarian reform law in 1962, efforts at land distribution were minimal until the peasant organizations pushed for them. A more effective law was adopted in 1975, which established maximum property ceilings and authorized the expropriation with compensation of idle lands.[36] The 1962 Honduran agrarian reform law contained provisions favorable to women that were maintained in the revised legislation. The land rights of widows and other female household heads were explicitly guaranteed (Honduras 1975: Article 79). Moreover, female household heads were given priority over male heads and single men if the women had also exploited land under indirect forms of tenancy or were agricultural wage workers (Article 81). Single women without dependents, however, were discriminated against relative to single men, who were included among the potential beneficiaries if over the age of sixteen, regardless of whether they were fathers and household heads. Assuming that the beneficiaries would be men, the inheritance provisions stipulated that, upon the death of a beneficiary, preferential right to the land parcel was to be given to the *wife* or partner or any of his children. For the land rights to be transferred to an adult child, that child had to "meet the family obligations of the *father*" (Article 84; our emphasis). These provisions were relatively more favorable to women (since wives and companions were at least mentioned) than the inheritance provisions of the original 1962 law. In that legislation beneficiaries were required to submit a rank-ordered list of heirs to the INA and could include among them whomever they wished (Article 89 in Escoto 1965: 51), a practice conforming to the civil code, which provided for full testamentary freedom.

Data for 1978 (which cover over half of the total number of beneficiaries in the Honduran reform) revealed that women constituted only 3.8 percent of the 33,203 beneficiaries (Callejas 1983: 3). In the mid-1970s, a reported 18.7 percent of rural households were headed by women (Honduras 1977: Table 5), suggesting that, notwithstanding the stated priority given to female household heads, women were drastically underrepresented as reform beneficiaries. A decade later, the proportion of female beneficiaries remained about the same, suggesting that women did not benefit either as household heads or by inheriting land rights from their spouses or partners (Martínez, Rosales, and Rivera 1995: 37–38).

Sara Elisa Rosales, a specialist on the issue, analyzes women's exclusion as follows: "Even though Article 79 assured women of access to land, in practice, the agrarian reform technicians did not promote it. Peasant women were organized in Housewives' Clubs by Caritas, and they did not think in terms of land. There was no proposal to allow women access to land. Some people were aware of this but it was not a priority. The priority was to organize [agrarian reform] enterprises, and it was men who organized and led these."[37] According to peasant leader Deisy Echavarría, "As women we have not been active in the cooperative model for it was aimed at the men . . . we have not been successful in penetrating the cooperatives."[38] An in-depth study of four Honduran *asentamientos* illustrates how the implementation of the law resulted in the virtual exclusion of female household heads (Safilios-Rothschild 1983: 19). Women were simply not considered to be agriculturalists. Although their participation in certain tasks was recognized, women were not considered capable of carrying out the heavier agricultural work. Male cooperative members thus felt that women could join the cooperatives only if they had sons to carry out the agricultural fieldwork (Bradshaw 1995a: 147). In cooperatives that do have a few women members (such as in Yoro, where there are two or three women out of a total membership of fifty to sixty-five), their membership is purely "symbolic"; the active member is the oldest son.[39]

In cooperatives that did have working women members, the gendered division of labor contributed to a devaluation of women's contribution to the collective effort. According to researcher Emma Mejía,[40] women members were assigned to the care of small animals while the men tended cattle; similarly, women worked on the crops destined for the cooperative's self-provisioning rather than on cash crops. Since the activities carried out by women were seen to be less important than those carried out by the men, the male members considered that women were contributing less than they were to the cooperative's success, and they resented women's right to participate in cooperative decision making. At the same time, women had to work on the cooperatives "with the same responsibilities as the men," meaning the same hours, a requirement that did not take into account women's additional responsibilities for domestic work and child care. The latter factor contributed to fairly high female drop-out rates on the cooperatives, reinforcing the prejudices of the male members against incorporating women.

The wives of cooperative members were at a disadvantage if they became widowed, for the family did not automatically inherit the right to cooperative membership; rather, the cooperative members themselves decided who, if anyone, was to be the beneficiary (Bradshaw 1995a: 147). As it was explained to us, "widows are few in the cooperatives because when a *compañero* dies, the cooperative purchases the share of the deceased member so that the woman does not bring a new man into the cooperative."[41] When the cooperative grants membership to a grown son, rather than to the widow, it can lead to the following situation: "In some cases the son then forms his own family and has expelled his own mother and small siblings from the land, a situation which would not happen if the law gave the mother the preferential right" (Martínez, Rosales, and Rivera 1995: 43).

The main gender-equitable change in Honduran land legislation came about in 1991, when the Permanent Women's Forum of the National Congress succeeded in modifying various clauses of the agrarian reform legislation that had discriminated against women (Martínez, Rosales, and Rivera 1995: 43). Articles 79 and 84, which addressed the designation of beneficiaries and inheritance, were rewritten in explicitly nonsexist language. Revised Article 79 also established for the first time that single women *or* men above the age of sixteen could be beneficiaries of the reform, irrespective of whether they were a household head (as in Mexico after 1971). Moreover, the revised legislation explicitly provided for land to be jointly allocated and titled to married couples or partners in consensual unions. Revised Article 84 established that the spouse or partner had rights of first inheritance to land ceded under the agrarian reform. These gender-progressive modifications were adopted just after the neoliberal government of Rafael Callejas came to office with the intention of ending the agrarian reform.

Turning to Ecuador, its agrarian reform passed through numerous phases after the initial Alliance for Progress legislation was promulgated in 1964. The first phase eliminated pre-capitalist relations of production on highland haciendas under a land-to-the-tiller program. In 1970 sharecropping was proscribed on coastal rice plantations, and these estates were expropriated and adjudicated collectively to production cooperatives. A second agrarian reform law was issued in 1973, and the pace of expropriations of underutilized estates increased; nonetheless, colonization programs in the Amazonian and coastal regions were more important than agrarian reform efforts.[42]

While Ecuador has never collected official data on beneficiaries by sex, most studies suggest that women were a very small proportion of those benefiting directly from either agrarian reform land allotments or the colonization program (Martínez 1992). In a study of rice cooperatives in the Guayas River Basin, it was found that women made up only 5.7 percent of the members; in another study of the coastal region, women constituted 8.8 percent of the cooperative membership (Phillips 1987: 113). In a study in the sierra, in the canton Machachi, it was found that only 5.3

percent of the agrarian reform beneficiaries were women (Stolen 1987: 43). The small share of women beneficiaries was largely due to two factors: the priority given to household heads, who were assumed to be male, and discriminatory provisions in the law on cooperatives. Article 84 of the initial agrarian reform law stipulated that priority be given to household heads whose principal activity was agriculture and who otherwise were landless or near-landless, a provision maintained in the 1973 law (García 1993: 6). Since culturally it is assumed that in a household composed of an adult man and woman, the man is the head, the vast majority of beneficiaries of agrarian reform and colonization allocations were male. This practice was supported by the civil code of the time, which stipulated that the husband was the administrator of all marital property. The law on cooperatives contained two discriminatory provisions: Article 18, which required married women to obtain the consent of their husbands to join an agricultural cooperative; and Article 19, which forbade both spouses from being members of the same agricultural cooperative. As Rosa Jordán (1996: 60) argues, this largely explains the very low percentage of women in the coastal agricultural cooperatives.

Colombia's 1961 Agrarian Reform Law No. 135 did not directly discriminate against women—the beneficiaries were to be sharecroppers, renters, and landless wage workers. However, in practice, only one person per household was designated the beneficiary and this was usually the male household head. This practice conformed to the civil code of the time, which stipulated that husbands represented the household in all family matters. The discrimination against women was reinforced by the point system devised by the agrarian reform agency, INCORA (Instituto Colombiano de Reforma Agraria) to evaluate potential beneficiaries. The point system favored those who had histories of residence or work in or near the expropriated farm and those peasants with more education, larger families, good reputations, and farming experience (Edwards 1980: 60). Women would certainly have been at a disadvantage compared to men in terms of educational attainment. Moreover, female heads of household might also suffer under the reputation criterion if failure to conform to the patriarchal family norm lowered their status in the eyes of the community. Women would also be disadvantaged by the farming-experience criterion since men are always considered to be the agriculturalists, with women simply regarded as their "helpers."

Inheritance provisions were another source of discrimination against women. The family farms distributed by INCORA did not necessarily pass to surviving spouses or companions upon the death of the beneficiary. Rather, it was left up to the agrarian reform agency to determine the "best qualified heir." (It might choose the surviving spouse or companion, but there was no legal requirement to do so.) If no suitable heir was found, INCORA was authorized to purchase the family's investment in the land (Findley 1973: 164).[43] Given the invisibility of women as agriculturalists, it is doubtful that very many women inherited agrarian reform beneficiary status. As a result of all of these factors, women derived limited direct benefits under Law 135. Through 1986 they constituted only 11.2 percent of the direct beneficiaries (León, Prieto, and Salazar 1987: 49).

In 1984 Colombia became one of the first Latin American governments to adopt an explicit policy regarding the incorporation of women into the process of rural development. The policy was motivated by the food crisis characterizing this decade, and the growing recognition of both the importance of peasant production to national food supplies and women's participation in agriculture. This recognition, in concert with the Integrated Rural Development (DRI, Desarrollo Rural Integrado) programs that characterized this period, improved rural women's access to credit and technical assistance, particularly for income-generating projects. But the series of measures adopted in favor of rural women in this period did not carry the force of law and implementation was uneven, depending greatly on personalistic factors.[44] Moreover, since national consensus in support of a thorough agrarian reform still had not been achieved, the new initiatives did not adequately address women's lack of land rights.

One of the main accomplishments of this period was the growing organization of rural women under the umbrella of the various projects promoted by the new policy regarding rural women. In 1985 this process led to the creation of the first national association of rural women, ANMUCIC (Asociación Nacional de Mujeres Campesinas e Indígenas de Colombia) (Gómez-Restrepo 1991; Villareal 1998). While initially charged with developing projects aimed at rural women, this organization soon realized that income-generating projects for women were insufficient measures and began demanding that the agrarian law spell out explicitly the land rights of women. Their demands were to play an important role in shaping Agrarian Law 30 of 1988.

During the mid-1980s the peasant movement in Colombia, although quite divided, was growing in strength, partly in response to the agricultural crisis characterizing these years, which coincided with the spreading guerrilla threat and the growing influence of drug traffickers and paramilitary groups. In response to the demand to deepen the agrarian reform, the government adopted Agrarian Law 30. The new law did not substantially modify the principles of the initial agrarian reform; rather, it was designed to speed its implementation. But it was a singularly important law for rural women because for the first time it explicitly recognized women's land rights. Among the main provisions of the law was that, henceforth, agrarian reform allotments and titles were to be issued in the name of couples, irrespective of marital status. In addition, special provisions were made for female heads of household, who were to be given priority access to unutilized national lands and be assisted in gaining membership in communal enterprises created under the agrarian reform.

Between 1986 and 1991, there was a dramatic increase in the average annual number of agrarian reform beneficiaries as compared with the previous twenty-five years. However, notwithstanding the provisions in Law 30 favoring the incorporation of women, the proportion of women beneficiaries nationally remained the same, 11 percent (Durán Ariza 1991, Appendix 3). This figure is considerably below the estimated share of female-headed households in rural areas in that period, 17.1 percent (Colombia 1993).[45] A number of difficulties were encountered in implementing the more gender-equitable norms of Agrarian Law 30. For example, in 1989 the executive committee of INCORA issued a directive that made joint titling of land mandatory when so requested by a man and his wife or companion, suggesting that the main resistance to joint titling came from INCORA's own functionaries. Moreover, in order to increase the proportion of female beneficiaries, INCORA issued another circular in 1991 giving priority to women who were in a state of "lack of protection" due to Colombia's increasing violence, which was associated with a rising incidence of widowhood and female abandonment. Women in such a situation were to be given an additional ten points on their application to become land beneficiaries (Medrano 1996: 7). These dispositions, which were incorporated into the next agrarian law, finally began to increase women's access to land in adjudications of the mid-1990s.

Under military rule Brazil adopted a mild agrarian reform law in 1964, the Estatuto Agrario, in part to co-opt what until the military coup had been a growing and increasingly radical peasant movement (the *ligas camponesas*) and in order to qualify for the benefits of the Alliance for Progress. The law established the following order of preference for agrarian reform beneficiaries: (1) the expropriated owner who wanted to work a land parcel with family labor; (2) workers on the estate who held a land parcel in usufruct or were wage workers; (3) peasants whose properties were less than those required for family farming in the region and did not provide for family subsistence; and (4) those with farming experience. Within these categories, priority was given to household heads with the largest families who had agricultural experience (Article 25, in da Luz 1996: 123). These criteria discriminated against women since, as in other Latin American countries, if a man resided in the household, he was always considered its head. The criteria regarding the size of the family labor force also introduced a bias against female-headed households since these, by definition, are smaller in size, given the absence of an adult male. Moreover, in selecting beneficiaries, the agrarian reform agency, INCRA (Instituto Nacional de Colonização e Reforma Agraria), applied a point system whereby men between eighteen and sixty years of age were awarded one point while women in this age group were awarded only .75 points. The discrimination by sex was maintained for children, with boys between the ages of fourteen and seventeen awarded .75 points and girls .50; boys between the ages of nine and thirteen were awarded .25 points and girls .20 (ibid.). This norm clearly discriminated against female-headed households as well as those households with large numbers of female children. The criteria regarding the length of experience in agricultural work also discriminated against women. As unpaid family labor, women's work in agriculture tends to be invisible and undervalued, even by women themselves. Moreover, it is difficult for women to prove their agricultural experience for, until recently, few women belonged to the rural unions (Albuquerque and Ruffino 1987: 325; Suárez and Libardoni 1992: 119; Siqueira 1991: 63).[46]

According to Lena Lavinas (1991: 6), the discrimination against women was such that "in the distribution of land plots in the colonization or agrarian reform projects single women, even if they were heads of household, were not taken into account unless they had a grown son who could serve as the representative of the household. Similarly, when women were widowed they lost their right to the land plot and had to leave the *assentamentos,* many times returning either to rent their plot or to work it as a temporary wage worker." Other scholars concur that it was customary for women who found themselves widowed with young children to lose their right to remain in an agrarian reform project.[47]

During the whole period of military rule in Brazil (1964–1984) only 185 estates, totaling 13.5 million hectares, were expropriated by INCRA for purposes of agrarian reform, benefiting 115,000 families (Cardoso 1997: 22). Priority in terms of solving the problems of landlessness and rural conflict was given to planned and spontaneous colonization of the Amazonian frontier, which coincided with the military's concern for securing Brazil's borders.

Upon Brazil's return to civilian rule in 1985, President José Sarney introduced a proposal for a National Agrarian Reform Plan of the New Republic (PNRA-NR) and created a new Ministry for Agrarian Reform and Rural Development (MIRAD). The landed oligarchy quickly organized themselves in opposition, and the PNRA-NR was redrafted twelve times before it became law in October 1985 (Hall 1990: 219). The debates over the PNRA-NR overlapped with the drafting of Brazil's new constitution, which was approved in 1988. The landlord's lobby was once again successful in making sure that provisions for agrarian reform were watered down and left vague. In this context, little progress was made in the late 1980s on agrarian reform (Suárez and Libardoni 1992: 110).

Nonetheless, among the reported objectives of the Sarney government's PNRA-NR was to distribute land more equitably between men and women. Thus in 1986 MIRAD issued a directive to INCRA recommending that beneficiaries be chosen "independently of sex" (Suárez and Libardoni 1992: 118–19).[48] However, it was not until the 1988 constitution that the main gender progressive step was taken. The new constitution established that in land to be distributed through the agrarian reform, "titles of ownership and use should be granted in the name of men, women or both, independently of their marital status" (Article 189, in da Luz 1996: 177). This article is noteworthy because this was the first time that it became explicit that women could be beneficiaries of the agrarian reform. Moreover, Brazil (along with Colombia in 1988) became the first country to provide for the possibility of joint titling of agrarian reform land. However, because the provision for joint titling was not made obligatory, its application was left to the whim of functionaries. Thus while this constitutional provision represented a major legal advance for gender equity, its application in practice was limited. Nonetheless, INCRA subsequently revised its beneficiary selection criteria, and equal weight was now to be given to male and female labor in the point system (Suárez and Libardoni 1992: 118).

INCRA still does not keep data on agrarian reform beneficiaries by sex or on the joint titling of land.[49] The first agrarian reform census in 1996 revealed that women made up 12.6 percent of the 159,778 beneficiaries on 1,425 *assentamentos* (INCRA/CRUB/UNB 1998: 26).[50] As a national average, researchers consider this figure to be high, given the discrimination to which women were subject until the 1988 constitution and subsequent changes in beneficiary criteria.[51] However, this figure is close to the 1991 census figure for rural female household heads, which was 12.2 percent (Brasil 1996: table 6.11). It is probable that since 1990 the selection of beneficiaries has become more gender equitable, and, according to the agrarian reform census, almost half of the beneficiaries were settled on *assentamentos* since that date (ibid.: 35). In sum, up until the late 1980s, agrarian reform and colonization efforts in Brazil were extremely limited in scope in addition to being discriminatory against women.

More Radical Reforms of the 1970s: Peru and Chile

Two of the agrarian reforms initiated under the Alliance for Progress were subsequently modified and deepened by progressive regimes in the 1970s, the radical military government of Peru and Chile under the Allende administration. While both reforms were notable in terms of their breadth, neither took into account gender-equity considerations and both proved to be as patriarchal as the other, more minimalist reforms in the region.

When the revolutionary military government in Peru came to power in 1968, its leaders were well aware of the political potency of the land issue for they had been called in time and again to repress the peasant land invasions in the sierra in the 1950s and 1960s. Moreover, the government of General Juan Velasco Alvarado was committed to national modernization, and structural reform of the agrarian sector was considered a prerequisite to needed social change. The main thrust of the military's agrarian reform was anti-feudal and based on the principle of "land for he who works it." In practice, the reform ended up being anti-capitalist as well, largely as a result of peasant militancy. Through Decree Law 17716 of 1969 some 427,000 households, approximately one-third of rural households, were allocated almost half of Peru's agricultural and forest land.[52] The vast majority of beneficiaries received land through various types of associative enterprises, including production cooperatives, peasant communities and groups, and *sociedades agrícolas de interés social* (SAIS), which combined production cooperatives and peasant communities into one profit-sharing unit. Less than 10 percent of the beneficiaries were allocated land individually, although in practice the majority of land farmed within peasant communities and groups was farmed individually (del Castillo 1997b).

Very few rural women benefited directly through the agrarian reform, primarily because beneficiaries were required to be household heads over eighteen years of age with dependents. In addition, beneficiaries had to be employed exclusively in agriculture, not own more land than the regionally defined family farming unit, and have worked under pre-capitalist forms of tenancy on a hacienda (Article 84, in Lafosse de Vega-Centeno 1969). In the case of the production cooperatives formed in what had formerly been capitalist enterprises, the primary beneficiaries were the permanent agricultural workers who were employed on the estates at the moment of expropriation. These permanent workers were generally men, although women were often an important component of the seasonal agricultural labor force. For example, Blanca Fernández (1982) shows that on the cotton plantations in the department of Piura, women represented up to 40 percent of the temporary labor, but few women held permanent jobs. As a result, women ended up constituting only 2 percent of the cooperative membership. The inability of the agrarian reform to benefit all seasonal agricultural workers was detrimental to both men and women. But whereas men were found in both categories of workers, permanent and seasonal, women were only a part of the seasonal workforce. Thus, for structural reasons, they were excluded as a social group as beneficiaries of the reform. In order to become cooperative members and thus potential beneficiaries of the reform, the few women who were permanent workers were subject to the requirement that they also be household heads, further reducing their participation.

The differential impact of the head-of-household criterion is clearly seen in the case of those agricultural enterprises where both men and women were employed on a permanent basis. For example, in the dairy region of the province of Cajamarca, women made up from 30 to 50 percent of the permanent workers on the dairy farms, since milking was still done manually and considered a female occupation. But of the fifteen cooperatives in the region, only five had female members, and overall women constituted only 2 percent of the cooperative membership (Deere 1977). National-level data, disaggregated by sex, were never collected by Peruvian reform officials since data-collection efforts focused on beneficiary households. Survey data for eighty-three production cooperatives showed that in a sample of 724 members, approximately 5 percent were women (Buchler 1975). As a national estimate even this figure may be high, for this 1971 survey excluded the coastal agro-industrial sugar cooperatives whose members were almost exclusively male. No estimates have been made of the proportion of women among those who received individual land allocations, but there is agreement that women were generally excluded as direct beneficiaries from the agrarian reform (Casafranca and Espinoza 1993: 18; Peru 1994b: 22; Macassi León 1996b: 38; del Castillo 1997a).

The main way that women might potentially acquire land rights through the reform was by inheriting them from a husband or partner upon his death. Article 88 of the law specified that, upon the death of a beneficiary who had not completed the purchase of his parcel, the agrarian reform authorities were to assign the parcel, without charge, to the spouse or permanent companion and the children under eighteen years of age, and that they were not obliged to pay for the land until the youngest child reached eighteen years of age (Macassi León 1996a: 17). This article was, thus, favorable to women since it assumed that women became the household head upon being widowed and also recognized the land rights of women in consensual unions even though the civil code of the time did not. But in the case of those who had finished paying for their parcel, the rules were different. If a beneficiary left a will, then the parcel would go to whoever was designated as the heir as long as that person worked the land directly (Article 104). This provision was also contrary to the civil code, but in a manner potentially less favorable to women since the civil code automatically guaranteed spouses and children one-third of the estate of the deceased. If the beneficiary died intestate, then it was up to the legal heirs (the spouse, children, and parents of the deceased) to decide to whom the parcel should pass. If they could not agree, this task fell to the agrarian reform authorities, who were to allocate the parcel among those heirs meeting the conditions of the law (i.e., that they be over eighteen, work the land directly, and be household heads). Lawyer Ivonne Macassi León (ibid.) argues that this article excluded permanent companions since, even after consensual unions were officially recognized, the civil code did not provide for partners in consensual unions to inherit from each other. This point is important, and works against women acquiring land rights, since consensual unions are very common in the highlands. In sum, the Peruvian agrarian reform may have appeared to be gender neutral in that it did not explicitly exclude women from being beneficiaries, but in practice legal, structural, and cultural factors served to exclude the great majority of rural women as direct beneficiaries.

The Chilean agrarian reform began in 1962, but not much land redistribution took place until the Christian Democratic government of Eduardo Frei took office in 1964. The election of the socialist Salvador Allende in 1970 rapidly increased the pace of the agrarian reform. Almost as many farms were expropriated in his first year in office as in the six-year term of Frei (Thiesenhusen 1995: 104). By 1973 the Chilean reformed sector consisted of approximately 40 percent of the country's agricultural land. Estimates of the number of beneficiaries vary widely, from a minimum of fifty-six thousand households (Echenique 1996: 74) to some seventy-six thousand (Silva 1991: 16) but in any case a figure amounting to 20 percent or less of the total number of landless families at the time.

Rural women were virtually excluded from the Christian Democratic agrarian reform primarily because beneficiaries were required to be household heads (Article 71, in Chile 1967: 35). In addition, an elaborate point system prioritized those who had agricultural experience and who lived and worked full-time on the estate—the *inquilinos* (tenant farmers) and permanent wage workers (Garrett 1982: 280). According to researcher Ximena Valdés (1995: 163), "Land rights were only conceptualized in terms of men. . . . Men's form of insertion on the *fundos* [farms] and haciendas, plus their familial situation and number of dependents, constituted the basis for their being given access to the expropriated lands in the reformed sector. Women were thus excluded from access to land. Through its policy, the state contributed to reinforcing the existing peasant practice of land only being transmitted through the male line." The practice of making male household heads the direct beneficiaries of the reform was also consistent with the provisions of the civil code whereby the husband was the administrator of the household's common property and its representative in dealings with third parties (Garrett 1982: 281). Moreover, female household heads were virtually excluded from the reform by the preference given to permanent workers on the estates. Although quantitative data are not available on the gender composition of the reform's beneficiaries, there is widespread agreement that few women benefited directly from the agrarian reform of either the Christian Democrat or Popular Unity (UP, Unidad Popular) governments (ibid.; Mack et al. 1987; Tinsman 1996: 323, 331–32).

Allende's UP government broadened the criteria for defining beneficiaries of the reform since it was concerned with expanding employment opportunities in the countryside as well as narrowing the gap that had developed between those who were members of the *asentamientos* and the temporary, seasonal workers they often employed. In place of the *asentamientos,* the UP began organizing new Centers of Agrarian Reform (CERAs), which grouped together several expropriated estates in the hope of achieving economies of scale. The idea was to include not only permanent and temporary workers as members of these new units but also their family members who were over eighteen years of age. All members were to participate in the general assembly of the CERAS and elect members to the diverse working committees, one of which was the social welfare committee. This committee, conceptualized as the means to provide collective solutions to common problems, was considered the most important vehicle to organize women and ensure their participation in the reform process (Garrett 1982: 283).

As the criteria for participation in the reform were broadened, the legal and structural impediments to women's participation were eliminated. Patricia Garrett argues, nonetheless, that the new agrarian reform structure had limited success in incorporating women. Women's participation in the CERAS was resisted by both men and women. Indeed, one of the most frequent criticisms of the CERAS was that they allowed the participation of women.[53] Women's resistance to participation in the CERAS was closely linked to cultural practices. Garrett (1982) points to the conservative influence of the strongest women's organization in the countryside at the time, the Mothers' Centers (CEMAS, Centros de Madres), organized by the Catholic Church, political parties, and the state under the Frei administration. The focus of the CEMAS was on women's domestic role, and they gave little attention to women's role in production. Moreover, they were not concerned with social problems since even these were considered inappropriate matters for women. But they did provide rural women with a form of social participation that drew them out of their homes into a forum where they could discuss ordinary problems. At their height in 1973 there were twenty thousand CEMAS nationwide with a membership of almost one million women (Tinsman 1996: 252).

As Garrett argues, neither men nor women considered that women should be concerned with problems that went beyond the domestic realm, and few rural women joined the social welfare committees. Moreover, the Allende government did not have the human resources required to organize rural women along lines different from what was already in place. This lack was partly due to the political difficulties it faced by 1973, but it also reflects the absence of a clear state policy regarding the incorporation of women. According to Heidi Tinsman:

> [W]hen it became clear that the CERA's inclusion of women jeopardized male support for the UP Agrarian Reform, government functionaries quickly capitulated. According to several oral accounts, while local INDAP [Instituto de Desarrollo Agropecuario] and CORA [Corporación

de Reforma Agraria] officials informed rural workers that CERAS were open to all campesinos regardless of sex, they did not push men to bring their wives to General Assembly meetings . . . the UP was willing to sacrifice its goals for rural women because of the expediency of maintaining men's allegiance. (Tinsman 1996: 418)

The two broadest experiments in Latin America under the legacy of the Alliance for Progress thus had results similar to those of their predecessors. Women were bypassed as direct beneficiaries of the reform for it was assumed that by granting land rights to household heads, all household members would benefit. The lesson of the Chilean experience appears to be that, in the absence of a women's movement with a feminist consciousness, even a progressive government interested in broadening beneficiary criteria would encounter strong resistance.

Land Reform and Civil War: The 1980s in Central America

The Sandinista revolution in Nicaragua and civil war in neighboring El Salvador once again drew attention to the pressing need for agrarian reform in Central America, and both countries subsequently carried out significant land-redistribution efforts. Guatemala remained immune to efforts to address the land hunger of the rural poor, its military governments in the decade of the 1980s engaging instead in brutal repression in the countryside. In Honduras land reform efforts wound down, and in Costa Rica low-key efforts at land distribution continued as usual.

The Sandinista agrarian reform began in 1979 with the confiscation of land owned by the deposed dictator, Anastasio Somoza, and his close associates. By the time the Sandinistas left office in 1990, over five thousand farms accounting for almost 3 million hectares had been expropriated and redistributed (Kaimowitz 1989: 386). The agrarian reform ended up affecting 46.2 percent of the nation's farmland, which was redistributed as follows: 13.9 percent of the total area was held by production cooperatives of various types; 11.7 percent was organized into state farms; 20.7 percent was allocated to individuals; and 2.1 percent was given back to indigenous communities (CIERA 1989, vol. 9: 39).

The Sandinista agrarian reform was the first in Latin America to include the incorporation of women among its initial objectives. The 1981 agrarian reform law stipulated that neither gender nor kinship status would hinder someone from becoming a beneficiary of the reform. More-over, the 1981 agricultural cooperative law established that a goal of the cooperatives should be to encourage the active participation of women, stating that they should be incorporated into the cooperatives under the same terms as men, with the same rights and duties (CIERA 1984: 27). The Sandinista experience underscores the point that an explicit state policy favoring the incorporation of women as beneficiaries is a necessary but not sufficient condition for women to acquire land rights. Between 1979 and 1989, a total of 5,800 rural women benefited directly under the Sandinista agrarian reform, representing 9.7 percent of the 59,545 beneficiaries (INRA-INIM 1996: 10). Women made up 11 percent of the members of the production cooperatives and 8 percent of those allotted individual land parcels.[54] Female-headed households constituted approximately 19 percent of the total in rural Nicaragua in the early 1990s (Valdés and Gomáriz 1997: 33), suggesting the extent to which women were discriminated against, notwithstanding the provisions favoring gender equity.

One of the main changes that took place during the decade of the 1980s was the growing presence of rural women in the Sandinista mass organizations. In 1984 the rural workers' association, the Asociación de Trabajadores del Campo (ATC), created a women's division and began organizing temporary and permanent women wage workers in both the state and private sectors. By 1989 women represented 40 percent of its membership of 135,000. Their growing weight in the union movement reflected the growing feminization of the agricultural labor force that occurred during the contra war and the concerted effort of the ATC to incorporate them (CIERA-ATC-CETRA 1987). It was not until 1986 that the peasant association UNAG (Unión Nacional de Agricultores y Ganaderos) organized a women's division and began to play a more active role in incorporating women as UNAG and cooperative members. By 1989 women constituted 12 percent of its membership of 125,000. In February 1989, when the first national meeting of peasant women leaders was held, one of the main demands that emerged was that land distributed through the agrarian reform be allocated and titled in the name of both spouses.[55] Rural women in this period also demanded that they be allowed to cultivate unused state land for self-provisioning purposes and that they be integrated into the cooperatives as members (CIERA 1989, vol. 7: 77–79; Pérez Alemán 1990: 90–95). By the end of the Sandinista period, two thousand women wage workers had been given access to self-sufficiency parcels on state farms and another thousand women had formed production collectives on lands borrowed from production cooperatives (INIM 1995: 75), illustrating the growing demand of women for access to land and for their incorporation as beneficiaries of the agrarian reform.

The gains rural women made in terms of land rights under the Sandinista government, however, were not much greater than those of their Central American neighbors (particularly in Costa Rica and El Salvador), which did not have gender-equitable agrarian laws in this decade. This result may be explained by the following factors: (1) the goal of gender equity was not broadly internalized by the Sandinista leadership and was not given priority in organizational efforts; (2) there was a considerable delay between the time when the agrarian reform was initiated and when the leaders of the Sandinista rural mass organizations were sensitized to gender issues; (3) and, finally, by the time the rural mass organizations began to internalize gender issues, the contra war and the deteriorating state of the economy paralyzed effective action.[56]

The main female beneficiaries of Sandinista agrarian reform efforts ended up being female heads of household, as in neighboring Honduras, El Salvador, and Costa Rica. The proportion of female beneficiaries was considerably greater in Nicaragua than in Honduras, suggesting that gender-equitable legislation did make some difference. But the fact that the share of female beneficiaries was similar to those in the Salvadoran and Costa Rican reforms also indicates the strength of the resistance to recognizing women's land rights. Moreover, rural women need to know of their rights and be in a supportive setting to claim them, and this, in turn, requires the strong support of both women's and peasant organizations (Deere 1983; Padilla, Murguialday, and Criquillón 1987). These conditions came together in a very different context in the 1990s.

Agrarian reform was not seriously considered in El Salvador until the country was in the midst of a profound social crisis related to the country's inegalitarian land-tenure structure and the rural poverty with which it was associated.[57] In response to the increasingly vocal demands of peasant organizations for agrarian reform, the Instituto Salvadoreño de Transformación Agraria (ISTA) was set up in 1975, but its initial efforts at land redistribution were extremely limited. After the victorious Sandinista revolution in neighboring Nicaragua, and at U.S. prodding, agrarian reform was initiated by a military-civilian junta in 1980. In Phase I (Decree 154), all farms larger than five hundred hectares were expropriated with compensation. On these lands, production cooperatives were constituted, primarily made up of the permanent workers on these estates. Phase III

(Decree 207), initiated in 1983, was a land-to-the-tiller reform.[58] All renters and sharecroppers on farms of less than a hundred hectares in size were to become the owners of the plots they worked up to a maximum size of seven hectares.

In May 1991, after a decade of agrarian reform, 81,799 households had benefited under Phases I and III, representing approximately 11 percent of the rural economically active population (Fund. Arias 1992: 31).[59] Women constituted 11.7 percent of the beneficiaries under Phase I, and 10.5 percent under Phase III (ibid.: 34).[60] While these figures compare favorably with what was accomplished under the Sandinista agrarian reform in Nicaragua, the full picture is somewhat more complicated. When the production cooperatives of Phase I were constituted, generally only one person per family could join, the household head (ibid.: 47).[61] Since, as elsewhere, an adult male residing in a household is always considered its head, the main group of women who benefited were single women with young children. Given the very high incidence of female-headed households in rural El Salvador, an estimated 21.2 percent in 1985 and 23.5 percent in 1992 (El Salvador 1985: Table B-39.3; El Salvador 1992: 292–94), it is apparent that women were under-represented among the beneficiaries.

Further, women cooperative members have not fared as well as men in terms of the benefits of cooperative membership. The great majority of production cooperatives assign some land to their members for their own self-provisioning efforts. In a survey of cooperative households in the mid-1980s, it was found that 82 percent of male-headed households had access to an individual land parcel compared to only 65 percent of female-headed households. Moreover, when women were assigned parcels within the cooperatives, they tended to get the poorest land and the smallest parcels—an average of .5 *manzanas* (one *manzana* equals .7 hectares) for women and .8 *manzanas* for men (Lastarría-Cornhiel 1988: 594–95).

Finally, in Phase III of the reform relatively more women ended up having their lands expropriated than emerged as beneficiaries. Women constituted 36 percent of those whose lands were expropriated[62] but only 10.5 percent of the beneficiaries. The great majority of those who lost land were elderly widows and single women who did not work the land directly themselves, but rather sharecropped it or rented it out (Fund. Arias 1992: 36). In their effort to generate the largest number of beneficiaries who might support the program of the military-civilian junta, the reformers failed to recognize the importance that women might place on owning land (as a source of food or income, or for old-age security). In general, this phase

of the reform had unintended negative consequences for many poor peasant households. Some campesinos had been forced to rent their land because they did not have the working capital to put it into production, while
others had migrated temporarily in order to earn wage income (Thiesenhusen 1995: 151). What is ironic is that absentee landowners who owned
between 150 and 500 hectares were totally exempt from the reform even if
they worked the land with sharecroppers or renters. Thus political expe-
diencies far outshadowed considerations of equity and, in particular, gender equity.

In gender terms, inheritance rights to cooperative membership were
the most favorable aspect of the Salvadoran agrarian legislation of the
early 1980s. If a member died, any family member could replace him in
the cooperative, but preference was supposed to be given to the spouse or
partner (*compañera de vida*).[63] Nonetheless, this did not always happen in
practice: "When a member died it was established that the spouse would
be the beneficiary, but there were problems in incorporating women and
generally the oldest son would replace him. But at some point the son
would form his own family and that woman would be left without a source
of support" (Fund. Arias 1992: 49). With respect to Phase III beneficiaries,
inheritance rights followed the norms of the civil code of the time, which
were not as favorable to women as the regulations governing the cooperatives. A beneficiary was at total liberty to will the land to whomever he
chose, so that the land rights of the spouse or partner were not guaranteed. If a beneficiary died intestate, the legal heirs included his spouse,
children, and parents, but not partners in consensual unions and "natural" children since consensual unions were not legally recognized at that
time (FAO 1990: 5; FAO 1992: 88). In sum, the agrarian reforms initiated in
the 1980s had disappointing results from a gender perspective. In both the
Sandinista and Salvadoran reforms, even the most likely group of women
to be included as beneficiaries, female heads of household, were considerably under-represented.

The Exclusion of Women

The Latin American agrarian reform experience leads to one overall conclusion: rural women were largely excluded as direct beneficiaries. Reformers intended to benefit peasant families, assuming that these processes were
gender neutral; instead, they ended up being gender-biased, primarily bene-

fiting male household heads. Table 3.2 summarizes the data on the female beneficiaries. Women's participation ranged from negligible or low (in Chile, Ecuador, Honduras, and Peru) to a high of one-third of the beneficiaries.[64] The mode was 11 to 12 percent, a figure much lower than the incidence of rural female household heads in most countries. The figures on the high end must be qualified, however, for in Mexico, Bolivia, and Cuba women were also a very low proportion of the direct beneficiaries in the initial years of these reforms, which was when the bulk of the land was distributed. In all three of the pioneering agrarian reforms, women's participation grew over time, partly as a result of inheritance, but also because of factors particular to each reform.

It is worth highlighting the fact that the percentage of female cooperative members in Cuba in the 1980s was almost double the share of women members in the other Latin American countries that promoted production cooperatives in this period. The high Cuban figure reflects the policy decision that all adult family members, irrespective of sex, could join the production cooperatives coupled with the efforts of the peasant organization, ANAP, to ensure that women actually did so. Nicaragua also enunciated such a policy, but then did little to implement it, suggesting how the guarantee of formal land rights is a necessary but not sufficient condition to ensure that women benefit directly from an agrarian reform and acquire effective land rights.

The difficulty in determining the number of female beneficiaries with precision is also worth noting. First, information on female beneficiaries shares all of the general problems of comparative agrarian reform data. Estimates for any given country often vary depending on which groups are counted as beneficiaries (e.g., whether squatters who benefit through titling efforts on public land are included). Second, government planners assumed that the intended beneficiaries of agrarian reform efforts were rural households or families, and some countries—such as Bolivia, Chile, Ecuador, and Peru—did not even ask the sex of the prospective beneficiary on the application form. In countries that did collect beneficiary data by sex, it was not until the 1980s, after prodding by feminist researchers, that this information was analyzed. In Honduras statistics on gender were processed for only one year, and the collection of such information never became routine. In Bolivia, where the gender variable was not reported on beneficiary forms, it has been possible to reconstruct this variable only through the analysis of given names for a sample of beneficiaries. In Chile, Ecuador, and Peru the application forms have long since disappeared, making such an effort currently impossible.[65] Only the most recent agrarian re-

TABLE 3.2. Percentage of Female Beneficiaries in Thirteen Latin American Agrarian Reform and Colonization Programs

Country/Years of Reform	Female Beneficiaries (%)		
Bolivia (1954–1994)	17.2 (1994)		
Brazil (1964–1996)	12.6 (1996)		
Chile (1964–1973)	low		
Colombia (1961–1991)	11.2 (1986)	11.0 (1991)	
Costa Rica (1963–1988)	11.8 (1988)		
Cuba (1959–1988)	Cooperatives: 34.7 Individuals: 5.5 (1979)	21.0 13.0 (1988)	
El Salvador (1980–1991)	Cooperatives: 11.7 Individuals: 10.5 (1991)		
Ecuador (1964–1993)	low		
Honduras (1962–1991)	3.8 (1979)		
Guatemala (1962–1996)	8.0 (1996)		
Mexico (1920–1992)	*Ejidos:* 1.3 (1970)	15.0 (1984)	
Nicaragua (1981–1990)	Collectives: 11.0 Individuals: 8.0 (1990)		
Peru (1970–1991)	low		

Sources: Bolivia: INRA, data made available to the authors, 1997; Brazil: INCRA/CRUB/UNB (1998: 26); Chile: Garrett (1982), Valdés (1995), and Tinsman (1996: 418); Colombia: León, Prieto, and Salazar (1987: 49), and Durán Ariza (1991); Costa Rica: Brenes Marín and Antezana (1996: 2); Cuba: Stubbs and Alvarez (1987: table 8.1) and Galán (1998: 17); Ecuador: Phillips (1987) and Martínez (1992); El Salvador: Fundación Arias (1992: 34); Guatemala: Rivas and Bautista (1997: 6); Honduras: Callejas (1983) and Martínez, Rosales, and Rivera (1995: 37–38); Mexico: Valenzuela and Robles (1996: 37), and Arizpe and Botey (1987: 71); Nicaragua: INRA-INIM (1996: 10); Peru: Deere (1985: 1040), Casafranca and Espinosa (1993: 18), and Peru (1994: 22); and authors' interviews.

form programs maintain registries of beneficiaries by sex.[66] In the great majority of countries the task of obtaining gender-disaggregated data is still laborious and is typically undertaken by the understaffed women-and-development units of the agrarian reform institutes, such as in Colombia, Costa Rica, and Honduras. The lack of systematic data collection attests to the low priority that has been given to women's land rights by the majority of Latin American governments, notwithstanding important changes in civil codes with respect to women's property rights.

Women were excluded from the Latin American agrarian reforms for legal, structural, ideological or cultural, and institutional reasons (Deere 1985, 1986, 1987; Galán 1998: 17). All these factors are interrelated, and have as their basis patriarchal ideologies embedded in concepts of masculinity and femininity and the proper gender division of labor in the public and private spheres. Most agrarian reform laws appear to be gender neutral in that the beneficiaries are defined in terms of certain social groups, such as the tenants and permanent wage workers on the expropriated estates. However, without exception, the agrarian reform legislation refers to these groups in the masculine form. The language of agrarian reform legislation, by failing to explicitly include women, has served to reinforce the cultural assumptions of both planners and beneficiaries concerning who would benefit. The expectation that the beneficiaries would be male was often made explicit in the inheritance provisions of the laws, when the widow (and not the widower) was designated as the potential heir of the agrarian reform parcel upon the death of her husband or permanent companion.

Two culturally charged concepts permeated the Latin American agrarian reforms: that of agriculturalist and household head. Irrespective of the amount of labor that rural women dedicate to agriculture—whether as unpaid family workers or as wage workers—agriculture in Latin America has been socially constructed as a male occupation. As a result, women's work in agriculture is largely invisible. If considered at all, it is usually seen as supplementary assistance to the principal male farmer. As Table 3.3 shows, almost all of the Latin American agrarian reform laws favored agriculturalists as beneficiaries of their reforms. A related cultural notion is that rural households must always be headed by an adult male if one resides within the household. In practice, the two concepts have been conflated so that, even in the agricultural censuses, the agriculturalist of the household unit is assumed to be the male household head.[67] As Table 3.3 also shows, a number of agrarian reform laws explicitly required beneficiaries to be household heads. Those that did not explicitly designate household heads as beneficiaries stipulated that only one person per household could be a beneficiary. In either case, following cultural norms, if an adult male is present within the family, he would be designated the household head or representative of the family for agrarian reform purposes.

By the 1960s most Latin American civil codes recognized the legal

TABLE 3.3. Beneficiary Criteria of the Agrarian Reforms

Country and Year of Law	Household Head	One Person per Household	Single with Dependents	Point System	Agricultural Experience
Bolivia					
1952	No	Yes	Yes	No	Yes
Brazil					
1964	Yes	No	No	Yes	Yes
Chile					
1967	Yes	No	No	Yes	Yes
1971	No	No	No	No	No
Colombia					
1961	No	Yes	No	Yes	Yes
Costa Rica					
1961	Yes	No	No	Yes	Yes
Cuba					
1959	Yes	No	No	No	Yes
Ecuador					
1961	Yes	No	No	No	Yes
El Salvador					
1980	Yes	No	No	No	Yes
Guatemala					
1952	Yes	No	No	No	No
1962	No	Yes	No	No	Yes
Honduras					
1962	Yes	No	Yes	No	Yes
1975	Yes	No	Yes	No	Yes
Mexico					
1920	Yes	No	No	No	No
1922	No	No	Yes	No	No
1971	No	No	No	No	No
Nicaragua					
1981	No	No	No	No	No
Peru					
1969	Yes	No	No	No	Yes

Sources: See Table 3.2.

right of married women to manage their own assets. However, with the exception of Mexico, husbands continued to be the sole representative of the family and were responsible for administering the property and economic affairs of the household. Thus, the agrarian reforms that privileged male household heads as beneficiaries conformed to the civil codes of the time. The women who could have benefited most directly from the reforms were female heads of household, particularly in those countries (Mexico, Bolivia, and Honduras) that explicitly included them as potential beneficiaries. But with few exceptions (Mexico, Costa Rica, and Brazil), rural women represented a much higher percentage of reported rural households heads[68] than they did of agrarian reform beneficiaries, suggesting that structural, cultural, and institutional factors were, indeed, overwhelming barriers to their incorporation as direct beneficiaries.

A number of agrarian reform programs established point systems to evaluate prospective beneficiaries (see Table 3.3). The systems utilized in Brazil and Costa Rica were blatantly discriminatory, granting more points to male- than female-headed households, and more to male family labor than to female family labor. In addition, point systems that privileged large families also tended to discriminate against households headed by women, which, by definition, lacked an adult male worker and were thus smaller than male-headed households. The point systems employed in Chile and Colombia also favored those with more education and with farming experience. Given the persistent inequalities in male and female schooling levels in rural Latin America, these provisions constituted another form of discrimination against women. Point systems or priority lists were also utilized to favor one group of potential beneficiaries over another, such as permanent over temporary workers on estates.

In the case of the production cooperatives in Chile and Peru, the structural characteristics of men's and women's labor force participation served as another barrier to rural women. At the time the reforms went into effect in these countries, the permanent agricultural wage workers on the expropriated estates were generally men, although women were often an important component of the seasonal labor force. The failure of many of these reforms to benefit the vast majority of seasonal agricultural workers affected both men and women; however, men were found in both categories of workers—permanent and seasonal—while the structural characteristics of women's labor force participation resulted in their being excluded as a social group. The few women permanent workers on the estates, and thus potential beneficiaries of the reform, were then subject to an additional criterion: that they be household heads. This requirement, of course, reduced their participation still further (Deere 1987: 174). Other structural factors, such as high population growth rates and unfavorable person-land ratios, were also used as arguments to deny women access to land through the reforms (Fund. Arias 1992: 49–50; Safilios-Rothschild 1983: 17).

Up through the 1980s in Latin America, the ministries of agriculture and the agrarian reform institutes were male bastions, with few women on their professional staffs. The men implementing these reforms generally assumed that only men could be agriculturalists. The only professional women employed in the agricultural sector were home economists, who beginning in the 1940s were employed in programs charged with enhancing the living standards of poor rural families. These programs targeted women in their domestic roles, a task facilitated by the organization of rural women into mothers' or housewives' clubs by the Catholic Church, political parties, and other groups throughout Latin America. These were a particularly effective means of organizing women around reproductive rather than productive concerns in countries such as Chile, Bolivia, Peru, and Colombia.

Compounding the institutional barriers to women's direct incorporation as beneficiaries was the composition of the peasant organizations that thrived in concert with the agrarian reforms. Until the 1980s the membership and leadership of these groups was almost always exclusively male, although women were often active participants in demonstrations and land take-overs, and often in the forefront of potentially violent confrontations with the military or police. They carried the banners of "Land to the Tiller" and "Agrarian Reform Now!" from Mexico in the early decades of this century (Ramos 1993), to Honduras (Rosales 1994: 53), Colombia (Villareal 1998: 63; Comisión Mujer 1990: 27), and Peru (CEIMME 1995: 27; Radcliffe 1993: 212), among other countries. Yet women rarely had a voice or a vote within these organizations, and they were in no position to press their own specific gender interests with respect to land rights. The main demand of all these peasant organizations was voiced in class terms: the demand for land to the tiller. These organizations also assumed that in allocating land to the male household head, all household members would benefit, an assumption that excluded women from land rights.

One of the main ways in which women could sometimes attain beneficiary status and thus land rights was through the inheritance provisions of some of the reforms. The agrarian reform laws of El Salvador, Honduras, Mexico, and Peru all stipulated inheritance rules more favorable to the land rights of widows than the inheritance provisions of their civil codes (FAO 1992). In other countries that provided for wives or companions to inherit land rights upon the death of their mates, adult children also qualified as potential heirs, with the agrarian reform institute ultimately responsible for choosing the heir. In most countries with this provision, sons were almost always given priority over widows, to the detriment of the economic security of the latter.

The incorporation of gender-equitable criteria in agrarian reform laws in Latin America proceeded at a very slow pace until the decade of the 1980s. Mexico was the first country to reverse the discriminatory criteria contained in its reform laws, doing so in 1971, a time when the distribution of land for all effective purposes had ended. Nicaragua right from the beginning established that agrarian reform beneficiaries were to be selected independently of their sex and marital status, but pro-active measures to assure effective land rights for women were not pursued during the Sandinista regime. Brazil and Colombia at the end of the 1980s and Honduras in the early 1990s also took steps to modify previously discriminatory provisions in their agrarian reform legislation and regulations. These three countries were also the leaders in the region in introducing the possibility of joint allocation and titling of land to couples, responding to a demand that was beginning to be heard in other countries as well. But it would not be until the decade of the 1990s that a confluence of factors led to changes in the agrarian codes of most countries and to a significantly different gender composition of agrarian reform beneficiaries.

four

Building Blocks toward
Gender-Progressive Change

The man feels bad if the woman has land. If the woman has land, it is to individualize ownership; if the man had land it is said that it is the family's land.[1]

THE BUILDING BLOCKS that prepared the way for gender and land rights to be considered an important issue have been set in place at the international, national, and local levels. Our entry point is the genesis and evolution of the field of women in development (or WID), for this field provided the framework that has oriented the priorities of international agencies and the actions of governments in addressing gender concerns over the past several decades. The influence of the WID field grew in tandem with the consolidation and expansion of the international women's movement, the latter facilitated by the United Nations Decade for Women and the four international conferences with which it is associated.

The UN Decade for Women was proclaimed under the banner of "Equality, Development, and Peace" at the First UN Conference on Women, held in Mexico City in 1975. Of course, by this time, the *second* UN Development Decade was well underway, underscoring the argument of WID pioneer Ester Boserup that development efforts had ignored women.[2] In her foundational text *Women's Role in Economic Development* (1970),

Boserup argued that women had been marginalized from the development process both relatively and absolutely. Women had been marginalized relatively by not being taken into account explicitly in development efforts and not enjoying the presumed gains from development on equal terms with men. Women had been marginalized absolutely by being displaced at times from their traditional roles and activities, thus suffering a loss in socioeconomic status. For Boserup the problem was that the development field had not taken into account women's productive role. What attention development practitioners had given to women was limited to welfare issues concerning the well-being of families, where women were acknowledged to play socially useful roles as mothers and homemakers.[3] By not recognizing that women were often also farmers, for example, development practitioners overlooked the fact that efforts to increase yields might depend on convincing women as well as men to utilize improved seed. Thus ignoring women resulted in errors of policy design as well as "development failures"—an inability to transform traditional practices to generate increases in output and income.

If the problem was that women had been marginalized from development, then the solution was to integrate women into the development effort. The concept was appealing for it combined arguments for social justice with those of economic efficiency. To quote Lucille Mair, the secretary general of the Second UN Conference on Women, "Women had been a 'missing link' in development, now they were being found; they could actually be a valuable resource, indeed were half, or more, of a nation's human resources, no longer to be wasted" (in Tinker 1990: 31). Moreover, the premises of WID fit neatly within the dominant development paradigm of the period whereby economic development was viewed as a relatively linear and benign process of economic change, one propelled by economic growth. What was required for women to benefit from this process on the same terms as men was to expand their educational and employment opportunities, as well as to change the legal frameworks that discriminated against women.[4]

In the United States, the WID field was legitimized by the Percy Amendment to the U.S. Foreign Assistance Act of 1973, which instructed U.S. programs "to give particular attention to those programs, projects and activities which tend to integrate women into the national economies of foreign countries, thus improving their status and assisting the total development effort" (Tinker 1990: 31). Notwithstanding official U.S. support, in the international environment of 1974 it was still a major struggle to convince the UN General Assembly to approve an international women's conference. When the conference was finally authorized, it was approved without funding, leaving organizers only one year to secure external sources of support.[5]

An estimated six thousand women attended the gathering of NGOs held in tandem with the official UN Conference in Mexico City. With respect to the impact of the meetings, Lucille Mair again comments, "Mexico City focused on some of the fundamental issues . . . but it also did something that, while less tangible, may be in some ways more important than anything else: It established a network of concern" (in A. Fraser 1987: 71). In Latin America the networks that grew out of the Mexico City conference provided the impetus for the development of the regional feminist and women's movements, the former to be centered in future years around annual gatherings known as the Encuentros Feministas.[6] Among academics in both the United States and Latin America, it spurred research to make women and the sexual division of labor visible in the development process.[7]

The foundations of the women in development field were barely in place and beginning to gain acceptance in mainstream development discourse[8] when feminist scholars raised the question of *what kind of development* women were to be drawn into. Drawing on the critical social science of the 1970s, Lourdes Benería and Gita Sen (1981), for example, criticized Boserup for failing to challenge the modernization paradigm— specifically, for assuming that the capitalist model of development was benign. They pointed out that Boserup was blind to the role played by class relations in her assumption that discrimination against women was rooted only in traditional values that could be overcome through access to education, employment, and improved technology. Further, Benería and Sen argued that women's role in both production and reproduction had always been part of the development process and, moreover, that it was central to capitalist development.[9] Within what emerged as the women *and* development (WAD) approach, the problem of women's subordination required a more fundamental change in the development process, one that tackled the inequities in the global economic system and focused on changing exploitative class relations as well as women's oppression.[10]

International efforts in this period to commit nation states to the goal of gender equality centered on the negotiations leading to the approval, by the UN General Assembly in December 1979, of the Convention on the Elimination of All Forms of Discrimination against Women. This convention garnered sufficient signatures by 1981 to gain the status of an international treaty. Subsequent UN conferences on women, in Copenhagen in 1980 and Nairobi in 1985, maintained the momentum both to ratify the 1979 convention and to adopt national legislation to implement its provisions.

By the early 1980s there was a growing disillusionment within WID ranks, for its focus on enhancing women's productive role through income-generating activities had too often resulted in marginal, underfunded, women-only projects. Moreover, donor agencies typically channeled their activities through existing organizations that were thoroughly embedded in the old welfare paradigm; they commonly viewed women as housewives who had free time to earn "pin money" (Tinker 1990: 38). These projects seldom resulted in viable income-earning opportunities for women. Sometimes they only increased the length or intensity of their working day, and most did little to enhance women's status relative to men (Buvinic 1986; Flora 1987). There was optimism for a time within WID circles that the International Labor Organization (ILO)–World Bank emphasis of the early 1970s on meeting basic human needs (itself a criticism of the earlier mainstream development focus on economic growth) would bring compatibility between development and WID objectives. In order to meet basic needs, the poor had to participate in development programs rather than being passive recipients of welfare; moreover, a poverty-reduction strategy had to include women since they were often among the poorest of the poor and were traditionally charged with providing their household's basic needs. But the basic-needs strategy proved difficult to implement and short lived. At best, in the integrated rural development approach that became popular among Latin American governments in the 1970s—many times, as an alternative to carrying out more fundamental agrarian reforms— basic needs were often marginalized along with rural women as the "social component add-on" to "real" development efforts (Chaney 1987).

As WID practitioners struggled with how to bring women into the mainstream of development efforts, advances within feminist theory shifted the focus of attention from the study of women to that of gender. For feminists the concept of gender highlighted the social rather than biological origins of the sexual division of labor. Joan Scott (1988a: 42) provided a widely cited definition of the concept, emphasizing two interrelated propositions: "gender is a constitutive element of social relationships based on perceived differences between the sexes, and gender is a primary way of signifying relationships of power." As Benería and Roldán conceptualize it,

Gender may be defined as a network of beliefs, personality traits, attitudes, feelings, values, behaviors, and activities differentiating men and women through a process of social construction that has a number of distinctive features. It is historical; it takes place within different macro and micro spheres such as the state, the labor market, schools, the media, the law, the family-household, and inter-personal relations; it involves the ranking of traits and activities, so that those associated with men are normally given greater value. (Benería and Roldán 1987: 11–12)

This approach opened up new venues of analysis in terms of how biological differences were socially constructed as gender differences and identities in diverse cultural contexts and economic systems.[11] Gender analysis also provided a more holistic view than the earlier WID or WAD approaches, since it highlighted the social relations between men and women in the workplace, home, community, and state.[12] Moreover, a focus on gender required theorizing the relations between production and reproduction and allowed a richer and fuller perspective on how "women are positioned as a subordinated group in the division of resources and responsibilities, attributes and capabilities, and power and privilege" (Kabeer 1994: 65).

By the time of the Third UN Conference on Women at Nairobi in 1985, the field was making a conceptual shift from WID and WAD to GAD, or gender and development. As thousands of women gathered from all over the world for the parallel NGO forum,[13] including a very large presence from the Third World, the question was no longer what development could do for women but rather how women (and men) could redefine development. The GAD perspective was best put forward in the position paper written by the DAWN (Development Alternatives with Women for a New Era) Collective for the Nairobi meetings (Sen and Grown 1985). DAWN panels at the NGO forum focused on the impact of the debt crisis and structural-adjustment policies (since these were having a devastating effect on the poor throughout the Third World at that time); violence against women; reproductive rights; women and the environment; and on the necessity of empowering women, among other pressing themes. The "forward looking strategies" adopted by governments at Nairobi constituted an acknowlegment that efforts to incorporate women into development up to then had been partial and ineffectual, partly because of insufficient political backing. Moreover, they reflected a growing consensus that women's issues had to be defined not only in terms of legal equality (the focus of the 1975 Mexico City conference) but also in terms of women's access to resources.[14]

One of the contributions that proved pivotal in consolidating the gender-and-development approach was Maxine Molyneux's (1985, 1986) distinction between women's interests and practical and strategic gender interests. Molyneux argued that the class differences among different groups of women made it impossible to talk about women's interests in general. Rather, she posited that what must be distinguished were those interests derived from the concrete conditions of women's positioning within the gendered division of labor and those derived deductively from an analysis of women's subordination. For example, given women's responsibility for domestic labor, women had a practical gender interest in the provision of resources that met basic needs. Strategic gender interests, in contrast, sought to transform women's position within the gendered division of labor and society.

Considerable work on gender planning was carried out by feminists in the late 1980s and early 1990s,[15] making its way into the language of official government documents in the decade of the 1990s. Gender analysis was readily accepted by most governments in Latin America, for it was more politically acceptable to deal with gender (defined as "women plus men") than with women's issues alone. Governments also found it acceptable to deal with practical gender needs and demands to the extent that these were based on efficiency and equity arguments. Under structural-adjustment programs and the rise to dominance of the neo-liberal paradigm in development, efficiency was raised to a new level of concern as governments sought to trim the size of the state and shift many state activities to the private sector.[16] In this context, women were rediscovered as managers of micro-enterprises, which fit well within the new development orthodoxy of reliance on free markets. Also, there was a new appreciation of women's participation in community labor and of the "elasticity" of women's domestic labor, both which allowed them to accommodate to external shocks. Few Latin American governments took the initiative with respect to strategic gender needs, and these concerns largely remained the province of the women's movement, NGOs, and the more progressive international development-assistance organizations.[17] As governments adopted the language of gender, they also stripped it of much of its transformative potential (de Barbieri 1996; Lamas 1996).

In the late 1980s, as the importance of sustainability was recognized within the development field, the focus of GAD gradually expanded into GED—gender, environment, and development (or WED, women, environment, and development) (Bradiotti et al. 1994; Jackson 1993a). Central to this approach has been recognition of the pivotal role of women in natural resource management. Another perspective, known as ecofeminism, is based on a rejection of Western development thinking, finding inspiration in indigenous systems characterized by a more benevolent relation between women and nature (Mies and Shiva 1994).[18]

The 1985 Nairobi meetings also provided the impetus for the creation or strengthening of a number of women's networks that would play pivotal roles in furthering the recognition of gender concerns and the elaboration of women's rights at four other UN conferences in the 1990s: the UN Conference on the Environment and Sustainable Development held in Rio de Janeiro, Brazil, in 1992, also known as ECO '92; the World Conference on Human Rights held in Vienna in 1993; the 1994 International Conference on Population and Development in Cairo; and the 1995 World Summit for Social Development in Copenhagen.[19] Each of these conferences provided an important building block toward gender equality with respect to a particular theme: ECO '92 for the recognition that gender equality was necessary for sustainable development; Vienna for the affirmation that women's rights were human rights and that these were as applicable in the domestic as in the public sphere; Cairo for the legitimation of women's reproductive rights; and Copenhagen '95 for recognition of the necessity of women's empowerment to attain gender equality, among other topics. These conferences also provided considerable momentum for the preparatory meetings for the Fourth UN World Conference on Women, which was held in Beijing, China, in September 1995. In Latin America, Beijing engendered the most significant preparatory process yet with respect to the involvement of NGOs; in a number of countries rural women's organizations participated in the process for first time. The objective of the Beijing conference was to evaluate the progress made with respect to the "forwarding looking strategies" adopted at Nairobi, and to define and adopt new measures with respect to twelve critical areas of concern (UN 1996). Even though the most debated topic at Beijing was that of reproductive and sexual rights, the official conference gave more attention to rural women and indigenous issues than had ever before been the case at an international women's conference.[20]

Property and Land Rights in the International Arena

A central aim of the 1975 World Plan of Action approved at the First UN Conference on Women in Mexico City was to secure constitutional and legislative guarantees of non-discrimination and equal rights, including the provision of parity in the exercise of civil, social, and political rights pertaining to marriage and citizenship.[21] Specifically, it was recommended that legislative measures be undertaken to "ensure that women and men enjoy full legal capacity relating to their personal and property rights, including the right to acquire, administer, enjoy, dispose of and inherit property."[22] No mention was made in the concluding report of women's access to land, although concern was expressed about the particular problems of rural women worldwide. In contrast, by the time of the 1995 UN World Conference on Women in Beijing, women's land rights formed an important component of the strategic objectives of the Platform for Action. Moreover, women's land rights had passed from being solely an element in efficiency arguments, a strategy for raising women's productivity, to being treated as an economic right, with clear recognition of the importance of land rights to rural women's empowerment and pursuit of economic autonomy.

A turning point in this evolution was the 1979 UN Convention on the Elimination of All Forms of Discrimination against Women. In Article 2 of the convention, signatory states condemned all forms of discrimination against women and agreed to eliminate these using all appropriate measures, including constitutional and legislative changes. Moreover, governments agreed to modify or abolish all existing laws, regulations, customs, and practices that discriminated against women.[23] Specific attention was given to the measures required to eliminate the discrimination against rural women and to assure that women participated and benefited from rural development on par with men. Women's access to land, nonetheless, was considered in the context of programs of agrarian reform, rather than as a general right. Women were to receive "equal treatment in land and agrarian reform as well as in land resettlement schemes."[24] The sections on property rights, however, make clear that efforts to end discrimination against women must include recognition of women's rights to own, inherit, and administer property in their own names: "State Parties shall accord to women, in civil matters, a legal capacity identical to that of men and the same opportunities to exercise that capacity. They shall in particular give women equal rights to conclude contracts and to administer property and treat them equally in all stages of procedure in courts and tribunals."[25] Moreover, within the family men and women are to be accorded "the same rights for both spouses in respect of the ownership, acquisition, management, administration, enjoyment and disposition of property."[26]

That same year rural women's issues were addressed for the first time by the Food and Agriculture Organization (FAO) at the World Conference on Agrarian Reform and Rural Development in Rome. A special section of that conference's Programme of Action was dedicated to "Integrating Women in Rural Development." Among its main recommendations were that governments should consider action to:

> (i) Repeal those laws which discriminate against women in respect of rights of inheritance, ownership and control of property and to promote understanding of the need for such measures. (ii) Promote ownership rights for women, including joint ownership and co-ownership of land in entirety, to give women producers with absentee husbands effective legal rights to take decisions on the land they manage. (iii) Adopt measures to ensure women equitable access to land, livestock and other productive assets. (iv) Repeal laws and regulations which inhibit effective participation by women in economic transactions and the planning, implementation and evaluation of rural development programmes. (v) Ensure full membership and equal voting rights for women in people's organizations such as tenants' associations, labour unions, cooperatives, credit unions and organizations of the beneficiaries of land reform and other rural development programmes. (FAO 1979: 10)

Subsequently, the mid-decade World Conference on Women was held in Copenhagen in 1980. In the Programme of Action for the second half of the UN Decade for Women, the following were among the priority areas of action with respect to rural women and land rights:

> (a) Eliminate from legislation on rural development, where necessary, provisions that discriminate against women; (b) Make rural women aware of their rights so that they can exercise and benefit from them; (c) Ensure access for rural women to the use, enjoyment and development of land, in conditions of equality with men, by according to women the same practical and legal rights as those of men in access to ownership and the use and management of land, in the production of goods from land by means of agriculture or grazing and in the disposal of any such products or of the land itself. (UN 1980: 39, par. 200)

The Nairobi Forward-Looking Strategies for the Advancement of Women approved in 1985 highlighted the fact that discriminatory legislative provisions—civil codes, in particular—continued to limit the legal capacity and status of women and their ability to inherit, own, and control property (UN 1986: 18, par. 50). The dismal record of most countries in ensuring women equal treatment with men in agrarian reform programs was recognized, as was the need for constitutional and legal changes to ensure that women benefited on a par with men:

> Agrarian reform measures have not always ensured women's rights even in countries where women predominate in the agricultural labor force. Such reforms should guarantee women's constitutional and legal rights in terms of access to land and other means of production and should ensure that women will control the products of their labour and their income, as well as benefits from agricultural inputs, research training, credits and other infrastructural facilities. (UN 1986: 20, par. 62)

Further:

> Rural women's access to land, capital, technology, know-how and other productive resources should be secured. Women should be given full and effective rights to land ownership, registration of land titles and allocation of tenancies on irrigation or settlement schemes and should also benefit from land reform. Women's customary land and inheritance rights under conditions of land shortage, land improvement or shifts into cash-cropping should be protected. Implementation of inheritance laws should be modified so that women can inherit a fair share of livestock, agricultural machinery and other property. (UN 1986: 45, par. 182)

Particular attention in the Nairobi "forward-looking strategies" was also given to the needs of female household heads and to the discriminatory nature of assumptions that households are always headed by men (UN 1986: 72, par. 295).

At the instigation of Queen Fabiola of Belgium and the International Fund for Agricultural Development (IFAD), the First Ladies of a number of Third World governments subsequently organized an initiative to draw world attention to the plight of rural women.[27] Concerned that most governments, development organizations, and international financial institutions had an urban bias and that the burden of poverty fell disproportionally on rural women, they convened a Summit on the Economic Advancement of Rural Women in Geneva in 1992. The resulting Geneva Declaration for Rural Women constituted a comprehensive set of strategies aiming "to arouse public opinion and mobilize all necessary political will and resources in order to transform the status and quality of life of rural women and their families" (UN 1992: 3, par. 9). The conferees recognized that improving rural women's access to resources required alternative policies that ensured a "more equitable gender-based distribution of land, labour, capital, technology, social services and infrastructure," and that created the conditions "for their social, political and economic empowerment" (ibid.: 4, par. 12 [iii] and [ix]). Moreover:

> new legislation and institutional procedures should be introduced and/or existing ones reformed in order to ensure that rural women have equitable and sustainable access to productive resources. Similar measures should be taken to ensure that women have equity in inheritance, marriage, divorce and child custody, with due regard for different legal systems. . . . Existing land legislation should be reviewed so that rural women are not discriminated against in gaining access to land. Institutions should be set up to promote a more equitable distribution of land, and to ensure the security of women's access to land of good quality. Women should be considered as direct beneficiaries of agrarian reform or settlement programmes and land property titles should be registered under the name of women tenants as well as men. Mechanisms should also be in place to reduce women's vulnerability to loss of land in cases of divorce, separation and widowhood. (UN 1992: 6–7, par. 13 [iii] and [vi])

The Geneva Declaration for Rural Women received relatively little attention internationally, perhaps because it was issued by the wives rather than by the heads of state themselves.[28] Nonetheless, subsequent UN conferences continued to recognize the importance of women's property rights and the specific problems of the land rights of rural women.

Inheritance rights were treated explicitly in the report of the 1994 World Conference on Population and Development in Cairo. The chapter titled "Gender Equality, Equity and the Empowerment of Women" recommended that "Governments at all levels should ensure that women can buy, hold and sell property and land equally with men, obtain credit and negotiate contracts in their own name and on their own behalf and exercise their legal rights to inheritance" (UN 1995a: 24, par. 4.6). Further, this document called attention to the need for leaders and opinion makers "to speak out and act forcefully against patterns of gender discrimination within the family, based on preference for sons" and to undertake special educational efforts and public-information campaigns to promote the equal treatment of girls and boys as well as "equitable inheritance rights" (ibid.: 26, par. 4.17). In the declaration of the 1995 Social Summit in Copenhagen, attention was called once again to the need to eliminate existing restrictions on women's access to land and their inheritance of property in order to achieve equality and equity between men and women (UN 1995b: 20, par. 5 [c]). Moreover, a forceful argument was made in terms of how the eradication of poverty required the strengthening of women's land rights (ibid.: 61, par. 26 [g]).

In the 1995 Beijing conference's Platform for Action, women's access to and inheritance of land was treated in the context of required strategic actions in four of the twelve critical areas of concern. In the section titled "Women and Poverty" it was argued that "Women's poverty is directly related to the absence of economic opportunities and autonomy, lack of access to economic resources, including credit, land ownership and inheritance, lack of access to education and support services and their minimal participation in the decision-making process" (UN 1996: 19, par. 51). Further, "The release of women's productive potential is pivotal to breaking the cycle of poverty so that women can share fully in the benefits of development and in the products of their own labour" (ibid.: 19, par. 55). Toward this end, governments should "revise laws and administrative practices to ensure women's equal rights and access to economic resources," and "undertake legislative and administrative reforms to give women full and equal access to economic resources, including the right to inheritance and to ownership of land and other property, credit, natural resources and appropriate technologies" (ibid.: 22, par. 61b). In the section on "Women in the Economy," women's land rights are treated as an economic right and seen as necessary to women's achieving economic autonomy. Governments are advised to "Undertake legislation and administrative reforms to give women equal rights with men to economic resources, including access to ownership and control over land and other forms of property, credit, inheritance, natural resources and appropriate technology" (ibid.: 69, par. 165e).

These sections delineating women's land rights in the Platform for Action were not controversial at the Beijing conference for most of the points had already been raised in the regional preparatory meetings the preceding year. It is worth noting, however, that the final language of the sections on "Women and Poverty" and "Women and the Economy" of the Beijing Platform for Action was an improvement over the language of the Latin American Regional Program of Action in that the former stressed women's ownership and control of productive resources such as land, instead of simply *access* to land (CEPAL 1994b: 12, 15–16, and 22). In addition, the Beijing platform clearly highlighted the importance of women's ownership and control of land not only to make women more productive (the efficiency argument) but also as an economic right that is necessary for women's well-being and for them to achieve economic autonomy and independence (the empowerment argument). The Latin American Regional Program of Action had largely focused on the efficiency argument for women's land rights (ibid.). The NGO document developed at the 1994 Mar del Plata preparatory meeting for Beijing, however, treated women's land rights in the context of their importance for women's economic independence, the perspective adopted in the Beijing Platform for Action. It is worth noting that rather than being developed in the section on "Women in the Economy," the discussion of land rights in the NGO proposal was most prominent in the section on "Violence against Women," with women's access to resources being considered essential to augmenting their bargaining power within the household (Foro 1994: 27).

What did generate controversy at the Beijing conference was the section regarding equality of inheritance rights for girls and boys (León 1997b: 12).[29] A number of Islamic countries, appealing for religious tolerance, argued that flexibility was required with respect to inheritance norms. The Koran establishes inheritance rights that guarantee girls only half the amount granted to boys. Such a division is considered equitable since men are required to provide economically for all of the women of their family. The Islamic position at the Beijing conference was thus to argue for equitable rather than equal inheritance rights between girls and boys. In the Latin American context, however, equitable inheritance provisions would have represented a major setback for women, since the default clause in civil codes provides for equality of inheritance among children irrespective of sex.[30] Moreover, acceptance of the principle of equity rather than equality would have contravened the UN Convention on the Elimination of All Forms of Discrimination against Women for it would have meant accepting policies based on traditional, stereotypical gender roles that discriminate against women and limit their human development (ibid.: 13–14).

The intense debate, which almost prevented the final signing of the declaration and platform for action, instead led to a compromise in language in the latter. The principle of equality was maintained but the statement was left sufficiently vague so that the Islamic states could interpret it as they saw fit. In the actions to be taken by governments to eliminate all forms of discrimination against girls, it was agreed to: "Eliminate the injustice and obstacles in relation to inheritance faced by the girl child so that all children may enjoy their rights without discrimination, by, inter alia, enacting, *as appropriate*, and enforcing legislation that guarantees equal right to succession and ensures equal right to inherit, regardless of the sex of the child" (UN 1996: par. 274d; our emphasis). The topic of inheritance, however, was deleted completely in the all-important final declaration of Beijing. In addition, compared to the specificity of the Platform for Action with respect to women and land rights, the final declaration is somewhat disappointing.

Following Beijing, the FAO convened the World Food Summit in Rome in 1996, and one of the objectives in its Plan of Action is "to ensure gender equality and empowerment of women." Governments committed themselves to support and implement the commitments made at the 1995 Beijing conference to mainstream a gender perspective in all policies and to "introduce and enforce gender-sensitive legislation providing women with secure and equal access to and control over productive resources including credit, land and water" (FAO 1997: 91–92, par. 16, a, b). The various UN plans of action thus show a steady evolution in thinking about the importance of women's access to and control over resources, particularly land rights. Whereas initially these were framed in productionist terms, the argument for women's land rights is increasingly made in terms of their economic autonomy and empowerment.

The Commitment to Equality
by Latin American States

Considering the amount of time that it took between the emergence of the first organized demands for women's full citizenship and the advent of women's suffrage (twenty years in Uruguay, Panama, the Dominican Republic, and Cuba; thirty in Brazil and Bolivia; forty in Argentina, Colombia, and Paraguay; and fifty years in Chile and Mexico [Valdés and Gomáriz 1995: 160]), the ratification by most Latin American states of the UN Convention on the Elimination of All Forms of Discrimination against Women was a relatively rapid affair. Its acceptance was no doubt facilitated by the momentum to achieve women's formal equality with men that was generated by the 1975 UN Conference on Women. Six Latin American countries—Cuba, Mexico, Nicaragua, El Salvador, Panama, and Uruguay—were among the first twenty-six to ratify the 1979 convention, allowing it to go into force in September 1981 (see Table 4.1). By the time of the 1985 UN Conference on Women in Nairobi, seventy-five countries had ratified the treaty worldwide, including sixteen from Latin America. Upon their return to democratic rule, Chile and Paraguay subsequently ratified the convention, as did Bolivia in 1990, so that by that latter year all nineteen Latin American countries had ratified the UN convention. As of 1996, it had been ratified by 152 of the 185 member countries of the United Nations (Binstock 1998: 13).

When it was first approved in 1979, only eight Latin American countries explicitly provided for gender equality in their constitutions (see Table 4.1).[31] After ratifying the UN convention, six additional Latin American countries adopted constitutions that explicitly guarantee men and women equal rights: Brazil, Colombia, Guatemala, Nicaragua, Paraguay, and Peru. It is important to stress, however, that constitutional reform was by no means a direct result of the ratification of the 1979 UN convention; rather, when for domestic political reasons (often a change in regime) a redrafting of the constitution was on the national political agenda, the political space was opened up for the incorporation of gender equality as a constitutional principle. That this opportunity was actually taken advantage of very much reflects the strength of the feminist and women's movement in Latin America by the decade of the 1980s and the growing presence of women professionals within the state and in public life generally.

New constitutions were also adopted in the 1980s in El Salvador and Argentina, which established that "all persons" or "all inhabitants" were equal before the law, although discrimination by sex was not explicitly prohibited. Costa Rica did not alter its constitutional language until 1998, when it established that "all persons are equal before the law" and prohibited discrimination "contrary to human dignity."[32] Chile adopted a new constitution under military rule in 1980 that retained sexist language, but this language was finally modified in the constitutional reform of 2000, which established that "all persons are born free and equal in dignity and rights" (SERNAM 2000: 21). Most countries that had not already done so, upon signing the 1979 UN convention proceeded to reform their civil and family codes to end the statutory discrimination against women in family

TABLE 4.1. Steps toward Gender Equality in Latin America

	UN Convention Ratified	Explicit Equality in Constitution
Argentina	1985	1994
Bolivia	1990	1967
Brazil	1984	1988
Chile	1989	2000
Colombia	1981	1991
Costa Rica	1984	1998
Cuba	1980	1976
Dominican Republic	1982	No
Ecuador	1981	1979
El Salvador	1981	1983
Guatemala	1982	1985
Honduras	1983	1965
Mexico	1981	1917
Nicaragua	1981	1987
Panama	1981	1972
Paraguay	1986	1992
Peru	1981	1993
Uruguay	1981	1967
Venezuela	1983	1961

Sources:

UN Convention to End All Forms of Discrimination against Women: Valdés and Gomáriz (1995: 139) and Ladin (1994). The reported date of ratification sometimes varies depending on whether it was the initial date of approval by the executive branch or the date when it was approved by the legislature. We report the first date indicated in either source.

Gender equality in the constitution: Valdés and Gomáriz (1995: 138), SERNAM (2000: 21), and authors' interviews.

matters. All but four Latin American countries now legally recognize the dual-headed household (see Table 2.1), and all but one (Chile) recognize consensual unions (see Table 2.4). Nonetheless, "the problem which persists is that of the effectivity of the norms which declare equality" (Binstock 1998: 43).

While national women's offices of various sorts had already been created by a number of Latin American governments, the ratification of the 1979 UN convention generated more effective state machinery to promote the advancement of women since the convention required signatory countries to submit within one year a report on the status of women to CEDAW (the UN Committee to Eliminate All Forms of Discrimination against

Women), as well as periodic reports on their efforts. It was thus largely in response to this international commitment that specialized, national-level offices focusing on women's and gender affairs were created or strengthened in the great majority of countries. During the 1980s national offices were established in Brazil, Costa Rica, Ecuador, El Salvador, Guatemala, Mexico, Nicaragua, and Peru, among other countries (see Appendix: Table 3). Their efficacy during this decade was mixed, depending among other factors on the degree of support—financial and political—they received from the presidency, the stature of their leadership, and their relationship to (and the strength of) the national women's movement. Some were important only at specific moments, such as the Brazilian National Council on Women's Rights (CNDM, the Conselho Nacional dos Direitos da Mulher) during the debates leading to the 1988 constitutional reform in that country. Others were distinguished by their overall irrelevance or ineffectiveness (Placencia and Caro 1998: 44).

During the 1980s the growth of the women's movement in Latin America largely took place outside of and in opposition to the state. A number of countries were still governed by authoritarian regimes, and in countries such as Brazil and Chile the women's movement grew and flourished in tandem with the struggle for the return to democratic rule, in which it was itself a leading participant (Jaquette 1994). It is worth noting that the most successful of these state offices in this period, the CNDM in Brazil, was the product of an agreement between the Brazilian women's movement and the democratically elected government of José Sarney to include representatives of civil society in policy making on gender concerns (Alvarez 1990).

In the 1980s the coordination between the national women's offices and the newly established women's offices within the ministries of agriculture was generally quite weak. Over that decade, nonetheless, there was a marked shift in the latter from a welfare approach, focused on women's domestic role (and largely carried out by home economists), to an approach emphasizing women's productive roles, albeit often through income-generating projects. Only a few countries during this decade attempted to develop sectoral strategies aimed at rural women. In Mexico PROMUDER (Programa de Acción para la Participación de la Mujer Campesina) was initiated with high expectations in 1983 under the Secretariat for Agrarian Reform (Arizpe and Botey 1987). Due to a number of difficulties, including insufficient financing and lack of political support, the focus of this program was limited to promoting small-scale, income-generating projects for women within the structure of the UAIMs (the Agro-industrial

Units for Women) on the *ejidos*. It had little impact in terms of addressing fundamental problems of gender inequality (Aranda 1991, 1993; Aranda, Botey, and Robles 2000). In Colombia what is known as the Policy for Rural Women was launched in 1984 under the Ministry of Agriculture. It was somewhat more successful than the Mexican initiative in terms of its impact upon national agrarian policies and as a catalyst in the creation of a national organization of rural women (León 1987).

In the 1990s a number of the national women's offices were elevated in status (CEPAL 1998a, 1998b). Offices with ministerial ranking currently include those in Chile, Costa Rica, Honduras, and Peru.[33] Their activities range from support of local-level projects for women, to the design of specific programs and campaigns, to national plans in favor of women; and their efficacy continues to vary. The most successful national women's offices have been those with a mandate to influence public policy and to engage civil society in policy formation, as in Chile and Costa Rica. In Chile it was not until after the restitution of a democratically elected government in 1989 that the state began to be concerned with women's issues. Its new interest has been attributed to the increasing influence of the women's movement (which grew out of women's active role in the democratization process) coupled with international pressure to comply with the UN convention, which Chile signed in 1989. The Servicio Nacional de la Mujer (SERNAM) was created with the charge of designing and coordinating public policy in order to eliminate all forms of discrimination against women (Chile 1995: 22). It was the first national women's office in Latin America to develop, in 1993, a comprehensive five-year plan to end the discrimination against women, the Plan of Equality of Opportunities for Women.

The Beijing UN Conference on Women thrust a number of the national women's offices into the spotlight, since these were responsible for coordinating the evaluation of the accomplishments with respect to the Nairobi "forward looking strategies" of the previous decade and the preparation of the various country and regional reports for the 1995 Platform for Action. In most cases these national offices worked closely with NGO national coordinating committees, broadening the space for discussion and evaluation of the status of women. Throughout Latin America, the meetings in preparation for Beijing served as a catalyst for the consolidation or, depending on the case, rejuvenation of the feminist and women's movements, and they marked a new moment of collaboration between civil society and the state. This moment must be placed in the context of the adoption of the neo-liberal economic model in most countries, which, among its many elements, included the decentralization of the state and a shift in many of its functions to the private sector and civil society—specifically, NGOs.

The Beijing Platform for Action subsequently committed Latin American states to develop detailed national action plans to promote gender equality and to end discrimination against women. The national women's offices were charged with elaborating these plans, which to date have been developed and approved, besides in Chile, in Argentina, Brazil, Colombia, Costa Rica, the Dominican Republic, Ecuador, El Salvador, Mexico, Paraguay, and Peru (WEDO 1998). These plans vary considerably in scope, ranging from a reiteration of general principles following international guidelines to the development of concrete measures to achieve gender equity to be undertaken by specific government ministries and agencies. Chile and Costa Rica have gone the furthest in this latter regard with their respective Plans for Equality of Opportunities (Binstock 1998: 44, 21).

The priorities that emerge from these national planning processes often reflect the burning issues of the national and international women's movements, and in the 1990s these centered on reproductive rights and on ending violence against women. Except for the adverse effect of structural adjustment policies on women and concomitant attention to women in poverty, there has been less concern for material issues relative to the attention these other issues have garnered. Moreover, the national plans elaborated thus far have tended to have an urban bias, as the national offices themselves have had. These factors largely explain why rural women's issues were generally of minor consequence or were only subsequently addressed in addendums to general, national plans.

El Salvador's national plan for women provides an example of both the urban bias and the very general nature of some of these plans. The National Women's Policy (PNM, Política Nacional de la Mujer) was elaborated in 1997 via a six-month process of negotiation between the Salvadoran Women's Institute (ISDEMU, Instituto Salvadoreño de la Mujer), other government functionaries, and representatives of the women's movement and NGOs. Of the ten chapters of the PNM, only one focuses on rural women. The strategic objectives are a very watered-down version of those contained in the Beijing Platform for Action. The only reference to women's land rights is a call to "promote, under conditions of equality, women's right to property and access to resources (land, credit, technology), . . . and to bring agrarian legislation and the legal framework of the agricultural cooperatives up to date" (ISDEMU 1997: 44). No specific actions are contemplated that might, in practice, enhance women's land rights or control over land. Why gender and land rights received relatively cursory treatment is partly related to the fact that, although agrarian reform remains a hot political issue, the government considers the agrarian reform to be over.

In Chile and Costa Rica, after the national plans had been approved, it became necessary to develop a plan specifically for rural women. SERNAM's Plan of Equality of Opportunities for Women gave little attention to the concerns of rural women, an oversight noted by the Women's Department of the Comisión Nacional Campesina (CNC, the National Peasant Commission of Chile) at its Second Meeting of Rural Women.[34] SERNAM subsequently decided to correct this deficiency by creating an advisory Working Group on Rural Women, which would bring together peasant and indigenous women leaders, researchers, and NGO and government representatives to develop a national plan for rural women. In 1997 SERNAM issued a detailed set of policy proposals to assure rural women equality of opportunity, a product of this consultative process. If fully implemented, the proposals will constitute an important step toward increasing rural women's access to credit, technical assistance, and training. But while the document stresses the importance of studying and analyzing the mechanisms to "regularize" women's land rights, particularly those of female household heads, it makes no reference to increasing women's ownership and control of land (SERNAM 1997: Proposition 1.4.8).

Researcher Ximena Valdés, a member of the working group that prepared the document, recognizes that "the Beijing Platform for Action is a lot more progressive than Chile's Plan for Equality for Rural Women."[35] When asked why women's land rights had not been given greater stress, another member of the Working Group, peasant leader Francisca Rodríguez, responded: "The topic of land is a topic which does not enter into the discussion today in this country . . . I believe it was the lack of practice of discussing a topic that was almost censored, silenced. . . . In addition, we wanted to write a document which would be effective and with which we could move forward quickly for one has to respond to popular demands."[36] Other participants in this Working Group concurred that the topic of gender and land rights had been absent in the formulation of the 1997 proposals for rural women: "No one thought of women and land, for it was to question relations of power."[37]

In Costa Rica, as in Chile, the national plan that was first produced, the PIOMH, the National Plan for Equality of Opportunities between Women and Men 1996–1998 (CMF 1996), was found to be deficient in terms of the attention it gave to the specific problems of rural women.

In the PIOMH these problems were only treated quite generally under the theme of gender and the environment. Thus the national women's office (CMF, Centro Nacional de la Mujer y Familia) subsequently elaborated an addendum to the national plan—known as the PIOMHICITO, or "little plan" —that focused on the agricultural sector and the environment (CMF 1997). Women's land rights figure prominently in the document, leading off the six thematic sections; moreover, women's land rights are justified not only to enhance their productivity (the productionist argument) but also to foster their empowerment. Among the specific goals delineated is that of meeting *all* of the requests for land or land titling presented by qualified women. These actions are considered necessary to overcome the history of discrimination against women in Costa Rica's agrarian reform program —one in which only 28 percent of women soliciting land benefited as compared to 61 percent of the men who did so (ibid.: 19). It is an important example of the potential of pro-active measures to create equality of opportunities for rural women.

It is interesting that Costa Rica was the pioneer in developing detailed and specific measures regarding women's land rights since it is a predominantly urban country and the national-level organization of rural women was still in its formative stages. The Association of Rural Women Producers (Asociación de Mujeres Productoras Rurales de Costa Rica) was only organized in 1996; however, the planning process gave this association a voice and considerable visibility, a fact that largely explains the very concrete measures that were incorporated into the plan for rural women. Moreover, Costa Rica is one of the countries with an ongoing, if weak, land-distribution program. In contrast, in Chile agrarian reform is considered to be over and done with, as reflected by the total lack of attention to land issues in the discussions leading to the plan for rural women. Moreover, the rural women's movement was quite fragmented and dispersed in the mid-1990s while the organization of rural women at the local level was quite weak.

The Organization of Rural Women

The emergence of the national and international feminist and women's movements, coupled with the new state machinery charged with integrating women into development and the proliferation of NGOs, led in the 1980s and 1990s to the growing organization of rural women at the local, regional, and national levels in Latin America. Until the 1970s, the primary form of organization of rural women had been local-level mothers' or housewives' clubs or centers. In a number of countries these emerged primarily at the behest of CARITAS, the Catholic Relief Agency, with the objective of distributing subsidized foodstuffs, as in Bolivia, Ecuador, and Peru. In some countries the mothers' clubs were the initiative of political parties (such as the ones in Chile promoted by the Christian Democratic Party [Garret 1982: 283]) or producer groups (such as the National Federation of Coffee Growers in Colombia). Everywhere they focused on women's reproductive roles, often providing an important space for women to gather to discuss their common problems as wives and mothers. In a few countries the local-level mothers' clubs were linked together in departmental or regional federations. In Bolivia the organizational structure reached the national level and provided some rural women with important training in leadership skills and organizational development, skills they would later use in other organizations (Udaeta 1993: 126). In this country, as throughout the Andes, by the 1970s their focus of activity had become local-level income-generating projects for women, a focus that would be replicated broadly in Latin America as a result of NGO external financing during the debt-ridden 1980s (Casafranca and Espinosa 1993: 28; Cuvi 1992: 162; Jordán 1996: 54, 109–13).

Another important root of the rural women's movement in Latin America is liberation theology. During the decades of the 1960s and 1970s Christian base communities flourished everywhere in Latin America, but especially in Brazil, the Andes, and Central America. These were perhaps the first mixed-sex organizations in Latin America that encouraged women's participation, including them in leadership positions as "delegates of the word." In a number of countries these committees were also closely involved in local and regional struggles over land, such as those carried out by the *ligas camponesas* in northeast Brazil in the early 1960s. In the next decade, the process of local-level *concientización* (consciousness raising) of rural men and women around social justice issues, and their subsequent involvement in land struggles and revolutionary activity, would be replicated in Central America (Golden 1991: 71–75; Stephen 1994: 204–9). Everywhere it seems rural women have been active participants in land take-overs and peasant demonstrations, yet they have been largely invisible within the main peasant organizations and rural unions that led the struggle for agrarian reform in Latin America in the 1960s and early 1970s.

The 1980s represent a watershed in that, through the convergence of the factors already mentioned—in addition to the growing and more visible participation of rural women in the agricultural wage labor force —women's secretariats and commissions began to appear within the mixed-sex peasant organizations and rural unions. In the 1970s few of the national peasant organizations had women's secretariats; by the end of the 1980s almost all of the major peasant organizations and rural unions had women's secretariats of some sort (see Appendix: Table 4). Most of these had as their explicit aim the incorporation of rural women into their membership as a means of strengthening the organization. Also, given the growing availability of international funding for women's projects in the 1980s, some of these secretariats were set up explicitly as a means of attracting these international resources.

With a few exceptions, the national rural women's organizations of the 1990s grew out of the women's secretariats and commissions of these mixed-sex peasant organizations. The national rural women's organizations in Bolivia, Brazil, Chile, Colombia, Ecuador, El Salvador, Honduras, Mexico, and Nicaragua all have their origins in mixed peasant organizations and rural unions; others have their origin in the Christian base communities (see Appendix: Table 5). In most cases, rural women found it necessary to create their own organizations in order to gain the autonomy to pursue their own practical and strategic gender interests. One of the earliest of these was FEMUC, the Federación de Mujeres Campesinas de Honduras, which in 1977 grew out of the Women's Secretariat of the UNC, the Unión Nacional Campesina. In 1980 the National Federation of Peasant Women of Bolivia "Bartolina Sisa" grew out of the CSUTCB, the Confederación Sindical Única de Trabajadores Campesinos de Bolivia (Confederation of Peasant Workers of Bolivia). While these organizations were founded in order to create a separate space to address gender concerns, at the same time they have maintained very close ties to the mixed organizations from which they emerged, which has sometimes hindered their autonomous development.[38]

Rural women's organizations have also been formed in opposition to the male-dominated, mixed-sex organizations, as was the case with the National Association of Rural and Indigenous Women of Colombia (ANMUCIC, Asociación Nacional de Mujeres Campesinas e Indígenas de Colombia) (Villareal 1998: 72). A similar initiative emerged at the departmental level in Puno, Peru (Radcliffe 1993: 214). In Peru, and until recently in Nicaragua, the male-dominated mixed organizations have been successful in preventing the emergence of an autonomous rural women's organization at the national level. Similarly, in countries with large indigenous populations, such as Ecuador, the priority given by indigenous organizations to ethnic issues, and their emphasis on ethnic unity around the demand for access to collectively held land and the preservation of traditional customs, has stymied the development of an autonomous rural women's movement.

The most successful of the endeavors to form a strong national movement—one having both a strong local-level base of support as well as a national presence—is that of the rural women workers in Brazil, the ANMTR, Articulação Nacional de Mulheres Trabalhadoras Rurais. The organization of rural women workers began within the rural union movement in the early 1980s, precisely because rural women began to demand the benefits associated with union membership: access to scarce jobs, health care, the possibility of retirement benefits, and, potentially, land. The subsequent creation of two regional associations in the mid- to late 1980s—the Movimento de Mulheres Trabalhadoras Rurais (MMTR-NE) in northeast Brazil, and the Articulação de Mulheres Trabalhadoras Rurais do Sul (AMTRS) in southern Brazil—was closely linked to the difficulties women faced within the rural unions. These included their lack of representation in union leadership positions and resistance to having their gender interests recognized as valid (Deere and León 1999b; Stephen 1997). Part of the success of the rural women's movement in Brazil stems from the close ties it developed with the urban women's movement, and the alliances that were built in the struggle for the gender-progressive reforms in the 1988 constitution. The ANMTR and its constituent regional, state, municipal, and local organizations are in the forefront in Latin America in pressing such issues as social security benefits for rural women (including maternity leave), reproductive rights, and an end to violence against women. While a number of gains have been made with respect to rural women's land rights, these have tended to take a back seat to the class-based demand to deepen the agrarian reform.

In Peru an NGO initiative laid the foundation for what may eventually become a national rural women's organization. In 1988 the Lima-based Centro de la Mujer Peruana "Flora Tristán" created the Rural Women's National Network (Red Nacional de la Mujer Rural) to bring together NGOs working with rural women in the various departments of Peru. It has helped to link NGOs, peasant women's organizations, and female leaders of the mixed-sex peasant organizations in the departments of Cajamarca, San Martín, Piura, Junín, Arequipa, and Lambayeque. In 1997, 120 organizations were directly affiliated with it.

Another important actor in fostering the organization of rural women has been the state. In Colombia the organization of ANMUCIC followed closely the Ministry of Agriculture's 1984 articulation of a national policy toward rural women and the convening of a national meeting of some 150 rural women later that year. It still is debated whether the decision to form a national organization was made by rural women themselves or by the state. What is evident is that the state's policy for rural women clearly needed a mass vehicle for its execution; moreover, the women leaders of the Secretaría Femenina of ANUC (Asociación Nacional de Usuarios Campesinos) were searching for a more autonomous space in which to pursue both class- and gender-based demands.[39] ANMUCIC was subsequently to play a major role in the late 1980s in introducing gender issues into the debates over the reform of Colombia's agrarian law, the topic of a later chapter.

In contrast to Colombia, Mexico—which since the early 1980s has attempted to integrate women into rural development through various programs—long discouraged the development of autonomous national organizations of rural women. The state's priority since the 1970s has been the UAIMs, the Agro-Industrial Units for Women, which until 1992 were required to be established on each *ejido*. In the late 1980s it was reported that over a hundred thousand peasant women benefited from the productive projects carried out on these (Comité Nacional 1995: 48). However, the project-by-project focus of Mexico's strategy for rural women—while perhaps serving to create loyalty to the then-ruling party, the PRI (Partido Revolucionario Institucional), and the official, government-supported peasant union, the CNC (Confederación Nacional Campesina)—did little to organize rural women beyond the local level.[40] In addition, UAIM projects have often overlapped with other state initiatives in the countryside, leading to a proliferation of efforts and demands on rural women's time as well as their political manipulation (Mingo 1996; López and Jarquín 1996).

The rise of autonomous, oppositional peasant organizations in the 1980s, such as the CNPA (Coordinadora Nacional Plan de Ayala) and UNORCA (Unión Nacional de Organizaciones Regionales Campesinas Autónomas)[41] did little initially to change the marginal nature of rural women's participation in the mixed-sex associations. Women's contributions were largely devalued and their demands, including for land rights, were ignored (Lara 1994: 79; Stephen 1998: 152–53). These experiences prompted the emergence in the 1990s of rural women's organizations as spin-offs from the mixed-sex organizations or as autonomous associations at the local and state level. Rural women's independent organizations are increasingly voicing demands that combine practical and strategic gender interests (J. Aranda 1993; Stephen 1998). This process has been assisted by feminist promoters of rural development who are affiliated with the Inter-regional Feminista Rural and the Red Nacional de Promotoras y Asesoras Rurales (National Network of Rural Development Promoters and Advisors), organizations that in the 1990s also strongly defended rural women's land rights (Alberti 1998: 204; Lara 1994: 86).[42]

Two national organizations of rural women have emerged, both with roots in mixed national organizations. UNORCA was the first to convoke, in 1991, a national meeting of peasant women's organizations, which was followed in 1993 by the creation of a national network of such organizations.[43] This led in 1997 to the creation of AMMOR (Asociación de Mujeres Mexicanas Organizadas en Red, the Association of Mexican Women's Networks) as an independent organization. The state followed suit that same year, supporting the creation by the CNC of the Federación Nacional de Uniones de UAIMs y Organizaciones Económicas de Campesinas (National Federation of the Unions of UAIMs and Peasant Women's Economic Organizations), an organization now operating in twenty-six of Mexico's thirty-one states.[44] Neither of these national-level organizations, however, has played a very effective role in articulating the demand for women's land rights.

In Costa Rica the first national rural women's organization also developed at the behest of the state. In 1996 the office of the First Lady, with backing from the FAO, convened the leaders of local-level women's groups.[45] From this gathering emerged the Asociación de Mujeres Productoras Rurales de Costa Rica (Association of Rural Women Producers of Costa Rica). While initially designed to facilitate the provision of state services to rural women, this organization has also spurred rural women's participation in the design of national-level policies and increased the national visibility of rural women farmers.[46]

Elsewhere in Central America, in the countries emerging from civil war in the 1990s, a national rural women's movement has been slow to emerge. This is partly due to the polarization of women's groups and partly because for over a decade gender interests were subsumed by revolution. In El Salvador one of the first rural women's organizations to emerge had its roots in the Christian base communities and Christian mothers' committees in the eastern part of the country. AMS, the Asociación de Mujeres de El Salvador, was founded in 1987 and had a reported membership of over four thousand rural members in the late 1980s (Stephen

1994: 208). After the signing of the peace accords, some of the women's groups affiliated with the various factions of the FMLN (Frente Farabundo Martí de Liberación Nacional)—such as the Mujeres por la Dignidad y la Vida, known as "Las Dignas"; the MAM, the Movimiento de Mujeres "Melida Anaya Montes"; and the IMU, the Instituto de Investigación, Capacitación, y Desarrollo de la Mujer)—declared their autonomy from the FMLN and begin to organize urban and rural women around gender concerns. The most active in rural areas has been Las Dignas. One of the newest rural women's organizations with a national scope is the Central de Mujeres Campesinas (CMC), which grew out of the Women's Secretariat of the ADC, the Alianza Democrática Campesina, the largest FMLN-affiliated peasant organization.

In Guatemala the peace process of the 1990s was singularly important for the reconstruction of civil society after three decades of repression, and it led to a proliferation of new civil society associations and NGOs. Of the organizations of women with some national scope, the oldest and most visible has been CONAVIGUA, the Coordinación Nacional de Viudas de Guatemala (National Coordination of Guatemalan Widows), founded in 1988 among the victims of the repression. A number of rural women's organizations have emerged as auxiliaries of the main Mayan groups. The rural women's organizations with the greatest autonomy are those that developed in the 1980s among the indigenous population in exile in Mexico, such as Mama Maquín and Madre Tierra.[47]

Of the various rural women's associations that have emerged in Central America, the most broad-based in terms of membership and national visibility is the women's division of UNAG, the National Union of Agriculturalists and Cattlemen of Nicaragua. By the mid-1990s about seventeen thousand rural women participated in UNAG, and the rural women's movement was considered to be "among the strongest elements of the national women's movement" in a country with a relatively strong women's movement, partly as a result of the Sandinista revolution.[48]

Another impetus to the consolidation of rural women's organizations in Latin America in the 1990s was provided by the preparatory activities for the 1995 Beijing women's conference. A main objective of the NGOs at the regional level was to increase the diversity of the women's movement, and thus each country's organizing committee was urged to ensure that rural and indigenous women would be well represented. According to Mercedes Urriolagoitia, the Bolivian national coordinator of the NGOs for Beijing, "For Beijing, a more pluralist discussion was generated in the

Andean countries, for the first time including peasant and indigenous women. . . . There was respect for the autonomy of the indigenous movement . . . for the first time, indigenous women, peasant women, and Guaraní women came together to discuss common problems. . . . This was the first time that Aymara women came together with indigenous women from the Beni."[49] During 1995 five regional meetings of peasant and indigenous women were held in Bolivia for the purpose of discussing the Plan of Action for Beijing and the Latin American preparatory document resulting from the Mar del Plata gathering, entitled "The Situation of Indigenous Women." A number of indigenous women from Bolivia subsequently attended the Beijing meeting. After Beijing discussions have continued on whether a national confederation of peasant women in Bolivia should be created, one that would be totally independent of the mixed-membership associations (Salguero 1996).

The Beijing process was also important in encouraging efforts in Chile to organize the first indigenous women's organization, the Coordinadora de Mujeres Mapuches. After the Beijing conference and their participation in the Rural Women's Working Group of SERNAM to prepare the proposals for a national plan for rural women, the leaders of the women's department of the CNC and the Coordinadora de Mujeres Mapuches, plus representatives of several mixed associations, came together in 1997 to form the Red Nacional de Mujeres Rurales e Indígenas, which the next year became the Asociación Nacional de Mujeres Rurales (ANAMURI).[50] The latter includes, besides the above-mentioned groups, organizations and syndicates of rural women wage workers and independent women. Similarly, in Ecuador following Beijing the National Council of Indigenous Women of Ecuador (Consejo Nacional de Mujeres Indígenas del Ecuador) was organized in 1996.[51]

Another initiative in September 1996 brought together rural women from organizations throughout Latin America, the Primer Encuentro Latino-Americano y del Caribe de la Mujer Trabajadora Rural (ENLAC, the First Latin American and Caribbean Gathering of Rural Working Women) (Cevasco 1996). The initiative for this meeting, held in Fortaleza, Ceará, in Brazil, came out of the fifth Encuentro Feminista held in San Bernardo, Argentina, in 1990. Of some three thousand women in attendance at that latter meeting, only eight were peasant women, prompting feminist leaders to worry about the lack of resonance of feminist concerns among rural women and making clear the need to build stronger ties between rural and urban women's organizations. Over the next several years a coordinating committee composed of organizations from six countries promoted this hemisphere-wide meeting of rural women. One of the main accomplishments of ENLAC—besides the feat of assembling a multilingual, interracial, and inter-ethnic meeting of peasant and indigenous women from twenty-one countries, and establishing dialogue between them, the rural NGOS, and feminists—was its contribution to strengthening national rural women's organizations in Latin America (ENLAC 1998: 87–91). While the makeup of these organizations varied, generally they were seen as weak, involved in complicated relations with the mixed-sex rural organizations and the women's movement, and unfocused in their demands. While it was proposed that a Latin American and Caribbean network of rural women workers should be created, and that a subsequent ENLAC meeting be held in the not-too-distant future, the first priority was to consolidate national-level organizations of rural women.

In the late 1990s a number of national-level networks were formed that brought together departmental or provincial rural women's associations, national women's organizations, and the women's secretariats of mixed peasant and union federations. These include REDNAMURH, the Red Nacional de Mujeres Rurales de Honduras; FEMUPROCAN, the Federación de Mujeres Productoras de Nicaragua; and the Mesa Permanente de Mujeres Rurales in El Salvador (Permanent Roundtable of Rural Women).[52] These networks have been formed with the explicit goal of fostering an autonomous rural women's movement—independent of the state and of the male-dominated mixed associations—to address gender concerns. Their significance is that they cross the boundaries of the political parties and revolutionary movements that have divided the peasant and women's movements in the past.[53] In 1998 a national Network of Rural Women's Organizations (Red de Organizaciones de Mujeres Rurales) was organized in Colombia as well, but through a different process than in Central America, one more closely linked to state planning initiatives.[54]

In sum, the dominant trend during the late 1990s was the strengthening of the national rural women's movement, in some countries through the creation of national networks and in others by the consolidation of a national organization of rural women. Almost everywhere the development of strong, autonomous rural women's organizations has been constrained by their relation to mixed-sex rural organizations and to the political parties of the left, and also by the often overriding goal of maintaining unity with class and/or ethnic-based demands, particularly in countries where agrarian reform is still a motivating issue. Also, the national rural women's organizations have often been created from the top down; only over time have they developed an organizational structure reaching down to the local level, and it still remains weak. The exception is Brazil, where the organization of rural women workers was built simultaneously from the ground up, at the local, municipal, and state levels, and through regional organizations representing various state organizations. This pattern of development partly accounts for the success of the AMTRS and the MMTR-NE in gaining a national voice in debates on agrarian and women's issues.

The national rural women's organizations also have mixed relationships with the national women's movement and to the state. In Brazil and Nicaragua these organizations have evolved in close association with the urban women's movement and are among the strongest pillars of the national women's movement. In other countries there is still a great distance between the national women's movement and rural women's organizations. Not surprisingly, it is in those countries with the strongest ties between the rural and urban women's movement where the rural women's organizations have focused most on strategic gender interests, including the empowerment of women in all of its dimensions.

In most countries women's access to land has emerged as both a practical and strategic gender interest, although the salience of the land rights issue has varied, depending on particular country situations. Nonetheless, issues of inheritance, joint titling of land to couples, and women's access to and control of land under the same conditions as men have been on the agenda everywhere.

five

Engendering the Neo-Liberal Counter-Reforms

The most extreme and ridiculous case was on one cooperative where on the day they were going to decide whether to parcelize the cooperative they called together all the women members and locked them in a room. The men then went off and held their assembly to decide how to divide up the lands. The opinion of the women members did not count at all and neither were they given land.[1]

DURING THE 1980s an extraordinary consensus was reached among the international financial institutions as well as Latin American governments concerning the virtues of neo-liberalism.[2] Import-substitution industrialization (ISI) and the state-driven policies of previous decades were largely discredited in favor of free markets and open economies. Facing daunting debt-service payments and large current-account deficits, Latin American countries adopted stabilization programs in order to bring about macroeconomic balance. These programs aimed to reduce the domestic fiscal deficit, establish equilibrium in the balance of payments, and reduce inflation while allowing for debt repayment. Structural adjustment was to establish the conditions for long-run growth by moving toward a free-market economy that favored tradeables at the expense of non-tradeables in the overall context of liberalization of trade regimes.[3]

It was argued that stabilization and structural-adjustment policies would be particularly favorable for the agricultural sector, which was judged to have suffered most under the ISI policies of previous decades. Cheap food policies, for example, were discarded in favor of market-determined prices that were expected to improve the terms of trade for agriculture. Consolidation of the exchange rate, in concert with devaluation, was expected to benefit agricultural exports. The latter were expected to profit from trade reform as well, such as through lower tariffs and the elimination of export taxes. Reduction of the fiscal deficit, however, meant that the agricultural sector stood to lose from an end to subsidized agricultural credit and reduced public investment. The privatization and closing of state agricultural banks, in addition, was to reduce the volume of resources channeled to this sector. The reduction in the size of the state often meant reductions in or the elimination of a number of other public programs that served the agricultural sector, such as state marketing and irrigation boards, extension services, and the like. Some of these changes were expected to have contradictory short-run effects. For example, devaluation should improve the competitive position of agricultural exports in foreign markets. However, to the extent that this sector also depended on imported inputs of machinery, spare parts, fertilizer, and so on, the devaluation could also increase costs. Moreover, the end of food subsidies, with their pro-urban bias, might advantage farmers by increasing agricultural prices, but their supply response also depended on the net impact of changes in their costs of production, public investments, and other structural factors (Rao and Caballero 1990).[4]

Neo-liberal agricultural policies could also be expected to have differential effects on different groups of agricultural producers, depending on whether they produced export crops or domestic foodstuffs, the degree of international competition they faced, and the extent to which they had previously relied on government subsidies and services. The differential effects of these policies on small and large farmers could thus be expected to have substantial distributionary consequences, generally favoring the latter over the former (Carter and Barham 1996).

In concert with the change in macro and sectoral policies came a concerted move to change the institutional structure of the agricultural sector, for the aim of neo-liberalism was to get prices *and* institutions right (Carter and Barham 1996: 1142). For a number of Latin American countries this meant the undoing of the agrarian reform of previous decades, and it is these policies that are the focus of this chapter. As Table 5.1 shows, a number of countries passed new agrarian laws that brought a formal end to state intervention in land expropriation and distribution for purposes of social justice. Of the twelve countries that are the focus of this study, in seven—Chile, Ecuador, El Salvador, Honduras, Mexico, Nicaragua, and Peru—agrarian reform efforts have now come to a close.[5] In the most extreme cases, the end of agrarian reform meant the restitution of land to former landowners who had been expropriated (Chile and Nicaragua). A more common feature of the counter-reforms has been privatization and the individualization of land rights. The neo-liberal model favors individual over collective land rights; they are considered to be more conducive to profit-maximizing behavior and, hence, to greater efficiency. Thus state farms have been privatized and support has been withdrawn from production cooperatives and other group-farming activities favored under the previous model. Under the new agrarian legislation the reformed sector may be divided up among the beneficiaries, and eventually—usually upon payment of the agrarian debt—these parcels may be sold. In some countries, such as Mexico and Peru, the move toward privatization has included land previously held collectively by indigenous and peasant communities. In other countries, in response to the mobilization of the indigenous movement, collective property rights have been guaranteed under the new agrarian legislation and even furthered, through the recognition of historic indigenous land claims.

In all of the countries studied here, privatization of land rights has been accompanied by land titling programs designed to enhance security of land tenure, promote investment, and rejuvenate the land market. These efforts have primarily focused on the new landowners emerging from the reformed sector, but they have also included the large group of traditional smallholders who lack formal land titles. Finally, in a number of countries the new role of the state in land distribution is to assist market-based transactions. In Table 5.1 the term "state-assisted land transactions" refers to state land banks of various types as well as state support to direct negotiations between buyers and sellers in the land market.[6] Activities now considered proper for the state include bringing large landowners and the landless together (to reduce transaction costs) and state provision of long-term credit and subsidies to the "resource poor" so that they can participate in the land market.

Before turning to the implementation of the neo-liberal model in agriculture and its gendered consequences, it is important to take into account a few structural features of the region (see Appendix: Table 6). In the 1990s Latin America's most rural countries in terms of population distribution were those in Central America and Paraguay and Bolivia. Those with the

TABLE 5.1. Institutional Change under Neo-Liberalism

Country/ Year of Law*	End of State Distribution	Restitution	Parcelization of Collectives	Land Titling	State-Assisted Land Transactions
Bolivia (1996)	No	No	No	Yes	Yes
Brazil (1985)	No	No	No	Yes	Yes (1995)
Chile (1974)	Yes	Yes	Yes	Yes	No
Colombia (1994)	No	No	No	Yes	Yes
Costa Rica (1961)	No	No	No	Yes	Yes
Ecuador (1994)	Yes	No	Yes	Yes	No
El Salvador	Yes (1995)	No	Yes (1991)	Yes	Yes (1991)
Guatemala (1964)	No	No	No	Yes	Yes (1999)
Honduras (1992)	Yes	No	Yes	Yes	No
Mexico (1992)	Yes	No	Yes	Yes	No
Nicaragua	Yes (1997)	Yes (1990)	Yes (1990)	Yes	No
Peru (1995)	Yes (1991)	No	Yes (1980; 1995)	Yes	No

Sources: Authors' interviews and for Bolivia, Bolivia (1996); for Brazil, Fernandes (1996) and Cardoso (1997); for Chile, Silva (1991) and Jarvis (1992); for Colombia, INCORA (n.d.); for Costa Rica, Román (1994); for Ecuador, Ecuador (1994) and Navarro et al. (1996); for El Salvador, Flores (1994) and Funde (1997); for Guatemala, Guatemala (1997, 1999); for Honduras, Honduras (1995); for Mexico, Calva (1993) and Tribunales Agrarios (1994); for Nicaragua, Enríquez (1991) and Stanfield (1995); and for Peru, Peru (1995), del Castillo (1997b), and del Castillo et al. (1995).

*Year of law refers to the most recent agrarian code; where blank means that the agrarian reform legislation has not yet been replaced by a comprehensive agrarian code. The other dates refer to the year specific policies were adopted.

highest percentage of the economically active population (EAP) working in agriculture include Guatemala, Bolivia, Honduras, Paraguay, and Peru. In most countries in the region the share of the EAP is larger than the share of agriculture in the gross domestic product (GDP), a reflection of the low productivity of this sector. The agricultural sector generates less than 20 percent of GDP in all countries except for Nicaragua, Paraguay, and Honduras. Nonetheless, except in Venezuela and Mexico, the agricultural sector continues to play an important, if not central, role in exports, generating at least one-third of the value of total exports in most countries in the region. Under the neo-liberal model, with its stress on comparative advantage, the agricultural sector was almost as important at the end of the twentieth century as it was in the beginning, notwithstanding the significant change in the sectoral composition of GDP and of the labor force. Nonetheless, partly because of the structural diversity of the region, the specific manner by which institutional change in the agricultural sector has been fostered has varied considerably.

Chile: The Neo-Liberal Pioneer

Chile was not only the pioneer, implementing neo-liberal strategies in the decade of the 1970s, but also the country where the counter-reform was most extreme and neo-liberal strategies were implemented most broadly. These involved the privatization not only of the reformed sector but also of water rights, agricultural credit, and research and extension services (Gómez and Echenique 1988). Chile is also the only country where these reforms have had a chance to mature over a period of decades, allowing analysis of their impact on rural labor markets and the gendered division of labor in agriculture.

One goal of the military regime that overthrew the Socialist president Salvador Allende in September 1973 was to foster the development of an internationally competitive agricultural sector. This was to be accomplished through the privatization of the reformed sector and the development of a vigorous land market, by external liberalization, and by withdrawal of the state from promoting and managing agricultural production. It was also to be accomplished by breaking the back of the trade union and peasant movements.

The first step was the dismantling of the reformed sector. Some of the land (28 percent) that had been expropriated under the Frei and Allende regimes was restored, in full or in part, to former owners; portions were individually titled to beneficiaries of the agrarian reform (41 percent); and portions were auctioned off to private entrepreneurs (Silva 1991: 23).

The aim of the parcelization process was to create a family farming sector. To be eligible for a "family agricultural unit" of ten standardized hectares, an applicant had to be a farm resident at the time of the initial expropriation of the farm, a household head, and someone who had not participated in an illegal land take-over during the previous two governments (Jarvis 1992: 192). Although the initial intent of the military was to benefit the worker-peasants (*inquilinos*) who had been agrarian reform beneficiaries, this aim was subsequently modified to allow university technicians, former administrators, public employees, and others to benefit as well. A system of points was created to rank the applicants for land titles;

it included "such categories as the relationship of the applicant to the land subject to distribution, age, number of family dependents, possession of certain university degrees, having administered or held a position that required the trust of the landowner, and so on" (Silva 1991: 26). As a result of this ranking, it is estimated that 10 percent of these new farms were allocated to persons of non-peasant origin.[7] In total, some 36,533 new farms were titled; beneficiaries had to purchase their parcel with thirty-year commercial mortgages (ibid.: 25).

The land that had been legally titled as collective property to production cooperatives under the previous regime (approximately 11 percent of the area in the reformed sector, with 9,907 beneficiaries) was left formally intact by the military government (Silva 1991: 21). Nevertheless, due to state neglect this sector also largely disintegrated, with the land devolving into individual holdings by the end of the 1970s (Jarvis 1992: 192). Besides the undoing of the reformed sector, another component of Chile's counter-reform was the parcelization and privatization of the lands of Chile's indigenous communities. The lands of the Mapuche people of southern Chile had been collective property, although most farming was carried out on individual parcels with only pasture lands utilized collectively. In 1979 the Pinochet government decreed that these individual parcels were to become private property that could be bought and sold (ibid.).

It is difficult to analyze the gender implications of the privatization process because data by sex of beneficiary were not collected for those who received land titles through the counter-reform. But since the pool of applicants was initially composed of those who had benefited from the previous agrarian reform, one can surmise that the beneficiaries were practically all male. Few women qualified to apply for land since most, including female heads of household, had been excluded as beneficiaries in the agrarian reform. As Sarah Bradshaw (1990) argues, the counter-reform was as patriarchal as the previous agrarian reform. The gendered implications of the counter-reform would largely depend on its indirect impact: whether the male head of household was designated a beneficiary and, in beneficiary households, how incomes generated by individual peasant proprietors compared to those generated in the former cooperative form of organization. Few beneficiary households were able to survive the competitive stress of the marketplace under neo-liberalism. For the majority of non-beneficiary households, the fate of both men and women largely depended on conditions in the labor market.

Under the military's neo-liberal model, Chile's economic growth was to result from a restructuring of the economy that would emphasize the country's comparative advantage in world markets. Chile's particular economic strength was seen as the natural resource sector, especially mining, agriculture, and timber. Liberalization, combined with the counter-reform of land tenancy, had the effect of substantially increasing the supply of agricultural labor. This produced the low wages needed to build a competitive edge for export agriculture. Approximately half of the previous agrarian reform beneficiaries were excluded from the parcelization process, and these marginalized households had few options. Given the high unemployment rates in the cities, most remained in the countryside, either moving to the new rural hamlets (*villorios rurales*) that began springing up along the roadways or becoming employees or sharecroppers working for those who did receive land (Silva 1991: 27).

The expanded fruit cultivation in Chile's central region also led to a new process of land concentration. Lack of access to credit and technical assistance (because of the state's withdrawal from provision of these services) meant that few of the beneficiaries of the counter-reform could compete with the larger commercial farms, and many were forced to sell their land and join the landless as workers on the large estates (Bradshaw 1990: 113). It is estimated that as many as half of the new property owners from the reformed sector lost access to land through these processes (Lago 1987: 24).[8] Finally, the opening of the economy to foreign food imports wreaked havoc on domestic food production, driving many small farmers into semi-proletarianization and seasonal migration or forcing them to sell their lands (Díaz 1990: 133–35).

The gender composition of the agricultural labor market did undergo a major change. Women workers came to predominate in fruit production and processing, the most dynamic and labor-intensive export activity (Lago 1987; Bradshaw 1990; Campaña 1990; Rebolledo 1993). By the late 1980s women constituted 52 percent of the estimated 250,000 temporary workers in Chilean agriculture (X. Valdés 1995: 62), and they made up the great majority of those employed in fruit-packing jobs. Women's work in this dynamic export sector, nonetheless, is characteristically unstable and part-time. The fruit industry, at best, provides jobs for only six to seven months out of the year. The majority of permanent positions (which were severely reduced over the 1980s) are occupied by males; women constitute only an estimated 5 percent of the 40,000 workers with permanent positions in the fruit industry (Venegas 1995: 123). For the remainder of the year, the women must resort to the informal economy, domestic service, or—if their family owns some land—the tasks of traditional agriculture. Venegas found that few of these temporary workers were able to find full-time, year-round employment by combining occupations (ibid.: 125). Another change in the gender division of labor prompted by the neo-liberal model has been rural women's increased responsibility for subsistence production on family plots, particularly in regions of non-export agriculture where generally men have been forced into seasonal migration in search of wage work (Bradshaw 1990: 117; Lago 1987: 27).[9]

A major characteristic of rural Chilean families in the neo-liberal period has been their impoverishment and their greater reliance upon multiple sources of income, requiring the active efforts of both men and women (de los Reyes 1990: 149). Rural poverty peaked in 1987, when 52.5 percent of the rural population experienced indigence or extreme poverty (X. Valdés 1994: 40). Since then, the incidence of rural poverty has been decreasing, although Chile continues to exhibit one of the more unequal distributions of income in Latin America (Morley 1995: Tables 2.1 and 2.4). Among the poorest social groups are rural women, particularly female household heads (Chile 1995: 32).[10] In addition, the incidence of rural female-headed households has been on the rise, increasing from 13.5 percent in 1982 to 17.2 percent of the total in the 1992 census (X. Valdés 1994: 40).

The gender-biased nature of the Chilean agrarian reform was thus reproduced in the counter-reform. Since few women were direct beneficiaries of the former, few women had the opportunity to acquire land under the parcelization process that dismantled the reformed sector. Moreover, Chile's agro-export growth boom was particularly exclusionary, leading to the absorption of part of the smallholder sector by larger commercial farms (Carter and Barham 1996: 1136–37). By the 1980s, the fate of most rural men and women was largely determined by events in the labor market. The labor-intensive character of Chile's most dynamic agricultural activity, fruit production for export, brought about a change in the gender division of labor, one that favored women's seasonal employment in agriculture. Permanent agricultural employment, although restricted in scope, continued to favor men. Even as they came to rely on multiple income earners, rural households earned extremely low incomes throughout this period. Few rural women or men could generate savings or obtain access to credit in order to participate in Chile's reinvigorated land market.

Neo-Liberal Agrarian Codes of the 1980s and 1990s: Peru, Mexico, Honduras, and Ecuador

Peru in the 1980s, and then Mexico, Honduras, and Ecuador in the early 1990s most closely followed the Chilean model. They all adopted new agrarian codes that appeared to be gender neutral, establishing that land could be owned by "natural or juridic" persons. Peru's counter-reform was initiated in 1980 with President Fernando Belaúnde's Law for the Promotion and Development of Agriculture, which allowed agrarian reform enterprises to be parcelized and these land parcels, once duly titled, to be sold. The only lands exempt from this measure were those allotted to the officially recognized peasant communities of the highlands and coast and the native communities of the tropical lowlands. By the end of 1986, approximately half of the production cooperatives had been or were in the process of being parcelized, accounting for one-third of the land allocated under this form of organization (Cuba Salerno 1993: 93). The relatively rapid disintegration of the cooperatives is largely explained by the lack of state support to these under the Belaúnde government, the large debts that many cooperatives had accumulated, and the unfavorable macroeconomic climate of the 1980s, which had produced an agricultural crisis. Their parcelization also responded to the internal difficulties of many of the production cooperatives and peasant demands for recognition of individual holdings (Kay 1998).

Little has been written about the gender implications of the undoing of Peru's agrarian reform, perhaps because—since so few women were direct beneficiaries of the reform—it was assumed that few women benefited directly from the parcelization of the collective enterprises. According to Laureano del Castillo (1997a), in those cooperatives with women members, the most common outcome of the process of parcelization was for women to be assigned smaller parcels than the men, particularly when they were the partner of a male member. Castillo explains that the process was quite heterogeneous:

> Different cooperatives followed very different criteria on how to divide up their lands. For example, if the average amount of land to be given to each member was five hectares, some gave five hectares to each male and female member, irrespective of whether they were married or formed part of a couple. In other cases, different criteria were utilized, such as the distribution of land to families. Thus if two mem-

bers were married they only got five hectares between them. In other cases male members got five hectares and female members only half that, so that a couple could only put together 7.5 hectares.[11]

When the production cooperatives in the coastal valley of Pisco were parcelized, for example, members were assigned four hectares apiece. But when both partners in a couple were members, they were assigned only five hectares altogether. No consideration was given to what might happen if the couple eventually split up; in fact, the end result was often that "men were titled land and the wives were dispossessed" (Méndez 1984a). In at least one case, however, a women member resisted this discriminatory treatment: "On one of the enterprises the process of parcelization came to a stand-still because one of the wives who was a cooperative member, who had been separated from her spouse for a number of years, refused to accept this option" (ibid.).

Decisions about what was a "just" distribution of land in the case of couples—whether separated or living together—ended up having prejudicial effects in some cases for women members who were household heads: "What often happened was that the membership rights of all of the women were disregarded, many of whom were widows or single mothers" (Revilla 1990: 44). According to Teresa Revilla, a group of these female household heads took their complaints to the National Institute of Cooperatives, which intervened in their behalf. They then received a regular allotment of land. But in most cases, couples did not get two shares, which, in her opinion, would have exacerbated inequalities in land distribution.

During this period little research was carried out on household decision making and whether there were differences by gender in how the process of privatization was perceived. María Julia Méndez, who participated in many of the discussions of the coastal cooperatives about whether to parcelize, indicates that husbands often consulted their non-member wives on this crucial decision: "It was difficult to conclude the sessions on the parcelizations in only one meeting, for the male members always asserted that they wanted to think over the decision. We found out that this often meant that they wanted to discuss the decision with their wives. In some cases, decisions were reversed once the men discussed the parcelization with spouses."[12] She also argues that wives were sometimes the protagonists in the decision to parcelize the coastal cooperatives:

It is curious that women were sometimes in the vanguard of the parcelization process, in the sense that they often pushed their spouses in favor of the division of the cooperative. . . . It was evident that women favored parcelization. I believe that women thought that they would have greater influence in decision-making on individual parcels. . . . In the cooperatives, they had little possibility of directly influencing decision making. In addition, women were an important share of the temporary labor force of the cooperatives [but were excluded from membership]. If they farmed individual parcels, they would have greater autonomy in organizing their work as they saw fit as compared to working for the enterprise.[13]

Not only women but also the grown children of cooperative members were an important part of the temporary labor force of these enterprises. In the early 1980s few new permanent jobs were being created on the cooperatives, leading to worries about the children's future. Méndez considers this another reason why women favored parcelization: "the illusion of having a family parcel that could incorporate the labor of all family members, following its own individual destiny, became a powerful motive to parcelize the cooperative."[14] Somewhat ironically, women's exclusion from the agrarian reform cooperatives may have ended up contributing to their demise.[15]

One of the main results of the parcelization of the cooperatives on the coast was that intensified family labor on individual parcels replaced seasonal wage workers on former cooperative lands, leading to a contraction in the demand for wage labor and a rural out-migration (Méndez 1984b). According to most accounts, the counter-reform in this period, complemented as it was by a general economic crisis (one that was very detrimental to the agricultural sector), did little to generate new employment opportunities for either men or women in the countryside.[16] While the Belaúnde and subsequently the Alán García government favored the parcelization of the cooperatives, relatively little progress was made with regard to land titling, inhibiting the development of a vigorous land market as well as the availability of credit through formal channels that would reinvigorate agricultural production. By 1990 only about 14 percent of the agrarian reform beneficiaries had received either individual or collective land titles (Casafranca and Espinoza 1993: Table II-8).

The officially recognized peasant communities were exempt from the 1980 law on parcelization,[17] and in 1987, under the García government, the Law of Peasant Communities (Law 24656) was passed, which once again guaranteed the integrity of communal property and recognized the relative autonomy of the peasant communities.[18] The state pledged itself to respect and protect "the customs and traditions of the community" (Article 1 in Peru 1987). This law is noteworthy because it clearly established for the first time that both men and women have the right to be community members. However, the law distinguished between general community membership and the category of *comunero calificado* (qualified community member). Under the latter category, one was required to be of legal age, to be a registered voter, to have maintained stable residence in the community for at least five years, to be inscribed in the community registry, and to meet whatever other prerequisites might be established in the community statutes (ibid.). While all *comuneros* have the right to use the goods and services of the community, one must be a *comunero calificado* to participate with voice and vote in the community assembly and to be elected to a position of leadership in the community. Theoretically the qualified *comunero* can be a man or woman, but in customary practice there is only one per family, and it is the man who as head of household represents the family before the community.

To accelerate the development of the rural land market, as well as the flow of capital into the agricultural sector, the Alberto Fujimori government in 1991 passed the Law to Promote Investment in the Agricultural Sector (Law 653). Formally ending the agrarian reform (by rescinding Decree Law 17716 of 1969), this law was intended to facilitate the development of a medium-sized capitalist agricultural sector by permitting either "natural or juridic persons" to acquire land, irrespective of whether they were direct producers. Various researchers consider the 1991 agrarian law a step forward for gender equity since land rights are no longer framed in terms of household heads; rather, all persons are, in principle, potential holders of land rights (Macassi León 1996a: 19; Casafranca and Espinoza 1993: 18; FAO 1996: 8). However, the special provisions governing inheritance in DL 17716 were rescinded, making inheritance subject to the provisions of the 1984 civil code. The agrarian reform inheritance provisions had been quite favorable to widows, automatically granting them land rights upon the death of their partners whether or not they were married.[19] In contrast, the civil code does not grant couples in consensual unions inheritance rights. Since rural women are almost as likely to form a consensual union as a marriage, this change could be potentially prejudicial to them.

The 1993 Peruvian constitution went a step further in guaranteeing the right of private property by specifying just two permissible grounds for expropriation: national security and public works. It also established, implicitly, the property rights of men and women whether the land is held in private, communal, or another associated form. But most controversially, the constitution established for the first time that peasant and native communities could freely dispose of their land, making possible the legal parcelization and sale of communal holdings. The 1995 land law (Ley de Tierras, law no. 26505) reinforced many of these points with the aim of increasing security to property owners.[20] This law is considered strongly neo-liberal because it attempts to minimize restrictions on the right of private property and dramatically reduces the role of the state in land issues.

One of the most positive aspects of the 1995 land law is that it guarantees the right of qualified agrarian reform beneficiaries to be titled the land they hold in usufruct. This is a very important provision for small farmers because many beneficiaries never received a formal title to their land. However, the law does not address women's land rights and leaves open the question of what will happen in the case of widows (particularly, those who had lived in a consensual union) who are in possession of an agrarian reform land parcel (del Castillo 1997a). A land law that was proactive in favor of gender equity would have explicitly guaranteed women the right to be titled the land they currently possess, irrespective of marital status.

The most controversial aspect of the land law has been its provisions permitting the privatization of the land of peasant and native communities (del Castillo 1996). These may now choose any form of "entrepreneurial organization" they please, without the permission of the state. On the Peruvian coast, community members may acquire their usufruct parcels as individual property by a simple majority vote of the community assembly (Article 10 in Peru 1995). The assembly can also decide to give the land to third parties in usufruct, or to rent, sell, or mortgage it. Communities in the sierra and *selva* (the eastern tropical lowlands) have the same options as do those on the coast; however, decisions must be made by a two-thirds majority vote of the qualified *comuneros* (Article 11).

The differing majorities required to privatize community holdings in the coast and sierra reflect the government's differing intentions for these two regions. The great bulk of coastal lands consist of desert and can only be brought into cultivation through irrigation. These are also the lands best suited for the future development of agricultural exports, and it is these that the government is most anxious to privatize and launch on the land market.[21] While the government may have less interest in privatizing the highland communities' land, the new law has stimulated within them considerable interest in parcelization.[22] But according to some, it is in the more recently formed peasant communities, not the ancestral ones, where interest in privatization is keenest.[23]

Particularly troubling from a gender perspective is that only qualified *comuneros* who are members of the community assembly—generally male household heads—will decide whether their communities are to be privatized, possibly without consulting their wives and partners (Macassi León 1996b: 38). A supposedly "gender neutral" law could very well result in women being excluded from secure access to land. It appears that little attention has been given thus far to the gender implications of parcelization of communal land. Comments one researcher, "What will happen in terms of women's right to participate in decisions? The topic of who is a qualified *comunero* has not even been brought up, let alone whether women will take part in the decision to parcelize community landholdings."[24] A high proportion of Peru's indigenous peasantry resides in the officially recognized peasant communities of the highlands, so that the most significant impact of the counter-reform on men and women may depend on what happens within these communities in terms of privatization. Because most of them limit voting in the community assembly to household heads, it is unlikely that the majority of women will participate directly in the crucial decisions governing the future of their communities. Moreover, if parcelization results in the individualization of land rights, what had been the family usufruct plot could become male private property, as is happening in Mexico.

The Mexican agrarian reform of 1917 officially came to a close in 1992 with the changes enacted to Article 27 of the Mexican constitution. Henceforth, the state would no longer intervene in the process of land distribution. Moreover, these changes paved the way for the privatization of the *ejidos,* the collective holdings that encompass approximately one-half of Mexico's agricultural land. By majority vote the *ejidos* may now decide to grant their members individual titles to their usufruct plots, and they can choose to disband as an *ejido* altogether. Once titled, *ejidatarios* may sell, rent, sharecrop, or mortgage their land.[25] The privatization of *ejido* landholdings launched by the Salinas government was designed to help modernize Mexico's agricultural sector and, in concert with the liberalization of the rest of the economy, allow the country to compete effectively in international markets. In removing the impediments to the creation of a land market, the neo-liberal legislation was meant to attract domestic and foreign capital to the agricultural sector through outright land sales, joint ventures, or contract agriculture. It also created the possibility for the reconcentration of land to create "efficiently" sized enterprises, if not the old latifundio of the past.[26]

Critics argue that Article 27 broke the agrarian social pact of the Mexican revolution. Furthermore, they argue that the aim of the counter-reform is to bring about a "depeasantization" of the countryside in favor of accelerated capitalist development (Calva 1993: 9–10; de Vries 1995). This outcome is forecast by the concomitant abandonment of state support for the *ejidos* in the form of subsidized credit and other inputs and technical assistance, and the gradual elimination of guaranteed prices for basic grains, the latter a consequence of Mexico's joining the North American Free Trade Agreement (NAFTA), which went into effect in 1994.[27]

There is general consensus among critics that the counter-reform is particularly prejudicial to rural women since it erodes their land rights in a number of ways (Encuentros 1992: 222–27; Stephen 1993; Zapata 1995; Esparza, Suárez, and Bonfil 1996; Bonfil 1996; Botey 2000). First of these is that all major decisions regarding the future of the *ejido* (whether to parcelize or dissolve the *ejido* or to enter into joint ventures) are to be made by the recognized *ejido* members (Article 28 in Tribunales Agrarios 1994). This means that the spouses and partners of *ejido* members are excluded from decision making. In effect, most women (since they make up only 17.5 percent of all *ejido* members)[28] have no direct role in determining the future of their communities. According to researcher Paloma Bonfil (1996: 71), "Experience suggests that women's participation in the *ejido* and communal assemblies, although it varies in magnitude, force and weight, will always be at a disadvantage as compared with men's participation. The changes introduced in Article 27 to the constitution exacerbate this disadvantage and leave peasant women without a legal framework of protection to guarantee their access to land."

A second provision eroding women's rights, and the most dramatic change introduced in the new legislation, is that upon a majority vote of *ejido* members, *ejidatarios* may acquire a title to this land and dispose of it as they see fit, including renting or selling it. What was considered a family resource—the *patrimonio familiar*—becomes the individual property of the *ejidatario* (Stephen 1996a: 289; Lara Flores 1994: 86; Esparza et al. 1996: 8, 25, 35). If an *ejidatario* decides to sell his parcel, his spouse or partner and children have what is called the "right of first buyer" (*derecho de tanto*);[29] however, they have only thirty days to make arrangements to purchase the land. Given the low wages and incomes of rural women, it is doubtful that many will be able to exercise this right should their husbands decide to sell the family plot (Esparza et al. 1996: 38). Lynn Stephen (1993: 16–17) found in her interviews in Oaxaca that many women were afraid that if their *ejidos* were parcelized, their husbands would, indeed, decide to sell their land. Yet, she notes, "most hoped that their husband would consult them if they wanted to sell land, but pointed out that there was no guarantee that they would do so. . . . Given an average wage of $4.00 per day, most women are unlikely to be able to purchase land."

Third, and a major departure from previous practice, inheritance provisions no longer assure that access to *ejido* land will remain within the family. Now *ejidatarios* may freely choose their heir, which may be the spouse or concubine, one of the children, a parent, or *any other person* (Article 17 in Tribunales Agrarios 1994; our emphasis). Moreover, the designated heir no longer has any responsibility to provide support to those who were economically dependent upon the deceased. This change in inheritance procedures places rural women in a much more precarious position than ever before with respect to land rights (Zapata, Mercado, and López 1994: 188; Ochoa Pérez 1998). Only when the *ejidatario* has not made out a will does the traditional preference ordering rule: the spouse or concubine, or in her absence, one of his children, a parent, or finally, any other person who depends economically on the *ejidatario* (Article 18). Carlota Botey (2000: 154) argues, further, that the new agrarian legislation violates the Mexican civil code. By allowing the *ejidatario* to designate non-family members as heirs to the *ejido* parcel, the law does not take into account that the civil code establishes that if a couple was married under the default marital regime (*sociedad conyugal*), half of the common property of the couple belongs to the spouse.[30]

A fourth aspect of the new agrarian law that is considered detrimental to rural women is that the *ejidos* are no longer required to set aside a parcel for women's productive activities, the UAIMs (Unidad Agrícola Industrial de Mujeres). While the efficacy of these was always subject to question, and few *ejidos* actually complied with this requirement, now the law allows the creation and maintenance of these to be voluntarily determined by each *ejido*'s general assembly (Article 71). The only provision that may favor some rural women is Article 48, which specifies that if an *ejidatario* has been absent from the *ejido* for more than five years, whoever has been in charge of the land parcel may claim it. According to Stephen (1993: 16–17), as Oaxacan men have migrated to northern Mexico and the United States to work as farm laborers in increasing numbers over the years, women and children have taken on growing responsibilities for sub-sistence production on the *ejido* plot. However, it is doubtful that many women will benefit from this provision since they often work the land with another male family member, typically a grown son, uncle, or cousin. In Stephen's estimation, only those abandoned women who have maintained direct control over their land parcel have the potential to be beneficiaries.

Surprisingly, there was relatively little public debate or open protest over the neo-liberal counter-reform (Fox 1994: 262–63). Under the leader-ship of the Permanent Agrarian Council (CAP, Consejo Agrario Perma-nente), the umbrella grouping of eleven national peasant organizations, various national forums were held and an alternative peasant agrarian law was drafted and presented to the Mexican Congress (Calva 1993: 92–93).[31] But President Salinas was not willing to compromise and used his skill at "divide and conquer" and his offer of tangible concessions on other issues to convince most of the CAP leadership to endorse the drastic changes in Mexico's agrarian law.[32]

It is worth noting some of the provisions of the alternative law cham-pioned by the CAP, even though it was not adopted. Besides arguing for the need to continue distributing land, the CAP's Women's Commission demanded that the *ejido* parcel be considered the "patrimony of the fam-ily" and not of the individual male *ejidatario* (Lara Flores 1994: 86). This provision was incorporated into the draft law. In addition, women and children were to be protected by a clause requiring the *ejidatario* to will land only to those who depended economically on him; moreover, the heir was required to provide maintenance to the other remaining dependents, as in the previous law. Another clause would have required the consent of all family members for *ejido* parcels to be transferred to a third party in whatever form.

Land rights are clearly an important issue for indigenous women in Mexico, as seen in the Zapatista struggle that erupted in January 1994 in the state of Chiapas. In their "Women's Platform for the Dialogue," adopted at the state convention of Chiapan women in May 1995, the fol-lowing demands were voiced: "Throw out the new Article 27 because it takes away women's right to inherit land"; "Women should have the right to own and inherit landed property"; "If a man abandons his family, the parcel should automatically pass to the woman"; and "in recognition of women's property rights and to protect the children, land adjudication and titles should explicitly include women as co-owners" (Rojas 1995: 203, 209). In the subsequent dialogue between the EZLN (Zapatista National

Liberation Army) and the Mexican government on "indigenous rights and culture" in November 1995, women's land rights figured prominently. The position paper of the EZLN states that "land should be redistributed in an egalitarian manner to men and women" and that "women must be included in the tenancy and inheritance of land" (ibid.: 251).[33]

Women's demands for land rights were also clearly voiced at the national meeting of the women of ANIPA (Asamblea Nacional Indígena por la Autonomía) in Chiapas in December of that same year, which included 260 indigenous women representing twelve organizations and coalitions. One of their specific demands was that when a couple separated the land should be divided equally between them (Rojas 1995: viii). And in the position paper prepared by indigenous women for the 1996 National Indigenous Congress, high on the list of demands was a change in the new Article 27, so that women's land rights would be recognized (Seminario 1996: 3). At the 1997 Seminar on Women and Access to Land held in Mexico City, the question was raised whether rural women themselves were the source of such demands, or whether these demands reflected the influence of feminists on the leadership of the various women's organizations.[34] According to researcher Paloma Bonfil, "The discussion of women and land rights represents the top leadership of indigenous women, but those documents [and demands] are quite distanced from the base" or grass roots. Further, it was argued that few rural women understood the changes implied by the modification of Article 27 of the Mexican constitution for few of them understood their legal rights under the previous agrarian law. According to agrarian lawyer Bárbara Zamora, "There was no state policy directed to inform people, neither before or after the changes. Therefore, there is great confusion in terms of the interpretation of the law."[35]

The implementation of the Mexican counter-reform initially produced considerable conflict at the local level as decades-old land disputes were revived among *ejidos,* neighboring communities, and landowners. Additional disputes arose as the *ejidos* decided whether to allow parcelization, and then, when they did, over the actual delimitations of the parcels to be titled. Moreover, discord has often erupted between family members over who is to be titled land (Stephen 1996b). The limited evidence thus far is mixed on whether the privatization and titling program is respecting the land rights of those women who currently have them, the *ejidatarias.* Elizabeth Katz (1999), citing anecdotal evidence, notes the concern that the titling agency, PROCEDE (Programa de Certificación de Derechos Ejidales y Titulación de Solares Urbanos), will dispossess women of their land rights due to its preference for those who work the land directly. Sarah Hamilton (2000a) reports that in the two *ejidos* she studied that have undergone the PROCEDE process, *ejidatarias* had been treated equitably by the ejidal authorities. She cites two cases of women who were assigned land rights in prior years due to the absence of their husbands from the *ejido;* they have been able to maintain these rights in the titling process. Hamilton also reports that the rural women she interviewed are not very concerned about the implications of going from family patrimony to individualized private property: "Most women appeared to be satisfied with their position as mothers in families that were expected to honor their rights to succession and subsequent disposition of land. Most did not seem to be troubled by the dependent, if not precarious, nature of their access to ejidal rights, nor by the fact that their menfolk were legally at liberty to disinherit them" (ibid.: 18). She concludes that "Despite legal provision for sale of land by individual *ejidatarios* and the disinheritance of wives and children, land continued to be viewed as a family resource" (ibid.: 26).

Nonetheless, as rural women become aware of their loss of land rights, they continue to protest against Article 27 and its erosion of the concept of family patrimony. According to a report of the National Coordinating Committee for Beijing '95, in regional and national forums rural women have risen in protest, particularly about the ability of husbands who are titled land to sell it without their consent (Costa 1995: 44). This report blames the lack of effective organization of rural women at the national level, as well as their lack of representation in the national congress,[36] for the neglect of women's land rights in discussions regarding possible revisions of Article 27. At the local level, rural women have also protested against the changes governing the operation of the UAIMs in cases where the *ejido* assembly has decided to dissolve the UAIMs without the consent of the women members.[37]

With the end of land distribution by the state, and disintegration of family patrimony on the Mexican *ejidos,* women's access to land will largely depend on inheritance practices and on their ability to participate in the land market as buyers. One of the tendencies of the last two decades has been the growing semi-proletarianization of rural women, a tendency that many consider will accelerate as *ejido* land is rented and sold. Moreover, many of the new agricultural exports have favored female wage employment, particularly in the production of winter fruits and vegetables and flowers, leading to a growing feminization of the agricultural labor force (Arizpe and Botey 1987). In addition, employment in the packing houses, such as those engaged in avocado and mango exports, has also favored women (B. Suárez 1995). The low wages that most women earn as farmworkers, however, will largely preclude them from saving sufficient funds to participate in the land market as buyers. It has been estimated that one-third of women agricultural wage workers earn less than the minimum wage (Esparza et al. 1996: 37). In addition, with the privatization of the banking system, the end of subsidized credit, and an underdeveloped rural financial system for mortgages, it is unlikely that rural women will benefit from the development of the land market.

Turning to Honduras, in 1992 the Agricultural Modernization and Development Law was approved amid heated national debate. The intent of policymakers was to invigorate the land and credit markets in hopes of stimulating investment and increasing agricultural production. But according to its critics, "the Agricultural Modernization Law brings the agrarian reform to an end and constitutes a counter-reform" (Martínez, Rosales, and Rivera 1995: xv). They argued that what was needed in Honduras was a deepening of the agrarian reform rather than its undoing: "without a renewed political compromise to carry out a genuine agrarian reform, one which is planned, broad, rapid and participatory, not only will social inequalities and structural disequilibriums increase, but also, social conflicts as well" (Noé, Thorpe, and Sandoval 1992: 211). Besides ending, for all practical purposes, the expropriation of land, other provisions of the law serve to bring closure to the process through which the landless could claim public lands. Individuals who had illegally occupied national lands for at least three years, and who paid the required fees, could claim this land and receive title to it (Article 5 in Honduras 1995). But those who currently lack land will be unable to obtain it by non-market means (Thorpe 1995). Agrarian reform beneficiaries granted provisional titles under the 1975 law were to receive full title within a period of six months, complete with an INA (Instituto Nacional Agrario) mortgage until full payment was made for the land (Article 65). These INA mortgages may be sold to third parties or used as collateral for a loan.[38] Production cooperatives are to be converted to "enterprises," with members receiving individual ownership shares (Títulos de Participación Individual, TPIS) based on their labor contribution. These TPIS may be passed on through inheritance and sold either to other cooperative members or to third parties.[39]

With respect to gender, public lands may be allocated to either men or women over the age of sixteen if single, or of whatever age if married or in a consensual union, irrespective of whether they have dependents (Article 64). The anomaly of the agrarian reform law, whereby only women who were mothers could be beneficiaries, was thus eliminated, a provision first introduced into agrarian legislation in 1991. However, whereas the 1991 legislation had required that, in the case of couples, land adjudications be jointly titled, in the Modernization Law joint titling to couples is no longer to be the norm. The possibility of joint titling of land was retained, but only *if a couple so requested it*, making this provision much less effective in terms of women's land rights (Martínez et al. 1995: 55; our emphasis).

The Agricultural Modernization Law triggered substantial sales of co-operative land.[40] A number of factors have been suggested to explain why the cooperatives and peasant groups responded so enthusiastically to the possibility of selling all or part of their land: the high level of debt they were carrying; the possibility of getting rid of "excess" land (which might be subject to expropriation if left unutilized); and pressures from local entrepreneurs and multinationals (Thorpe 1995). Women were such a small proportion of the agrarian reform beneficiaries (an estimated 3 percent) that the undoing of the agrarian reform cooperatives will have minimal direct effects on them. Rather, the effects are more likely to be indirect, depending on the fate of male family members who were former cooperative members, and on whether the capitalist enterprises that replace the cooperatives generate more or less demand for female labor.

There is evidence that women family members sometimes opposed the sale of the cooperatives, particularly those that had been profitable (largely located in the northern, commercial agricultural region of the country). Researcher Mirta Kennedy observes:

> There's been an interesting process of mobilization of women. . . . It was reported in the press that women protested the dismantling of the cooperatives because such was decided upon only by the men [since the women were not cooperative members]. When the cooperative was dismantled no one asked their opinion. Then the men sold the land and pocketed the money. At that point, the discord was such that some of these couples separated, even after twenty-five years together. It was very interesting how the women mobilized in protest and that there was a clear confrontation between the sexes. . . . The women denounced what their partners were doing, but they had no legal rights since they were not members of the cooperative, and moreover, the majority are in consensual unions.[41]

The neo-liberal law thus has had contradictory effects for different groups of rural women. On one hand, while it provided for women to be beneficiaries of state titling efforts on the same terms as men, this provision was applicable only to squatters already occupying public lands. Moreover, the fact that joint titling of lands distributed under the agrarian reform was an option rather than a requirement greatly reduced the potential in this legislation for enhancing gender equality. On the other hand, since women were not members of the cooperatives and peasant groups of the reformed sector, they were excluded from the crucial decision making about the fate of this sector under neo-liberalism, to the possible detriment of wives and partners.

According to one of its advocates, Ecuador's 1994 Law for Agrarian Development, passed under the conservative government of Sixto Durán, "is an absolutely liberal law that legitimizes the ownership of property under whatever scheme, be it private, communal, or in a partnership . . . it does not have restrictions on whether men or women have access to land."[42] Its critics assert that the law brings to an end the period of agrarian reform: "It is clear in this law that the State definitively renounces its duty to administer justice, to distribute the national wealth, to look out for the interests of the poor and to orchestrate society" (Navarro, Vallejo, and Villaverde 1996: 39). It differs from the neo-liberal laws previously discussed in that it was the result of intense negotiation and compromise between business interests and CONAIE (Confederación de Nacionalidades Indígenas del Ecuador), the main national indigenous organization.

The 1994 law has potentially favorable and unfavorable aspects in terms of peasants' and indigenous peoples' land rights.[43] Among its main provisions is one permitting communal lands to be parcelized and sold if two-thirds of the community members so wish (Article 22 in Ecuador 1994). A two-thirds majority vote is also required to transform the community into another form of association. CONAIE claimed victory for forcing the provision that any change in tenure or structure would require a two-thirds vote, rather than a simple majority, of community members. Also, at its insistence, the law stipulates that communal pastures at high elevations and forest land cannot be subdivided. CONAIE was also successful in blocking the attempt to privatize water rights; water is recognized as a public good that cannot be sold (Article 40). The text of the law refers to "perfecting" the agrarian reform, rather than ending it, by making available credit, training, and technical assistance to beneficiaries. However, land can be expropriated only under very restricted conditions (Article 30). CONAIE succeeded in retaining "great demographic pressure" as a condition for expropriation, although this is considered largely a symbolic victory. The right of indigenous, Afro-Ecuadorian, and Montubian[44] communities to their ancestral lands is recognized, and they are to be adjudicated such land free of charge (Article 36). Up to this time, only indigenous communities had been adjudicated ancestral lands.

The law also recognizes multiple ways of organizing production including individual, family based, cooperative, associated, communal, and other forms (Article 17). These forms must serve a social function, which is defined as keeping land in production while conserving natural resources and protecting the ecosystem (Article 18). That a goal of agricultural development should be to assure domestic food security (and not only exports) is considered another victory of CONAIE, as is the provision that land may be farmed collectively and not just individually. The national agrarian reform institute, IERAC, was abolished and replaced by the National Institute for Agrarian Development, INDA. In theory, INDA performs most of the functions of the previous institute except those of a judicial nature; any land conflicts are now to be resolved by civil judges. In practice, it is a skeleton of its old self, with a much reduced budget and staff. Its main function now is to legalize the actual land tenure situation through land titling efforts.[45]

From our vantage point, Ecuador's agrarian development law pretends to be gender neutral in that property owners, "be they natural or juridic persons," are guaranteed land rights (Article 19). In the regulations implementing the law, the beneficiaries are further defined as "peasants, indigenous people, Montubians, Afro-Ecuadorians, agriculturalists in general, and agricultural entrepreneurs" (Article 1 of Regulations in Ecuador 1994). The only explicit mention of women is in the section on training, where it states that "training should take into account women's participation in agriculture and should incorporate them actively in the respective programs" (Article 3). Worthy of note is that while ethnicity and race are mentioned explicitly in the law and in its regulations, gender does not merit parallel treatment in terms of land rights. This reflects the fact that in the debate over the agrarian development law, gender was never an issue, for the main demand of CONAIE centered on securing government recognition of indigenous territories as collective units and guaranteeing the right to collectively held land. Thus, the main accomplishment in gender terms of the Ecuadorian legislation was its intended neutrality in vesting land rights on "natural or juridic persons" rather than on household heads.

Special Cases: Neo-Liberalism and the Peace Processes in Central America

Nicaragua and El Salvador represent special cases. In the early 1990s their governments implemented neo-liberal reforms while they attempted, at the same time, to secure the conditions for lasting peace. In both countries support was withdrawn from the reform sector of the previous decade, leading to the parcelization and privatization of agrarian reform production cooperatives. Land continued to be redistributed, but it went primarily to the former combatants in their civil wars. Guatemala in the 1990s had no significant agrarian reform sector to undo. As a result of the peace accords ending its guerrilla insurgency, however, it was also forced to address the agrarian question as well as gender issues.

In Nicaragua Violeta Chamorro's coalition of opposition forces (UNO, the Unión Nacional Opositora) defeated the incumbent Sandinista government in 1990, and, as it began implementing the neo-liberal model, it reversed many of the policies of the Sandinista revolution. The main objectives of the new government with respect to the agrarian sector were: (1) the resettlement of the contra forces and former soldiers of the Sandinista army; (2) land restitution to those it considered to have been unfairly expropriated under Sandinista rule; (3) privatization of the state farm sector; and (4) the provision of individual land titles to members of the production cooperatives and to those who had been granted lifetime usufruct rights to individual plots (Enríquez 1991: 174–75; Fund. Arias–CIPRES 1992: 77).

The UNO government moved relatively quickly with respect to the resettlement of former combatants, redistributing lands of the state farms and purchasing additional farms for this purpose (Stanfield 1995: 4). Of the 10,493 contras or contra supporters who received land between 1990 and 1992, only 6 percent were women (INIM 1993: 11). An estimated 10 to 15 percent of the contra combatants had been women (Kampwirth 1998: 1–2), suggesting that they were under-represented among the beneficiaries. Of the 8,300 former members of the Sandinista army who received land in this period, only 7 percent were women, a figure approximately equivalent to their representation in the armed forces in this period.[46]

A National Review Commission was also set up to correct the situation of land that had been illegally usurped from prior owners. The commission was flooded with requests and issued some 2,200 decisions in favor of former owners, generating considerable instability and conflict in the countryside. After 1992 government policy focused more on issues of compensation than on dislodging current occupants in cases where the initial land expropriations were deemed illegal (Stanfield 1995: 7).

With respect to the state farms, by 1992 the great majority had been privatized. Of 436,804 *manzanas* in the state sector, by that year 30.6 percent of the land had been returned to the previous owners, 17.3 percent had been redistributed to ex-Sandinista army soldiers, 20.2 percent went to demobilized contras, and 31.9 percent of the land had been or was in the process of being purchased by workers on the state farms (ibid.: 11). Women workers lost out in the process of privatization since they tended not to participate in the decision-making process on state farms and thus were excluded from the discussions regarding privatization and worker-controlled areas (Renzi and Agurto 1994: 38–39). While women had represented 45 percent of the members of the rural worker's union (the ATC) and 35 percent of the permanent workers on state farms (CIERA, ATC, CETRA 1987: 104), it is estimated that they now constitute only 24 percent of those permanent workers who are part of the new workers' cooperatives created on many of the former state farms (Fund. Arias–CIPRES 1992: 87).[47]

The severe structural adjustment program implemented by the Chamorro government also caused considerable instability in rural areas. One of the government's initial actions was to reduce the size of the state, and thousands of government workers were fired. This had a dramatic impact on the agricultural sector, and on the production cooperatives in particular, since the latter had been dependent on a network of government agencies and sizable government support under the Sandinistas. In addition, the policy of providing small farmers and cooperatives cheap credit ended in early 1992.[48] The production cooperatives were particularly hard hit by this move since they had relied on credit to pay their members' wage advances.

A case study by Dorien Brunt (1995: 11–12) of the Jalapa region highlights how the unfavorable macro-economic situation and the changed legal framework led to the undoing of the production cooperatives and to a fall in women's participation (from 27 percent of the membership in 1989 to 7 percent in the cooperatives remaining in this department in 1995). Her insightful analysis shows how difficult it was to incorporate women into the production cooperatives due to male opposition, and how a substantial female participation was achieved only because of strong state support for the cooperatives and for women's incorporation into them. In addition, Jalapa is a coffee region, and women have traditionally harvested this crop.

Moreover, it was a militarily contested region throughout the 1980s and many men were involved in defense efforts, requiring the active participation of women in production. According to Brunt, once the state withdrew its support, discussion in the production cooperatives intensified over the rights of male and female members. The male members argued that women were not as productive as men and that they missed too many days of work because of sick children. Maternity leave also became a source of dispute. Brunt comments, "In many ways it was made clear to the women that they were of no use anymore for the cooperative. Facing all these problems together with the fact that the economic situation of the majority of cooperatives is deplorable, many women 'choose' to leave the cooperative" (ibid.: 12). Single mothers were among those most likely to have left the cooperative in search of wage employment. In general it is reported that throughout Nicaragua, when the cooperatives were parcelized there were fewer women members than in previous years.[49]

The parcelization of the cooperatives gained support because of the uncertainties regarding state policies in this period and because it was a strategy to prevent the return of expropriated land to former landowners. Poorly defined inheritance rights to cooperative membership were another factor sometimes inclining women cooperative members toward parcelization. One observer remarked, "One of the problems with which women were very concerned was inheritance . . . this worried the men members as well, but it was particularly strong among the women. They wanted to make sure that their children would have a claim on the property. We find this on all of the cooperatives. It has been one of the causes behind the disintegration of the cooperatives."[50] For those who remained in the cooperatives in Jalapa, in the process of parcelization women tended to receive land of the poorest quality (Brundt 1995). Moreover, nationally it is reported that women received not only the worst land but also smaller plots than male members (Fund. Arias–CIPRES 1992a: 83–84).[51] Even so, in the Jalapan case many women now regret having left the cooperatives. As one woman put it, "If I had known that they were going to parcel the land, I never would have left the cooperative. I would have seen it through" (Brunt 1995: 12).

The former production cooperatives in Jalapa now operate as credit and service societies. Land is individually cultivated, although some of them still maintain an area for collective production. Subsequently, the National Development Bank waged an aggressive campaign to recover bad debts and placed an embargo on the land of several cooperatives in Jalapa, as a prelude to foreclosure. Also, many cooperatives discovered they did not have sufficient resources to work all of the land they controlled, and they began to sell portions of their land in what also appears to be a national trend (Brunt 1995: 14; Fund. Arias–CIPRES 1992). By 1994 it was estimated that 90 percent of the land that was once worked collectively had been parcelized. Additionally, a 1994 study of four departments of the country revealed that 14 percent of the land allocated through the agrarian reform had already been sold to third parties.[52] One observer commented, "This process of parcelization has not finished yet. Every day we see that cooperatives are being parcelized because of the problem of the agrarian debt, a problem known as 'the Cobra.' They are having to sell part of their land to pay these debts, or at least to pay the interest on the debt."[53]

Sometimes it has been the wife who has urged her partner to sell his share of the cooperative land. One researcher observed, "The women were often those who encouraged members to sell land—'rather than ending up with nothing, let's sell the land to a neighbor or whomever.'"[54] The process of parcelization sometimes also provided the opportunity for other rural women to acquire land. According to another researcher, "These lands are thrown on the market and thus some women have the opportunity to obtain them, but then comes another problem. Where are women going to get the funds so that they can participate in this land market? Some of the projects we have been working with have funding for this purpose, so that women can take advantage of this opportunity, but in general these funds are limited."[55]

Overall, women ended up at a disadvantage in the dismantling of the production cooperatives and state farms. Many women had dropped their membership in the production cooperatives by the time these were parcelized due to the difficulties they experienced in this period. Of those who were able to claim individual land parcels, they usually got smaller parcels and lands of poorer quality than the male co-op members as a result of their weaker bargaining position, itself a reflection of the undervaluation of women's labor within the cooperatives. Nonetheless, as this process was taking place, the Chamorro government was developing a gender perspective, and the titling of land to former agrarian reform beneficiaries was to take place under much more favorable terms for women than the initial process of land distribution.

In El Salvador the neo-liberal agenda was adopted in 1989 under the Cristiani government. The aim, as in other countries, was to liberalize the economy so that market forces would orient all economic activity (FUNDE 1997). With respect to land, Decree 747 of 1991 formally allowed Phase I cooperatives to be parcelized and individually titled at the request of the cooperative membership (Flores 1994: 6). Cooperatives were now basically free to choose whatever form of association they preferred: to continue as traditional production cooperatives; to opt for a mixed system that included some collective property alongside titled, private parcels; to form what is known as a shareholding cooperative (*cooperativa asociativa de participación real*); or to dissolve and parcelize the property altogether. Phase III beneficiaries were also now allowed to sell, rent, or mortgage their properties, although land sales and rentals could only legally be made to landless peasants (Fund. Arias 1998a: 18).

Relatively little research has been carried out on the process of parcelization of the cooperatives, although as of September 1994, 28,428 individual land titles had been distributed on 217 cooperatives (Lastarria-Cornhiel and Delgado 1994: 15). It has been noted that when it came time to discuss the future of the cooperatives, few women members participated in the decision-making process, for they did not understand the options available to them.[56] It is generally held that on those cooperatives that were parcelized women members got the worst land and the smallest and most poorly situated parcels (Fund. Arias 1992: 51). In the case of the San Andrés cooperative, for example, when it was parcelized women members received the least favorable parcels in the distribution.[57]

After twelve years of civil war—one that killed an estimated seventy-five thousand people and produced a profound economic crisis—Salvadorans were ready for *concertación,* the process of negotiation that led to the 1992 Chapultepec peace accords between the national government and the FMLN (Farubundo Martí National Liberation Front) and the designation of the latter as a legal political party.[58] One of the pressing issues in the negotiations was the resettlement of the population displaced by the war, estimated as approximately 14 percent of the Salvadoran population,[59] in addition to the reintegration of the FMLN combatants and excess military personnel into civilian life. Another critical issue was the future of the agrarian reform, and this was resolved in favor of its continuation.[60] But Article 105 of the constitution was reaffirmed; earlier it had set 235 hectares as the maximum size of the farms whose excess lands were subject to expropriation, limiting the scope of any further land redistribution.[61] The focus of future agrarian reform efforts was now to be on the sale of national lands[62] and state purchase of lands voluntarily offered by their owners at market prices. Other relevant aspects of the accords included consensus on the need to develop a new agrarian code that would consolidate all the various and assorted land decrees within a year of the signing of the accords; the participation of peasant organizations in the implementation of development policies; and the distribution of land to ex-combatants and squatters in the zones of conflict.[63]

The Land Bank (Banco de Tierras), which had been legally created in 1991, became the main vehicle for distributing land to former combatants, through what subsequently was known as the land transfer program or PTT, Programa de Transferencia de la Tierra. It was funded primarily by the U.S. Agency for International Development (USAID) and was to compensate landowners in cash. Potential beneficiaries assumed a thirty-year debt, with a four-year grace period and a subsidized interest rate of 6 percent (CEPAL 1993b: 64). Priority among potential beneficiaries was given to former combatants from both sides of the conflict who had an agricultural "vocation" and were landless, followed by squatters (tenedores) in the zones of conflict. Special considerations were to apply in the zones of conflict, the most important being that the current land tenure was to be respected until a final resolution could be reached. This was important because in the FMLN-controlled zones many farms had been abandoned by their owners during the war and were occupied by squatters, usually displaced peasants and FMLN supporters. It was agreed that the squatters could not be dispossessed, and the FMLN was given responsibility for carrying out an inventory of these properties. During 1992 it enumerated 5,884 occupied properties in thirteen departments of the country, with some 27,671 squatters (Alvarez 1997: 3). Landowners were given the choice of selling these properties at market prices through the Land Bank or of retaining their lands. In the former case, the squatters could then purchase the land; in the latter case, they could remain on the property until another farm was offered for sale in the region (Flores 1994: 10). Beneficiaries were issued provisional, collective titles to these properties, known as *indiviso* titles (where the group owned the farm, although internally land could be worked either collectively or individually, depending on the group's preferences).

The in-depth study of women and land rights carried out by the Arias Foundation called attention to the fact that in the peace accords' discussion of agrarian issues, no mention was made of women and their rights to land (Fund. Arias 1992: 67–68). Somewhat ironically, the implementation of the land transfer program in the zones of conflict proceeded very slowly, and while these delays caused hardship for former combatants and FMLN supporters, the delays also allowed concerns regarding gender discrimination to be addressed (Luciak 1999). The manner in which this process evolved and its outcome is discussed in the next chapter.

In 1994 a new land policy was announced, one based on assuring security of land tenure. The top priority became the development of a land cadastre and the titling and registering of land. The World Bank loaned the Salvadoran government $50 million for the former purpose, while USAID is financing the latter (World Bank 1996b: 4–5, 27). To address the pressing problem of rural poverty,[64] the government of Armando Calderón Sol focused on education and on generating non-agricultural employment in the countryside. As the vice-minister of agriculture explained, "It has been shown that a land program does not offer high levels of welfare."[65] She was of the opinion that the agrarian reform efforts in El Salvador had been a disaster, partly because they have always been politically motivated:

> The first phase was carried out to deprive the left of a potent issue. The second, the land-to-the-tiller phase, was carried out without any consideration for efficiency or the proclivity of the farmers for farming. The PTT program was a political compensation program. Land was again given to those who did not have an agricultural vocation. In none of these programs has production been a consideration. Moreover, El Salvador does not have enough land to satisfy the demand of all who want it, and yet those that have it [the cooperatives and the PTT beneficiaries] are not working what they have.

According to Vilma de Calderón, "The agrarian reform is over. The task now, the policy of the government, is to make sure that the land is worked." This is to be accomplished by giving owners a secure title so that they may invest, rent, or sell their land.

In the view of most peasant organizations and other critics, however, the agrarian reform is not yet over. Among the unresolved problems are the share of the agrarian and agricultural debt that is to be forgiven,[66] and the excess land of Phase II properties that has not been expropriated and redistributed.[67] Moreover, the promised agrarian code has still to be issued, leaving some space for debate over the future of unutilized land on farms above 100–150 hectares in size. The government presented a proposal to the Salvadoran congress in 1993, but there was such strong opposition to the proposed code that it was sent back to be reworked, and as of late 2000 agreement had still not been reached on a new agrarian code.

To summarize, the counter-reform in El Salvador was as unfavorable to female production cooperative members as was that in Nicaragua. However, the PTT program of land distribution to former combatants and squatters that resulted from the peace process coincided with the growth of the women's movement in El Salvador, and this was to have a much more favorable gender outcome.

Guatemala continued with its minimalist policies regarding land distribution through the mid-1990s. The main issue in this decade was how to achieve national reconciliation after the guerrilla war and severe repression in the countryside by military governments during the 1980s.[68] It has been estimated that between 1981 and 1984 the army destroyed 440 towns, villages, and hamlets; that one million people were displaced internally and 150,000 fled to Mexico; and that between 100,000 and 150,000 persons died in the conflict (Berger 1992: 196). Civilian rule returned to Guatemala in 1986 with the election of a Christian Democratic government and provided a new political opening for rural organizing. The main demand of the majority of rural organizations was for agrarian reform. There was also a resurgence of ethnic-cultural awareness among the majority Mayan population, demanding their historic right to Mayan territory and recognition of their own culture. In 1994 five of the main Mayan organizations came together to form COPMAGUA, the Coordinadora de Organizaciones del Pueblo Maya de Guatemala. The political opening of this period finally culminated in the peace accords of the mid-1990s, with broad consensus on the need for pacification of the country and the reintegration of the thousands of refugees and displaced persons. A main force in the conclusion of the accords was the new role of the Mayan organizations in Guatemalan society coupled with an increase in women's organizational activities (Fund. Arias–Tierra Viva 1993: 148).[69]

Three accords between the government of Guatemala and the URNG (Unión Revolucionaria Nacional Guatemalteca) address the agrarian question as well as the issue of gender and land rights.[70] First is the 1994 Accord on the Displaced Population (Acuerdo para el Reasentamiento de las Poblaciones Desarraigadas por el Enfrentamiento Armado). This accord is a broader version of the 1992 accord establishing the conditions and guarantees for the Guatemalan exiles in Mexico to return to their communities of origin or other comparable locales. This earlier accord specified that "it is understood that the term 'returned' refers to returned men as well as returned women," explicitly giving women the same rights as men. To facilitate the return of the exiles, the government, through its agency

FONAPAZ (Fondo para la Paz), was to provide subsidized credit that would allow the returnees to purchase land, and the government was to make available to them either public lands or private land purchased through FONATIERRA (Fondo Nacional de Tierras).[71] The 1994 accord is broader since it covers not only those who lived in exile but also the population displaced internally by the armed conflict. (Henceforth, both groups will be referred to as refugees.) This accord provided for the refugees to resettle in their communities of origin or other comparable locales under conditions of dignity and security. The government agreed to facilitate the return of land the refugees had abandoned because of the armed conflict. If this should prove impossible, the government was to purchase lands to resettle them in another location, also to be financed by FONAPAZ (MINUGUA 1995: 10).

The discrimination that women have traditionally faced in access to land and housing is mentioned explicitly in this accord, and the government committed itself to utilizing a gendered approach in its plans and actions: "The government promises to eliminate any form of discrimination, in practice or legally, against women in terms of facilitating their access to land, housing, credit, and participation in development projects. A gender focus will be incorporated into all policies, programs and activities of the global development strategy" (Section III [8]). In addition, in the section on the guarantees to be provided to the refugee population, the government committed itself to "give particular attention to the situation of female-headed households, particularly, widows and orphans, who have been the most affected" (Section II [2]).

The second accord was the 1995 Accord on the Identity and Rights of Indigenous Peoples (Acuerdo sobre Identidad y Derechos de los Pueblos Indígenas). With respect to land, the government promised to take measures to "recognize, title, protect, provide restitution to, and compensate" indigenous people, and it recognized the right to individual, communal, or collective land tenancy (Section IV.F). In addition, the accord recognized the right of indigenous communities to maintain their historic system of land administration. The state also agreed to protect indigenous communities from land grabs, and to prevent the titling of lands taken from these communities in the past by private parties. The government also promised to publicize and comply with the UN Convention on the Elimination of All Forms of Discrimination against Women, a convention it had signed in 1982.

The third accord was the 1996 Socio-Economic Accord (Acuerdo sobre

Aspectos Socio-Económicos y Situación Agraria). This accord represents the core of the peace process for it envisions a new model of development, one designed to serve the interests of the majority of the population. In the preamble, the accord recognizes that to achieve this goal it is necessary to eliminate poverty and indigence, discrimination, social marginalization, and those policies that have distorted the socio-economic, cultural, and political development of the country. These are recognized as the basis of the conflict and instability in Guatemala in the past. It affirms that social justice must be the basis for any lasting peace (Guatemala 1997: 59). The accord also recognizes that land rights have been at the heart of the conflict, and that an integrated strategy is necessary to facilitate the peasantry's access to land and other resources, provide legal security to all, and to address potential conflicts in rural areas.

The main way that landless and near-landless peasants are to gain access to land is through a land bank that provides mortgages and other credit. The land bank is to prioritize *peasant men and women* who are organized for the purpose of acquiring land (Section III, B.34, our emphasis). It is to be initiated with land from the following sources: (1) public lands and the remaining national farms; (2) public lands that were adjudicated irregularly in the colonization zones, particularly in El Petén and the Franja Transversal del Norte; (3) unused lands that may be expropriated in accordance with Article 40 of the constitution; and (4) land to be purchased from willing owners with funds either donated or lent to the government as well as its own internal resources. The accord goes into considerable detail regarding the legal reforms necessary to provide security of land tenure, including the need for a comprehensive rural cadastre and land-registration system.

Another section of this accord is dedicated to women's participation in socio-economic development and once again commits the state to promote an end to all forms of discrimination against women. It recognizes that women's contributions in all spheres of economic and social life have been undervalued, and that women's participation must be strengthened at all levels under conditions of equality (Section I.B., pars. 11 and 12). Committing the state once again to take into account gender differences in all development strategies, plans, and programs, and to train the civil service in gender analysis, it stresses the need to: "Recognize the equality of rights of women and men in the home, in the workplace, in production, and in social and political life, and to assure her the same possibilities as a man, particularly with respect to access to credit, the adjudication of land and other productive and technological resources" (Section I.B., par. 13). It is also recognized that all national legislation and implementing regulations would have to be revised in order to eliminate all forms of discrimination against women.

The separate accords went into effect with the signing of the final peace accord (Acuerdo de Paz Firme y Duradera) on 29 December 1996.[72] A fairly detailed implementing schedule had been agreed upon, to be overseen by a newly created Follow-up Commission (Comisión de Acompañamiento). This commission will also oversee the $1.9 billion in aid pledged by the international community to implement the peace process (SAIIC 1997: 3). In order to meet its various commitments under the accords to resolving the land issue, in April 1997 the government set up a technical-legal unit known as PROTIERRA (Comisión Institucional para el Desarrollo y Fortalecimiento de la Propiedad de la Tierra) to coordinate all state activities regarding land, involving seven institutions or groups.[73] The other two pillars of the coordinated plan involve agricultural and rural development, both to be under the direction of a restructured Ministry of Agriculture and Livestock (MAGA). The accords also provided for strengthening and broadening the participation of peasant organizations, rural women's organizations, indigenous organizations, cooperatives, and NGOs in the National Agricultural Development Council (CONADEA). This is to be the principal mechanism of consultation, coordination, and social participation in decision making with regard to rural development and will be linked to PROTIERRA (Guatemala 1997: 157). PROTIERRA is also a member of the various ongoing commissions that deal with land issues.

In January 1998 the institutional structure for implementing the provisions of the accords related to land was still in a state of flux. There were credible rumors that the agrarian reform institute, INTA, might shortly disappear, with many of its functions to be absorbed by FONTIERRA. But on the day we visited FONTIERRA, its personnel had been dismissed, leaving the future of the land-bank program uncertain.[74] As of mid-1998 this institution had still not been funded (Spence et al. 1998: 36). According to experts on Guatemala, "how much more land will eventually be freed up for sale to peasants by mechanisms such as the Land Fund is uncertain given the apparent paucity of idle state lands, the unwillingness of the private sector in the past to sell land to the government, and uncertainty over the political will needed to implement the Fund's objectives" (ibid.).

These problems, of course, stymie the good intentions regarding gender and land rights that were written into the accords. In addition, notwithstanding the efforts to conduct gender training among INTA and MAGA personnel, few of these are interested in issues of gender equality. They continue to view women agriculturalists "as invisible" and assume that by benefiting male household heads, the women within these households will benefit as well.[75] The staff of PROTIERRA had not really begun to think about how to address gender issues in the titling program. Said one official, "The plan is to title in the name of whoever has the paper."[76] Joint titling of land to couples had not even been raised as a possibility. The problem is that the theme of gender and land rights was not in the public discourse. This was partly because the international agencies, rather than national consensus, were responsible for issues of gender equality figuring so prominently in the accords.[77] Another factor is that land itself is such a controversial issue and fundamental land redistribution is still a taboo topic.[78]

Special Cases: The Market and Social Justice in Colombia, Bolivia, and Brazil

In those countries where agrarian reform was still on the agenda in the 1990s, it was in large measure because of pressure from the grass roots: in Colombia, because of the level of rural strife associated with the guerrilla forces, drug traffickers, and paramilitary groups; in Bolivia, due to the militancy of peasant and indigenous groups; and in Brazil, where the organized movement of the landless has resulted in a continuing "land reform from below." In all three countries land redistribution is taking place through legislation that addresses gender equity, albeit with varying degrees of specificity.

The escalating violence and political crisis characterizing Colombian society in the 1980s[79] prompted initiatives for national reconciliation, leading to the constitutional assembly that produced the exceptionally progressive constitution of 1991. The new constitution emphasized participatory democracy, redefined human rights to include social justice, upheld equality of rights and opportunities among men and women, and explicitly prohibited discrimination against women. The new constitution provided the context for Agrarian Law 160 of 1994, passed under the Gaviria government. While Gaviria's initial intention had been to follow the neo-liberal model, focusing agrarian reform efforts on strengthening the land market, political pressure from below in the context of a severe agricultural crisis led to a law that was both redistributive and neo-liberal. On one hand, it sought to broaden access to land by fostering a private land and credit market. On the other hand, it maintained the role of the state as the key intermediary in relations between the market and peasantry in the interest of assuring a modicum of redistributive justice.

The law sought to expand peasant and landless workers' access to land through two avenues, market-assisted purchases and direct interventions by INCORA, the land reform agency.[80] Market-assisted purchases begin with peasant initiatives to identify and purchase land on the regular land market. INCORA then steps in to assure that both parties agree upon an acceptable price. Direct interventions involve INCORA's traditional role of purchasing or expropriating land, the latter for considerations of social interest.[81] Under either approach beneficiaries receive a state grant equivalent to 70 percent of the value of property; the remaining 30 percent must be acquired on commercial terms through the banking system. Potential beneficiaries cannot have been previous beneficiaries of the agrarian reform, have credits in arrears, or have defaulted on previous bank debts. Moreover, in order to receive the full state subsidy, they must work the land directly for twelve years; only then will they receive title to the property, assuming they have canceled their commercial mortgages.

The main provisions that favor women reinforce or extend the changes initially introduced in the 1988 agrarian law. Potential beneficiaries are explicitly defined as poor peasant men or women who are household heads and who do not own property. Land is to be allocated jointly to couples irrespective of their marital status (Article 24). Beneficiaries are selected through a point system that reflects the objectives of the land redistribution program.[82] Priority is given to female household heads and other women who are socially or economically vulnerable because of political violence, abandonment, or widowhood, and who lack access to sufficient land. They are given the maximum number of points in the determination of beneficiary status.[83] The law also provides for the participation of the peasant women's association, ANMUCIC (along with the main mixed peasant organizations), on the executive committee of INCORA and on the regional and local committees charged with selecting the beneficiaries and implementing the reform.

The 1994 law is noteworthy for committing the Colombian state to furthering agrarian reform in a period when this process is in reversal in much of the rest of Latin America. It also, in principle, guarantees women's land rights through the two most important avenues: assuring female household heads as well as other adult women priority in land distribution efforts, and re-affirming the principle that land allocated to households should be titled in the name of both spouses or partners. Nonetheless, according to agrarian expert Absalón Machado, the law suffers from a number of deficiencies and ambiguities.[84] He considers it to lack coherence since it was a product of compromise between the competing projects put forth by traditionally antagonistic groups (such as the landlord's lobby, peasant groups, and the unions representing state workers). For example, the law seeks to reform the institutional structure behind state intervention in land distribution. However, it does this in such a way as to reduce the power of INCORA, which was considered to be quite corrupt, without clearly specifying a new chain of command and one with the capacity to coordinate actions at the national, regional, and local levels. At the same time, the law sought to broaden participation in the process of agrarian reform, but in fact ended up creating an unwieldy structure of decision making, making its implementation even more unwieldy. Moreover, Machado considers that the law failed to create the mechanisms necessary for a successful market-oriented strategy, principally an effective system of taxation and clearer regulations governing land rental.

The market-assisted program got off to a shaky start amid renewed charges of corruption within INCORA.[85] Subsequently, a $50 million loan was secured from the World Bank to implement a pilot project in five municipalities.[86] A major aim of the project was to decentralize agrarian reform planning and implementation and to broaden participation by reducing the power of INCORA. This was to be done by shifting resources to the regional and municipal levels; giving municipal agrarian reform councils primary responsibility for assessing the supply and demand for land and for screening and selecting beneficiaries; and by involving the private sector, particularly NGOs, in a number of activities previously carried out by INCORA. Another element differentiating the pilot project from the agrarian reform of the past was its emphasis on the elaboration of feasible production plans as a precondition for peasant groups to receive a state subsidy for purchase of a farm (Deininger 1999: 656–62).

Whereas during the 1994–95 period direct intervention by INCORA continued to be the dominant mode through which land was allocated, by 1996 market-assisted transactions predominated. And while the average number of beneficiaries in 1996–97 surpassed the average number allotted land under the previous administration, it was evident that this pace could not be sustained. This new phase in Colombia's agrarian reform was taking place under highly unfavorable circumstances. Over the preceding decade, drug traffickers had undertaken a counter-reform of their own in the countryside. They accomplished what the 1961 agrarian reform was never able to do: to take land away from the landed oligarchy. It is estimated that some three to four million hectares of land have been taken over by the drug traffickers,[87] at least twice if not three times as much land as was redistributed by the Colombian state over the preceding thirty-five years. In the face of this illegal counter-reform (in addition to the heavy-handed pressure emanating from the United States for Colombia to take stronger measures against the drug trade), in December 1996 the Colombian national congress approved Law 333, which allows property acquired through illegal means to be expropriated by the state (*extinción de dominio*).[88] The expropriated lands are to pass to INCORA for redistribution. While this measure suggests that the government is committed to continuing the agrarian reform, effective implementation of Law 333 will be a challenge.[89]

By the time Law 160 was five years old, it had proved incapable of reforming Colombia's agrarian structure. The government of Andrés Pastrana once again opened up the debate over agrarian reform in the context of its 1998 proposals for a new peace process. Most sectors of Colombian society agree that the agrarian problem continues to be one of the principal roots of the country's armed conflict, but they offer different solutions.[90] While there is no consensus on furthering the agrarian reform even within the Pastrana government,[91] it constitutes one of the central issues in peace discussions between the government and the largest guerrilla group, the FARC (Fuerzas Armadas Revolucionarias Colombianas).[92] It obviously will not be an easy task to establish the conditions under which poor rural women and men get access to greater amounts of land.

In Bolivia the need for a new law to govern land rights and land distribution dates from the early 1980s and the dramatic changes that had taken place in the eastern and Amazonian area of the country and the rise of the new latifundia in those regions. Additionally, the lack of coordination between government agencies concerned with granting land, forest, and mineral rights had resulted in a mosaic of overlapping land rights and titles. Moreover, these different land claims had begun to encroach seriously on the territory of indigenous people in the Amazonian basin and Chaco regions. Compounding the problem was the fact that thousands of temporary migrants from the highlands had decided to stay in these regions, often becoming squatters on public land or on indigenous territory.[93] It is reported that anywhere between 30 and 60 percent of Bolivia's territory is subject to overlapping claims (Ybarnegaray 1997: 11). While during the 1980s there was consensus on the need to revise the 1953 agrarian reform law, the main issue was whether the new legislation would adopt the neo-liberal approach—making land a commodity that could be bought and sold—or whether it would protect and extend collective land rights and maintain the central role of the state in land distribution, an issue that took over a decade to resolve.

The 1996 Ley INRA (INRA law)[94] embodies an unusual combination of neo-liberal and social justice principles, one that according to Miguel Urioste and Diego Pacheco (1999: 11) did not satisfy anyone. Overall, the law gave more attention to the issue of equitable access to land than it did to issues of land market liberalization, through its prioritization of collective land adjudications (Muñoz and Lavadenz 1997: 2). What also stands out, in contrast to other Andean countries (with the partial exemption of Colombia), is that the role of the state in land redistribution is to continue. Specific highlights of the law are as follows: The right of indigenous peoples and communities to originary communal land (*tierras comunitarias de origen*) is guaranteed. Land titles were to be issued immediately to indigenous peoples and communities recognized by previous supreme decrees. This land cannot be sold, subdivided, used as collateral, or expropriated by the state. Moreover, the internal distribution of usufruct rights to individuals and families is to be governed by traditional customs and practices (Article 3). Also guaranteed in the law is the continued existence of peasant homesteads (*solares campesinos*), small farms, and collectively held land as long as the land continues to serve a social function, assuring the welfare of peasant families. Medium-sized properties and agricultural enterprises also received legal recognition; only latifundia are not legally recognized (Article 3). The former are also expected to serve a socioeconomic function, defined in terms of land being put to its best use while the need for sustainability, land conservation, and protection of biodiversity are acknowledged.

Agricultural land, whatever the form of property, cannot be legally subdivided in portions smaller than the area defined as "small property" (the acreage necessary to meet subsistence needs) for the particular region. Inherited small property is thus indivisible (*indivisión forzosa*) although several heirs can share ownership of the land (as *co-propietarios*) (Article 48). Small property, the peasant homestead, originary communal land, and land titled collectively to peasant communities also cannot be used as collateral or expropriated by the state (Article 53). The peasant homestead and small property were given the legal status of family patrimony and cannot be used as collateral or sold while there are children under eighteen years of age living in the household (Article 41). Originary communal land and land titled collectively cannot be sold under any circumstances. In addition, all these forms of property are exempted from taxes (Article 4). The method of calculating taxes on medium-sized property and agricultural enterprises was revised in order to make effective tax collection more feasible.

Abandoned land can be expropriated by the state without indemnification (*reversión*). One of the criteria used in determining whether land has been abandoned is whether taxes have been paid over two or more periods (Articles 51 and 52). Land can be expropriated with compensation (based on the self-declared tax value) for other reasons—if it does not meet a socioeconomic function, in order to regroup land for redistribution, to conserve and protect the environment, and for other projects of public interest (Articles 58 and 59). Land expropriated by the state and public land will either be allocated collectively free of charge (*dotación comunal*) to indigenous people or indigenous or peasant communities without sufficient land, or sold at market value at a public auction. Priority in the distribution of land is to be given to collective allocations and to those who currently reside upon it (Articles 42 and 43). It is these provisions that establish that agrarian reform will continue; nonetheless, the possibility of the state fostering the development of a land market (through public auctions) constitutes the neo-liberal element of the law.[95]

Another innovation in the Ley INRA is that it explicitly calls for criteria of gender equity to be applied in the distribution, administration, tenancy, and use of land; moreover, it establishes that women have land rights independent of their civil status (Article 3, par. 5). This law is, thus, more gender-progressive than the typical neo-liberal law, which at best pretends to be gender neutral by assigning land rights to natural or juridic persons. However, the legislation contains no specific mechanisms to assure a gender-equitable outcome, such as joint allocation and titling of land. Moreover, other aspects of the 1996 law may be directly prejudicial to peasant women, such as the effort to combat the minifundia by not allowing peasant homesteads and smallholdings to be legally subdivided. While the possibility of *co-propiedad,* or joint ownership by heirs, may facilitate inheritance by women, it is unlikely that such co-ownership will increase women's control of land if there is a male heir.

Among the concerns of those interested in furthering the agrarian reform is how much land will be available for redistribution. Since not much public land is left, the availability of land for distribution will very much depend on political will: whether the state expropriates land that is not being used productively. The vast majority of the idle lands consists of neo-latifundia in the eastern region of the country that prior governments gave away free of charge (AOS/AIPE/TIERRA 1996: 19). The worry is that the large landowners might pay the taxes on the land and then sell it to the highest bidder. This would, of course, reduce still further the land available for distribution to peasant groups (Ybarnegaray 1997: 45). Another concern is that the tax rate on these lands may still be too low, providing a disincentive to sell land. Seen in its best light, the land tax and increased tenure security should encourage landholders to invest more and sell idle portions, and—perhaps by expanding the land market—reduce land prices (Muñoz and Lavadenz 1997: 22).

Another concern has to do with whether peasant squatters will be able to organize themselves into communities in order to gain access to land.[96] Without such collective organization, peasant migrants to the Amazonian and eastern region will not be eligible for land and may end up having to participate in the state's land auction, where they undoubtedly will be at a disadvantage. Nonetheless, one of the provisions of the subsequent implementing legislation, designed to "level the playing field," is that land can only be auctioned off in blocks of a hundred hectares; a landlord, for example, wanting to purchase a thousand hectares would have to participate in the auction successfully ten times.

With respect to gender, the law is admirable in its intent to comply with the provisions of the Bolivian constitution (Article 6) by guaranteeing women equality in the distribution and tenancy of land, independent of their civil status. However, as noted, no specific provisions of the law or its regulations are pro-active in this respect. While the law prioritizes collective land titling to peasant communities or indigenous peoples in future land redistributions, access to land is to be governed by time-honored customs and practices, and these generally are not gender neutral. While it is argued that traditional practices are the only reasonable way to govern access to collectively held land, given the great heterogeneity that exists among indigenous communities in Bolivia, tradition will not necessarily guarantee women's access to land under the same conditions as men. But perhaps the greatest worry in the late 1990s was whether the government of Hugo Banzer (elected in 1997) would implement the Ley INRA at all.[97] This concern was voiced by the Bolivian Episcopal Conference, which spoke out for the first time in its history on agrarian issues (Conferencia Episcopal 1999). Moreover, besides urging that the agrarian reform continue, in another historic move it called for women's land rights to be respected and taken into account (ibid.: 40).

Given the extent of landlessness in Brazil and the degree of concentration of land, it is not surprising that with the return to democratic rule in the 1980s there was a resurgence in the organization of landless rural workers and an increase in the number of conflicts over land. These events took place in the context of the development of the "new unionism,"[98] the organization in 1982 of the first workers' party in Brazil, the Partido dos Trabalhadores (PT), and the organization of a new movement of landless workers, the Movimento dos Trabalhadores Rurais Sem Terra (MST) (Fernandes 1996: 67). The MST first emerged in the state of Rio Grande do Sul in the early 1980s around a series of land occupations. Its origins are found in the Catholic Church's Christian base communities (CEBs, *comunidades eclesiais de base*), which began proliferating in rural areas and in the shantytowns in the 1960s. During the military regime the CEBs often represented the only space where the poor could seek solace and reflect upon their condition, and where they received assurance that they too were entitled to land and housing. The land invasions that grew out of this conciousness-raising process were supported by the CPT, Comissão Pastoral da Terra—organized by the National Council of Catholic Bishops in 1975—which increasingly publicized and gave coherence to these struggles (ibid.: 70–71). The CPT played a crucial role during the early 1980s in organizing landless workers from different states and in spurring their national organization into the MST.[99]

Today the MST is organized in twenty-two states, and according to its founders, "it has become the required point of reference in the struggle for agrarian reform and is recognized both by the federal and state governments as the representative voice of the demands of landless rural workers" (in Fernandes 1996: 242). According to John Hammond (1999: 1), "The MST is strong because it has a strategy which manages to combine a moderate and legalistic image with militant mobilization of its base. The former gives it credibility in public opinion and some claim to legitimacy while the latter gives it clout." Between 1990 and mid-1998 the MST had organized some 785 land occupations involving over 200,000 families and over 21 million hectares of land (Deere and León 1999a: Table 3). This is almost as much land as was allocated by the government to agrarian reform and colonization settlements between 1964 and 1994. The number of occupations has escalated since 1995. At the end of 1999 there were 538 *acampamentos* nationwide with 69,804 families awaiting INCRA (Instituto Nacional de Colonização e Reforma Agraria), the agrarian reform institute, to allocate land to them.[100]

In his electoral campaign for the 1994–98 term, Fernando Henrique Cardoso (1997: 24) stressed relatively modest targets for the agrarian reform—to give land to 280,000 families.[101] The aim would be to make productive farmers out of the beneficiaries. Once elected Cardoso created the position of Special Minister of Agrarian Reform (Ministro Extraordinario de Política Fundiaria) in order to streamline and expedite the activities of INCRA, which is now subordinated to this office, and he increased the budget for agrarian reform from $.4 billion in 1994 to $2.6 billion in 1997 (Deininger 1999: 663). The Cardoso government committed itself to providing agrarian reform beneficiaries with a complete package of credit and technical assistance, and the financing package per beneficiary has averaged $7,500, which includes an effective subsidy of around 70 percent (ibid.: 670). To complement the credit, a new decentralized technical assistance service was created (Project Lumiar). The idea was that for each group of three hundred families, there would be a permanent local team of four professionals to work with them with the aim of making the *assentamento* self-sustaining in the shortest period of time possible. Another goal of the Cardoso government has been to "emancipate" many of the older agrarian reform and colonization projects that still depend on government support. A settlement is to be considered ready for emancipation when it has reached its maximum capacity of settlers, land titles have been distributed, its basic infrastructure and services are in place, and the community is socially and economically integrated into the local and regional economy (Cardoso 1997: 33–34).

Another of Cardoso's initiatives is to decentralize and speed up the execution of agrarian reform projects. The idea here is that municipalities and state governments in cooperation with INCRA will carry out a census of the landless at the local level and identify what municipal or state land is available or what private land might be acquired for agrarian reform purposes. The federal government will guarantee the credit and share the costs of financing the local infrastructure for these new settlements. The primary vehicle for the decentralized reform is to be the state agrarian reform commissions, to be composed of representatives of the government, the private sector, and the social movements. In the first eighteen months after this initiative was announced, only one state commission had been created, in the state of Pernambuco, primarily because of the resistance of the social movements to decentralization. They were worried that the federal government would abdicate responsibility for the cause of agrarian reform. Moreover, they were also concerned that the power of landlords would be sufficient at the local level to stop any significant redistribution of land if the initiative was left to state and municipal governments.[102]

The World Bank has financed another pilot project, entitled "Programa Cédula da Terra." This program provides credit lines for land acquisition through the market, so that the state may eventually reduce its role in land expropriation and redistribution. It functions as follows: a group of peasants identify the land they would like to buy and present a plan to the state technical unit. If their plan is approved, the group then receives the financing to purchase the land with a twenty-year mortgage. In its first stage, the program operated through the Banco do Nordeste; the Brazilian government provided the funds for land acquisition and the World Bank contributed those for infrastructure investments (Cardoso 1997: 34–35). The hope was that beneficiaries would purchase unproductive lands and invest in them, maximizing the social gain (Deininger 1999: 663–64).

During 1996 several new federal laws were passed to foster more efficient use of land and to encourage landowners to sell unproductive land for agrarian reform purposes. The most important incentive concerned taxation: the tax on unused land was raised substantially, from a maximum of 4.5 percent of the declared value of the property for farms larger than fifteen thousand hectares, to 20 percent for all farms larger than five thousand hectares. Moreover, the tax rate is to be calculated not only according to farm size but also according to the degree of land utilization (Cardoso 1997: 83).

During Cardoso's second term in office it became evident that the pilot land bank, the Programa Cédula da Terra, was to become the model nationally for land reform efforts, and his government negotiated a $1 billion, four-year loan from the World Bank for this purpose. However, the degree of opposition by the MST and the rural unions to the land bank program was such that in early 2000 the World Bank sent a commission to investigate the pilot program as well as rural violence in the countryside and reduced its loan to $200 million until an accord between the government and the opposition could be reached.[103] Although the MST continues to oppose the expansion of the land bank program, the agricultural workers' confederation, CONTAG, subsequently agreed to support it.

The main concern of the MST is that the land bank will totally replace federal land-expropriation efforts even though the amount of unused and underutilized land potentially subject to expropriation is still large.[104] Moreover, the MST contends that the new taxes designed to encourage land-owners to offer their land for sale have been ineffective and have not resulted in either an increase in the supply of land on the market or a lowering of its price. In addition, the MST does not consider it just that the resource-poor are expected to purchase this land at relatively high interest rates. Also, those participating in the land bank program are not eligible for the subsidized credit available to beneficiaries on *assentamentos* organized by INCRA. Finally, the MST leadership fears that the land bank approach, combined with the decentralization of land reform efforts, will result in a program under the control of and run in the interests of the landlord class, who continue to hold power at the local level.[105] No new developments have taken place in Brazil with respect to gender and land rights issues in the years since the progressive clause was adopted in the 1988 constitution (that land distributed under the agrarian reform be allotted to men, women, or couples, irrespective of civil status), partly because agrarian reform remains such a controversial issue in Brazil.

IN BROAD STROKES, Latin American governments have followed one of two paths. Those more ideologically committed to the neo-liberal model —Chile, Peru, Mexico, Honduras, and Ecuador—have formally brought agrarian reform to an end. With the partial exception of the latter two, the state may no longer expropriate land to meet social justice goals. Nicaragua and El Salvador are also closely associated with this group of countries; although they continued redistributing land in the 1990s as part of peace processes ending civil wars, land distribution has for all practical purposes now concluded. All of these countries have engaged in the process of counter-reform, opening up the reformed sector to parcelization, including, in most cases, the collectively owned holdings of peasant and indigenous communities. In Colombia, Bolivia, Brazil, and Guatemala, countries pursuing the second path, agrarian reform efforts of some sort continue and the state may still expropriate land for purposes of redistribution. The role of the state, nonetheless, is shifting from a focus on expropriation to various forms of state-assisted land transactions. The implementation of pro-distributionary legislation requires a political will that currently seems to be absent among the governments of most of these countries, with the partial exemption of Brazil, where the pace of the agrarian reform is largely being determined by the landless movement.

In the first group of countries, where production cooperatives were parcelized, the direct effect of this process on women depended on the extent to which they had been beneficiaries of agrarian reform efforts. Women constituted a much higher percentage of production cooperative members in Nicaragua and El Salvador than in Chile, Peru, or Honduras. Case study evidence suggests that in Nicaragua female members began abandoning the cooperatives even before they were parcelized as a result of the withdrawal of state support to this sector. It is thus likely that women ended up as an even lower proportion of the beneficiaries of parcelization efforts than they were of cooperative membership. In addition, in Nicaragua as well as El Salvador there is evidence that female members were at a disadvantage—having less bargaining power than their male counterparts —when the cooperatives were broken up, and they received smaller parcels as well as the worst land. In these countries, as well as in Peru, couples were also penalized in the parcelization process, usually receiving land as a family unit; the amount of land they received on a per capita basis was thus less than that received by individual cooperative members. With respect to the indirect effects of parcelization, in large measure these depend on whether the male cooperative member was able to acquire a good land parcel; whether independent household production generates higher or lower incomes than the income previously earned through work on the cooperative; and on possible changes in who controls household income. In some cases, wives favored the parcelization of the production cooperatives precisely because they envisioned that they would play a much greater role in decision making in family-based production than they had as temporary workers on the cooperatives. In other countries, they opposed the parcelization of the cooperatives, particularly where these had been profitable and presumably a reliable source of household income. For those who subsequently sold or lost their land through indebtedness or inability to compete under the new conditions of production, the outcome of the process will largely depend on its labor market effects and on how these are gendered.

In the case of the parcelization of the *ejidos* in Mexico, the changes brought about have less to do with the reorganization of production than with the transformation of family patrimony into individual male property. This outcome resulted from the policy of vesting effective land rights on only one person per household, the household head. It is somewhat ironic that Mexico, which in 1971 was the first to formally guarantee rural women the same land rights as men within the *ejidos*, is now the retrograde among the countries studied here. The vesting of land rights on "natural and juridic persons" is not gender neutral. While it may seem like an advance over the agrarian reform legislation, the practices of the past condition how the process of individualization plays out in the present, tending to reproduce gender inequality. In contrast, in the countries where agrarian reform efforts continue (Colombia, Bolivia, Brazil, and Guatemala), governments have committed themselves to the goal of gender equity in future land distributions. Costa Rica, Honduras, and Nicaragua have done so as well, which could be important for land titling efforts. These countries differ, however, in the extent to which the goal of gender equity is backed up by mandatory measures of inclusion, such as provisions for joint titling or for prioritizing female household heads.

six

The Struggle for Women's Land Rights
and Increased Ownership of Land

*During the revolution we women were asleep and didn't demand
that we be adjudicated land. If an agrarian reform process were to
come now, we would fight for land of our own. The current struggle is that we be included in land titles.*[1]

THE NEO-LIBERAL AGRARIAN CODES that provide for formal equality in
men's and women's land rights have come about through the combined
actions of three groups of social agents, what feminist scholars Virginia
Vargas, Saskia Wieringa, and Geertje Lyclama (1996) have called "the triangle of empowerment": women active in social movements (urban and
rural), women in the state, and women in formal politics. We would add
a fourth actor, the international agencies. It is the interaction of these four
groups, facilitated since the mid-1970s by myriad international and regional conferences and networks, that has generated consensus on the
content of gender-progressive public policies and specifically on the need
for recognition of rural women's land rights. The international agencies
have also played a key role in funding much of this activity and have intervened at key political moments in favor of women's land rights in certain

countries. It is this strategic alliance that successfully carried out the battle within national legislatures and political parties to change the content of Latin America's agrarian codes in the 1990s. Nonetheless, the degree of involvement of rural women's organizations in the process has varied. Equally heterogeneous has been the extent to which this strategic alliance of feminist agents has been able to maintain momentum, once gender-progressive provisions are adopted, to make sure that these are implemented, actually increasing rural women's ownership of land.

In order to guide our comparative analysis, Table 6.1 summarizes the main changes in favor of women's land rights that have been incorporated in recent agrarian codes. Seven countries have adopted provisions that state explicitly that men and women have equal land rights. In four of these (Bolivia, Brazil, Costa Rica,[2] and Nicaragua), land rights are independent of marital status. Colombia stipulates that male and female household heads have equal rights to be allotted land, while Honduras and Guatemala vest potential land rights on peasant men and women. In those new codes following strict neo-liberal principles, potential land ownership is vested in all natural or juridic persons; they establish only implicitly that men and women may own land independently of their civil status (Ecuador, Mexico, and Peru).[3] This legislation is, thus, the least favorable for gender equity. It is worth noting that almost all of these new laws, irrespective of the strength of their commitment to gender equity, are still written in sexist language that privileges men. In the detailed provisions of these laws it still is left implicit that they apply to women, for the beneficiaries are designated in the masculine form, such as *agricultores* and *campesinos*. The exceptions are Honduras's 1992 Agricultural Modernization Law and Guatemala's 1999 legislation creating a new land bank, in which beneficiaries are explicitly referred to throughout the text as peasant men and women, *campesinos* and *campesinas*.

Among the most important advances in favor of gender equity in six of the twelve case studies are provisions for the joint allocation and titling of land to couples. Such provisions were first adopted in Brazil and Colombia in 1988, then in Costa Rica (1990), Honduras (1991), Nicaragua (1993), and Guatemala (1999).[4] However, in Brazil and Honduras joint titling is an option only if requested by the couple; in the other countries it is mandatory with respect to the allocation and titling of lands distributed by the state. Three countries, Colombia, Nicaragua, and Guatemala, give priority to female household heads in the distribution and titling of agrarian reform or public land. In addition, Colombia's 1994 law gives priority

TABLE 6.1. Changes in Agrarian Codes with Respect to Gender, Twelve Countries

Country	Explicit Equality	Non-Sexist Language	Joint Titling	Priority to Female Household Heads	Special Groups
Bolivia					
1996	Yes	No	No	No	—
Brazil					
1988	Yes	No	Optional	No	—
Chile	No new code	—	—	Land titling project	—
Colombia					
1988	No	No	Yes	Yes	—
1994	Yes	No	Yes	Yes	Unprotected women
Costa Rica					
1990	Yes	No	Yes	No	Women in Consensual Unions
Ecuador					
1994	Natural persons	No	PRONADER project	No	—
El Salvador	No new code	—	—	—	Women combatants
Guatemala					
1999	Yes	Yes	Yes	Women refugees	—
Honduras					
1991	Yes	No	Yes	No	—
1992	Yes	Yes	Optional	No	—
Mexico					
1971–92	Yes	No	No	No	—
1992	Natural persons	No	No	No	—
Nicaragua					
1981	Yes	No	No	No	—
1993	Yes	No	Yes	Yes	—
Peru					
1995	Natural persons	No	No	No	—

Sources: Bolivia (1996); da Luz (1996); Gómez-Restrepo (1991); INCORA (n.d.); CMF (1994); Ecuador (1994); Honduras (1995); Martínez et al. (1995); Guatemala (1999); Arizpe and Botey (1987); Tribunales Agrarios (1994); Deere (1983); INIM (1996); Peru (1995).

to all rural women who find themselves without protection due to the violence ravaging that country. Colombia's law is thus the most inclusive of women, for "unprotected" single women may constitute a priority group for land distribution whether or not they are also mothers and household heads.

A few other countries have given special attention to women within certain groups, such as El Salvador's priority under the peace accords for the women combatants in the civil war and female squatters in the zones of conflict. Under the PTT (Programa de Transferencia de Tierra), women's land rights were honored independently of their civil status, resulting in individual allocations to men and women who formed a couple. Chile, under its 1992–96 land titling program for smallholders, also gave priority to female household heads. Ecuador, in a special program for smallholders, PRONADER, gave priority to the joint titling of land to couples.[5] In the sections below, we discuss how gender-progressive change was achieved, analyze the difficulties in implementing these provisions in practice, and compare the outcomes of these measures.

Joint Allocation and Titling

The joint allocation and titling of land to couples is an advance for gender equity for it establishes explicitly that property rights are vested in both the man and woman forming a couple. In countries that have reformed their civil codes to establish gender equality in household management, it serves to reinforce the principle that both spouses represent the family and may administer its property. In those countries that have not instituted such reforms, it serves to protect women from losing access to what is often the household's most important asset in case of separation or divorce. In either case, joint titling guards against one spouse making decisions with which the other spouse is not in accord—such as sale or mortgage of the property —and prevents the dispossession of a spouse through a will. Moreover, joint ownership increases the bargaining power of women by improving their fall-back position, and it should enhance their role in household and farm decision making. Joint allocation and titling can also be seen as a strategy to defend the peasant family and the family farm by reducing the probability that a couple will separate. To the extent that it promotes family stability, it has been favored by conservative regimes otherwise enamored of neo-liberal principles that privilege individuals. Establishing joint allocation and titling of land to couples has not been easy, even when such a provision is compatible with the reformed civil codes. Its implementation has been resisted by agrarian reform functionaries as well as peasant men and women, for it goes against patriarchal norms. Thus, for dispositions regarding joint titling to be effective, they must be mandatory, as is shown in the cases below.

BRAZIL: CONSTITUTIONAL CHANGE

Brazil was one of the pioneers in instituting the possibility of joint allocation and titling to couples of land distributed through the agrarian reform. Moreover, joint titling was made possible irrespective of whether a couple was married or in a consensual union. However, joint titling was not made mandatory but rather was introduced as an option that could be requested by a couple; as a result, this measure has not proven very effective. Nonetheless, the changes introduced in Brazil's constitution in 1998 —which established that agrarian reform land could be assigned to men, women, and couples—probably increased the percentage of female beneficiaries of agrarian reform efforts in the 1990s.

The women's movement in Brazil developed in the 1970s on two parallel fronts: as part of the national movement struggling for a return to democracy, and as a new social actor fighting for recognition of women's rights and an end to the discrimination against women (Barsted 1994: 40; Alvarez 1990). One of its main accomplishments with the return to democratic rule was the creation of the Conselho Nacional de Direitos da Mulher (CNDM, the National Council on Women's Rights) under the Sarney government in 1985. The CNDM, a commission operating under the jurisdiction of the Ministry of Justice, brought together women from a diverse cross-section of civil society, including many feminists. It played a critical role in the debates regarding the new constitution, influencing its content in a gender-progressive direction.

The rural women's movement emerged in the context of the democratic opening of the 1980s. It developed around two central demands: that women be admitted into rural unions and that social security benefits, including paid maternity leave and retirement pensions, be extended to rural women workers (Siqueira 1991: 58). These demands reflected the growing participation of rural women in the agricultural labor force and the discrimination that women faced both as wage workers and within the rural unions. CONTAG (the Confederação Nacional dos Trabalhadores na Agricultura), the largest union confederation of agricultural workers in Brazil, addressed rural women's issues for the first time at its fourth congress in

1985, where it resolved to incorporate more women into its membership and to take steps to end the discrimination against women. One of the factors that explains the opening of CONTAG to women members at this point in time was the growth of the new unionism and the competition between CONTAG and the leftist Central Única dos Trabalhadores (CUT, the Central Workers' Union) for new members. Within CONTAG, where contested local-level elections were often taking place for the first time in many years, women were viewed as a potential positive force for change within the traditional union structure.[6] During this same period the CUT, at its second national congress in 1986, organized a women's commission, the Comissão Nacional sobre a Questão da Mulher Trabalhadora, to address the concerns of both urban and rural women. Subsequently, in 1988 it organized its first national meeting on the "women's question."

The national women's council, CNDM, working in tandem with the growing rural women's movement, was largely responsible for the enhanced state attention to rural women's issues during this period.[7] The Ministry of Agriculture organized the first National Congress of Rural Women in 1986. The demand for the allocation of agrarian reform land to female household heads and for the joint allocation and titling to couples was clearly put forth. According to the recommendations of the Northeast working group, "When the agrarian reform arrives, land should be distributed without discrimination to the men and women who want to work it. Female heads of household should not be excluded, those separated women and single mothers. . . . Land titles should have the names of husbands and wives" (EMBRATER 1986: 16). Throughout this period, the women of the Movimento das Mulheres Trabalhadoras Rurais (MMTR) of Brejo, Paraíba, in the Northeast were among the most vocal in demanding the joint allocation and titling of agrarian reform land to couples (Albuquerque and Ruffino 1987: 324–25).

It was as a result of all the seminars and congresses of this period, and the interaction between the CNDM, the female leadership of the unions, and the growing movement of rural women, that a number of gender-progressive propositions were placed before the constitutional convention in 1988, including the already-noted clause stipulating that land distributed through the agrarian reform could be assigned and titled "in the name of a man, woman, or both, independent of their civil status" (Article 189, in da Luz 1996: 177). This provision reached the national congress as a result of a popular amendment to the constitution, one brought about by a national signature campaign coordinated by the CNDM.[8]

The importance of this provision was that for the first time it was explicitly stated that women could be beneficiaries of the agrarian reform. As a result INCRA, the agrarian reform agency, was forced to change some of its more discriminatory practices. In October 1988 the point system utilized to select beneficiaries was revised so that equal weight would be given to male and female family workers (Suárez and Libardoni 1992: 118). Other selection criteria remained the same, however, including family size, size of the family labor force, and length of experience in agricultural work. Thus the factors favoring large families continued to discriminate against female household heads, and most women were disadvantaged by the criteria favoring prior agricultural experience.

Another gain for rural women in the 1988 constitution was that it established for the first time that rural and urban men and women had the same labor rights and were entitled to similar social security benefits. This meant that permanent as well as temporary wage workers, peasant producers as well as unpaid family workers, had the same rights to unemployment and disability insurance and the retirement system.[9] Women who were unpaid family workers in peasant production would be eligible for retirement benefits directly and no longer only as a dependent of a male household head; in addition, they were eligible for 120 days of paid maternity leave. A number of the new constitutional rights acquired by women in 1988 required enabling legislation to become law. In subsequent years, attaining these rights in practice would became the main priority for the rural women's movement. But with the election of President Fernando Collor in 1989, the CNDM went into a period of decline. Its budget was cut and it lost considerable autonomy (Barsted 1994: 42). As a result, most feminists resigned. Not until after Fernando Henrique Cardoso took office in 1994 was the CNDM revitalized, although by the end of the decade it still had not regained the dynamism or prestige that it enjoyed in the mid-1980s.[10]

At the Fifth CONTAG Congress in 1991 (where women were 10 percent of the delegates), women's issues were clearly on the agenda, including how to achieve in practice the new rights accorded to women in the constitution. Among the demands made by the commission on agrarian reform at that congress was that women be allotted land in their own names, or jointly with their spouse or partner (Suárez and Libardoni 1992: 135–36). In 1990 the CUT organized a Rural Women's Commission linked to its Departamento Nacional de Trabalhadores Rurais to better address what was considered to be the low participation of rural women in unions and the lack of recognition of rural women as workers (CUT 1991: 23–24). Among the main demands of rural women at the Second National Meeting of Women Workers of the CUT in 1991 was that women's names appear on agrarian reform land titles (Godinho 1995: 165). The demands at these meetings suggest that INCRA had been slow to implement the gender-progressive constitutional norms.

INCRA still does not keep systematic data on agrarian reform beneficiaries by sex, nor on the joint titling of land,[11] but according to data from the first agrarian reform census undertaken in 1996, the share of female beneficiaries is a relatively modest 12.6 percent (INCRA/CRUB/UNB 1998: 26). Almost half of the 159,778 beneficiaries were allotted land since 1990 —that is, since the 1988 constitution went into effect—suggesting that the incorporation of women as beneficiaries probably dates from this period. The fact that data on joint titling of land were not even sought in the agrarian reform census suggests how limited this practice must be in reality.

While recognition of the land rights of female household heads and the joint titling of agrarian reform land have been among the issues raised in the various meetings, congresses, and platforms of the rural unions and women's organizations, these have not been their primary demands (Deere and León 1999b). This fact is partly related to the multi class composition of the rural women's movement, which includes, in addition to landless workers and temporary and permanent rural wage workers, peasant producers and semi-proletarians. Their unified, gender-based agenda has been for recognition as rural women workers—the position they all share—and to attain in practice the social security benefits guaranteed them in the constitution. Thus one of the main activities of the ANMTR has been a national campaign to obtain documents for rural women so that they can join the social security system.[12] Moreover, given the relatively meager efforts at agrarian reform in Brazil, compared with the demand for land, the rural women's movement has joined the mixed organizations in making the deepening of the agrarian reform their primary demand. In this context, where the rural social movements and unions are pitted against the government, women's land rights issues seem divisive.

Since 1998, however, all the social movements have begun to give greater attention to the issue of women's land rights in the agrarian reform, partly due to the high visibility of women in land occupations throughout Brazil, partly because the pace of the agrarian reform has stepped up in response to the occupations, and partly as a result of the greater attention to gender concerns within the mixed-sex rural organizations. To demand joint allocation and titling of land to couples now constitutes a policy of the MST, along with the goal that the leadership of the *acampamentos* and *assentamentos* be 50 percent female (MST 2000: 58). At its seventh congress in 1998, CONTAG once again passed a resolution to demand that INCRA allocate land jointly to couples and not just to men (CONTAG 1998: 124). And this was one of the main demands of the Marcha das Margaridas in August 2000, a march on Brasilia organized by that confederation's National Women's Commission in partnership with the MMTR-NE and other groups (CONTAG et al. 2000: 6). During what has been called the largest gathering of rural women ever to be held in Brazil (some fifteen to twenty thousand women from throughout the country attended), their representatives met with President Cardoso and his staff to present their list of demands. At that meeting the president of INCRA agreed to institute the joint allocation and titling of land to couples; as of December 2000, however, instructions had not been issued making joint allocation and titling mandatory.[13]

COLOMBIA: THE LONG STRUGGLE FOR GENDER EQUITY

Colombia first recognized women's land rights in 1988. Henceforth, agrarian reform allocations and titles were to be made in the name of couples, irrespective of their marital status. In addition, special provisions were made for female heads of household, such as priority access to unutilized national lands or membership in the communal enterprises created under the agrarian reform. Also, peasant women's groups were to be given representation equal to that of men on the regional and national committees of the agrarian reform agency, INCORA. These gender-progressive changes in Colombia's agrarian law were the result of the Policy toward Rural Women adopted by the Ministry of Agriculture in 1984 (itself a product of the presence of a number of feminists within the federal government) and of the role this office played in assisting in the creation that year of the first national association of rural women, ANMUCIC (Gómez-Restrepo 1991; Villareal 1998).

ANMUCIC initially focused on promoting income-generating opportunities for women in the context of integrated rural development projects; but it soon became aware that such measures were insufficient, and the organization turned its attention to the discriminatory aspects of the agrarian reform that denied women land rights. According to ANMUCIC, the 1961 agrarian reform law had led to the allocation of land predominantly to men, under the assumption that by benefiting household heads all household members would benefit as well. ANMUCIC activists pointed to numerous cases of separations in the countryside where women in male-headed households lost all access to land, and they began demanding that land be assigned to couples irrespective of whether they were married or in consensual unions. In addition, they drew attention to the growing number of rural households headed by a woman and their need for land. Their demands played an important role in shaping Agrarian Law 30 of 1988.[14]

Notwithstanding the provisions favoring the incorporation of women, the share of women land-reform beneficiaries during 1988–91 remained the same as in the previous period, 11 percent (Durán Ariza 1991, Appendix 3). Unfortunately, the available data for this period do not report the extent of joint titling, so it is impossible to draw any firm conclusions regarding the efficacy of this provision. (Joint titling might still be reported under the category of male household heads.) Nonetheless, it was clear that the gender-balancing provisions of Law 30 were not being implemented.[15] According to the founding president of ANMUCIC, the "struggle to enforce the law" pitted her organization against peasant men's associations, which often resisted having women be represented on INCORA's beneficiary-selection committees.[16] The very creation of a national rural women's organization had been viewed suspiciously by the main mixed peasant organization, ANUC (Asociación Nacional de Usuarios Campesinos), who saw it as divisive for class-based demands and as a competitor for resources (Villareal 1998: 72). ANMUCIC also had to confront an unfriendly bureaucracy within INCORA; local-level functionaries simply resisted allocating land to women together with men.

Indicative of the degree of male opposition was that even after a strongly worded letter by the director of INCORA instructed the regional offices to implement the law's provisions favoring women (written as a result of ANMUCIC pressure),[17] a year later in its annual report INCORA failed to make any mention of the provisions of the law favoring the incorporation of women as beneficiaries. Moreover, none of these provisions were explicitly listed among its goals, which still focused on benefiting rural families (Ministerio de Agricultura 1989). The lack of compliance with joint allocation and titling was such that the executive committee of INCORA in 1989 was forced to issue a new resolution that made joint titling of land mandatory when so requested by a man and his wife or partner.[18] The wording of this resolution suggests that the primary resistance to joint titling did not come from peasant families but rather from INCORA's local functionaries. Nonetheless, it represented a step backward, since the resolution did not require functionaries to implement the law as fully intended, which was to apply joint titling *in all cases* and not just when it was requested by a couple.

The fact that Law 30 was applied inconsistently at the local level was related to the lack of political will nationally to promote comprehensive gender-equity provisions during the decade of the 1980s (Gómez-Restrepo 1991: 224). This situation began to change, however, during the debates leading up to the approval of the 1991 constitution. The women's movement played a major role in assuring that the new constitution stressed equality of rights and opportunities between men and women and prohibited discrimination against women. The country's civil code was reformed at the same time so that the rights of consensual unions were fully recognized.

There was also growing recognition in this period that the number of female heads of household was increasing rapidly as a result of the escalating violence in the country and the growing number of households being displaced and forced to migrate to urban areas.[19] In 1991, at the initiative of ANMUCIC and with the support of Colombia's First Lady, Ana Milena Muñoz de Gaviria,[20] INCORA issued another resolution with respect to women that went beyond the provisions of Law 30. It instructed its offices to give priority in land distribution efforts to women who were in a state of "lack of protection" due to the widespread violence in the country, which was associated with an increasing incidence of widowhood and abandonment.[21] Women in such a situation were to be given an additional ten points on their application to become land beneficiaries (Medrano 1996:7). While this measure seems quite patriarchal (in its assumption that a woman without a man requires the protection of the state), it was innovative since for the first time it included among the potential beneficiaries single women who were not necessarily mothers. Moreover, it can be interpreted as a measure of positive discrimination in favor of gender equity since men were still required to be household heads to qualify as beneficiaries.

In 1994 the Gaviria government passed Agrarian Law 160. The then-president of ANMUCIC indicates that the original draft law presented by INCORA omitted all of the gains achieved for women by her organization in the 1988 law and since then, whether intentionally or not.[22] This happened notwithstanding the existence since the early 1980s of an Office for Rural Women in the Ministry of Agriculture and Rural Development and the many gender-sensitivity training courses it had promoted within

INCORA. Only through ANMUCIC's intense lobbying, coupled with support from its allies within the government, were the gender-equity provisions retained and strengthened in the new legislation. According to INCORA's legal advisor,

> The leaders of ANMUCIC arrived in my office, and they asked me to include two things in the law: priority to female household heads and to women who were in a state of lack of protection due to the violence, widowhood, and abandonment. Why should we protect female household heads in the land distribution process? These leaders emphasized how the problem of unprotected women had become more acute— the increase in the number of widows, the disintegration of the rural family not only for traditional reasons of abandonment (men's inability to meet their obligations to the family) but because of the disintegration of the peasantry.[23]

As a result of these efforts, the 1994 law specifies that its beneficiaries are to be peasant men or women who are household heads, who live in conditions of poverty, and who do not own property. The supporting legislation incorporates the provision, first introduced in 1991, that not only female household heads but also other women who are without protection are to be given the maximum number of points in the determination of beneficiary status.[24] This measure went beyond any previous Colombian law in seeking to promote the access of poor women to land. In addition, the 1994 law affirmed the provision, first enacted in the 1988 agrarian law, requiring the *mandatory* joint allocation and titling of lands to couples.[25]

The 1994 law has several deficiencies that displeased ANMUCIC and its allies. For one, only persons who are credit-worthy are potential beneficiaries. While this may seem like a reasonable provision, women are not on a level playing field when it comes to seeking credit from commercial banking institutions and may have more difficulty than men in convincing bankers that they are indeed farmers and credit-worthy. Also, a woman can be disqualified if a former partner has ever defaulted on a loan.[26] Another issue, given the preference in the law for family farming, is the status of communal enterprises or associative groups under the new legislation. In some cases women's groups have organized cooperative production schemes, only to find themselves rebuffed at the moment of soliciting land collectively.[27] In addition, in the regulations regarding the World Bank's market-assisted land project, the mechanism by which female heads of household and those who lacked protection were to be given priority was not very clear.[28] In interviews it became apparent that female household heads would be given priority over men only when all else was equal.[29] It seems that there is a growing general awareness, nonetheless, that INCORA's mandate is to favor female household heads, for sometimes women who are not household heads have solicited land claiming that they are. In the department of Magdalena, for example, a group of women claiming to be widows petitioned for land, but as ANMUCIC's president observed, "they had their partner standing behind them, so that the women would appear as head of household. The opportunism of men has to be restrained so that real female household heads don't lose that preferential right because of such actions."[30]

Following the enactment of the 1994 law, the allocation of land to couples increased steadily. As Table 6.2 shows, the share of couples being given land parcels increased from 18 percent in 1995 to 78 percent in 1998, for an average of 57 percent of the total allocations over the 1995–98 period. Over this period women alone represented 13 percent of the land allocations, only slightly higher than the historic 11 percent figure. This suggests that while some attention has been given to the demand for land by female household heads and perhaps other single women,[31] the priority has been the joint allotment of land to couples. No significant trends have emerged in the average amount of land allotted to men and to women, or to individuals versus couples. As Table 6.2 also shows, after 1995 the majority of beneficiaries acquired land through market-assisted transactions rather than through purchases by INCORA. Also worthy of note is the sharp fall in the number of beneficiaries in 1998, which does not bode well for the future of the land distribution program.[32]

The Colombian case illustrates how a coalition of state planners and a vocal national rural women's organization succeeded in bringing pressure to bear upon lawmakers to favor gender equity when new agrarian reform laws were being drafted. Their success was very much linked to the political moment at the time and the efforts of a coalition in favor of deepening the agrarian reform process and broadening the categories of beneficiaries. This case also illustrates how difficult it can be to implement gender-progressive change in practice. Such change was resisted by state functionaries charged with implementing the reform, by male peasant leaders, and sometimes by peasant men and women. Notwithstanding the fact that ANMUCIC was represented on the national, regional, and local commissions charged with selecting beneficiaries, it took a concerted effort of consciousness raising to get INCORA functionaries to implement the law, as well as almost ten years before joint allocation became the

TABLE 6.2. Beneficiaries of Law 160, Adjudications during 1995–1998, Colombia

Modality	Female Beneficiaries	Male Beneficiaries	Couple Beneficiaries	Total Beneficiaries
		1995		
Market Assisted	170 (17.8%)	704 (73.6%)	83 (8.7%)	957 (100%)
Direct Intervention	626 (19.5%)	1,928 (60.0%)	661 (20.5%)	3,215 (100%)
Total	796 (19.1%)	2,632 (63.1%)	744 (17.8%)	4,172 (100%)
		1996		
Market Assisted	743 (15.3%)	1,094 (22.6%)	3,007 (62.1%)	4,844 (100%)
Direct Intervention	202 (12.2%)	455 (27.6%)	993 (60.2%)	1,650 (100%)
Total	945 (14.5%)	1,549 (23.9%)	4,000 (61.6%)	6,494 (100%)
		1997		
Market Assisted	273 (7.9%)	120 (3.5%)	3,064 (88.6%)	3,457 (100%)
Direct Intervention	212 (11.3%)	624 (33.0%)	1,054 (55.7%)	1,890 (100%)
Total	485 (9.0%)	744 (14.0%)	4,118 (77.0%)	5,347 (100%)
		1998		
Market Assisted	94 (7.4%)	198 (15.5%)	986 (77.2%)	1,278 (100%)
Direct Intervention	9 (11.1%)	—	72 (88.9%)	81 (100%)
Total	103 (7.6%)	198 (14.6%)	1,058 (77.8%)	1,359 (100%)
		TOTAL 1995–98		
Market Assisted	1,280 (12.1%)	2,116 (20.1%)	7,140 (67.8%)	10,536 (100%)
Direct Intervention	1,049 (15.3%)	3,007 (44.0%)	2,780 (40.7%)	6,836 (100%)
Total	2,329 (13.4%)	5,123 (29.5%)	9,920 (57.1%)	17,372 (100%)

Source: Provided to the authors by the Office of Planning and Regional Offices, Subgerencia de Ordenamiento Social, INCORA, as of September 1999.

Notes: For 1996, the land-market data by sex was reported by 21 out of the 21 regional offices with this program; the data for direct intervention was reported by 13 out of 16 regional offices with this modality. For 1997, land-market data was reported by 24 out of 24, and direct intervention data by 12 out of 15 regional offices with these programs. For 1998, the corresponding figures were 19 out of 24 and 6 out of 6, respectively.

norm in practice. In addition, by prioritizing female household heads to the detriment of single women affected by the violence, ANMUCIC passed up an important opportunity to press for individual titling to women who were not necessarily mothers, one of the more innovative aspects of the law in terms of the promotion of gender equality.

COSTA RICA: THE LAW TO PROMOTE
THE SOCIAL EQUALITY OF WOMEN

Gender-progressive change in Costa Rica's land distribution program came about through proactive legislation designed to reverse the discrimination to which women have traditionally been subject. The 1990 Law to Promote the Social Equality of Women, passed at the end of the Arias administration, established that land and housing were to be considered family property, giving both spouses equal property rights.[33] The law also recognized consensual unions for the first time, and privileged the women within them in terms of the allocation and titling of property facilitated by the state (Guzmán 1991: 199, 208; Campillo 1995: 360–61). This historic piece of legislation made joint titling of land or housing distributed through state programs mandatory in the case of married couples; in the case of consensual unions, such property was to be titled in the name of the woman alone. According to Article 7, "All property distributed through social development programs should be inscribed in the name of both spouses in the case of married couples, in the name of the women in the case of consensual unions, and in the name of the individual in any other case, be it male or female" (CMF 1994: 8).

This was the first time ever in Latin America that legislation provided for a pro-active measure involving positive or reverse discrimination. It was defended on the basis of the lack of protection that women in consensual unions have traditionally faced and the importance of giving continuity, stability, and cohesion to the family unit: "Society and the judicial apparatus had never given women in consensual unions any rights whatsoever. To balance such an unequal relation among couples required strong measures . . . the law wished to protect such women to assure their children continuity and permanence in the home or land parcel" (Molina et al. 1992: 42).

Among the factors that led to the passage of this law was Costa Rica's signing in 1984 of the UN Convention to Eliminate All Forms of Discrimination against Women. Advocates argued that to achieve equality, the historic discrimination against women must be reversed directly, giving unmarried mothers, in this case, an advantage over their partners (Molina et al. 1992: 42). Article 7 was largely the result of the organized demands of urban women, voiced through NGOs and the national women's office, the CMF (Centro Nacional de Desarrollo de la Mujer y la Familia). Although the law was to have very important repercussions for rural women, rural women's organizations—which consisted primarily of local-level groups at the time—played a minimal role in its formulation and approval.

Since the 1980s poor urban women were organizing housing committees (*comités de vivienda*) to press for increased state subsidies for the construction of urban housing. In concert, they challenged the practice of titling subsidized housing in the name of the male head of household. They argued that if a couple broke up, it was the woman and children who would find themselves homeless; the man would remain with the home since it was registered in his name. Another problem was when men took out a loan, using the home as collateral, without their partner's consent; they could even sell the home without the partner's knowledge. Sometimes the men failed to pay the monthly charges on the state mortgages, leading these homes to be reclaimed. The activists argued that women were much more responsible, and if the homes were registered in their name, they would go to great lengths to make sure that their children were not left homeless (Molina et al. 1992: 42; Sagot 1997; Blanco 1997: 51).

The feminist NGO, CEFEMINA (Centro Feminista de Información y Acción), played a key role in articulating these concerns of urban women. It was joined by feminists within the CMF, whose mandate was to advocate for and coordinate all public policies to end the discrimination against women. CEFEMINA and CMF found strong support for this initiative in the office of the First Lady. Margarita de Arias had been quite involved in promoting women's issues internationally, including the initiative of First Ladies that led to the 1992 Geneva declaration regarding the enhancement of the position of rural women. It was largely at her instigation that the urban housing initiative ended up being applied to all state programs dealing with the distribution of property, including the agrarian reform.

Article 7 of the law was taken quite seriously by agrarian reform functionaries, who began allotting land to women whether or not they had been the one to submit the request for land (Madden 1992: 80). According to an internal document of the agrarian reform institute, "IDA [the Instituto de Desarrollo Agropecuario], in order to apply the legislation, takes into account—in the process of selection of the beneficiaries—the civil status of the person filling out the request form. In the case of a woman in a consensual union, the parcel is allocated to her, even if her partner was the one to have filled out the form . . . we call this the indirect modality" (Villalobos 1993: 6). As a result of Article 7, in 1990 women constituted 38.7 percent of those assigned land parcels by IDA. As Table 6.3 shows, this figure represents a considerable increase over the share of female beneficiaries in the 1986–89 period, when they averaged only 13.2 percent. Women continued to be favored in land adjudications over the next two years, reaching 65 percent of those allocated land in 1992, and 45 percent over the three-year period during which this provision was applied.

The application of the law, however, sowed confusion in rural areas. Rural women had not been involved in its formulation, were taken by surprise by it, and sometimes feared its ramifications. One organizer reported, "Many men started to blame the women . . . this was a problem for them for their partners would protest, 'Why in her name?' . . . The women would say, 'I don't want it registered in my name.' It was too much responsibility that fell on them all of a sudden, without having any kind of information or support. . . . It wasn't the case with all women, but at least some women were afraid, because this situation came out of nowhere."[34] Nonetheless, other peasant women immediately recognized the importance of Article 7: "This law is for the good of both the man and woman; if it [land] was only in his name, he could sell it and leave, and I would be left with my children wandering around, suffering a great deal. . . . It's a form of protection for women in case their men turn out to be drunks and beat them, for in case he leaves, the woman can continue to work the parcel" (in Chiriboga et al. 1996: 99–100).

The constitutionality of Article 7 was soon challenged by a group of peasant men from the *asentamiento* of Huetares, in Río Frío.[35] They had solicited land from IDA and had expected it to be assigned in their names. When they realized that the land would be allocated in the name of their partners, they filed suit against IDA. They argued that Article 7 violated Article 33 of the constitution, which established that "all *men* are equal before the law" (our emphasis) and which prohibited discrimination "against human dignity."[36] The men had been involved in land take-overs in the Río Frío region for the previous twelve years and pointed out that their partners had never participated in these. They thus felt that Article 7 was also in clear violation of another constitutional article, which established that "no law can be applied retroactively to the detriment of the established patrimonial rights of another person" (Article 34). IDA responded to this latter argument noting that since land distribution was a social program,

TABLE 6.3. Land Allocations by Sex, 1986–1992, Costa Rica

Year	Men		Women		Total	
	No.	%	No.	%	No.	%
1986	579	(91.2)	56	(8.8)	635	(100)
1987	1,172	(88.0)	161	(12.0)	1,333	(100)
1988	1,297	(81.1)	303	(18.9)	1,600	(100)
1989	1,079	(90.7)	110	(9.3)	1,189	(100)
Subtotal	4,127	(86.8)	630	(13.2)	4,757	(100)
1990	490	(61.3)	309	(38.7)	799	(100)
1991	170	(60.3)	112	(39.7)	282	(100)
1992	104	(35.0)	194	(65.0)	298	(100)
Subtotal	764	(55.4)	615	(44.6)	1,379	(100)

Source: Compiled by the authors from data provided by the Junta Directiva, Instituto de Desarrollo Agrario, as of October 1997.

it was socially just to redistribute land to a family group, or through joint titling. Nonetheless, the agency was forced to admit that there might be discrimination in assigning land only to women in the case of consensual unions.

The suit was heard by the Supreme Court, which concluded that the exclusion of men from land adjudication and titling in the case of consensual unions was unconstitutional, notwithstanding the historical vulnerability of women in consensual unions. Moreover, in its opinion, if one accepts the principle of positive discrimination in favor of women in consensual unions, one is accepting the premise that men in consensual unions always abandon their partners. Even if this might usually be the case, the court reasoned, this does not justify excluding men from land adjudication and titling on the basis of their sex. The Supreme Court thus settled the suit in the men's favor, and subsequent land allocations involving consensual unions were to be titled in the name of the couple. IDA continued assigning land to women in consensual unions through 1992; then, because of this suit, it stopped giving lands to couples in consensual unions altogether. Land titling to such couples did not resume until 1994.[37]

Whether Article 7 will significantly increase women's ownership of land in Costa Rica depends on a number of factors. First, it is unclear that the political will exists to undertake significant land redistribution. Under the current neo-liberal model—which favors economic efficiency over social justice—it is doubtful that a thorough redistribution of landed property will soon be on the national agenda. Second, since 1987 IDA's budget for purchases of land has been greatly reduced, leading to a slowdown in the rate of land adjudications. Whereas between 1986 and 1989 IDA allocated land to an average of 1,189 beneficiaries annually, after the Law to Promote the Social Equality of Women was passed, between 1990 and 1992, there were only 460 adjudications per year (see Table 6.3). This suggests that women's land rights are being recognized only as land distribution slows down to a trickle, greatly diminishing the redistributionary potential of the law.

A 1996 report by the coordinator of IDA's Women's Office was quite pessimistic that large numbers of women would gain access to land (Víquez Astorga 1996). Besides the above factors, she notes that few rural women are aware of their rights and hardly ever apply for land, which she attributes to the fact that they do not see themselves as farmers. Moreover, despite the significant number of gender-training courses that have been held, government functionaries in the agricultural sector do not value women as agricultural producers. Thus even though IDA is applying the law with respect to joint titling, the institution does so "in a formal way, so that it really is not making a difference in terms of women's control over land" (ibid.: 5). Nonetheless, several studies suggest that peasant women do wish to become landowners and that their demand for land is still largely unsatisfied. Of the women who applied to IDA for land in 1991, only 28 percent were assigned land; the comparable figure for men was 68 percent (CMF 1997: 19). A study of rural women's organizations revealed that of the 176 groups interviewed, one-third needed access to land to carry out their productive projects. This study concluded that "the large number of groups that need land shows that actual land distribution policies have been insufficient to meet the demand forthcoming from women's organizations" (Fund. Arias 1997a: 47).

Until recently, rural women in Costa Rica have not had a national voice of any kind. Although peasant men have a long history of struggle and organization (Román 1994), it was not until 1996 that a national peasant women's organization was created. Up until then rural women's organizations could only be found at the local level, and generally they were organized around income-generating projects for women.[38] The Asociación Nacional de Mujeres Productores Rurales de Costa Rica was founded in 1996 as an outcome of a meeting co-sponsored by the Office of the First Lady and FAO. Among its activities, the association has sought to promote women's awareness of their land rights. According to its president, women "have been ignored when it came time to distribute land." In addition, they are unaware of their property rights under the civil code and of inheritance laws. As she confesses, "I, myself, was not aware that I, too, was the co-owner of my parcel. Nonetheless, I don't have access to credit because the parcel is registered in my husband's name."[39]

Among the first activities of the association was to participate, under the coordination of the CMF and the Ministry of Agriculture, in the development of a national plan for rural women producers, the PIOMHICITO or "little plan," as it is known (CMF 1997: 19–22). One of the plan's six goals is equality between men and women in access to and control over land. A set of very concrete actions was recommended with respect to the agrarian reform, including a complete reassessment using a gender lens of the regulations and methods used to select the beneficiaries; and an evaluation of the information, legal advice, and training made available to rural women regarding the land-distribution programs of the agrarian reform institute, IDA. Moreover, the specific goal was set of meeting all of the requests for land or land titling presented by women who qualify for IDA's programs as a means of compensating for the discrimination against women in previous years.

Unfortunately, there was a change of government in this period, and under the new administration of Miguel Ángel Rodríguez the implementation of both the PIOMH and the PIOMHICITO has been a low priority.[40] For example, no efforts have been made to improve the data-collection procedures of IDA with respect to the sex of those requesting land or land-titling services, suggesting that the objectives of the PIOMHICITO are being ignored.[41] Moreover, the rural women's association, which had been created under the auspices of the previous government, lost official support, and this has weakened its visibility and effectiveness. In addition, the women's movement has largely withdrawn from cooperation with the state, and at the moment progress toward gender equity in Costa Rica is at a standstill.

NICARAGUA: WHAT A FEMALE PRESIDENT
CAN DO WITH FEMINIST ALLIES

Joint titling of land had been a demand of the Women's Division of the Unión Nacional de Agricultores y Ganaderos (UNAG) since the late 1980s, but it was not until after the election of President Violeta Barrios de Chamorro in 1990—and the consolidation of the women's movement in Nicaragua—that the conditions were in place for more equitable practices in land distribution and titling to be adopted. From the mid-1980s on, growing groups of women had become critical of AMNLAE (Asociación de Mujeres Nicaragüenses "Luisa Amanda Espinoza"), the Sandinista mass organization for women, calling for it to democratize its structure and to confront feminist issues directly. But it was not until after the defeat of the FSLN in the February 1990 elections and the end of the civil war that the space was created for the development of an autonomous women's movement (Stephen 1997: 60–61).[42] With respect to rural women, a prominent woman jurist commented in 1998, "The work with rural women was basically promoted by women linked to the Sandinista Front. . . . Since then women from other political forces have joined the movement, which I feel is stronger each day. I believe that the women's movement in rural areas is among the strongest forces of the women's movement."[43]

The membership of rural women in UNAG continued to grow, reaching seventeen thousand in the mid-1990s.[44] Since its first congress in 1989, the Women's Division of UNAG has demanded joint titling of land to couples and priority in assigning and titling land to female household heads (UNAG 1993). According to UNAG leader Marta Valle, "In 1990 the women's movement gained momentum and it was realized that land had not been distributed equally, that we women were at a disadvantage when it came to property. 'The floor shook beneath us' with the problem of women's property. We realized that we didn't own anything, that we don't have access to or control over resources. . . . It is the work of the women's movement that joint titling or titling of women is now being considered."[45]

The women's movement worked closely with INIM (Instituto Nicaragüense de la Mujer, created in 1983 under another name) to promote gender issues among the women in the UNO (Unión Nacional Opositora) leadership, including President Violeta Barrios de Chamorro. The president took gender issues seriously enough that she held a two-day retreat with all of her ministers and their spouses to discuss the incorporation of gender considerations into state policy. Such an unusual step reflects the strength and unity reached by the women's movement in Nicaragua after 1990.[46] INIM was also strengthened in 1993 by new legislation that gave it greater autonomy and by the creation of an advisory board composed of representatives from all branches of government as well as from civil society. In addition, an Inter-institutional Commission on Women and Rural Development (CMYDR) headed by INIM, with representatives from INRA and the Ministry of Agriculture and Livestock plus other ministries, was created to promote rural women's integration into development initiatives and increase their access to productive resources (INIM 1996: 3, 5).

At the same time, a priority of the Chamorro government had become that of fortifying the legal framework of the agrarian reform through a massive land titling effort. It was estimated that approximately 60 percent of the property in the reformed sector was characterized by titling problems, and this was judged to be a major source of instability in the countryside (INIM 1993: 6). Thus, with World Bank funding, the land titling and land distribution program known as PNCTR (Programa Nacional de Catastro, Titulación y Regularización de la Propiedad) was initiated in 1993. This program was to carry out a rural cadastre, modernize the national system of land registry, and regularize the situation of Sandinista agrarian reform beneficiaries and of ex-combatants ceded land (INRA-INIM 1996: 16).

In October 1993 CMYDR convened the first national conference on women and land tenancy with the explicit goal of sensitizing INRA officials to the importance of including women among the beneficiaries in the land titling program. It was argued that joint titling would promote the stability of the rural family and that men were more likely to sell the land than women, so that joint titling "would in a sense tie him down, and put women in a better position if it came down to discussing sale of the land."[47] Also noted was the high proportion of female household heads in rural areas, 18.8 percent in 1992 (Valdés and Gomáriz 1997: 33). At the conference, President Chamorro instructed INRA to begin giving preference to joint titling of land (*mancomunado*) distributed under the agrarian reform and to promote the titling of female heads of households (INIM 1996: 5). An INRA functionary comments on how this directive was experienced in the field:

> This instruction fell from the sky. . . . There was no kind of training of the technical personnel of how the titles would be made out in the names of men and women. The explanation given at that moment was that one had to protect the children, the woman, the family. When the man was the owner, what happened was that the women and children were often left unprotected. If he got involved in another relationship, he would keep the land, and leave the children and woman unprotected. . . . Later on, everything was more institutionalized, more organized, and there were gender-training sessions for the technicians.[48]

The UNAG Women's Division was aware that legal changes by themselves would be insufficient to guarantee women's land rights. At its fourth congress in 1993, it adopted the following resolution: "Women need to initiate an aggressive process of persuasion with men in order to make sure that titling efforts allow her to be a co-owner of property" (UNAG 1993: 22). Joint titling of land to couples (whether married or in consensual unions) was made official by Law No. 209 of December 1995. The legislation was made retroactive to cover all those who received land under the agrarian reform.[49] That same year the PNCTR program, with external funding, began giving gender-sensitivity training not only to its functionaries but also to peasants demanding access to land or the legalization of their parcels (INRA-INIM 1996: 17).

Between September 1992 and December 1996, women constituted 25.5 percent of the 37,613 persons who benefited from the Chamorro government's land-titling program for agrarian reform beneficiaries, as Table 6.4 shows. While the pace of land titling initially slowed down under the government of Arnoldo Alemán, the gender-progressive policies continued in place, and under his government (through August 2000) women represented 42 percent of the 21,258 beneficiaries. All told, during the period in which gender-progressive policies were in place (1994–2000) women represented 33.5 percent of the beneficiaries. Comparing this figure with the data on agrarian reform beneficiaries of the 1980s—where women represented 10 percent (INRA-INIM 1996: 10)—one sees that significant changes in favor of gender equity have taken place.

During the 1992–96 period, 25 percent of the titles were issued to individuals, 60 percent were joint titles, and 16 percent were collective titles issued to cooperatives.[50] Women constituted 40 percent of the 8,745 recipients of individual titles but only 17 percent of the 5,666 members of cooperatives who received collective titles. It appears that the practice of joint titling tended to favor male pairs, such as fathers and sons or brothers, rather than marital couples, for women represented only 21 percent of the 21,134 beneficiaries of joint titling. Although joint titling of couples had been discussed with INRA functionaries at the local level, the notion of *mancomunado* was not very well understood: "At the central level, people assumed that it meant a man and a woman, but *mancomunado* can refer to a couple or to two people, *mancomunado* means that 'the two of us are tied together,' thus the two can be two men, or two women, or a couple . . . thus, *mancomunado* titling does not necessarily include a woman. In the Women's Unit of INRA it was assumed that everyone would understand that *mancomunado* meant a couple, but the technicians who are out there in the field . . . they understood *mancomunado* as two persons."[51]

TABLE 6.4. Adjudication and Titling by Sex, 1992–2000, Nicaragua

Year	Number of Titles	Area (mzs.)	Men No.	Men %	Women No.	Women %	Total No.	Total %
			Beneficiaries					
1992–93	4,444	140,557	5,228	(87.6)	741	(12.4)	5,969	(100)
1994	5,843	182,539	7,592	(81.4)	1,738	(18.6)	9,330	(100)
1995	6,337	255,550	6,960	(70.1)	2,971	(29.9)	9,931	(100)
1996	6,391	255,533	8,255	(66.7)	4,128	(33.3)	12,383	(100)
Chamorro govt. subtotal	23,015	834,179	28,035	(74.5)	9,578	(25.5)	37,613	(100)
1997	3,372	137,899	3,306	(58.2)	2,370	(41.8)	5,676	(100)
1998	1,362	87,128	1,781	(59.1)	1,231	(40.9)	3,012	(100)
1999	—	—	4,869	(56.5)	3,748	(43.5)	8,617	(100)
2000*	—	—	2,405	(60.8)	1,548	(39.2)	3,953	(100)
Alemán govt. subtotal	—	—	12,361	(58.1)	8,897	(41.9)	21,258	(100)
Total, period of gender-progressive policies, 1994–2000	—	—	35,168	(66.5)	17,734	(33.5)	52,902	(100)

Source: Derived from "Consolidado General de Títulos" as of December 20, 1996, provided to the authors by the Dirección Legalización y Titulación, Sistema de la Propiedad, INRA; for 1997, from "Consolidado del Período Enero–Diciembre 1997," División de Titulación, INRA; and for 1998–2000, from "Datos de titulación de tierra en Nicaragua, según sexo, por año, 1998–2000," Oficina de Titulación Rural, Ministerio de Hacienda y Crédito Público, December 2000.

* Data for 2000 are as of August. Another two thousand titles were expected to be issued by year's end. E-mail communication to the authors from Patricia Hernández and Paola Pérez Alemán, 4 December 2000.

The fact that the 1995 law requiring joint titling of couples was not being taken into account was rectified by 1997, as a result of the efforts of the Women's Unit in INRA and local-level efforts by UNAG activists.[52] In that year 45 percent of the 3,372 titles issued went to couples consisting of a man and woman; only 4 percent were issued to other pairs, such as fathers and sons; 45 percent were issued to individuals; and cooperative members accounted for 6 percent of the titles.[53] Moreover, a new property law was approved by the Congress in December 1997, and it incorporated the portions of Law 209 that provided for the joint titling to couples of land distributed by the state.[54] However, a new agrarian code remains the subject of intense debate.

After almost two decades, the progressive intent of the 1981 agrarian reform law—which established that neither sex nor kinship position should hinder one from being a beneficiary of the agrarian reform—is finally being applied in Nicaragua, partly because of the relatively high proportion of rural female household heads, and partly because joint titling was made retroactive to cover previous land distributions. However, the difficulty of overcoming patriarchal attitudes and the invisibility of women in agriculture is quite evident in Nicaragua's initial experience with joint titling, which local functionaries assumed was meant to apply to two males rather than to spouses. It took the concerted efforts of both the UNAG Women's Division and the state—and intense gender consciousness-raising training at all levels—to rectify this situation.

HONDURAS: HALF MEASURES AVAILED US NOTHING

The main gender-progressive change in Honduran land legislation came about in 1991, when—as a result of pressure by international agencies, NGOs, feminist groups, and some of the rural women's organizations—the Permanent Women's Forum of the national congress succeeded in modifying various clauses of the agrarian reform legislation that had discriminated against women.[55] The arguments for doing so were based on the government's ratification of the UN Convention to End All Forms of Discrimination against Women and the Nairobi "forward looking" strategies, as well as the need for consistency with Honduras's recently approved (and short-lived, due to a change in government) National Women's Policy.

The reform included a re-writing of Articles 79 and 84 of the agrarian reform law, which addressed the designation of beneficiaries and inheritance in explicitly non-sexist language. Revised Article 79 established for the first time that single women *or* men above the age of sixteen could be beneficiaries of the reform, irrespective of whether they were a household head. Moreover, the revised legislation explicitly provided for joint titling in the case of spouses or couples in consensual unions. Revised Article 84 established that the spouse or partner had first rights of inheritance to land ceded under the agrarian reform (Martínez et al. 1995: 55). These gender-progressive modifications were adopted just after the neoliberal government of Callejas came to office intent on pushing Honduras through a classical structural-adjustment program, one designed to create the conditions favorable to export agriculture. It seemed as if the momentum for gender-progressive change was being maintained, nonetheless, for the Agricultural Modernization Law of 1992 was written in non-sexist language, explicitly denoting that peasant men and women could be beneficiaries, and most of the modifications approved by the Congress in 1991 were maintained.

The main setback for gender equity was that in the new law joint titling to couples was no longer to be required; rather, it was only a legal possibility *if a couple so requested it* (Article 64 in Honduras 1995). In other words, joint titling would depend on cultural norms that are decidedly patriarchal. In addition, consensual unions, which characterize the majority of households in rural Honduras (see Table 2.4), may apply for a joint title only if the relationship is duly registered, a process that is both costly and time consuming (Acosta and Moreno 1996: 3). Moreover, other discriminatory aspects were maintained in the legislation, such as requiring potential beneficiaries to work in agriculture on a full-time basis (Roquas 1995: 6–7; Martínez, Rosales, and Rivera 1995: 55). As one women peasant leader noted, "Women are not involved in agricultural production activities on a full-time basis and consequently according to the law, they do not qualify for obtaining land from the Honduran government" (in Roquas 1995). This disposition ignores the inter-relationship between rural women's productive and reproductive work as well as their important role in the seasonal agricultural labor force. It is also discriminatory as well as contradictory since the modernization law allows for land to be owned by juridic figures (i.e., corporations), who do not have to prove that they are agriculturalists.

The gender-regressive aspects of this law are partly attributable to the failure of the national organizations of rural women to speak with one voice. By the mid-1990s there were six peasant women's associations in Honduras, and each of the main national peasants' organizations with mixed membership had an active women's division (Brenes Marín and Antezana 1996: 19). Two of the mixed-sex peasants' organizations participated in the negotiations with the state over this law and had women representing them. Nonetheless, as one organizer explained, while "there were two women in the negotiations, they were not representing gender interests, but rather, other interests. . . . They added *la colita* [the qualifier, if the couple requests it] . . . we were not there, the most conscious women of the movement were not present . . . gender interests were not represented."[56] One of the main demands of several of the national rural women's organizations has been that the joint titling of land be made mandatory (Martínez et al. 1996: 37). Nonetheless, while there was a proposal in the national congress that would make it so, it had not been lobbied for by peasant women's organizations. This woman added, "We haven't made any progress on the reform of Article 79 because the women's movement has not made it a priority, lobbying for it in an organized and systematic manner."[57]

The rural women's organizations recognize that land rights are key for bettering their condition and improving their bargaining power with men. Nonetheless, the proliferation of peasant women's associations and the competition between them—partly related to the competition between the mixed peasant associations with which they are affiliated and their divisions over state policy—has hampered their ability to come up with a unified program of action for gender equity. A step in the right direction was taken in 1997 with the formation of REDNAMURH, the National Network of Rural Women's Organizations. The members of this network realize that land distribution has for all practical purposes concluded in Honduras; that the attention of the state is centered on various land-titling programs (the parcelization of the reformed sector, the titling of squatters on national or *ejido* land, and the titling of traditional smallholders); and that women's ownership of land now largely depends on the outcome of these titling efforts. They have thus made the mandatory titling of land to couples, irrespective of marital status, one of their main priorities. This priority is reflected in the proposed Policy for Gender Equity in Honduran Agriculture, which was being debated in early 1999 (PRO-EGEDAGRO 1999). In addition, the Plan for Gender Equity in Agriculture, 1999–2002, developed by the new national women's office, is quite comprehensive and includes such demands as the allottment of new lands to rural women's groups and the opening up of membership in cooperatives to couples, in addition to the mandatory joint titling of land to couples.

A Parcel of One's Own: The Peace Accords in El Salvador

Although a number of Latin American countries now specify in their agrarian legislation that men and women, independent of their civil status, may be beneficiaries of agrarian-reform or land-titling projects, few programs have individually benefited both husbands and wives (or both partners in a consensual union) at the same time. El Salvador is the only country to have experimented with the individualization of land rights in such a way as to include both members of a couple. This experiment was a result of the Land Transfer Program, PTT, which was negotiated as part of the 1992 peace accords.

Rural women did not fare particularly well in the agrarian reform of the 1980s. While a number of women's organizations emerged during that decade, none of these developed a feminist agenda, and class-based demands took precedence over all other issues during the civil war. Moreover, during the negotiations leading to the peace accords, gender issues never emerged, even though three high-ranking female commanders of the FMLN participated in the process (Fund. Arias 1992: 67–68). Ilja Luciak (1999), in his interviews with these former commanders, found that they recognized that gender issues had been ignored during the war, and they understood that a gender perspective was absent from the design of the reinsertion programs, particularly the land program. Rosario Acosta, a FMLN congressional deputy representing the peasant sector, reflects upon this as follows:

> If the socio-economic theme [in the accords] was barely included, still less could a space be expected for gender concerns: that is, "we have to assure that a certain proportion of women get land, or that a certain portion of land goes to benefit women." But, in practice, in the majority of households in the zones of conflicts (or of the former combatants) there were many women, many widows, orphans, mothers, wives, etc. Thus, in practice, a good number of women benefited from access to land, credit, training programs. But I confess that it was not a planned outcome, rather, the land transfer program was a general program. . . . There was no gender thinking in the peace accords.[58]

The attention given to gender issues in the PTT was largely due to the efforts of the formerly FMLN-affiliated women's organization "Las Dignas," which in early 1993 launched a national campaign opposing discrimination against women in the land transfers. They argued that priority should be given to female household heads and that in the case of couples, each partner should receive his or her own individual land title (Las Dignas 1993). The government had planned to award land solely to household heads (with the intention of benefiting families). The FMLN, at the prodding of Las Dignas and the top-level FMLN female commanders who supported them, pressured the government for land to be allocated on an individual basis, so that women with partners or husbands could nevertheless be direct beneficiaries. While subsequent official guidelines provided for land to be allocated to individuals, local officials and FMLN cadres continued to favor family groups, and in the case of couples, they continued allocating land to the male household head. Moreover, these local functionaries often added requirements of their own, such as literacy or the possession of official documents (birth certificates or voter registration cards); women were over-represented among those not meeting any of these criteria (Luciak 1999; Las Dignas 1993). It took a concerted effort by top-level female ex-commanders and Las Dignas to partially overcome these barriers when beneficiary lists were revised in late 1993.

Of the 20,432 beneficiaries (ex-FMLN combatants and squatters in the zones of conflict) who had obtained land through the reinsertion program as of December 1997, 34 percent were female; moreover, women were assigned a proportional share of the 81,769 *manzanas* allotted to this group (A. Álvarez 1998). Luciak (1999) argues that discrimination against women was largely overcome inasmuch as women represented 29 percent of FMLN combatants at the time of demobilization, and as of March 1996 they represented 26 percent of the FMLN ex-combatants who were beneficiaries of the land-transfer program. While it is certain that a much higher proportion of women benefited from the PTT program than did so under the previous agrarian reform process, some still believe that women were discriminated against:

> Talking with my *compañeras* in the Frente [FMLN], it seems that some feel that they were excluded from this program. Why? Because many of them at the end of the war had to leave because they were pregnant or had some specific problem. Thus the women missed out on the benefits given to the other combatants. It appears that there is no discrimination, but not taking into account those specific problems of women, such as giving birth to a child, means that the women, irrespective of the years which they gave to the struggle, were forgotten.[59]

Others estimate that the majority of women who received land were female household heads and believe that few women actually benefited from the provision allowing each partner in a couple to receive land individually. A member of Las Dignas reports her experience as follows:

> A group of us women squatters grabbed a parcel of six *manzanas*. We planted it collectively, and expected it to be adjudicated to us, but

when the time came, the lands were given in the names of our husbands. Because if one had a husband, it was in the husband's name; only if one did not have a husband was it in the woman's name. For women to be benefited directly was a real struggle. . . . There was subtle pressure for women who did have a partner to receive land jointly or *mancomunado*. There was a housing construction program, and the idea was that the houses would be constructed on the basis of one house per couple. Some women opposed this, saying that they wanted their own land and their own house. But there was a certain amount of pressure, as I mentioned, subtle pressure so that the women would be convinced to accept a house and parcel jointly with their partner.[60]

Antonio Álvarez, who was the FMLN representative to the PTT, nonetheless argues that:

Women's rights and men's rights were not dependent on each other; each had their own individual right. We did not legally establish a relation of dependence. Where we were building houses, and it was a husband and wife, a couple, what we did was to build the houses side by side, but with separate rights, the women's right and the man's right to a home. Why? Because when it came time [for the couple] to separate, so that each could maintain their own property rights. What happens if you combine these rights? Usually it is the man who finds another woman, and the woman leaves with her bags to see where she might find a place to sleep.[61]

Álvarez also reports that it has been difficult to make men understand that women have rights equal to those of men, and admits that sometimes women have been discriminated against in the assignment of individual land parcels: "At the moment of land distribution there was a tendency for the men to impose a distribution scheme that marginalized women—not in the sense of not giving them land, but rather, in giving them less productive land."[62]

Through a process of negotiation and struggle, independent land rights for men and women were established under the special PTT program in El Salvador. The novelty of such an approach is evident both in the resistance it confronted and by comparing the number of female beneficiaries under the PTT program (consisting of FMLN ex-combatants and supporters)—34 percent—with the share of women who benefited under the agrarian reform, which averaged 11 percent. At the same time, the principle of individual land rights was not accepted as the law of the land;

rather, it only applied to a specific group, the FMLN beneficiaries of the PTT program.

Also, the land that was allotted under the PTT amounts to only 6 percent of El Salvador's arable land, significantly less than the 22 percent that has been adjudicated to the agrarian reform sector (Gómez Cruz 1997: Tables 6 and 7). Moreover, most PTT beneficiaries have found themselves in quite precarious conditions. The lands that were available for the PTT program were generally considered to be of poor quality and lacking in basic infrastructure.[63] As a result, the government was forced to forgive their agrarian debt in late 1996.[64] PTT beneficiaries have still not received land titles, which has generated considerable insecurity (FUNDESA 1997: 7). Most are hoping for individual land titles to their specific plot of land within the farm that was collectively assigned to them. Rosa Linees, a member of Las Dignas, comments, "The document which we now have is provisionary; it does not guarantee that we are the owners or that our debts have been canceled. We need security to say 'this is my parcel'. . . that I can do with it as I please."[65]

As part of the peace accords, the government promised to issue a new agrarian code within a year of the accord's signing. The code was drawn up and presented to the Salvadoran congress in 1993, where it encountered such strong opposition that it was referred to a special commission for revision. An impasse ensued, following which the Alianza Democrática Campesina (ADC, the FMLN-affiliated peasant organization) presented its own version of a new agrarian code in 1996. Both versions of the proposed code are an advance over previous legislation with respect to women's land rights. Three provisions in the section regarding the peasant family enterprise are similar in both versions and are favorable to women.[66] Proposed Article 24 states that whenever one member of a family concludes an agrarian contract, all members of the household are to benefit, even though the contract may not have been written in the name of all family members. Proposed Article 25 specifies that when a contract is concluded for the individual allocation of land, the title will be in the name of *both* spouses or partners unless the person is a single household head. And proposed Article 27 states that the dissolution of marital ties, or abandonment by whoever is listed as the primary beneficiary on a rental contract or in a land adjudication transfer, should not compromise the rights of the members of the family unit. It is noteworthy that there appears to be consensus between the government and the main peasant organization that land adjudicated under the agrarian reform should be titled to a couple.

In the case of associative enterprises, proposed Article 31 stipulates that "all else being equal, it is prohibited to discriminate against women or children of working age in favor of some other person in the admission of new members, access to work, or the enjoyment of the benefits or rights derived from the enterprise" (Orellana 1996: 34). This article is also identical in both versions of the code. The phrase "all else being equal," of course, leaves the door open to discrimination against women for cultural, ideological, and structural reasons, in the absence of strong measures to overcome perceptions that women are not agriculturalists or that their responsibility for domestic labor prevents them from participating in cooperative work on the same terms as men. Nonetheless, this is a much stronger statement of women's rights to participate in production cooperatives than characterized the cooperative law of the past.

Thus far, ISDEMU, the Salvadoran Women's Institute (which was created in 1996, after the two drafts of the agrarian code had already been prepared), has not played any role in the negotiations over the agrarian code.[67] A Permanent Roundtable of Rural Women, however, was organized by peasant women leaders and IMU, an NGO, to allow rural women to influence debates over the agrarian code. One of their main demands was that "the Agrarian Code be widely discussed and reviewed by rural women so that we are not discriminated against" (IMU 1998: i). After many months of discussion, the roundtable participants issued a document summarizing their views and setting forth a proposal for an alternative agrarian code with a gender perspective (IMU 1999). One of their contributions was to rewrite the bulk of the ADC proposal in nonsexist language to make it absolutely clear that "the social subjects" of rural El Salvador consist of men and women. Their document maintains the same articles favoring gender equity contained in the ADC and the government proposals, but also improves their language.[68] For example, in Article 16 on the family enterprise, it specifically defines the head of the family group as both members of the couple; in the absence of one partner, the household head is to be "the man or woman who in effect has responsibility for living arrangements, feeding and care of the unit." In addition to providing for the joint allocation of land to couples, the document stipulates that in state adjudications made before the new code goes into effect, and where the land title is in the name of only one spouse or partner, the permission of the other is required to sell the land (Article 18). Its proposed wording also strengthens women's role in associative enterprises, "guaranteeing the participation of women under conditions of equity as members and in decision-making bodies and leadership" (Article 28). Just as in the ADC proposal, it sees the state's role in agrarian reform as continuing, including the expropriation of land that is abandoned or serves no social function (Articles 62–64). The beneficiaries are to include tenants working on the farm, and men and women who need land. The proposal adds that, "in all of the above situations, under equal conditions, priority is to be given to female heads of household responsible for satisfying the needs of their families" (Article 125).

What is interesting is that the Roundtable of Rural Women's proposed agrarian code makes no reference to a "a parcel of one's own," the individual allocation of land to each member of a couple. This is perhaps because, irrespective of the PTT experiment, it is still so difficult to conceive of family farms where land rights might be individual. What is heartening, given the fact that all three versions of the proposed agrarian code provide for joint allocation and titling of agrarian reform land to couples, is that this soon might become the law of the land in El Salvador. However, the code is still at an impasse since agreement has not been reached on continuation of the agrarian reform, the fundamental issue.[69]

The Peace Accords and the Process of Empowerment among Guatemalan Women Refugees

The peace accords in Guatemala differed from those adopted in Nicaragua and El Salvador in terms of their much greater gender content. The intention to guarantee women's land rights and access to other resources is expressed repeatedly in the various documents. The most specific provision with respect to women's land rights is contained in the Accord on the Displaced Population, which prioritized female household heads in the distribution of land; no mention, however, was made of the possibility of joint allocation or titling of land to couples. The attention given to gender considerations in the accords was largely due to two factors: the role of the women's bloc within the Assembly of Civil Society (ASC, Asamblea de la Sociedad Civil) during the peace negotiations, and the pressure of international organizations.

The ASC was created in 1993 after a stalemate had been reached in the peace negotiations between the government and the National Guatemalan Revolutionary Union (URNG). It was organized according to sectoral interests, but while there were numerous women in the assembly, they initially had not formed a bloc to press gender interests (ONAM 1997b: 10). It was only after women's issues were ignored or marginalized in the discussions that considerable political work was undertaken to convince the rest of the assembly that women's organizations constituted "a sector" that merited a voice in the peace process (Aguilar and Pellecer 1997).[70] According to the National Women's Office, "If it [the creation of a women's sector] hadn't happened this way, the deepest needs of women would not have been taken into account in the peace accords. . . . The space gained by the women's sector represents an enormous gain in terms of the participation of women in the resolution of national problems from their own particular perspective, and in terms of the recognition of their participation" (ONAM 1997b: 10). The women's sector activists, besides making sure that gender concerns appeared prominently in the accords, were instrumental in the creation of a women's forum as a mechanism to monitor all of the promises contained in the accords concerning women's rights. The forum is organized as a three-tiered process of consultation, at the local, regional, and national levels (Guatemala 1997: 158).[71]

Another factor in the consolidation of the women's sector within the ASC, the attention to gender issues in the accords, and the creation of the women's forum was the organization and mobilization taking place in preparation for the 1995 UN World Conference on Women in Beijing. Particularly prominent in the preparations for Beijing were NGOs, many of whom were also members of the ASC's women's sector. The women's sector also received considerable advice and support from international NGOs and the various representatives of United Nations organizations who were accompanying the peace process.[72]

With respect to the demands of rural women's groups, the greatest gender consciousness developed among the refugees in Mexico, where at least three relatively strong women's groups were formed: Mama Maquín, Madre Tierra, and Flores Unidas.[73] In the context of discussions regarding their reintegration into Guatemala, one of their demands became that not only should they and their families be assured of access to land upon their return but that the land should be granted and titled in the name of the couple (Fund. Arias–Tierra Viva 1993: 153). According to Paula Worby (1999: 7), who worked with these women's groups as a consultant to the UNHCR (the UN High Commission for Refugees, or ACNUR, as it is known by its Spanish acronym), "it was not immediately evident that women should also struggle for land joint ownership. This issue became meaningful only by analyzing the outcome for women abandoned by their partners (and often deprived of the land or belongings of the family) and the vulnerable situation that women and their children often find themselves in." The demand for joint titling of land was also an "outgrowth of their new awareness of women's rights in general," or the process of empowerment they experienced as a result of being part of organized women's groups in exile.

The projects of the refugee women's groups in Mexico were multifaceted and supported by NGOs and the UNHCR. These included a literacy campaign designed to raise women's self-esteem, the introduction of time- and labor-saving devices for domestic chores, reproductive health services, communication-skills training, and training in legal literacy and human rights (Worby 1999: 6). Mexican anthropologist Mercedes Oliveira was among the feminists who worked with these groups. She noted that several factors favored the process of feminist consciousness raising in the refugee camps. Women's traditional domestic realm had been destroyed along with their communities by the repression in Guatemala. In exile it was impossible "to recreate the same models and cultural patterns. . . . The women were left with big holes [in their lives] because when the community structure was broken, the kinship structure and rituals that work to preserve values, cultural modes, and also women's subordination were also broken" (in Chinchilla 1998: 486). Further, "The repression caused much damage, but it also gave rise to something very positive for women, for it allowed them to change, to have their ears opened to new alternatives and possibilities. Thus, when we arrived with a gender perspective, the women heard us. The fact that we managed to organize 12,000 women in the camps seems like a miracle, but in reality it was the fact that the women needed a new perspective to fill the voids in their lives that opened the way for a new way of participation and different relations" (ibid.: 487).

In the refugee camps in Mexico, groups called permanent commissions (*comisiones permanentes*) constituted the main organizational structure, and the male leadership of these thwarted the autonomous organization of the women. According to Oliveira, "In the workshops the women would hear a gender perspective, they would discuss it, develop it, and it would begin to work its way into their discourse" (in Chinchilla 1998: 487). The male leaders considered this very divisive for they wanted the women's groups to focus on the incorporation of women into the war effort and, later, the return to Guatemala. "The demand for equality between men and women would end up being muted. . . . Even with these obstacles, we managed to raise consciousness among the women, even the leaders. But what happened was that equality became a slogan, more than a practice. Thus there were advances, but these were very limited, because a real transformation was not achieved" (ibid.).

With respect to land issues: "One of the demands that we introduced with respect to the return [to Guatemala] was the right to land. We asked, 'And what of the women, where do they stand in the plan?' We began to work this topic with the women, to see that it was very important for them to have the security of land, and that this would only happen if they were co-owners of their parcels. We saw that they would have to become members of the cooperatives which were being formed and be equally responsible for the repayment of the credits—as they always are, although this is not recognized" (in Chinchilla 1998: 488). A member of Mama Maquín recounts the process in the following terms: "After the [8 October 1992] accords were signed we held various meetings . . . in order to analyze the content of the accords, and we realized that women who are married or in common-law unions were not being taken into account in regards to the right to land, only men, widows, and single mothers. . . . That is when we decided to fight for the right to be joint owners of the land, for our own security and that of our daughters and sons, so that we will not be left out in the street if the man sells the land or abandons his partner" (Mama Maquín 1998: n.p.).

Oliveira was responsible for organizing one of the first returns of a refugee group to Guatemala. She checked on the possibility beforehand of women being designated as co-owners of the land to be acquired in the new community and their co-signing the bank credit. The Guatemalan authorities assured her, "No, no, there is no problem; on the contrary, this gives us even greater assurance that the credits will be repaid." Thus the women signed the credit requests along with their partners. Then, "Those responsible in the Comisión Permanente took the papers and when they returned, a new list had been drawn up that didn't include the names of the women. They argued that it had been the only way that they could get the papers [for the land]. Nonetheless, the seed was planted, and now, two, three years later, women have incorporated this demand as their own. In the latest returns they are being included as members of the cooperatives and as co-owners of the land" (in Chinchilla 1998: 488).

As a result of the lobbying of the women's groups, and the support they received from the UNHCR, recognition of women as property owners eventually become part of the general agenda of the refugee organizations. But co-ownership was to prove a difficult struggle, resisted not only by refugee men but also by Guatemalan officials and policy makers. Some of the returning refugee women found that government functionaries were principally interested in organizing male households heads as members of the cooperatives, and it was they who were being given credit to purchase a farm and whose names appeared on the collective land titles. The only women directly included as beneficiaries were widows and single mothers, but even they were sometimes denied membership in the cooperatives. At a workshop organized by UNHCR in late 1995, representatives of the refugee women's organizations presented the following demands, which reveal the problems they were encountering:

- That the institutions guarantee the participation of women as members of the cooperatives with the same rights as men, and accept our signature from the time of the request for the credit to purchase the land;

- That in the regulations of these institutions it be clearly stated that women have a right to land tenancy;

- We ask INTA to give widows and single mothers the same right to land tenancy as men;

- That property titles to land be in the name of men and women;

- That INTA not require that we be formally married to have a right to land.[74]

As these demands make evident, the returning women refugees found a number of obstacles to their full participation.[75] Many government officials assumed that since under the Guatemalan civil code at the time the man represented the family, it made perfect sense that only the man should be given credit to purchase land and have it titled in his name. Other functionaries, more willing to include women on land titles, assumed that only married women could be co-owners of land with men, thus excluding women in consensual unions. In those cooperatives willing to consider the membership of both spouses, a major problem developed in terms of the dues structure for cooperative membership. Sometimes it was considered that if both members of a couple joined, each should pay the same dues as other individual members. The women argued that there should be only one dues quota per family, although each spouse should have an individual voice and vote within the cooperative and be eligible to be elected to its executive committee. Other disputes concerned the amount of land that a couple (as compared to an individual) would be assigned in usufruct.

The women's groups insisted that couples should be granted more land than individuals. On some cooperatives, the men argued that if wives wanted to join the cooperative, they would have to work for the cooperative on equal terms with the men. The wives' position was that these men were not taking into account the time involved in domestic labor, and that reproductive duties were as important to the success of the cooperative as productive work.

The UNHCR was actively involved in trying to solve these disputes and in urging compliance with the UN Convention on the Elimination of All Forms of Discrimination against Women (which Guatemala had previously signed) as well as Article 4 of the Guatemalan constitution, which recognizes the equality of men's and women's rights (ACNUR 1995; Pacay 1995: 77). The UNHCR argued forcefully that in the granting of credit for the purchase of land there should be two representatives per family, the adult man and woman, considering this to be the precondition for women to be co-owners and for them to become members of the cooperatives with both voice and vote. Further, "to protect women and their dependents in the long run . . . their full participation in decision making is a prerequisite to secure any kind of real advance within the community" (ACNUR 1996: 5). As a result of the mobilization of the women returnees in demand of their rights together with the mediating role of UNHCR, in the regulations governing the use of financial resources signed in 1996 by FONAPAZ and the members of the Permanent Commission the following agreement was reached: "It will be understood that a beneficiary family will be represented by a couple (whether married or in a consensual union), and that both partners have equal rights with respect to the land assigned to the family unit as co-owners."[76]

Similar demands were taken up by the Coordinator of Displaced Women[77] in that group's October 1997 proposal to CTEAR (the Comisión Técnica de Reasentados) and the National Women's Forum with respect to the implementation of the Peace Accord on the Displaced Population:

- It is necessary to facilitate access to land. The majority of displaced women are denied access to this productive resource. . . ;
- In the case of projects . . . that have as their goal the acquisition of assets such as housing and land, that a regime of co-ownership between a man and a woman, whether or not they are legally married or in a consensual union, be required so that the woman not end up unprotected in the case of abandonment. . . ;

- That single mothers and divorced or abandoned women who live with other family members be beneficiaries of projects, independently of the family that has taken them in, to allow them to maintain their own families;

- In the case of family members who have been detained-disappeared, it is necessary to create a fund to cover the legal costs of the transfer of the land title to the wife or partner; this procedure takes a long time and is costly. Many women cannot enjoy the benefits of projects because they are not the legal owners of the land left to them by their husbands (ACPD 1997: 4–5).

It is considered highly unlikely that the government will be able to re-settle and give access to land to all of the refugees who might otherwise have a right to it under the terms of the accords.[78] With this in mind, the bulk of the report of the Coordinator of Displaced Women focuses on income-generating projects for women, training, and technical assistance (ibid.).

In July 1998 the negotiating committee (Comisión Paritaria) charged with this task finally presented a draft law to the Congress to create the promised new land bank, to be called FONTIERRAS (Fondo de Tierras). Its role would be to define and implement government land policy, administer public financing for the acquisition and allocation of land, and facilitate "access to land by peasant men and women" (Guatemala 1998: Article 20). In keeping with the peace accords, peasant women were mentioned explicitly as potential beneficiaries of this program. Moreover, priority was to be given to the most vulnerable social groups, including "single mothers, widows, the returned population, the internally displaced, the demobilized and the rural population in a situation of poverty" (ibid.). However, in the next paragraph, the draft law returned to the ways of the past, specifying that beneficiaries would be household heads (Article 21). No mention was made of the possibility of land being allocated and titled to couples. As a close observer of the process noted, "the discriminatory language was included because it seemed 'natural' to speak about *jefes de familia* and no one saw it as contradictory with the part about promoting land access by 'campesinas.'"[79]

Subsequently, the UNHCR, drawing on its experience with the refugee women's organizations, developed a critique of the draft law and suggested alternative language. They argued that to be compatible with the constitution, the proposed law should drop the reference to household heads; that beneficiaries should always be referred to as peasant men or women; and that land and credit should be allocated jointly to couples, irrespective of their marital status. These recommendations were circulated broadly and received the support of the National Women's Forum, which until then had not been following closely the developments regarding the land bank project. It was finally the URNG representatives who took up the issue of joint titling at the negotiating table, and succeeded in having new language introduced to make joint allocation and titling of land to couples mandatory. The government representatives on the Comisión Paritaria were concerned with other aspects of the law and did not object to the new language.[80]

Thus in Decree No. 24-99 of May 1999 creating FONTIERRAS, beneficiaries are to be peasant men and women and "with the exception of those cases where the beneficiary family has a single father or single mother, the titles should be issued in the name of the couple or *convivientes* who are the heads of the beneficiary family" (Guatemala 1999: Article 20). The priority in access to land given to the displaced population under the peace accords was retained for the next ten years, "with special emphasis on families headed by single mothers and widows" (ibid.: Article 47).

While the wording of this legislation is very favorable for women's land rights, we have several concerns regarding the land bank program. First, the gender-progressive aspects of the legislation were in large measure the result of pressure from international agencies. It is not clear that a gender-progressive agenda has been internalized either by the state or by the mixed peasant and indigenous organizations involved in the negotiations and oversight of the program. It will no doubt require a major effort by organized rural women's groups and their urban allies to insure that the provisions of the legislation are actually implemented. However, the National Women's Forum, which was set up to oversee the implementation of the accords, has not yet played a very important role in making sure that the state meets its gender commitments. Moreover, the national women's office, ONAM (Oficina Nacional de la Mujer), remains weak and has not been capable of exercising much leadership. In addition, the rural women's organizations are small and fragmented. Second, notwithstanding the passage of legislation creating a land bank, it is not clear that the political will exists in Guatemala to adequately fund its operations so that the program significantly increases poor peasant men's and women's access to land. A related concern is whether sufficient land will be offered for sale at reasonable prices to meet the demands of the refugee population, let alone other landless groups. Finally, given the generally adverse conditions facing the agricultural sector, it is not clear whether a land mortgage program will be viable, particularly one offering near-commercial interest rates.

ONE OF THE MAIN questions this chapter sought to answer was how gender-progressive change actually comes about. The experience of the five countries that up through 1995 had adopted provisions for the joint allocation and titling of agrarian reform land suggests the importance of a "triangle of empowerment"—that is, coalitions that link the rural and urban women's movements with their allies within the state. The strength of these coalitions explains how joint titling was incorporated in the agrarian reforms or national constitutions of Brazil, Colombia, Nicaragua, and Honduras. In all four countries, joint allocation and titling had been a demand of rural women's organizations and these had a national presence as well; in Brazil and Nicaragua, in particular, rural women's groups are an integral part of the national feminist and women's movements. The Costa Rican case is the exception to this trend; at the time that the Law for the Promotion of Social Equality for Women was adopted, a national rural women's organization had yet to be created. The joint allocation and titling of land to couples was a spin-off of the demand by urban women for joint titling of housing to couples. What is similar between the Costa Rican and other four processes is the active role played by feminist scholars and NGOs in articulating the demand for joint ownership by couples before the state. Moreover, when these gender-progressive measures were adopted, there were close links among the women working in the national women's offices, in the legislature, and in the national women's movement.

Another element that has been important, directly and indirectly, in support of women's land rights has been the international agencies. Their work in strengthening rural women's organizations, urban and rural NGOs, and the state's women's offices is often not visible; but the pay-off is apparent when these coalitions succeed in bringing about legislative changes, such as the recognition of women's land rights. Of the cases studied here, they played the largest direct role in Honduras and also in helping to negotiate and implement the Guatemalan peace accords. The support of the UN agencies largely explains why rural women refugees won their demands regarding joint allocation and titling of land to couples, and why joint titling is mandatory in Guatemala's 1999 land bank legislation. The negative side is that their direct involvement is usually short lived, and if the "triangle of empowerment" is not in place to maintain steady pressure on the state, gender-progressive policies are not implemented.

Experience also suggests that, to be effective, provisions for the joint allocation and titling of land to couples must be mandatory rather than optional. The very idea of co-ownership is so counter to patriarchal tradition that it is strongly resisted at all levels, particularly by local officials. This resistance is especially evident in the cases of Colombia and Nicaragua, where compliance with this norm took years. Numerous gender-sensitivity training courses for local-level functionaries (and in Nicaragua, for potential beneficiaries) had to be sponsored before the law was effectively applied. The case of the Guatemalan refugees also demonstrates the difficulties in getting male peasant leaders and local-level functionaries to accept the principle of joint titling.

In quantitative terms the main countries where women have been a significantly growing share of the beneficiaries of land allocation and titling efforts—through both mandatory joint titling and the priority given to female heads of household—are Colombia and Nicaragua; in El Salvador, as well, women are a much higher proportion of the beneficiaries of the PTT than they were of previous agrarian reform efforts. In contrast, in Brazil and Honduras, where it is not mandatory, joint titling has hardly been applied; without other mechanisms of inclusion of women as beneficiaries, few gains have been made in increasing women's ownership of land. In both countries the pursuit of women's land rights by the rural women's organizations has taken a back seat to the need for solidarity with the mixed peasant organizations and unions in support of the general demand for agrarian reform in a generally confrontational political situation.

The case for joint allocation and titling of land to couples is closely tied to arguments for the defense of the peasant family: co-ownership of property fosters the stability and security of women and children by lessening the likelihood that women will be abandoned by their spouse or companion. Explicit property rights for women increase their bargaining position in the household by enhancing their fall-back position. If abandoned, they are legally entitled to half of the property, thereby reducing the probability that the man will induce such a rupture in the family unit; but if such a rupture takes place, women retain some economic security. Irrespective of the particular marital regime or civil code, joint titling of land requires the couple to be in accord to undertake major transactions such as renting or selling the property. Moreover, joint titling of land should increase women's access to other resources, such as credit and technical assistance, as well as strengthen their role in household decision making.

At the same time, joint titling may be a necessary but not sufficient condition for women to share in agricultural decision making and control over the use of land and its fruits. Joint assets do not necessarily require shared decision making, nor do they necessarily benefit all household members. In the absence of strong institutional support (whether from women's organizations or the state) and an ongoing process of empowerment, women may be de jure rather than de facto owners. That is, ownership alone may do little to reduce women's subordination to men. This is where the argument for individualization of land rights comes in. If women own their land outright, rather than through a joint title with men, it is more likely that ownership will result in their direct control of it and its benefits. Moreover, in case a couple should split up, there are fewer problems involved if a woman owns her land individually rather than jointly. Such women are less likely to be badgered by former husbands or partners, for example, to give up the best land, or to give up their land rights altogether in exchange for other forms of compensation. As Agarwal (1994a) argues, the individualization of land rights probably carries the greatest potential benefits for women.

Nonetheless, independent land rights for women in couples has not been articulated as a demand by women's organizations in most Latin American countries, primarily for three reasons. One reason is structural, related to the relatively small amount of land available for land distribution in most countries, considering current political constraints.[81] Given the extent of land hunger, the very notion of individual land rights is potentially quite divisive, both among claimants and land reform advocates. A second reason is strategic. The defense of the peasant family is an issue upon which the left and right can both agree. The abundant evidence of family instability and female dispossession, and the growing incidence of female-headed households and evidence of their relative poverty, has given this issue great currency in public debates. To the extent that joint titling of land promotes family stability, it is supported, in principle, by all sides. In contrast, the individualization of land rights is viewed as potentially harmful for family unity. This is perhaps why in the debate over the new agrarian code in El Salvador, the individualization of land rights, even though it was a basic principle of the PTT program, does not even appear on the agenda. All sides seem to agree on the joint titling of land to couples, and the issue has been left at that, even by organized rural women.

A third, related reason has to do with the level of development of the national rural women's organizations. These organizations are relatively new, and the process of empowerment of the women within them is still incipient. It is one thing to argue for the protection of women because they are more vulnerable—as in the case of female household heads—or as a means to protect the family; it is quite another to argue for individual land rights to empower women per se. If joint titling is seen as potentially threatening to patriarchal authority, individual titling is much more so: "the man feels bad if the woman has land." But as noted in the epigraph to this chapter, rural women in Nicaragua would do things differently today if they had the chance. They would demand land on their own, for after fifteen or so years of organization they have a gained a voice and sense of empowerment to demand strategic gender changes.

seven

In Defense of Community: Struggles over Individual and Collective Land Rights

> *The priority for indigenous women is their struggle as a people and not only as women. . . . We belong to a people, to a collective entity, thus the struggle of indigenous women is different from that of the women's movement. . . . indigenous men and women demand to be recognized as peoples, to be recognized as subjects with collective rights.*[1]

THE RISE TO DOMINANCE of neo-liberal governments in Latin America coincided with the growth and consolidation not only of the women's movement but also of the indigenous movement. Besides their timing, they share a number of other factors in common. Both social movements challenged the traditional conception of universal human rights, drawing attention to its exclusionary biases. Both movements grew simultaneously at the international, national, and local levels, with the growth in the latter contexts supported by international conventions to end discrimination based on sex and ethnicity. And both movements, although in diverse ways, challenged neo-liberal legislation that sought to end the agrarian reforms of previous decades. As a result, institutional change in the agricultural sector in the neo-liberal period has been quite heterogeneous on at least two counts: in terms of the gains and losses with respect to women's land rights and in terms of collective land rights.

    Some of the countries with the largest indigenous populations have had the slimmest gains or actual reversals in women's land rights. While the 1996 Bolivian Ley INRA has a strong preamble favoring gender equality in land rights, no specific provisions of the law guarantee women access to land on the same terms as men. Both the 1994 Ecuadorian and 1995 Peruvian land laws profess to be gender neutral in that land rights may be vested in natural or juridic persons, but this legislation does not explicitly guarantee even formal gender equality. Among the cases analyzed here, the 1992 Mexican agrarian code represents the main setback with respect to women's land rights, since what was the family patrimony has become the individual private property of household heads, the great majority of whom are male. Of the countries with large indigenous populations, only Guatemala has professed its intention to guarantee gender equity in future land distributions, incorporating specific mechanisms of inclusion in its recent land-bank legislation.

The main demands of the indigenous movement in the debate over land rights in the neo-liberal period have been as follows: (1) recognition of their historic land claims, including the recognition of their status as indigenous territories; (2) recognition and/or affirmation of collective property rights, including the inalienability of collective property; and (3) recognition of customary law—that is, the right of peasant and indigenous communities to follow traditional customs and practices. The outcome with respect to the defense of collective property rights has also varied, these rights having been strengthened in the 1990s in Ecuador and Bolivia and weakened in Mexico and Peru.

The focus of this chapter is on the tension between the demand for recognition of collective land rights and the demand for gender equality in land rights. In principle, collective land rights should promote gender equity to the extent that they guarantee all members of a community access to land. In other regions of the world, such as South Asia and Africa, it has been argued that women's access to land was much more secure under traditional, communal landholding systems as compared with the post-colonial period, which has been characterized by the individualization of land rights (Agarwal 1994a; Lastarria-Cornhiel 1997). We argue that in the Latin American case collective land rights do not necessarily guarantee all members of a community secure access to or control of land. Rather, how collective land is distributed—the rules through which it is allocated to families and to the men and women within them—and who participates in determining these rules, are governed by traditional customs and practices (*usos y costumbres*), which often discriminate against women. Moreover, most Latin American countries that protect the right of indigenous and peasant communities to collective property also recognize the right of these communities to allocate land as they see fit, following traditional customs and practices. This tension between the rights of women and the rights of indigenous communities to follow their own traditional customs and practices is at the center of the debate between the feminist and cultural relativist critiques of universal human rights and is also apparent in the international agreements regarding indigenous peoples.

Feminist and Cultural-Relativist Critiques of Universal Human Rights

Under international law universal human rights are defined "to be rights held equally by every individual by virtue of his or her humanity and for no other reason" (Howard 1993: 316).[2] What the feminist and culturalist critiques of human rights share is that they both challenge the *universality* of human rights as derived from liberal thought. They contend that liberal thought, which originated the concept of the universality of human rights, is a product of Western philosophy and politics, and as such it has been historically exclusionary of other cultures and groups, such as women and indigenous groups (Brems 1997: 142–47; Pollis 1996: 318). For human rights truly to be universal, they must be inclusive of all groups. However, whereas feminists use a gender lens, cultural relativists use a cultural perspective, each challenging on different terms how human rights are to be defined, prioritized, and applied.

The main claim of cultural relativists is that there is no such thing as a universal morality; rather, morality is said to be conditioned by cultural and historical context. They argue that the doctrine of the universality of human rights is based on a Western notion of rationality that has elevated the concept of individualism to a level of abstraction incompatible with other cultures.[3] An alternative notion of morality may be found in other, non-Western cultures that privilege the collectivity over the individual. Within these non-Western cultures, collective rights and obligations place limits on individuals in favor of the collective (Brems 1997: 146). For most Latin American indigenous cultures, the validity of moral principles rests on ancestral authority and longevity. From the perspective of cultural relativists, the history of colonialism can be summarized as the displacement of ancestral or collective authority. At the same time, the introduction of the concept of individual rights was limited, for it was applied only to the conquerors—at the expense of indigenous peoples. The indigenous position in the debate over land rights is thus that collective rights to land must be privileged over individual rights, for two reasons. First, given the history of colonialism, there is a moral argument to be made for restitution of land and territories to indigenous communities and peoples. Second, collective land rights are the basis of indigenous cultural identity and are necessary to the very survival of indigenous peoples. Both of these points have now been incorporated into International Labor Organization (ILO) Accord No. 169, as we discuss below.

The feminist critique of universal human rights, besides calling for women's inclusion in the system of production of human rights, stresses the need to break the dichotomy between the public and the private domains (Brems 1997; Garay 1996). It highlights how in the liberal tradition, human rights were defined in order to regulate the relations between men and the state in the public sphere, a sphere from which women were excluded. In addition, since the subordination of women occurs in large measure within the private sphere—that is, in the practices and traditions of family life—human rights must be extended so that the "personal is political" or the "private is public" (Brems 1997: 139). Thus, the demand to bridge the private and public must be understood as having dual objectives: to extend rights to private relations, and to include women as participants in rights in the public sphere.

When the discourse on human rights is limited to the public (civic and political) sphere, the condition of women is not all that has been excluded. The social, economic, and cultural rights of both men and women are also left unrecognized. Feminists have challenged the privileging of civil and political rights over socio-economic rights since the latter are so necessary to improve women's condition. Among the rights that feminists want to include as priorities, which have long been stressed by socialists as well, are the rights to food, clothing, shelter, work, health, and education, as well as the general right to economic development. Additionally, feminists argue that, because of women's differences from men, "the catalog of human rights" has to be revised to include new rights, such as reproductive and sexual rights (Brems 1997: 139–40; Facio 1996: 81–82). The slogan "women's rights are human rights" best sums up this effort, as was recognized in the Geneva Declaration of Universal Human Rights (UN 1993).

Where the feminist and cultural-relativist critique of universal human rights come into conflict is that in most societies women and culture are closely connected. As Amanda Garay (1996: 24) explains, "women are most frequently the transmitters of culture to their children and are often responsible for maintaining cultural traditions in the home and maintaining links to the community. . . . The close connection of women to culture makes it difficult to recognize that the human rights specific to women are part of the atomistic rights regime." The close connection between indigenous women and culture in Latin America is particularly apparent in terms of language and dress. Until recent decades indigenous women remained monolingual whereas their partners became increasingly bilingual; and while men dress in Western clothing, women maintain traditional dress. Since women have a greater responsibility than men in terms of the preservation of culture and the socialization of children, cultural relativists are particularly wary of any attempts to expand the concept of universal human rights to include women's rights. Similarly, the close identification of women and culture and the gender inequalities that this has produced have made feminists wary of ceding grounds to cultural relativists, particularly the strong strand of cultural relativism in which culture is seen as the sole authority by which to validate moral principles.[4] Feminists have been particularly wary of constructions that link women to culture and nature, for these have often been based on a biological determinism that defines women as being "closer to nature" than men, limiting women's options and human development (Ortner 1974: 67–87).

Indigenous Rights in the International Arena

International Labor Organization Accord No. 107 of 1957 was the first international agreement specifically developed to safeguard the rights of indigenous and tribal peoples. There is general agreement that it was based on an ethnocentric conceptualization in which indigenous populations were considered in need of integration into national societies (OIT 1987: 4). That is, the overall objective was "to reduce them to civilization," since indigenous groups were seen as inferior, temporary societies destined to disappear under the forces of modernization.[5] The role of the state was paternalistic, to protect these vulnerable groups during the transition. The dominant national ideologies in Latin America in this period upheld economic modernization and racial *mestizaje,* and the concepts of integration and assimilation were accepted by advocates of indigenous rights from both the right and left: Indians were to be transformed into

peasants and citizens (Dandler 1996; Black 1998; Hvalkof 1998). One of
the main contributions of Accord No. 107, nonetheless, was with respect
to indigenous land rights. States were obligated to recognize and protect
"the right of ownership, collective or individual, of the members of the
populations concerned over the lands which these populations traditionally occupy" (Article 11, in OIT 1987). According to indigenous law expert
Roque Roldán, the accord played a very important role in terms of the
norms that were developed in the period of the agrarian reforms in 1960s
for indigenous groups in Latin America.[6]

A major factor that led to the revision of ILO Accord No. 107 in 1989
was that since the 1950s indigenous people worldwide had been forming
organizations to protect their own interests, and these began to receive international support in the late 1970s and 1980s (CIT 1988). Since 1982 one
of the main spaces for indigenous participation at the international level
has been the UN Working Group on Indigenous Populations. This annual
international forum brings together indigenous organizations, government
representatives, international agencies, and NGOs (Dandler 1996: 3–6). Due
largely to its efforts, Accord No. 169 represents a fundamental change in
approach to indigenous issues on a number of counts. Rather than considering indigenous populations as temporary societies, doomed to disappear,
it assumes that indigenous peoples constitute permanent societies. Indigenous and tribal peoples are given status equal to that of other nationali-
ties of a given country in terms of fundamental rights. This is why the
accord may be considered an instrument of inclusion rather than of integration, for it is based on the recognition of cultural diversity. The accord
stipulates that indigenous and tribal peoples should enjoy the same human
rights and fundamental liberties as others without discrimination. In addition, it specifically mentions that the provisions of the convention should
be applied without discrimination to both men and women (Article 3.1,
in Sánchez 1996, Appendix).[7] At the same time, the convention strongly
affirms and supports traditional rights. It recognizes that for indigenous
social, economic, and cultural rights to be fully effective, there must be so-
cietal respect for indigenous identities, traditional customs and practices,
and institutions (Article 2.2b). But it also makes clear that traditional customs and practices cannot be incompatible with fundamental rights as
defined in the national juridical system, nor with recognized international
human rights (Article 8.2).

Worth highlighting are the following points with respect to indigenous land rights:

1. The accord recognizes the special relation of indigenous people to the land and territory they occupy or use and, in particular, "the collective aspects of this relation" (Article 13.1).

2. In its use of the term "lands," it specifically includes "the concept of territories, which covers the total environment of the areas which the peoples occupy or otherwise use" (Article 13.2).

3. It also recognizes indigenous peoples' right of property and possession of the lands they traditionally occupy, and in appropriate cases, the right to use lands that are not of their exclusive occupation, but to which they have long had access for traditional activities and subsistence (Article 14).

4. With respect to inheritance, following the norms already established with respect to traditions and customs, the convention requires respect for the procedures for transmission of land rights established by indigenous peoples (Article 17.1).

5. In terms of agrarian reform programs, indigenous and tribal peoples are to be assigned additional lands on the same terms as other groups when the lands they are possess are insufficient (Article 19).

ILO Accord No. 169 has been ratified by nineteen countries, including ten of the nineteen Latin American countries listed in Table 7.1. The main Latin American countries with sizable indigenous populations that had not signed the accord as of early 1999 were Chile, El Salvador, Venezuela, and Brazil. Ratification of Accord No. 169 was one of the objectives of the many hemisphere-wide activities that were carried out by Latin American indigenous organizations as part of the "Five Hundred Years of Indigenous Resistance" commemorations that led up to the 1992 quincentennial of Columbus's arrival in the Americas. As a result of these activities and the pressure of the UN Working Group, the UN designated 1993 as the International Year of Indigenous Peoples, 1995–2004 as the International Decade of the Indigenous Peoples of the World,[8] and August 8 as the International Day of Indigenous People.

One concern of the women's movement is whether countries that are signatories to Accord No. 169 will undertake serious efforts to end the many forms of discrimination against indigenous women, particularly the forms that are firmly established in tradition. It is worth noting that in the preamble to Accord No. 169, mention is made of a number of the international accords that proscribe discrimination,[9] but no specific mention is made of the UN Convention to Eliminate All Forms of Discrimination against Women, a convention that has had the force of international

TABLE 7.1. Ratification of ILO Convention No. 169 and Indigenous
Population in Latin America, early 1990s

Country	Year of Ratification	Indigenous Population	Indigenous Share of Total Population (%)
Argentina	2000	350,000	1.0
Bolivia	1991	4,900,000	71.0
Brazil	No	300,000	0.2
Chile	No	1,000,000	8.0
Colombia	1991	600,000	2.0
Costa Rica	1993	35,000	1.0
Cuba	No	—	—
Dominican Republic	No	—	—
Ecuador	1998	4,100,000	43.0
El Salvador	No	400,000	7.0
Guatemala	1996	5,300,000	66.0
Honduras	1995	700,000	15.0
Mexico	1990	12,000,000	14.0
Nicaragua	No	160,000	5.0
Panama	No	140,000	6.0
Paraguay	1993	100,000	3.0
Peru	1994	9,300,000	47.0
Uruguay	No	4,000	0.2
Venezuela	No	400,000	2.0
Latin America		approx. 40 million	

Sources:

Ratification of ILO convention: International Labour Office, Norms Department, Geneva, February 1999; made available to the authors by Jorge Dandler, senior specialist on rural employment and indigenous people, ILO, San José; updated 28 November 2000.

Indigenous population and share of total population: Oficina Internacional del Trabajo, Equipo Técnico Multidisciplinario, "Estimación de la Población Indígena en América Latina," on http://www.oit.or.cr/mdtsanjo/indig/cuadro.htm, accessed 19 February 1999.

law since 1981. Moreover, while the accord states that its provisions are to be applied equally to men and women, in the section on inheritance no explicit mention is made of women's land rights, so that inheritance practices are left to the customs of the indigenous and tribal communities. Specifically, Accord No. 169 seems to ignore the all-important clause of the 1981 Women's Convention that obliges signatory states to modify or abolish all existing laws, regulations, *customs, and practices* that discriminate against women (Article 2f, in UN 1980: 2–3), a commitment that was again reiterated in the 1995 Beijing Platform for Action (paragraphs 230g and 232d, in UN 1996: 93, 96).

It might be argued that Accord No. 169 is compatible with both the 1981 Women's Convention and the Beijing Platform for Action since the accord states (Article 8.2) that traditional customs and practices cannot be incompatible with fundamental rights as defined in the national juridical system nor with recognized international human rights. This was apparently the majority position at the Beijing Conference, for the 1995 Platform for Action explicitly endorses Accord No. 169 (paragraph 61c), calling for governments to consider ratifying this international treaty.[10] Nonetheless, the lack of an explicit guarantee of women's land rights remains a weakness in Accord No. 169, particularly since gender-discriminatory customs regarding land rights are so difficult to change. Indigenous rights expert Jorge Dandler concedes that "There is probably a gender bias [in Accord No. 169]. Gender issues could be made more explicit, particularly on the topic of land. The emphasis of the convention was on collective rights to land; it was based on an advanced conceptualization of peoples and their rights to territories."[11]

The Defense of Community under Neo-Liberalism: Ecuador and Bolivia

One of the main demands of the indigenous movement in Latin America has been for the recognition of indigenous territories. The concept of territory must be distinguished from that of land rights since the former implies the right to self-determination and self-government, being related to the notion of nation and nationhood (Hvalkof 1998: 8). The rationale for this demand was expressed by women participants in a 1995 gathering of "first peoples":

> It is vitally important to the survival of indigenous people to have our own physically defined space, the space that we have occupied since ancestral times in harmony with our own *cosmovisión*. We think of our territories not just as utilitarian or productive spaces, but rather as intimate and sacred spaces. This is why we demand the recognition of our territories, so that we can exercise autonomy; have our own traditional authorities; and our own economic, social, political, legal, and cultural systems, with the objective of guaranteeing an integrated

and balanced development that benefits our societies. (CONAIE and CONAMIE 1995: 66)

The concept of territory as employed by Latin American indigenous groups also includes the right to control the use of the subsoil (for example, the granting of mineral rights), and this, in fact, has been a highly controversial issue. Most Latin American governments see territorial recognition as a breech of national sovereignty, since the subsoil is considered to be part of the national patrimony.[12] Nevertheless, most governments have signed ILO Accord No. 169, which recognizes indigenous peoples' right of property and possession of the land and territory they occupy. This is because in Accord No. 169 the concept of territory was left undefined, since the issue was so controversial. According to the technical committee that drew up this convention, "the use of the term *territory* will not have any implications whatsoever with respect to national property and sovereignty" (OIT 1996: 15).

Table 7.2 summarizes the main gains and losses of the indigenous movement in recent Latin American constitutions and agrarian legislation and shows that significant gains have been made since the late 1980s with respect to the recognition of historic indigenous land claims and collective property rights. Brazil appears as the exception to the latter trend; its 1988 constitution grants indigenous groups the right to the collective *use* in perpetuity of the lands they have traditionally occupied, but this land remains federal property (Van Cott 1999). Also, most of the new constitutions acknowledge that their nations are "pluri-cultural" and multi-ethnic, and they recognize customary law to the extent that it does not conflict with other constitutional guarantees or national legislation. The exceptions are Brazil, Chile, Honduras, and, to a certain extent, Mexico.[13] Just as varied among countries, and even more controversial in recent years, is whether peasant and indigenous collective landholdings are inalienable and whether this form of property may be dissolved. In recent decades collective landholdings that once were inalienable were opened up to privatization under neo-liberal legislation in Chile, Mexico, Peru, and Ecuador. Such legislation was subsequently reversed in Chile and Ecuador, and in Bolivia this proposal was defeated almost as soon as it was proposed.

Chile, in the vanguard of the neo-liberal movement, was the first country to change its position on the collective land rights of indigenous people. A 1979 law passed during the Pinochet regime authorized the individual titling of usufruct plots in indigenous communities and subsequently allowed these plots to be bought and sold. It is estimated that

TABLE 7.2. Collective Land Rights in New Constitutions and Agrarian Codes

| Country | Recognition of Indigenous Land Claims | | Recognition of Collective Indigenous Lands | Recognition of Customary Law | Possibility of Privatizing Collective Land |
	Constitution	Code			
Bolivia	1994	1996	Yes	Yes	No
Brazil	1998	No	No	No	No
Chile	No	Yes (1993)	No	No	Yes (1979); No (1993)
Colombia	1991	1994	Yes	Yes	No
Costa Rica	No	—	—	—	—
Ecuador	1998	1994	Yes	Yes	Yes (1994); No (1998)
El Salvador	No	—	—	—	—
Guatemala	1998	—	Yes	Yes	No
Honduras	No	1992	Yes	No	No
Mexico	1992	—	Yes	Partial	Yes
Nicaragua	1987	—	Yes	Yes	No
Peru	1993	1995	Yes	Yes	Yes

Sources: On constitutions, Van Cott (1999). On agrarian codes, see Table 5.1.

between 1979 and 1987, some 70 percent of the 2,100 indigenous communities divided up their collective holdings (Echenique 1996: 86). While Chile was the pioneer in privatizing collective holdings in the name of efficiency, in that country, too, the 1990s brought a resurgence of the indigenous rights movement. Its main accomplishment was the passage of the 1993 Ley Indígena, which affirms collective rights to land. The sale of indigenous land—whether it is owned collectively or individually—to non-indigenous persons is also now prohibited (CONADI 1995).

The 1992 reform of Article 27 of the Mexican constitution is also considered a setback for collective land rights. Under the Mexican agrarian reform, the *ejidos* had been ceded collective land rights by the state in perpetuity, and *ejido* and indigenous community lands could not be used as collateral, sold to a non-*ejido* member, or rented to outsiders. Under the counter-reform, upon a majority vote of *ejido* members individuals holding usufruct rights may acquire a title to this land and subsequently rent or sell it. Land may be sold to non-*ejido* members, however, only if the *ejido* as a whole has decided to pass to full private property. By early 1998, 81 percent of the 27,144 *ejidos* in Mexico were participating in the Ejido Rights Certification Program, PROCEDE, the first step toward full privatization of *ejido* land rights (Estadísticas 1998: n.p.).

In the case of Peru, although the counter-reform was initiated in 1980 under the government of Fernando Belaúnde, the officially recognized peasant and native communities had been exempt from the law on parcelization. It was the 1993 constitution that established for the first time that these communities could freely dispose of their land, thereby opening up the legal possibility of their parcelization and sale. The 1995 land law made this possibility explicit, establishing that these communities may now choose any form of "entrepreneurial organization" they please, without the permission of the state. Members of the coastal communities, by a vote of 50 percent of the *comuneros,* may acquire their parcels as individual private property. The community assembly is also empowered to give, rent, sell, or mortgage community lands. Communities in the sierra or *selva* have the same options as do those on the coast, although any changes require a two-thirds majority vote of the qualified *comuneros* (del Castillo 1996).

In neither Mexico nor Peru was there strong organized opposition to the neo-liberal land laws, largely reflecting the weakened state of national peasant organizations at the time, and the failure of these organizations to build strong ties to the indigenous movement growing in various regions of these countries. In contrast, in Ecuador and Bolivia—where indigenous Amazonian groups built strong organizations during the 1980s, and where they and the highland peasant and indigenous organizations were able to act in a unified way—not only were attempts to weaken collective forms of property beaten back but collective rights were strengthened and extended in scope. We examine these two cases in more detail and then consider how the demand for women's land rights either did not arise or was subsumed in the discussion of indigenous demands.

In 1986 the two main peasant and indigenous organizations in Ecuador —ECUARUNARI, formed in 1972 of peasant federations in the sierra, and CONFENIAE (the Confederación de Nacionalidades Indígenas de la Amazonia Ecuatoriana), formed in 1980 of indigenous organizations in the Amazon region[14]—joined together to form CONAIE, the Confederación de Nacionalidades Indígenas del Ecuador. During the late 1980s CONAIE grew in strength through the actions leading up to the 1992 quincentennial. It consolidated its role as the legitimate voice of the indigenous people during the "Indigenous Uprising of 1990" (*levantamiento indígena*), which centered on conflicts over land and the demand for recognition of indigenous territories.[15] The uprising began with the peaceful occupation of the Santo Domingo church in Quito in May of that year. This action was followed by a national strike in which women were very active participants

(Red de Educación Popular 1992). Indigenous communities in the high-lands and Amazonian region closed down markets and set up roadblocks until the government was forced to negotiate. One of the main issues in the negotiations was the legal recognition of indigenous territories in the Amazon. Other issues included the settlement of some seventy-two specific land conflicts pending before IERAC, the agrarian reform institute; the creation of a land fund to subsidize land purchases; and the continuation of the agrarian reform (specifically, a demand that large landholdings be expropriated in areas of high population pressure).

According to Chad Black (1998: 2), CONAIE pursued a three-part agenda of land, culture, and national identity: "The centrality of cultural claims, mediated through an alternative conception of the nation, and the organizational process that gave birth to CONAIE and a unified national Indian movement represented a significant break from traditional leftist and popular social movements." Moving beyond land reform and traditional labor concerns, CONAIE pushed the concept of multi-nationality onto center stage, "going beyond recognition of the diversity of cultures and languages within Ecuador to a redefinition of the very nature of national-democratic participation" (ibid.: 22).

Although the *levantamiento indígena* had broad support from civil society, the Social Democrats who had negotiated with CONAIE lost the 1992 elections, ushering in the neo-liberal government of Sixto Durán Ballén. This government promptly promulgated a very neo-liberal land law —one that envisaged the break-up of the indigenous communities—and this act provoked another rebellion by peasants and indigenous people in June 1994, one in which the presence of women was again quite noticeable. This uprising, called the "Mobilization for Life," included demonstrations in all the major cities of the highlands and the occupation of major oil wells in the Amazonian region (Macas 1995). As one of CONAIE's women leaders explained,

> The indigenous peoples could not accept a law that would promote the concentration of land in the hands of those who have always held it, and that would make it prohibitive for indigenous communities to get access to land. Without any means of expanding [the land base], we would die of hunger and misery in the large cities. . . . Land can't be sold or negotiated. A people without a territory is a dead nation. That is why one of our fundamental objectives is the defense and recuperation of our territories.[16]

After ten days the government was again forced to negotiate for the courts had declared the neo-liberal law unconstitutional on procedural grounds. The main actors in the negotiations were CONAIE and the various regional chambers of agriculture representing business interests.

CONAIE's main victory was in having the state recognize the right of indigenous, Afro-Ecuadorian, and Montubian communities to their ancestral lands; moreover, these lands would be adjudicated to them free of charge. This is considered to be one of the most positive aspects of the 1994 Law of Agrarian Development (discussed in chapter 5), and it is innovative in the case of Afro-Ecuadorian and Montubian communities since up to this time only the ancestral lands of indigenous communities had been legally recognized. CONAIE had wanted the state to recognize the territory they defined "as a geographic area or natural space under the cultural influence and political control of a people" (de la Cruz 1995: 8). Ecuador is an oil-producing nation, and the government was not about to give up control over the subsoil. Also, it may be one thing to recognize indigenous territory in the *selva* (particularly in non-oil-producing regions) but quite another thing to contemplate doing so in the highlands. Recognition of a Quichua territory in the highlands would challenge the very legitimacy of private property rights and, probably, the very concept of the nation state as traditionally defined.

Among the various forms of organization of production recognized in the 1994 land law are communal forms, which CONAIE had also insisted upon. However, the law allows communal lands to be parcelized and sold if two-thirds of the community members so wish; a similar vote is required to transform the community structure into another form of association. CONAIE claimed victory in that it forced the provision that any change in tenure or structure would require a two-thirds rather than a simple majority vote of community members. Also at its insistence, the law provides that communal pastures at high elevations and forest land cannot be subdivided, and attempts to privatize water rights in the legislation were defeated (Ecuador 1994; Macas 1995).

No explicit mention is made of gender or of women's land rights in the Law of Agrarian Development. The law presumes to be gender neutral in that property owners, "be they natural or juridic persons," are guaranteed their right to work the land (Article 19). In the regulations supporting the 1994 law, the beneficiaries are defined as "peasants, indigenous people, Montubians, Afro-Ecuadorians, agriculturalists in general and agricultural entrepreneurs" (Article 1). The only explicit mention of women is in the section in the regulations on training, where it states that "training should take into account women's participation in agriculture and should incorporate them actively in the respective programs" (Article 3). That ethnicity and race were mentioned explicitly in the law and its regulations, but that gender did not merit parallel treatment, reflects the fact that during the whole debate over the agrarian development law women's land rights were never an issue. The main demand of CONAIE centered on securing government recognition of indigenous territories and guaranteeing the right to collectively held land; why CONAIE paid no attention to gender issues is explored in the subsequent section. Another reason that the issue of gender did not figure at all in the discussions surrounding the 1994 law was that land rights were not a primary concern of DINAMU (Dirección Nacional de la Mujer), the national women's office, whose priority at that time centered on passage of a law against domestic violence.[17] In addition, in that year, as part of President Sixto Durán's effort to trim the size of the state, the Department of Peasant Women in the Ministry of Agriculture had been eliminated. Thus there was no strong lobby within the ministry either.[18]

The omission of gender concerns from the Law of Agrarian Development was partly corrected in the section of the 1998 constitution that affirms, "the State will guarantee the equality of rights and opportunities of women and men in access to resources for production and in economic decision making with respect to the administration of the conjugal society and property" (Article 34 in Ecuador 1998). This measure was largely the result of the efforts of the revamped national women's office, CONAMU (Consejo Nacional de las Mujeres), which had recently been elevated in status. It had launched a vigorous lobbying effort to introduce gender concerns throughout the constitution. Moreover, CONAIE continued to lobby for the inalienability and indivisibility of collective property in the debates regarding Ecuador's constitutional reform, and it was successful in securing these in the 1998 constitution (Article 84, ibid.) as well as Ecuador's ratification of ILO Accord No. 169. In addition, Ecuador was officially recognized in the constitution as a pluri-cultural and multi-ethnic state, although not one that was pluri-national, as CONAIE had wanted.[19]

Peasant and indigenous organizations played a key role in the effort to place the discussion of a new agrarian reform on the Bolivian national agenda. The CSUTCB (Confederación Sindical Única de Trabajadores Campesinos de Bolivia), which led this effort, had been characterized up through the 1970s by its traditional, class-based demands; by the 1980s

CSUTCB was marked by the influence of the Katarista indigenist movement, an Aymara-based movement that privileged ethnic identity. Also, during the early 1980s a number of regional organizations had been consolidated that also privileged ethnic identity: the Central Indígena del Oriente de Bolivia, the Central de Pueblos Indígenas del Beni, and the Asamblea del Pueblo Guaraní. The main demand of all of these groups—particularly after they joined together in 1982 to form CIDOB (Confederación Indígena del Oriente, Chaco, y Amazonia)—was recognition of the territories they had traditionally occupied. In contrast to Ecuador, however, at the moment of discussion of the new agrarian code, the highland and *selva* organizations had not structurally merged to form one, united indigenous organization.

With the return to democratic rule in 1982, the CSUTCB proposed a new agrarian reform law that would uphold the principle of land for those who work it directly and strengthen the legal standing of communal property. At the same time, the other indigenous groups began pressing for recognition of their right to the territory they have traditionally occupied. Throughout the next year there were large peasant mobilizations in support of a new agrarian reform, and a presidential commission was appointed to study CSUTCB's proposal (Urioste 1992: 137–41). Then in 1985 Víctor Paz Estensoro became president, and in the context of structural adjustment, neoliberal ideas began to gain currency in government circles. There was discussion of the need for a new land law, but one quite different from that envisioned by the CSUTCB, one that would focus on making land a commodity (that could be bought and sold without impediment) and subject all rural property to taxation. Both ideas met with tremendous peasant opposition.[20]

The land issue exploded during 1990, when the first indigenous march—the forty-day "Indigenous March for Territory and Dignity" from Trinidad to La Paz—took place in the context of hemispheric preparations for the "Five Hundred Years of Indigenous Resistance" campaign.[21] Up until then, the Bolivian state had not recognized the rights of indigenous peoples and communities to their original territory, and this became the main demand of the increasingly vocal association of indigenous peoples, CIDOB. The group also called for respect for their traditional practices and customs and demanded bilingual, multi-cultural education. In response, the government of Jaime Paz Zamora was forced to issue four supreme decrees in September 1990 recognizing the major indigenous peoples of the Amazonian region and their right to their original lands. In 1991 the government also ratified ILO Accord No. 169. However, the government refused to recognize these lands as indigenous territories, calling them "original communal land" and reserving for itself the right to the subsoil. Moreover, several years went by without the government developing the necessary implementing regulations.

In 1992 there was another major indigenous march from the lowlands to La Paz and, in response, the government issued eight supreme decrees recognizing the ancestral lands of various other indigenous groups (Muñoz and Lavadenz 1997: 6). The 1994 constitutional reform also made explicit the right of all indigenous people to their original communal lands and the inalienable character of collective property (Article 171), and it explicitly recognized Bolivia as a multi-ethnic and pluri-cultural state (Article 1). During this period there were major accusations of corruption against the two institutions charged with agrarian reform and colonization, the CNRA (Consejo Nacional de Reforma Agraria) and the INC (the Instituto Nacional de Colonización). In late 1992, in the face of these myriad problems and contending positions, President Jaime Paz Zamora directly took over these two institutions. The Interventora Nacional (National Intervention), as this process (and commission) was known, was charged with drafting a new law to govern land rights and land redistribution, settling the morass of overlapping claims, and reorganizing the agrarian reform institute. Meanwhile, a moratorium was placed on the titling and allocation of any new land.

The new law project was developed in the context of a contentious national discussion involving peasants, indigenous peoples, medium and large growers, the political parties, and other sectors of civil society. While there was recognition of the need for consensus, finding it was a difficult process. When the law was about to be discussed in the national congress, in August 1996, there was another massive march, the "March for Land and Territory." This action by peasants and indigenous people included significant numbers of rural women (Ybarnegaray 1997: 32). The main issue of indigenous groups from eastern Bolivia was the titling of territory, including full rights over the subsoil, and not just the titling of their original, communal land. Peasant groups (Aymara and Quechua) continued to demand that land be for those who work it directly.[22]

Strangely absent from this national debate over land, until the last minute, were gendered perspectives. None of the rural women's associations raised the issue of gender and land rights. This is somewhat surprising given the level of organization of rural women over the decade of the

1990s and the high visibility of rural women in the various peasant and indigenous marches to La Paz. (It is said that at least half of the protestors have been women.) But the central demand of these mobilizations has been for access to and the titling of indigenous territory, or communal access to land. The traditional practices and customs by which the land would be redistributed internally did not emerge as an issue. The main issues raised by women in these national mobilizations were access to health care and education.[23]

An NGO, TIERRA (Taller de Iniciativa en Estudios Rurales y Reforma Agraria), was largely responsible for the fact that there was any recognition at all of gender issues in the proposed legislation.[24] TIERRA and the under-secretary for gender issues of the Ministry of Human Development held a workshop on the issue, and, subsequently, a consultant's report was commissioned by TIERRA. This report (A. Camacho 1996) served as the basis for discussions between the under-secretariat and the Interventora Nacional and for the workshops that were then conducted for congresswomen and others to generate consensus on the best way to introduce gender equity into the law. The consultant's report argued that Bolivia's ratification in 1989 of the UN Convention to Eliminate All Forms of Discrimination against Women provided the basis for affirmative actions regarding women's access to land: "The objective of Article 5 of Law 1100 [ratifying the UN Convention] is to modify socio-cultural patterns in the behavior of men and women in order to eliminate prejudices and traditional practices . . . that are based on . . . stereotypical notions of the sexes. . . . Article 14 of the Convention proposes equal treatment for women in plans of agrarian reform and resettlement" (A. Camacho 1996: 1–2). The main recommendation of this report—which was incorporated into the law—was that mention be made of gender equity, independent of a woman's marital status, in the distribution, administration, tenancy, and use of land. The consultant's report made several additional recommendations, including that an Office for the Integration of Women be created within INRA, Bolivia's agrarian reform institute, whose representatives would be voting members on the National Agrarian Commission overseeing implementation of the law. It also recommended such representation in departmental-level bodies. The report stressed that changes in language were required in several parts of the law so that mention would be made explicitly of men and women. And it recommended that all women be exempt from expropriation (A. Camacho 1996). None of these latter recommendations were adopted.

According to Isabel Lavadenz, then the director of INRA, by the time this report was prepared and the subsequent workshops were held, it was quite late in the process to introduce major modifications in the proposed law. The Coordinadora de la Mujer—a feminist network that had played a crucial role several years earlier in drawing the attention of the Ministry of Agriculture to gender issues—also weighed in at a late stage in the proceedings.[25] According to another participant in the process, "The topic of women's rights was raised when the law project was already being debated in the congress. It was thus not a central topic, because there were more general topics of debate, those pertaining to the interests of the mass of peasants and agricultural entrepreneurs."[26] There was consensus, nonetheless, that a paragraph on gender equity should be introduced into the law. The Parliament approved this paragraph without much discussion or dissension.[27]

The main achievements of the indigenous movements in Bolivia and Ecuador have been with respect to the recognition of historic land claims in the Amazon region, although neither movement succeeded in having these recognized as indigenous territories. What is interesting is that although there was greater unity between highland and *selva* organizations in Ecuador than in Bolivia—a joint organization, CONAIE, having been formed rather than an alliance—the potential gains to the peasantry and indigenous movement from the new legislation are far greater in Bolivia. In Ecuador CONAIE basically had to run a defensive campaign aimed at preventing the dismemberment of Andean highland communities. While this was also an issue in Bolivia, in this country there was a stronger consensus favoring the maintenance of collective property and continuation of the agrarian reform. Moreover in Bolivia, in redistributing public lands and private lands to be expropriated by the state, priority is to be given to the collective allocation of land to indigenous or peasant communities who lack sufficient land. In Ecuador the state, for all practical purposes, is no longer to be involved in the expropriation of land. With respect to gender, the Bolivian land law is more favorable than that of Ecuador, since it states explicitly that women have land rights independent of their marital status and that gender equity criteria are to be applied in the distribution of land. However, this provision was not a demand of organized indigenous and peasant women; rather, it resulted from pressure by the urban women's movement and their allies within the state.

Organized Indigenous Women, Defense of Collective Land, and Traditional Customs and Practices

Although women were very visible participants in the indigenous protests of the 1990s in Ecuador and Bolivia, in neither country in the negotiations leading to the new agrarian codes were gender and land rights raised as an issue by the national peasant and indigenous organizations or by indigenous women leaders. According to Nina Pacari, a national leader of CONAIE, the whole topic of gender and land rights is irrelevant, for "the indigenous people have not taken up the individual demand [for land]; it has always been collective, from the perspective of the community" (in Torres G. 1995: 79). The topic seems irrelevant because the preservation of indigenous communities—their very identity as indigenous people—is based on communal access to land. To question how that communal land is then going to be distributed—through what rules it will be allocated to families and to the men and women within them, and who will participate in determining those rules—is considered divisive and a threat to indigenous unity. It is argued that issues of class and ethnicity—issues that unite peasants and indigenous people—must come before all other issues because it has been as peasants and indigenous people that men and women in Ecuador have been exploited over the centuries. Blanca Chancoso (n.d.: 22), a secretary general of ECUARUNARI in the 1980s, explains the position of organized indigenous women this way: "[I]ndigenous women do not have their own demands, as women, for we are not separate from the people. Our indigenous people are exploited and discriminated against, and together with the people, we suffer this same discrimination."

The position of the mixed peasant and indigenous organizations, which is shared by most of their female members, may be summarized as follows: "To incorporate gender-equity criteria in the discussion of land, water, and access to resources is not a problem of the indigenous people. That is a problem of women of the middle class. It is not relevant to us. We want to struggle and fight for the problems of the people as a whole."[28] Two issues must be distinguished here: the issue of class and the distrust among indigenous women leaders of feminist demands; and the reasons why collective demands are so important to indigenous women. With respect to the first issue, the main point of contact between indigenous and middle-class women has been in the domestic realm, where the former are employed as servants and exploited by the latter. The women's movement is viewed as being concerned only with mestizo interests and as ignoring issues vital to indigenous women, such as the perpetuation of poverty and discrimination. Moreover, indigenous women leaders do not share the same priorities as middle-class feminists. Demands by the latter for reproductive rights, for example, are sometimes viewed by indigenous women leaders as a call for ethnocide (Minnaar 1998: 71).

Indigenous women leaders argue that their primary interest must be the defense of the community, which in turn is based on the defense of collective access to land, for it is this factor that gives cohesion and meaning to indigenous identity. Thus one of the principal demands in the 1994 Forum of Indigenous Women, which preceded the debate on Ecuador's agrarian law, was as follows: "Ask the leaders of our *cabildos* [local councils], of the provinces, regions, and nationally, that communal lands not be divided nor sold. They are for the benefit of all and were acquired through great sacrifice. These should be maintained communally, for the family. Our *compañeros* have to assume responsibility for the care of land and women, for to divide the land is the same as dismembering a woman" (CONAIE 1994: 41).

The defense of land (*la tierra madre*) is equated with the defense of women, for women are seen to be identified more closely with culture and nature. The defense of culture is, in turn, based on an appeal to a mythical ancestral culture where women where venerated as the source of life, together with land. This worldview is quite evident in the following testimony: "Land and the woman is one and the same mother; both produce, give life; they feed us and clothe us. We say that it is one and the same mother, because for us indigenous women, land is what gives us life. . . . We women are similar to land for we give life, we are the reproducers. Since land is our mother, it cannot be divided. It would be like dividing our own mother" (CONAIE 1994: 38). This analogy between women and land, or the identification of women with nature, means that women have very specific duties linked to biology. Just as the Earth feeds and reproduces life, the role of indigenous women is defined in terms of physical and cultural reproduction. In our view, this limits their human development (Minnaar 1998: 75–76).

While CONAIE is made up of representatives of diverse indigenous cultures—ranging from the majority Quichua populations of the highlands and *seja de selva* (foothills of the eastern Andes) to heterogeneous tribal groups in the Amazon basin—this theme of the relation between woman and land and of the centrality of both to the reproduction of indigenous culture is often generalized as the "essence" of indigenous culture. In Andean indigenist discourse this mythical ancestral culture was based on the complementarity of male and female roles.[29] The basis of complementarity was the alleged equality between men and women, linked to the essential role that each played in the process of production and reproduction. Each gender had authority derived from these complementarity roles, and each engaged in decision making in their respective spheres (Perrin and Perruchon 1997). In this analysis, it was colonialism and/or capitalism that introduced gender inequality: "Before in our culture, when our society was free [Aymara] men and women had the same rights. Women had authority. . . . The current system tries to impose that 'men are superior to women.' In the traditional system men and women both participated and made decisions. Since this traditional system has been under attack for over four centuries, our objective is to defend it and protect it" (ISIS International 1987: 45). As Renee Minnaar (1998: 74) argues, "Just because in the *cosmovisión* of Andean peoples the universe was divided into masculine and feminine halves, it is insufficient to deduce from these the existence of egalitarian gender relations." She notes that complementarity was based on symmetry rather than equality, and that symmetry maintains gender differences and hierarchical gender relations.

Whether such an egalitarian ancestral culture ever existed is beyond the scope of our inquiry; our concern is with how, within this discourse, gender equality is to be attained. According to a Bolivian indigenous women leader, "Once we are able to break with colonial structures, we can live in complementarity. . . . In the society in which we live, colonialist and patriarchal, it is impossible to ask a man to show solidarity to a woman, it is impossible to ask a woman with a *machista,* patriarchal, and colonial mentality to show solidarity to another poorer, indigenous woman. We have to break with all this."[30] In other words, since patriarchy is a European import, and men and women complement each other in the division of labor, there is no need for gender-specific demands in current struggles.[31] Class and ethnic solidarity must come foremost, for what is necessary in the present context is collective access to land and autonomy for indigenous communities so that they can eventually return to the ways of the past, a past in which complementarity in the gender division of labor was synonymous with gender equality. This is one of the reasons why the growth of the indigenous movement and the increasing participation of women within it has not led to an automatic questioning of women's role within indigenous society. Rather, the participation of women is a consequence of the need to strengthen the indigenous organizations, for women are key players (as reproducers of life and culture) in the resistance offered by indigenous peoples to assimilation into the dominant culture (Prieto 1998: 15–16; Moya 1987).

In a detailed study of indigenous female leaders undertaken in Ecuador, it is suggested that one of the reasons that these leaders promote the discourse "that in complementarity there is equality" is that "the same process of revaluation of one's culture, of the traditional, that is used to reclaim the values, knowledge, and identity of indigenous people is being used to revalue the position of women" (Cervone 1998: 185). According to Emma Cervone, indigenous women leaders have to defend two spaces simultaneously: first, the ethnic space in which respect for cultural difference and equality of rights must be maintained in the face of challenges by white/mestizo society; and second, their space as women leaders within the indigenous movement, in which they must be validated by male indigenous leaders. She thus argues that the equality ideology, "highlighting the feminine in the symbolic order of the value system," can be seen as a strategy by women leaders to defend their space as women (ibid.: 186). Nonetheless, there are a number of contradictions in this position, as Cervonne recognizes, including the fact that the revaluation of the position of women is taking place more at the symbolic than at the political level. As Minnaar (1998: 78) argues, the valorization of women through their link to nature and culture "will not gain them more power of decision in the redistribution of work, in automatic access to resources, and in decision-making"; rather, it serves to exclude women from arenas outside the reproductive realm.

In addition, the gender-equality discourse is often at odds with the fundamental lived experience of indigenous women at the base, particularly with respect to such issues as domestic violence. For this reason Cervone warns that a rupture between the female leadership at the national and local levels could occur over issues of inequality (Cervone 1998: 186–87). In both Bolivia and Ecuador, local-level organizations of women have proliferated over the past two decades, but the male-dominated local institutions have been slow to accept greater participation by women. In Ecuador the primary form of local-level organization in the highlands has been the *comunas,* associated with communal access to landholdings and local governance. By law membership in these is open to all men and women over eighteen years of age; however, in practice, households are represented by the male household head. It was estimated that in the mid-

1980s less than 10 percent of the members were women, the vast majority of whom were widows or abandoned women (FIDA 1989: 166). The leadership of the *comunas* has traditionally been all male, and while in recent years there appears to be an increase in the number of women in leadership positions, it is estimated that women constitute less than 1 percent of the elected leaders in mixed base-level organizations.[32] The main form of local-level governance in the Bolivian highlands has been through the village peasant syndicate structure, where representation is based on one member per household, again usually the male household head (Sostres and Carafa 1992; Paulson 1996).[33] As in Ecuador, although indigenous women are increasingly participating in their own women-only groups, this has not automatically led to their growing representation in traditional structures of governance and power within their communities, although in recent years their participation in these has also been growing.

Some indigenous women leaders argue that the lack of participation by women in community decision-making structures is not a problem because the vote of the male household head is not an individual vote but rather a collective one representing the interests of the family (Pacari 1998: 64). However, there is not much evidence supporting this proposition.[34] Moreover, indigenous women raise very different issues in their own local organizations and women-only meetings from those presented to the mixed associations, including issues of domestic violence and women's lack of land rights. For example, in Bolivia during the NGO preparations for the 1995 Beijing conference, women's land rights emerged as a problem in three of the regional meetings of peasant and indigenous women, in the following terms:

- The agrarian syndicates prefer men when it comes to distributing lands and property rights. We women don't have our own lands. Many times if the husband dies our lands are returned to the community. Parents give preference to male sons, discriminating against women.

- Among our proposals to enhance our situation are the following: access to education for women at all levels; technical training and credit; the right to landed property . . .

- Women have a right to land, and we want this to be legalized for we are the ones who work the land: land belongs to whoever works it.

- Families own the land although we don't have formal titles. Nonetheless, we women suffer because we don't have the right to our own land, to plant our own crops, which is what we need for economic survival. (Salguero 1995: 23, 25, 28, 35)

The problems associated with women's lack of land rights become most apparent in the case of male migration, for often access to credit or technical assistance depends on the applicants' being landowners or having land in their own name. Moreover, when seasonal migration by the spouse turns into permanent migration, women without secure land rights are placed in a precarious situation; sometimes the family's usufruct plot reverts to the peasant syndicate or community. Under traditional practices, there is no certainty that community authorities will assign land to women who are abandoned.

What is worth noting here is that when the concerns expressed by indigenous women at the local and regional level were taken to the national meeting, what was privileged was the general demand for recognition of indigenous territories and defense of communal land. Of the various concerns regarding women's land rights that had been expressed earlier, only one—regarding inheritance—was preserved in the final recommendations: "We indigenous and originary people have been the owners of our lands and territories and we shall continue struggling in order to leave our children 'free' lands and territories. . . . When it comes to inheritance of these territories from parents and spouses, we want to have property rights over these" (Salguero 1995: 48).

According to the coordinator of these meetings, "Many indigenous women emphasized the role of complementarity and how with complementary roles there is no discrimination. . . . Nonetheless, nothing is clearer in terms of challenging the idea that in complementarity there is no discrimination than the issue of inheritance of land rights."[35] This observation suggests the following points: that traditional patterns of inheritance based on customary law and practices often discriminate against women; that indigenous women are increasingly aware of this discrimination; and that there is often a great distance between the concerns of indigenous women at the grass roots and what is expressed by their leaders in national-level meetings, particularly in meetings where the male leadership of the mixed associations is also present.

There is recognition among organized indigenous women leaders that they suffer discrimination within the mixed indigenous organizations. They are under-represented in numbers both within the membership and in leadership positions. One of the main demands of women within CONAIE, for example, is for equal participation by men and women in the organization: "We demand that we be taken into account so that participation in assemblies, congresses, etc. is egalitarian between men and women; i.e., if ten people are to participate, it should be five men and five women" (CONAIE 1994: 7). In Ecuador until recently there was little consideration that indigenous women should perhaps form their own organization, as a precondition to equal participation with men in the public sphere.[36] According to the general coordinator of the Indigenous Women's Commission of the Ecuadorian Amazon, "We indigenous women in Ecuador have not organized ourselves with the goal of creating an organization apart from that of the men, but rather, we have seen the necessity for women to work jointly with men to address the conflicts we confront."[37]

The situation in Ecuador contrasts with that in Bolivia, where the Bolivian Federation of Indigenous and Peasant Women "Bartolina Sisa" was born under the protective wing of the CSUTCB in the early 1980s. The Bartolinas have emphasized a mix of class- and ethnic-based demands, following the priorities of the mixed peasant organization. When gender demands emerged in the late 1980s, even as secondary issues, they were sufficient to generate conflict with the parent organization. This tension, which has surfaced with varying degrees of intensity in different moments, has still not been resolved, suggesting that organizational autonomy—having one's own women's organization—does not necessarily produce the space to make specific gender demands.[38] However, a women-only organization may provide other benefits, such as the opportunity for women to gain organizational and leadership experience and to attract international funds for their projects.

In Ecuador a national organization of indigenous women, CONMIE, the Consejo Nacional de Mujeres Indígenas del Ecuador, was finally formed in 1996 against the strong objections of CONAIE. Teresa Simbaña, one of its founders, says that the main reason the women formed their own organization was that the mixed-sex organizations were dominated by men and they provided women with little opportunity to participate in decision making.[39] Moreover, the women saw that funds coming to the organization for women's projects were being poorly managed and often redirected toward general purposes rather than their intended use. They had also seen that indigenous women in other countries were successfully developing their own organizations. They thus called a national congress of indigenous women in October 1996. Simbaña recalls, "The men didn't like it at all that we were going to form our own organization. They called me seven times to tell me to cancel the congress. They threatened the women of CONAIE with expulsion if they supported me in forming the organization. . . . They said the idea of a women's organization wasn't an indigenous idea, that it was a copy of the mestizas. . . . The women of CONAIE got scared and left."[40] Today CONMIE has fifty base organizations of rural women affiliated to it as well as numerous independent women members. Among its objectives, according to Simbaña, is to raise women's self-esteem so that they have their own voice as women "with dignity, as persons, so that they are not objects." In terms of land, since the agrarian reform is now over in Ecuador, the current struggle, in her opinion, is making women aware of their property rights in marriage and with respect to inheritance.

It is difficult to discern what, if any, impact the existence of an autonomous national indigenous women's organization has had on CONAIE and its leadership. But there are some indications that CONAIE's female leaders have become more open to feminist concerns. Nina Pacari (1998: 66), for example, acknowledges that

> The struggle of the women's movement is very important. . . . It's a movement that is growing and has large goals to change society. But for indigenous women it is different because we must prioritize the perspective of indigenous people without this meaning that we exclude the topic of women's rights. . . . It would not be prudent for us, as an organization or as leaders, to forget the problems we have as women. It also would not be prudent to separate ourselves and for us to go as indigenous women with the exclusive struggle of women, and on the other hand, the men with the struggle as peoples.

Pacari argues that the demand must be for state policies that are coherent with both a gender and ethnic perspective (ibid.), and she is credited, as a member of the 1998 Constituent Assembly, with arguing for gender considerations to be incorporated in Ecuador's new constitution (Ayala 1999: 1). This evolution in thinking is probably the product of a combination of factors: the emergence of a gender perspective among indigenous women in other parts of the continent, particularly in Mexico and Guatemala; the growing influence of this perspective in regional meetings of indigenous women leaders; and the internalization of the discourse of difference within the Latin American women's movement. Contributing to the former trend has been growing awareness of the impact of the neo-liberal counter-reform on indigenous women in Mexico.

The best case that can be made for why it is important to specify women's individual land rights within collective forms of property ownership is by reference to what is happening to women's access to land under the counter-reforms underway in Mexico and Peru. In both countries neo-liberal agrarian legislation now allows for collective landholdings to be divided and sold.[41] Before the counter-reform, women's rights to collective land were much more explicit in Mexico than in the Andean countries, for Mexico in 1971 was the first Latin American country to establish formal legal equality between men and women in its agrarian legislation. Nonetheless, *ejido* regulations specified that each household was entitled to be represented by only one member, and following traditional customs and practice this was the male household head. Thus while the state had granted all adult women land rights, *ejido* membership and effective land rights were limited to female household heads. Nevertheless, usufruct rights on the *ejido* were considered to be the family patrimony, entitling each member within the household access to land and other resources. Inheritance provisions on the *ejidos* protected this family patrimony by restricting the inheritance of *ejido* parcels, in the case a will was made out, to the spouse or partner and/or a child, or in the case there was no will, by giving first preference to the spouse or partner.

In the current counter-reform, all major decisions regarding the future of the *ejido* (such as whether to parcelize and/or dissolve the *ejido*) are being made by recognized *ejido* members. This means that spouses of *ejido* members are excluded from decision making, which in effect excludes most women (since women represent less than one-fifth of total *ejido* membership) from participating directly in determining the future of their communities. Moreover, upon a vote of *ejido* members, individuals holding usufruct rights may acquire a title to the family parcel and dispose of it as they see fit, either renting or selling it. Further, changes in inheritance provisions no longer assure that access to the parcel will remain within the family since the *ejidatario* now has testamentary freedom. What we want to highlight is that what was a family resource—the *patrimonio familiar*—has given way in the counter-reform to a process of individualization of land rights that has excluded women. This is because state legislation has combined with traditional norms and practices to grant household representation to only one sex. Since married women have no rights of direct representation within the *ejido*, they have no direct voice and vote in the decisions determining the privatization of communal land, and thus the family patrimony has become the individual property of the male household head.

A similar process may take place in Peru. There, since 1987, men and women have had equal formal rights to be members of the officially recognized peasant and indigenous communities. However, the Law of Peasant Communities, which obligated the state to respect and protect "the customs, practices, and traditions of the community," also distinguished between community membership and the category of qualified *comunero,* with only the latter being able to participate with voice and vote in the community assembly and be elected to a position of leadership (Peru 1987: Article 1). While theoretically the *comunero calificado* can be a man or woman, in customary practice there is only one qualified comunero per family, and it is the man who as head of household represents the family before the community. Traditionally, the only women who participate in communal decisions are widows (del Castillo 1997a). As explained by researchers Susan Bourque and Kay Warren, referring to the highlands in the Department of Lima:

> Mayobamba men say that each family is represented by a single *comunero* and as long as there is a male to take on this role, it should be done by a man. In any given family, brothers become *comuneros* while sisters must gain access to representation and resources through their fathers and husbands who are *comuneros*. Only when a woman has been widowed or when she is a long-term single mother and no longer attached to her father's family does she receive *comunera* status. (Bourque and Warren 1981: 157)

In some cases, if widows remarry, they lose their right to represent their family and their direct access to land (Casafranca and Espinoza 1993: 19, 26). Other researchers have also concluded that the highland peasant communities are characterized by widespread "discrimination with respect to the usufruct of land by sex, age, and civil status (i.e., women, younger sons, orphans, widows, and the elderly)" (Bonilla 1997: 72).

While it is only since the 1995 land law in Peru that peasant communities in the highlands or native communities in the *selva* may freely choose their form of association and decide on the disposition of communal land, this decision is to be made by a two-thirds majority vote of the qualified *comuneros*. As in Mexico, married women will not participate in this crucially important decision-making process regarding the future of their communities; and if the individualization of land rights takes place, they may also see the family usufruct parcel transformed into male private property. In Peru relatively little attention has been given thus far to the gender implications of the parcelization of communal land. A 1997 report by a

Working Group on Communities and Titling was concerned, nonetheless, about what would happen to the land rights of widows, who often face discriminatory treatment when it comes to honoring their land rights: "The latter might turn out to be a significant problem in those zones of the sierra that have been affected by the social and political violence and where the number of widows is quite high"(Coordinadora Nacional 1997: 3). If widows within peasant communities do not have assured land rights as household heads, the probability is slim that the interests of wives and daughters will be fully considered in the parcelization process.

Among the countries with large indigenous populations, it is in Mexico—where the privatization of communal land has proceeded the farthest—that indigenous women have been most vocal in demanding land rights. As participants explained at the 1994 NGO meeting in preparation for Beijing, the revision of Article 27 of the Mexican constitution, which opened the way for privatization of the *ejido,* "affects us indigenous women because we cannot decide on the fate of our lands; it allows land to be sold, when previously it was inalienable, it couldn't be mortgaged. . . . Now they can take away our lands. Besides, this Article does not take us into account. . . . We do not count. . . . Parallel to the struggle for land is the struggle for women's rights."[42]

In Chiapas indigenous women have been particularly vocal and specific about their demands. As a result the EZLN became the first indigenous movement to support the call for women's effective land rights (Rojas 1995: 251). Now indigenous women throughout Mexico are beginning to demand land rights and to recognize that traditional customs and practices discriminate against women, particularly those that exclude them from inheritance and from the structures of participation and decision making. Indigenous women at a 1996 seminar organized by ANIPA explained their reasoning as follows: "In the communities women's rights are violated by traditional customs and practices that affront women's dignity" and "Indigenous women are stating their demands and revindicating their rights, not to go against their culture or group, but rather, so that customs are rethought from a perspective that includes them" (Seminario 1996: 2–3). In sum, there is growing recognition that the demand for respect of traditional customs and patterns is rarely, in practice, a call for gender equality based on complementarity. Rather, this demand is a often a call for the reproduction of practices that subordinate women to men. As the Mexican experience suggests, the only way to guarantee that men and women will have equal and effective land rights within collective forms of landholding is if the rights of individuals to land are clearly guaranteed within the collectivity. This in turn requires that both men and women have effective rights of representation within their communities.

Reconciling Culturalist and Feminist Perspectives

The importance of community for indigenous people, and of collective rights over land and territory for indigenous identity and survival, are clear. But it is one thing to support the demand for collective property rights and quite another to defend traditional customs and practices in allocating that land to families and the individuals within them. As feminists we are concerned with those instances when respect for custom violates the individual rights of indigenous women. Accepting the strong cultural relativist position—that culture is the principal determinant of moral right and rule—requires accepting the subordination of women; it negates their individual human rights. While we are respectful of indigenous worldviews that link women and land as sources of life, and while we appreciate the appeal of the complementarity thesis in evoking a past where men and women might have been equal, we worry about where all this leads: to arguments for the preservation of all aspects of a culture, no matter how discriminatory.

Besides idealizing the past and requiring the acceptance of a closed cultural system, the strong cultural relativist position ignores internal inequities and relations of power (Howard 1993: 329). Traditional authority is based on a complex network of economic, social, and political factors. By not recognizing the relations of power in which authority derived from tradition is based, this vision can claim that the problems of indigenous women arise from factors other than traditional culture. But the argument that the subordination of women is a product of external forces, whether of colonialism or *machista* acculturation, is a way of deflecting attention from current inequities and injustices. This strong cultural relativist position is beginning to be challenged by indigenous women intellectuals. According to Amanda Pop, a Kichie Mayan scholar in Guatemala,

> It is important to know the history of the atrocities to which our people have been subjected, but if I am consistently going to interpret the present according to some mystical past, which is not even a real history, then where is this going to lead? I have to analyze what is currently most important, and the present is the most important task. If

I do not question whether there is discrimination, then other people are deciding the question for us, and those are our men. . . . It really is not important how it [discrimination against women] came about; more important is that it exists.[43]

When women such as Pop express these ideas, demanding recognition of the rights of women, they have been denounced by male Mayan intellectuals for engaging in ethnocide, as occurred in a 1996 journalistic debate in Guatemala:

According to some Mayan men, when we Mayan women claim our rights as women, we are committing ethnocide. Very interesting this discourse of our men, for they are appropriating the right to decide what Mayan culture should be, what the stereotypical Mayan woman should be. I find it interesting because they are doing exactly what they criticize in others: not recognizing the value and richness of diversity and difference. . . . We will only be "pure Mayan women" if we do not question the unequal relations between men and women that have up to now predominated in our communities. . . . It is said that in the Mayan *cosmovisión,* Mayan women were equal to men. That might have been the case in the *cosmovisión,* but among Mayan men and women today inequality is pervasive. (Alvarez 1996: 26)

Can the differences between cultural relativists and feminists be reconciled? The writings of Boaventura de Sousa Santos (1997) suggest that they might be reconciled theoretically by a shift in focus away from universal human rights to what he calls multi- or transcultural human rights. Santos argues that the debate between universalists and relativists is basically a false one, in addition to being prejudicial to the development of an emancipatory conception of human rights. Whereas universalism hegemonizes one voice to represent human diversity (what he terms "the struggle of the West against the rest of the world"), relativists essentialize their own monolithic cultural view in seeking to legitimize their own conceptions at the expense of others. He argues that what is needed is a transcultural, horizontal dialogue between different cultures to expand our comprehension of human diversity and dignity.

Santos (1997: 10) proposes that all cultures are basically incomplete in terms of their conception of human dignity. This incompleteness is evident in the fact that there is a plurality of cultures; if each was as complete as it pretends to be, then there would be only one culture. He argues that this incompleteness is most visible from the outside, from the perspective of another culture. The task of elaborating a transcultural conception of human rights begins by raising consciousness of this fact, of the incompleteness of cultures. The aim of this exercise is not to achieve completeness but rather to establish a horizontal dialogue, one in which the aim is not to dominate or impose but to broaden the conception of human dignity. He argues that all cultures have conceptions of human dignity, some of which are broader than others or have a larger element of reciprocity than others. The challenge is to look for the common preoccupations or the aspirations that are mutually intelligible, what he terms "the constellation of local signifiers that are mutually comprehensible" (ibid.) He proposes that, in this manner, a transcultural dialogue on human dignity might generate a hybrid or "mestiza" multicultural conception of human rights.

Feminist theory and practice embarked on such a course almost two decades ago with the emergence of the "feminism of difference"—that is, the recognition of diversity within the category of "women" and of women's myriad experiences and interests arising from the intersection of class, race, ethnicity, and nationality, among other factors (Molyneaux 1985; Barret 1990; Fraser 1997). The feminism of difference within the international women's movement has required not only the recognition of diversity but also a recognition of values and lifestyles different from the dominant Western ones, on the terrain emphasized by Santos, through a horizontal dialogue across the women's movement. This process has led to a consensus that not all cultural differences are worthy of respect or revindication while not all practices can be universalized (Subirats 1998: 58). In addition, this process of dialogue has begun to generate shared, cross-cultural criteria to evaluate policies beneficial to women—for example, those that enhance women's bargaining power within the household and community and improve women's default options.

Dialogue between the Latin American women's movement and indigenous women leaders did not really begin until the 1990s, although the discourse of the politics of difference has figured in the annual Encuentros Feministas since the previous decade. According to an indigenous woman leader, "Before I thought that it was impossible or contradictory to be indigenous, a woman, and a feminist. Now I wouldn't say that because feminism has helped me to recognize my identities. . . . When within feminism we began to talk about identity, I began to recognize myself as an indigenous woman, an intellectual, and a feminist."[44] As a practice, the politics of difference began to come to fruition with the preparatory events among NGOs in the region for the 1995 Beijing women's conference. Its most profound expression was probably the 1996 ENLAC (Encuentro Latinoamericano y del Caribe de la Mujer Trabajadora Rural) meeting in Brazil, which brought together peasant and indigenous women and feminists from twenty-one countries in the largest inter-racial, inter-ethnic, and multi-lingual meeting to date among women in Latin America and the Caribbean (ENLAC 1998). It is this constellation of factors that has encouraged indigenous women leaders to re-examine their own foundational myths and to recognize the limitations of upholding a past that is discriminatory today. This process is best seen in the evolution of the demands emanating from regional meetings of indigenous women leaders over the past decade.

Indigenous women began to question relations of power when they began to demand equal participation in the mixed indigenous organizations (Hernández and Muiguialday 1993: 132). These demands were made very timidly at the 1989 Meeting of Latin American Peasant and Indigenous Organizations, organized in the context of the planning for the Five Hundred Years of Resistance campaign. The few women who attended this meeting first had to explain to the men that they were not against them before they spoke out about concerns regarding their participation: "[O]ur struggle is not against men, but rather against a system of domination and exploitation that mutilates both men and women. In solidarity we raise the criticism that in other events [of indigenous peoples], women's organizations in Latin America be taken into account; that the indigenous organizations include women's delegations; and that the participation of women be taken into account in the coordinating committees of such events" (Comisión Mujer 1990: 29).

It was apparently at the second continental meeting of the Five Hundred Years campaign, held in Guatemala in 1991, that indigenous groups first recognized the triple oppression of indigenous women (Hernández and Murguialday 1993: 157). One of the resolutions of this meeting acknowledged that, "The struggle for women's emancipation must take place in an integral framework that takes into account the struggle against class inequality, ethnic inequality and gender inequality." By 1995, in the context of the preparatory activities for the Beijing UN Conference on Women, indigenous women in the various regional meetings were increasingly vocal regarding the mechanisms that reproduce gender inequality. For example, the following statement emerged from the 1995 Seminar of Indigenous Women of South America, held in Bogotá:

We women have begun to criticize the [indigenous] organizational structures for being exclusionary, for not being autonomous models, for not being internally democratic, and more than anything else, for ignoring and belittling our contribution. We have been very clear in expressing our wish to work together with the men within our organizations, even if we continue to face obstacles that lead us to be discriminated against within them. It hurts us that on many occasions we have to put up with excuses to maintain us in inferior positions from which we can't exert leadership, that our contributions are not taken seriously, and that our work with indigenous women is the first to be interrupted if there are financial problems. . . . This is why it has become increasingly clear that we must struggle for the space in which to participate at all the different levels of power, where the vital decisions are made that affect the life and future of women and of the people. (ONIC 1996: 35–36)

In the process of demanding the right to full participation within the mixed indigenous organizations, there is growing recognition of the complexity of factors that reproduce women's subordination to men, down to the community level: "In terms of politics, indigenous women recognize that in their communities many aspects of the dominant ideology are reproduced which emphasize that women should be maintained in a subordinate position in all spheres. This generates relations of power and inequality between men and women that go against the idea that women should be incorporated into the structures of decision making . . . [and] that consider that women are not capable of leadership" (ONIC 1996: 86).

As indigenous women leaders begin to challenge the structure of decision making within indigenous communities, they are demanding a voice in how "customary" rules are determined and defined. At the same time, the demand for women's land rights remains rather muted in most of these regional meetings, perhaps because these must be considered, in the first instance, part and parcel of the broader struggle for indigenous land and territories. Nonetheless, at the second continental meeting of the Five Hundred Years of Indigenous Resistance campaign, the Commission on Women and Life demanded that the campaign support its struggle to attain "the same rights as men to the property of land and housing, access to credit, the creation of jobs for women, and equal remuneration for equal work" (in Hernández and Murguialday 1993: 158). Among the conclusions of the forum on Indigenous Women and Political Participation at the NGO preparatory meeting held at Mar del Plata in 1994 was "[t]o demand the right of indigenous and peasant women to land" (CEIMME 1995: 136). And at the 1995 Seminar of Indigenous Women of South America, the following recommendation was approved: "That indigenous women, whether widowed or not, be given access to land and credit" (ONIC 1996: 55–56). Thus while the issue of women's land rights has not always emerged as a primary demand, as organized indigenous women have begun to question in public forums the structure of gender inequality within their mixed organizations and communities, the relationship between material factors and relations of power are beginning to be uncovered, examined, and resisted.

eight

Inheritance of Land in Practice

National laws requiring an equal division of the estate among all the children, when not evaded, are said to have increased litigation and sown confusion.[1]

ONE OF THE DISTINCTIVE ASPECTS of Latin American society, compared to many other regions of the world, is the legal tradition inherited from colonial rule whereby all legitimate children, irrespective of sex, inherit equally from both of their parents.[2] Another is that the foundational myths of a number of the major pre-Columbian civilizations were based on the notion of the complementarity of men and women. This belief system is associated by some with traditions and customs that are relatively gender egalitarian, such as bilateral or parallel inheritance systems.[3] Given such a favorable heritage, one might expect the actual distribution of land between men and women to be relatively equitable. Yet one of the salient features of Latin America today is that most land is owned by men, suggesting the disjunction that exists between women's legal inheritance rights and local practices.

Gender inequality in the inheritance of land in Latin America has been attributed to a number of factors, among the most important being patrilineality, patri- or virilocality,[4] and what may be called the logic of peasant household reproduction. In peasant societies inheritance of land is a fundamental condition of peasant household reproduction, for access to land is what guarantees the continuity of the unit of production and reproduction between generations (Deere 1990). Where access to land is limited (by natural or socio-economic conditions, such as the pattern of land tenure), inheritance has often constituted the primary means through which new units of production and reproduction are formed, and through which patrilineality is reproduced over time. The logic of patrilineality is that the community is maintained over time by means of the allocation of women to men through patri- and virilocal residency. Inheritance systems that prioritize the eldest or youngest son in providing access to land and that disinherit daughters are argued to have as their objective assuring the continuity of the family patrimony as well as guaranteeing security to elderly parents (Carneiro et al. 1998: 5).[5] It is sometimes argued that enforcement of the rules of the Latin American civil codes would lead to the rapid fragmentation of land and the end of viable peasant economies in several generations. That is, enforced gender equality in inheritance of land might precipitate a process of depeasantization. Moreover, equal inheritance of land among all children might require selling off the family patrimony, leading to the end of the unit of production and reproduction and the demise of peasant communities. These conditions have been used to justify male privilege and the custom of prioritizing one son in inheritance (ibid.).

Another factor favoring male privilege in inheritance of land is gender socialization and stereotyping. Many regions of Latin America are characterized by a gender division of labor that defines agriculture as a male occupation; women are seen primarily as housewives regardless of their contribution to family agriculture. Moreover, often the right to inherit land is considered an "earned" right, following the principle that land should belong to those who work or earn it (Woortmann 1995; Carneiro 2000; Hamilton 2000). Women's nonparticipation in agriculture, or society's failure to acknowledge the agricultural work they actually perform, may serve to exclude women from land rights. In many cases both factors —the locale of post-marital residency and gender stereotypes—combine to produce particularly strong systems of patrilineal land rights.

There is also abundant evidence that inheritance practices among the Latin American peasantry are not uniform nor static. These have changed over time in response to a myriad of factors, and it is these changes—and the question of whether inheritance is becoming more or less gender equitable—that is our primary interest in this chapter. Given the rich tradition of anthropological studies on the Latin American peasantry, it is somewhat surprising that there are few national-level summaries of inheritance practices in peasant communities.[6] Below, we sketch such summaries with respect to children's inheritance of land for six countries, these cases having been chosen because of the greater availability of data. In order to explore whether countries with large indigenous populations are characterized by more egalitarian practices, we first consider three Andean countries and then three predominantly mestizo or ethnically mixed countries.

The Mixed Evidence on Bilateral Inheritance in the Andes

The literature regarding inheritance practices in the Andes in the preconquest period is rather slim. One often-cited account of land distribution under the Incas, sometimes assumed to be the norm for inheritance practices, is provided by the Inca Garcilaso de la Vega in his 1509 *Comentarios Reales de los Inca*. When sons were born, households received from local chiefs (*kurakas*) an additional one *topo* of land, whereas for daughters they received only one-half a *topo* (in Figallo Adrianzen 1990: 414), suggesting gender asymmetry was the norm. On the other hand, Silverblatt (1980) argues that parallel systems of kinship and inheritance were widespread in the Andes and that these were disrupted under Spanish colonial rule. There seems to be consensus that in contemporary Peru inheritance in the highlands tends to be bilateral, with both sons and daughters inheriting land and animals from both parents (de la Cadena 1995).

According to Bernd Lambert (1977: 13), "Animals are regularly inherited by children of both sexes, and consequently accrue to the herd of the descent group that attracts the young couple. . . . Rules governing the inheritance of land are more variable and complicated, but tend to concentrate both cultivated fields and pastures in the hands of the resident members of the descent group." Patri- or virilocal residence is the most common practice, favoring inheritance of land by sons. The locale of residency of a young couple, nonetheless, tends to be determined by which one's parents have more land, uxorilocal residency (with a woman's parents) not being uncommon: "[E]verywhere some married men reside uxorilocally, usually because they have several brothers, while their wives have few or none, or because their wives come from families wealthier than their own" (ibid.: 15).

Data for the province of Cajamarca (in the department of the same name), a region characterized today by a predominantly mestizo peasantry, provides good evidence of bilateral inheritance, and of men and women inheriting approximately equal shares of land. A 1975 survey of 105 households found that only one-third of these households had been constituted as units of production primarily through inheritance, land purchases being the dominant form of acquiring land (Deere 1990: 193). However, of the thirty-six households where inheritance was the primary form, 42 percent represented inheritance primarily by women and only 33 percent were constituted through inheritance by men; in 25 percent of the households, men and women inherited and brought into the household approximately equal shares of land. In the 1970s it was common in this region for one sibling to purchase the inheritance shares of those who had migrated; women were just as likely as men to purchase land from the other heirs. It was also customary for the youngest child—son or daughter—to remain living at home, caring for the parents in their old age, and to inherit the parental home and surrounding land. This latter practice has been widely reported throughout highland Peru (Lambert 1977: 11).

Susan Bourque and Kay Warren's (1981: 3, 140) study of two rural districts in the highland province of Cajatambo in the department of Lima also found that inheritance of land was bilateral. However, sons tended to inherit parcels that were larger and better endowed than those passed on to daughters. In contrast, Norman Long and Bryan Roberts (1978: 305) report that in the Mantaro Valley of the department of Junín, inheritance was predominantly bilateral, with male and female offspring receiving approximately equal shares of land. Nonetheless, one child would usually reconcentrate the family holdings under his or her control, compensating the other siblings with cash, animals, or shares of future harvests. Long and Roberts do not report whether sons were more likely than daughters to consolidate the family farm, but they do stress that "property passes through both the paternal and maternal sides of the family," implying that women usually owned land to pass on to their children. Such is also the case in the district of Jarpa in Huancayo (de la Cadena 1988: 38).

Farther south, in the largely indigenous Quechua district of Chuschi in the department of Ayacucho, parallel patterns of inheritance prevail, where sons inherit the property of their fathers and daughters that of their mothers (Isbell 1978: 75, 79).[7] There is also a predilection to favor the eldest, whether a son or daughter, with a larger share of the distributed property, as well as the child, usually the youngest, who resides with the parents the longest and serves them the most. Billie Jean Isbell provides a revealing anecdote about the clash between indigenous and mestizo norms of inheritance in this region:

> In 1959 the notary public in Cangallo, the province capital, informed me that Chuschi and three other villages—Quispillaqta, Ochuri, and Chacoya—persisted in this peculiar parallel inheritance pattern. He stated that he has battled since his arrival in 1921 to teach them that Peruvian constitutional law requires that all siblings inherit equally. He refused to record wills that did not conform to the law. The notary was especially dismayed by the possibility that women could inherit greater estates from their mothers than their male siblings if the woman was richer than her husband. This can happen and has happened. Villagers simply register a will that complies with the law, return to the village, and institute the traditional inheritance, sealing the agreement with a solemn oath and mutual drinking. (Ibid.)

Contrasting patterns of inheritance have been reported in the department of Cuzco. In the Quechua-speaking community of Alccavitoria in the province of Chumbivilcas, "the bilaterality of inheritance corresponds to the bilaterality of descent. Marriage involves not only the starting of a new family but at the same time the formation of a new capital-holding partnership for its support. This capital is in the form of land and animals brought into the marriage by both partners" (Custred 1977: 127). In the indigenous community of Chitapampa in Cuzco, Marisol de la Cadena (1995) found that up through the early decades of the twentieth century the custom was for the eldest son to inherit the vast majority of the family's land, what she estimates as approximately 80 percent of the holdings. A second son might inherit another 10 to 15 percent of the land. All the other children, male or female, would inherit and divide among them the remaining land. She also found that over the course of this century inheritance of land has became increasingly more egalitarian, as Table 8.1 shows. De la Cadena argues that as land has lost its value as a source of income and of power within the community, its ownership has been increasingly "feminized." She also attributes the growing fragmentation of land to the growing equality in inheritance shares. The latter is quite apparent in this table, with the average amount inherited after 1970 being half of the amount that was common in the early twentieth century.

TABLE 8.1. Inheritance of Land in Chitapampa, Department of Cuzco, Peru

	Men No. %		Women No. %		Total Heirs No. %		Average Size (topo)
1900–20	53	(78)	15	(22)	68	(100)	1.14
1940–70	112	(69)	49	(31)	161	(100)	0.91
1970–87	141	(60)	94	(40)	235	(100)	0.68

Source: "Censo comunal y genealogías de herencia, 1987," in de la Cadena (1995), table 2.

Note: The topo is equal to 0.3 hectares.

Other scholars have also observed this tendency toward greater equality in inheritance of land over the course of the twentieth century (Bourque and Warren 1981: 9). According to Lambert (1977: 15), "The inequality of the sexes in matters of inheritance was probably greater in the last century than it is now, especially among the Aymara and around Lake Titicaca. In some Aymara communities, all the daughters traditionally inherited a share of the parental lands equal to that of a single son."

Another factor that has encouraged more egalitarian inheritance practices, besides the growing inviability of peasant farming and increasing awareness of national laws (itself a product of rising literacy rates and internal migration), has been the growing number of female-headed households in rural areas. In some regions of the highlands, such as Cajamarca, it is socially acknowledged that female inheritance of land is one of the best insurance policies in maintaining a modicum level of security for women and their children in case of their abandonment, an increasingly frequent phenomenon over the course of the twentieth century (Deere 1990).

Sarah Hamilton (1998: 205), surveying the literature for highland Ecuador, concludes that "equal inheritance is observed in communities where land reform favoring males did not affect freeholders . . . ; where indigenous forms have been reinstated in the generation that is now inheriting parcels granted during the land reform initiatives of the 1950s and 1970s . . . ; and where indigenous patterns were maintained despite laws favoring males." She argues that in the central sierra province of Cotopaxi, inheritance of land tends to be bilateral; that sons and daughters tend to inherit land of equal quantity and quality; and that women's inheritance rights do not depend on whether they remain in their communities of origin upon marriage. In a survey of seventy households in Chachaló, in the canton Salcedo, she found that more than three-fourths of the adult women owned land, a slightly higher proportion than men. Of these women landowners, the largest share, 39 percent, reported owning land jointly with their husbands; another 25 percent owned land both independently and with their husbands; and 13 percent only owned land independently. Whereas independently owned land was largely the result of inheritance, jointly held land was usually the result of land purchases. In this survey the average amount of land owned independently by men (2.3 hectares) was slightly larger than the average amount owned by women (1.8 has.) (ibid.: 202).

Hamilton (1998: 204) argues that her data are consistent with the finding that inheritance of land in the sierra tends to be gender blind. Drawing on a number of ethnographic studies of the indigenous, highland population, she concludes that "women are likely to own, or control the usufruct of, land and animals independently from their husbands" and that this pattern is largely due to bilateral inheritance. She argues that the usual pattern is that upon marriage, each spouse receives at least a part of the land they will eventually inherit. These lands will be worked in a joint enterprise; but neither spouse can unilaterally control the holdings of the other. Moreover, husbands and wives do not inherit land from each other. Rather, land is held individually for the children, who inherit from both sides. By tradition, the youngest child, irrespective of gender, is expected to take care of the aging parents and will inherit the familial home and surrounding land.

Kristi Stolen's (1987: 57–58) study in the sierra community of Caipi, in the canton Machachi, concurs with Hamilton's findings regarding equality of inheritance of land shares among all children. Another study in the province of Cotopaxi by Hernán Ibarra and Pablo Ospina (1994: 92–94) suggests more heterogeneity in inheritance patterns, but that the norm is for all children to receive some land in inheritance. They stress the variety of mechanisms that are used to avoid excessive sub-division of land, such as the purchase of the inheritance shares of siblings who have migrated by the child who remains at home, caring for the elderly parents. In some but not all communities, this remaining child is by custom the youngest, irrespective of sex.

In discussions with agrarian experts, the hypothesis emerged that inheritance patterns in the highlands today largely depend on whether agricultural production is still a viable activity among smallholders.[8] Where land is still valuable, because agricultural production is still profitable (as in the case of potato production in the department of Cachi), inheritance practices tend to favor sons. By contrast, in the south, in such predominantly indigenous departments as Cañar and Lojas, where soils are depleted and agriculture is a much less profitable activity and where there are high rates of male out-migration, bilateral inheritance practices appear to be the norm. In the opinion of one peasant women leader, with such high rates of migration to the cities among both sons and daughters, the most important factor governing contemporary inheritance practices is which child is willing to stay on the land to farm it.[9] Thus while there is strong evidence of the predominance of bilateral inheritance practices in the Ecuadorian highlands, it is difficult to disentangle the influence of indigenous customs and practices from the changing conditions of production and tenancy over the course of the twentieth century.

A recent survey of inheritance practices in Bolivia suggests considerable heterogeneity in inheritance patterns nationally, and different practices among different ethnic groups (Pacheco 1999).[10] On the Bolivian altiplano, where the indigenous Aymara population is concentrated, inheritance of land is reported to be primarily patrilineal. The largest amount of evidence for bilateral inheritance practices comes from the central Andean valleys, where the indigenous Quechua and mestizo peasantry are largely located. But even within one ethnic region, there may be wide variation in inheritance patterns, reflecting (among other factors) different forms of insertion by indigenous communities into the regional economy as well as differing class relations. Jorge Balán and Jorge Dandler (in Paulson 1995: 103), for example, distinguish three different modalities in the Quechua region of Cochabamba: (1) in the indigenous communities that operated relatively independently of colonial society and the hacienda system, inheritance was usually bilateral and work roles and rituals were organized around the principle of complementarity; (2) in the indigenous communities that were enmeshed in the hacienda system, only male household heads generally received usufruct plots on the hacienda, with inheritance of these rights and obligations being patrilineal; and (3) in the independent indigenous communities integrated into commercial agriculture and in greater contact with mestizo cultural influences, notwithstanding the fact that women often had more diversified economic roles (such as participating in commerce), inheritance also tended to be patrilineal. Susan Paulson (ibid.: 103–5) argues that over time—through the agrarian reform, greater commercialization of agricultural production, and internal migration—these divisions in Cochabamba have become blurred. She suggests that the general tendency has been in support of male inheritance of land.

The Aymara community of Chari illustrates the difficulties of rigidly characterizing contemporary inheritance systems (Spedding and Llanos 1998). In this community access to ancestral community land is governed by the peasant syndicate, and usufruct rights to agricultural parcels are distributed to peasant families following patrilineal norms. Since this area is characterized by exogamy and virolocal residency, women do not have any right to inherit agricultural land. Access to pasture land, which is utilized communally, is governed by a woman's kinship position to the male household head, as wife or daughter. However, within this patrilineal community, women may inherit small parcels of land, called "residuals," which are usually marginal plots outside of the principal land distribution system of the peasant syndicate. These residuals are passed along the female line, from mothers to daughters. Cattle is also inherited following a parallel system by gender, with sons inheriting from fathers and daughters from mothers.

It is again difficult to disentangle traditional inheritance norms and practices from changes resulting from such factors as demographic pressure on a static land base and the growing commodification of land. It has been suggested that excessive land fragmentation on the Bolivian altiplano may have led to a change over the course of the twentieth century from the old system of bilateral or parallel inheritance to one favoring either the oldest or youngest son. Denise Arnold (1997: 345–49) describes an Aymara community near Oruro where daughters used to inherit land and animals. Now, because of land scarcity, they rarely inherit any land at all if there are sons in the family. Sheep constitute the main property that is inherited, and both sons and daughters receive them in approximately equal shares beginning when they are small. The size of this herd increases over time and constitutes the daughter's dowry when she marries and leaves home; for sons it represents the capital enabling them to start their own families and independent units of production.

Moreover, although inheritance practices governing land among the Aymara on the altiplano are generally held to be patrilineal and associated with patri- and virilocal residence, in the regions where they have migrated in large numbers and where access to land was not initially constrained, bilateral inheritance practices currently predominate. Alison Spedding (1997: 325–25) reports that in the northern Yungas region, as a result of bilateral inheritance, approximately one-third of the households reside uxorilocally. These case studies suggest the hypothesis that ancestral norms among the Aymara might have favored bilateral and/or parallel rather than patrilineal land inheritance practices, and that the latter system has evolved over the course of the twentieth century in response to land scarcity.

In contrast, in other regions of Bolivia, such as Tarija, Chuquisaca, and parts of Cochabamba, it has been suggested that land scarcity and associated male migration as well as the decline of peasant agriculture and livestock production have favored more gender-equitable inheritance practices. There is also now a tendency for land inheritance in these regions to favor the youngest child, irrespective of sex, who remains at home caring for the elderly parents.[11]

Much more research is obviously required before one can safely generalize about inheritance practices in Bolivia in the past or today. Nonetheless, overall there is more evidence of the prevalence of patrilineal systems in Bolivia than in the Peruvian or Ecuadorian highlands, where bilateral inheritance of land appears to be the norm. However, in all three countries bilateral inheritance practices do not necessarily result in equal inheritance of land by sons and daughters; rather, these often favor sons in terms of parcel size and quality.

Strong Male Preference in Land Rights: Mexico, Chile, and Brazil

Mexico, Chile, and Brazil are ethnically mixed countries, but largely mestizo in composition and governed by different inheritance regimes. While Mexico is characterized by full testamentary freedom, Chile and Brazil are governed by civil codes that provide for egalitarian inheritance by children. Nevertheless, in all three countries there is a strong male preference in inheritance practices regarding land. In one of the few comprehensive, national-level reviews of land inheritance patterns, María de la Soledad González (1992: 412–13) argues that in Mexico generally only sons inherit land. She found this to be the case across ethnic groups, including among the numerically dominant mestizo population and the Nahuas of central Mexico, the Mayas of Chiapas, the Mixtecos of Oaxaca, and the Purepechas of Michoacán. Paloma Bonfil and Raúl del Pont (1999: 230–31) confirm this finding, arguing that patrilineal inheritance is as strong in indigenous communities organized under communal forms of land tenancy as in communities governed by the *ejido* system. There are, nevertheless, exceptions to this trend. Pilar Alberti (1998: 193), for example, describes inheritance among the Nahuas of the Sierra de Puebla as being based on equal land rights for all children, although daughters tend to inherit less land than do sons.

González (1992: 409) describes the most common pattern across Mexico—and in the community she studied in the state of Mexico—as that where the youngest son inherits the parents' home and sometimes the largest parcel of land in return for the care he is expected to provide to elderly parents.[12] The division of farmland rarely takes place until the father's incapacitation or death, although older sons may receive a small parcel of land upon which to build a house when they marry. She argues that this pattern serves to maintain the father's position as head of the family and to assure that sons meet their obligations to the parents. Her review also suggests that the amount of land each son receives is closely related to his contribution to the parental household, be it in labor or cash. Daughters rarely inherit land from their fathers unless there are no male heirs. If the father is a fairly large landowner a daughter may inherit some land, but she always inherits less land than her brothers. In contrast, if mothers own land independently, they tend to pass it on to their daughters (González 1992: 379, 382, 390).

Rosío Córdova Plaza (1999) argues that the main structural factor limiting women's access to land in Mexico has been patri- and virilocality. Since wives move to their husband's community, they lose all claim to land. Married daughters remain, at best, as residual heirs; if they receive something of their parents' patrimony, it is usually much less than what their brothers receive. Unmarried daughters, on the other hand, are more likely to inherit some land; and if they are the youngest child and there are no male heirs, they will inherit the parents' home and the primary land parcel. Another factor favoring patrilineality in Mexico has been the rules of *ejido* membership and inheritance, which specify that the *ejido* parcel is indivisible and that land rights can only be transmitted to one person.

González (1992: 414–20) also argues that inheritance practices are undergoing some change. Bilateral inheritance of land is becoming more common in regions where agriculture is no longer the primary household activity and where some occupational diversification has occurred. She also finds bilateral inheritance to be increasing where there has been long-standing male and female out-migration, with sons and daughters inheriting land based on their contribution to maintaining the parental household through remittances. In this context it is also becoming more common for daughters to inherit the family home and to assume care for elderly parents. Moreover, it is reported that there is an increased interest by daughters in inheriting land for the security it offers them, and that they are beginning to contest land rights (Castañeda 2000).

In Chile the norm is for all children to inherit from their parents, although sons are privileged with respect to the inheritance of land. Ximena Valdés (1995: 150) argues that rural women were generally the first migrants to urban centers as population pressure upon the land increased in the early twentieth century (partly due to the great concentration of land in latifundios) and that this pattern reinforced a tendency toward male inheritance of land. She considers rural women to be more likely than men to inherit houses, rather than land, while men more often inherit the family farm, a pattern that contributes to the concentration of land in hands of men.

A detailed study of wills in two communities during the first three decades of the twentieth century offers some interesting contrasts, suggesting the heterogeneity that must exist on a broader scale (Rebolledo 1995). In Santa Cruz, in the province of Colchagua, in the early decades of the twentieth century, men tended to favor sons in wills, particularly the eldest son. Women, in contrast, tended to favor daughters and other women in their wills. A different pattern prevailed in San Felipe, in the province of Putaendo. Here either sons or daughters inherited land, usually receiving it at the moment of marriage. Interestingly, both men and women who left wills tended to favor women in inheritance, whether daughters, sisters, or wives: "In general among the women who are beneficiaries of wills, there is an attempt to better the situation of those who are single or underage, as well as those who are in a precarious situation, be it because of health or a bad marriage. In this way, the will serves as an economic guarantee of the subsistence of those persons considered to be socially vulnerable" (ibid.: 171). Daughters were especially favored by being willed the parental home. The common practice in San Felipe, where men tended to migrate more than women, was for one daughter, often unmarried, to remain in the parental home, caring for her elderly parents. Rebolledo concludes that "the recognition of women's capacity to be owners and administrators of economic goods is seen in their being named as the executors and holders of goods in various testaments at the beginning of the century; in some cases, even elder brothers were passed over, indicating that the economic role and the possibility for female autonomy in San Felipe was recognized early on" (ibid.: 172). This proposition is also supported by Rebolledo's (ibid.: 159) data on the visibility of women in local land markets. Single women or widows often bought property, particularly from siblings (male or female), suggesting that they sought to consolidate the family farm, which perhaps had been left to all siblings in equal shares.

Contemporary studies, nonetheless, stress the male bias in inheritance of land. For example, Sarah Bradshaw (1990: 117) reports that because "land rights automatically go to any males in the family, and male labor is seen, in general, to be indispensable, whilst female labor is considered as secondary, then the sons remain working the land. Hence daughters may be forced to migrate whilst sons face parental pressure to remain." In general, young rural women are much more likely to migrate permanently to urban areas than young men, resulting in high male-to-female ratios in rural areas (Aranda 1992: 7–8). Christopher Scott (1990: 85–87), based on national-level fieldwork in rural areas, reports that inheritance of land is formally considered to be bilateral, with all children having the right to inherit from fathers and mothers. In practice, however, women find it difficult to claim a share of land:

> Dealings between male claimants commonly take the form of market transactions, as when one brother buys the share of another, or where a single resident male heir pays rent to absentee male heirs for the use of the entire property. By contrast, female claimants seem particularly vulnerable to pressure from male siblings to renounce their legitimate rights of ownership. This pressure may take the form of physical intimidation or of an expressed expectation that female heirs will not exercise their entitlements, particularly after marriage.

Ximena Aranda (1992: 7–8) notes that to avoid creating microfundios there is an increasing tendency for a single child—always a son—to inherit the family farm. According to agrarian expert Jorge Echenique, if the family parcel is divided among all the siblings, women do inherit land; but when the whole farm is given to only one child, it is always to a son: "It goes against the woman, because they migrate to be employed in domestic service, or they become proletarians in the fruit industry."[13] In other words, alternative income-generating opportunities and locale of residence are also important factors in influencing inheritance patterns.

In the indigenous region of southern Chile, the tradition of exogamous marriage and patrilocal residence favors patrilineal inheritance and the concentration of land by men.[14] Mapuche leader Isolde Renque Paillalef describes these practices:

> Generally when one gets married [the woman] leaves her community, going to that of the husband. He thus inherits land, and the woman who leaves her community generally receives artisan products, animals, chickens, all those domestic things that are movable. Land obviously

can't be moved to her place of residence. So what happens at the time of inheritance? The brother or sister who inherits the land gives her the equivalent of what should be her legal share, an animal or whatever.[15]

According to Renque, if a woman brings her partner to her own community, or if the husband is not a Mapuche and they do not have land elsewhere, "then they live in her community and that is where they will receive an inheritance share, that is the difference." In other words, the locale of residence upon marriage plays a crucial role in determining inheritance practices.

An important point in terms of women's property rights versus control over land was raised by peasant leader Francisca Rodríguez at the 1997 Seminar on Gender and Land Rights: "Women's inheritance of land has to be considered along with one other factor, which is their right to administer land. Women might inherit land, but who administers the land is not the heir . . . that is, a woman is the heir on paper, but not in management."[16] Under the default marriage regime in Chile, the husband is still the legal manager of household property, including land inherited by the woman.

Researchers in Brazil have also found considerable discontinuity between the norms of the civil code, which limit testamentary freedom and provide for equal inheritance of property among all children, and local inheritance practices. Miriam Nobre (1998: 58) summarizes the situation: "In the countryside there is no law; what is relevant is custom. And the custom is not to give women land. She is not entitled to inherit land." As in other countries, inheritance patterns in Brazil vary widely by region, ethnicity, race, and class position, among other factors, but patrilineal inheritance is the dominant pattern. The region that has been most studied in Brazil is the south, a region characterized by substantial immigration of German, Italian, and Polish settlers during the late nineteenth and early twentieth century. According to Maria José Carneiro (1998), the inheritance custom that these colonists brought with them to the New World was that of primogeniture, that is, the oldest son inherited the family patrimony of land. Over time, however, this custom evolved into an inheritance system favoring the youngest son (known as *minorato*). This change was the result of the initially favorable conditions the colonists found in southern Brazil: an agricultural frontier that encouraged the formation of new settlements and allowed families to acquire additional land over time upon which to settle all the sons who wanted to farm. As the older sons left the homestead, the youngest one remained at home with the obligation to take care of the parents in their old age, maintaining the tradition of the indivisible family farm, but leading to the *minorato* system.

Most students of the German colonies in Rio Grande do Sul report that daughters were generally excluded from the inheritance of land. Inheritance of land was strongly associated with those who worked it directly, and women were not considered "to work" in agriculture. Moreover, it was expected that upon marriage they would move away, since patri- or virilocality was the usual practice, and that they would be supported by their husbands. While daughters were given a dowry consisting of animals and household goods, its value was generally less than what a land share would have been worth (Carneiro 1998; Woortmann 1995). Inheritance patterns among the Italian immigrants to Rio Grande do Sul followed a similar pattern of patrilineal inheritance. Sons generally received their inheritance of land at the time of marriage; daughters received a dowry consisting of household goods and a calf. Usually youngest sons would be favored with the largest endowment of land in return for the care they were expected to provide elderly parents (van Halsema 1991: 99–100). Of the different ethnic groups who populated this most southern state, only in Brazilian Portuguese households were women likely to inherit land (Stephen 1997: 212).[17] Moreover, Lynn Stephen reports that inheritance of land was closely correlated with women's participation in household and farm decision making, with landed women of Portuguese heritage having a much stronger bargaining position in household affairs than other women in this region.

Ellen Woortmann (1995: 193), who worked among the German colonists in this state, observed a growing tendency in recent decades toward daughters inheriting land, although it was always a smaller parcel than that inherited by their brothers. However, sometimes they were expected to sell this inheritance to a brother. Woortmann observed that when they did retain ownership of a land parcel, "in practice, this land passed to the control of their husbands." This led to a contradictory situation, according to Woortmann, for when women only inherited animals, they acquired an economic resource and could engage in dairy-processing activities that gave them an independent income. As inheritance of land by women became more common, inheritance of animals has diminished, and at the same time women have tended to lose the basis of their relative economic autonomy: "The woman who before enjoyed the usufruct of the product of her dowry no longer enjoys the usufruct of her inheritance" (ibid.: 194).[18]

Recent changes associated with the modernization of agriculture, the increase in both male and female educational opportunities, and the expansion of alternative income-generating opportunities have prompted a number of other changes in these southern colonies.[19] For one, inheritance shares have increasingly taken the form of family investments in education. Children with higher levels of education than their siblings who migrate to urban areas are expected to renounce any other claim to inheritance. This has allowed the more entrepreneurial son to consolidate the family holding and attempt to meet the challenges of commercial farming. Second, increasing numbers of families find themselves without any willing heir, or with only a single daughter remaining at home. Third, more and more daughters are claiming their inheritance of land, a product of rising educational levels. Whereas in the past an unmarried daughter (*solterona*) might have no choice but to become the live-in maid of her brother, this is no longer the case, as women become aware of their rights as well as the broader range of opportunities available to them.

One of the most detailed studies of past and expected inheritance practices was carried out in western Santa Catarina, a farming region largely colonized by German-Brazilian families who migrated there from the 1930s from the neighboring state of Rio Grande do Sul (Abramovay et al. 1998). The most common practice in this region until recent years was for the youngest son to inherit the family homestead, although parents attempted to endow all sons with land. Under current conditions, the *minorato* system is weakening; only 13 percent of the fifty-three households studied reported this intention. Most fathers in this survey were unsure who would be willing to take over the family farm, but most expected to bequeath land and capital to their sons and daughters in equal shares. While parents predicted that their daughters would be as likely to inherit land as sons, daughters reported a much lower expectation of inheriting land than did sons. This region of southern Brazil has been characterized by a much higher rate of rural out-migration by young women than by young men. Ricardo Abramovay and his colleagues (ibid.: 74) argue that this is not due to more favorable employment conditions for women in the cities; rather the trend is a consequence of push factors. The difficulties of maintaining family farms under the present productive conditions (increased competition from foreign imports due to liberalization, for example) and relative land shortage, have encouraged parents to urge daughters to seek alternative opportunities elsewhere since it is no longer certain that they can aspire to become prosperous farm housewives. And while they expect to bequeath land to their daughters, patterns of socialization have not changed, so that daughters are rarely trained as are sons to become future farm managers, another factor contributing to the female exodus from rural areas.

Carneiro et al. (1998) argue the general point that as agriculture becomes less important as a source of peasant household reproduction, inheritance of land tends to become more equitable. This was the case in the municipality of Novo Friburgo in the state of Rio de Janeiro, which they studied. In this region, initially populated by Swiss-Italian and German colonists in the early nineteenth century, agriculture has been in decline for several decades. At the same time, land values have increased due to the development of the tourism industry. The prevailing inheritance practice now is equal inheritance shares among siblings, which has exacerbated the pattern of land fragmentation. It has also encouraged the development of the land market, as it is now common for land to be sold to outsiders (ibid.: 9).

Relatively little research has been carried out on inheritance patterns in the Northeast of Brazil, the least prosperous region of this vast country and the one characterized by the greatest racial diversity. In the state of Sergipe (municipality of Lagoa da Mata) in the Northeast, the customary pattern until recent decades was for women to be excluded from the inheritance of land, following the norm of patrilocality (Woortmann 1995: 275–75). Nonetheless, women were provisioned with a dowry at the time of marriage, usually consisting of calves. Since cattle-raising is a male activity in this area (in contrast to the South, where women are involved in dairy production), the wife's dowry would usually be incorporated into the husband's herd, so that women lost direct control over their inheritance. With a growing land shortage in this region, there has been a tendency toward the individualization of grazing rights as well as a switch toward endogenous marriage patterns, including cross-cousin marriage. In these new circumstances, women have begun to acquire land rights. However, Woortmann (ibid.: 278) argues that what appears to be a transformation in women's status is simply a change in the rules of inheritance: "Land continues in practice to be the domain of men. The woman, who is effectively traded among households in support of viri/patrilocal residency, is the instrument of land exchange between men." In other words, although women increasingly own land in their own names, they rarely control its use.[20]

Who Will Control the Family Farm?
Inheritance of Land by Wives

Whether a widow is legally able to maintain controlling ownership of the family farm upon the death of her husband depends on a number of factors: the marital regime under which the couple contracted marriage and the default regime governing in that country; whether the husband wrote a will, the share of his patrimony he may will freely, and whether he wills that share to her; whether the civil codes provide for widows automatically to receive a share of their husband's estate, irrespective of the provisions of his will; and in the case the husband dies intestate, whether wives are included in the first order of succession, receiving an equal share with children, or whether they receive only a marital share. Table 8.2 summarizes the factors influencing the possibility that a widow may retain controlling ownership of the family farm, with controlling ownership defined as more than a 50 percent share, so that she cannot easily be persuaded to sell the farm if she opposes such a decision. This would be most likely to occur in countries were the default regime is either full common property or participation in profits (since widows retain half the common property of the union).

In the best of circumstances—marriage under the common-property regime—widows are guaranteed ownership of half the family farm. In cases when the husband dies intestate, only in those countries where wives automatically form part of the first order of inheritance would they be guaranteed a controlling share of the property. The only country meeting these favorable conditions is El Salvador. Nonetheless, if the husband makes out a will, there is no provision requiring that the widow will inherit from his share of the estate, and thus no guarantee that she will end up with the controlling share of the farm.

Under the participation-in-profits regime the likelihood of widows retaining control of the family farm is even more variable for it depends on whether (1) they themselves brought land to the marriage; (2) the relative amount of land each spouse brought to the union; and (3) the relative amount of land that was jointly purchased by the couple rather than acquired individually. For simplicity, let us assume a situation in which all the land was jointly acquired and the widow can prove joint ownership. In this case she is in the best position in Bolivia and Peru, for in both countries wives are in the first order of inheritance should the husband die intestate, and they are protected in case the husband left a will. In these countries she

TABLE 8.2. Factors Influencing the Possibility of Wives Retaining Controlling Ownership of Family Farms

Country	Favorable Default Marital Regime	Protection of Wives under Wills	Wives in First Order of Intestate Succession
Bolivia	Participation in profits	Yes	Yes
Brazil	Participation in profits	No	Yes
Chile	Participation in profits	Marital Share	Marital Share
Colombia	Participation in profits	Marital Share	Marital Share
Costa Rica	No	No	Marital Share
Ecuador	Participation in profits	Marital Share	Marital Share
El Salvador	Common property	No	Yes
Guatemala	Participation in profits	No	Marital Share
Honduras	No	Marital Share	Marital Share
Mexico	Participation in profits	No	Marital Share
Nicaragua	No	Marital Share	Marital Share
Peru	Participation in profits	Yes	Yes

Sources: Tables 2.3 and 2.4 and authors' interviews.

always inherits a share equal to that of one of the children, which, added to her half of the family patrimony, would give her controlling ownership of the farm.

In Brazil the widow is in a less favorable position, for if the husband dies intestate she inherits a fixed one-quarter of his estate but only in usufruct and only as long as she does not remarry. While this may give her sufficient bargaining power to dissuade the children from breaking up and selling the family farm, it reduces her options relative to a situation in which she had full property rights. In practice, this system has contributed toward the view that widows only temporarily "hold" the farm for the children and has weakened their effective land rights even over their half of the common property.

In the other countries with a favorable default marital regime (Chile, Colombia, Guatemala, and Mexico), widows are guaranteed a marital share if their husband dies intestate, but the terms of this share vary. In Mexico if a wife has no property she inherits the same share as one child; otherwise she inherits the difference between the value of a child's share and that of her own estate. Under our assumptions (that the farm was jointly purchased, there being no other property), it is unlikely that the widow will gain any more than her half of the farm. In Chile the marital portion is more generous in that it may equal up to twice the size of a child's share. However, unless she renounces the *gananciales*, she only receives the difference between the *porción conjugal* and the value of her estate (including her 50 percent share of the common property). As these examples are meant to illustrate, the marital portion is primarily meant to take care of glaring inequalities in the value of each spouse's individual property.

Let us now assume that all of the land in the family was inherited by the husband, that the wife brought no land to the marriage, and that the couple purchased no other land together. In this case the common property of the couple (the *gananciales*) would consist only of the value of any improvements to the land that took place during the union. Only this value would automatically be divided in equal shares between the estate of the deceased and the widow. Let us further assume that the widow forsakes her share and thus is propertyless and eligible for the maximum share of the *porción conjugal*. In Colombia, Guatemala, and Mexico she would then inherit a share equal to that of a child; in Chile, she would be entitled to a share double that of a child, or if there were only one child, to a share equal to the child's. Under these conditions a widow might inherit one-half of the family farm only in the case that she has only one child; but in no case would she acquire a controlling share.

What these examples illustrate is that the inheritance provisions of most Latin American civil codes are antithetical to the possibility of wives retaining control over the family farm in case of widowhood. They demonstrate that the marital share was primarily conceived to ensure that the widow would not be left destitute in cases where there was great inequality between the spouses in terms of the property each had brought to the union. The *porción conjugal* was not intended to provide women with economic autonomy, our primary concern. In most countries whether widows are guaranteed a modicum of security in old age ultimately depends on social practices and the goodwill of judges, husbands, and children. In those countries with testamentary or near-testamentary freedom, husbands could will their wives full control of the family farm; in the other countries, husbands could will their wives controlling ownership if they so chose.

Given the differing implications of different marital regimes, and the differing rules governing inheritance by wives depending on whether the husband makes out a will, it should come as no surprise that, in practice, these rules are not well understood. Moreover, there has been scant research on local practices regarding inheritance of land by widows. The available data suggest that there is also a large gap between the legal norms protecting wives and local practices. In Bolivia and Peru, countries in which widows are in a relatively strong legal position vis-à-vis inheritance rights, usufruct rights within peasant and indigenous communities are governed by traditional customs and practices that are enforced by the governing board of *comuneros,* which is elected by and made up of male household heads. When a household head dies, the household's usufruct parcel formally reverts to the community, and it is up to the governing board to determine whether usufruct rights pass on to the wife or to the oldest son. In the case of peasant communities in highland Peru, "Traditionally, the right of widows to maintain a land parcel to sustain herself and her children has generally been respected; however, cases are found where widows have more restricted rights, such as access to less land than is usual, or the poorest land, or even where they are not given any land rights at all" (Coordinadora Nacional 1997: 3). There is also considerable heterogeneity in the traditions that govern the rights of widows within indigenous communities in Bolivia. It is a question of some debate whether in the Aymara communities that received land collectively under the agrarian reform, the widow inherits the family usufruct parcel upon the death of her spouse, or whether this depends upon her having a son capable of working the land.[21] Cases have been cited of widows losing their right to the family parcel, with this land reverting to the community (Salguero 1995).

In Mexico, as well, older women sometimes attest that "since land is collective, when the husband dies it reverts to the community and not the widow. This is not the case if there is a son who can inherit" the land (in Alberti et al. 1998: 33). Since 1940 the rules governing inheritance on the *ejidos* made wives and partners the preferential heirs if the *ejidatario* died intestate; if he left a will, he could designate either his wife or one of the children. Córdova Plaza (1999: 11) argues that up to thirty years ago it was primarily the oldest son who inherited the position of *ejidatario,* and thus the family patrimony, since this position could only be held by one member per family. She argues that one of the main changes in inheritance patterns is that wives and partners are increasingly being designated the main heir upon death of the *ejidatario.* She studied an *ejido* in Tuzamapán, Veracruz, where women made up 24 percent of the members and virtually all inherited this position; the great majority inherited their position from their husbands upon being widowed. She attributes this change to a growing recognition of women's role in agriculture—accentuated in this region of Veracruz by a switch from sugar cane to coffee production: "wives have become the preferential heir of agrarian rights and this has favored her becoming the formal head of household upon the death of her husband, often concentrating all of his lands in her hands. While eventually her heirs will be sons, the new arrangement has meant that widows are in control of the family resources for a certain period of time. . . . In these circumstances, the titling of a parcel to a woman is not just a formal affair, but rather, gives her real prerogatives. Once a widow is in possession of the agrarian certificate, she effectively assumes control of family production. Given her knowledge of agricultural work and crop management, women are capable of working, hiring peons, supervising the means of production and contracting with agro-enterprises" (ibid.).

Other case studies emphasize how difficult it has been to change traditional inheritance practices that favor sons to the benefit of widows. Dorien Brunt's (1992: 82–99) research in Guadalajara demonstrates how women's land rights are often challenged by male relatives. In addition, if faced with opposition, women find it difficult to claim land rights successfully for they have to convince those in power of the legitimacy of their claims. This means using the right arguments—such as not claiming land rights for themselves as women, but rather on behalf of their sons as future household heads—and mastering and manipulating patron-client relationships on par with men.

Quantitative evidence on current inheritance practices is available for 14,099 *ejidatarios* who filed their wills with the Agrarian Reform Secretariat during the years 1993–1995. As Table 8.3 shows, *ejidatarios* were just as likely to will their land to wives or partners as to sons.[22] Since the data by gender are incomplete (other relatives not being specified by sex), we cannot conclude that women are currently favored over men in inheritance provisions. Still, the evidence does suggest that women in the future will have greater access to land in their own names than is currently the practice among certified *ejidatarios*. However, the great majority of these women will have direct control over land for only a relatively short period —during widowhood—in effect making them a bridge in the transmission of land between generations.

Particularly discouraging in terms of gender equity are the comparative data in Table 8.3 by generations: sons are designated the heir in 38.8 percent of the cases as compared to only 8.8 percent for daughters, a more than four-to-one advantage in favor of men. While *ejidatarias* also prefer to designate sons as heirs, they are more likely to designate daughters as heirs

TABLE 8.3.   Registered Heirs of *Ejidatarios,* 1993–1995, Mexico (percentage)

Females		
Wives/partners	38.5	
Daughters	8.8	
Granddaughters	0.4	
Subtotal		47.7
Males		
Sons	38.8	
Grandsons	2.5	
Subtotal		41.3
Other relatives		10.0
Non-relatives		1.0
		100.0
		(N = 14,099)

Source: Compiled from Valenzuela and Robles (1996: 49–51), based on Sistema Informativo del Registro Agrario Nacional (RAN).

than are male *ejidatarios;* 19 percent of *ejidatarias* designated daughters as their heirs as compared with only 5 percent of the *ejidatarios* (Valenzuela and Robles 1995: 52). As Table 8.3 also shows, the gender inequality is reproduced in the third generation, with grandsons more likely to be designated beneficiaries than are granddaughters.

A representative sample survey of 515 *ejidatarias* undertaken in 1998 revealed that the majority were widows who had inherited their land from their husbands (Robles et al. 2000: 59). Of those who had made inheritance plans and expected to bequeath their land to only one heir (as required by *ejido* regulations), there was a strong male preference with 51.5 percent designating a son, 19.8 percent a daughter, 15.8 percent another family member, and 2.8 percent a non-family member; 5.5 percent favored their spouse or companion. Conforming to the case study evidence, there was a strong preference for the youngest son, followed by the oldest, and then any other son. The youngest daughter was favored among the daughters, although she still fell behind any son in the ranking. This survey also revealed that women were more likely to have inherited land when it was bequeathed to more than one heir, a practice that is technically illegal. Of the 402 *ejidatarias* who inherited their land parcel, one-quarter did so as a result of a partible inheritance (ibid.: 41). Over one-third of these *ejidatarias* planned to will their land to more than one heir. Daughters represented over one-third of the beneficiaries in these cases as compared to only 20 percent when only one heir was planned (ibid.: 59), suggesting that partible inheritance favors gender equity.

Turning to Chile, the only evidence on inheritance by wives is from Rebolledo's (1995) archival study in two municipalities. She found that by the 1930s in both Santa Cruz and San Felipe, men and women tended to favor their spouse in wills. The most marked change was in Santa Cruz, where in earlier decades fathers had favored their eldest sons. She concludes that the tendency to bequeath land to wives reflects the greater recognition that women acquired over time for their potential role as farm managers (ibid.: 175). This change in favor of spouses could also be due to the increase in life expectancy among both men and women over the course of the twentieth century.

With respect to Brazil, Carneiro (2000: 4–5) argues that wives are excluded from the inheritance of land in three ways: because they do not inherit from their fathers; because their work in family agriculture is seen only as an extension of their role as wives; and because they are not socially recognized as capable of being the head of a productive unit. Thus even though wives are automatically entitled to half of the common property of the household, they rarely exercise this right, with management and control of the family farm passing instead to sons. Also, according to Nobre (1998: 58), "When widows receive land they usually don't assume control and administration of the property. This responsibility passes to their second husband, to the eldest son or sometimes the family unit of production is broken up." However, participants in the 1998 Workshop on Gender and Land Rights in the state of Pernambuco[23] reported that it is becoming more common for the family farm to be managed by the widow upon the death of her husband, or for at least half of the land (that which corresponds to her half of the common property) to remain under her control until her death. Obviously, this is an area of inquiry worthy of further research, as are the potentially contrasting inheritance practices in northeastern and southern Brazil.

THIS REVIEW OF inheritance practices in six countries, besides demonstrating their great heterogeneity, illustrates the large gap that often exists between the egalitarian norms of most Latin American civil codes with regard to the inheritance rights of children and local practices governing the inheritance of land. Overall, inheritance of land in Latin America favors sons, even where bilateral inheritance practices are the norm. This pattern was supported, until recently, by patri- and virilocal marital residence, the logic of peasant household reproduction, and gender socialization and stereotyping that privileges men's work in agriculture, socially legitimizing inequality in land inheritance in favor of men. With regard to ethnicity, it is difficult to discern on the basis of the existing literature whether bilateral inheritance is any more closely associated with indigenous communities in comparison with those made up by the white or mestizo peasantry, although bilateral inheritance is more common in Peru and Ecuador than in Bolivia, Mexico, Chile, or Brazil. Moreover, it is only in the Andean region that vestiges of parallel inheritance systems are found, alluding to a past where perhaps the distribution of land was more equitable between the sexes. In the Andean case bilateral inheritance of land is also supported by the greater visibility and social recognition of women's work in agriculture. Working against it have been patri- and virilocality,[24] and patriarchal forms of representation within indigenous communities that grant community membership and thus decisions over land rights only to male household heads. In Mexico, institutional factors (testamentary freedom combined with *ejido* regulations prohibiting partible inheritance) also strongly support patrilineal inheritance norms; and, of the four countries with large indigenous populations, Mexico is the one most strongly characterized by patrilineal land inheritance.

It is difficult to identify ancestral inheritance practices given the many forces of change that have impacted for centuries upon indigenous communities. It is also difficult to gauge the influence of gender-equitable civil codes in fostering more equitable inheritance patterns over time, since other factors have also been at work, such as growing land scarcity, that may also alter the logic of peasant household reproduction. Nonetheless, such factors as increased schooling, internal migration, and integration of local peasant economies into the national economy have fostered greater awareness of national legal norms, contributing toward more equitable inheritance for all children. Without doubt, one of the factors precipitating change has been a relative land shortage, but the evidence suggests that this may work in two directions. Increasing land pressure over time may provoke a change from a system of equitable inheritance to concentration of land under the male line, as suggested in the case of the Aymara on the Bolivian altiplano as well as among the Chilean peasantry. At the same time, growing land scarcity may force families to engage in multiple income-generating activities, and to rely less on farm activities. Data from Peru, Ecuador, Bolivia, Mexico, and Brazil all support the proposition that as agriculture becomes less important as the primary source of peasant household reproduction, inheritance of land becomes more equitable.

With respect to the impact of migration, the evidence is mixed. Greater opportunities for female migration undoubtedly favor inheritance of land by sons, as reported in Chile. On the other hand, the spread of schooling, growth of alternative employment opportunities, and migration by both young men and women may reduce gender bias. The most important factors in who inherits land may become who wants to remain in the community and farm, or who contributes the most through remittances to parents' security in old age. Similarly, demographic change in support of smaller rural families has reduced the number of potential heirs, a factor probably also contributing to gender equality. Under these conditions it is more difficult to justify male privilege in land inheritance and to deny opportunities for women to accumulate capital or become agriculturalists. Where bilateral inheritance has predominated, growing land scarcity within peasant communities has also prompted a change from patri- or virilocality to uxorilocal or neo-local residency. This, in turn, has been associated with enhanced bargaining power for women (since wives are not under the direct or indirect control of their in-laws) and a subsequent tendency toward greater gender equality in inheritance of land. But these propositions require further research.

With regard to the inheritance rights of spouses, the available evidence suggests that, until recently, it was only in special circumstances that widows inherited the family patrimony of land. Indigenous communities seem to be even less generous to widows than mestizo peasant communities more influenced by national legal norms, but this subject also merits further study. Another topic worthy of further empirical work is the relationship between different marital regimes and formal inheritance norms in fostering greater or lesser land ownership by widows and, particularly, their greater effective control over land. The material analyzed here supports the proposition, argued by Bina Agarwal (1994a and 1994b), that access to land is not the equivalent of control over land. In many situations women's inheritance of land simply serves as a vehicle for land to pass to brothers, husbands, or sons.

The data for Chile and Brazil, in particular, suggest that whether women are able to exercise control over land is largely related to whether they are viewed as potential agriculturalists. In the other countries women play a larger role in agricultural production, and there is greater evidence that they may manage their own inheritance of land and, in case of widowhood, become the principal manager of the family farm. For women to exercise effective control over land requires a number of factors. To start with, they must be aware of their rights, not only with respect to marital regimes and inheritance but as citizens with rights to manage their own economic affairs and to make demands upon the state. Moreover, for women to become effective farm managers might require not only a change in socialization, so that women are trained and view themselves as agriculturalists, but also changes in the practices of the state, so that women farmers are supported appropriately, a topic taken up in the next chapter.

Although rural women are often unaware of their inheritance rights, and even "resist comprehending that there is a law which protects their right to inheritance,"[25] organized rural women throughout Latin America are increasingly becoming more cognizant of these rights and demanding them, whether as daughters or wives. Moreover, where civil codes are unfavorable to inheritance by wives, rural women's organizations are beginning to press for their reform. At the First National Meeting of Rural Women in Chile in 1985, organized by the Women's Department of the National Peasant Commission (CNC), among the main demands was reform of inheritance and property legislation (CNC 1985; GIA 1985: 9). One of the main concerns in Mexico with regard to the changes in Article 27 of the Mexican constitution regarding the *ejidos* was the abrogation of the inheritance provisions that protected wives. Since 1992 *ejidatarios* may freely choose their heir, with this choice not limited to wives or a child as was the case in the past, a change denounced by the Women's Commission of the Permanent Agrarian Council (CAP) (Lara Flores 1994: 85), among other groups, such as at meetings of indigenous women in Chiapas. The EZLN has included this demand in its position papers: "that women must be included in tenancy and inheritance of land" (Rojas 1995: 203, 251; Stephen 1998: 150).

During regional meetings leading up to the 1995 World Conference on Women in Beijing, Bolivian rural women also voiced their discontent with the discrimination they faced with respect to inheritance. They denounced both the dispossession of widows from communal lands and the preference given to sons in inheritance: "When it comes to inheritance of these lands from parents and spouses, we want to have property rights over these" (Salguero: 48). The Beijing conference helped focus attention on women's land rights in general, and inheritance rights in particular. In most countries, the Platform for Action adopted at Beijing was widely distributed by the national women's offices, serving as the basis for post-conference activities organized primarily by NGOs. In Peru, for example, at a post-Beijing conference held in Cajamarca, one of the main demands of the peasant women leaders in attendance was compliance with Peru's legal codes, so that all children, male and female, could inherit land equally from their parents (de Jong 1997). In this fashion, the demand for equality of inheritance rights among men and women is beginning to enter the public discourse.

nine

Women Property Owners: Land Titling, Inheritance, and the Market

[Señora Rosa] is very upset because the land titling regularization project is for female household heads. She has a husband and thus does not qualify under this category. She's furious she has a husband; she says he's worthless to her and can't accept that because of him there will be a delay in getting the title. . . . What is clear is that the land title is much more important to her than her husband.[1]

ONE OF THE PILLARS of neo-liberal thinking about the future of the agricultural sector is the necessity of providing security of tenure to producers. This has been addressed in two ways: through the formal end to agrarian reform efforts involving the expropriation of land; and by land titling projects and efforts to modernize cadastral systems and land registries. In the 1990s almost every single Latin American country was undertaking land titling programs of some sort, with most of these projects partly financed by the World Bank or the Inter-American Development Bank (IDB) (Echeverría 1998: 5–8). The focus on land titling activities stems, in part, from the large number of smallholders in Latin America who do not hold formal titles to their land, particularly the agrarian reform beneficiaries of previous decades. In most countries land titling and registration procedures have been costly, bureaucratic, and time-consuming, discouraging land transactions from being officially recorded.[2] Also, the lack of cadastral surveys has often led to multiple and overlapping land claims, exacerbating conflicts over land.[3]

Foremost among the reasons for the land titling programs has been their economic rationale, which is three-fold (Feder and Feeny 1991; Binswanger et al., 1995: 2719–20; Melmed-Sanjak 1998). First, it is hoped that security of tenure will stimulate investment and thus improve agricultural productivity, increasing agricultural production. A secure title is expected to lead to greater investment since it increases the probability that the farmer will reap the benefits of capital accumulation.[4] Moreover, in order to obtain credit from commercial banking institutions farmers must have clear titles to their properties, which serve as collateral against loans. It is the combination of increased ability to secure capital and farmers' greater incentive to do so that is expected to increase their long-term capital investments and use of variable inputs, leading to productivity gains (Dorner 1992: 77). One of the factors that has made land titling such a pressing issue in the neo-liberal period is that the state has largely withdrawn from the provision of subsidized credit to farmers, making the agricultural sector more dependent upon the private banking system.

Second, it is expected that land titling programs will fuel a more "effective" land market, making it easier for land to be bought and sold as well as rented. Land titling and registration enhances the transparency of transactions and improves the process of transferring and marketing land since it reduces uncertainty or the risk of challenges to land rights. Third, a precondition for unused land to be put on the market is an effective system of land taxation; without it there is less incentive for landowners to offer land for sale, particularly in countries prone to high rates of inflation. The ability to design an effective and equitable system of land taxation depends, in turn, on the existence of a rural cadastre, a modern registry system, and on the majority of land being titled and registered.

According to its advocates, an effective land market should result in the transfer of land from less to more efficient farmers and should favor small farmers.[5] Skeptics, on the other hand, worry whether land titling and the fueling of the land market will lead to accelerated depeasantization and further land concentration (Carter and Mesbah 1990; 1993; Carter and Zegarra 1997). This outcome might result from increased peasant indebtedness brought by their greater reliance on markets or because, if long-term credit is unavailable, the resource-poor will be unable to compete in the land market on the same terms as other buyers. There is also concern that for the land market strategy to be an effective means of reducing rural poverty, *all* of its elements must be in place: not just formal land titles but also the rural cadastre and land registry system, an effective taxation system, and the availability of long-term credit at reasonable terms. Otherwise, governments will be diverting scarce resources (and increasing their external indebtness) for programs, which if only implemented partially, will not have the expected pay-offs.[6]

In many ways, the land titling programs that began in the 1990s represent the defining moment in terms of property rights, for in a number of countries these programs are being carried out on a massive scale. Once properties are measured and mapped, and titles are registered, land ownership will be more difficult to contest. Hence the urgency of our main question: To what extent are women's property rights being respected as ownership of land is formally demarcated and registered? Of particular concern is whether the gender-progressive norms of many of the agrarian codes of the 1990s are being taken into account in the implementation of land titling projects. Is land that was jointly acquired by a husband and wife being jointly titled in the name of the couple? Are titling procedures respecting individual inheritance of land by wives or husbands, or only ceding one title per household and issuing it in the name of the household head? Are widows receiving preferential rights to family lands?

Gender Outcomes of Land Titling Projects

Gender-disaggregated data is available for six land-titling projects—in Honduras, Colombia, Mexico, Peru, Ecuador, and Chile. These countries differ as to whether they have adopted measures favoring gender equity in their agrarian legislation. Both Honduras and Colombia provide for the joint allocation and titling of land to couples, although in Honduras such is voluntary; Colombia also gives priority to female household heads in state programs. In Mexico, Peru, and Ecuador recent agrarian legislation purports to be gender neutral and gives no specific attention to women's land rights. In Ecuador, nonetheless, joint titling of land to couples was adopted as the norm in a rural development project in twelve zones of the country. In Chile female household heads were prioritized in its titling program, but no provisions were made for the joint titling of land to couples.

Honduras's titling project for public lands during the 1980s was a precursor for broader-scale efforts through the region. During the 1960s and

1970s, the main way the landless or land-poor in Honduras got access to land was not through the agrarian reform but rather by squatting on public land. This was facilitated by a 1973 decree that validated previous land occupations, allowing individuals to possess and use national lands for agricultural purposes without formally applying to the state for permission. A subsequent 1975 decree transferred the right of municipalities to allocate lands within their domain (known as ejidal land) to the National Agrarian Institute (INA). Thereafter, INA was charged with the administration of national and ejidal lands and given responsibility for assigning private ownership rights to individuals. Nonetheless, formal titling of these lands was a low priority during the agrarian reform period; it was estimated that by the early 1980s over 60 percent of the agricultural land in Honduras was being worked without a formal title (Stanfield et al. 1990).

In 1982 a pilot project, the Land Titling Project for Small Farmers, PTT (Proyecto de Titulación de Tierra para los Pequeños Productores), was launched with support from USAID to title forty thousand farmers in seven departments of the country. The rationale for this project has much in common with current land-titling initiatives. Insecurity of tenure was considered to be a major constraint on agricultural development, and it was hoped that issuing formal land titles would improve farmers' access to credit, increase investment and productivity, and enhance the efficiency of the land market (Stanfield et al. 1990). The project targeted squatters whose parcels were between five and fifty hectares in size, although smaller parcels planted with coffee were also eligible. Government titling and cadastral services were provided free of charge. Project beneficiaries, however, were required to purchase their parcel from INA, but at a price usually below the going market rate.[7] They automatically received a twenty-year, interest-free mortgage to do so (ibid.).

Between 1982 and 1989 some 32,029 titles were issued, representing around 22 percent of the parcels delineated on public land in six departments (Stanfield et al. 1990: Table 2). Up through the late 1980s, data on the sex of the beneficiaries were not collected. A preliminary study of the gender implications of the titling project in the two departments where the project had been initiated (Santa Barbara and Comayagua) attempted to enumerate the sex of the beneficiaries from the names listed in the property registry. This analysis revealed that only 16.7 percent of the titles were issued to women (León, Prieto, and Salazar 1987: 38–39).

Honduras's 1992 Law for the Modernization of Agriculture allowed those who could prove that they had illegally occupied national or ejidal land for at least three years to claim these parcels, purchasing them from INA (Thorpe 1995). A new program was subsequently launched, known as the PTMT (Programa de Titulación Masiva de Tierras). Under this initiative beneficiaries also receive an interest-free mortgage to purchase their land from the state. The main change in the regulations is that land-titling beneficiaries may now sell these mortgages to third parties or use their titles to secure a loan; that is, beneficiaries are no longer under the tutelage of INA until they fully pay for their land (Melmed-Sanjak 1998: 42). The modernization law also established that public lands were to be allocated in a nondiscriminatory manner to either men or women and that such lands could be jointly titled to a couple, although only if the couple requested it.

Most studies informed by a gender analysis stress the difficulties women face in participating in the titling program on the same terms as men and in being titled land either in their own names or jointly with their spouses or partners. Given the predominant gendered division of labor, women are not taken seriously as agriculturalists. Their capacity to combine productive and reproductive work is questioned, as is their ability to manage wage workers and be efficient producers. Women's low level of independent income is another problem, for PTT functionaries question their ability to pay for the land or meet mortgage payments (León et al. 1987; Rosales 1994: 51–52, 56–57). A 1996 INA report noted that one of the main factors preventing women from being granted land titles under the titling program was that women were rarely aware of their rights to be titled land—either jointly with their spouses, when they had acquired the land together, or in their own names, when they had inherited the parcel or worked it directly. There has been little publicity regarding the rights of women under the Law of Modernization, partly because of the lack of consensus within civil society on whether women should even have land rights (Acosta and Moreno 1996: 4).

The available data indicate that efforts at joint titling of land to couples have been extremely meager. Between September 1995 and May 1997, only twenty-six titles (covering 689 hectares) had been registered as jointly titled property in the whole country.[8] Besides the fact that joint titling is voluntary, other obstacles make this practice unlikely. First, the application form for titling services does not even provide space for the applicant to list his marital status nor the name of his wife or partner. Second, if a couple lives in a consensual union, this relationship must be officially registered, a process that is both costly and time consuming. According to an

INA official, "If a couple is interested in having both names on a title, taking land as a family patrimony, the application must include a marriage certificate or a certificate that the couple lives in a consensual union. We have proposed a reform to make it easier for couples who live together to be jointly titled land. The application forms are also being changed to include the names of both the man and the woman."[9]

The data nonetheless suggest that the proportion of women benefiting from the land-titling initiative continues to increase moderately. According to a World Bank (1996c, Annex B: 2) report, between 1982 and 1995 women were 20 percent of the sixty thousand beneficiaries of the titling effort. In one region where land titling was carried out massively during the period 1994–96, women represented 23 percent of those receiving land titles (Acosta and Moreno 1996: 2). As Table 9.1 shows, of those who registered their titles to formerly public lands between 1995 and 1997, women represented 25 percent.[10] These data indicate that women have fared significantly better under the land titling program than under the agrarian reform of the 1970s and 1980s, where they represented less than 4 percent of the beneficiaries (see Table 3.2).

The rather impressive difference in the share of female beneficiaries under these two state initiatives may reflect a combination of the following factors: (1) an increase in the number of female household heads in rural areas; (2) a slow but growing acceptance over time that women are agriculturalists and perhaps less social opposition to recognizing women as individual farmers than accepting them as cooperative members (*asentamientos* having been the primary form of land distribution in the 1970s); and (3) the fact that rural women have increasingly demonstrated their desire for land, both by squatting on national lands and subsequently demanding that such land be titled in their names.

Nonetheless, the fact that a relatively high proportion of women have been beneficiaries of the titling program may be a statistical artifact, a re-

TABLE 9.1.   Titles Registered by Sex, Non-Reformed Sector, 1995–1997,
Honduras

	Number	Hectares	Average Size (has.)
Women	27,378 (25%)	115,678 (21%)	4.23
Men	82,784 (75%)	442,635 (79%)	5.35
Total	110,162 (100%)	558,313 (100%)	5.07

Source: Compiled by the authors from data provided by the División de Titulación de Tierras, Instituto Nacional Agrario, Tegucigalpa, January 2001.

sult of the arbitrary manner in which the project has been implemented at the local level. Evidence for this hypothesis is provided by a detailed study of the titling project in the department of Santa Barbara. Kees Jansen and Esther Roquas (1998) show how arbitrary rules and practices sometimes had unintended consequences. In this region the PTT worked with the rule that each person could be issued only one title, and that one title could not contain more than two or three parcels. Official INA policy was supposedly that one title could contain up to ten parcels, but since INA brigade members implementing the project were evaluated according to the number of titles they issued per day, it was in their interest to combine only a few parcels per title. This caused problems since land in this community is highly fragmented. The brigade members attempted to solve this by "advising people to title remaining parcels in the names of other household or family members, for example, a wife, son, brother or *compadre*" (ibid: 95). This practice undoubtedly increased the number of women reported as beneficiaries of the land titling program, and thus could have inflated their numbers.

On the other hand, Jansen and Roquas also report that some women lost legal claim to their own parcel when it was titled, for convenience, under the name of the husband. Moreover, in this region INA functionaries did not accept joint owners, forcing couples or siblings owning land together to title it in only one name. Land conflicts increased when the titled owner decided to sell the land without the consent of the other owner, which he or she was now legally entitled to do. According to Jansen and Roquas (1998: 96), "After receiving the INA title, some women considered these parcels to be their own property, and took control of decisions (such as renting, selling or refusing to sell, transferring to children, and so on) which went against the wishes of the original holder" (ibid.: 96).

A bill that would require joint titling to couples of public land has been pending in the congress for a number of years,[11] and this provision is one of the proposed changes in Honduras's draft Plan for Gender Equity in Agriculture (1999–2002) (PRO-EGEDAGRO 1999). Mandatory joint titling was finally approved as part of the Law for Equality of Opportunities for Women in April 2000 (Honduras 2000: Article 73). Mandatory joint titling of land to couples is particularly critical to assuring women's land rights in Honduras because the default marital regime in this country is that of separation of property. If a land parcel acquired by a couple is titled in the husband's name, that parcel becomes his individual property. It is his to dispose of as he sees fit; his wife's signature is not required to rent or sell the land, and he may will the land to whomever he pleases. While the inheritance provisions of Honduras's civil code are unfavorable to wives (they provide for full testamentary freedom), wives and partners have some protection under the Law of Modernization when an owner who has been titled public lands dies intestate. In this case the wife or partner is the preferred heir. Nonetheless, it is likely that under the land-titling program in Honduras, until recently a good number of rural women were being dispossessed of their land rights.

Since the start of Colombia's agrarian reform process in the early 1960s, the agrarian reform agency, INCORA, has been more successful in titling land on the agricultural frontier—lands settled both spontaneously and through government-sponsored colonization projects—than in land redistribution. Up through the mid-1990s, INCORA titled 12 million hectares of national land (known as *baldíos*) but acquired only 1.3 million hectares through expropriation and purchase for redistribution (Fajardo and Mondragón 1997: 52). As part of its efforts to modernize its agrarian programs, the government launched a new land-titling program in 1995 known as "Titular."[12] The idea is to streamline and better coordinate the activities of the different agencies involved in the regularization of property rights, including the modernization of the cadastre and property-registry systems. In addition, many of the activities involved in these systems are to be privatized and decentralized in hopes of improving their efficiency. Supported by a $38.5 million loan from the IDB, this program is meant to provide security of tenure through mass land-titling activities, titling a hundred thousand rural properties by 2001.[13]

It was not until 1996 that data on the sex of the beneficiaries and on individual versus joint titling of land to couples began to be collected in the titling program. In the three years for which complete data are available, couples accounted for 28.4 percent of the land titles issued, and individual women for 27.9 percent, as Table 9.2 shows. If we compare these figures with those on beneficiaries in the agrarian reform program, we see that women were a relatively larger share of those persons individually titled national lands compared with those allocated land (the share of women beneficiaries in the latter program being only 13 percent). This might reflect a much higher incidence of unprotected single women or female household heads in the zones of recent settlement than in the rest of the country and, thus, compliance by INCORA with this relatively new provision of the agrarian code. On the other hand, joint titling to couples is a much less frequent phenomenon in the titling than in the agrarian reform

TABLE 9.2. Titling of Public Lands by Sex, 1996–1997 and 1999, Colombia

	Number	Hectares	Average Size (has.)
Women	6,153 (27.9%)	127,606 (23.0%)	20.7
Men	9,620 (43.7%)	261,806 (47.2%)	27.2
Couples	6,247 (28.4%)	165,166 (29.8%)	26.4
Total	22,020 (100%)	554,578 (100%)	25.2

Source: Provided to the authors by the Office of Planning and Regional Offices, Subgerencia de Ordenamiento Social, INCORA, Bogotá, July 2000.

Note: In 1998 10,435 titles were issued for 378,798 hectares, and individual women were 32.5 percent of the beneficiaries; unfortunately, data were not reported on individual men or on joint titles.

program (28.4 versus 57 percent). It is difficult to explain these different patterns, which may also only be the result of incomplete reporting. Nonetheless, the data do indicate considerable headway in Colombia in implementing gender-progressive change.

The great majority of Mexican *ejidos* have opted to join the process of individual land titling. As of March 1998, of 27,144 *ejidos* 81 percent were participating in the *ejido* rights certification program known as PROCEDE (Programa de Certificación de Derechos Ejidales y Titulación de Solares) ("Estadísticas sobre el avance de Procede" 1998: n.p.). As of January 1999, 18,031 *ejidos* (66 percent of the total) had completed the certification process and 2.2 million *ejidatarios* and other individuals had received titles to individual land parcels, communal lands, or urban plots within the *ejidos*, encompassing 40 million hectares (Robles et al. 2000: 19).

Privatization of the *ejido* actually involves two steps. The first consists of certification by PROCEDE, which allows an *ejidatario* to rent his or her land, to give it in usufruct to a third party as a guarantee against a loan, or to sell it to another *ejidatario*. Such land remains part of the *ejido* regime and is subject to its regulations. The second step in the process, the conversion to full private property (*dominio pleno*), requires a two-thirds majority vote of the *ejido* membership and the filing of the *ejido* plan with the National Agrarian Registry. This process involves a number of costs, whereas the certification process is free. These costs may explain why few *ejidos* have converted to full private property (where land can be freely sold to third parties); another impediment is that once former *ejido* land is privately held, it is subject to taxation. However, without *dominio pleno* the landowner cannot seek credit from the private banking system.[14] In any case, it seems that agricultural entrepreneurs have favored renting land rather than buying it, particularly in northern Mexico. The most

TABLE 9.3. Titling in the *Ejido* Sector by Form of Holding and Sex, 1993–1998, Mexico

	Women		Men		Total	
	No.	%	No.	%	No.	%
Ejidatarios	213,410	(17.6)	999,177	(82.4)	1,212,587	(100)
Posesionario	38,856	(22.4)	134,749	(77.6)	173,605	(100)
Avecindados	148,868	(30.6)	338,016	(69.4)	486,884	(100)
Total	401,134	(21.4)	1,471,942	(78.6)	1,873,076	(100)

Source: Compiled from "Estadísticas," *Estudios Agrarios: Revista de la Procudaría*, no. 10 (1998): n.p., in http://www.pa.gob.mx/publica/pu071011.htm, accessed 19 January 2000.

frequent legal sales have been of *ejidos* located near urban areas or the beaches, which represent prime real estate.[15]

The certification process has produced reliable data for the first time on the gender composition of *ejido* members and others with land rights on the *ejidos*. As Table 9.3 shows, data for 1.5 million individuals who had completed the certification process as of early 1998 revealed that women made up 21.4 percent of the beneficiaries. Women, nonetheless, represented a lower share of those titled land as *ejidatarias* (17.6 percent)—those who have voice and vote in the *ejido*—as compared to those titled land plots who are not *ejido* members, the *posesionarios*[16] (22.4 percent), or those titled urban house plots, the *avencidados* (29.8 percent). In absolute terms, the majority of the 401,134 women who received titles were *ejidatarias* (53 percent), followed by *avecindadas* (37 percent) and *posesionarias* (10 percent).[17]

In terms of the regional distribution of *ejidatarias,* women constituted a higher share than the national average in the states of Baja California, Puebla, Morelos, Michoacán, Nayarit, Tlaxcala, Sonora, and Sinaloa, representing over 20 percent. They were considerably underrepresented in the Yucatán peninsula (in the states of Campeche, Quitana Roo, and the Yucatán), where they amounted to less than 10 percent of the *ejidatarios* (Robles et al. 2000: 20). On average *ejidatarias* were titled less land than *ejidatarios:* 7.9 as compared with 9.0 hectares; the majority of women (53 percent) received a title to less than five hectares of land (Valenzuela and Robles 1996: 40–41).[18] *Ejidatarias* were also generally older than their male counterparts, 68 percent being over fifty and 36 percent over sixty-five years of age, as compared to 54 percent and 23 percent, respectively, for the men (Robles et al. 2000: 21). A nationally representative sample survey of 516 *ejidatarias* carried out in 1998 revealed that 43 percent were widows and 41 percent were married, with the remainder being single, divorced, or in consensual unions (ibid.: 47). Almost two-thirds of the *ejidatarias* were economically active, one-fourth being the principal or sole income earner in their households. With respect to land use, 6.6 percent farmed their parcel alone while 40.5 percent did so with the help of family members. In 22.7 percent of the cases the land was worked by other family members; in 25 percent it was sharecropped, rented, or loaned out; and in only 5.2 percent was it not worked at all (ibid.: 64). The majority of those sharecropping the lands of *ejidatarias* were also family members. These data suggest that, contrary to what is often reported, a relatively high share of *ejidatarias* are actively involved in working or managing their plot of land.

The Mexican land-titling process stands out for its scale (involving approximately half of Mexico's land surface) and the rapidity with which it has been carried out, particularly given the conflicts it has reportedly unleashed.[19] It is interesting that in the whole process no serious discussion arose about whether, in this defining moment for private property rights, land should be jointly titled in the name of couples. That this is the case largely reflects the previous terms of *ejido* membership: although land was considered to be family patrimony, only one member of the family could be the official *ejido* member, with effective land rights. Thus the individualization of land rights proceeded with this practice largely unchallenged, although in certain cases it may violate married women's property rights under Mexico's civil code.[20]

In Peru the Special Project for Titling (PETT, Proyecto Especial de Titulación y Catastro Rural) is designed to bring order and stability to the land-tenure situation through the completion of a full rural cadastre and the listing of all properties in the National Land Registry. Begun in 1992, the project was initially intended to provide titles to the thousands of agrarian reform beneficiaries who had never completely legalized their situation. With a $21 million loan from the IADB, the project was extended to include the four million or so land parcels lacking titles; the aim became to "sanitize" one million land titles by the year 2000 (del Castillo 1997b: 69), a target that was largely met.[21] This project purports to be gender neutral. According to the vice-minister of agriculture, "there is no discrimination against women" and no further measures are necessary to pursue gender equity.[22] The attainment of gender equity has not been an objective of Peruvian agrarian legislation. Nor has there been any kind of gender sensitivity training among ministry officials or functionaries implementing the PETT. Moreover, national-level data by sex of the beneficiaries are not being collected.

According to lawyer Ivonne Macassi León (1996b: 38), women landowners are often at a disadvantage when it comes to land titling, given their monolingualism, low levels of literacy, and lack of legal documentation. In order to participate in the titling program one must have *capacidad civil,* that is, be registered to vote (Millones 1996). Macassi León argues that the PETT program recognizes women's right to land when they are the direct producers, "but only after asking a woman, Where is your husband? Where is your son?"[23] Even though land is being titled by parcels and not the farm unit, one concern is that women who are not household heads will lose their ownership rights to parcels they have inherited. According to an official of the Ministry of Agriculture in the Department of Cajamarca, "Among the peasantry it is the man who assumes all responsibility with regard to land tenancy except for exceptional cases, where the woman —whether because they are single, widowed, a single mother, or because of the incapacity of the man—assumes responsibility" (Millones 1996). However, this observation may only reflect the predilections of government functionaries. Fieldwork undertaken in this region in the mid-1970s revealed that women were very much involved in the administration of their land parcels (Deere 1990).

A second concern is that, until recently, no attention had been given to the joint titling of land to couples. Until 1996 applicants for land-titling services were not even asked their marital status.[24] PETT officials then realized that in order for these titles to be entered in the public registry—and thus conform to Peru's civil code—it was necessary to report this information. As a result, the application form for land-titling services was revised and new instructions were issued, as follows:

- If the applicant is married, the wife's name should be included;
- If the applicant lives in a consensual union, without any impediment to marriage, the partner's name should be included;
- If the applicant lives in a consensual union and has an impediment to marriage, but he has children with this partner who also lives on the farm, then their names should be included.[25]

Beginning in 1997 land titles were to include the name of the applicant and his wife or partner. At the 1997 Seminar on Gender and Landed Property,[26] there was agreement that in the case of marriages, the names of both spouses were now appearing on the titles; that is, joint titling was becoming the norm for married couples in most regions. But there was considerable disagreement over whether titles were being issued to couples in consensual unions. Some participants argued that the problem is that people in consensual unions report that they are single, since that is the marital status listed on their identity document. In such cases, the name of the companion would not even be asked when the form was filled out. Others argued that the problem was that those living in consensual unions must show proof that they have lived together for two years and do not have impediments to marriage (such as already being married to someone else). Few couples in consensual unions have such documentation, and it is expensive and time consuming to obtain. In order to get around this problem, a lawyer with the PETT reported that in the titling program in the department of Lima, "We opted to declare people who lived together as co-property owners . . . that is, we got around the problem of proving that you were in a consensual union by not declaring it and writing down that they were single . . . and the documentation supported this marital status. We then declared them to be co-property owners."[27]

The participants at the seminar concluded that co-ownership might be the easiest way of obtaining joint titling of land for unmarried couples, for it would certainly be easier for government functionaries to implement. Meanwhile, it is apparent that very different practices are being followed in different parts of the country. In the department of Cajamarca, for example, the director of the PETT is convinced that only married couples can be titled land: "If an unmarried couple is living together, that is a complication. I advise them to get married. That way, both of their names appear on the land title and one partner cannot sell the land without the other's permission."[28] Cajamarca is also one of the few departments keeping data on land-titling beneficiaries by sex. According to the PETT director, they started collecting such data only after being pressured to do so by a local network of NGOs.[29] This effort revealed that between 1993 and 1996, women made up 20 percent of the 18,242 beneficiaries of the titling effort. However, data are not being collected on the joint titling of couples. When asked why not, the director replied, "No one has ever asked me for it until now."[30]

Since 1988 the activities of organized rural women, their associations, and the NGOs that work with them have been coordinated by the Red Nacional de la Mujer Rural, a network organized by the Lima-based Centro de la Mujer Peruana "Flora Tristán." The Red has been successful in organizing departmental-level networks of NGOs, peasant federations, and rural women's organizations in Cajamarca, San Martín, Piura, Junín, Arequipa, and Lambayeque. At a 1996 forum co-sponsored by the Red in Cajamarca, one of the main demands of the 130 peasant women leaders in attendance was that land titles be issued in the name of both spouses, whether they were married or in a consensual union.[31] Another demand was for legal recognition of receipts made out to women for the purchase of land.[32] According to Rosa Guillén, a member of the Red's rural women's team:

> It was at meetings of women . . . in that space, where women demand their recognition as producers. They demand the right to land, it is a clear demand . . . we saw it at the meeting in Arequipa and in Cuzco. The topic of land rights and land titling was also very much in evidence in Piura and Junín. This is why the Information Network of Arequipa decided to center their campaign for the recognition of women producers on the theme of peasant women's land rights. They, along with the NGOs, are negotiating with the PETT in Arequipa in order to obtain joint titling of couples. . . . I believe that the recognition of women as producers leads clearly to the problem of access to resources and control over them.[33]

In 1998 the Red Nacional de la Mujer Rural decided to launch a major national campaign in support of women's land rights under the PETT. They began to lobby PETT officials for a clarification of the land rights of women in consensual unions, arguing that such women should be recognized as co-property owners, and they circulated a draft of administrative guidelines with a gender perspective.[34] Subsequently, campaigns in favor of women's land rights were launched by three of the departmental networks affiliated with the Red, in Cajamarca, Cuzco, and Tacna (Fernández et al. 2000). These campaigns included, among other actions, discussions with departmental PETT officials regarding the draft administrative guidelines and, in some cases, gender-training sessions with their personnel and an evaluation of the titling program from a gender perspective.

These studies revealed a number of impediments to the recognition of women's land rights. First, the titling program was primarily directed to men, and only their associations (such as irrigation commissions) were targeted for publicity, making it difficult for women to learn of the program. Second, there was a general lack of compliance by local PETT technicians with the instructions regarding the marital-status data to be furnished on the application form for titling services. If an applicant's identity document listed him as single, the technicians rarely checked to see if in fact he was married or living in a consensual union. Such expedience was encouraged by the fact that the technicians were paid according to the number of cases resolved each day. Third, women were rarely aware of their rights under Peru's default marital regime of *gananciales,* and failed to "see that they are being dispossessed" when their husbands or partners registered jointly acquired land as their own property (ibid.: 37).[35] Moreover, in regions such as Cajamarca, over 60 percent of rural couples live in consensual unions, and not only the women but also PETT functionaries typically consider that such women have no property rights at all. Fourth, women are sometimes unable to get their property titled either because they lack official documents or because, if married and separated from their spouse, they need his signature to complete the paperwork and he cannot be found (ibid.: 55). The departmental-level studies also found that PETT data-keeping was deficient and that it was difficult to estimate the number of women or couple beneficiaries with any degree of accuracy. While as a result of the departmental-level campaigns there have been some advances in recognizing women's land rights, the lack of a national policy in support of these—either by the Ministry of Agriculture or the national PETT office—has greatly hampered efforts. As of late 2000 the PETT still had not clarified the situation of couples living in consensual unions.

As in Peru, in Ecuador women's land rights were totally invisible in its 1994 neo-liberal agrarian legislation. One of this country's major rural initiatives since 1988, nonetheless, has been the National Program for Rural Development (PRONADER) in twelve zones of the coast and sierra, and this program did have a gender and land-titling component. During 1994 and 1995 an effort was launched to bring PRONADER's land-titling practices in line with the recent changes in Ecuador's civil code.[36] The default marital regime in Ecuador is that of participation in profits; thus any property acquired during the marriage should belong to the couple. In addition, since 1982 consensual unions are afforded the same property rights as marriages. Project personnel attempted to convince the agrarian reform and colonization institute, IERAC, that land titles should be issued in the name of couples rather than to household heads. They argued that although the sale of any real estate theoretically requires the signature of the spouse, this regulation is often ignored, resulting in women losing access to land without their consent or knowledge. If a land title included the name of the co-owners, then both would have to be in agreement to conclude any official land transaction, giving wives much more security.

PRONADER's efforts included consultations by an expert on gender and land rights as well as training seminars with IERAC-PRONADER personnel.[37] Although IERAC never adopted an explicit policy favoring joint titling to couples, it did change the application form for land-titling services so that the marital status of the beneficiary was clearly designated and a space was provided for the name of the wife or companion. PRONADER functionaries were instructed, after they verified this information and other requirements, to issue land titles in the name of couples. As Table 9.4 shows, couples were issued 70 percent of the land titles given under the PRONADER program.[38] Among those titled individually, men exceeded women, but by a relatively small margin (17 percent versus 13 percent of total titles). With respect to marital status, the overwhelming majority of those titled land jointly were married couples as opposed to consensual unions. Among those titled individually, women were more likely to be widows or divorced compared to men, the majority of whom reported that they were single.[39]

TABLE 9.4. Land Titles Issued by PRONADER by Sex and Marital Status, 1992–1996, Ecuador

	Number	Hectares	Avg. Size	% of Total
Women				
Single	941	941.0	1.00	
Widows	527	300.5	0.57	
Divorced	128	59.9	0.47	
Subtotal	1,596	1,301.4	0.81	12.8
Men				
Single	1,855	2,188.5	1.18	
Widowed	218	288.2	1.32	
Divorced	62	71.6	1.15	
Subtotal	2,135	2,548.3	1.19	17.2
Couples				
Married	8,062	8,803.2	1.09	
Consensual Unions	623	1,684.4	2.70	
Subtotal	8,685	10,487.6	1.21	70.0
Total	12,416	14,337.3	1.15	100.0

Source: Derived from a table provided to the authors by the Consejo Nacional de las Mujeres, Quito, August 1997; based on data compiled by Cecilia Chávez G. from the files of INDA-PRONADER.

The attempt to promote gender equity through joint titling did have unforeseen consequences. PRONADER functionaries who had gone through the gender-awareness program always attempted to speak with the women to learn of their needs in terms of titling—many times because of the absence of their partner due to migration. It was noted that this practice later caused problems for the couple, sometimes leading to domestic violence, because the women had initiated the titling process. PRONADER was not in any way prepared to deal with this situation and to give assistance to the battered woman.[40]

The PRONADER experience also demonstrates that while much can be done at the level of individual projects, gender training and awareness do not necessarily become institutionalized; moreover, the pursuit of gender equity requires sustained political will. As noted by the consultant to this project, "There was institutional inertia . . . we never got joint titling accepted as the norm. What we accomplished was always a result of good faith. In addition, when Ecuador's National Institute for Agrarian Development (INDA) was created, the team left, and no standardized procedure remained."[41] Unfortunately, data at the national level are still not collected for the sex of the individual titled land or for whether land was jointly titled.[42]

During 1997 the national women's office was elevated in status and renamed CONAMO (Consejo Nacional de la Mujer). With more resources and a stronger team, this institution took on a much higher profile in public debates, including over constitutional reform. One major accomplishment was that in the 1998 constitution, gender equality in access to resources became a goal (Ecuador 1998: Article 34). As a result of CONAMO's subsequent lobbying, in 1999 INDA revised its administrative procedures for the allocation and titling of land to make these compatible with Ecuador's civil code and constitution.[43] Joint titling is now to be the norm for married couples and those in consensual unions. For couples who live together but do not meet the official requirements for consensual unions (such as having no impediments to marriage), the institution plans to title them land as co-owners (as a form of business society). CONAMU plans to mount a major gender-training program with INDA functionaries and the NGOs contracted to collect data for titling purposes to make sure that these new regulations are implemented properly. Joint titling of land is a major step toward gender equity in Ecuador, which has been one of the laggards among the twelve countries examined in this study.

As it is elsewhere in the region, a characteristic of Chile's smallholding sector is the absence of registered land titles. In order to regularize the situation in the countryside, since 1992 the Ministry of National Property has been carrying out a program of massive land titling, partly financed by the World Bank. The rural poor are the target population for this program of free titling services. At the initiative of SERNAM (the National Women's Service), female household heads were to be targeted as well (Min Bienes 1996, vol. 1). Among the first activities of SERNAM when it was founded was the development of a program to support female heads of households with low incomes (Chile 1995: 35). From its initial focus on increasing their access to urban housing and its titling in their names,[44] this program expanded to include land-titling activities. In 1991 SERNAM signed an agreement with the Ministry of National Property to ensure that in the National Land Titling Project about to be undertaken priority in titling efforts would be given to rural female heads of household (Barria 1992: 19).[45]

As of 1996 some twenty-six thousand land titles had been issued in rural areas, but data were not collected on the sex of the beneficiary (Min Bienes 1996, vol. 1). In that year the ministry commissioned a sample survey of the beneficiaries of the rural titling project in order to evaluate the efficacy of the program. We were given access to this data set in order to analyze its results by sex. These results were indeed surprising, for in this sample 42.8 percent of the beneficiaries of land-titling services were women.[46] The survey may have over-sampled women since female heads of household were designated a priority group in the sample frame, consistent with the agreement between SERNAM and the ministry to prioritize female household heads.[47] However, the consultant who designed and supervised the survey does not consider women to be grossly over-sampled. Rather, he considers the results to reflect the high demand existing among rural women for title to land. In addition, the titling program was free and involved relatively little paperwork, other factors that could explain why women property owners were eager to be titled their land.[48]

At the 1997 Seminar on Gender and Land Rights, in discussions about how so many women could be beneficiaries of the titling program, it was hypothesized that since the sample included both those who were titled their plots or homesteads (sitios, defined as being under five thousand square meters in size) as well as those titled farms or larger land parcels (parcelas), women were probably concentrated in the former category. As Table 9.5 shows, women were in fact better represented among those who were titled the smaller land plots, being 46 percent of the beneficiaries, as compared to 40 percent of those titled farms.[49]

It is worth considering some of the other characteristics of those who

TABLE 9.5. Land Titling of Plots and Farms by Sex, 1993–1996, Chile

	Women		Men		Total	
	No.	%	No.	%	No.	%
Plots	359	(45.4)	432	(54.6)	791	(100)
Farms	272	(39.8)	411	(60.2)	683	(100)
Total	631	(42.8)	843	(57.2)	1,474	(100)

Source: Compiled by the authors from "Encuesta de Evaluación del Impacto del Programa de Saneamiento y Regularización de la Pequeña Propiedad Rural," data tape provided by the Ministerio de Bienes Nacionales, July 1997.

own farms. Women landowners were slightly older than the men, 56 percent of the women being over fifty years of age as compared with 51 percent of the men. In terms of primary occupation, only 12 percent of the women identified themselves as farmers as compared to 45 percent of the men. The largest group of women, 45 percent, considered themselves to be unemployed, as compared to only 6 percent of the men. An additional 25 percent of the women reported that their occupation was not specified, perhaps because the category of "housewife" was not included among the options. These data suggest that rural women find it difficult socially to recognize their own work, perhaps because agriculture is still considered to be a male occupation. This latter proposition is suggested by the fact while only 12 percent of the women considered their main occupation to be farming, 49 percent of the women reported that their farms were currently cropped, dedicated to fruit tree cultivation, or engaged in animal production. Farming activities could be the primary responsibility of someone else within the household; unfortunately, the occupation, sex, and age of other household members were not reported on the survey data tape, barring us from exploring this important issue further.[50] Male-owned farms were more likely to be in production, characterizing 58 percent of the cases. Slightly more women (39 percent) than men (33 percent) reported that the primary use of the farm was as their place of residence. The remaining farms were made up of either natural or commercial forests or were nonproductive.

The Chilean survey also provides some insight into how peasant men and women view the importance of a land title. Before this land-titling project began, men were slightly more inclined than were women (87 percent versus 82 percent) to consider that having a clear title to land was important or very important.[51] After participating in the project, the proportion of both men and women who considered it important or very important increased significantly, to 94 percent and 93 percent, respectively, with the gender gap disappearing. Both men and women value the security a title gives them and also consider that the value of their properties has increased now that they are titled.[52]

These case studies of land-titling projects illustrate a number of points. First, these projects have lacked conceptual clarity about the bundle of property rights embedded in the household. They have often ignored the property-rights provisions of their countries' civil codes by not taking into account that a household might contain at least three different types of property: that of the wife, the husband, and common property. Moreover, they have been designed without attention to the fact that marital regimes vary according to how property acquired before marriage or through inheritance is treated. They have often not taken into account that property acquired by the couple during the union almost always constitutes common property, a norm reinforced in most countries by the provisions for the dual-headed household. As we have argued, joint titling of land is not a redundant measure but rather a necessary measure to guarantee married women and those in consensual unions effective ownership rights to land that has been jointly acquired.

Second, the titling projects in Honduras, Mexico, Peru, and Chile all initially intended to promote the individualization of land rights. For this reason they titled only one person per household—the household head, who was usually the principal farmer. While in the Chilean case, this practice worked in favor of some women—since female household heads were prioritized (their land claims were favored over those of their children, for example)—it trampled upon the rights of married women and those in consensual unions. This problem has probably been most severe in Mexico, where the land-titling process followed the principles of *ejido* membership, which had vested land and voting rights on only one person per household, the household head. The individualization of land rights was guided by the assumption that women are not agriculturalists and thus have no interest in owning land. Another barrier was the requirement that one have an identity document such as a voting card to be titled land, which women—given their higher rates of illiteracy and monolingualism—are less likely to have than men. A further problem has been that the land-titling projects have generally been promoted to men and their associations. Women have been less likely to learn of such projects or to be aware of the benefits that titling may offer them. This is related to the general lack of legal literacy among rural women, both regarding land rights as well as the property rights pertaining to different marital regimes. The case studies mentioned above nonetheless attest to the interest of rural women in being titled land once they become aware of their rights and of the existence of land-titling programs.

Third, the cases reviewed also illustrate the special problems that women in consensual unions experience in being jointly titled land with their partners. Even when these unions have the same legal rights as marriages, establishing their existence legally is expensive and time consuming. Colombia seems to be the only case among the ones examined here where the existence of a consensual union was taken at face value, without cumbersome requirements put in the way of establishing joint ownership rights over land. A relatively easy administrative solution to this problem, being followed now in Ecuador, is to title land to two single people who co-habit and own land together as co-owners or *co-propietarios*.

Finally, the data suggest that the recent land-titling programs have been more gender equitable than the state interventions of the past. That they have succeeded partially in overcoming the gender bias of the previous agrarian reforms is partly due to the more gender-equitable agrarian legislation of the neo-liberal period, itself a product of the impact of the women's movement on the state. But the relatively high share of female beneficiaries of titling programs also reflects the fact that the number of existing women property owners is not negligible.

Women's Acquisition of Land: Inheritance versus the Market

How have rural women property owners acquired their land? Notwithstanding over twenty years of efforts by researchers and others in the gender and development field to encourage the collection of better data, few agricultural censuses report the sex of their principal farmers or how their property was acquired, severely limiting any comprehensive analysis of gender and property. Only two of the twelve countries analyzed in this study have reported the former data. In Guatemala, in its last agricultural census (for 1979), women made up only 6.6 percent of that nation's farmers (Guatemala 1985: 369–72, Tables 10 and 11). Peru is the only country that has reported the sex of their nation's farmers over two census periods, allowing some analysis of trends.[53] In Peru the share of women farmers increased from 13.3 percent in the 1972 census to 20.3 percent in 1994

TABLE 9.6. Ownership of Land by Sex, Regional Comparisons, Ecuador and Brazil (percentage)

Ecuador

	Sierra	Coast
Women	23	6
Men	20	66
Couples	57	28
Total	100	100
	(n = 75)	(n = 75)

Brazil

	Santa Catarina	Paraná
Women	6	6
Men	42	67
Couples	46	15
Other	6	13
Total	100	100
	(n = 50)	(n = 50)

Source: For Ecuador, compiled from Jordán (1996: 157); for Brazil, from Sisto (1996: 309, 348).

(Peru 1975: 3, Table 3; MinAg 1998: 14). This increase is no doubt associated with a rise in the proportion of female-headed households in rural areas, particularly in the highland zones where the guerrilla conflict led by Sendero Luminoso (Shining Path) in the 1980s was concentrated.[54]

To get some idea of the share of rural property owners who are women in most countries, and how they obtained their land, one must rely on survey and case study data. The only attempt to collect data on women farmers and their ownership of land regionally was the IICA-BID study of rural women food producers in eighteen Latin American and Caribbean countries undertaken in the mid-1990s.[55] In most countries small surveys were undertaken in different regions; unfortunately, few of the published reports from this study include this disaggregated data, limiting this study's usefulness.[56] The disaggregated data for Ecuador and Brazil are presented in Table 9.6.

The highland and coastal regions of Ecuador are characterized by strikingly different ownership patterns, this regional variation being one of the main characteristics of all Andean countries. Women's ownership of land as well as joint ownership by couples is a much more frequent phenomenon in the more indigenous highland region than on the coast, where land is overwhelmingly owned by men. These data support Hamilton's

TABLE 9.7. Form of Land Acquisition by Sex, Peru (percentage)

	Women	Men	Total
Inheritance	39.4	26.7	29.3
Purchase	22.1	24.1	23.6
Agrarian Reform Allocation	6.2	9.5	8.8
Other	3.6	4.8	4.6
None of the above	28.7	34.9	33.7
Total	100.0	100.0	100.0
	($n = 351,929$)	($n = 1,379,835$)	($n = 1,731,764$)
Percentage of Owners	20.3	79.7	100.0

Source: Data made available to the authors by the Oficina de Información Agraria, Ministry of Agriculture, from III CENAGRO 1994, Question 42.

Note: "None of the above" probably refers to holdings within peasant communities.

(1998) findings (discussed in Chapter 8) that land ownership in the Ecuadorian highlands is relatively gender equitable. The data for southern Brazil suggest how land-ownership patterns may vary dramatically even within a culturally homogeneous region. While few women own land individually in either southern state (suggesting that inheritance of land is particularly male-biased), joint ownership of land is much more common in Santa Catarina than in Paraná.[57]

National-level data by sex on how land was acquired is only available for four countries, Peru, Chile, Nicaragua, and Mexico. As Table 9.7 shows, according to unpublished data from the 1994 Peruvian agricultural census, the primary means by which women landowners acquired their land was through inheritance, characterizing 39 percent of the women farmers.[58] This option was followed in importance by those who reported "none of the above" (most likely because they were comuneras with permanent usufruct rights to a land plot within Peru's peasant communities)[59] and then by those who purchased their land in the market. The most frequent form of land acquisition by men was as comuneros, followed by inheritance and then market purchases. While in absolute terms men were more than three times as likely as women to have inherited land—demonstrating the degree of male privilege in inheritance—inheritance was by far more important to women than men as the principal way they became landowners. If we assume that all of those reporting "none of the above" were comuneros, the gender differences in the acquisition of land rights within the peasant communities were also significant, with men being more than five times as likely as women to have these land rights. The agrarian

TABLE 9.8. Form of Acquisition of Plots and Farms by Sex, Chile (percentage)

Form	Plots			Farms		
	Women	Men	Total	Women	Men	Total
Inheritance	30.4	22.0	25.9	84.2	65.4	72.9
Donation by State	22.3	20.1	21.1	1.8	2.7	2.3
Purchase	17.5	29.2	23.9	8.1	25.1	18.3
Other	29.8	28.7	29.1	5.9	6.8	6.5
Total	100.0	100.0	100.0	100.0	100.0	100.0
	(n = 359)	(n = 432)	(n = 791)	(n = 272)	(n = 411)	(n = 683)

Source: Compiled by the authors from "Evaluación del Impacto del Programa de Saneamiento y Regularización de la Pequeña Propiedad Rural," data tape provided by the Ministerio de Bienes Nacionales, July 1997.

Notes: The category "inheritance" includes *sucesión,* defined as the joint inheritance of a land parcel by several heirs. In this case, the land was apparently titled to the administrator of the family plot or farm. No statistically significant difference was found by gender, and given the small number of cases, these were pooled in the general category of inheritances. The category "other" includes what are termed imperfect donations by private parties and other responses.

reform of the 1970s appears as a much less important means for either men or women to have acquired ownership of land than other forms, perhaps because, after almost three decades, a significant share of agrarian reform sector land is held by those who inherited it from their parents.[60]

Turning to Chile, the survey data from the land-titling project discussed earlier also reveal gender differences in how land was acquired. With respect to plots, women were more likely than men (30 percent versus 22 percent) to have acquired their plot through inheritance, as Table 9.8 shows. While this is consistent with reports that women often inherit the parental home as compensation for the care they provide to elderly parents, the survey questionnaire did not ask from whom the plot was inherited, which could be a parent, spouse, or other relative; thus we cannot substantiate this proposition. Men, on the other hand, were more likely than women (29 percent versus 17.5 percent) to have purchased their land plot, a difference that is statistically significant. There was no significant difference in the other ways of acquiring plots, women and men being equally likely to have acquired these through state or private donations.[61]

These gender differences are accentuated in terms of the acquisition of farms. Women were much more likely (84 versus 65 percent) to have acquired their farms through inheritance, whereas men were more likely than women (25 versus 8 percent) to have acquired their farms on the land market, findings that are statistically significant. While more men than women inherited both plots and farms in absolute numbers, the data indicate the very important role inheritance has played in terms of women's access to land. The data also suggest that participation in the land market is quite skewed, with men more likely to participate in it than women. Nevertheless, the data also show that women are not adverse to entering this market when their financial circumstances allow; that is, they are interested in owning land for all the benefits that owning property bestows, a conclusion reinforced by the relatively high proportion of women who participated in the land-titling program.

A nationally representative sample survey of 3,015 rural households undertaken in Nicaragua in 1995 revealed that only 32 percent of these households owned land, 17 percent worked land under various forms of indirect tenancy, and 51 percent were landless (Renzi and Agurto 1998). Among those who owned land, women were the primary landowners in only 13 percent and men in 68 percent of the households, illustrating the high degree of gender inequality in land ownership in this country. Jointly titled land characterized only 3 percent of the households, and those who owned land collectively (principally as members of production cooperatives) made up the remaining 16 percent of landowners. Table 9.9 shows the form of acquisition of land by sex. These data also suggest that inheritance is by far the most important means through which women acquire land. As in Peru and Chile, there is a strong male bias in absolute terms (men being four times as likely as women to inherit land); but inheritance is relatively more important for women than for men. Unfortunately, the data do not allow us to explore further whether women are more likely to inherit land as daughters or as widows. The survey data do show that men are much more active participants in the land market than

TABLE 9.9. Form of Land Acquisition by Owners by Sex, Nicaragua (percentage)

Form of Access	Women	Men
Inheritance	57	32
Purchase	33	52
Agrarian Reform	10	16
Total	100	100
	(n = 125)	(n = 656)

Source: Constructed from data reported in Renzi and Agurto (1998: 75), based on the 1995 FIDEG survey of 3,015 rural households.

are women. They also confirm that the agrarian reform privileged men over women.

The importance of inheritance as the primary means through which women acquire land is also evident in Mexico. A nationally representative sample survey (Robles et al. 2000) of *ejidatarias* revealed that 76 percent had acquired their land through inheritance; only 14.6 percent had acquired land in their own right from the *ejido* assembly, while 9.4 percent had purchased their land. As Table 9.10 shows, of those who inherited land, half had done so from their husbands. Those who inherited from their parents were more likely to have received land from their fathers than from their mothers.

Case studies from different parts of Mexico also demonstrate the importance of inheritance in women becoming *ejidatarias* and confirm that men are much more likely than women to have acquired land through the land market. In the *ejido* El Rancho in the state of Guadalajara, women constituted 18 percent of the *ejidatarios* and almost all of them inherited this position. In contrast, the majority of the men were either among the original founders of the *ejido* or became members by vote of the assembly when this *ejido* acquired additional land in the 1950s. Only 20 percent of the men acquired their land rights through inheritance whereas almost one-quarter purchased them from another *ejidatario* (Brunt 1992: 80). In an *ejido* in Tuzamapán, Veracruz, women constituted 24 percent of the members and virtually all inherited this position.[62] No women purchased

TABLE 9.10. Source of Land Acquired by *Ejidatarias,* Mexico

	Beneficiaries		Total	
Source of Land	No.	%	No.	%
Inheritance				
from husband	204	(50.8)		
from father	102	(25.4)		
from mother	46	(11.4)		
from other family	48	(11.9)		
from non-family	2	(0.5)		
Subtotal			402	(76)
Allocation by *ejido* assembly			77	(15)
Purchase			50	(9)
Total			529	(100)

Source: Compiled from Robles, Artís, Salazar, and Muñoz (2000: 37, 118).

Note: The category "inheritance" includes those who have formally inherited their parcel as well as those who have been given a plot as a pre-inheritance (*cesión*).

their land rights, and only two acquired these directly from the *ejido* assembly, one because of abandonment by her husband and the other because her husband became disabled due to alcoholism (Córdova Plaza 1999: 11).

Above we established the importance of inheritance as the primary means through which rural women have acquired ownership of land. The available data also suggest that inheritance practices have been more gender equitable than past programs of state intervention in the distribution of land. But this does not mean that inheritance of land is anywhere near being gender equitable. Rather, significant differences exist in the probability that daughters as opposed to sons will inherit land and in the actual amount of land which they inherit. Table 9.11 presents data on the average amount of land owned by men, women, and as jointly titled property in six countries. What is striking is that in every case men own more land, on average, than do women.[63]

Whether land was acquired predominantly through inheritance or purchase, or through state distribution or titling, gender inequality in the amount of land owned is the norm. With respect to land distributed by the state, a survey in the department of Jinotega, Nicaragua, of those benefiting from the titling of agrarian reform land also revealed that women landowners received less land.[64] The author of this study argues that this trend was the result of "unconscious discrimination" due to predominant norms regarding the gender division of labor: "It is assumed that women do not need greater amounts of land than what is necessary to produce for household food security" (Rocha 1998: 40). A similar logic governs inheritance practices and is tied to the expectation that sons rather than daughters will be farmers. Another factor explaining the gender inequality in the amount of land owned is that daughters are more likely to inherit land in a partible inheritance process—that is, where land is divided among more than one heir. In contrast, if the land is bequeathed to only one heir, the sole heir is much more likely to be male than female.

Will the Land Market Be Gender Neutral?

One of the main purposes of land-titling programs is to enhance the functioning of rural land markets, and advocates argue that more effective land markets should facilitate the transfer of land to small farmers. Will participation in this market be gender neutral? If so, one would expect poor rural women to face no more obstacles than those encountered by poor

TABLE 9.11. Differences by Sex in the Amount of Land Owned, 1990s

Chile, 1992–96

	Plots	*Farms*
Women	939.7 sq. meters	4.6 has.
Men	1071.9 sq. meters	6.0 has.

Ecuador, 1992–96

	PRONADER Program
Women	0.81 has.
Men	1.15 has.
Joint	1.21 has.

Honduras, 1995–2000

	Non-Reformed Sector
Women	4.23 has.
Men	5.35 has.

Mexico, 1993–96

	Ejidatarios
Women	7.9 has.
Men	9.0 has.

Colombia

	Agrarian Reform Programs 1996–98	*Colonization Program* 1996–97 and 1999
Women	13.4 has.	20.7 has.
Men	17.7 has.	27.2 has.
Joint	14.5 has.	26.4 has.

Peru, 1994

	Total
Women	6.59 has.
Men	9.36 has.

Sources: Tables 6.2, 9.1, 9.2, 9.4, and 9.5; for Mexico, Valenzuela and Robles (1996: 40); and for Peru, INEI (1995: 18).

rural men. As buyers poor peasants are constrained by their limited financial resources and lack of access to credit on terms they can afford. In addition, poor rural men and women would be equally discouraged from participating in the land market by high transaction costs and the relatively high land prices resulting from supply constraints in this market, such as a limited offer of land for sale. Moreover, if the land market were gender neutral we would expect men and women to be able to buy land at a similar price. Similarly, as sellers, we would expect peasant landowners, whether male or female, to offer their land for sale for similar reasons, and with the same outcome. For example, we would expect that one of the effects of land-titling programs would be to increase the value of titled land relative to untitled land of similar quality. If motivations for participating in the land market were gender neutral, we would expect male and female landowners to offer their land for sale at a similar rate. If, on the other hand, men and women value ownership of land for different reasons or have differential access to the other resources required to be productive and efficient farmers, participation as sellers might differ significantly by gender. Unfortunately, until recently little systematic information has been collected on the functioning of land markets in Latin America, and specifically on whether participation in these differs by gender.[65] Here we summarize the available case study evidence on women as buyers and sellers in the land market.

One of the earliest studies of women's participation in the land market was carried out in the northern Peruvian department of Cajamarca in the context of sales of hacienda lands as these were parcelized by private initiative in the 1950s and 1960s, prior to Peru's agrarian reform (Deere 1990). The importance that women place on owning land in their own names or in being co-property owners is quite evident: in a sample of 374 land transactions on nine haciendas, 25 percent of the purchases were made by a woman and another 24 percent were made by a couple. Fourteen percent were by a family group, which often included a widow and her grown children. Only 37 percent of the purchases were made by men alone (ibid.: Table 24).

The large number of land purchases made by women or in which women participated reflect a relatively high incidence of female household heads (both de facto and de jure) and the importance at that time of female economic activities. Sheep raising, a female activity in this region, served as a critical source of savings for the purchase of land; nonetheless, few female household heads were able to purchase land solely on the basis of their own earnings. Given differential labor-market opportunities, it was generally men who migrated to other regions to earn wage income for the land purchase. But it was often women who came up with the final payment for the land parcel because the household's animal stocks were under their care and control. In some of the cases in which a woman is listed as the buyer, this was because her spouse was absent at the time the sale was concluded. Other women buyers were household heads whose sons contributed to the land purchase but who bought it in their own names. Whether peasant women were able to buy land in their own names or jointly with their husbands or partners, however, did not depend only on their own desires and capabilities. The whims and prejudices of the landowning class were also important here, as evidenced by a contrasting pattern of sales on different haciendas. Some landlords refused to sell land or only rarely sold land to a woman, considering it inappropriate to do so given gender norms; others were eager to sell land to whoever could produce the full payment in cash, given the impending agrarian reform.

On all except one hacienda, men bought significantly larger parcels, on average, than did women. Moreover, women not only purchased smaller quantities of land but also paid a higher price per hectare, in part because of the inverse relation between parcel size and per-hectare price. But in five of the nine haciendas studied, women paid more per hectare than any other group of buyers, reflecting their weaker bargaining power vis-à-vis landlords as compared to peasant men (Deere 1990: 199–201). This case study illustrates some of the ways in which land markets are not gender neutral. Whether women were able to participate at all depended on the predilection of those offering land for sale. Moreover, women did not participate in the market under the same terms as men; rather, these terms were conditioned by a host of other factors, some economic—such as the resources at their disposal—and others non-economic—such as their desperation to buy land and their greater degree of subservience to landlords, factors that lowered their bargaining power in this market.

As we saw in the previous section, women landowners have been much less likely to acquire land through purchases in the land market than have men. In the Chilean survey of land-titling beneficiaries, only 8 percent of the women acquired their farm through purchase as compared to one-quarter of the men. In the 1995 Nicaraguan survey, where it was even more common than in Chile for peasant farmers to have acquired land through the market, the gender differences were notable as well, with only one-third of the women owners having acquired their land through purchase as compared to one-half of the men. Among the economic factors that impact upon unequal participation in the land market are purchasing power (particularly the ability to generate savings) and/or access to credit. These, in turn, are conditioned by the income-generating activities and income levels that men and women may generate. The abundant literature on rural labor markets in Latin America has demonstrated the persistent differences in men's and women's agricultural labor market participation, with men having much greater access to permanent employment opportunities than do women. Even in cases in which female labor is preferred for certain tasks or crops, female employment is overwhelmingly concentrated in seasonal or temporary tasks. Moreover, when men and women are employed for similar activities, women tend to be paid less than men.[66] Given the low wages characterizing agricultural work and the pattern of women's employment, few rural women generate sufficient savings to participate in the land market as buyers.

With respect to the availability of credit for land purchases, until recently few Latin American state agricultural-credit programs provided loans for the purchase of land, and mortgage activities within the private financial system were generally undeveloped. If a rural mortgage market existed at all, it was usually geared toward large commercial farmers. Over the last couple of decades there has been growing interest among international agencies, governments, and NGOs in experimenting with land-credit programs oriented to the rural poor. One of the oldest and most successful NGO programs has been that of FEPP (Fondo Ecuatoriano Populorum Progresso) in Ecuador, initiated on a small scale in 1977. Since 1990, when its funding was expanded, it has been operating what is known as the Rotating Fund for Access to Land and Its Use by Peasant Organizations. Since one of its aims is to strengthen local peasant organizations, FEPP only provides loans for the collective purchase of land; these go to groups who have been engaged in land conflicts, have exhausted all legal means of solving them, and are attempting to negotiate the purchase of a property (Navarro, Vallejo, and Villaverde 1996).[67] Between 1990 and 1995 199 organizations took advantage of this fund, purchasing or legalizing 382,324 hectares of land on behalf of 7,884 families (ibid.: 139). FEPP considers that it is benefiting peasant families, as represented by the household head. In this period 14 percent of the direct beneficiaries of the program were women (ibid.: 168), a relatively low share if compared with other data on women's ownership of land in highland Ecuador (see Tables 9.4 and 9.6). No effort has been made in this program to title land jointly to couples once they cancel their debt and receive their parcel as individual private property.

A much more modest program has been carried out in Guatemala by the private foundation FUNDACEN (also known as the Penny Foundation). It began funding land purchases by the rural poor in 1984 in a project supported by USAID. Its mode of operation is to purchase farms on the market and then to subdivide and resell them as small parcels.[68] In order to qualify as a beneficiary of this program, one must be a household head and an agriculturalist, be among the poorest of the poor, and have a child of working age living at home. It is estimated that women make up only 1 percent of the direct beneficiaries of this program, which as of the early 1990s had benefited only around twelve hundred families (Fund. Arias–Tierra Viva 1993: 130–36). Obviously this program has not been gender neutral and even less successful in incorporating women as direct beneficiaries than the meager state agrarian reform efforts in Guatemala.

These private-sector initiatives suggest that, unless given an explicit gender content, land-market programs by themselves will do little to increase women's ownership of land. Many of the same factors—cultural, structural, and institutional—that constituted mechanisms of exclusion of women in state agrarian reform programs are likely to bias their participation in these programs. Moreover, these factors may even be aggravated in private-sector programs since these must operate under market conditions. To the extent that greater emphasis is placed on the need for beneficiaries to be credit-worthy and to generate profitable activities to repay their mortgages, this will work against the participation of women since it is difficult for them to meet these requirements on the same terms as men. As the Colombian experiment with market-assisted land transactions shows, for women to be direct beneficiaries requires an explicit policy favoring their participation, including, as a minimum, provisions for the joint allocation and titling of land to couples, and/or affirmative-action measures such as those prioritizing female household heads.

Finally, there is ample evidence of rural women's interest in participating in the land market for all the benefits that ownership of land confers. Acquiring a parcel of one's own is widely recognized as one of the best forms of security for women and their children and as a means of obtaining some economic autonomy. Rural women go to great lengths to attempt to purchase land, including saving from their meager earnings while employed as domestic servants in urban areas. It took one Guatemalan woman fifteen years as a domestic servant to save enough to purchase a small parcel of land in her community of origin (Fund. Arias–Tierra Viva 1993: 72–73). A case study in Mexico revealed that acquiring land of their own is an aspiration of even young, single women whose greater level of education has allowed them to obtain non-service-sector employment: "Different from what was the case in the past, . . . single women, if they have their *dinerito* [small sum of money], can acquire land to secure their own future" (Castañeda 2000: 8–9). They are aware of the potential increase in bargaining power within marriage that ownership of assets, particularly land, conveys: "To have land allows them to negotiate within the household . . . but it also gives them a certain ability to participate in community decision making, even if only indirectly. To own land strengthens them, it gives them security with respect to the present and the future. This is why if women receive other goods [besides land as an] inheritance they often will sell them in order to begin accumulating the funds to purchase a land parcel, however small" (ibid.: 18).

One of the worries about land-titling programs is that, by fueling the land market, rather than benefiting small farmers they will provoke depeasantization and greater concentration of land; another is that the process will be gender biased, with women landowners more likely to sell their land than men. Chile, which initiated the process of counter-reform in the 1970s, provides strong evidence in support of the first proposition. Slightly over half of the agrarian reform beneficiaries of the 1960s and 1970s lost access to land when these reformed estates were privatized and parcelized by the Pinochet regime. The expansion of fruit cultivation in the central region of Chile then led to a new process of land concentration. Lack of access to credit and other technical assistance (itself a result of the state's withdrawal from support to the agricultural sector) allowed few of the beneficiaries of the counter-reform to compete with larger farms that had access to capital. Also, the opening of the economy to foreign food imports wreaked havoc on domestic food production, forcing many small farmers into semi-proletarianization and seasonal migration or to sell their lands (Díaz 1990: 133–35). According to Echenique (1996: 88), by 1978 15 percent of the beneficiaries of the counter-reform had sold their parcels; this figure increased to 45 percent by 1983, and 57 percent by 1991. Unfortunately, for our purposes, these data were not collected by gender, although in general there were few female beneficiaries of either the agrarian reform or counter-reform parcelization process.

The only other case of large-scale land sales by agrarian reform beneficiaries for which data are available is the process currently taking place in Nicaragua. It has been reported that approximately one-third of the area of the reformed sector (one million *manzanas*) has now been sold, with perhaps half of these sales having been made by the most recent beneficiaries, the former combatants (the contras and FSLN soldiers) who received land as part of the peace accords of the early 1990s. Another major source of sales has been the cooperative sector (Sedo 1999: 24). A study in fourteen municipalities found that the number of production cooperatives had been reduced by half and that 70 percent of their lands had been sold.[69] A case study of agrarian reform beneficiaries in the department of Jinotega confirms these national trends (Rocha 1998). The main groups of sellers were members of the agrarian reform cooperatives or ex-contra and ex-army reform beneficiaries who had been allocated land even though they lacked an agricultural vocation and had not wanted to live in the area. Many of the cooperatives in Jinotega had been formed, for political purposes, in the war zone, and they were not economically viable. In this region it is generally held that female cooperative members were even more likely to sell their land share than the male members, either because they distrusted the worth of their land title or because they were pressured to do so by their spouses or companions (ibid.: 42). One community member said, "Due either to a lack of orientation or ignorance, many people do not have faith in the land title. They think that when another government comes to power their land will be taken away, and that it is better to sell the land now than to lose it later." Another remarked, "The women let themselves be bossed around by men, and because of this, they sell their land. They do not think of the children, only of the *reales* [money] that they will get by selling the land. They don't think about the future." Said a third, "Many of those men who forced their women to sell are no longer with them, they abandoned them and left the *comarca* [district]. Those poor women and their children have ended up having to live off relatives" (ibid.: 43).

In contrast, in Chile, where the land-titling program is taking place decades after the agrarian reform and counter-reform, there is no evidence of a gender bias. Of those titled land between 1993 and 1996, women were no more likely than men to sell their land upon receiving their land titles. In fact, only eight cases were reported of beneficiaries subsequently selling their land in a survey of 1,492 titling beneficiaries. There was also no statistically significant difference between men or women (3.2 percent versus 4.9 percent) selling, renting, or ceding their land to others after it was titled. Moreover, men and women were equally likely (each representing only 5.6 percent of the total) to report that they expected to sell or rent their land sometime in the future.[70]

At the 1997 Seminar on Women and Land Rights in Mexico, it was noted that the parcelization and titling of *ejido* land had not yet stimulated the formal land market. This was because most *ejidos* had not moved to the second step in the process, *dominio pleno,* partly because of worries over the tax burden they might incur by doing so. Despite the low level of legal sales thus far, there was consensus among the participants that illegal land sales (of *ejido* lands having only certificates) were taking place all over Mexico. There was speculation that women might be more likely to sell their land than men. According to an agrarian lawyer, "Women sell easier, they are often pressured to do so by their children, by the *ejido* commission, and by buyers."[71] Among the reasons that *ejidatarias* might be more susceptible to pressures to sell their land is their more advanced age as compared to *ejidatarios,* as was reported earlier. If they do not have a grown child interested in working the land parcel, elderly women may find it difficult to put together the resources to hire wage labor to do so. However, even if an older woman is no longer in a position to work the land, either by herself or with the assistance of wage labor, land is an important asset that, with a functioning rental market, could prove to be a significant source of income. Thus even if land prices were to rise, it would not necessarily be in the interest of elderly women to sell their land. Moreover, in the case of widows, if they sold their land rights on the *ejido* they might feel obliged to divide the proceeds with their children. It would not be in the widow's interest to do so unless she felt quite confident that in subsequent years, a child would come to her assistance if she was in need. In one of the few studies that has addressed this issue, Hamilton (1999) found that in the four *ejidos* she studied women were not any more likely than men to want to sell their land. She also did not find pressure on *ejidatarias* by their children to sell the family patrimony.

Whether smallholders once titled will fuel the land market through their sales will likely depend on whether they can become viable agriculturalists. Ironically, one of the main factors that might lead to greater peasant dispossession is increased use of formal-sector credit, precisely what neo-liberal planners hope will facilitate greater investment among smallholders and hence productivity and production gains. While it is not yet clear that massive land titling will lead to greater private-sector lending to smallholders—due to the higher transaction costs (and thus lower profitability) of small-scale loans—whether smallholders can productively use such credit very much depends on the broader economic milieu: pricing, tariffs, exchange-rate policies, and other factors under the neo-liberal model. If this model, with its bias toward agricultural exports, is unfavorable to smallholders (in that the production of food crops is unprofitable), it is unlikely that smallholders will seek credit for investment purposes; and if they do so, the likelihood that they will be able to use this credit productively is low. This is the basis of the prediction that greater reliance on formal-sector credit will lead to greater peasant indebtedness, and if such loans are secured by land, by their eventual dispossession.

Will this process be gender neutral? There is a growing literature demonstrating that female farmers in Latin America are at a disadvantage as compared to male farmers. They generally have less access to credit,[72] technical assistance, irrigation,[73] and marketing services than do men.[74] The baseline survey of the twelve PRONADER zones in Ecuador revealed, for example, that at the start of that program, although women made up 21 percent of the farmers, they were only 15.3 percent of those with access to modern technology, 12.4 percent of those with access to credit, and 9.4 percent of those who had passed through training programs (Camacho and Prieto 1995: 68–69).

Peruvian census data also illustrate the unequal position of male and female farmers. As Table 9.12 shows, women were almost as interested as men in receiving technical assistance. While less than 10 percent of Peruvian farmers received any technical assistance at all, men were slightly favored over women. Perhaps as a result, a slightly higher share of men than women used improved seed. Less than 10 percent of farmers applied for credit and even fewer received it, with this share being slightly higher for male than female farmers. Similar reasons were given by both men and women who applied for credit for not having received it: the lack of sufficient guarantees for a loan or the lack of a land title, and the high cost of credit. Nonetheless, a higher proportion of women had registered land titles than did men, suggesting that if all else were equal, they should have been better candidates than men for loans.

With the growing impact of the gender-and-development field and the commitment by states to gender equity, ministries of agriculture in

TABLE 9.12. Characteristics of Male and Female Farmers, Peru, 1994

	% Women	% Men	% Total
Need technical assistance	75.6	80.5	79.5
Receive technical assistance	6.8	9.8	9.2
Use improved seed	14.8	17.1	16.7
Applied for credit	4.6	8.8	8.0
Received credit	3.6	6.8	6.1
Possess registered land titles	81.3	67.5	70.3
Illiteracy rate	49.8	18.8	25.0
Over 65 years of age	23.3	14.9	16.6
Total	351,929	1,379,835	1,731,764
	(20.3)	(79.9)	(100)

Source: Ministerio de Agricultura (1998), various tables; based on the 1994 Agricultural Census.

most Latin American countries have begun to recognize that farmers are also women. During the 1980s eight of the twelve countries studied here set up rural women's offices of various sorts, either within these ministries or in their agrarian reform institutes.[75] Most of these focused on developing income-generating projects for rural women or on designing women's components for integrated rural-development projects. The most ambitious effort of this period was in Colombia, which in 1984 attempted to develop an integral state policy toward rural women that took into account their role as producers and reproducers (León 1987). This effort in many ways foreshadowed the national plans of the 1990s.

The establishment and strengthening of national women's offices in the 1980s led to the development of national plans to achieve equality of opportunities for women in the 1990s. While the initial plans often suffered from an urban bias, subsequent plans in Chile, Costa Rica, and recently Honduras and Colombia focus specifically on rural women (SERNAM 1997; CMF 1997; PRO-EGEDAGRO 1999).[76] On the whole, their main objective has been to institutionalize and mainstream a gender-sensitive approach to state planning, addressing rural women's issues (such as lack of access to resources) across government ministries, institutes, and other agencies, and setting up specific targets within them to end the discrimination against rural women. Central to all of these plans has been improving women's access to credit, training, and technology.

A different approach has been taken in El Salvador, where efforts directed at rural women are based in CENTA (Centro Nacional de Tecnología Agropecuaria y Forestal), formerly a unit of the Ministry of Agriculture but now an autonomous state agency. After undertaking an evaluation of gender and institutional performance in the early 1990s, CENTA decided to disband its rural women's program and to mainstream gender in all of its activities, under the guidance of an Office on Gender Coordination.[77] The focus now is on male and female farmers and on assuring that women have equality of opportunity in the training and technical assistance provided by this institution.[78] CENTA has also embarked on a policy of recruiting female researchers and extension agents. Most analysts consider these to be major steps forward in terms of attending to the needs of rural women producers (Girón and Halsband 1995: 33; Orellana 1996: 47).

As yet there is no comprehensive summary of the activities of NGOs directed at rural women in Latin America. Such a review would probably show a proliferation of local rural women's groups in the 1980s and that the number of rural women participating in such organizations probably exceeded those benefited directly through state programs. This tendency has undoubtedly been accentuated in the 1990s, as various countries have attempted to decentralize as well as privatize state services to the rural sector, with local-level NGOs often assuming these functions. In Bolivia, for example, NGOs have become the major source of credit and technical assistance in rural areas. While the NGOs do not focus exclusively on them, rural women represent an increasing number of the clients for NGO services as these institutions also attempt to mainstream women into their primary activities (Ranaboldo 1997). Another emphasis of the 1990s has been on micro-credit projects for women, often following the group-solidarity model of backing for loans (Solario et al. 1996).

This brief review has aimed to illustrate some of the efforts that have been undertaken to reduce the discrimination to which rural women have traditionally been subject in terms of their access to resources other than land. But it is evident that women still remain at a competitive disadvantage as farmers, and face a higher probability of failing at farming than men. If being a successful commercial farmer was the only reason that ownership of land was important to women, we would have to conclude that women would be more likely than men to enter the land market as sellers. However, land ownership is important to women for reasons other than commercial farming. It remains a poor household's best insurance policy in terms of meeting basic food requirements through subsistence production. Moreover, land is a critically important asset that can be rented to generate income to meet household needs. And as we have attempted to demonstrate, ownership of land is crucial to women's bargaining position within the household, family, and community. All of these factors might mitigate any tendency for women property owners, if they are in fact less successful farmers than men, to sell their land.

ten

Land and Property in a Feminist Agenda

A CENTRAL THEME of this book has been the continuing disjuncture between men's and women's formal equality before the law and the achievement of gender equality in actual practice, a theme that is well illustrated by the gap between women's property rights and their ownership of land. The struggle for formal equality before the law and for women's property and land rights has been a contentious process over the course of the twentieth century, and these goals still have not been attained in all Latin American countries. While much has been accomplished in the legal realm, women in Latin America are still much less likely to own land than men, and when they do so, their holdings are smaller and more marginal. A central purpose of this study has been to examine why the ownership of land is so unequal, and we have pointed to several important reasons: male privilege in marriage; male preference in inheritance; male bias in state programs of land distribution and titling; and gender bias in the land market, with women less likely to participate successfully in this market as buyers than men. Within peasant and indigenous communities governed by communal tenure of land, traditional customs and practices also discriminate against women, so that most women are denied effective land rights.

This inequality is prejudicial to women's well-being, since there is a positive association between the assets and income controlled by women and their own and their children's welfare. Women's direct ownership of productive assets greatly reduces their risk of poverty. For rural women, ownership of land is the best guarantee they will be able to provide at least some portion of their household's food requirements. Also, land ownership is often a precondition to increasing women's productivity, since it mediates their access to credit and other services. Ownership of land both improves women's fall-back position within marriage and gives them greater marital options. By increasing women's bargaining power, ownership of land is also associated with women's greater role in household and farm decision making. There is little question that an increase in women's bargaining power is necessary to empower women, to change gender relations, and to achieve real equality between men and women. Hence, the importance of our central question. In this chapter we summarize our answers to the other questions posed in Chapter 1, considering first what the contemporary women's movement has accomplished with respect to women's land rights, and then discussing what we have learned in the process and the challenges that lie ahead.

Significant strides were made toward formal gender equality in the last half of the twentieth century. Among the gains were the establishment of formal equality between the sexes in almost all Latin American constitutions and the reform of most civil codes so that the dual-headed household, consensual unions, and civil divorce were legally recognized. These reforms were usually spearheaded by the national women's offices, and their adoption was facilitated by the commitment of Latin American states to establish equality between men and women and by international pressure to abide by the UN Convention on the Elimination of All Forms of Discrimination against Women. During the 1990s a growing number of Latin American states also adopted national plans to achieve equality of opportunities for women. These plans recognize that women's lack of access to resources constitutes one of the main forms of inequality between the sexes. At the same time, with the important exception of Costa Rica, these plans have fallen short of recommending concrete measures of affirmative action to increase women's access to property. Thus, while considerable gains have been made in strengthening women's property rights in pursuit of formal gender equality, there has been relatively little substantive progress toward remedying gender inequality in asset ownership. Moreover, these national plans have generally had an urban bias. Efforts to address the question of women's land rights in most countries have generally taken place outside this national planning framework.

The neo-liberal agrarian codes that provide for formal equality in men's and women's land rights are a product of "the triangle of empowerment," the coordinated action between the urban and rural women's movements, women in government, and women in formal politics, assisted in many cases by the international agencies (Vargas et al. 1996). Through strategic alliances these groups have successfully carried out the battle within national legislatures and political parties to change the content of Latin America's agrarian codes in the 1990s. The new agrarian codes are more gender progressive, not because of neo-liberalism, but rather because of their timing. When neo-liberal regimes embarked upon institutional reform of the agricultural sector, they created the space for the women's movement to press for legislation that supports gender equality.

One of the main accomplishments of the neo-liberal agrarian legislation has been the burial of the concept of the male household head as the focus of state land-distribution and titling efforts—one of the principal mechanisms of exclusion of women as direct beneficiaries in the agrarian reforms of previous decades. The neo-liberal agrarian codes have followed two paths in doing so. In one group of countries (Peru, Mexico, Ecuador, and Honduras), the new codes vest land rights on natural and juridic persons rather than on household heads, in keeping with the neo-liberal emphasis on the right of individuals freely to pursue their self-interest. In another group of countries (Bolivia, Brazil, Colombia, Costa Rica, Guatemala, Nicaragua, and again, Honduras, since it does both), the legislation of the neo-liberal period explicitly establishes equality of land rights between men and women. The adoption of explicit equality is certainly preferable to the presumed neutrality suggested by the vesting of land rights on natural and juridic persons, for the latter assumes a level playing field, hardly the case. But it is also insufficient simply to guarantee women's formal land rights. Without concrete mechanisms of inclusion —such as mandatory joint titling to couples or affirmative action measures—it is difficult, if not impossible, to increase women's ownership of land. Thus among the major accomplishments in securing women's land rights have been provisions for the mandatory joint allocation and titling of land to couples irrespective of their marital status, a measure consistent with the dual-headed household and necessary to its implementation in practice.

Between 1988 and 1995, five countries made provisions in their agrarian legislation for the joint allocation and titling of land to couples. In Colombia, Costa Rica, and Nicaragua joint titling became mandatory for married couples and those in consensual unions. In Brazil and Honduras it was only an option that couples could request; moreover, in Honduras it was only an option for married couples and couples formally registered as living in consensual unions.

Since the Beijing UN Conference on Women, Peru under its titling program for previous agrarian reform beneficiaries adopted mandatory joint titling of land, but only for married couples. The Dominican Republic in 1998 adopted mandatory joint titling for both married couples and those in consensual unions, in legislation that covered former agrarian reform beneficiaries. Guatemala adopted mandatory joint allocation and titling, irrespective of marital status, in its 1999 legislation creating a new land bank. Ecuador in its 1999 regulations governing the titling activities of its agrarian institute also made joint titling of land mandatory for married couples, with couples living in consensual unions to be designated as co-owners.

Efforts continue in Peru to extend the benefits of joint titling to partners in consensual unions as co-owners, as in Ecuador. In Honduras efforts now focus on making joint titling mandatory in practice and facilitating joint titling for couples in consensual unions. In El Salvador joint titling of land to couples irrespective of marital status has been proposed in all three draft versions of the agrarian code still under discussion there. Changes in titling norms are not on the agenda, to our knowledge, in Mexico or Chile, countries whose land-titling programs privilege individuals and have practically concluded. Nor are they under consideration in Bolivia, which has not yet commenced large-scale land-titling efforts.

The importance of mandatory joint titling becomes apparent if one reviews what has been accomplished in terms of women's increased ownership of land. Table 10.1 summarizes the data presented in earlier chapters on beneficiaries by sex in recent land adjudications and titlings.[1] It is apparent that recent programs are laudatory from a gender perspective if their results are compared with those shown in Table 3.2, which lists the share of women beneficiaries in the agrarian reform period. In Colombia in the period of agrarian reform dating from 1961 to 1991, women represented only 11 percent of the beneficiaries. Once joint titling and priority to female heads of household were mandated (1988) and enforced (1995) in land distribution efforts, this share increased to 45 percent in the 1995–98 period. Under the Sandinista agrarian reform in Nicaragua, which intended to benefit women irrespective of their marital status, women were only 10 percent of the direct beneficiaries in the period 1979–89. Once mechanisms of inclusion were implemented (joint titling and priority to female heads of household) beginning in late 1993, this figure increased to 33.5 percent (1994–2000).

Unfortunately, Costa Rica has not made public its data on land adjudications by sex beyond the two years following the initial passage of the Law to Promote the Social Equality of Women. In the brief period in which land was allocated in a woman's name if the couple lived in a consensual union, or in the names of both members of a married couple, the female share of beneficiaries rose from 12 percent (1962–88) to 45 percent (1990–92). In El Salvador the share of women beneficiaries rose from 11–12 percent under the agrarian reform (1980–91) to one-third under the land-transfer program associated with the peace accords; under the latter program, each member of a couple received individual allocations of land, the policy of "a parcel of one's own." The only other country to be distributing new land for agrarian reform purposes in this period is Brazil. Although its constitution states that land is to be distributed to men, women, or couples, implementing regulations have not been issued with explicit mechanisms of inclusion. The fact that women make up only 12.6 percent of the direct beneficiaries on the *assentamentos* well illustrates the point that explicit formal equality does not automatically translate into significant gains for women if not accompanied by explicit mechanisms of inclusion.

The second section of Table 10.1 summarizes the available data on land-titling programs among smallholders. In the first two programs, in Chile and Ecuador, the percentage of women beneficiaries was quite high as a result of two different mechanisms of inclusion: in Chile, the priority the land-titling program gave to female household heads; and in Ecuador, the emphasis given by the PRONADER project to the joint titling of land to couples, irrespective of their marital status. Such high shares of female beneficiaries would not have been possible in either case had it not been for the relatively large number of existing women property owners, a situation primarily attributable to favorable inheritance practices. Notwithstanding the fact that inheritance of land generally favors men, the

TABLE 10.1. Proportion of Beneficiaries by Sex and Form of Title in Land Allocation and Titling Programs in Latin America, 1990s

	Beneficiaries %	Titles %
Land Allocations		
Colombia	1995–98	1995–98
	Women 45	Individual 43
	Men 55	Joint 57
	Total 100	Total 100
	(n = 27,292)	(n = 17,372)
Nicaragua	1994–2000	1997
	Women 33.5	Individual 45
	Men 66.5	Joint 45
		Other 10
	Total 100	Total 100
	(n = 40,332)	(n = 3,372)
Costa Rica	1990–92	
	Women 45	—
	Men 55	—
	Total 100	—
	(n = 1,279)	
El Salvador	1993–96	1993–96
	Women 34	Individual 100
	Men 66	Joint —
	Total 100	Total 100
	(n = 20,432)	(n = 20,432)
Land Titling Programs		
Chile	1993–96	1993–96
	Women 43	Individual 100
	Men 57	Joint —
	Total 100	Total 100
	(n = 1,474)*	(n = 1,474)
Ecuador	1992–96	1992–96
	Women 49	Individual 30
	Men 51	Joint 70
	Total 100	Total 100
	(n = 21,101)	(n = 12,416)
Honduras	1995–2000	1995–2000
	Women 25	Individual 100
	Men 75	Joint —
	Total 100	Total 100
	(n = 110,162)	(n = 110,162)
Mexico	1993–98	1993–98
	Women 21	Individual 100
	Men 79	Joint —
	Total 100	Total 100
	(n = 1.9 m.)	(n = 1.9 m.)

Sources: See Tables 6.2, 6.4, 6.3, 9.5, 9.4, 9.1, and 9.3; and for El Salvador (A. Alvarez 1998).
* Survey data

main way rural women acquire land is through inheritance, which positions them to be formally titled land when other obstacles, such as institutional sexism and the opposition of male relatives, can be overcome. Relatively gender-equitable inheritance practices are also reflected in the data on beneficiaries in the land-titling programs in Honduras and Mexico. Nonetheless, the less favorable outcomes for women in both these countries, as compared to Chile or Ecuador, suggest how important it is that titling programs contain explicit mechanisms for the inclusion of women, and that joint-titling provisions be mandatory.

Once concrete mechanisms of inclusion are contained in legislation, there is still no guarantee that these will have the effect of increasing women's ownership of land. Each step of the process becomes a point of contention because it involves nothing less than contesting patriarchy. Recall that in Colombia perpetual vigilance by the national rural women's organization, ANMUCIC, and its allies in the state and urban women's movement was required to assure that mechanisms to increase women's ownership of land would be maintained in the various revisions of the agrarian code and, most importantly, finally implemented from 1995 on, a process that took eight years. In Nicaragua efforts to implement mandatory joint titling to couples were initially subverted by the titling of land to pairs of men, and it took almost four years to secure compliance with this provision. Among the measures pursued to attain compliance by the agrarian reform agencies were staff training sessions in gender sensitivity, which in Nicaragua were also extended to potential beneficiaries of titling services. In Colombia this process was also facilitated by ANMUCIC's membership in local and regional beneficiary selection committees and the support for these gender-progressive policies by the agency's female director during her 1996–97 term.

The case of Honduras illustrates both the importance of perpetual vigilance on the part of the women's movement and the non-linearity of gender-progressive change. Here, a coalition of the women's movement and female parliamentarians (backed by representatives of the international organizations) had succeeded in rewriting agrarian reform legislation in 1991 to reverse previously discriminatory practices against women who were not household heads, as well as to favor widows in inheritance provisions, and to institute mandatory joint allocation and titling of agrarian reform land. Most of these provisions were maintained in the 1992 Law of Modernization of Agriculture, except one: mandatory joint titling. In the final drafting of the law, the infamous *colita* (tail, or rider) was added making joint titling voluntary, an option "if the couple so requested it." Notwithstanding the large numbers of organized rural women in this country, it has been impossible to reverse this setback to date. This is partly related to the lack until recently of a strong national women's office within the Honduran government. While in the early 1990s female legislators were partly able to compensate for this deficiency, their initiative in the legislative realm could not be sustained. Moreover, the lack of unity among rural women's organizations (reflecting, in large measure, the lack of unity among the mixed-sex peasant organizations with which they were allied) and the perceived divisiveness of gender issues in the overall struggle against the neo-liberal counter-reform were other contributing factors. The lesson here is of the importance of each element of the triangle of empowerment and of the need to sustain this alliance over time, but particularly of the need for an autonomous rural women's movement, able to effectively articulate women's strategic gender interests.

The Costa Rican case also illustrates the non-linearity of the struggle for gender equality and how it is conditioned by the state's overall commitment to policies of redistribution. The 1990 Law for Social Equality of Women was followed by a fairly comprehensive Plan for Equality of Opportunities and a subsequent Addendum for Rural Women, the latter the initiative of a strong national women's office. The Rural Women's Plan was the most comprehensive set of actions to be undertaken by a Latin American state to date in favor of rural women, and it included affirmative action measures intended to increase women's ownership of land. Recall that the agrarian reform institute, IDA, was instructed to approve all requests for land made by eligible rural women. This policy was to be complemented by a revision of the beneficiary-selection criteria to assure that greater numbers of women would be eligible for the land-distribution program, and by a major publicity effort to increase rural women's awareness of their land rights. But then a new government was elected that placed low priority on achieving women's real equality with men. Although its formal structure was left intact, the top-level staff of the Women's Office was changed and few efforts were made to operationalize the Rural Women's Plan. The inaction on the part of IDA has been such that they have successfully refused to make public gender-disaggregated data on their land-distribution and titling activities, even though this is required by law. The state's lack of political will—both on gender issues and with respect to agrarian reform—has seemingly prompted a retreat on the part of the women's movement from any engagement with the state at all, with the consequence that there has been no pressure on it and virtually no action on the progressive elements of the Rural Women's Plan.

These experiences raise the question of how to make gender-progressive gains irreversible. The importance of sustaining the strategic alliances that initiated these changes is evident. Further, it seems clear that the women's movement cannot afford the luxury of ignoring the state. Whatever the government in power, it must be held accountable to the international commitments in favor of gender equality assumed by the state. This means that the women's movement will have to negotiate an accommodation with the women's machinery within the state even when these positions are staffed by non-feminists. Another challenge is to maintain an open-ended, horizontal dialogue among the different constituencies of the women's movement—urban and rural, indigenous, white, black, and mestizo, and from across the social classes. Respect for difference is not a one-shot proposition but rather an on-going process of negotiation among equals in the elaboration of strategies and priorities, or the construction of democracy within the movement. It is also clear that a critical mass needs to be built within civil society in support of gender-progressive policies and the changes they can be expected to bring about.[2] A critical mass can include an expansion in the number of people favoring gender-progressive change; it can also refer to an accumulation of processes that themselves become irreversible. Important in the former is when a growing number of men join women in support of these policies. Basic to the latter are qualitative transformations that result from previous initiatives. These include the empowerment of rural women and the strengthening of their organizations, which may come about through struggles for land rights. Another related, qualitative transformation is rural women's increased bargaining power within the household and community derived from their ownership and control of land.

This brings us to the issue of property ownership, and which form— individual, joint, or collective—is most conducive to enhancing women's bargaining power and empowerment, and under what circumstances. It is somewhat of a paradox that in certain circumstances the individualization of land rights seems perfectly natural and acceptable, as in the case of inheritance of land, which is usually on an individual basis. Moreover, the liberal notion of property rights privileges the individual, as when neo-liberal agrarian codes convey property rights on natural and juridic persons. Yet the individual ownership of land by women appears to challenge the natural order of things. To quote María Elena Reynoso once again, "If the woman has land, it is to individualize ownership; if the man has land it is said that it is the family's land."[3] Two associated notions underlie this natural correspondence between male ownership and control of family land: an ideology of familialism and the patriarchal logic of peasant household reproduction.

The ideology of familialism is premised on the notion of a benign male household head whose actions are motivated by altruism rather than self-interest. This ideology has permeated both neo-classical economists' and political theorists' views of the household and family, and it has been translated into public policy that assumes that by benefiting male household heads, all members of the family benefit as well. One of the main contributions of feminist analysis in recent decades has been to challenge these assumptions, demonstrating that households are more accurately characterized by hierarchy and inequality, and that to benefit male household heads does not necessarily benefit women and children on a par with men. The logic of peasant household reproduction follows a reasoning similar to that of familialism, but it is grounded in the perceived need to maintain the family patrimony of land from generation to generation through patrilineality (and usually patri- or virilocality) in order to guarantee the survival of the family as the basic unit of production as well as the continuity of the community. Underlying community struggles over the maintenance of collective property is a similar logic, but one that places primary emphasis on the defense of community, with patrilineality seen as the best mechanism to guarantee it. What makes the demand for recognition of women's land rights so radical is that it contests patriarchy on two levels: (1) its material base—property ownership; and (2) its ideological system, which holds that the subordination of women is natural and serves higher principles, such as the unity and cohesion of the family, the continuation of the peasant family farm, and the reproduction of peasant and indigenous communities.

Because the demand for recognition of women's land rights is so radical, it has been much easier to press for joint allocation and titling of land to couples than for individual land rights for women (particularly married women) or a parcel of one's own. The argument for joint titling of land to couples is made most successfully as a defense of the peasant family—that is, that joint titling fosters family stability and enhances the security of women and children by reducing the likelihood that they will be abandoned by the male household head. It does this by enhancing women's fall-back position, which raises the costs of a potential separation to men, and by increasing women's bargaining position within the household. And while joint titling reduces the options of men, this is justified in public policy discourse on the grounds of the welfare of children.

A similar line of reasoning, concern for the welfare of children, has supported the recognition and priority that have been given to the land rights of female household heads. Rural female household heads can no longer be seen as an aberration; while the incidence of female household headship is strongly associated with civil wars, its link to male semi-proletarianization and migration (and the factors that cause it, land scarcity and rural poverty) is generally recognized. The land rights of female household heads are thus accepted as part of an anti-poverty strategy, one that addresses the short-term welfare of women and children and perhaps contributes toward family stability in the longer run. What is novel in the recognition of the land rights of female household heads is that it implicitly requires recognition of women as farmers. It thus helps to reduce the invisibility of women in agriculture and challenges the gender stereotype of the occupation of agriculturalist. Thus the demand for priority to female household heads in land distribution programs has several strategic elements: on one hand, it challenges traditional gender roles; and on the other, it opens the way for a discussion of the individual land rights of all women.

There is little question but that independent land rights for all women should be the goal for feminists. Independent land rights broaden women's options as to whether to form a union and with whom, and they give women the strongest fall-back position and degree of security within a union. Although more research is required on these questions in Latin America, independent land rights should give women the strongest bargaining power within the household, and they are probably a precondition for married women to exercise effective control over land. Moreover, women's ownership of land is critical, whether or not women are farmers, for the security that owning an asset conveys as well as the particular association between ownership of land, power, and women's empowerment.

A pressing issue in countries with large indigenous populations and communal forms of land ownership is women's right to representation in communal governance structures. Traditional customs and practices discriminate against women by limiting membership in community governance as well as effective land rights to one person per household, the household head. In practice, this system has served to exclude married women from the crucially important decisions governing the future of their communities. Under the counter-reform in Mexico, it has had the deleterious consequence of facilitating the conversion of family patrimony into individual, male private property. This experience demonstrates dramatically the need for all adults to be voting members of peasant and indigenous communities if processes within them are to be democratic. It also illustrates that land rights must be vested individually (in all adult members of the family and community) both to protect women's access to land and to secure the basis for their empowerment and exercise of citizenship.

Finally, a word needs to be said about women's ownership of land as members of production cooperatives. In the early 1980s it was thought that production cooperatives would be an ideal vehicle for establishing women's land rights, for they would seem to offer women a number of advantages over farming on their own or as a member of a family farm (Deere 1983, 1986). One of the benefits of production cooperatives is the larger pool of land and labor they make available. These advantages would favor mechanization, the specialization of the labor force, and a more diversified set of productive activities. It was hoped that the greater possibilities for training and specialization of labor might help to break down traditional gender roles. Another benefit the production cooperatives were expected to offer was recognition of women's individual land and membership rights. That is, when they joined cooperatives, even as members of family groups, membership was recognized on an individual basis, and their earnings were related to their individual labor effort, providing rural women with a basis for economic autonomy. The realization of these potentialities has differed broadly across Latin America, related to the mixed success of the cooperative movement in different countries. But what we have learned is the difficulty of incorporating women into cooperatives on the same terms as men, of changing the traditional gender division of labor, and of having women's work be valued on the same terms as men's (CIERA 1984). Partly as a result of these factors, women had little bargaining power within the cooperatives, being viewed by the male members as second-class workers and members. Thus when the production cooperatives were broken up under the counter-reforms, women everywhere have been at a disadvantage; their land rights have been trampled upon when they receive less land and land of poorer quality than the male members. This is probably one of the main negative consequences for women (besides the dispossession of married women from land rights on the Mexican *ejidos*) of the neo-liberal counter-reform in Latin America.

This result is partly related to lack of support that women cooperative members received from the rural unions and peasant organizations that pretended to represent them, as well as the latter's lack of attention until recently to gender issues.

Women have also acquired ownership and control of land as part of all-women collectives or production cooperatives, and rural women's organizations have demanded these in Colombia, Honduras, Costa Rica, and (in the past) Nicaragua. This form of organization of production potentially offers women many of the benefits of cooperative production without the constraints enumerated above. It may be a particularly promising approach to training women, such as when they do not consider themselves to be agriculturalists and capable of managing an independent land plot. The problem is that such women-only initiatives have often resulted in only marginal income-generating projects, such as the UAIMS in Mexico; they have rarely received the kind of sustained assistance from government agencies or NGOs required to be successful over time. The fact that there is not greater evidence of success of women's collectives is perhaps because they have not yet been part of an integrated strategy by rural women's own organizations to empower women in all dimensions. It is a strategy deserving of further consideration.

Turning to the broader issues of women's property rights, in most countries the women's movement has given insufficient attention to the implications of different marital regimes for women. But these can have enormous consequences for women in case they are widowed, separated, or divorced. There is no straightforward answer to the question of which marital regime is most favorable for women, since much depends on a woman's class position and her relative earnings and assets as compared to those of her spouse. The only general policy we would advocate is that countries allow couples to choose from among the broadest array of options (full common property, participation in profits, and separation of property). Moreover, a high priority for the women's movement as well as the national women's offices must be efforts to increase women's legal literacy so that they are aware of the options open to them and the implications of their choices.[4] While it is important that a range of marital regimes be made available, in most countries the default option usually pertains since couples are rarely aware that they have any other choices. The default option is thus what affects the greatest number of women, particularly rural women. Under existing conditions of inequality in the ownership of assets and in the life-time earnings prospects of men and women, the most favorable default option for the majority of poor women is that of full common property; the least favorable is the separation-of-property regime. In countries where the latter is the default regime (Costa Rica, Honduras, and Nicaragua), it will be important for the women's movement to question why this is the default regime and to study carefully its consequences for the economic position of wives and women in consensual unions.

The reform of inheritance laws in support of the rights of widows is one of the most critical tasks facing the women's movement, particularly in those countries with testamentary freedom (Costa Rica, El Salvador, Guatemala, and Mexico); where women in consensual unions do not have inheritance rights (Peru and Chile); or where a widow inherits from her husband's estate only in case of economic need. While the majority of countries provide for a *porción conjugal,* the objective of this provision is to protect widows from destitution, particularly in cases where the individual patrimonies of husband and wife are severely unequal. It was not designed to provide widows with economic autonomy. Under current inheritance legislation, it is unlikely that widows can maintain a controlling share of the family farm or business, or in some cases even the home. Whether they are able to do so largely depends on the goodwill of judges, husbands, and children, a situation that makes women particularly vulnerable.

With weak social security systems (particularly in terms of coverage of the rural population), their privatization in many countries under neoliberalism, the weakening of kinship and community networks, and the gender gap in the lengthening of life spans, older women are likely to be a growing share of the most economically vulnerable population. Moreover, the bargaining power of parents over children is closely associated with the former's control over property. Strengthening the inheritance rights of widows—such as by placing them in the first order of inheritance (along with children) should the spouse die intestate—could thus be one of the most effective means of strengthening the safety net of this vulnerable population, both by directly increasing the resources under their command and by enhancing their ability to command the assistance of children. Strengthening the inheritance rights of widows—to the extent that it brings about a redistribution of assets from men to women—could have other benefits with respect to changing gender relations and roles. While women's ownership of assets received through inheritance may be temporary or short lived, supporting the ability of widows to remain in control of the family farm or business enhances their economic autonomy and provides a role model for other women. In addition, there is evidence that women are more likely than men to will their property to daughters or to include all of their children as heirs. Thus, strengthening the inheritance rights of widows is likely to support a longer-run trend in favor of gender equity in inheritance of property.

The other great advantage in focusing on the inheritance rights of widows is that it is an issue of interest to both rural and urban women, and one that could potentially unite their movements. Along with the joint titling of land and housing to couples, irrespective of marital status, improving the inheritance rights of widows is among the issues that could benefit the greatest number of women in terms of increasing their ownership of assets and bargaining power. This coincidence of interests is absolutely necessary since, as the long century of struggle to enhance women's civil and property rights shows, reform of civil codes is not an easy task to achieve.[5]

Another measure specific to rural women is enhancing their inheritance rights in the new agrarian codes. Recall that the rules of inheritance in the agrarian reform laws were often more favorable to widows and women in consensual unions than the civil codes. With the exception of Honduras, this is no longer the case today, with neo-liberal agrarian legislation usually deferring to the civil codes in this matter. In Honduras widows have preferential right to any land distributed by the state, including the titling of public lands and, presumably, other land distributed in the past under the agrarian reform. Such a retroactive measure would be most beneficial in those countries of recent state land distribution programs (such as Colombia, Nicaragua, and El Salvador); but it is relevant in all countries engaged in the titling of public lands or where the state is supporting land banks with public funds. Preference to widows in the inheritance of lands adjudicated by the state would be particularly important in those countries (e.g., Colombia and Bolivia) where legislation forbids the sub-division of family units of production.

Another challenge facing the women's movement is how to foster a culture of equality with respect to inheritance by children. The Latin American legal tradition of equal inheritance among all children has not resulted in anything approaching equality between men and women in the ownership of land, although it has contributed toward inheritance being the primary means through which women have acquired land. The fact that sons are more likely to inherit land than are daughters and, when both receive land, to inherit larger and better plots reflects the manner in which inheritance is conditioned by gender roles. Since sons are expected to become agriculturalists and daughters housewives, land has been concentrated in the male line while female inheritance sometimes takes the form of other assets, such as animals. These gender-differentiated forms of inheritance, however, have rarely resulted in inheritance shares of equal value, with capital accumulation favoring sons.

There is considerable evidence suggesting that where agriculture is no longer the primary source of income in peasant economies, inheritance of land among children tends to become more equitable, with other factors besides gender (such as who remains to care for elderly parents or contributes the most through remittances) influencing the division of the family property. The main challenge, thus, is how to promote gender equity when agriculture is still an important source of livelihood. Among the measures that could be important in creating a culture of equality are those promoting the valorization of women's work in agriculture and the recognition of women as citizens, with the right to pursue agriculture as a vocation and to demand equality in inheritance. A starting point in this direction are campaigns for the documentation of rural women, such as that being carried out in Brazil. Strong rural women's organizations are obviously necessary both to support changes in gender roles and to promote rural women's achievement of effective citizenship.

Turning to the other prospects for increasing women's ownership of land, we have identified two trends in land distribution in the neo-liberal era: those countries where agrarian reform efforts have come to an end (Chile, Ecuador, El Salvador, Honduras, Mexico, Nicaragua, and Peru) or are practically dormant (Costa Rica), and those countries where in the 1990s a role for the state in land redistribution was still envisioned— Colombia, Bolivia, Brazil, and Guatemala. It is in this latter group where the state may still expropriate land for purposes of social justice, although, at the close of the twentieth century, the only country in which expropriation of unutilized land was still taking place was Brazil, due to pressure from the landless movement and rural unions. In Bolivia the promise of its 1996 Ley INRA has yet to be realized, as the Banzer government (elected in 1997) has largely failed to implement it. Under Colombia's 1994 law on agrarian reform, efforts switched in 1996 from an emphasis on state purchases of land to market-assisted land transactions. But by 1998 even the latter program had virtually come to a complete halt due to a lack of political will, the escalating violence and non-governability of the country, and the absence of consensus regarding the implementation of agrarian reform measures. Driven by the momentum of the peace accords, Guatemala appears to be moving forward with plans for land redistribution via a new land bank. In Brazil the Cardoso government announced its intention of converting the experimental land bank program carried out in the Northeast into the new model for agrarian reform efforts, suggesting that the state's role in land expropriation and distribution is soon to diminish. How likely is it that these land-bank programs will increase women's access to land?

The land market is not gender neutral, an observation related to the fact that the form of land acquisition in Latin America has been quite gender differentiated. While market purchases are often the primary means that men acquire land, among women inheritance is a much more important mechanism. Women are at a disadvantage as buyers in the land market for a number of reasons. The ability to participate in this market is a function of savings and access to credit, which in turn depend upon the array of income-generating activities in which men and women engage and their respective rates of remuneration. The lower rate of female participation in the land market reflects their lesser income-generating opportunities, which limit their capacity to save as well as their creditworthiness. Moreover, holding economic factors constant, women and men are not on a level playing field when it comes to negotiating in this market; gender-role socialization makes it is difficult for women to bargain as equals with men, as suggested by case study evidence that women pay higher prices for land. Overall, though, there has been insufficient research carried out on land markets from a gender perspective, making this a topic ripe for attention. With the growing interest in the functioning of land markets, it will be important for future studies to take into account not only who owns each parcel of land but how it was acquired, from whom, and on what terms.

What would it take to increase women's participation in the land market? Past programs to provide subsidized credit for land acquisition have been directed to male household heads with the objective of benefiting poor households. The main program where significant numbers of women have benefited has been Colombia's market-assisted land reform, where participation in the subsidized credit program was conditioned on mandatory allocation and titling to couples and where priority was also given to female household heads. These experiences suggest that the state will continue to have a crucially important role to play if markets are to produce more gender-equitable outcomes.

The new Guatemalan legislation creating a land bank looks excellent from a gender perspective, for it explicitly designates peasant men and women as potential beneficiaries. Moreover, the legislation includes specific mechanisms of inclusion, providing for mandatory joint allocation and titling of land and priority inclusion of female household heads in the program. The projected land-bank program in Brazil is much more problematic from a gendered perspective. While women and couples are potential beneficiaries of agrarian reform efforts, no specific mechanisms have been adopted to insure that this will be the case; thus it is highly unlikely that an expanded land-bank program will increase women's ownership of land under these conditions. A major effort would be required by the national rural women's movement to make women's land rights a state priority, which in turn depends on women's land rights becoming a top priority for the ANMTR, as well as for the MST and the rural unions. It is unlikely that this will happen while the future of the agrarian reform and the very proposal for an expanded land bank remain such contentious issues.

Land banks are an unsatisfactory alternative to agrarian reform for a number of reasons. First, by providing an alternative means for some peasant households to acquire land, they serve to absolve the state of responsibility for assuring that the distribution of land meets social-justice objectives. Second, they potentially reward landlords who otherwise might have been expropriated (for having holdings above a certain size and/or unproductive lands) with payment at market prices, often in cash. This makes them both unjust in class terms and an expensive proposition for the state. Third, for significant numbers of the landless to benefit depends on sufficient land being offered for sale at reasonable prices. As long as land remains a source of power and prestige, as well as a hedge against inflation, it is doubtful that large numbers of landlords will voluntarily offer their land for sale. Powerful incentives—such as a progressive system of land taxation—must be in place, in an overall context of macro stability, to reasonably expect landlords to participate in a competitive land market. Fourth, for significant numbers to benefit also depends on the availability of long-term credit at reasonable terms. Given the adverse conditions for non-export agriculture in most countries, it is doubtful that a land-mortgage program will be viable at near-commercial interest rates. Thus the impact of a land-bank program in meeting the demand for land ultimately depends on political will: the will to tax land so that it is offered for sale in sufficient quantities and so that enough revenues are generated to allow the state to adequately subsidize land purchases by the poor. If, in addition, a goal of a land-bank program is to reduce rural poverty, then the complementary resources (social and productive infrastructure, credit for working capital, technical assistance, and so forth) have to be made available to potential male and female beneficiaries as well.

At the close of the 1990s, land titling programs were the main state initiative in the agricultural sector in most Latin American counties. We highlighted the lack of conceptual clarity with respect to ownership rights in the design of these programs. Few began with any notion about the bundle of property rights potentially encompassed within the household: that land might belong to the husband, the wife, or be jointly acquired property. Little thought was given to the need to make land-titling procedures consistent with the marital regimes of the civil codes, let alone to new provisions establishing the dual-headed household. Inattention to the land rights of married women and those in consensual unions has been a major source of gender inequity, particularly in the programs in Mexico, Honduras, and initially Peru. Vesting land rights in only one person per household, the household head, may have served to dispossess married women in those countries of ownership rights over the common property of the union. An additional problem in Peru and Honduras has been the difficulty of legally recognizing couples in consensual unions and by extension, their property rights.

Nonetheless, the land-titling programs to date have been more gender equitable than previous programs of state intervention. A comparison of outcomes in countries having specific mechanisms to include women with outcomes in countries that pretend to be gender neutral shows that gender-equitable legislation does make a difference but that such provisions have to be mandatory. That the percentage of women beneficiaries in all countries is higher than the share of women who benefited directly from the agrarian reforms of the past also reflects the fact that the number of existing women landowners is not negligible and that inheritance has been the primary way by which rural women acquire land.

Although land-titling programs are coming to a close in Chile and Mexico, in other countries there is still a long way to go in satisfying the demand for land titles. But there is little time to waste in implementing inclusionary measures, for once land is titled, ownership rights are most difficult to contest. The tasks facing the women's movement differ by country. In Bolivia, El Salvador, and Brazil the need is to develop mandatory mechanisms of inclusion of women. In Honduras and Peru these mechanisms have been partial and incomplete, and the main task is to secure co-ownership titles for couples in consensual unions. Also in Peru, if highland communities vote to parcelize their communal lands—an option open to them since 1995—a major effort of consciousness raising will be required to assure that as the land is "individualized," women are not be excluded from ownership rights, as has happened in Mexico. In Nicaragua, Colombia, Ecuador, Guatemala, and Costa Rica perpetual vigilance will be necessary to make sure that gender-progressive norms are in fact implemented. In all countries, the active involvement of rural women's organizations will be required to make sure that rural women are aware of their land rights and are supported to take advantage of them. In addition, the rural women's movement and national women's machinery will have to remain perpetually vigilant to make sure that female farmers are not discriminated against in access to credit, training, and technical assistance, which in turn will help assure that they do not become a disproportionate number of those selling land on the land market.

A central concern of this book has been how to eliminate or reduce the distance between formal and real gender equality through a redistribution in the ownership of assets. The range of policy interventions upon which we have focused—joint titling of land to couples; the use of affirmative action measures to favor specific groups of women, such as female household heads; strengthening the inheritance rights of wives; and establishing effective land rights for women within peasant and indigenous communities—should all contribute toward a more gender-equitable redistribution of land ownership. Most of these policies have the advantage of combining redistribution with issues of recognition—in particular, promoting the recognition of women as full and equal citizens. Promoting the land rights of women within peasant and indigenous communities also requires that issues of representation in governance be directly addressed and challenges the distribution of power within these communities as well as within the household. But while crucially important, these interventions may be of relatively limited scope in terms of the actual amount of land to be redistributed. What could potentially do the most to enhance rural women's ownership of assets (particularly for landless rural women) would be a policy of fundamental land redistribution—that is, a policy of redistribution that was not only gender based but also involved the redistribution of land among social classes.

At the close of the twentieth century land in Latin America was as concentrated as ever. The main change over the last half of that century was that the agricultural frontier was greatly reduced in size, leading to the expansion of potentially cultivable land but little change in its distribution. A notable feature of many countries continues to be the large amount of unproductive land. Moreover, the problems of landlessness, under- and unemployment, and associated rural poverty continue. Because of extensive rural-urban migration, poverty is now concentrated in urban centers, but rural areas remain among the poorest in the region. Another important change is that agriculture is no longer the main source of wealth in most countries, as evidenced by the dramatic fall in the share of agriculture in GDP. One would think that under these conditions land would be much easier to redistribute. However, in most Latin American countries agricultural exports are still key (see Appendix: Table 6), and, indeed, are the focus of the neo-liberal model, providing one explanation for why the political will continues to be missing to carry out a fundamental redistribution of landed property.

Nonetheless, it would seem to be fairly obvious that the policy that could do most to alleviate rural poverty would be to redistribute idle land to the men and women willing to work it. While agrarian reform no longer has the same economic logic that it did under the period of import-substitution industrialization (when land distribution was seen as necessary to enlarge the internal market and increase domestic foodstuff production to keep real wages low for the industrialization effort), the social logic is just as compelling. With urban areas unable to absorb the excess supply of rural labor (coupled with high crime rates and the deteriorating quality of life in the cities), a rural solution to the problem of persistent high rates of poverty and inequality is increasingly critical, if not indispensable, in many countries. The question is how to create the political will for land redistribution under these new circumstances. Another issue is what kind of land reform to pursue and how to learn from the shortcomings of past efforts.

We are only certain of one aspect: the women's movement must be a part of any solution to the agrarian question. Without the mobilization of women in support of land redistribution, it is unlikely to happen. The new factor in the political equation in most countries is the growing organization of rural women and of their national organizations and networks. Rural women also have the most to gain from a new wave of land reform, one to be carried out under new terms, designed to promote gender equality. Their active participation could be what tips the scales in favor of land redistribution and social justice in the new millennium. Moreover, social justice with redistribution and recognition is necessary to broaden women's citizenship, to deepen democratic processes in most countries, and to sustain a culture of equality.

Appendix

Notes

References

Index

Appendix

TABLE I. Form of Acquisition of Land for Agrarian Reform and Colonization, Thirteen Latin American Countries

Country and Year	Expropriation with Compensation	Landlord Reserves	Public Lands	State Purchases
Bolivia				
1953	Yes	Yes		
1967			Yes	
Brazil				
1964	Yes	Yes	Yes	
Chile				
1967	Yes	Yes		Yes
Colombia				
1961	Yes	Yes	Yes	Yes
1988	Yes	Yes	Yes	Yes
Costa Rica				
1961	No expropriation		Yes	Yes
Cuba				
1959	Yes	Yes		
Ecuador				
1964	Yes	Yes		
1970	Yes	Yes		
1973	Yes	Yes	Yes	
El Salvador				
1980	Yes	Yes		
Guatemala				
1952	Yes	Yes	Yes	
1962	No expropriation		Yes	
1986				Yes
Honduras				
1962	Yes	Yes	Yes	
1975	Yes	Yes	Yes	
Mexico				
1917	Yes	Yes	Yes	
Nicaragua				
1981	Yes	Yes	Yes	
Peru				
1969	Yes	Yes		

Sources: Thiesenhusen (1989; 1995), Dorner (1992), Escoto (1965), and Menjívar (1969); and for Bolivia: Villarroel and Barrios Ávila (1969); for Brazil: Hall (1990), Fernandes (1996), and Cardoso (1997); for Chile: Silva (1991) and Kay and Silva (1992); for Colombia: Edwards (1980) and Fajardo (1983); for Costa Rica: Barahona (1980) and Román (1994); for Cuba: INRA (1960) and Valdés Paz (1997); for Ecuador: Barsky (1984) and Zavallos (1989); for El Salvador: Diskin (1989); for Guatemala: Pedroni (1991), Berger (1992), and Paz Carcamo (1997); for Honduras: Salgado (1996, 1997) and Honduras (1962, 1975); for Mexico: Alexander (1974) and Otero (1989); for Nicaragua: CIERA (1989); and for Peru: Deere (1990).

TABLE 2. Form of Distribution to Beneficiaries of Agrarian Reform and Colonization Programs, Thirteen Countries

| Country/ Year | Individual | Collective Adjudications | | | Land Payment |
		Existence of/Form	Individual Usufruct	Production Cooperative	
Bolivia					
1953	Yes	Yes	Yes		No
1967	Yes				Yes
Brazil					
1964		*assentamentos*	Yes	Yes	Yes
Chile					
1967		*asentamientos*	Yes	Yes	Yes
1970		CERAS	Yes	Yes	Yes
Colombia					
1961	Yes				Yes
1973		*empresas comunitarias*	Yes	Yes	Yes
Costa Rica					
1961	Yes	*asentamientos*	Yes	Yes	Yes
Cuba					
1959	Yes	state farms	No	(1959–61)	No
1963		state farms	No		No
1977		CPAS		Yes	Yes
Ecuador					
1964	Yes				No
1970		Yes	Yes	Yes	Yes
1973		Yes	Yes	Yes	Yes
El Salvador					
1980		Yes	Yes	Yes	Yes
1983	Yes				Yes
Guatemala					
1952	Yes	Yes			Yes
1962	Yes	Yes	Yes	Yes	Yes
1986		Yes	Yes		Yes
Honduras					
1962	Yes				Yes
1975		*asentamientos*	Yes	Yes	Yes
Mexico					
1920		*ejidos*	Yes		No
1934–40		*ejidos*	Yes	Yes	No
Nicaragua					
1981	Yes	CAS	No	Yes	Yes
		state farms	No	No	
Peru					
1964	Yes				Yes
1969	Yes	SAIS, CAPS	Yes	Yes	Yes

Sources: See Appendix: Table 1.

TABLE 3. National Offices on Women and Gender Affairs, Twelve Countries

Country	Year	Name	Dependency of
Bolivia	1993	Subsecretaría de Asuntos de Género	Ministerio de Desarrollo Humano
	1997	Dirección General de Asuntos de Género, Generaciones y Familia	Ministerio de Desarrollo Sustenible
Brazil	1985	CNDM, Conselho Nacional de Direitos da Mulher	Ministerio de Justicia
Chile	1991	SERNAM, Servicio Nacional de la Mujer	Ministerio de Planificación y Cooperación
Colombia	1990	Consejería de Juventud, Mujer y Familia	Presidencia
	1995	DINEM, Dirección Nacional de Equidad para Mujer	Presidencia
	1999	Consejería para la Equidad de la Mujer	Presidencia
Costa Rica	1980s	Dirección General de la Mujer y Familia	
	1986	CMF, Centro Nacional de la Mujer y Familia	Ministerio de Cultura, Juventud, y Deporte
	1998	Instituto Nacional de la Mujer	autonomous
Ecuador	1980	Oficina Nacional de la Mujer	Ministerio de Bienestar
	1986	DINAMU, Dirección Nacional de la Mujer	Ministerio de Bienestar
	1997	CONAMU, Consejo Nacional de la Mujer	Presidencia
El Salvador	1989	Oficina de la Mujer	Secretaría para la Familia
	1996	ISDEMU, Instituto Salvadoreño para el Desarrollo de la Mujer	Presidencia
Guatemala	1981	ONAM, Oficina Nacional de la Mujer	Ministerio de Trabajo y Seguridad Social
Honduras	1994	Oficina Gubernamental de la Mujer	Presidencia
	1999	INAM, Instituto Nacional de la Mujer Hondureña	autonomous

TABLE 3.

Country	Year	Name	Dependency of
Mexico	1980	PRONAM, Programa Nacional de Integración de la Mujer al Desarrollo	Comisión Nacional de Población
	1996	Programa Nacional de la Mujer	Secretaría de Gobernación
	1998	CONAM, Coordinación General Programa Nacional de la Mujer	Secretaría de Gobernación
Nicaragua	1983	Oficina Nacional de la Mujer	Presidencia
	1987	INIM, Instituto Nicaragüense de la Mujer	Presidencia
	1998	INIM	Ministerio de la Familia, Mujer y Juventud
Peru	1983	Oficina Nacional de la Mujer	Ministerio de Justicia
	1996	PROMUDEH, Ministerio de Promoción de la Mujer y Desarrollo Humano	

Source: Valdés and Gomáriz (1995: 185), CEPAL (1998), and authors' interviews.

TABLE 4. Rural Women's Offices and Secretariats in Mixed Peasant Organizations, Twelve Countries

Country	Peasant Organization	Rural Women's Secretariats/Year
Bolivia	CSUTCB, Confederación Sindical Única de Trabajadores del Campo de Bolivia	Vinculación Femenina, 1979
	CIDOB, Confederación Indígena del Oriente Boliviano	Departamento Mujer, 1990s
	Confederación Sindical de Colonizadores de Bolivia	Vinculación Femenina, 1980s, and five regional women's federations, 1990s
Brazil	CUT, Central Única de Trabalhadores	Comisão Nacional da Questão da Mulher Urbana e Rural, 1986
	CONTAG, Conferação Nacional de Trabalhadores Agrícolas	Comisão Nacional de Mulheres Trabalhadoras, 1997
	MST, Movimento dos Trabalhadores Sem Terra	Colectivo Nacional de Mulheres do MST, 1996
		Colectivo Nacional de Gênero, 1999
Chile	CNC, Comisión Nacional Campesina	Departamento Femenino, 1984
	Confederación El Surco	Departamento Femenino, 1986
	Confederación Triunfo Campesino	Departamento Femenino, 1986
	Confederación Unidad Obrero Campesina	Departamento Femenino, 1986

TABLE 4.

Country	Peasant Organization	Rural Women's Secretariats/Year
Chile	MUCECH, Movimiento Unitario Campesino y de Etnias de Chile	Secretaría de Mujer Rural, 1995
Colombia	ANUC, Asociación Nacional de Usuarios Campesinos	Secretaría Femenina, 1977
	FESTRACOL, Federación de Trabajadores Agrarios de Colombia	Secretaría Femenina, 1981
	FEMSUAGRO	Secretaría de la Mujer, 1985
	FANAL, Federación Agraria Nacional	Secretaría de Asuntos Femeninos, 1986
	ANDRI, Asociación Nacional de Usuarios de Proyectos de Desarrollo Rural	Comité Femenino, 1986
	ANUC Reconstrucción	Programa Mujer y Familia, 1987
	ACC, Acción Campesina Colombiana	Secretaría de la Mujer, 1989
	ONIC, Organización Nacional Indígena de Colombia	Secretaría de Mujeres, 1990
Costa Rica	UPA, Unión de Pequeños y Medianos Productores Agropecuarios	Proyecto de la Mujer y Jóven, 1990
	Mesa Campesina	Coordinadora Nacional para el Trabajo con la Mujer Campesina, 1995
Ecuador	ECUARUNARI	Secretaría de la Mujer, 1978
	CONFENIAE, Confederación de Nacionalidades Indígenas de la Amazonia Ecuatoriana	Comisión Nacional de Mujeres, 1982–85
	CONAIE, Confederación de Nacionalidades Indígenas del Ecuador	Comisión Nacional de Mujeres Indígenas del Ecuador, 1986
El Salvador	ANTA, Asociación Nacional de Trabajadores Agropecuarios	Secretaría de la Mujer, 1985
	ADC, Aliànza Democrática Campesina	Secretaría de la Mujer, 1990s
	ACCO, Asociación Comunal Campesina de Occidente	Secretaría de la Mujer, 1994
Guatemala	CUC, Comité Único Campesino	None
	COPMAGUA, Coordinadora de Organizaciones del Pueblo Maya de Guatemala	Consejo de Mujeres Mayas, 1990
	CONIC, Coordinadora Nacional Indígena y Campesina de Guatemala	Secretaría de la Mujer, 1993
	CONAMPRO, Coordinadora de Pequeños y Medianos Productores	Comisión de la Mujer, 1996
	CNOC, Coordinadora Nacional de Organizaciones Campesinas	None

TABLE 4.

Country	Peasant Organization	Rural Women's Secretariats/Year
Honduras	UNC, Unión Nacional Campesina	Secretaría de Asuntos Femeninos, 1963
	ANACH, Asociación Nacional de Campesinos de Honduras	JUFEDECO, Juntas Femeninas para el Desarrollo Comunal, 1975
		ANAMUC, Asociación de Mujeres Campesinas, 1982
	CNTC, Central Nacional de Trabajadores del Campo	Secretaría del Programa de Desarrollo Integral de la Mujer Campesina, 1980s
	COCOCH, Consejo Coordinador de Organizaciones Campesinas	Secretaría de la Mujer, 1988
	UTC, Unión de Trabajadores del Campo	Equipo Nacional de la Mujer, 1991
	COCENTRA, Confederación Centroamericana de Trabajadores	Comisión Regional de Mujeres de Centro America, 1991
		Comité Femenino Nacional de la Mujer, 1994
Mexico	CNC, Confederación Nacional Campesina	UAIMS, 1970s+
	CNPA, Coordinación Nacional Plan de Ayala	Comisión de la Mujer, 1984
	UNORCA, Unión Nacional de Organizaciones Regionales Campesinas Autónomas	Red Nacional de Mujeres, 1993
	CAP, Consejo Agrario Permanente	Comisión de la Mujer, 1990s
	ANIPA, Asamblea Nacional Indígena por la Autonomía	Comisión de Mujeres, 1990s
Nicaragua	UNAG, Unión Nacional de Agricultores y Ganaderos	División de la Mujer, 1986
	ATC, Asociación de Trabajadores del Campo	Secretaría de la Mujer, 1984
Peru	CCP, Confederación Campesina del Perú	Secretaría de la Mujer, 1979
		Comisión Nacional de Asuntos de la Mujer, 1987
		+ Asociaciones Departamentales de Mujeres Campesinas, 1985+
	CNA, Confederación Nacional Agricultores	Secretaría Femenina, 1988
		+ Asociaciones Departamentales de Mujeres Campesinas

Sources: Sources cited in text and authors' interviews.

TABLE 5. National Rural Women's Organizations, Twelve Countries

Country	Date	Name	Origins
Bolivia	1980	Federación de Mujeres Campesinas de Bolivia "Bartolina Sisa"	CSUTCB
	1987	Central de Mujeres Indígenas del Beni	Central de Pueblos Indígenas del Beni, CIDOB
	1990s	Federación de Mujeres del Trópico de Cochabamba	Federación de Colonizadores de Cochabamba, Confederación Sindical de Colonizadores de Bolivia
	1995	Federación de Mujeres Productores de Coca	Federaciones de Productores de Hoja de Coca
Brazil	1980s	AMTRS, Articulação de Mulheres Trabalhadoras Rurais do Sul	CONTAG, CUT, MST, Comisão Pastoral da Terra, CEBs, autonomous women
	1980s	MMTR-NE, Movimento Mulheres Trabalhadoras Rurais-NE	CONTAG, Comisão Pastoral da Terra, CEBs, autonomous women
	1995	ANMTR, Articulação Nacional de Mulheres Trabalhadoras Rurais	AMTRS, MMTR-NE, state-level MMTRs, women's commissions of mixed organizations, such as MST
Chile	1997	Red Nacional de Mujeres Rurales e Indígenas	CEDEM, Departamento Femenino de la CNC, Coordinadora de Mujeres Mapuches, and others
	1998	ANAMURI, Asociación Nacional de Mujeres Rurales e Indígenas	Red Nacional de Mujeres Rurales e Indígenas plus others, including women's unions
Colombia	1984	ANMUCIC, Asociación Nacional de Mujeres Campesinas y Indígenas de Colombia	State, ANUC
	1998	Red de Organizaciones de Mujeres Rurales	State, plus national and regional women's organizations
Costa Rica	1996	Asociación de Mujeres Productoras Rurales de Costa Rica	State, local-level women's organizations
Ecuador	1996	CONMIE, Consejo Nacional de Mujeres Indígenas del Ecuador	Independents, local and regional women's organizations
El Salvador	1987	AMS, Asociación de Mujeres Salvadoreñas	CBCS, FMLN
	1990	Asociación de Mujeres por la Dignidad y la Vida	FMLN-RN
	1993	CNC, Central de Mujeres Campesinas	ADC

TABLE 5. National Rural Women's Organizations, Twelve Countries

Country	Date	Name	Origins
	1995	Asociación para el Desarrollo Integral de la Mujer	Independents
	1998	Mesa Permanente de Mujeres Rurales	INU, Las Dignas, CNC, and others
Guatemala	1987–88	CONAVIGUA, Coordinación Nacional de Viudas de Guatemala	CBCS
	1990	Mama Maquín	Exile
	1993	Madre Tierra	Exile
	1993	Organización Ixmucane	Exile
Honduras	1977	FEMUC, Federación de Mujeres Campesinas of Honduras	UNC, Clubes de Amas de Casa
	1982	ANAMUC, Asociación Nacional de Mujeres Campesinas	ANACH
	1985	CODIMCA, Consejo para el Desarrollo Integral de la Mujer Campesina	FEHMUC
	1990	AHMUR, Asociación Hondureña de Mujeres Urbanas y Rurales	FEHMUC
	1991	AHMUC, Asociación Hondureña de Mujeres Campesinas	Independents
	1994	ENMUNEH, Enlace de Mujeres Negras	Independents
	1997	UMCAH, Unión Campesina de Mujeres de Honduras	Independents
	1996	REDNAMURH, Red Nacional de Mujeres Rurales de Honduras	FEHMUC, CODIMCA, AHMUR, ENMUNEH, and others
	1999	Confederación Hondureña de Mujeres Campesinas	Five peasant women's federations
Mexico	1997	ANMOR, Asociación de Mujeres Mexicanas Organizadas en Red	Red Nacional de Mujeres de UNORCA
	1997	Federación Nacional de Uniones de UAIMs, y Organizaciones Económicas de Campesinas	CNC
Nicaragua	1998	FEMUPROCAN, Federación de Mujeres Productoras de Nicaragua	UNAG and ATC Women's Secretariats, Resistance Women, independents
Peru	1987	Red Nacional de la Mujer Rural	Departmental networks of NGOs, departmental and provincial peasant women's organizations, Centro de la Mujer Peruana "Flora Tristán"

Sources: As cited in text and authors' interviews.

TABLE 6. Comparative Sectoral Data, Latin America, mid-1990s

Country	Land Area (millions sq. km)	Population (millions)	Rural Population (%)	Labor Force in Agriculture (%)	Agriculture as Share of GDP (%)	Agriculture as Share of Total Exports (%)
Argentina	2.78	35.7 (1997)	13.4 (1996)	10.4 (1997)	5.5 (1993)	54.1 (1995)
Bolivia	1.1	7.8 (1997)	40.3 (1996)	45.0 (1997)	15.3 (1996)	31.3 (1995)
Brazil	8.46	163.1 (1997)	17.8 (1996)	18.5 (1997)	12.2 (1995)	34.4 (1995)
Chile	0.76	14.6 (1997)	11.9 (1996)	16.6 (1997)	9.3 (1990)	37.2 (1995)
Colombia	1.14	37.1 (1997)	25.7 (1996)	22.2 (1997)	12.9 (1995)	35.7 (1995)
Costa Rica	0.05	3.6 (1997)	50.7 (1996)	21.8 (1997)	15.5 (1996)	71.3 (1995)
Dominican Republic	0.05	8.1 (1997)	33.6 (1996)	18.9 (1997)	14.6 (1990)	42.6 (1992)
Ecuador	0.27	11.9 (1997)	38.3 (1996)	28.0 (1997)	11.9 (1996)	56.0 (1995)
El Salvador	0.02	5.9 (1997)	50.7 (1996)	31.1 (1997)	12.9 (1996)	52.2 (1994)
Guatemala	0.11	11.2 (1997)	55.4 (1996)	48.1 (1997)	n/a	69.3 (1995)
Honduras	0.11	5.9 (1997)	51.3 (1996)	34.5 (1997)	22.1 (1996)	84.6 (1994)
Mexico	1.97	94.2 (1997)	24.8 (1996)	22.3 (1997)	5.9 (1996)	9.0 (1995)
Nicaragua	0.12	4.4 (1997)	25.3 (1996)	22.4 (1997)	33.8 (1996)	77.8 (1995)
Panama	0.08	2.7 (1997)	44.6 (1996)	22.0 (1997)	8.1 (1996)	75.4 (1995)
Paraguay	0.41	5.1 (1997)	47.9 (1996)	35.7 (1997)	25.4 (1996)	85.8 (1995)
Peru	1.28	24.4 (1997)	29.0 (1996)	31.8 (1997)	7.2 (1996)	34.2 (1995)
Uruguay	0.18	3.2 (1997)	13.4 (1996)	13.1 (1997)	10.0 (1996)	59.5 (1995)
Venezuela	0.91	22.8 (1997)	5.5 (1996)	9.1 (1997)	4.1 (1996)	2.9 (1995)

Sources: For land area, rural population, agriculture as share of GDP, and agriculture as a share of exports, Inter-American Development Bank, *Basic Socio-Economic Data: Statistics and Quantitative Analysis* (Washington, D.C.: IADB, 1998), various tables; and for population and share of labor force in agriculture, FAO, *Production Yearbook 1997,* vol. 5 (Rome: FAO, 1998), table 3.

Notes

Preface

1. Deere also received a small grant, the Healey Faculty Research Grant, from the Graduate School of the University of Massachusetts at this time to conduct follow-up field work on women's land rights in Cajamarca, Peru, the locale of her doctoral dissertation research in the mid-1970s.

2. These are cited in the bibliography as Deere and León (1997; 1998c; 1998d; 1998e; 1999a; 1999b; 1999c) and León and Deere (1999).

Chapter 1: The Importance of Gender and Property

1. Excerpts from interviews in the state of Oaxaca, Mexico, by Josefina Aranda (1993: 187). Unless indicated, all translations from a Spanish source to English are our own.

2. Mayan woman NGO worker in Guatemala, in Fundación Arias–Tierra Viva (1993: 58).

3. We use the terms "property" and "assets" interchangeably. Assets are defined as all personal property that may be used in the payment of debts, including real estate (land, housing, and buildings); other productive assets (machinery and equipment); financial assets (savings accounts, stocks, and bonds); and consumer durables (automobiles and appliances). Assets are distinguished from income in that the former represent a store of wealth; that is, it is a stock rather than a flow concept. Income in any given period, of course, may contribute to increasing the stock of assets if it is saved rather than consumed.

4. We examined almost every agricultural census published since 1960 for the nineteen Latin American republics. Only four countries have published data on the gender of their farmers. Up until the 1980s most census questionnaires did not even ask the sex of the farm operator, it was so taken for granted that only men

were agriculturalists. Most agricultural censuses now include the sex variable in the questionnaire, but then do not process and publish this information in the census volumes.

5. Tenancy arrangements, such as land rental or sharecropping, also involve land rights since such agreements usually consist of mutually enforceable claims. We focus primarily on land rights governing the ownership of individual private property or the usufruct of communal land and give less attention to tenancy arrangements.

6. The above definition of land rights parallels the standard definition of property rights. As a legal concept, property refers to *rights* in or to things, with rights defined as an enforceable claim. Thus a "given system of property is a system of rights of each person in relation to other persons" (MacPherson 1981: 4) or an institution. Property rights are commonly thought of as the rights of ownership; however, in legal thinking some elements of ownership are not rights (Becker 1997: 18–19; Reeve 1993: 558–67). Moreover, many rights may be associated with any given asset, and, to complicate things, subsets of rights can be possessed or owned by different persons (Demsetz 1998: 145). There is consensus that the owner of a right must control at least three elements of the bundle of possible rights: (1) to use a resource; (2) to exclude others from doing so without his/her permission; and (3) to transfer control of this bundle of rights to others (ibid.). Thus, ownership means that "the owner has an entitlement bundle that includes the exclusive, alienable right of use" (ibid.). It should be apparent from this elaboration that the concept of ownership refers to a specific set or form of property rights.

7. An excellent summary of the activities of the international women's movement and the UN conferences in support of women's equality is given by Moghadam (1998).

8. The per capita Gross Domestic Product (GDP) growth rate for twenty-six Latin American and Caribbean countries fell by an average of 1.1 percent during the 1980s, compared with an average annual 3.5 percent growth rate in the decade of the 1970s (IADB 1997: table B-2).

9. On the transfer of surplus see Pastor (1987); on the shift in the costs of reproduction of labor, see Wyss (1995), Bolles (1983), Antrobus (1989), Deere et al. (1990), Elson (1991), and Benería and Feldman (1992).

10. A gender-neutral policy is one that does not have any impact on gender relations; a gender-blind policy is one assumed not to have any impact on gender. A gender-biased policy is one where the benefits or costs fall unduly on one gender. As Judith Astelarra (1995: 29) argues, almost every public policy has some impact on women's lives, whether intended or unintended.

11. On women in what are known as the *máquilas* or export-processing zones, see Fernandez-Kelley (1983), Nash and Fernandez-Kelley (1983), and Safa (1995); on women in the informal sector, see Benería and Roldán (1987) and Scott (1991); and on the feminization of agricultural labor see the articles in Deere and León (1987b) and Lara Flores (1995).

12. The second-generation reforms aim to reform institutions and include all those initiatives to make the state more efficient, including decentralization. A good summary of these, as well as an evaluation of the first round of reforms, is provided in IADB (1997).

13. See Deere (1985, 1986, 1987) and León, Prieto, and Salazar (1987).

14. In Latin America property rights are the domain of the civil and family codes whereas land rights are usually determined by specific legislation. Enhancing women's property rights within the civil codes has not always been accompanied by women attaining land rights in the agrarian codes and vice versa.

15. On the variety of factors that contributed to the consolidation of the women's movement in Latin America, see Vargas (1989, 1992); Jaquette (1989); Alvarez (1990, 1998a, 1998b); Kirkwood (1990); Sternbach et al. (1992); León (1994); and Aguilar et al. (1997). While we will sometimes refer to the women's movement as if it had a unified agenda and a single voice, its composition and priorities at any given moment are quite diverse at the country level. In a twelve-country, comparative analysis, we must necessarily stress the points of commonality.

16. On the new social movements in Latin America, see Escobar and Alvarez (1992) and Alvarez, Dagnino, and Escobar (1998).

17. Under the marital regimes where the property jointly acquired during marriage is common property (i.e., formally owned by husband and wife), this joint property until recently was administered by the husband. The achievement of dual household headship was to make explicit that the administration of this common property corresponded to both members of the couple. If the asset is not titled under the name of both partners, however, the husband can often dispose of this property without permission of the wife and use the proceeds as he sees fit.

18. See Sacks (1974: 208–11) for a good summary of Engels's evolutionary analysis.

19. On the status of the debate over the origins of women's subordination see Silverblatt (1991). For the numerous critiques of Engels's thesis see the references in Agarwal (1994a: chap. 1, n. 24).

20. On the influence of this idea in the socialist societies of the twentieth century, see Molyneux (1981) and Larguía and Dumoulin (1983).

21. See Safa (1995: 37–46) and Benería and Roldán (1987: 160) for a flavor of some of the issues in this debate. There is consensus that there is no automatic link between women's independent access to and control over income, changes in gender relations, and women's awareness of their subordination to men.

22. Recall here a basic axiom of Marxian political economy: that it is lack of access to means of production that compels proletarianization, or the need to sell one's labor power for a wage.

23. Today human capital assets may be as important a factor as inheritance in determining the endowments of men and women. The evidence regarding the differential schooling attainments of men and women in Latin America, nonethe-

less, suggests that this has not yet been a forceful leveling mechanism. The greatest gender differential is found in rates of illiteracy and the population with no schooling at all; the gender differential decreases as one goes up the educational scale. While the level of educational attainment across Latin America is quite heterogeneous, Valdés and Gomáriz (1995: 100) conclude that the general tendency is for the level of schooling of women to be inferior to that of men while their illiteracy is higher.

24. In a survey of smallholders in Costa Rica, for example, it was found that men spent 38 percent of the income they earned on their own personal needs whereas women spent 20 percent or less on themselves. Among smallholders in Honduras, men spent 32 percent of their income on their own, individual expenses while women pooled almost all of the income they earned (Elson et al.: 1997: 111, 243, 323).

25. In 1950 the average life span for women in Latin America was 53.5 years, increasing to 71.4 years in 1990. For men the increase was less pronounced, from 50.2 in 1950 to 66.2 years in 1990, so that the gender gap in favor of women widened (Valdés and Gomáriz 1995: 115).

26. In a study summarizing the rural household income surveys carried out in the 1970s, Deere and Wasserstrom (1981) found that the poorest households were those with limited access to wage work rather than those lacking access to land. But not all of these surveys included landless households. In rural El Salvador, for example, landless households were much poorer than those with access to some land (Deere and Diskin 1984).

27. See Facio (1996) for an excellent discussion of the implications of having men as the reference point for what is human. Besides Nancy Fraser (1997, 175–86), upon whom we rely for a summary of this debate, see Scott (1988b), Young (1990), and Subirats (1998), and for an insightful discussion of the Latin American version, Schutte (1998).

28. Androcentrism is defined as "the authoritative construction of norms that privilege the traits associated with masculinity" (N. Fraser 1997: 20).

29. Nancy Fraser (1997: 181–82) argues that in the United States the subsequent debate centered on group identity and cultural differences, with the main protagonists being anti-essentialist versus multi-culturalist positions. Both of these focused almost exclusively on cultural misrecognition to the neglect of issues of political economy.

30. Real equality is also referred to as substantive equality, meaning equality in terms of material goods, or economic equality (Bobbio 1993: 76). For feminists real equality encompasses more than just economic equality, including the non-economic dimensions.

31. Feminists are equally critical of a second, conservative view in which non-discrimination means to treat all groups the same, under the assumption that if all groups have the same rights, then differences will not turn into inequalities. The criticism of this position is that the only way toward equality among different groups is to treat each group differently, according to their specific character-

istics. Hence, "the demand for equality thus requires unequal treatment that takes into account differences" (Astelarra 1995: 33).

32. The term "affirmative action" has its origin in the civil rights legislation of 1965 in the United States, whose objective was to end discrimination based on race. Affirmative action was explicitly applied to sexual discrimination in 1967. In Europe, the preferred term for measures to correct gender discrimination is "positive action." Both terms encompass the possible use of discriminatory measures to correct given inequalities (Osborne 1995: 300).

33. Thus, according to Article 4 of the 1979 UN Convention to End All Forms of Discrimination against Women, "Adoption by State Parties of temporary special measures aimed at accelerating *de facto* equality between men and women shall not be considered discrimination as defined in the present Convention, but shall in no way entail as a consequence the maintenance of unequal or separate standards; these measures shall be discontinued when the objectives of equality of opportunity and treatment have been achieved" (UN 1980b).

34. It might also require a change in the social valuation of the work that men and women do. That is, due to differences in physical strength as well as agility and dexterity, men and women might be more productive at different tasks; a recognition of difference would require that women's tasks be valued as much as those performed by men.

35. Generic male forms of nouns and pronouns, for example, have gone out of style in favor of supposedly gender-neutral language such as the use of "men and women" or "persons." Okin (1989: 8–9) argues that they generate a false gender neutrality that can be just as or even more misleading than the blatantly sexist male terms of reference of the past.

36. The seven principles, which must be respected simultaneously for gender equity to be achieved, are: anti-poverty, anti-exploitation, income equality, leisure time equality, equality of respect, anti-marginalization, and anti-androcentrism (Fraser 1997: 45–47).

37. The first part of this section is largely based on León (1997a), the introduction to a collection of influential articles in Spanish translation.

38. See the reflections written by a group of the participants at the Taxco meeting, cited as Collective (1997) and Lamas (1998).

39. Lamas (1998: 10) goes on to note that, "Even though feminism recognizes ethnic, class and age differences among women, it implicitly denies any differences in intellectual capacity, ability and sensitivity. . . . This militant egalitarianism has led to a paralyzing practice that diminishes the effectiveness and political presence of the movement. The myth fuels womanism, which idealizes and mystifies the relation among women and hinders leadership."

40. See Schuler (1997: 34) on the influence of Paulo Freire's (1970) work on feminist concerns regarding the creation of gender consciousness.

41. A good example of a process of empowerment is provided by Alberti (1998) with respect to an indigenous women's organization in Mexico; also see Alberti et al. (1998) on the use of an empowerment approach methodology.

42. See Sen (1980, 1990) and for a summary of this literature, Seiz (1991), Agarwal (1997), and Summerfield (1998).

43. This is partly because of the deterioration in access to communal resources and the erosion of traditional external social supports in recent decades in South Asia. Similar processes have been at work in Latin America. In addition, Agarwal (1994a: 65) argues that access to wage employment and other, non-farm income-generating opportunities is often linked with access to land, so that "effective rights in land thus have the potential for strengthening women's fall-back position not only directly but also indirectly by improving returns from other income sources."

44. On rural Mexico on these same points see Castañeda (2000: 15). In the urban context, Ann Varley (1994: 129) also argues that home ownership gives women more bargaining power in terms of garnering assistance from their children. She also cites cases in Mexico of widows being evicted from their homes by children who have been given title to the property.

Chapter 2: Gender, Property Rights, and Citizenship

1. Article 132 of the 1855 Chilean Civil Code, in Claro Solar (1978, vol. 1, tome 2: 7).

2. We use the term "consensual union" rather than "common law marriage" precisely because the latter was not recognized under the Latin American legal tradition until recently.

3. The evidence is provided by studies of illegitimacy. For example, among the white population in the Lima parish of San Marcos in the seventeenth century, 45.6 percent of the registered births were illegitimate, whereas the corresponding figure for the indigenous population was 72 percent (Mannarelli 1991: 78). In eighteenth-century Buenos Aires, the illegitimacy rate was 32 percent among whites and 44 percent among blacks (Socolow 1989: 232). See Dueñas (1997) on the late colonial period in Colombia and Lewin (1992: 362) on the historically high rates of illegitimacy in Brazil.

4. The trajectory of the Hispanic American legal tradition is based on the following codification: the *Siete Partidas de Alfonso X, el Sabio* (dictated in the mid-thirteenth century); the *Ordenamiento de Alacalá* of 1348; the *Leyes de Toro* of 1505, which codified inheritance rules; the *Nueva Recopilación de las Leyes de Castilla of 1567*; and the *Novíssima Recopilación de las Leyes de España* of 1805 (Ots y Capdequi 1969: 44). That of Brazil is based on Portugal's 1603 *Código Philippino* (Mendes de Almeida 1870). In general terms, the Portuguese and Hispanic traditions were similar with respect to family and property law and specifically the property rights of married women. The salient differences are noted in the text.

5. Women could not hold public office, for example, or even be guardians or adopt children, for the governance of children was considered a "public ministry" only suitable for men. Neither could they witness a will or act as an advocate in

court (Arrom 1985a: 58). Nonetheless, there was always a difference between law and practice. On this disjuncture, see Graubart (2000).

6. Although the age of majority was twenty-five, daughters as well as sons were under a father's tutelage until he died, he specifically emancipated them, or they married (Arrom 1985a: 57).

7. Unless otherwise indicated, this summary is based on Arrom (1985: 62–68), whose analysis of women's legal capacity and property rights is applicable throughout the Spanish colonial empire, Ots y Capdequi (1969: 54–56), and Bernal de Bugeda (1975).

8. By law, the *arras* was limited to 10 percent of the assets of the groom at the time of marriage, supposedly to protect the assets of any children by a husband's previous marriage. In colonial Hispanic America the *arras* was much less common than the dowry (Lavrin and Couturier 1979: 284; Lavrin 1978: 34).

9. Equal inheritance shares for all children regardless of sex was established in Law XXVI of Toro. The distribution need not be completely equal since one child or several children could be favored with what was termed the *mejoras,* but this could not exceed one-fifth of the estate. According to Lavrin and Couturier (1979: 286), the value of the dowry was deducted from a daughter's inheritance whereas the cost of a son's education was deducted from his share.

10. This definition is from Article 132 of the 1855 Chilean civil code (in Claro Solar 1978, vol. 1, tome 2: 7).

11. The exception is provided by the "community property system" which developed in the southern and western territories of the United States in the early nineteenth century. In this system, whatever money and property was acquired by either spouse during marriage constituted community property, defined as jointly owned property that was divided equally among the spouses in case of separation or divorce (Nicholas et al. 1986: 40).

12. See Wells (1925) for an insightful discussion of the origins, similarities, and differences governing women's property rights in Latin America and the United States in the eighteenth and nineteenth centuries. For him, the main difference in the two traditions is that "The marriage relation in the Spanish (civil law) conception may be likened to a partnership; in the feudal (common law) conception, to a servitude" (ibid.: 235). He also stresses the flexibility in Spanish marriage law in comparison to the rigidity of English common law.

13. In Latin America this was termed *patria potestad* and defined as the power that fathers had over the person and property of their children.

14. Flexner and Fitzpatrick (1996: 59) date the impulse for the Married Women's Property Acts to the 1839–1850 period. They attribute this reform to the pressure from wealthy landowners who wanted to protect their bequests to their daughters, in addition to that of liberal-minded men and a few vocal women.

15. In the early nineteenth century the position of married women in England initially got worse (Whittick 1979: 18); for example, after 1833 married women in that country did not even retain control of their dowries if they were widowed or separated (Arrom 1985a: 83).

16. In the linguistic structure of the Spanish language, the male form is the generic term. Feminists have criticized this usage, arguing that it is sexist since there is a word for a female citizen, *ciudadana* (Thomas 1997; Facio 1996: 79).

17. The frequency of constitutional change was related to the often rapid turn-over in the executive, with twenty-five governments holding power between 1824 and 1890, only one of which was elected through contested elections (Sharat 1997: 62).

18. Other countries, however, did not go through such a tortuous path to exclude women. The 1824 Mexican constitution granted citizenship and suffrage to all Mexicans without the requirement that they own property or be literate, yet women were excluded. According to Arrom (1980: 496), "This exclusion was considered so natural that it did not even have to be specified in the Constitution."

19. The reasoning behind *potestad marital* and the relative incapacity of married women was as follows:

> A woman is not incapable because she is a *woman*, but rather, because she is married. Her state is not a state of being incapacitated, but rather, one of dependence. . . . The conjugal society, just as every other society, needs a head and due to the way things have developed, the head can be none other than the husband. The woman is incapable, because nature has made her dependent. . . . The incapacity of women is justified as a consequence of the community of interests that is created in marriage and of the necessity to give just one person the direction of these interests. Potestad marital appears as the manner to assure, from both the economic and moral side, the unity of the family. (Claro Solar 1978, vol. 1, tome 2: 74–75)

Thus the incapacity of the married woman is based on the need to maintain the authority of the husband and prevent any antagonism that might arise between two equal beings; the supposed objective is to maintain the unity of the family and, thus, coherence in society. Women's legal capacity was diminished not only to protect her economic and moral interests—as the "weaker" or more vulnerable sex—but also those of the husband and the family, thereby concealing a defense of patriarchy.

20. See, for example, Article 131 of the 1855 Chilean code (Claro Solar 1978, vol. 1, tome 2: 7).

21. Church-state relations were also a critical factor in limiting the adoption of divorce and recognition of the legal rights of "natural" or illegitimate, as well as adoptive, children in Latin America.

22. Civil marriage was first recognized independently of marriage by the Catholic Church in Brazil in 1890 (Lewin 1992: 362), Peru in 1897 (Quiroga León 1990: 85), and Ecuador in 1903 (García 1992). Indicative of the power of the church in Colombia, civil marriage in that country was not recognized until 1974 and only became a legal requirement in 1991 (FAO 1992: 76).

23. References to the Mexican Civil Code of 1870, as well as the subsequent 1884 code, are based on the civil code of the Federal District and Territory of Baja California. This civil code was subsequently replicated by most of Mexico's other states.

24. Elizabeth Dore (2000: 6, 20) makes a provocative argument regarding the regressive tendencies of liberalism with respect to gender equality, arguing that "women lost their legal protection to family property" partly because of the "abolition of the requirement that the property of married couples be jointly owned." This is a misrepresentation of the introduction of the separation-of-property regime in Mexico since it was introduced at this time only as an option, and, moreover, it was not the default option. In several Central American countries, as we will later show, it was subsequently introduced as the default option—that is, binding if no other regime was chosen.

25. Another important change in the 1870 code that was in keeping with liberalism (by augmenting individual freedom) was the lowering in the age of majority from 25 to 21. While single daughters gained a new freedom to manage their economic affairs, they required their parents' permission to move out of the parental home, a restriction not placed upon sons. In addition, the grounds for legal separation were expanded to include incompatibility; however, a double standard was introduced with respect to the role of adultery as grounds for separation. Another major innovation in this code with respect to women's rights was the granting of *patria potestad* to widows, single mothers, and those mothers legally separated due to their husbands' misbehavior (Arrom 1985b: 307–12, and Arrom 1980). Mexico was preceded by Costa Rica's Civil Code of 1841 in this latter innovation (Rodríguez 2000: 104).

26. Limitations on universal male suffrage in Latin America, such as requiring ownership of property, service in the army, or literacy, continued well into the 1930s (Lavrin 1994: 185), and several countries retained a literacy requirement until the 1980s (Valdés and Gomáriz 1995: 160).

27. See Miller (1991) for the most complete comparative treatment of the process of attainment of female suffrage and civil-code reform. Also see Chaney (1979) on Peru and Chile, and Lavrin (1994 and 1995) on the Southern Cone. There are also excellent country studies of the struggle for female suffrage; see Kirkwood (1990) on Chile; Luna and Villareal (1994) on Colombia; Stoner (1996) on Cuba; and Sapriza (1985) on Uruguay.

28. Although the civil codes of most states tend to conform to that of the Mexican Federal District, in at least three states, as of the early 1990s, the household was still represented solely by the husband, who is charged with its administration (FAO 1992: 26).

29. The Socialist Party, founded in 1896, always included in its platform the demand for equality between the sexes and universal suffrage (Little 1978: 243).

30. According to Lavrin (1995: 210), however, if a woman did not register her desire to administer her own property, this right fell to the husband by default.

31. A number of Latin American countries did precede France in abolishing *potestad marital*. In that country the Napoleonic Code was not modified until 1938 and 1942 (Mazeaud and Mazeaud 1976).

32. The share of women who were illiterate around 1950 ranged from a low of 10 to 21 percent (in ranked order, Uruguay, Argentina, Cuba, Chile, and Costa Rica) to a high of 61 to 77 percent (in Nicaragua, El Salvador, Honduras, Guatemala, and Bolivia), with the remaining countries in the midrange of around 50 percent. Illiteracy was always much higher in rural areas than urban and greater among women than men, the only exceptions to this latter trend being Uruguay and Cuba, where the illiteracy rates were similar (UNESCO 1966: table 4, 38–41.)

33. The influence of the IACW within the Pan American Union was first felt at the Eighth International Conference of American States in 1938 in Lima, when that organization adopted a resolution in favor of the equal civil rights of men and women. It was this precedent that facilitated the adoption of "the equal rights of men and women" clause in the United Nations Charter in 1945. The IACW delegation at the founding meeting of the UN in San Francisco—which included Bertha Lutz, Amalia Caballero de Castillo Ledón (its chairwoman and also an official Mexican delegate at the conference), and Minerva Bernardino of the Dominican Republic—is largely credited for the inclusion of this historic commitment to equal rights (Miller 1991: 116).

34. A few countries did adopt restricted female suffrage in this period. For example, the 1933 Peruvian constitution granted suffrage to women in municipal elections; similarly, in 1934 women in Chile could vote in local elections. In that latter year some provinces in Argentina also granted women the vote (Miller 1991: 99).

35. In Mexico, Chile, and Costa Rica the attainment of suffrage was largely due to the lobbying efforts of the women's movement. In other countries, such as Colombia, the Dominican Republic, Nicaragua, Peru, and Paraguay, conservatives or authoritarian regimes gave the vote to women in hopes of currying their favor. In many countries women got the vote in the context of revolutionary processes that broadened the base for democratic rule; included in this group are Bolivia, Costa Rica, Guatemala, Argentina, and Venezuela (Valdés and Gomáriz 1995: 159–60).

36. Interview with lawyer Elizabeth García, CIDES, 23 July 1997, Quito.

37. Colombia's adoption of divorce in 1976 was only partial, since it applied only to those who had contracted civil marriage, having repudiated any religious faith. Those married by the Catholic Church could not divorce for civil purposes until 1992, in a process termed "the cessation of civil effects of matrimony," rather than divorce. Telephone interview with lawyer María Cristina Calderón, Profamilia, 10 February 2000, Bogotá.

38. Among the earliest countries to establish divorce were Costa Rica (1888), Nicaragua (1904), Uruguay (1907), and Mexico and Cuba (1917). See Lavrin (1995) for a detailed account of the struggle over divorce in the Southern Cone.

39. This section builds upon, updates, and expands FAO (1990 and 1992).

40. See Article 189 of the 1928 Civil Code (in Lexadin 1996). Few couples, nonetheless, make use of the capitulaciones. E-mail communication to the authors from lawyer Martha Torres Blancas, 11 April 2000, Mexico City.

41. Article 204 (in Lexadin 1996) and e-mail communication, Martha Torres Blancas, 11 April 2000, Mexico City.

42. This second variant was introduced only in 1994. The national women's office, SERNAM (Servicio Nacional de la Mujer), lobbied for it to become the default option in marriage, but this effort failed. Interview with Claudia Uriarte, legal advisor, SERNAM, 16 July 1997, Santiago.

43. In El Salvador the separation-of-profits regime was the default regime until the 1994 reform of the civil code. Interview with lawyer Silvia Guillén, FES-PAD, 16 January 1998, San Salvador. On the other hand, in Brazil full common property was the default option until divorce was legalized in 1977. Interview with lawyer Leila Linhares Barsted, CEPIA, 12 July 2000, Rio de Janeiro.

44. The other countries with a double-signature provision are Brazil and Ecuador. Colombia only adopted the double-signature provision in 1996 (Law 258) and only for the sale of a couple's principal residence. Interview with lawyer Luz Margot Pulido, 31 August 1997, Bogotá.

45. Articles 323 and 731 of Peru's civil code (1984). In interviews, nonetheless, it seemed that this was a little-known provision and probably not consistently applied, if at all.

46. Articles 111 and 112 of civil code, in Iñíguez de Salinas and Pérez (1997).

47. Interview with Teresa Simbaña, founder of the Consejo Nacional de Mujeres Indígenas del Ecuador, 24 February 2000, Quito.

48. Interview with lawyer Hilda Morales Trujillo, former advisor to ONAM, 6 January 1998, Guatemala City.

49. Interview with lawyer Carlos Fradique Méndez, cited in "La rapiña del divorcio," El Tiempo (Bogotá), 21 November 1999: 8A.

50. The census data reported in Table 2.4 probably understate the proportion of couples living in consensual unions as opposed to marriage. It is highly improbable that census takers ask to see the identity card of women to verify their marital status and may find it convenient simply to report that women living with a man are married.

51. For example, in rural Peru 40 percent of the women who report living in a couple are in a consensual union (Peru 1994a: table 18). In rural El Salvador 63 percent of couples are, reportedly, living in a consensual union (FAO 1990: 20).

52. The exceptions are El Salvador and Nicaragua. In the former, the default regime for consensual unions is that of participation in profits whereas the default regime for marriages is full common property. In the latter, the default option for these is full common property whereas that for marriages is the separation-of-profits regime. The reason for these anomalies is not at all clear.

53. Costa Rica's 1995 reform went further than most other countries by recognizing the legal rights of "irregular" consensual unions, defined as those with legal impediments to marriage (i.e., one partner being married to someone else),

if the couple had children and met the time stipulation. This provision was strongly opposed by the Catholic Church and was struck down in 1999 by the Supreme Court on the grounds of unconstitutionality, presumably because the constitution protects the family. E-mail communication from Lara Blanco, researcher at the Fundación Arias, San José, 23 November 1999.

54. The exception to the requirement that consensual unions be registered to receive the same benefits as couples is Brazil. In this country recognition of paternity (a common child) is sufficient to prove the relationship if it is of at least five years' duration and there are otherwise no impediments (CFEMEA 1996: 62).

55. According to Arrom (1985a: 63), "Widows normally received half the community property, but an impecunious widow could inherit a larger share if the probate judge determined that she was in greater need of it than the other heirs." In her review of approximately one hundred Mexican wills from the 1800–1850 period, Arrom found that it was exceedingly rare for children to end up in a more favorable economic position than widows. E-mail communication to the authors, 14 April 2000.

56. The *porción conjugal* was calculated in terms of the difference in the relative value of each spouse's estate, subject to other limitations such as that the marital portion not exceed twice the inheritance share of a legitimate child, or if there was only one child, that it not be greater than this share (Articles 1176, 1177 and 1178, in Chile 1961).

57. If the deceased had no legitimate children (or descendents), the inheritance was divided between the spouse, parents (or ascendants), and any natural children. The marital portion in this case was limited to one-fourth of the deceased's estate. In the absence of legitimate or natural children, ascendants, or siblings, the full inheritance fell to the surviving spouse (Article 1178, Chile 1961).

58. "Mensaje del Ejecutivo al Congreso proponiendo la aprobación del Código Civil" of 22 November 1855 in Chile (1961: 38). That the Chileans thought they were innovating on Spanish colonial law in this respect is quite apparent in this preamble by President Manuel Montt.

59. The Chilean Civil Code of 1855 is said to have been virtually replicated by Colombia, Ecuador, and Venezuela in their codes of this period and to have heavily influenced the Argentine Civil Code of 1869 (Claro Solar 1978, vol. 1, tome 2: 21; Leret 1975: 57).

60. On the decline of the dowry in Mexico since the late colonial period, see Lavrin and Couturier (1979: 293–94). On its decline in Peru over the course of the nineteenth century, see Hünefeldt (1997: 390–91).

61. According to Arrom (1985b: 313–14) testamentary freedom increased the individual freedom of both fathers and mothers and could be considered a countervailing force to the decline of parental authority provided for in other reforms of this period, such as those which lowered the age of majority and enhanced children's freedom of choice of marital partners. It also served to prevent the dispersal of capital, and was seen by its proponents as stimulating both incentives to work and to accumulate and concentrate capital, factors indispensable for capitalist development.

62. Arrom (1985b: 314) argues that the greater vulnerability of daughters as compared to sons was recognized in the 1884 code by the provision that a pension (*alimentos*) had to be automatically provided to unmarried daughters; sons were only guaranteed a pension if they were still minors or were incapacitated.

63. As Dore (2000a.: 21) also argues, the gendered effects of land privatization within the indigenous communities were quite heterogeneous, largely depending on whether women had any direct rights at all within the communal-property regimes. Her own case study of Diriomo, Nicaragua, shows how the process of land privatization favored the acquisition of land by indigenous women (Dore 2000b).

64. We assume that the husband is the deceased for in Latin America the average life expectancy of women exceeds that of men by between five and six years (UNDP 1998: table 2). The same rules apply in terms of men inheriting from their wives.

65. In El Salvador, however, if a wife or a daughter is excluded from the man's will they may demand a monthly pension or a settlement from the heirs (Fundación Arias 1998a: 9). In Costa Rica, where the default marital regime is separation of property, judges have considerable discretion to modify wills to favor the surviving spouse, particularly with the distribution of *gananciales* generated during the marriage. E-mail communication from Lara Blanca, Fundación Arias, 2 February 1998, San José.

66. In Brazil during the colonial period and up until 1907, testamentary freedom was restricted to one-third of a person's estate. Nazzari (1995: 801) argues that the share that could be freely willed was raised in order to encourage the greater circulation and accumulation of capital, a factor also encouraging the establishment of full or near-testamentary freedom in other countries.

67. In Bolivia, if there are no living children, one-third of the estate may be freely willed, with two-thirds of the estate automatically passing to the spouse and/or parents (Bolivia 1991). Peru is more generous to spouses; if there are no living children, the share that may be freely willed remains as one-third, with two-thirds of the estate passing automatically to the spouse. Only in the case in which there are no living children or spouse do parents inherit automatically, and then only 50 percent of the estate with the other half to be willed freely by the testator (Peru 1984).

68. Not all countries, nonetheless, give illegitimate and natural children the same inheritance rights as legitimate children; for example, in Honduras and Nicaragua the inheritance share of illegitimate children is smaller than that of legitimate children.

69. This phrase is practically identical in all of these codes; see, for Ecuador, Article 1218 in Larrea (1996); for Colombia, Article 1230, Código Civil (1996); Article 1150 in Honduras (1997b); and Article 1201 in Nicaragua (1997a).

70. In the case of Mexico a widow inherits a share equal to that of a child only if she owns no property; otherwise she is entitled only to the difference between the value of a child's share and her own property, including her half of the common property (Article 1624, Lexadin 1996). In Costa Rica and Nicaragua

there is also some limitation on the size of the widow's share as compared to the children, with the wife usually inheriting a smaller share (Costa Rica 1985; Nicaragua 1997a).

71. Mexico is the exception to this trend since it recognized the inheritance rights of women in consensual unions in its 1928 Civil Code but did not give men these same inheritance rights, or give these unions the other rights of married couples until much later (Carreras and Montero 1975: 120).

Chapter 3: Gender Exclusionary Agrarian Reform

1. Participant in the National Seminar of Rural Women, July 1997, Yoro, Honduras, in CODIMCA and Fundación Arias (1997: 22).

2. The first agrarian reform in the hemisphere was carried out in Haiti in the early nineteenth century, following the successful slave rebellion that led to that country's independence from France. In 1809 the large plantations were broken up and distributed among former slaves (Meyer 1989: 3).

3. Some of the signatory governments to the Alliance for Progress, such as Argentina and Uruguay, did not even go this far, taking refuge in the clauses (see the quote, above) exempting countries if their land-tenure system was not considered "unjust" (Montgomery 1984: 122, 126).

4. By 1967 the only countries that had redistributed some private property were Bolivia, Chile, Colombia, Costa Rica, and Venezuela (Montgomery 1984: 125).

5. The exception among the Alliance for Progress agrarian reforms was the 1962 Honduran law, which provided for land expropriations to be compensated in cash (Article 52, in Escoto León 1965: 47).

6. In Ecuador these properties consisted of those formerly owned by the Asistencia Pública, public charities initially organized by religious orders. In Guatemala they consisted of properties expropriated by the state from their German owners during World War II.

7. See Thiesenhusen (1989: table 1), Meyer (1989: table 1.1), and Kay (1998) for attempts to quantify and compare the impact of the agrarian reforms. The main difficulty in comparing their magnitude is that the agrarian reform agencies were quite inconsistent in their reporting on beneficiaries. For example, sometimes they included among the beneficiaries squatters on the agrarian frontier who were titled lands; in other cases, only those benefiting from state colonization efforts were included. Another difficulty is in estimating the total number of rural households who potentially qualified as beneficiaries, since the criteria employed by the various countries differed. Also, the agricultural censuses do not always correspond to the period of reform. Another problem is that the area reported in farms was a moving target during the period of agrarian reform due to the expansion of the agricultural frontier in most countries.

8. The distinction between *ejidos* and indigenous communities has to do with the origin of the landholding. The *ejidos* were constituted through the ex-

propriation of latifundios. The approximately two thousand indigenous communities were ones where land that had in the past belonged to them was returned (Mackinlay and de la Fuente 1996: 75).

9. Estimates on the scope of the Mexican reform differ widely, illustrating the measurement problem. Botey (2000: 119) and Mackinlay and de la Fuente (1996: 75) report that 106.8 million hectares were expropriated under the reform. Tellez (1994) reports that the reform encompassed 102.9 million hectares, or 48 percent of Mexico's total land area, and 2.9 million beneficiaries. According to a 1986 Inter-American Development Bank report, as of 1970 42.9 percent of family farmers were reform beneficiaries, and they held 43.4 percent of the land in farms (in Thiesenhusen 1989: table 1).

10. The potential scope of an agrarian reform is largely a product of the pre-existing concentration of land and the proportion of the population that was subject—in these early reforms—to pre-capitalist relations of production. The available data indicate that in Mexico at the end of the "Porfiriato" (1876–1910), eleven thousand haciendas controlled 57 percent of Mexican national territory (Thiesenhusen 1995: 30, 35). The 1950 Bolivian agricultural census revealed that 3.8 percent of the total number of landholdings (the latifundia) held 81.8 percent of the agricultural land (Urioste 1992: 82). The majority of these haciendas were located in the western, highland region of the country.

11. That such a huge state farm sector was constituted so quickly is largely explained by the pre-revolutionary pattern of land use and tenure, since the majority of Cuba's farmland was concentrated in large sugar cane plantations and cattle haciendas.

12. Tenants were allocated up to 27 hectares of land free of charge; they were entitled to purchase additional land up to a maximum of 67 hectares (five caballerías). By the end of 1963, the private sector in Cuban agriculture consisted of some 154,000 peasant households who held approximately 26 percent of the nations' farmland; another 3 percent was held by non-peasant households (Trinchet 1984).

13. In the majority of ejidos constituted during the Cárdenas regime, lands were worked collectively, resembling production cooperatives. They also received considerable state support in this period in the form of subsidized credit and technical assistance. Beginning with the Alemán regime (1946–52), state support to collective production was de-emphasized and most land that was subsequently redistributed was worked individually, with only pastures and forests utilized collectively. By 1970 it was estimated that only 12 percent of ejidos were worked collectively, a figure that fell to around 3 percent by the 1990s (Otero 1989: 290; Thiesenhusen 1995: 40–41).

14. Brunt (1992: 81) and Arizpe and Botey (1987: 70) report that discrimination was first introduced as a result of a 1927 law. We have followed Baitenmann's (1997) reconstruction, given her more detailed research into the matter.

15. However, ejidatarias continued to be favored by the provision that they were not required to work their land directly if they were prevented from doing so

by domestic obligations and the care of small children, being able to rent their land and/or to hire wage workers (Article 76).

16. Elaborated from Mexico (1992: tables 47 and 48) based on inhabitants in communities of less than 2,500 people. The proportion of female-headed households nationally was 17.3 percent.

17. Article 77 of Supreme Decree no. 03464 of August 1953, in Villarroel and Barrios Ávila (1969); our emphasis.

18. By that time farms larger than a hundred hectares in size (3.8 percent of the total) controlled 91 percent of the land (Ybarnegaray 1997: table 8).

19. Data provided to the authors by Isabel Lavadenz, director of INRA, 7 August 1997. This figure is based on a random sample of 17,099 out of a total of 49,684 individual land application forms (*expedientes*). The sex of the beneficiaries was estimated by an analysis of first names, and thus this estimate probably contains a small margin of error. This is one of the problems of not including the variable sex on agrarian reform documentation.

20. This explanation was suggested by Paulino Guarachi, Sub-secretariat for Rural Development, Secretariat of Popular Participation, interview of 15 July 1997, La Paz.

21. Interview with Luz Marina Calvo, sub-secretary for indigenous affairs, Secretariat for Human Development, 10 July 1997, La Paz.

22. E-mail communication to the authors from Isabel Lavadenz, 7 June 1998.

23. Interview with Pepe Ramírez, founder of ANAP (Asociación Nacional de Agricultores Pequeños), during the Conference of the 40th Anniversary of the Agrarian Reform, 12–14 May 1999, Havana.

24. This estimate is based on the share of women landowners among ANAP members in 1979; at that point they constituted only 5.5 percent of the individual landowners (Stubbs and Alvarez 1987: table 8.1). Surely in the twenty years that had passed since the promulgation of the land-to-the-tiller decree, a good number of women had become landowners through inheritance as either wives or daughters, suggesting that the share of women beneficiaries in their own right in 1959 was much less than the 5 percent figure.

25. Rural women in Cuba had an exceedingly low rate of participation in the economically active population compared to other countries, only 5 percent, irrespective of errors of measurement (Larguía and Dumoulin 1983: 141).

26. These female brigades were largely responsible for solving the seasonal agricultural labor shortages in both the state and private sectors. It is estimated that by the mid-1970s women constituted over half of the temporary labor force for the sugar cane, coffee, tobacco, and fruit harvests (FMC 1975). By this time brigade work was no longer unremunerated, as a result of FMC demands; moreover, women were paid a wage equal to that of men for comparable work. In order to encourage women's participation as wage workers, it was necessary to make provisions for women's domestic responsibilities, and the FMC also played a key role in promoting the development of child care centers and communal eating facilities at rural work centers.

27. Interviews with ANAP and FMC officials, 9–15 June 1980, Havana. This section draws largely on Deere (1986).

28. What we do not know is what share of women titleholders joined the production cooperatives, finding the expected benefits of group farming to be more attractive than the prospects of independent production as a female household head. Also, data are not available on the female production cooperative members with respect to whether they owned land in their own name or joined the production cooperative together with their spouse, partner, or parent.

29. On the changes in the Cuban agricultural sector since 1989 see Deere, Pérez et al. (1998).

30. Curiously, wives and partners did not receive favored treatment, however, upon the death of the beneficiary. If a beneficiary died intestate and before fully purchasing the land parcel, the legal heirs (which according to civil code included the wife, children, and parents of the deceased) had to agree on who was to manage the parcel on behalf of the family since the parcel could not sub-divided. If they could not agree, this decision fell to ITCO (Article 69).

31. Madden (1992:44) reports women as being 13.4 percent of the beneficiaries, but in another Fundación Arias report (cited in the text, above), this figure was apparently corrected.

32. Unutilized lands could legally be expropriated under Decree 1151, but so many restrictions were placed in the way that, in practice, this alternative was impossible (Berger 1992: 112–14).

33. Based on Registros de Adjudicación del INTA, Unidad de Planeamiento y Programación, November 1996.

34. Over half of the allotments to women have been made in three departments, in descending order: Alta Verapaz, Escuintla, and Guatemala (INTA 1996: graphic 1). These are also the departments where the lots distributed by INTA are concentrated. The greatest number of women benefiting by being included in the allocation of collectively owned farms are concentrated in the department of Alta Verapaz.

35. Interview with Fermina López Cabrera and Hilda Cabrera, Women's Commission of CONIC, 6 January 1998, Guatemala City.

36. Ramón Salgado (1996:106), summarizing the accomplishments of the agrarian reform between 1962 and 1992, reports that some 60,000 beneficiaries were allocated a total of 409,000 hectares of land, representing approximately 12 percent of the agricultural land and 13 percent of the rural population of the country. The vast majority of this land consisted of either national or *ejido* land, or foreclosed farms mortgaged to BANDESA, the state agricultural bank. Very little private-sector land was ever expropriated. The beneficiaries of the reform belonged to 2,641 base groups affiliated with twelve different peasant organizations. One of the differentiating characteristics of the Honduras reform was the active role played by these various peasant organizations, and they are usually credited with the fact that any land distribution took place at all.

37. Interview of 15 January 1998, Tegucigalpa.

38. Presentation at the Seminar on Gender and Land Rights organized for the authors by CODIMCA and Fundación Arias, 16 January 1998, Tegucigalpa.

39. Intervention by Rosaura García, INA functionary, Seminar on Gender and Land Rights, ibid. Also, in a survey of 32 *asentamientos,* only in two was there a relatively high proportion of women members (12 and 18 percent), but the women did not work the land themselves, relying upon their sons and/or wage workers (Safilios-Rothschild 1983: 18).

40. Researcher with ADP (Acciones para el Desarrollo y Población), interview of 15 January 1998, Tegucigalpa.

41. Intervention by Sara Elisa Rosales, Seminar on Gender and Land Rights, 16 January 1998, Tegucigalpa.

42. Eighty-eight percent of the land distributed between 1964 and 1993 was adjudicated through the colonization program. Some 221,689 households benefited, with slightly more households (52 percent) benefiting through agrarian reform than through the colonization program (48 percent). Data provided to the authors by the Oficina de Estadística, Instituto Nacional de Desarrollo Agrario, July 1997, Quito.

43. It is interesting that Findley (1973: 165) objects to this provision on the grounds of a paternalistic state limiting the options of a peasant family but does not see it as limiting the options of women.

44. For a detailed description of the 1984 measures favoring the incorporation of rural women and the debate regarding the efficacy of these policies, see León (1987); León, Prieto, and Salazar (1987); Gómez-Restrepo (1991); and Durán Ariza (1991).

45. Unfortunately, the available data for this period do not report the extent of joint titling, so it is impossible to draw any firm conclusions regarding the efficacy of this provision (since joint titling might still be reported under the category of male household heads).

46. Other supplementary criteria employed in the selection of beneficiaries included length of residency in the municipality; distance between the home and the expropriated property; household income (with the poorest to be favored); and organizational affiliation (with organized peasants to be favored).

47. Interview with Maria José Carneiro, researcher at the Centro para el Desarrollo Agrícola, Universidad Federal Rural de Rio de Janeiro, 19 June 1998, Rio de Janeiro; and with Edelcio Vigna de Oliveira, researcher at INESC, 22 June 1998, Brasilia.

48. According to Albuquerque and Ruffino (1987: 324–25), this directive was issued as a result of the pressure coming from the Movimento das Mulheres Trabalhadoras Rurais (MMTR) of Brejo, Paraíba. The main demand of the MMTR was for the joint allocation and titling to couples of land distributed through the agrarian reform.

49. Interview with Bruno Ribeiro, president of the Agrarian Reform Commission of the State of Pernambuco, 17 June 1998, Recife; and with Edson Teofilo, Nucleo de Estudios Agrarios y Desenvolvimento, Ministerio Extraordinario de Política Fundiaria, 25 June 1998, Brasilia.

50. There was significant regional variation in the number of female beneficiaries, with women's participation being highest in the states of Rio de Janeiro (17.9 percent), Paraíba, Amazonia, Pernambuco, Amapá, and Sergipe. The lowest proportions of female beneficiaries were reported in Paraná (7.2 percent), Santa Catarina, Ceará, Rondonia, Tocantins, and Goiás (ibid.).

51. Discussion by participants at the Seminar on Gender and Land Rights organized for the authors by INESC, 24 June 1998, Brasilia.

52. Beneficiaries as of January 1990; based on "Reforma Agraria en Cifras, enero 1990," in Casafranca and Espinoza (1993: table II-8).

53. There was also resistance to the CERA structure (because they broadened the categories of potential beneficiaries of the reform, bringing together *inquilinos,* sharecroppers, the landless, and others with no previous working relationship to one another) and to the amalgamation of different farms into one centralized unit. As a result of this opposition in many cases the CERAS differed from the *asentamientos* of the previous government in name only (Thiesenhusen 1995: 104).

54. According to earlier estimates of the Sandinista government, women made up only 8.6 percent of the membership of the production cooperatives (the CAS, Cooperativas Agropecuarias Sandinistas) in early 1989 (CIERA 1989, 7: 222). A mid-1989 survey undertaken by the peasant's association, UNAG (Unión Nacional de Agricultores y Ganaderos), gives a somewhat higher figure, 12.3 percent; it draws on a greater number of production cooperatives, 1,221 as compared to 1,120 in the earlier-mentioned study. Taking into account all forms of collective production, women represented 12 percent of the beneficiaries (Fundación Arias–CIPRES 1992: 31). According to these sources, women were less well represented among the members of Credit and Service Cooperatives (CCS), made up of long-standing property-owning farmers as well as beneficiaries of the reform who were allotted land individually: they represented 10.6 percent of CCS members in the UNAG survey, as compared to only 7.3 percent in the official data bank (the latter, which also included fewer CCSs).

55. Interview with Martha Eriberta Valle Valle, UNAG leader and FSLN deputy to the National Congress, 30 January 1997, Managua.

56. A rural women's research team was created within CIERA (Centro de Investigación y Estudio de la Reforma Agraria) in 1980 as part of the agrarian reform institute, INRA (Instituto Nicaragüense de Reforma Agraria), and researchers continually lobbied for a gender perspective. While this team was successful in influencing the language of the agrarian reform law to be inclusive of women, there was tremendous resistance among INRA functionaries to its implementation. On the resistance to women joining the production cooperatives, see Deere (1983) and CIERA (1984).

57. Some token land redistribution through colonization projects had taken place in the 1960s in response to the Alliance for Progress, but El Salvador remained the Central American country with the highest degree of rural landlessness. An estimated 65 percent of the rural population was landless or land poor (with access to less than 0.7 has.) according to the 1971 census. At the other end,

2 percent of the nation's farms held 60 percent of its farmland (Thiesenhusen 1995: 139–40).

58. Initially, three phases had been planned. Phase II, which would have affected farms between 100–150 (depending on land quality) and 500 hectares in size, was never implemented. Moreover, in the 1983 constitution the lower limit on farm size was increased to 245 hectares. Farms in the 245–500 range were given three years to sell or transfer excess farm land.

59. Approximately one-fifth of El Salvador's farmland was transferred to the reformed sector, with 73 percent of this accruing to the Phase I cooperatives, 24 percent to individual ex-tenants, and the remainder (consisting of voluntary farm sales) to peasants in various forms of tenancy (Thiesenhusen 1995: 153). According to this source there were 85,227 beneficiaries. Seligson (1995: 64) reports 85,000 beneficiary households with approximately 125,000 workers who, according to his calculations, represent 21 percent of the population economically active in agriculture.

60. Figures on the proportion of female beneficiaries also vary widely. A World Bank report (1996b: 29) cites three differing estimates for Phase I female beneficiaries: 12 percent, by the Agrarian Reform Evaluation Project (PERA) for 1991 (the source used in the Fundación Arias report, cited above); 6 percent, reported in the 1993 Land Tenure Survey; and 5 percent, reported in a Ministry of Planning document.

61. The household-head criterion for agrarian reform beneficiaries was stipulated in the 1975 law creating ISTA (Article 52, in Fundación Arias 1998a: 13).

62. FAO (1992: 90) puts this figure even higher, reporting that 70 percent of those expropriated were women. In addition, of the 3,500 women who received land parcels, some 2,800 renounced them according to this report, perhaps because of the civil war.

63. Article 19, "Reglamento Regulador de Estatutos de las Asociaciones Cooperativas Agropecuarias," in Mendoza (1997): 121.

64. Besides the thirteen agrarian reforms discussed in this chapter, quantitative data on the female beneficiaries are available only for the Dominican Republic, where they represented 5 percent of the total in 1995 (Galán 1998: 49). Some information is available for Panama, but the data reported refer to land-titling efforts in colonization zones (Fund. Arias–CEASPA 1995: 145).

65. In all three countries we attempted to locate these application forms, unsuccessfully.

66. Nonetheless, in El Salvador, as late as 1985, data were still not processed by the sex of the beneficiary, even though this agrarian reform was financed by USAID (Deere 1987: 187). Since 1972 the Percy Amendment to the foreign-aid legislation has required that all U.S. foreign-assistance programs take into account the impact of such programs on women.

67. In the questionnaires used in most of the Latin American agricultural censuses, the sex of the farmer is not even included as a variable; and when it is included, this information is not processed by the statistical agency and reported in the census publication.

68. On the conceptual problems in enumerating female household heads and the difficulties this poses for comparative analyses, see Buvinic and Youssef (1978); Chant (1997: 724, 704); and Desai and Ahmad (1998).

Chapter 4. Building Blocks toward Gender-Progressive Change

1. Interview with María Elena Reynoso, Agrupación de Mujeres Tierra Viva, 7 January 1998, Guatemala City.

2. According to Irene Tinker (1990), no specific mention was made of women in the Declaration of the First UN Development Decade (1961–70). In 1962 the UN General Assembly instructed the UN Commission on the Status of Women to prepare a report on the role of women in development. But even the commission assumed that "economic and social development would bring about any desired changes for women" (ibid.: 29); that is, it was assumed that the benefits of development would eventually trickle down to women as well as men. It was not until the Second UN Development Decade (1971–80) was proclaimed that mention was made of the need to encourage the "full integration of women in the total development effort." In 1967 the UN General Assembly had adopted the "Declaration to End the Discrimination against Women"; however, this was not a binding accord, and it was largely ineffectual (Binstock 1998: 10).

3. By the time of the publication of Boserup's book, the international family-planning community was also realizing that women played a key role in decision making over family size, a key element in efforts to reduce population growth in the Third World. See Hartmann (1995) on how they quickly incorporated WID concerns into population-control programs.

4. See Rathberger (1990), Young (1993), Kabeer (1994), Razavi and Miller (1995), Feldman (1998), and Luna (1999) for a more detailed treatment of the theoretical premises behind WID, WAD, and GAD and of the development policies for women that were derived from them.

5. See Tinker (1990: 28) on the difficulties of the UN Commission on the Status of Women just in getting an International Women's Year proclaimed at the United Nations, let alone a conference or a decade. Also, on the background of the Mexico City conference and a summary of the contents of the World Plan of Action resulting from it, see A. Fraser (1987).

6. We do not attempt to distinguish between the feminist and women's movements, since their development has been parallel and overdetermined. For a useful attempt to distinguish between them and a discussion of their inter-relationship, see Aguilar et al. (1997: 13). On their development in Latin America, see Kirkwood (1990); Vargas (1989; 1992); Sternbach, Navarro, Chuchryk, and Alvarez (1995); León (1994); and Alvarez (1998a and 1998b).

7. Under the leadership of June Nash, Helen Safa, and Elsa Chaney, the Social Science Research Council sponsored the first Conference on Feminine Research in Latin America, in Buenos Aires in 1974 (see Elu de Leñeros [1975] and Nash and Safa [1976]). The SSRC also funded the first training seminar for graduate students on Feminine Perspectives on Social Science Research in Latin Amer-

ica in Cuernavaca, Mexico, that same year. The first major intellectual gathering of scholars on WID themes is usually considered to be the 1975 Wellesley Conference that resulted in the special issue on "Women in Development" of the new feminist journal *Signs: A Journal of Women in Culture and Society* (1977). Reviews of the growth of feminist scholarship in Latin America include Navarro (1979), Feijoo (1989a, 1989b), Bonder (1998), and Luna (1999). By the mid-1990s, at least sixty gender or women's studies programs had been established in universities throughout Latin America (Valdés and Gomáriz 1995: 190).

8. See Staudt (1985) on the difficulties of WID concerns being taken seriously within USAID and other bureaucracies.

9. See Deere (1976), for example, on the role of women's subsistence production and its usefulness to capital accumulation. The view that women had been marginalized by development also ignored the important role of women beginning in the early decades of this century in the labor union movement in Latin America (Luna 1999).

10. Naila Kabeer (1994) calls the shift in thinking introduced by the WAD perspective the "structuralist perspective." She divides this perspective into three camps: (1) dependency feminists, who viewed gender inequality as part of the larger picture of global economic inequality; (2) feminists focused on global capitalist patriarchy, a radical feminism that gave gender subordination precedence over class inequities; and (3) a perspective that focused on capital accumulation and the social relations of gender. Our own early work (Deere 1977; León 1980; Deere, León, and Humphries 1982) could be considered a contribution to "dependency feminism," inspired as it was by Latin American dependency analysis (itself a powerful critique of modernization theory). However, it was also based on a framework that drew linkages between changes in the sexual division of labor, the social relations of production, and changes in national and international modes of capital accumulation, calling into question Kabeer's proposition that those who employed such a framework represented a different approach from dependency feminism. The unifying point was socialist feminism. The WAD perspective was widely circulated in Latin America through the translation into Spanish of a number of articles by U.S. and British feminists, in the three volumes edited by León (1982).

11. Among other pioneers in gender analysis were Oakley (1972) and Rubin (1975). Important in the diffusion of this concept in Latin America were contributions by Lamas (1986), de Barbieri (1992), and Oliveira Costa and Bruschini (1992). On the difficulties of translating the term "gender" into Spanish, see Schutte (1998).

12. See Young (1993) for a concise summary on how the use of gender was distinguished from the WID and WAD approaches.

13. It is estimated that fourteen thousand women participated in the NGO forum at Nairobi in addition to the approximately three thousand who attended the official conference (Tinker and Jaquette 1987: 419).

14. See Tinker and Jaquette (1987: 42–42) for an excellent analysis of the UN Conferences on Women during the decade and how their outcomes were condi-

tioned by the dominant UN agenda and North-South confrontations on such questions as the new international economic order and the condemnation of apartheid and Zionism.

15. Particularly influential in Latin America was the work by Kate Young (1988, 1991, 1993) and Caroline Moser (1989, 1991, 1993). Moser, drawing on Molyneux (1985), had translated the concepts of practical and strategic gender interests for planning purposes into gender needs. Young focused on the difference between women's condition and position, and framed the problem in terms of practical necessities and strategic interests. Whereas women's condition refers to the material and practical aspects needed to achieve a decent level of living, women's position refers to the status of women in relation to men. The problem of development planning was that it did not differentiate between these two levels. Young (1997: 107–9) also introduced the concept of transformative potential to focus on how practical necessities can be transformed into strategic interests and have the potential to transform gender relations and the structures of women's subordination.

16. On the critique of structural adjustment in Latin America and the Caribbean from a feminist perspective see Deere et al. (1990), Benería and Feldman (1992), and Benería (1995). The most influential feminist theoretical critiques are Elson (1991) and Kabeer and Humphrey (1994).

17. See Luna (1999) for an insightful discussion of the inter-relationship between the feminist NGOs, the women's movement, and the international funding agencies.

18. For a critique of ecofeminism see Molyneux and Steinberg (1995) and Jackson (1993b). Ecofeminism has been more influential in Asia than in Latin America; nonetheless, in the latter a growing appreciation of indigenous issues has coincided with the recognition of the importance of sustainable development and GED.

19. On the development of international women's networks, see Alvarez (1998a and 1998b) and Guillén (1996); on the development of the network on violence against women see Keck and Sikkink (1998).

20. This is with the exception, of course, of the Geneva Conference on Rural Women, convened by the First Ladies of Heads of State and discussed in the next section. Rural women are mentioned more than fifty times in the Beijing Platform for Action (Correia 1998: 159).

21. World Plan of Action, pars. 37 and 46–48, in A. Fraser (1987: 38–39).

22. World Plan of Action, pars. 120–30, in ibid.

23. UN (1982: 2–3), Article 2, pars. a and f.

24. UN (1980: 7), Article 14, par. 2 (g).

25. UN (1980: 7), Part IV, Article 15, par. 2.

26. UN (1980: 8), Part IV, Article 16, par. 2 (h).

27. The coordinating committee consisted of the First Ladies of Colombia, Egypt, Turkey, Senegal, Nigeria, and Malaysia. The Geneva meeting was attended by sixty-nine First Ladies from throughout the world. This was the first time the First Ladies had met at an international level to focus on a concrete eco-

nomic problem. The First Ladies of Latin America had first begun meeting in 1991, but the Geneva meeting shifted their attention from welfare issues (the traditional concern of First Ladies) to economic problems as well. Interview with Ana Milena Muñoz de Gaviria, former First Lady of Colombia, 25 March 1999, Washington, D.C.

28. The follow-up to Geneva among the First Ladies of Latin America resulted in a comparative study of rural women food producers in eighteen Latin American and Caribbean countries under the auspices of the Inter-American Institute for Agricultural Cooperation (IICA) and the Inter-American Development Bank (IADB). The results of this study were published as Kleysen and Campillo (1996); Chiriboga, Grynspan, and Pérez (1996); and Kleysen (1996).

29. On this and other points of debate at the Beijing Conference on Women also see Marina Subirats (1998), the Spanish head of the delegation of the European Union.

30. The legal principle of gender equality in inheritance rights is taken for granted in Latin America, to the point that inheritance was not even mentioned in the regional preparatory documents for Beijing (CEPAL 1994b and Foro 1994). Nonetheless, as we will subsequently show, there is a significant gap between legal inheritance norms and social practice.

31. Following its revolution of 1910, Mexico was the first Latin American nation to establish in its Constitution of 1917 that men and women were equal before the law, in the following terms: "All individuals shall enjoy the guarantees of this Constitution" (Carreras and Montero 1975: 71). Nonetheless, women were excluded from suffrage until 1953. The guarantee of equal rights was further amplified by reform of constitutional Article 4 in 1974 (Binstock 1998: 19). In the 1960s Venezuela, Honduras, and Bolivia adopted constitutions that explicitly prohibited discrimination based on sex or race, and Uruguay adopted a constitution establishing that "all persons" were equal before the law. In the decade of the 1970s Cuba and Ecuador adopted constitutions that explicitly declared that women enjoy the same rights as men, and Panama adopted a constitution prohibiting discrimination based on sex and race (Valdés and Gomáriz 1995: 138).

32. E-mail communication to the authors from Ana Isabel García, director of Fundación Género y Sociedad, 30 August 1999, San José.

33. Nicaragua's National Women's Institute (INIM) also had ministerial status until 1998, when the Alemán government moved it into a new Ministry of the Family.

34. Interview with Ximena Valdés, researcher at CEDEM, 20 July 1997, Santiago, and SERNAM/INDAP/CEDEM/FAO (1994: 13).

35. Intervention at the Seminar on Gender and Land Rights, organized for the authors by CEDEM, 18 July 1997, Santiago.

36. Intervention at the Seminar on Gender and Land Rights, ibid. Francisca Rodríguez also noted that ours was the first seminar in many years to focus on land rights, suggesting how socially sensitive this topic remains in Chile twenty-five years into the counter-reform.

37. Intervention at the Seminar on Gender and Land Rights, ibid.

38. According to Rosario León (1990: 141), in the organization's initial years, the demands of the Bartolinas (as its members are known) did not differ much from those of the CSUTCB, being focused on ethnic identity and class. "Gender demands began to appear once they had discovered their right to a public life and to engage in public action" (ibid.: 142). Important to this process were the links that soon developed between the Bartolinas and other women's grassroots associations, such as the Housewives' Committees in the mining communities. The Bartolinas were to play a very important part in the social movement in the transition to democracy in Bolivia in the early 1980s; but their organization was weakened, along with the other social movements, in the subsequent period, and they never developed strong roots at the base (Ardaya 1992, 1993).

39. Villareal (1998: 72–73) and interviews with Rosa Inés Ospinal, 10 June 1998, and Leonora Castaño, 12 June 1998, Bogotá. ANMUCIC was formally registered as a union with a juridic character in 1986. It should be noted that state officials were not of one mind whether it was appropriate to create an autonomous organization of rural women. Some INCORA functionaries, for example, argued that such an organization would be divisive to the main peasant organization, ANUC, and moreover, that it would split peasant families, for often the female leaders were the spouses of prominent male leaders.

40. An exception to this trend is the Women's Council of the Ejido Unión Lázaro Cárdenas in Nayarit, formed in 1987 by UAIMs from fourteen indigenous communities. See Stephen (1996c) for an interesting case study of the development of the Women's Council and its relationship to the official peasant organization, the CNC, and to the PRI.

41. A good overview of the development of the main national peasant organizations in Mexico and the relationship between them is provided by García (1994).

42. The organizations of rural promoters have been, in turn, assisted by feminist scholars of the group Mujer y Familia of CEICADAR–Colegio de Postgraduados en Ciencias Agrícolas (Alberti 1998).

43. Affiliated to this network in 1996 were twenty-six rural women's organizations in twelve states, with 16,400 members. These organizations have been relatively successful at promoting credit lines for women's productive projects in concert with empowerment issues (Alonso and del Pardo 1997).

44. Telephone interview with Beatriz Rivera, Federación Nacional de Uniones de UNAIMs, 10 December 1999, Mexico City.

45. In the mid-1990s there were over two hundred local-level rural women's organizations and groups active in the five regions of Costa Rica (Fund. Arias 1998f: 19). Most of these are project oriented, and, until recently, there was little communication between them.

46. Interview with Liliana Méndez, president of the National Association of Women Producers of Costa Rica, 20 January 1998, San José.

47. Discussion at the Seminar on Gender and Land Rights organized for the

authors by the Fundación Arias and the Fundación Guatemala, 8 January 1997, Guatemala City; and interview with feminist activist Ana Leticia Aguilar, 9 January 1997, Guatemala City.

48. Interview with Josefina Ramos, Supreme Court judge, 22 January 1998, Managua. The Fundación Arias (1998f: 26) report also notes that "in contrast to the other countries in the [Central American] region, there is a good deal of collaboration and interaction between organized rural women and the rest of the women's movement."

49. Intervention at the Seminar on Rural Women and Land Tenure, hosted for the authors by CEDLA (Centro de Estudios de Desarrollo Laboral y Agrario), CIDEM (Centro de Información y Desarrollo de la Mujer), and Consultores "rym, a.c.," 11 July 1997, La Paz.

50. Interview with Francisca Rodríguez, coordinator of the Departamento de Mujeres de la CNC, 17 July 1997, Santiago; and Ximena Valdés (1999: 13).

51. The struggle to form this organization in the face of strong opposition from CONAIE (Confederación Nacional de Indígenas de Ecuador) is described in Chapter 7. Interview with Teresa Simbaña, founding member of the National Council of Indigenous Women of Ecuador, 24 February 2000, Quito.

52. The move to form these national networks in Central America has been assisted by the Fundación Arias, which since the early 1990s has been carrying out research and drawing attention to the issue of gender and land rights. During 1996 and 1997 it held a series of national-level workshops and meetings in each of the Central American countries to encourage the development of such national networks and an eventual regional network. See Fundación Arias (1997b and 1998f), and CODIMCA and Fundación Arias (1997).

53. For example, as Table 5 in the Appendix shows, Honduras has an exceptionally large number of rural women's organizations. These are affiliated directly or indirectly either to COCOH, the main oppositional umbrella grouping, or the CNC, which generally supports the government, but most have joined together to form REDNAMURH. E-mail communication to the authors from Sara Elisa Rosales, 13 April 2000.

54. Various rural women's organizations had begun meeting in the context of discussions for a national plan for the agricultural sector (Misión Rural) and to prepare a rural women's agenda for the National Development Plan (Ospina 1998). The Rural Women's Office of the Ministry of Agriculture, concerned that there were other regional and national rural women's organizations besides AN-MUCIC and that these had not been receiving state support, convened all these rural women's groups to a meeting; the network was created as a by-product of this meeting. From the initial sixteen, there are now twenty-four organizations that meet periodically to discuss rural women's issues, including the incorporation of their concerns into Colombia's Plan for Equality of Opportunities and the National Development Plan.

Chapter 5: Engendering the Neo-Liberal Counter-Reforms

1. Interview with agrarian lawyer Laureano del Castillo, researcher at CEPES, 6 July 1997, Lima.

2. Since the IFIS (the IMF, World Bank, and Inter-American Development Bank) are located in Washington, D.C., neo-liberal policies were dubbed the "Washington consensus." See Green (1995) on how this consensus was internalized by Latin American governments.

3. The formal logic behind stabilization and structural adjustment policies is explained in Corbo and Fischer (1995).

4. The agricultural policies implemented by the different Latin American countries under neo-liberalism are summarized in Weeks (1995). He also provides an assessment of Latin American agricultural performance through the early 1990s. See de Janvry and Sadoulet (1993) for an assessment of the 1980s.

5. The agrarian codes of Peru (1991) and Mexico (1992) officially ended the process of agrarian reform. The new codes of Ecuador (1994) and Honduras (1992) clearly changed the institutional model while retaining the possibility of expropriating land for purposes of social justice; nonetheless, in both countries the agrarian reform is considered to be over. Neither Chile, El Salvador, nor Nicaragua have officially promulgated comprehensive new agrarian codes, but recent governments have ended (or confirmed) the end of agrarian reform efforts. No new elements have been introduced in Costa Rica in the period of neo-liberalism, except for a noted slow down in agrarian reform activities since 1990, and this case will not be discussed further in this chapter.

6. The World Bank has dubbed the experiments of this latter nature, which it is supporting in Brazil and Colombia, as "negotiated" or "market-assisted" land reform (Deininger 1999).

7. Because of the restrictions and ranking process—which excluded former temporary workers on the estates as well as activists who had been granted beneficiary status by the Allende government—33,085 former beneficiaries (50.2 percent of the total) were denied access to land in the privatization process (Silva 1991: 27).

8. Echenique (1996: 88) reports that by 1978, 15 percent of the households that had been beneficiaries under the counter-reform had sold their parcels; this figure increased to 45 percent by 1983, and 57 percent by 1991. Also see Gómez and Echenique (1988: 96–97).

9. The regions oriented toward production for the internal market were extremely depressed during the 1970s due to liberalization policies, since domestic producers could not compete with imported wheat and corn. After a major agricultural crisis in 1980–83, the government was forced to raise tariffs on basic foodstuffs, which allowed a partial recuperation of peasant and capitalist production in the non-fruit and lumber regions (Lago 1987: 23). The lumber region in southern Chile has been characterized by a very different gender composition of the labor force. Here gender norms have restricted employment to males, providing both permanent and seasonal employment to men. Lumber production,

however, is a much more capital intensive activity than fruit production, and has generated relatively few employment opportunities.

10. According to a 1997 study, in 1987, only a slightly higher proportion of female-headed households (45 percent) as compared to male-headed households (44 percent) were below the poverty line. By 1994 the share of male-headed households in poverty exceeded those of women (28 percent versus 26 percent) (Anríquez and Buvinic 1997: table 3). These data are not broken down by rural and urban areas; moreover, the definition of household head is based on the main income earner of the household and thus may not be comparable with the earlier de jure classifications of headship and poverty estimates reported by Valdés (1994) and Chile (1995).

11. Interview with Laureano del Castillo, 6 July 1997.

12. Interview with María Julia Méndez, employee of a regional cooperative association in the 1980s, 6 July 1997, Lima.

13. Ibid.

14. Ibid.

15. Elsewhere it has been noted that in cooperatives with a large female membership, and particularly where kinship ties among members were strong, women have been a force of cohesion within the cooperatives, preventing their disintegration (Deere 1983, 1987).

16. Some labor-intensive, non-traditional agricultural exports have been developed in recent years, such as asparagus and flower production, but the scale of these has been limited. Peru has thus not experienced the same growth in seasonal agricultural wage employment that Chile did as a result of the implementation of the neo-liberal model. Neither has it experienced a feminization of the agricultural labor force, as has happened in Chile or Mexico. Interview with researcher Efraín González, Instituto de Estudios Peruanos, 6 July 1997, Lima.

17. According to the 1994 agricultural census, there were 5,680 peasant communities and 1,192 native communities in Peru. The great majority of the peasant communities (96 percent) are located in the sierra whereas the native communities are all located in the *selva*. These communities account for 751,130 farms units, representing 43 percent of the national total of 1.7 million, 68 percent of the total farm surface, and 32.5 percent of the agricultural land (Valera 1997).

18. According to this law, the land of peasant communities cannot be used as collateral or rented to non-community members and it is inalienable. Only by exemption can communal land be sold, through a process requiring the agreement of two-thirds of the qualified members of the community meeting in a special assembly convoked for this purpose. The buyer has to pay for the land in advance of the sale.

19. This provision governed beneficiaries who had not completed paying for their parcels; the provisions for those who had completed payment were not as favorable to wives and spouses. However, the great majority of agrarian reform beneficiaries who received land individually never paid for this land.

20. This section draws primarily on del Castillo, Gallo, and Montes (1995);

del Castillo (1996 and 1997b); and interviews with Laureano del Castillo, 6 July 1997, and Guillermo Valera, director, Instituto Rural Peruano, 9 July 1997, Lima.

21. Interview with Efraín González, 6 July 1997.

22. In most highland communities, agricultural land tends to be farmed individually, and it is primarily the pasture land that is communally shared. Moreover, an informal, internal land market has also existed for some time (del Castillo 1996).

23. Interview with Guillermo Valera, 9 July 1997. One factor that may hamper parcelization is that few of the communities actually have communal land titles, which they presumably would need before a communal property could be formally subdivided (Coordinadora Nacional 1997).

24. Interview with researcher Manuel Glave, GRADE (Grupo de Análisis para el Desarrollo), 9 July 1997, Lima.

25. In order to sell land to non-*ejido* members, however, the *ejido* must convert totally or partially to another regime, known as *dominio pleno*.

26. Maximum size limits on landholdings are still in effect, however, and include the following: 100 hectares for irrigated land; 200 hectares for non-irrigated land of decent quality; 300 hectares for plantations; 400 hectares for pastures of good quality, or 800 for those of bad quality or for forests (Tribunales Agrarios 1994: Article 117).

27. See de Janvry et al. (1997: 21–22) for a discussion of the reorganization of the institutional apparatus serving the agricultural sector and of the agricultural policy reforms intended to open markets to international competition.

28. Data as of January 1997, in Warman (1997: table 33).

29. After family members, others who have the *derecho de tanto* include those who have worked the parcel for at least one year, other members of the *ejido,* and residents of the urban nucleus of the *ejido* (Tribunales Agrarios 1994: Article 84).

30. Whether the provisions of the civil code are violated depends on how the usufruct parcel was initially acquired. If the parcel was acquired as a purchase during the marriage, it probably constitutes common property. However, if the parcel was inherited by the *ejidatario,* then it probably forms part of his individual property, which he is free to dispose of as he sees fit. E-mail communication to the authors from lawyer Martha Torres Blancas, El Colegio de México, 11 April 2000.

31. The alternative peasant agrarian law and the neo-liberal law are compared and contrasted, clause by clause, in Calva (1993: 181–244).

32. For example, one of the demands of the CAP was that the government deal with the "backlog" (*rezago agrario*) of lands that had been officially ceded to *ejidos* but were still in the possession of their private owners. In many cases, the *ejidos* or claimants received a cash compensation for these "lost" lands (Fox 1994: 262).

33. As of early 2000, the dialogue between the EZLN and the Mexican government was still at a stand-still. Agreement was reached on only one point, in

January 1996, regarding the autonomy of indigenous communities; but then the government failed to present it to the legislature for approval.

34. This seminar was organized for the authors by the Centro de Estudios Sociológicos, Colegio de México, 16 January 1997, Mexico City.

35. Intervention at the Seminar on Women and Access to Land, 16 January 1997, Mexico City.

36. Of 500 deputies in the Mexican congress in the 1991–94 period, there were only 44 women, and of these only 5 were from rural areas (Costa 1995: 45).

37. Some eight complaints of this order were before the Procuraduría Agraria (the office of the Agrarian Attorney General, a newly created institution) in early 1997. Another case in Guanajuato was pending because the executive committee of the *ejido* sold the UAIM land parcel (because it consisted of excellent lands) without the consent of the women members. A general problem seems to be that the UAIMs were rarely legally registered but rather consisted of informal arrangements between groups of women and the *ejido* executive committee. Now, in the process of certification of *ejido* lands, few UAIMs quality for formal certificates of possession. Discussion at the Seminar on Women and Access to Land, 16 January 1997, Mexico City.

38. Previously, provisional titles could only be used as collateral for loans from state credit agencies. Also, land adjudicated under the agrarian reform could not be subdivided or sold without the authorization of INA.

39. The Agricultural Modernization Law was also the first Honduran legislation to address the situation of its ethnic minorities. Ethnic communities were to be titled the lands they traditionally have occupied free of charge (Article 65), a provision potentially important to the Miskito and Afro-Caribbean population of the country. These lands could be adjudicated to them collectively, if they so requested it, or individually.

40. Of the 2,694 officially recognized "peasant bases," 9 percent entered the land market as vendors in the initial years after the modernization law was passed, selling 6.5 percent of the 470,572 hectares that had been adjudicated to the reform sector (Thorpe 1995: 6–7). A number of cooperatives sold all of their land to the Standard Fruit Company, which was in the process of reconstituting a banana plantation. See Rubén and Fúnez (1993) for a detailed analysis of the sale of agrarian reform cooperative land.

41. Interview with Mirta Kennedy, researcher at CEMH (Centro de Estudios de la Mujer Hondureña), 30 January 1997, Managua, Nicaragua.

42. Interview with Neftalí Bonifaz, director of IDEA, 25 July 1997, Quito. Also see Camacho and Navas (1992) on the neo-liberal analysis of the agrarian question.

43. The following discussion of what the indigenous and peasant groups lost or gained in the 1994 law is based on Navarro, Vallejo, and Villaverde (1996: 35–39); Macas (1995); and our analysis of the law in Ecuador (1994). It also draws on the opinions expressed in the seminar on women's land rights organized for the authors by CEPAM, 24 July 1997, Quito.

44. The Montubians are descendants of the indigenous groups historically located in the *selva* region of Ecuador's Pacific coast, and are generally of mixed blood.

45. Interview with Wilson Sánchez, director of land planning, INDA, 23 July 1997, Quito; and with Emerita Burbano, INDA, 25 July 1997, Quito. Sánchez reported that IERAC previously had some 2,800 employees nationally; INDA currently has around 300 employees and only four local offices. Now they must rely on contracts with NGOs and consulting firms to carry out the necessary titling studies, rather than having their own staff for such purposes. According to him, this has not improved the agency's efficiency.

46. No exact figures are available, however; in 1980 women represented less than 10 percent of Sandinista military personnel (Luciak 2000: 17) and this figure probably fell during the contra war since only men were drafted for the war effort.

47. A main feature of the process of structural adjustment in Nicaragua has been the massive displacement of women from agricultural work. Whereas in 1989 there were an estimated 15,355 permanent women agricultural workers, this figure decreased to 1,285 by March 1991 (Fund. Arias–CIPRES 1992: 86).

48. Whereas in the late 1980s some eighty thousand producers received credit, by 1993 only sixteen thousand did so (Renzi and Agurto 1994: 36). See Enríquez (1999) for an in-depth analysis of the impact of neo-liberal policies on small farmers.

49. Participants in the Seminar on Women and Landed Property in the Latin American Counter-reforms, organized for the authors by the Fundación Arias, CIPRES, and CESADE, 23 January 1998, Managua.

50. Participant in the Seminar on Women and Landed Property, 23 January 1998, Managua.

51. Interview with Olympia Torres and Annete Backhaus of the GTZ, 22 January 1998, Managua.

52. Nitlapán (1994: 17–34). The sale of cooperative land was made possible by Law 88 of 1990, passed by the Sandinistas, which transformed provisional agrarian reform titles into full property titles that could be registered even though the initial land expropriation had never been officially legalized and constituted as land of the state. With full property rights, this land could now be sold, inherited, and mortgaged (Stanfield 1995: 4). Nonetheless, uncertainty over whether these property rights would be recognized constituted an important motivation for land sales by former agrarian reform beneficiaries. The sale of lands within the reformed sector is further discussed in Chapter 9 in the context of Nicaragua's current land-titling program.

53. Intervention by Melba Reyes, CESADE, at the Seminar on Women and Landed Property, 23 January 1998, Managua.

54. Intervention by Marta Luz Padilla at the Seminar on Women and Landed Property, 23 January 1998, Managua.

55. Intervention by Melba Reyes at the Seminar on Women and Landed Property, 23 January 1998, Managua.

56. Discussion at the Seminar on Gender and Land Rights, organized for the authors by IMU, 13 January 1998, San Salvador.

57. Participant from the San Andrés cooperative at the Seminar on Gender and Land Rights, 13 January 1998, San Salvador.

58. See Boyce (1996) and Wood (1996) on the process leading to the accords.

59. There were an estimated 400,000 internally displaced people plus another 285,000 Salvadorans living in exile in Guatemala, Mexico, Honduras, and Nicaragua; at least three-quarters of these were women and children (CEPAL 1994a: 6)

60. Other issues settled in the accords included reform of the military, the creation of a new national police force to be made up of ex-combatants of the FMLN and the government, and reform of the judicial system (Wood 1996: 79–84).

61. Nonetheless, the government was forced to agree to enforce the maximum-size provision as a result of the militancy of the ADC, the Alianza Democrática Campesina. During 1990–1991 ADC members occupied 49 properties that exceeded 245 hectares. In direct negotiation with the ADC, the government finally agreed to redistribute these properties to ADC squatters (many of whom were people recently repatriated to the country) (Salazar 1997). The ADC agreed, in turn, not to engage in any more land take-overs. This agreement was incorporated into the 1992 Chapultepec Peace Accord but it was not fully implemented until 1995 (Gómez Cruz 1997).

62. These national lands include lands expropriated under Phase I of the initial agrarian reform but where cooperatives were never formed due to the civil war.

63. Interviews with Rosario Acosta, FMLN deputy to the National Congress, 12 January 1998, San Salvador; and with Antonio Álvaro, FMLN representative to the PTT (Programa de Transferencia de Tierras), 14 January 1998, San Salvador.

64. According to a 1997 survey, poverty characterized 63.4 percent of the rural population, with 31.4 percent being characterized by extreme poverty (FUSADES 1997). Unfortunately, this study does not include gender-disaggregated data.

65. Interview with Vilma de Calderón, Vice Minister of Agriculture and Livestock, 12 January 1998, San Salvador.

66. Two decrees passed in 1996 were intended to clear up the outstanding debts. Decree 698 focused on the agricultural (working capital) debt and forgave all debts below 5,000 *colones*. If the remaining debt was paid within a year, the cooperative (or individual) would receive a 70 percent discount. Decree 699 focused on the debt incurred for land under the agrarian reform. Any debt of 16,665 *colones* or less was condoned. Again, if the balance was paid within a year, the cooperative (or individual) would receive a 70 percent discount (FUNDE 1997: 39–50). Critics contend that these decrees are aimed at fortifying the land market because few cooperatives are sufficiently profitable—given the negative macroeconomic climate for the agricultural sector—to be able to come up with the 30 percent needed to cancel their debts (ibid.; Foley et al., 1997; PRISMA 1996).

67. The 1983 constitution set the maximum size of farms at 245 hectares and

gave owners three years to sell or divest themselves of "excess" lands. Then in 1998 DL 895 established that these excess land were to be taken over by ISTA, a factor raised again in the peace accords, due to ISTA's lack of compliance. During 1994–95 the ADC conducted its own investigation of such properties and found 360 farms with excess land, totaling 46,263 hectares. As of August 1996, 42 properties had been certified with excess land, for a total of 12,482 hectares (Gómez Cruz 1997).

68. Between the years 1978–82 Guatemalan life was dominated by the counter-insurgency campaign of President Romeo Lucas García; then in 1982–83 by the scorched-earth policy of Gen. Efraín Ríos Montt; followed in 1984–85 by the model villages and development poles of Gen. Humberto Mejía Victores.

69. Women have been particularly active, including as leaders, in the organizations that developed among those who suffered the most during the repression and civil war: the Coordinadora Nacional de Viudas de Guatemala (CONAVIGUA), the Comisiones Permanentes de Representantes de los Refugiados en México (CCPP), the Grupo de Apoyo Mutuo (GAM), the Comunidades de Población en Resistencia (CPR), the Consejo Nacional de Desplazados de Guatemala (CONDEG), and the Consejo de Comunidades Étnicas "Runujel Junam" (CERJ) (Fund. Arias–Tierra Viva 1993: 101). One of the main demands of these organizations is for the recovery of the lands from which they were displaced during the war or the allocation of similar lands.

70. Unless otherwise noted, this section draws on Guatemala (1997) and ONAM (1997b); the former includes the full version of the text of all of the peace accords, while the latter includes the six accords most germane to gender issues.

71. FONATIERRA was created in 1992 as a special fund for the purchase of land from those willing to sell it. Land is then allocated collectively to peasant groups. It differed from the previous land bank within INTA in that the latter had actually sold land very cheaply and the program was not sustainable. Under FONATIERRA land was to be sold at market prices (Fund. Arias–Tierra Viva 1993: 153–54; Rivas and Bautista 1996: 6). Between 1993 and 1995 FONATIERRA assigned 9,072 hectares to 2,540 families in nine departments (ASIES 1995: 12).

72. In contrast to El Salvador or Nicaragua, no special programs were designed for ex-combatants (of either the URNG or the armed forces) in terms of access to land. The focus of the accord on the reinsertion of ex-combatants of the URNG is on their demobilization and re-training for entrance into civilian life, which is assumed to be urban based. It is estimated that approximately 25 percent of the URNG ex-combatants were women, although they were a lower share of those who appeared at the demobilization camps; it is thought that many of the female ex-combatants chose simply to return to their families rather than formally demobilize. Interview with María Asunción García, MINUGUA, 9 January 1998, Guatemala City.

73. These include: (1) the National Geographic Information System (SIGN), which is to compile a national database on land use; (2) the Registry and Cadastre System, which is charged with carrying out a massive land titling and mapping

program; (3) the Presidential Dependency for Conflict Resolution (CONTIERRA), which is to settle all current land disputes and those that might emerge in the process of titling; and (4) the land bank (FONTIERRA), which is to coordinate the financing for the acquisition of land by peasant groups from the new BANRURAL and to identify (in coordination with the Registry and Cadastre System) potential lands for sale. Also, the Property and Unused Land Tax is being decentralized, so that taxes are collected at the municipal level. New legislation is being proposed so that taxes penalize the under-utilization of land (PROTIERRA 1997).

74. FONTIERRA (Fondo de Tierras Acuerdo de Paz) replaced the former program, FONATIERRA, in May 1997. BANRURAL also replaced BANDESA in 1997 as the main source of funding of land mortgages and of short- and long-term credit for small farmers. FONTIERRA's role is to assist in the technical operations, advising peasant groups who find land to buy in negotiating their loans from BANRURAL. The latter are for ten years at a subsidized interest rate of 13 percent. Interview with Víctor Augusto Taracena, FONTIERRA, 5 January 1998, Guatemala City. In 1999 new legislation was passed creating FONTIERRAS (Fondo de Tierras); see Chapter 6.

75. Interview with Berta Falla, MAGA, 5 January 1998, Guatemala City.

76. Interview with Luís Felipe Telaque, PROTIERRA, 5 January 1998, Guatemala City. During 2000, however, a consultant was hired to assist PROTIERRA in applying gender-equity criteria in the national cadastre to be undertaken. (E-mail communication to the authors from Ana Leticia Aguilar, Guatemala City, 8 July 2000.)

77. Interview with María Elena Reynoso, Tierra Viva, 7 January 1998.

78. Interview with Edelberto Torres-Rivas, researcher at FLACSO, 7 January 1998, Guatemala City.

79. Besides an alarming increase in the death rate due to the activities of guerrilla groups, drug traffickers, and paramilitary forces, there was declining public confidence in the institutions and credibility of the state. This was also manifested in an internal crisis within the leading political parties (Leal Buitrago 1991). In this void, new political actors, including women's groups, rose to the forefront, demanding a new national political project and model of development.

80. This section is based on INCORA (n.d.); the law went into effect on 3 August 1994.

81. The state hoped to stimulate voluntary land sales through the use of financial incentives. Voluntary sales to peasant groups are to be paid half in cash and half in government bonds; acquisitions by INCORA are paid 40 percent in cash and 60 percent in bonds; and INCORA expropriations are compensated for fully in bonds.

82. The point system is described in Acuerdo 01 of 1995, article b (in INCORA n.d.: 259).

83. Acuerdo no. 012 of 1995, article 6, in INCORA (n.d.). Chapter 6 discusses why unprotected women are to be given priority in land allocation and how this provision came about.

84. Director of the Project in Support of the Agrarian Reform Program,

Ministry of Agriculture, INCORA, DNP, and World Bank, interview of 30 July 1997, Bogotá.

85. Internal memo of the Ministry of Agriculture and Rural Development, "Informe de Comisión de Evaluación Procesos de Negociación y Adjudicación Predios por Ley 160 de 1994," December 1997.

86. The Colombia program is one of three "negotiated" or market-assisted land reforms being financed by the World Bank; the other experiments are in Brazil and South Africa. These are described in detail in Deininger (1999).

87. Interview with Alejandro Reyes, researcher at the Institute of Policy Studies and International Relations of the University of Colombia, 30 May 1996, Bogotá, Colombia. Also see El Tiempo, "Narcos se adueñan del campo," 30 November 1996: 1. In this article it is estimated that as much as half of Colombia's productive lands are now in the hands of drug traffickers.

88. Articles 3 and 5 of Law 333 maintain the same gender-favorable criteria of Law 160 of 1994: they designate men and women as potential beneficiaries and continues to give priority to female household heads and those women facing a lack of protection due to the violence in the countryside.

89. One worry is that if these lands are expropriated and sold to peasants—given the alliance between the drug traffickers and the paramilitary groups—the result will be to escalate rural violence and political instability. Another concern is that if the drug traffickers are expropriated, the very same landlords who sold their land to them at sky-high prices might be able to recover these lands from the state, continuing the traditional pattern of land concentration (Molano 1997).

90. For a sampling of these positions see "Los ganaderos ofrecen tierras a cambio de paz," El Tiempo, 8 November 1997: 4B, and the polemic it aroused in this newspaper during that month; "Agenda pública, FARC-EP, Plataforma de un gobierno de reconstrucción y reconciliación nacional. Punto 7: Política agraria," Revista Dinero, 27 April 1998; and the alternatives suggested by Darío Fajardo (1998; 1999).

91. "Entrevista con el Ministro de Agricultura Carlos Murgas," El Tiempo, 19 November 1998: 13A, and Presidencia-DNP (1998).

92. Point no. 3 in the common discussion agenda is an integral agrarian policy that would include the redistribution of unproductive land; the appropriation and redistribution of lands acquired by the drug-traffickers; the democratization of credit, technical assistance, and marketing; and territorial reorganization (Gobierno Nacional, FARC-EP 1999: 21). The FARC has pressured for a "real" agrarian reform since its inception in the 1960s.

93. Interview with Miguel Urioste, director of TIERRA, 10 July 1997, La Paz.

94. Ley del Servicio Nacional de Reforma Agraria of 18 October 1996, commonly known as the Ley INRA. In this discussion of the law we draw upon AOS/AIPE/TIERRA (1996); Bolivia (1996); and INRA (1997).

95. A number of new institutions were created by the new legislation: INRA, the National Institute of Agrarian Reform, is to be a decentralized unit of the Ministry of Sustainable Development in charge of implementing land policies.

INRA is to undertake a massive land-titling project (*saneamiento*) over the next ten years with the aim of legalizing, on the basis of cadastral surveys, the status of all landholdings and solving the over-lapping claims to land. INRA is to work alongside the Agrarian Superintendency, within the same Ministry, which is charged with overseeing land use and protecting biodiversity. A National Agrarian Commission (CAN) is constituted as the maximum consultative body on agrarian policy; it is to be composed of four government representatives, one representative of private enterprise, and three representatives of peasant and indigenous groups. Finally, a special Agrarian Judiciary, independent of the executive branch, is set up to solve agrarian disputes.

96. Nonetheless, that land should be distributed to communities and not individually had been a major demand of the national peasants' association. Interview with Paulino Guarachi, 15 July 1997, La Paz.

97. By mid-1998 the technical studies for the process of regularizing land titles linked to the cadastre had been completed in Santa Cruz, the department most characterized by land conflicts, but these had not yet been approved by INRA (Muñoz 1999: 21). In addition, a government agency had begun a study to determine what market-determined prices might look like (ibid.). However, as of late 1999, land had yet to be redistributed (e-mail communication to the authors by researcher Annelies Zoomers, CEDLA, 17 January 2000).

98. The largest and oldest rural workers' organization is CONTAG, the Confederação Nacional dos Trabalhadores na Agricultura, formed in 1963, which in the mid-1990s had over 5 million members organized into 3,200 syndicates and 24 state federations (Cardoso 1997: 41). Until recently, it was considered a "reformist" union, in that it collaborated with the military government during its twenty-one years in power. Its traditional concern was with organizing permanent agricultural wage workers and securing and dispensing social benefits to them in coordination with the state (Tavares 1995: 24). Since the country's return to democratic rule, CONTAG has become much more radical in terms of voicing its demand for agrarian reform and in defending peasants from dispossession by landowners. The degree of its radicalism, however, varies greatly by state. The radicalization of CONTAG is partly due to the fact that in the 1980s two "confrontational" national organizations were formed, the CUT (Central Única dos Trabalhadores) and the MST. The CUT, formed in 1982, is an autonomous union which through its National Department for Rural Workers (Departamento de Trabalhadores Rurais) focused on organizing temporary agricultural wage workers, among others, and securing benefits for them. In 1998 CONTAG joined the CUT, and the latter's Department of Rural Workers was closed.

99. Among the general objectives adopted by the MST at its founding meeting in 1984 were the following: to promote the ownership of land by those who work it; to struggle for a society without exploiters and exploited; and to become an autonomous mass movement within the union movement in pursuit of agrarian reform (Fernandes 1996). Its first national congress was held in 1985, during which it was constituted as a national organization. Over the next decade it would de-

velop autonomously from the church and organize successful land occupations throughout Brazil, in effect carrying out a land reform from below. By 1988 it had organized more than eighty occupations in the south, involving thirteen thousand families (Hall 1990: 213).

100. Data obtained from http://www.mst.org.br/bibliotec/acampam/acamp99.htm (accessed 18 November 2000). These squatter camps have been constructed on public land or by-ways after a land occupation has taken place and the squatters have been evicted. According to Decree 2250/97 of 1997, INCRA will not inspect a property while it is occupied, thus requiring those carrying out the occupation to remove themselves to a nearby location.

101. Between 1995 and August 1998, 238,530 families were allocated land in *assentamentos* (NPOC 1999: 67).

102. In Pernambuco it was possible for such a state agrarian commission to be created primarily because of the positive relations between the leadership of the social movements and the state governor, and the faith of the former in the governor's candidate for the presidency of the commission. Interview with Bruno Ribeiro, presidente da Comissão da Reforma Agraria do Governo do Estado de Pernambuco, and Regina Piechocki, asistente da Comissão, 17 June 1998, Recife. See Deere and León (1999b) on the frustrations this commission experienced in trying to carry out its mandate before it was abolished altogether in August 1998 upon the demand of the social movements.

103. "Informes: Publicação Diária da Liderança do PT na Câmara dos Deputados," no. 2041, 18 April 2000: 1.

104. The amount of underutilized land potentially available for redistribution is a subject of considerable debate. A 1992 INCRA survey identified 55,000 large farms with 150 million hectares; however, according to this report there were only 25 million hectares of productive lands that could potentially be used for agrarian reform projects (Cardoso 1997: 38, 48–51). According to other studies, just on estates larger than 50,000 hectares, there were 35.3 million unproductive hectares (OAS 1997: 115). The range of estimated landless households is between 2.5 and 7 million.

105. "Cédula da Terra: mais uma mentira do governo," *Jornal Sem Terra*, December 1998: 10–11. Also see Martins de Carvalho (1999) and "O governo quer acabar com o INCRA" in "Artigos reforma agraria," http://www.mst.org.br/-bibliotec/textos/reformagr/incra.htm, accessed 18 November 2000.

Chapter 6: The Struggle for Women's Land Rights and Increased Ownership of Land

1. Participant in the seminar "Strengthening the Organization of Rural Women in Nicaragua," Fundación Arias (1997b: n.p.).

2. Costa Rica in its 1990 Law to Promote the Social Equality of Women established explicit equality between men and women in all state programs involving the distribution of assets, legislation that amends its agrarian reform legislation.

3. Honduras's legislation actually falls into both categories, vesting land rights on natural and juridic persons but also establishing that peasant men or women may be beneficiaries of state land distribution or titling programs.

4. Although not one of our case studies, it is worth noting that the Dominican Republic amended its agrarian reform legislation in 1997, and its new agrarian law also provides for mandatory joint titling for married couples and those in consensual unions (Article 39, in DGPM 1998); it is also written in non-sexist language. Land distribution efforts in the Dominican Republic have been at a standstill for some time; the new regulations will primarily apply to the titling of land previously adjudicated under the agrarian reform. E-mail communication to the authors, Pável Isa, Santo Domingo, 11 August 1999.

5. The experiences of Chile and Ecuador, since they involve strictly land titling programs, are discussed further in Chapter 9.

6. Interview with Paola Cappellin, professor of sociology at the Universidade Federal do Rio de Janeiro, 1 March 1999, Amherst, Mass.

7. In 1985 a special program, the Programa de Apoio a Mulher Rural, was created in the Ministry of Agriculture and, the next year, the Comissão de Apoio a Mulher Trabalhadora Rural was created in MINRAD, the Ministerio da Reforma Agraria e Desenvolvimento (Barsted 1994: 63). These offices were closed during the subsequent Collor government. Gender issues in the context of agricultural policy initiatives were not again addressed until the Cardoso government, and then only at the apparent prodding of the FAO (FAO-INCRA 1998).

8. It was an initiative that resulted from the 1987 seminar "Mulher rurais: Identidades na pesquisa e na luta política" organized by Lena Lavinas at the Federal University of Rio de Janeiro (Lavinas 1987), and coordinated with the CNDM. Interview with researcher Heleithe Saffioti, 28 June 1998, São Paulo.

9. The age of retirement for rural women was set at 55 years and for rural men at 60 years (Suárez and Libardoni 1992: 124–25).

10. Also, in contrast to its counterparts in other countries, the CNDM did not play a galvanizing role with respect to the 1995 Beijing Conference on Women. Moreover, in the aftermath of that world conference it appears to be doing little follow-up work on behalf of the rights of women. Interview with Silvia Camuco and Ana Paola Portella, SOS Corpo, 17 June 1998, Recife.

11. Interview with Bruno Ribeiro, president of the Agrarian Reform Commission of the state of Pernambuco, 17 June 1998, Recife; and with Edson Teofilo, Nucleo de Estudos Agrarios e Desenvolvimento, Ministerio Extraordinario de Política Fundiaria, 25 June 1998, Brasilia.

12. Personal documents, such as a birth or marriage certificate, identity card, or voter's registration card, are also necessary to be a beneficiary of the agrarian reform, so this campaign may also be establishing an important pre-condition for greater numbers of rural women eventually to be beneficiaries. The critical card for peasant women to join the social security system is the Bloco de Trabalhador Rural, obtained by paying a sales tax on the sale of agricultural products.

13. "FHC recebe agricultoras," Correio do Povo (Porto Alegre), 10 August

2000, and Deere's interviews with INCRA's superintendents in six states during the period September–December 2000.

14. Interview with Leonora Castaño, president of ANMUCIC, 13 June 1996, Bogotá.

15. The subsequent analysis draws on Gómez-Restrepo (1991), Medrano (1996), and interviews with Norma Villareal, expert on women and rural development, 17 April 1996, Bogotá, and with Diana Medrano, former head of the Office of Rural Women of the Ministry of Agriculture and Rural Development, 29 May 1996, Bogotá.

16. Interview with Leonora Castaño, 13 June 1996, Bogotá.

17. Memorandum no. 09784 of 6 April 1988 by director of INCORA, Dr. Carlos Ossa Escobar, to all regional offices.

18. Acuerdo no. 05 of 1989.

19. Interview with Otilia Dueñas de Pérez, director of INCORA, 2 August 1997, Bogotá.

20. Ana Milena Muñoz de Gaviria was involved in organizing the first international summit of First Ladies in support of rural women's issues (see Chapter 4). Interview with Leonora Castaño, former president of ANMUCIC, 19 November 1998.

21. In 1994 it was estimated that 30.8 percent of the displaced households were headed by a woman and that women constituted 58.2 percent of the displaced persons (Meertens 1998: 26–27). In a 1996 study, of an estimated 165,000 displaced households, it was found that 36 percent were headed by a woman (Caro et al. 1997: 42). By 1997 the number of displaced persons was on the order of 1.2 million representing approximately 2.5 percent of the population (Meertens 1998: 26–27), and these numbers continue to escalate.

22. Interview with Leonora Castaño, 13 June 1996, Bogotá.

23. Interview with Manuel Ramos, INCORA, 2 August 1997, Bogotá.

24. Acuerdo no. 012 of 1995, Article 6.

25. Acuerdo no. 023 of 1995, Article 15, on state distribution of land. INCORA has internalized this as applying to all three modalities of land distribution: by the state, through market-assisted adjudications, and the land-titling program on public lands.

26. "Estudio para identificar los cuellos de botella que limitan el libre acceso a la oferta de crédito de la caja agraria y a los recursos de redescuento de Finagro por parte de las mujeres rurales y establecer mecanismos para superarlos," internal report prepared for the Office of Rural Women, Ministry of Agriculture and Rural Development, n.d.

27. Interviews with Alba Lucía Zuluaga, consultant to the Office of Rural Women, Ministry of Agriculture and Rural Development, 6 June 1996, Bogotá; and with Pilar Vidal, consultant to INCORA, 3 June 1996, Bogotá.

28. "El mercado de tierras, Ley 160 de 1994, Manual operativo de prueba," internal report of the Proyecto de Apoyo al Programa de Reforma Agraria (Fase Experimental), Ministry of Agriculture and Rural Development, INCORA, DNP,

and World Bank, May 1997. This report mentions that female household heads have priority over others (p. 14) and that they can join the groups of peasant beneficiaries if they have at least 65 points (p. 23). The minimum required to be a beneficiary is 60 points (p. 13), and being an unprotected woman does not seem to merit points.

29. Interviews with Absolóm Machado, 30 July 1997; with Otilia Dueñas de Pérez, 2 August 1997; and discussion at the Seminar on Gender and Land Rights, organized by the Center for Documentation on Women and Gender, National University of Colombia, 30 July 1997, Bogotá.

30. Interview with María Ema Prada, president of ANMUCIC, 12 June 1998, Bogotá.

31. It is worth noting that even ANMUCIC seems unclear about the provision to be beneficiaries for single women who are characterized by a lack of protection (and not just female household heads) and has given it scant attention. Their priority has remained assuring the land rights of female-headed households and joint titling of land to couples. Group interview with the ANMUCIC leadership, 1 August 1997, Bogotá.

32. In the fall of 1999 a new agrarian reform law, backed by the main national peasant and indigenous organizations (including ANMUCIC) and the unions of state workers in the agricultural sector, was presented in the national congress. It would end the market-assisted program and refocus the efforts of INCORA on land expropriation, strengthening the institution. The main gender-progressive changes discussed above are maintained with the exception of the provision for single women characterized by a lack of protection to be given priority in land adjudication. The new provision gives priority to "female household heads who are victims of the violence or in a state of social unprotection." Article 52 in "Proyecto de Ley número 183 de 1999 Cámara," *Gaceta del Congreso*, no. 480, 29 November 1999.

33. For a brief history of this law and the various versions it went through before it was finally approved see Ansorena (1997). The most controversial aspects of the "Law Project to Promote Women's Real Equality," as it was initially known, were the establishment of a quota system for women candidates in the municipal and national legislature and a measure requiring mandatory day care centers in private enterprises. While both of these measures were removed from the final version of the law, those regarding property rights caused little controversy at the time.

34. Intervention by a rural promoter at the Seminar on Gender and Land Rights organized for the authors by the Fundación Arias, 20 January 1998, San José.

35. This case is reported in Voto no. 0346-94, no. 1237-90 of *Boletín Judicial*, no. 75 (1994): 2–3. Our analysis also draws on interviews with Judge Ricardo Zeledón and lawyer Magda Díaz, Supreme Court of Justice, 19 January 1998, San José.

36. Note that discrimination was prohibited in a constitutional article clearly written in sexist language, in which men are considered the equivalent of the

human race. This constitutional article was subsequently modified in 1998; now, "all persons are equal before the law." E-mail communication to the authors from Ana Isabel García, former director of CMF, 30 August 1999.

37. Interview with Judith Vísquez, Lorena Villalobos, Vicky Arroyo, and Carmen Rodríguez, IDA, 19 January 1998, San José. Unfortunately, IDA has not systematized its data-collection efforts by sex, and disaggregated data are not available for more recent years.

38. The strong bias in Costa Rica toward income-generating and other micro projects for women is seen in the most recent initiative of IDA. In order to deal with the growing number of young people as well as female-headed households on the *asentamientos,* it has engaged in a program of allocating small plots for housing and home gardens. Between 1996 and 1998 some 2,695 persons were beneficiaries of this program, receiving an average of 0.18 hectares of land; many were female household heads. Interview with Vicky Arroyo, Oficina de Huertos Familiares, IDA, 19 January 1998, San José.

39. Interview with Liliana Méndez, president of the National Association of Rural Women Producers of Costa Rica, 20 January 1998, San José.

40. Interview with Ana Isabel García, former director of CMF, 21 February 1999, San José.

41. The Plan for Equality of Opportunities for Rural Women included a comprehensive monitoring plan. The government formally complied with this plan, in the case of IDA reporting that progress had been made on a number of its objectives (CMF 1998). But IDA refused to make available any data supporting this claim. IICA, the InterAmerican Institute for Agricultural Cooperation, under our urging, even allocated funds to assist IDA in data collection efforts by sex, but this overture was rebuffed.

42. The first national Women's Meeting, attended by some eight hundred women, was held in January 1992. A number of networks were created, focused on specific themes such as health and violence against women, but there was no consensus on whether to create a new, autonomous national women's organization. Several months later the National Feminist Committee was created consisting of some twenty-five collectives and women's groups who wanted to build an autonomous feminist movement, and in October of that year they held the first national Encuentro Feminista, followed by the first Central American Encuentro Feminista. Although the National Feminist Committee disbanded in 1993, many of its members continued to be active in the loose regional network "Corriente Feminista Centroamericana." Corriente members throughout the region played an important role in preparing their countries' respective platforms for the World Conference on Population and Development in Cairo in 1994 and the Fourth UN World Conference on Women in Beijing in 1995 (Stephen 1997: 61–62). It is considered that "the women's movement has gained much more evident degrees of autonomy in the 1990s" (Asociación 1996: 15).

43. Interview with Josefina Ramos, Supreme Court judge, 22 January 1998, Managua.

44. Interview with Marta Valle, UNAG representative in the National Congress, and Matilde Rocha, UNAG's Women Section, 23 January 1998, Managua.

45. Intervention at the Seminar on Gender and Property Rights, organized for the authors by the Fundación Arias, CIPRES, and CONADE, 23 January 1998.

46. Interview with Malena de Montis, director of CENZOTLE, 29 January 1997, Managua.

47. Intervention by Patricia Hernández, INRA, at the Seminar on Gender and Property Rights, 23 January 1998.

48. Intervention at the Seminar on Gender and Property Rights, 23 January 1998.

49. Interview with researcher Lca Montes, Nitlapán, 31 January 1997, Managua.

50. This break-down is only available for the 22,096 titles issued to 35,545 individuals as of 4 November 1996 (INRA-INIM 1996), and thus the absolute numbers differ from those reported in Table 6.4 for the Chamorro government, which are based on titling activities as of 20 December 1996.

51. Interview with researcher Sonia Agurto, FIDEG, 22 January 1998, Managua.

52. Discussion at the seminar on Gender and Property Rights, 23 January 1998. In addition, by this time the program "Capacitación Técnica a Productoras Agropecuarias al Proceso de Titulación de Tierras" had been launched within the Ministry of Agriculture and Livestock with financial support from NORAD, to publicize women's right to be included in land titles. See MAG-NORAD (n.d.) on their dissemination efforts.

53. "Consolidado del período enero–diciembre 1997," División de Titulación, INRA. We could not verify the information on the composition of couples for subsequent years.

54. Article 49, Law no. 278, "Ley sobre Propiedad Reformada Urbana y Agraria," published in La Gaceta, Diario Oficial, no. 239, 16 December 1997.

55. Interview with researcher Sara Elisa Rosales, 15 January 1998, Tegucigalpa. Given the absence of a national women's office, in the 1990–93 period government initiatives on gender issues were centered in the legislature. The Permanent Women's Forum in the congress received technical assistance from UNICEF and other international agencies. E-mail communication to the authors from Rocío Tabora, UNDP-Honduras, 13 September 1999.

56. Intervention by a participant in the Seminar on Gender and Land Rights organized for the authors by the Fundación Arias and REDNAMURH, 16 January 1998, Tegucigalpa.

57. Ibid.

58. Interview with Rosario Acosta, 12 January 1998, San Salvador.

59. Interview with Lety Méndez, Women's Secretariat of the FMLN, 14 January 1998, San Salvador. See Hipsher's (1998) interviews as well for the opinion of former FMLN combatants and other women that they were ignored in these programs.

60. Interview with Carmen Arqueta, Las Dignas, 13 January 1998, San Salvador.

61. Interview with Antonio Álvarez, 14 January 1998, San Salvador.

62. Ibid.

63. A 1994 census of 420 properties transferred under the PTT found that only 49 percent of the land was potential agricultural land; 22.5 percent was being farmed individually, 4 percent collectively, and 23 percent was not being used at all. That potential farmland was going idle is associated with the high rate of absenteeism on these, which in turn was related to the poor conditions on many farms. Less than 40 percent of the beneficiaries had any housing on the property, only 11 percent had electricity, and fewer than 1 percent had access to potable water. Moreover, while PTT beneficiaries were to be provided with credit, as of 1995 only one-third of the ex-combatants and 11 percent of the former squatters had received loans for working capital. Moreover, the technical assistance they had received was also considered to have been deficient (Hernández and Dada 1997: 14, 21–22).

64. The cancellation of the debt was facilitated by the fact that the purchase of these farms had been financed by a donation from USAID and the European Economic Community.

65. Interview with Rosa Linees, member of Las Dignas, 13 January 1998, San Salvador.

66. The articles refer to the government's version of the code; see Orellana (1996: 33–34). In the ADC proposal these are articles 48, 49, and 51 in ADC (1996).

67. Interview with Patricia Alfaro and Rosalío Joven, ISDEMU, 12 January 1998, San Salvador. Recall that an objective of the National Women's Policy (PNM), approved in May 1997, was to promote women's property rights and access to land in conditions of equality with men (ISDEMU 1997: 44).

68. Those articles that are similar in this proposal to the other two proposals on gender issues are articles 16, 17, 18, 19, 20, and 24. The new articles that focus on gender are nos. 2, 22, and 28 (IMU 1999).

69. The alternative agrarian code with a gender perspective was submitted to the national congress in November 1999, but a year later had still not been discussed by this body. E-mail communication to the authors by Deysi Cheyne, director of the IMU, San Salvador, 28 November 2000.

70. Some eighteen organizations were represented in the women's sector of the ASC. Among those associated with agrarian and rural women's issues were the Agrupación de Mujeres Tierra Viva; FAMDEGUA (Asociación de Familiares Detenidos-Desaparecidos de Guatemala); CONAMPRU (Comisión de la Mujer de la Coordinadora Nacional de Pequeños y Medianos Productores); CERJ (Consejo de Comunidades Étnicas "Runujel Junam"); and CONAVIGUA (Coordinadora Nacional de Viudas de Guatemala) (ONAM 1997b: 11).

71. On the prospects of the women's forum see Aguilar and Pellecer (1997: 16).

72. Interview with Berta Falla, MAGA, 5 January 1998, Guatemala City.

73. Interview with María Asunción García, MINUGUA, 9 January 1998, Guatemala City.

74. Internal document, "Requerimientos de acciones presentados por las organizaciones de mujeres retornadas y refugiadas," workshop on El Acceso de la Mujer al Crédito, a la Tierra y a la Organización, 6 December 1995, ACNUR, Guatemala City. The organizations represented included Mama Maquín, Madre Tierra, CCPP, IXMUCANE, and Cooperativa El Arbolito.

75. Interview with Patricia Wohlers, MINUGUA, 9 January 1998, Guatemala City, and with Clara Arenas, director of AVANCSO, 9 January 1998. Also see Worby (1999).

76. "Reglamento para la concesión de recursos financieros a grupos retornados mayores de cincuenta familias suscritos entre FONAPAZ y los miembros de las comisiones permanentes, en base a los acuerdos del 8 de octubre de 1992," memo dated June 1996, made available to the authors by MINUGUA, Guatemala City.

77. This group, which is part of the Consultative Assembly of the Displaced Population (ACPD), was formed in 1996 and includes, among others, Mama Maquín, Madre Tierra, CONAVIGUA, CERJ, and GAM. Interview with María Asunción García, MINUGUA, 9 January 1998, Guatemala City.

78. The returnees are generally considered to be among the more privileged within the refugee population since they were the earliest focus of government and UN attention and were given priority in the assignment of land. In 1997 it was estimated that the total refugee population numbered approximately 55,000 families with 325,000 persons; of these, 11,179 families had returned from exile. Data of CEAR, Comisión Especial para Atención a los Refugiados, made available to the authors by MINUGUA, January 1998.

79. E-mail communication to the authors by Paula Worby, UNHCR consultant, 2 September 1999.

80. Ibid.

81. That is, assuming that any fundamental redistribution of land through broad-sweeping expropriation is more or less out of the question.

Chapter 7: In Defense of Community: Struggles over Individual and Collective Land Rights

1. Nina Pacari (1998: 60, 66), national leader of CONAIE and vice president of the Ecuadorian Congress.

2. The Universal Declaration of Human Rights was adopted by the UN General Assembly in 1948. It was designed to reaffirm and reinforce the provisions of the UN Charter that in its preamble affirmed the equal rights of men and women and prohibited discrimination based on sex, race, language, and religion. Nonetheless, the writing of the Universal Declaration of Human Rights in relatively gender-neutral terms required a major struggle. Early versions of the declaration had begun with "All men are brothers." After considerable lobbying, the UN Commission on the Status of Women managed to introduce language focusing on "all human beings," which was eventually adopted (Tomasevski 1993: 98–100).

3. More specifically, according to Santos (1997: 8–9), the concept of universal human rights is based on the following assumptions of Western liberal theory: that there is a universal human nature that can be rationally known; that human nature is different from and superior to all other realities; that individuals have an absolute dignity that needs to be defended from society and the state; and that individual autonomy requires a non-hierarchical organization of society. The consequences of this set of assumptions were that the 1948 Universal Declaration of Human Rights focused on individual rather than collective rights and gave priority to political and civil rights over economic, social, and cultural rights. Moreover, among economic rights, the right to private property received privileged treatment.

4. The "strong" version of cultural relativism is also referred to as cultural absolutism (Howard 1993). It is often distinguished from a "weak" or non-essentialist version whereby culture is seen as an important but not the sole source of validity of moral right or rule (Donnelly 1984: 400).

5. Interview with Jorge Dandler, senior specialist in rural employment and indigenous peoples, ILO, 21 February 1999, San José.

6. Executive director of CECOIN (Centro de Cooperación Indígena), Bogotá; interview of 15 September 1998. Colombia and Peru were among the countries that went furthest in this period in recognizing communal land rights. In the Peruvian agrarian reform the same principles governing the recognition of peasant communities in the highlands were applied to the Amazonian indigenous peoples, who were organized and ceded land collectively as "native communities," a move that Hvalkof (1998) argues fit well with the overall objective of the time of transforming Indians into peasants. In Colombia the Agrarian Reform Law 135 of 1961 provided for national lands to be assigned to indigenous groups with insufficient land (OIT 1987: 52).

7. For the English translation of the phrases noted in quotes below we have drawn upon "C169 Indigenous and Tribal Peoples Convention, 1989," memo, ILO, 14 April 1999.

8. Responding to the concerns of the UN Decade, the Inter-American Commission of Human Rights of the OAS approved a draft in 1995 of an Inter-American Declaration on the Rights of Indigenous Peoples that drew and expanded upon the provisions of Accord No. 169. With respect to gender, its main provision guarantees indigenous women the ability to "exercise their civil, political, economic, social and cultural rights without any form of discrimination," but no mention is made of women's land rights (Article 6 in Sánchez 1996: 329–41). This draft is still pending approval by the OAS heads of state. E-mail communication to the authors from Jorge Dandler, OIT-San José, 24 April 2000.

9. The precedents that are mentioned in its preamble include the Universal Declaration of Human Rights; the International Covenant on Economic, Social, and Cultural Rights; the International Covenant on Political and Civil Rights, "and the many international instruments on the prevention of discrimination."

10. Overall the 1995 Beijing conference is considered a victory for feminists over cultural relativists with respect to women's human rights. The Beijing Plat-

form for Action explicitly adopted the key principles on women's human rights of the Vienna Declaration and Programme of Action. Moreover, the debate over whether the goal was equality or equity between men and women was resolved in favor of equality (Brems 1997: 150–52).

11. Interview, 21 February 1999, San José.

12. On the issue of granting indigenous people autonomy with respect to self-governance—which will not be treated here—see the essays in Sánchez (1996) and Van Cott (1994). A number of countries, such as Bolivia, Colombia, and Ecuador, have made provisions for self-governance through more general processes of decentralization of the state, which grant considerable autonomy at the municipal level.

13. The pluricultural composition of the Mexican nation is recognized in its 1917 constitution, as amended, as is the obligation of the Mexican state to promote the development of indigenous languages, cultures, and customs. (Article 4 in Van Cott 1999.) A proposed amendment to the constitution, resulting from the 1996 San Andrés Peace Accords with the EZLN (Ejército Zapatista de Liberación Nacional), goes much further, recognizing the right of indigenous communities to practice customary law and granting these autonomy with respect to their "internal forms of living and social, economic, political, and cultural organization" (ibid.). But this proposed reform of the Mexican constitution was never submitted by the Zedillo government to the legislature for approval.

14. On the development of ECUARUNARI and its transformation from a peasant-oriented organization to a self-identified indigenous organization, see Zamosc (1994) and Black (1998). Also see the latter on the development of CONFENIAE from nine ethnic-based organizations in the Amazon, and on the evolution of their demands.

15. Prior to the uprising, some 600,000 hectares in the provinces of Napo and Pastaza had been titled to the Huaorani people. Now the OPIP (Organization of the Indigenous People of Pastaza) demanded that the bulk of the province of Pastaza be titled as the territory of the indigenous people who inhabited it (Navarro, Vallejo, and Villaverde 1996: 28–30).

16. Carmelina Porate, national women's leader of CONAIE, at the workshop "Mujer Indígena y Participación Indígena," NGO preparatory meeting for Beijing in Mar del Plata, Argentina, 1994, in CEIMME (1995: 68–69).

17. Interview with Rocío Rosero, researcher at DINAMO, 25 July 1997, Quito.

18. This office was reconstituted as the Division of Women and Youth in 1996 after the First Lady attended the Beijing Conference and returned convinced that priority attention had to be given to rural women. Interview with Dolores Casco, director of the Office of Peasant Development of the Ministry of Agriculture and Livestock, 23 July 1997, Quito.

19. See Andolina (1998) on the process leading to the constitutional assembly of 1998 and on CONAIE's role in securing indigenous rights in the new constitution.

20. Interview with Miguel Urioste, director of TIERRA, 10 July 1997, La Paz.

21. Interview with Paulino Guarachi, Sub-Secretariat of Rural Development, 15 July 1997, La Paz. Guarachi was a former secretary general of the CSUTCB.

22. Interview with Julia Ramos Sánchez, executive secretary, and Emiliana Sarcido, general secretary, Federación Nacional de Mujeres Campesinas de Bolivia "Bartolina Sisa," 15 July 1997, La Paz.

23. Discussion generated at the Seminar on Rural Women and Land Tenure, organized for the authors by CEDLA, CIDEM, and Consultores "rym, a.c.," 11 July 1997, La Paz.

24. According to the director of legal affairs of the Sub-secretariat of Gender Affairs, the initiative came from deputy Miguel Urioste, a specialist in agrarian matters and the founder of TIERRA. He reportedly said to the Sub-secretariat, "Do something: the law is about to be approved and there is no gender content." Interview of 14 July 1997, La Paz.

25. Letter from Jocelyn Olmos, Coordinadora de la Mujer, to Isabel Lavadenz, Interventora Nacional de CNRA, 3 July 1996, La Paz; and letter from Isabel Lavadenz to Jocelyn Olmos, 11 July 1996, La Paz. Archives of the Coordinadora de la Mujer.

26. Interview with Roxana Ibarnegaray, researcher at CONALSE, Ministry of Agriculture, 11 July 1997, La Paz.

27. The director of INRA thought that several of the other recommendations of the consultant's report, such as gender-neutral language, could be dealt with in the subsequent regulations to accompany the law. However, in the subsequent regulations, no additional gender-specific content was added (INRA 1997). In retrospect, Isabel Lavadenz considers that "It would have been interesting to have analyzed the topic of joint titling of small property and the family lot. . . . Maybe it is not required in the case of formal unions and consensual unions since if the peasant owns the land, land is considered a *ganancial* [profits, which are divided between the couple in case of separation]. But I am aware that certain cultural values need to be declared explicitly." Interview of 14 July 1997, La Paz.

28. Summary of the discussion on this topic by non-indigenous participants at the Seminar on Women's Rights to Land, organized for the authors by CEPAM, 24 July 1997, Quito.

29. Billie Jean Isbell (1978: 11) defines the notion of complementarity in terms of one entity's relation to another entity: "sexual complementarity is perhaps the most pervasive concept used to classify cosmological and natural phenomena. It also symbolizes the process of regeneration. Phenomena are conceptualized as male and female and interact with one another in a dialectic fashion to form new syntheses, such as new cycles of time and new generations of people, plants, and animals." She has called this dialectic the concept of "the essential other half."

30. Interview with Clara Flores, congressional deputy and indigenous leader, 12 July 1997, La Paz.

31. Interview with researcher Gloria Ardaya, 13 July 1997, La Paz.

32. Interview with Dolores Casco, director of the Peasant Development Division of the Ministry of Agriculture and Livestock, 23 July 1997, Quito. The es-

timate was made by Julia Almeida of the Division of Peasant Organizations of the Ministry of Agriculture and Livestock, on the basis of a review of the data on executive committees reported to the Ministry by 2,253 *comunas,* 1,985 cooperatives, and 1,382 other base-level organizations. These data are not gender-disaggregated, however, so this estimate is based on an analysis of first names in order to determine sex.

33. In the four Mizque communities studied by Susan Paulson (1996: 138), women represented 17 percent of the syndicate members, largely because they were widowed or separated from their partners. But a few of the women representing their households did so because they were the owners or administrators of the household's land, illustrating the potential importance of women's land ownership to changes in their bargaining position and political representation.

34. The only convincing evidence of joint household decision-making in most realms comes from Sarah Hamilton's (1998) case study of the central Ecuadorian sierra. Otherwise, the literature tends to show that within the majority of peasant and indigenous communities in the Andes, gender inequality is pervasive, as seen in inheritance patterns, land tenure, the structure of power and representation, and in daily life.

35. Mercedes Urriolagoitia, NGO national coordinator for Beijing, intervention at the Seminar on Rural Women and Land Tenure, 11 July 1997, La Paz.

36. There has been a Women's Secretariat within CONAIE since its creation in 1986, and one was subsequently established within CONFENAIE. However, in most of the indigenous organizations in the Amazon region, women's secretariats were not developed until the mid-1990s. In the case of FOIN (Federación de Organizaciones Indígenas del NAPO), which resisted creating a women's secretariat, the women formed their own women's organization and then petitioned for membership in FOIN. Subsequently, they were granted a permanent vice-presidency in the mixed-group organization (CEPLAES 1998: 154, 96).

37. Yolanda Vargas at the workshop on Indigenous Women and Participation, NGO Preparatory Meeting for Beijing, Mar del Plata, September 1994 in CEIMME (1995: 54–55).

38. Interview with Gloria Ardaya, 13 July 1997, La Paz.

39. Simbaña is a former national secretary of FEINE (Federación Ecuatoriana de Indígenas Evangélicos). Interview of 24 February 2000, Quito.

40. Ibid.

41. In Peru the decision to parcelize the peasant communities requires a 50 percent majority vote in the coast, and—as in Ecuador—a two-thirds vote in the highlands. In Mexico this decision only requires a simple majority vote.

42. Sofía Robles, "Grupo Iniativa Indígena por la Paz," San Cristóbal, Chiapas, in CEIMME (1995: 52–53).

43. Interview of 7 January 1998, AVANCSO, Guatemala City.

44. Victoria Álvarez, Quiché indigenous leader, Guatemala, in Chinchilla (1998: 451).

Chapter 8. Inheritance of Land in Practice

1. Anthropologist Bernd Lambert (1977: 15), referring to the Andean region.

2. This is the default rule in all twelve countries studied here should the deceased die intestate. Recall from Chapter 2 that four countries (Costa Rica, El Salvador, Guatemala, and Mexico) allow full testamentary freedom and two (Nicaragua and Honduras) allow near testamentary freedom.

3. Bilateral inheritance is characterized by children inheriting from both parents; it thus assumes that women own and inherit property that they can pass on to their children. Parallel inheritance refers to sons inheriting through the male and daughters through the female line.

4. Patrilocality refers to the residence of a young couple in the paternal home of the groom, while virilocality refers to residence on lands provided through the male line. Both are often associated with exogamy, where women marry outside their community of origin. The locale of post-marital residency is one of the strongest factors associated with different inheritance systems cross-culturally. In Agarwal's (1994a: 140–44) exhaustive study of inheritance systems in South Asia, for example, she found women's land inheritance rights in matrilineal and bilateral systems closely associated with women marrying and living within their natal villages.

5. As Maria José Carneiro (2000) argues, land has more than economic value in peasant societies, and inheritance systems also need to be studied from the point of view of their symbolic value in reproducing the family patrimony. She suggests that only in this way can the hierarchies and unequal relations within the family be fully understood, as well as the way that individual interests are subsumed to the collective interests of the family.

6. In Central America and Colombia there has also been scant attention to inheritance practices in community-level studies of the peasantry. For brief summaries of the available evidence see Deere and León (1999c) on Guatemala and (1998d) on El Salvador; CIERA (1989, vol. 7: 43–46) on Nicaragua; and Camacho (1999) on the Afro-Colombian region of Colombia.

7. Other evidence of the existence of parallel inheritance systems in Peru comes from Jane Collins's study of the Aymara in the Department of Puno (cited in Hamilton 2000: 6).

8. Interview with researcher Mercedes Prieto, 22 July 1997, Quito, and discussion at the Seminar on Women's Land Rights organized for the authors by CEPAM, 24 July 1997, Quito.

9. Interview with Rosita Cabrera, former women's leader of ECUARUNARI, 22 July 1997, 'O la Toglla, Quito province.

10. This survey of community inheritance practices was carried out by local-level NGOs in sixteen municipalities of seven departments of Bolivia. The study was based on a questionnaire filled out by community leaders, and is only indicative of general trends at the local level.

11. Discussion at the Seminar on Rural Women and Land Tenure, organized

for the authors by CEDLA, CIDEM, and Consultores rym a.c., 11 July 1997, La Paz, and interview with anthropologist Luz Marina Calvo, 10 July 1997, La Paz.

12. Virilocal residency and the inheritance pattern privileging the youngest son with the parental home in return for the care he is expected to provide to elderly parents is also reported to characterize the neighboring state of Tlaxcala (Castañeda 2000: 3).

13. Interview of 16 July 1997, Santiago.

14. Discussion at the Seminar on Gender and Land Rights, organized for the authors by CEDEM, 18 July 1997, Santiago, and comments on León and Deere (1999) by Álvaro Bello, researcher at CEDEM.

15. Intervention at the Seminar on Gender and Land Rights, 18 July 1997, Santiago.

16. Ibid.

17. Carneiro (2000) reviews the skimpy data available for other southern and central states, which nonetheless suggest that the more common pattern in land inheritance is patrilineality.

18. In the past it was generally mothers who provided a daughter's dowry. With the reduction in women's autonomous economic activities, they are also less likely to be able to provision their daughters for marriage (Woortmann 1995: 193).

19. Interview with researcher Maria José Carneiro, Centro para el Desarrollo Agrícola, Federal Rural University of Rio de Janeiro, 19 June 1998, Rio de Janeiro; also see Carneiro (2000).

20. In other regions of the Northeast, such as in the state of Pernambuco where a larger share of the rural population is mulatto, patrilineality and patri- and viri-locality also prevailed in the past. Land inheritance practices today are reported to be quite heterogeneous but generally more equitable between the sexes. Participants at the Workshop on Gender and Land Rights, organized for the authors by SOS Corpo, 15 June 1998, Recife.

21. Discussion at the Seminar on Rural Women and Land Tenure, La Paz, 11 July 1997.

22. There was considerable regional variation, nonetheless, with over 50 percent of the *ejidatarios* willing their land to wives or partners in the northern states of Baja California, Nuevo León, and San Luis de Potosí; in contrast, in the central and southern states of Mexico sons tended to be favored as heirs over wives and partners (Valenzuela and Robles 1996).

23. 15 June 1998, Recife.

24. It would seem that locale of marital residence would have less of an impact in constraining gender-equitable inheritance practices in the Andes than in other regions, since geography has imposed land-use patterns involving access to parcels at different elevations and thus locales. That is, family farms rarely consist of contiguous land parcels.

25. Participant at the Seminar on Rural Women and Land Tenure, La Paz, 11 July 1997.

Chapter 9: Women Property Owners:
Land Titling, Inheritance, and the Market

1. Excerpt from the novel by Marcela Serrano (1997: 106), *El albergue de las mujeres tristes*. It is situated in Chile, where female household heads were given priority in the national land-titling program.

2. For example, in Colombia it has been estimated that the inscription of a land title in the public registry, because of notarial and registry fees and taxes, can cost as much as 20 percent of the value of the transaction; in Ecuador these costs may be as high as 25 to 35 percent of the value of the land (Jaramillo 1998: 101).

3. This has been a particular problem on the agrarian frontier of a number of countries. In Bolivia, for example, the lack of a modern cadastral and registry system has aggravated conflicts between colonizers, ranchers, and indigenous groups (Urioste and Pacheco 1999: 12).

4. For example, a clear title should enhance the time horizon of farmers, making them more willing to make costly investments such as in irrigation systems or in tree crops that take years to mature. Also, it should increase the incentive for farmers to invest in more ecologically benign agricultural practices and land conservation measures.

5. This is because of the inverse relationship between farm size and productivity, a result that assumes a perfectly competitive market (Binswanger et al. 1995).

6. E-mail communication to the authors from Professor Billie R. Dewalt, University of Pittsburgh, 9 April 2000.

7. The requirement that landholders pay for this land proved a major source of resistance to the titling project since many of the targeted beneficiaries were second- and third-generation "owners," having purchased the rights to these usufruct parcels from third parties (Jansen and Roquas 1998).

8. Data provided to the authors by INA, División de Titulación de Tierras, Base de Datos, January 1998.

9. Interview with Rosario García, head of the Department of Women and Youth, INA, 15 January 1998, Tegucigalpa.

10. Land-titling beneficiaries have six months after being issued their title to register these in the public registry; only then are these legal titles (of *dominio pleno*). It is unclear whether the data reported by Acosta and Moreno (1996) refer to titled or registered lands.

11. One of the problems in Honduras has been that, until recently, there has been a proliferation of rural women's organizations with little coordination between them in attempts to influence state policy. This was beginning to change with the 1997 organization of REDNAMURH, the Red Nacional de Mujeres Rurales de Honduras. (Discussion at the Seminar on Gender and Land Rights, organized for the authors by CODIMCA and the Fundación Arias, 16 January 1998, Tegucigalpa.) While their lobbying efforts have been successful in calling attention to rural women's issues at the executive level, the contentious nature of women's property rights blocked further action at the legislative level until recently.

12. The full name of this program is the "Programa Presidencial para la Formalización de la Propiedad y Modernización de la Titulación Predial."

13. Titling activities under this project are provided for a modest fee, and beneficiaries do not pay for the land. They do have to pay a departmental land tax and a fee for registration of the title. Although these costs do not amount to more than 20 percent of the minimum salary in Colombia, they have been a source of grievance among potential beneficiaries, who claim that they cannot afford to pay them. Interview with Silvia Salamanca, Titular, 31 August 1997, Bogotá, who also made available to us the following internal documents: "Manual de procedimientos de titulación de baldíos," n.d., and "Informe presentado al Señor Presidente de la República," February 1998.

14. This explanation of the difference between PROCEDE certification and *dominio pleno* was provided by Judge Arely Madrid Tovilla, Superior Agrarian Commission, and Carlota Botey, chair of the Agrarian Commission of the National Congress, at the Seminar on Women and Land Rights organized for the authors by the Colegio de México, 16 January 1997, Mexico City; and in an interview with agrarian lawyer Juan Carlos Pérez, Mexico City, 17 January 1997. As of September 1998, of the 16,561 *ejidos* that had been certified, only 3.2 percent had opted to convert either fully or partly to *dominio pleno* (Rodríguez 1998).

15. Interview with rural sociologist Horacio Mackinlay, 17 January 1997, Mexico City. Rodríguez (1998) reports that of the 536 *ejidos* that had converted to *dominio pleno* as of September 1998, only 28 (5 percent) have sold the majority of their lands. He argues that expectations that privatization of the *ejidos* would lead to massive land sales, as well as that such a conversion would rapidly attract private investment, were both misplaced.

16. The *posesionarios* had usufruct rights on the *ejidos*, although they were not official members of these. The great majority of these were family members of an *ejidatario* and, although technically illegal, were the result of partible inheritance practices. During the PROCEDE program the *ejido* assemblies were encouraged to recognize their permanent land rights.

17. Robles et al. (2000: 20–21) report data on 479,991 women who received titles as of March 1999; of these, 52.4 percent were *ejidatarias,* 10.7 percent *posesionarias,* and 36.9 percent *avecindadas.* We report earlier figures in Table 9.3 because this more recent study does not report data on men titled land on the *ejidos.*

18. Robles et al. (2000: 115) report that *ejidatarias* were titled an average of 8.47 hectares, but no comparable data are presented on *ejidatarios.*

19. A reported 61,072 complaints were filed during the PROCEDE process (1993–98) relating to inheritance rights on the *ejidos.* Of the 24,347 declared conflicts, the great majority were solved through conciliation and arbitration, with only 6,509 resulting in suits before the agrarian tribunals. Unfortunately, the fact that no data are reported on the sex of the participants in these conflicts makes it impossible to discern if they were gender related (Zepeda 1998: n.p.).

20. Whether this is potentially the case depends on the marital regime and on how the property was acquired. In the case of the default marital regime (a *sociedad conyugal* based on participation of profits), if the parcel was acquired as a purchase during marriage, then it should constitute common property, legally belonging to both spouses. If the parcel was inherited by an *ejidatario*, then it probably forms part of his individual property, which he is free to dispose of as he sees fit.

21. E-mail to the authors by Laureano Castillo, CEPES, 1 December 2000.

22. Interview with Dr. Josefina Takahashi, Vice Minister of Agriculture, 9 July 1997, Lima.

23. Interview with Ivonne Macassi León, director of the Centro para la Mujer Peruana "Flora Tristán," 7 July 1997, Lima.

24. Interview with Ing. Miguel Suárez, Director de Procesamiento y Estadística, PETT, 9 July 1997, Lima.

25. "SUNARP: Aprueban directiva que establece lineamientos para la inscripción del derecho de posesión sobre predios rurales," *El Peruano*, 25 December 1996: 145439.

26. Seminar organized for the authors by the Red Nacional Mujer Rural of the Centro para la Mujer Peruana "Flora Tristán," 8 July 1997, Lima.

27. Intervention by a lawyer with PETT in the Seminar on Gender and Landed Property, July 1997, Lima.

28. Interview with Manuel Cerna, director of PETT, Dirección Sub-Regional Agraria Cajamarca, 4 July 1997, Cajamarca. That couples in consensual unions are not being jointly titled land is also reported in de Jong (1997: 5).

29. This network, CIPDER (Consortio Interinstitucional para el Desarrollo Regional), held a conference in Cajamarca on "Mujeres Cajamarquinas después de la Conferencia Mundial de Beijing" in September 1996 and had requested that a representative of the ministry present a paper on the PETT.

30. Interview with Manuel Cerna, 4 July 1997, Cajamarca.

31. Forum on Mujeres Cajamarquinas después de la Conferencia de Beijing, in de Jong (1997).

32. In Peru the default marital regime is that of participation in profits. Thus any land purchased during a marriage or consensual union should be the joint property of the couple. However, if the parcel was purchased before marriage, it would constitute part of the individual's patrimony.

33. Intervention at the Seminar on Gender and Landed Property, July 1997, Lima.

34. "Normas para el proceso de titulación y saneamiento de la propiedad rural"; the final version of the guidelines are in Fernández et al. (2000: 19–22).

35. Among their recommendations to overcome the problem that people are usually characterized in their identity documents as being single when they live in a consensual union was that the spouse or partner be required to be present when cadastral information is collected and that marital status information be verified with local justices of the peace.

36. Interview with Mercedes Prieto, former consultant on gender issues to IICA-PRONADER, 22 July 1997, Quito.

37. See García 1994. Several reports were also issued that for the first time included gender-specific variables (e.g., Ministerio de Bienestar Social/SSDR/PRONADER/IICA 1995).

38. The data presented in Table 9.4 were obtained as a result of a request by the authors to CONAMU (Consejo Nacional de las Mujeres), and the personal intervention of Mercedes Prieto, then a consultant to CONAMU. This office hired someone to review all of PRONADER's land-titling records and to compile the data by sex (estimating such from first names), civil status, and by individual and joint titling.

39. In a small, follow-up study of beneficiaries carried out by CONAMU in 1998, it was found that there had been several types of irregularities in the PRONADER land-titling process that, had they been corrected, would have resulted in an even higher proportion of joint titling. For example, a number of cases were found of beneficiaries (male and female) who reported that they were single when, in fact, they lived with a permanent companion (García 1999: 88–91).

40. Interview with Mercedes Prieto, 22 July 1997, Quito.

41. Ibid.

42. Interview with Wilson Sánchez, INDA (Instituto Nacional de Desarrollo Agropecuario), 23 July 1997, Quito, and confirmed by our inspection of recent lists of beneficiaries.

43. E-mail to authors from Elizabeth García, CIDES, 29 September 1999.

44. It did this by including an additional point on the application of female household heads for a government housing subsidy (Valenzuela 1997: 201).

45. In practice, the criteria for selecting beneficiaries for land titling varied by region, although in all, poor households were targeted. Other criteria employed were having been in possession of the parcel for five years; having the property fenced; being a beneficiary of or applicant to the housing-subsidy program; and being a member of the Junta de Vecinos. Only one region, the fifth (Valparaiso), actually reported that it targeted female household heads, although this does not necessarily mean that other regions did not do so (Min Bienes 1996, vol. 2, appendix 2: 232). In some regions, as illustrated in the epigraph to this chapter, female household heads apparently received titling services first.

46. According to the publication prepared by the consultancy group AGRARIA, which designed and carried out the survey, 39.3 percent of the beneficiaries in the sample were rural women (Min Bienes 1996, vol. 1: 3). Our results differ since they were apparently working with a sub-sample, rather than the full sample size of 1,492. The survey is known as the "Encuesta de Evaluación del Impacto del Programa de Saneamiento y Regularización de la Pequeña Propiedad Rural."

47. According to an official of the Ministry of National Property, women probably represent closer to 30 percent of those benefiting from the titling program. Interview with César Talavera, 30 April 1997, Santiago, Chile.

48. Interview with Jorge Echenique, AGRARIA, 16 July 1997, Santiago.

49. On the regional differences in the incidence of land titling (and hence ownership of land) by gender see León and Deere (1999: tables 1 and 3).

50. For this same reason we were not able to estimate how many of these women are household heads due to the absence of an adult male or as a result of their relative contribution to household income.

51. Calculations by the authors from the survey data tape, "Evaluación de la gestión y medición de impacto del programa de saneamiento y regularización de la pequeña propiedad rural," Ministry of National Property, Santiago, 1996.

52. The only other survey evaluating the impact of a land-titling project, that carried out in Honduras by the Land Tenure Center in the 1980s, reached this same conclusion, but the survey failed to report the gender of the respondents (Stanfield et al. 1990). For a taste of the debate regarding the efficacy of the Honduran titling project in terms of its goals (increasing access to credit, investment, stimulating the land market, reducing conflict over land), see Fandiño (1993), Salgado (1996), and Jansen and Roquas (1998).

53. The only other countries to publish data from which the share of women farmers can be discerned did so for only one year. In the Dominican Republic in 1960 women made up 11.4 percent of the farmers (República Dominicana 1966: 44, table 7a), and in Paraguay in 1981 women made up 11.9 percent of the farmers (Paraguay 1985: 2–39, table 1).

54. Census data are not all that helpful in substantiating this trend, since the figures on female heads of household were not broken down for rural and urban residency in the 1972 census, when female heads represented 22.3 percent of all households nationally (Peru 1975: 849–50, table 47). Moreover, since then, the national figure has remained more or less constant, being 22.1 percent in the 1981 census and 23.3 percent in that of 1993. The share of rural female household heads has fallen slightly over this period, from 21.1 percent to 20.1 percent (Peru 1984b: 1153–54, table 46; Peru 1994a: 551–53, table 6). On the problems of measuring female household heads, see Chant (1997: 7–24, 70–74).

55. This study was the result of the initiative of the First Ladies of Latin America following the 1992 Geneva Declaration on Rural Women, discussed in Chapter 4. One of their goals, for which they obtained a large grant from the IADB, was to improve data collection on rural women. Interview with Ana Milena Muñoz de Gaviria, 25 March 1999, Washington, D.C.

56. The published country studies that we examined included Bolivia (Llanos de Vargas 1996); Colombia (Gaitán 1996); Ecuador (Jordán 1996); Peru (Casafranca 1996); and the Southern Cone (Sisto 1996). With the exception of this latter study and that of Ecuador, all of these aggregate the survey data from the various locales into one over-all "national" figure. This information is virtually meaningless since the surveys were not nationally representative and were based on only 150 observations per country. This aggregated data by country was published by Kleysen and Campillo (1996: table 18) and reproduced in Wilkie et al. (1998: table 618); it should be used with great caution, given the discussed limitations.

57. This is a curious result, since the full-common-property marital regime

was the default option throughout Brazil until 1977. One would have expected land to have been reported as jointly owned with more regularity. The counter-intuitive survey results could be due to the small sample size.

58. The Peruvian census questionnaire assumes that the principal farmer of owner-operated farms is the owner in not asking to whom in the family the land actually belongs. It can probably be assumed that the only women who report themselves to be the principal farmer of owner-operated farms are in fact the landowners, given the gender stereotyping of roles.

59. Such was the explanation given by the Oficina de Información Agraria of the Ministry of Agriculture. This was obviously an error in the design of the census questionnaire, which should have specified this alternative more clearly among the options.

60. Since the agrarian reform benefited approximately one-third of Peruvian rural households, we would expect its impact to be more notable in the data in Table 9.7, leading us to the above explanation. Another explanation is that many of the beneficiaries of the agrarian reform were peasants residing in the peasant communities, and they may have reported the latter as the main form of acquisition of land, rather than the agrarian reform. Irrespective of these difficulties, the gender bias in the agrarian reform can be deduced from these numbers. Of the 152,906 farmers who reported that they acquired their land through the agrarian reform, only 14 percent were women. This figure probably includes a good number of widows who inherited the land parcel from their husbands, since the inheritance regulations of the agrarian reform law were relatively favorable to widows.

61. The category "state donation" refers to public land, usually belonging to municipalities, that has been ceded to squatters. The category "other" consists principally of imperfect donations by private parties that include gifts of land (such as by landowners to their workers) and private land that has been ceded as a result of land invasions during previous decades. Interview with Jorge Echenique, 16 July 1997, Santiago.

62. Two-thirds of the *ejidatarias* inherited their parcel from their husbands and one-fourth from their fathers; only 4.5 percent inherited from other family members and 1 percent from non-family members (Cordova Plaza 1999: 11). Ahlers's (1998b) study of an *ejido* in the Comarca Lagunera in north-central Mexico also supports the proposition that the primary means through which women acquire land rights is through inheritance. Also see Baitenmann (1997: 326) and Hamilton (1999).

63. This trend, of women owning smaller farms than men, is reported cross-culturally (Quisumbing 1998: 263).

64. Whereas the average amount of land titled to individual women owners ranged between 0.5 and 10 *manzanas,* the corresponding average for men was 0.5 to 20 *manzanas*. And whereas the average amount of land jointly titled to a couple ranged from 1 to 14 *manzanas,* the average amount titled to two men (*mancomunado*) was between 1.6 and 32 *manzanas* (Rocha 1998: 40).

65. The Land Tenure Center at the University of Wisconsin, under contract to USAID, pioneered the study of rural land markets in Latin America; see Shearer et al. (1991) for a summary of some of the pilot studies undertaken in the 1980s. Some of the more recent land market studies have been financed by the FAO and are included in the collection edited by Reydon and Ramos (1996). None of these, however, include a gender focus.

66. On rural women's labor market participation and the evidence behind these propositions, see the collection of articles in Deere and León (1987b) and Lara Flores (1995) and the discussion of the rural labor market under the neo-liberal model in Chile and Mexico in Chapter 5.

67. The terms of the mortgage are as follows: it is a ten-year loan (with the possibility of a two-year grace period on the repayment of principal) at interest rates set between 8 and 18 percent. Groups must come up with at least 10 percent of the value of the purchase from their own funds. FEPP holds the mortgage on the property until the loan is repaid. The program is financially quite successful. By 1995 it had recovered 25 percent of the funds loaned out, and only 5 percent of the loans were in arrears (Navarro et al., 1996: 191). A condition of the FEPP program is that land be held and worked collectively; in practice, the majority of groups have assigned each family their own usufruct plot, although some land is still used collectively.

68. Beneficiaries had to pay a 10 percent down-payment plus legal fees; they had twelve years to repay the mortgage at market interest rates (Fund. Arias–Tierra Viva 1993: 130–31).

69. "Veinte años después ¿qué pasó con la reforma agraria?" *El Observador Económico,* no. 89, June 1999: 17. Another study found that only 20 percent of these lands had been sold to other peasants, such as neighbors and family members. Instead, the buyers are generally members of "the new economic groups" that have arisen through ties to the past three governments as well as former landlords, suggesting that a new process of land concentration is underway (Sedo 1999: 24).

70. Compiled by the authors from the database "Evaluación de la gestión y medición de impacto del programa de saneamiento y regularización," Ministerio de Bienes Nacionales, 1996.

71. Interview with Juan Carlos Pérez, Mexico City, 17 January 1997.

72. For example, in the case of Colombia, women received 13 percent of the credit disbursed by the Caja Agraria, the state agricultural development bank, in 1996 (data made available to authors by the Caja Agraria, August 1997, Bogotá). In Chile, women made up 11 percent of the 65,872 persons of low resources who received credit through the government agency, INDAP (Instituto de Desarrollo Agropecuario) in 1995, and they accounted for 9 percent of the credit disbursed that year (SERNAM-INDAP 1997: 38). In 1997 they represented 14 percent of credit beneficiaries but received only 9 percent of the credit disbursed by INDAP (Valdés 1999: 19).

73. On the difficulties of women joining irrigation schemes even when they

are landowners, see Ahlers (1998a); these difficulties are compounded when they do not own land in their own names since water rights are often tied to land rights (Deere and León 1998b). On Peru, see Lynch (1991), Roeder (1994, 1996), and Valcarcel (1997); on Ecuador, see CIDCA-CESA-SNV-CAMAREN (1996) and Arroyo and Rutgerd (1997); and for Mexico, after the privatization of water rights, see Ahlers (1998b).

74. See the summaries of the IICA-BID case studies: Kleysen and Campillo (1996: 61–82), Ochoa and Campillo (1996: 183–92), Sisto (1996: 347–52), and Chiriboga et al. (1996: 51–55).

75. The exceptions were Chile, Guatemala, Peru, and Nicaragua, countries in which initiatives aimed at rural women producers are only a product of the 1990s.

76. Approved in July 2000, the Colombian Plan for Equality of Opportunities for Rural Women is a project of the Ministry of Agriculture rather than of the national women's office, as in the other countries, but it is to form part of the national Plan for Equality of Opportunities for Women, which is pending approval. Phone interview with Myriam Gutiérrez, advisor on rural women's issues to IICA, 5 July 2000, Bogotá.

77. This switch in focus is considered to have been at the behest of the World Bank, which has been CENTA's main funder. Interview with Margarita Ledesma, Coordinación de Género, CENTA, 12 January 1998, San Salvador.

78. CENTA is organized into four Technological Development Centers (CDTs) at the regional level. Each has a gender monitor charged with making sure that all programs are directed at both men and women farmers. At the local level peasants are organized into Neighborhood Producer Circles (CVPs, Círculos Vecinales de Productores), each of which has around ten members. These meet biweekly with an extension agent. Four or five CVPs are grouped together in the GYTT (Generación y Transferencia de Tecnología) program, which focuses on specific agricultural or technical problems. CENTA's policy has been to encourage the formation of mixed groups of men and women at the community level, although in some cases the former Housewives Clubs were converted into all-women CVPs. In 1997 male-only CVPs still predominated, although women made up almost a quarter of the membership of the mixed CVPs. All told, in that year women made up 12 percent of the 71,626 farmers belonging to the CVPs. Data provided to the authors by CENTA, Coordinación Nacional de Género, "Resumen-monitoreo de la participación por género en la organización de la comunidad (CVP registrados y atendidos), enero a diciembre 1997."

Chapter 10. Land and Property in a Feminist Agenda

1. The figures presented in Table 10.1 differ in some cases from those in the country-specific tables presented in earlier chapters. For comparative purposes, we have converted the data into similar units and distinguished between the dis-

tribution of beneficiaries and land titles; in countries with joint titling the absolute numbers differ, with the former always exceeding the latter.

2. The concept of a critical mass for gender-progressive change is developed by Dahlerup (1993) in the context of women's formal political participation.

3. Member of Agrupación Mujeres Tierra Viva, interview of 7 January 1998, Guatemala City.

4. NGOs in El Salvador, Honduras, and Nicaragua have developed campaigns to inform women of marital-regime options; for an example of some of the materials they have produced, see CEMUJER-Instituto de Estudios de la Mujer (1994a, 1994b, and 1994c), CDM (n.d.), and Centro de Derechos Constitucionales (1996a and 1996b).

5. Moreover, feminists have continued to expand the definition of citizenship, making the unified voice of the movement essential if progress is to be achieved. On the contemporary feminist view of citizenship in Latin America and what it requires, see, for example, Aguilar et al. (1997) and Vargas (1998).

References

Abramovay, Ricardo (Coordinator), Milton Silvestro, Nelson Cortina, Ivan Tadeu Baldissera, Dilvan Ferrari, and Vilson Marcos Testa. 1998. *Juventude e agricultura familiar: Desafios dos novos padroes sucessorios*. Brasilia: Ed. UNESCO.

ACNUR (Alto Comisonado de las Naciones Unidas para los Refugiados). 1995. "Dictamen jurídico sobre el acceso de la mujer desarraigada a la propiedad de la tierra y a créditos para la compra de la misma." Memo, September. Guatemala City.

———. 1996. "Las mujeres retornadas y el acceso a la tierra." *Revista Breves* (internal bulletin of ACNUR) no. 5, n.p.

Acosta, Ismalia, and Welber Moreno. 1996. "Informe de Honduras: Situación de la mujer rural y tenencia de la tierra." Paper prepared for the First Central American Conference on Intercambio de Experiencias sobre Sensibilización de Género con Demandantes de Titulación Agraria. December 9–10, Managua.

Acosta Díaz, Felix. 1994. "Los estudios sobre jefatura de hogar femenino y pobreza en México y América Latina." In Grupo Interdisciplinario sobre Mujer, Trabajo, y Pobreza, ed., *Las Mujeres en la Pobreza*, pp. 91–117. Mexico City: Colegio de México.

ACPD (Asamblea Consultiva de las Poblaciones Desarraigadas). 1997. "El enfoque de género en el Acuerdo para el Reasentamiento de la Población Desarraigada: Propuesta de la Coordinadora de Mujeres de la Población Desarraigada de la ACPD." Memo, Guatemala City.

ADC (Alianza Democrática Campesina). 1996. *Anteproyecto Código Agrario*. El Salvador: ADC.

Agarwal, Bina. 1994a. *A Field of One's Own: Gender and Land Rights in South Asia*. Cambridge: Cambridge University Press.

———. 1994b. "Gender and Command over Property: A Critical Gap in Economic Analysis and Policy in South Asia." *World Development* 22, no. 10: 1455–1478.

————. 1997. "'Bargaining' and Gender Relations: Within and Beyond the Household." *Feminist Economics* 3, no. 1: 1–51.

Aguilar, Ana Leticia, and Carmen Lucía Pellecer. 1997. "El foro de la mujer: ¿Un ejercicio posible?" *Malabares: Revista Centroamericana de la Corriente* (Managua) 7 (June): 16–17.

Aguilar, Ana Leticia, Blanca Estela Dole, Morena Herrera, Sofia Montenegro, Lorena Camacho, and Lorena Flores. 1997. *Movimiento de mujeres en Centroamérica*. Managua: Programa Regional La Corriente.

Ahlers, Rhodante. 1998a. "Indirect Access and Informal Networks: Gender Issues in Irrigation: A Latin American Overview." Paper presented at the Conference on Contribuciones de las Mujeres en la Planeación y Manejo de los Recursos Hídricos. May 21–22, Mexico City.

————. 1998b. "Moving In or Staying Out: Gender Dimensions of Water Markets." Paper presented at the Latin American Studies Association Congress, September 24–26, Chicago.

Alberti M., Pilar. 1998. "La organización de mujeres indígenas como instrumento de cambio en el desarrollo rural con perspectiva de género." *Revista Española de Antropología Americana* (Madrid) 28: 189–213.

————, et al., eds. 1998. *Empoderamiento y la mujer rural en Mexico: Informe del taller realizado en Tapalehixoxocatla, Morelos, en junio de 1995*. Mexico City: Colegio de Postgraduados en Ciencias Agrícolas.

Albuquerque, Ligia, and Isaura Ruffino. 1987. "Elementos que dificultam a participação da mulher no processo da reforma agrária." In Lena Lavinas, ed., *Anais do seminario mulheres rurais: Identidades e na luta política*, pp. 320–339. Rio de Janeiro: IPPUR/UFRJ.

Alexander, Robert J. 1974. *Agrarian Reform in Latin America*. New York: Macmillan.

Alonso R., Patricia, and Roberto del Pardo E. 1997. "La mujer campesina en el combate a la pobreza: El caso de la Red Nacional de Mujeres, UNORCA." *Estudios Agrarios* no. 8 (n.p., accessed on 19 January 2000 from http://www.pa.gob.mx/publica/pao70901.htm).

Álvarez, Antonio. 1997. "Programa de Transferencia de Tierras (P.T.T.), Chapultepec, 1992–1997." Memo, FMLN, September, San Salvador.

————. 1998. "Informe de mujeres beneficiarias P.T.T." Memo, FMLN, January, San Salvador.

Álvarez, Francisca. 1996. "Las mujeres mayas etnocidas." *El Periódico* (Guatemala City), 24 November, p. 26.

Alvarez, Sonia. 1990. *Engendering Democracy in Brazil: Women's Movements in Transition Politics*. Princeton, N.J.: Princeton University Press.

————. 1998a. "Latin American Feminisms 'Go Global': Trends of the 1990s and Challenges for the New Millennium." In Sonia Alvarez, Evelina Dagnino, and Arturo Escobar, eds., *Cultures of Politics, Politics of Cultures*, pp. 293–324. Boulder: Westview Press.

————. 1998b. "Feminismos latinoamericanos: Reflexiones teóricas y perspectivas comparativas." *Revista Estudos Feministas* 6, no. 2: 265–285.

Alvarez, Sonia, Evelino Dagnino, and Arturo Escobar, eds. 1998. *Cultures of Politics, Politics of Cultures.* Boulder: Westview Press.

Alvear, María Soledad. 1987. "Situación de la mujer campesina frente a la legislación: Estudio comparativo de Chile, Guatemala, Perú y República Dominicana." In FAO, ed., *Mujeres campesinas en América Latina: Desarrollo rural, migración, tierra y legislación,* pp. 145–212. Santiago, Chile: FAO.

Amezquita de Almeida, Josefina. 1977. "Condición de la Mujer en el Derecho de Familia." In Magdalena León de Leal, ed., *La mujer y desarrollo en Colombia,* pp. 273–315. Bogotá: ACEP.

Andolina, Robert. 1998. "CONAIE (and others) in the Ambiguous Spaces of Democracy: Positioning for the 1997–8 Asamblea Nacional Constituyente in Ecuador." Paper prepared for the 1998 Congress of the Latin American Studies Association, September 24–26, Chicago.

Angarita Barón, Ciro. 1975. "Potestad marital, patria potestad e igualdad de derechos." *Revista Cámara de Comercio de Bogotá,* no. 18: 63–74.

Anriquez, Gustavo, and Mayra Buvinic. 1997. "Poverty Alleviation for Male-Headed and Female-Headed Households in a Fast Growing Economy. A Case Study of Chile, 1987–1994." Memo. Paper prepared for "Social Effects of Macroeconomic Policy in LAC." United Nations Development Programme project in collaboration with IADB and CEPAL.

Ansorena M., Aixa. 1997. "Negotiating Women's Legal Equality: Four Versions of a Law." In Ilse A. Leitinger, ed., *The Costa Rican Women's Movement: A Reader,* pp. 111–118. Pittsburgh: University of Pittsburgh Press.

Antrobus, Peggy. 1989. "Gender Implications of the Development Crisis." In George Beckford and Norman Girvan, eds., *Development in Suspense,* pp. 145–160. Kingston: Friedrich Ebrt Stiftung with the Association of Caribbean Economists.

AOS/AIPE/TIERRA (Ayuda Obrera Suiza, Asociación de Institutiones y Educación, and Taller de Iniciativas en Estudios Rurales y Reforma Agraria). 1996. *Con los pies en la tierra: Reflexiones sobre la ley inra.* La Paz: Gráfica Latina.

Aranda, Josefina B. 1991. "Mujeres campesinas y políticas públicas en Mexico." In IICA, ed., *Mujer y modernización agropecuaria: Balance, perspectivas y estrategias,* chap. 2. San José: IICA.

————. 1993. "Políticas públicas y mujeres campesinas en México." In Soledad González Montes, ed., *Mujeres y relaciones de género en la antropología latinoamericana,* pp. 171–222. Mexico City: El Colegio de México.

Aranda, Josefina B., Carlota Botey, and Rosario Robles. 2000. *Tiempo de crisis, tiempos de mujeres.* Oaxaca: Centro de Estudios de la Cuestión Agraria Mexicana, Universidad Autónoma Benito Juárez de Oaxaca.

Aranda, Ximena. 1992. *Mujer rural: Diagnóstico para orientar políticas en el agro.* Santiago: Ministerio de la Agricultura, FAO, INDEP, and SERNAM.

Ardaya, Gloria. 1992. *Políticas sin nosotras: Mujeres en Bolivia*. Caracas: Ed. Nueva Sociedad.

———. 1993. "Las relaciones de género en las organizaciones políticas y sindicales bolivianas." In Soledad González Montes, ed., *Mujer y relaciones de género en la antropología*, pp. 253–273. Mexico City: El Colegio de México.

Arizpe, Lourdes, and Carolota Botey. 1987. "Mexican Agricultural Development Policy and Its Impact on Rural Women." In C. D. Deere and M. León, eds. *Rural Women and State Policy: Feminist Perspectives on Latin American Agricultural Development*, pp. 67–83. Boulder: Westview Press.

Arnold, Denise, with Juan de Dios Yapita. 1997. "La lucha por la dote en un ayllu andino." In Denise Y. Arnold, ed., *Mas allá del silencio: Las fronteras de género en los Andes,* pp. 345–383. Research Series, no. 27. La Paz: ILCA/ CIASE.

Arrom, Silvia M. 1980. "Cambios en la condición jurídica de la mujer mexicana en el siglo XIX." In José Luis Soberanis Fernández, ed., *Memoria del II Congreso de Historia del Derecho Mexicano*, pp. 493–513. Mexico City: UNAM.

———. 1985a. *The Women of Mexico City, 1790–1857*. Stanford, Calif.: Stanford University Press.

———. 1985b. "Changes in Mexican Family Law in the Nineteenth Century: The Civil Codes of 1870 and 1884." *Journal of Family History* 10, no. 3: 305–317.

Arroyo, Aline, and Boelens, Rutgerd. 1997. *Mujer campesina e intervención en el riego andino*. Quito: SNV (Servicio Holandés de Cooperación), CESA (Central Ecuatoriana de Servicios Agrícolas), and CAMAREN (Sistema de Capacitación en el Manejo de Recursos Naturales Renovables).

ASIES (Asociación de Investigación y Estudios Sociales). 1995. *Tenencia y uso de la tierra*. Guatemala City: ASIES.

Asociación de Mujeres Profesionales por la Democracia en el Desarrollo "Las Bujías." 1996. *Los derechos de las mujeres en Nicaragua: Un análisis de género*. Managua: Asociación de Mujeres Profesionales.

Astelarra, Judith. 1995. "La igualdad de oportunidades como condición de la democracia moderna." In SERNAM, ed., *Encuentro internacional: Políticas de igualdad de oportunidades, 20–23 octubre 1993, Santiago, Chile*, pp. 27–40. Santiago: SERNAM.

AVP (Asociación para la Vivienda Popular), ENDA América Latina, and FEDEVIVIENDA (Federación de Vivienda). 1995. *Análisis con perspectiva de género de la política de vivienda y del subsidio habitacional*. Bogotá: AVP and ENDA América Latina.

Ayala M., Alexandra. 1999. "El Protagonismo de las Indígenas." *Revista mujer/ fempress*, no. 214: 1.

Badilla, Ana Elena, and Lara Blanco, eds. 1996. *Código de la mujer*. San José:

CECADE (Centro de Capacitación para el Desarrollo), Editorial Porvenir, and Fundación Arias.

Baitenmann, Helga. 1997. "Rural Agency and State Formation in Post-revolutionary Mexico: The Agrarian Reform in Central Veracruz (1915–1992)." Ph.D. diss., New School for Social Research, New York.

Banco Mundial. 1997. "El Salvador, estudio de desarrollo rural, reporte principal, resumen ejecutivo." San Salvador: World Bank Report 16253 ES, vol. 1.

Barahona, Francisco. 1980. Reforma agraria y poder político: El caso de Costa Rica. San José: Universidad de Costa Rica.

Barret, Michele. 1990. "El concepto de diferencia." Debate Feminista 2: 311–325.

Barria, Liliana. 1992. Mujer rural: Políticas y programas de gobierno, 1990–1992. Santiago: MinAg, FAO, IDA, SERNAM.

Barrig, Maruja, ed. 1988. De vecinas a ciudadanas: La mujer en desarrollo urbano. Lima: SUMBI (Servicios Urbanos y Mujeres de Bajos Ingresos).

———. 1998. "Los malestares del feminismo Latinoamericano: Una nueva lectura." Paper prepared for the International Congress of the Latin American Studies Association, September 24–26, Chicago.

Barsky, Osvaldo. 1984. La reforma agraria ecuatoriana. Quito: Corporación Editora Nacional and FLACSO.

Barsted, Leila de Andrade Linhares. 1994. "Em busca do tempo perdido: Mulher e políticas públicas no Brasil 1983–1993." Revista estudios feministas (CIEC/Escola de Comunição UFRJ), no. especial (October): 38–53.

———. 1996. "Informe nacional: As condições jurídicas das mulheres rurais no Brasil, acesso a terra, ao credito, a capacitação e organização." Memo, April.

Barsted, Leila Linhares, and Elizabeth Garcez. 1999. "A legislação civil sobre família no Brasil." In CEPIA (Cidadania, Estudo, Pesquisa, Informaçõe e Ação), ed., pp. 9–26. Rio de Janeiro: CEPIA.

Batliwala, Srilatha. 1997. "El significado del empoderamiento de las mujeres: Nuevos conceptos desde la acción." In Magdalena León, ed., Poder y empoderamiento de las mujeres, pp. 187–212. Bogotá: TM Editores and Universidad Nacional, Facultad de Ciencias Humanas.

Baumeister, Eduardo, and Cor J. Wattel. 1996. "Una visión de conjunto de la estructura agraria hondureño." In Eduardo Baumeister, ed., El agro hondureño y su futuro. Tegucigalpa: Centro de Estudios para el Desarrollo Rural.

Becker, Lawrence. 1977. Property Rights: Philosophic Foundations. London: Routledge and Kegan Paul.

Benería, Lourdes. 1995. "Los costes sociales del ajuste estructural en América Latina: ¿Está superada la crisis?" Mientras Tanto (Barcelona) 61: 109–125.

Benería, Lourdes, and Shelley Feldman, eds. 1992. Unequal Burden: Economic Crises, Persistent Poverty, and Women's Work. Boulder: Westview Press.

Benería, Lourdes, and Martha Roldán. 1987. *The Crossroads of Class and Gender: Industrial Homework, Subcontracting, and Household Dynamics in Mexico City*. Chicago: University of Chicago Press.

Benería, Lourdes, and Gita Sen. 1981. "Accumulation, Reproduction and Women's Role in Development." *Signs* 8, no. 2: 279–298.

Bengelsdorf, Carollee, and Alice Hageman. 1977. "Emerging from Underdevelopment: Women and Work in Cuba." In A. Eisenstein, ed., *Capitalist Patriarchy and the Case for Socialist Feminism*. New York: Monthly Review Press.

Bengoa, José. 1992. "The Mapuche Peasants under the Military Regime." In Cristobal Kay and Patricio Silva, eds., *Development and Social Change in the Chilean Countryside*, pp. 233–246. Amsterdam: CEDLA.

Berger, Susan. 1992. *Political and Agrarian Development in Guatemala*. Boulder: Westview Press.

Bernal de Bugeda, Beatriz. 1975. "Situación jurídica de la mujer en las Indias Occidentales." In Universidad Nacional Autónoma Mexicana, *Condición jurídica de la mujer en México*. Mexico City: UNAM.

Binstock, Hanna. 1998. "Hacia la igualdad de la mujer: Avances legales desde la aprobación de la Convención sobre la eliminación de todas las formas de discriminación contra la mujer" (pamphlet). Serie Mujer y Desarrollo no. 24. Santiago: Unidad Mujer y Desarrollo, CEPAL.

Binswanger, Hans P., Klaus Deininger, and Gershon Feder. 1995. "Power, Distortions, Revolt and Reform of Agricultural Land Relations." In Jere Behrman and T. N. Srinivasan, eds., *Handbook of Development Economics,* vol. IIIB, pp. 2661–2772. Amsterdam: Elsevier.

Black, Chad T. 1998. "The 1990 Indian Uprising in Ecuador: Culture, Ethnicity and Post-Marxist Social Praxis." Paper prepared for 1998 International Congress of the Latin American Studies Association, September 24–26, Chicago.

Blanco, Lara. 1997. "Las políticas de tierra en Centroamérica: Una visión desde las mujeres." *Revista Perspectivas Rurales* (San José) 2 (September): 42–52.

Blutstein, H. I., et al. 1977. *Area Handbook for Colombia*. Washington, D.C.: American University.

Bobbio, Norberto. 1993. *Igualdad y libertad*. Barcelona: Universidad Autónoma de Barcelona and Ed. Paidos.

Bolivia, República de. 1990. *Código de familia*. La Paz: Ed. Gilbert.

———. 1991. *Código civil de 1975*. La Paz: Ed. Gilbert.

———. 1993. *Censo nacional de población y vivienda, 1992: Resultados finales*. La Paz: Ministerio de Planeamiento y Coordinación, Instituto Nacional de Estadística.

———. 1996. *Ley del servicio nacional de reforma agraria, Ley no. 1751, 18 octubre 1996*. La Paz: *Gaceta Oficial*.

Bolles, Lynn. 1983. "Kitchens Hit by Priorities: Employed Working-Class Jamaican Women Confront the IMF." In June Nash and María Patricia Fernández-Kelly, eds., *Women, Men and the International Division of Labor*, pp. 138–160. Albany: State University of New York Press.

Bonder, Gloria, ed. 1998. *Estudios de la mujer en América Latina*. Washington: Consejo Interamericano para el Desarrollo.

Bonfil Sánchez, Paloma. 1996. "Las familias rurales ante las transformaciones socioeconómicas recientes." *Estudios Agrarios: Revista de la Procuraduría Agraria* 5: 64–78.

Bonfil Sánchez, Paloma, and Raúl Marco del Pont Lalli. 1999. *Las mujeres indígenas al final del milenio*. Mexico City: Secretaría de Gobernación and Comisión Nacional de la Mujer.

Bonilla, Jenifer. 1997. "¿Tercer intento modernizador?" In Colectivo de Autores, eds., *Segundo encuentro regional por la agricultura: Contexto económico y pequeña producción rural andina*, pp. 67–74. Cusco: COINCIDE.

Boserup, Ester. 1970. *Women's Role in Economic Development*. New York: St. Martin's Press.

Botey, Carlota. 2000. "Mujer rural: Reforma agraria y contrarreforma." In Josefina Aranda, Carlota Botey, and Rosario Robles, *Tiempo de crisis, tiempos de mujeres*, pp. 95–154. Oaxaca: Centro de Estudios de la Cuestión Agraria Mexicana, Universidad Autónoma Benito Juárez de Oaxaca.

Bourque, Susan, and Kay Warren. 1981. *Women of the Andes: Patriarchy and Social Change in Two Peruvian Towns*. Ann Arbor: University of Michigan Press.

Boyce, James K., ed. 1996. *Economic Policy for Building Peace: The Lessons of El Salvador*. Boulder: Lynne Rienner Publishers.

Bradiotti, Rosi, et al. 1994. *Women, the Environment, and Sustainable Development: Towards a Theoretical Synthesis*. London: Zed Books and INSTRAW (International Research and Training Institute for the Advancement of Women).

Bradshaw, Sarah. 1990. "Women in Chilean Rural Society." In D. Hojman, ed., *Neo-Liberal Agriculture in Rural Chile*, pp. 110–126. New York: St. Martin's Press.

———. 1995a. "Women's Access to Employment and the Formation of Female-headed Households in Rural and Urban Honduras." *Bulletin of Latin American Research* 14, no. 2: 143–158.

———. 1995b. "Female-headed Households in Honduras." *Third World Planning Review* 12, no. 2: 112–131.

Brasil, República de. 1996. *Censo Demográfico 1991*. Vol. 1, *Familias e domicilios*. Rio de Janeiro: Fundação Instituto Brasileiro de Geografía e Estadística.

Brems, Eva. 1997. "Enemies or Allies? Feminism and Cultural Relativism as Dissident Voices in Human Rights Discourse." *Human Rights Quarterly* 19: 136–164.

Brenes Marín, May, and Paula Antezana. 1996. "El acceso de la mujer a la tierra en Centroamérica: Comparación de seis diagnósticos." Working paper prepared for the Fundación Arias Regional Workshop on El Acceso de la Mujer a la Tierra en Centroamérica, May 30, 1996, San José.

Brunt, Dorien. 1992. *Mastering the Struggle: Gender, Actors and Agrarian Change in a Mexican Ejido*. Amsterdam: Centro de Estudios y Documentación Latinoamericanos.

———. 1995. "Losing Ground: Nicaraguan Women and Access to Land during and after the Sandinista Period." Paper presented to the conference "Agrarian Questions: The Politics of Farming anno 2000," May 22–24, University of Wageningen, The Netherlands.

Buchler, Peter. 1975. *Agrarian Cooperatives in Peru*. Berne: Sociological Institute.

Buvinic, Mayra. 1986. "Projects for Women in the Third World: Explaining their Misbehavior." *World Development* 14, no. 5: 653–664.

Buvinic, Mayra, and Nadia Youssef. 1978. "Women-Headed Households: The Ignored Factor in Development Planning." Report submitted to the Office of Women in Development, USAID. Washington, D.C.: International Center for Research on Women.

Callejas, Cecilia. 1983. "Examination of Factors Limiting the Organization of Rural Women in Honduras." Master's thesis, Department of Sociology, University of Florida, Gainesville.

Calva, José Luis. 1993. *La disputa por la tierra: La reforma del Artículo 27 y la nueva Ley Agraria*. Mexico City: Distribuciones Fontamara.

Camacho, Aida. 1996. "Incorporación del componente género en el Proyecto de Ley de modificación del Servicio Nacional de Reforma Agraria." Consultancy report to TIERRA, April, La Paz.

Camacho, Carlos, and Mónica Navas, eds. 1992. *Evaluación del proceso de cambio en la tenencia y mercado de la tierra en la Sierra Norte y Central (1964–1992)*. Documento técnico no. 41. 2 vols. Quito: IDEA.

Camacho, Carlos, and Mercedes Prieto. 1995. *Género y desarrollo rural: Manual de autocapacitación para operadores de proyectos y guía para el facilitador*. Quito: PRONADER-Ministerio de Bienestar Social-DRI-DINAMU-IICA.

Camacho, Juana. 1999. "'Todos tenemos derecho a su parte': Derechos de herencia, acceso y control de bienes en comunidades negras de la costa Pacífica chocoana." In Juana Camacho and Eduardo Restrepo, eds., *De montes, ríos y ciudades: Territorios e identidades de la gente negra en Colombia*, pp. 107–142. Bogotá: Fundación Natura, ECOFONDO, and Instituto de Antropología.

Campaña, Pilar. 1990. "Mujer y agricultura en América Latina y el Caribe." *Estudios Rurales Latinoamericanos* 13, no. 3: 243–274.

Campillo, Fabiola. 1995. "Sesgos de género en políticas públicas para el mundo rural." In Ximena Valdés, Ana María Arteaga, and Catalina Arteaga, eds.,

Mujeres: Relaciones de género en la agricultura, pp. 339–379. Santiago: Centro de Estudios para el Desarrollo de la Mujer.

Cardoso, Fernando Henrique. 1997. *Reforma agraria: Compromiso de todos.* Brasilia: Presidencia da República, Secretaria de Comunicação Social.

Carneiro, Maria José. 1998. "Memoria, esquecimento e etnicidade na transmissão do patrimonio familiar." In Maria José Carneiro, et al., eds., *Campo Aberto: O rural no Estado do Rio de Janeiro*, pp. 273–296. Rio de Janeiro: Contra Capa Livreria.

———. 2000. "Herança e identidade de gênero entre agricultores familiares brasileiros." Paper presented at the Latin American Studies Association meetings, March, Miami, Florida.

Carneiro, Maria José, Kryssy de Freitas, and Gislaine Guedes. 1998. "Valor da terra e padrão de herança entre pequenos agricultores familiares." Paper presented at the 21st meeting of the Associação Brasileira de Antropologia, April, Vitoria, Salvador.

Caro, Blanca, Mauricio Gómez, and Luisa Manosalva. 1997. *Mujer rural en cifras*. Bogotá: Dirección Nacional de Equidad para la Mujer and Oficina de Mujer Rural, Ministerio de Agricultura.

Caro, Elvia. 1982. "Programas de desarrollo y la participación de la mujer en Colombia." In Magdalena León, ed., *La realidad colombiana*, pp. 190–207. Bogotá: ACEP.

Carreras Maldonado, María, and Sara Montero Duhalt. 1975. "Condición de la mujer en el derecho civil mexicano." In *Condición jurídica de la mujer en México*. Mexico City: Universidad Nacional Autónoma de Mexico.

Carrión, Eduardo. 1991. *Compendio de derecho sucesorio*. Quito: Pontificia Universidad Católica del Ecuador.

Carter, Michael, and Dina Mesbah. 1990. "Economic Theory of Land Markets and Its Implications for the Land Access of the Rural Poor." In Land Tenure Center Paper no. 141, Annex 1, of April 1991. Madison: University of Wisconsin.

———. 1993. "Can Land Market Reform Mitigate the Exclusionary Aspects of Rapid Agro-Export Growth?" *World Development* 21, no. 7: 1085–1100.

Carter, Michael, and Brad Barham. 1996. "Level Playing Fields and Laissez Faire: Postliberal Development Strategy in Inegalitarian Agrarian Economies." *World Development* 24, no. 7: 1133–1149.

Carter, Michael, and Eduardo Zegarra. 1997. "Land Markets and the Persistence of Rural Poverty: Post-Liberalization Policy Options." In Ramón López and Alberto Valdés, eds., *Rural Poverty in Latin America*, pp. 125–152. Washington, D.C.: World Bank.

Casafranca, Jazmine. 1996. *Las mujeres productoras de alimentos en Perú: Diagnóstico y políticas*. San José: IICA-BID.

Casafranca, Jazmine, and Cristina Espinoza. 1993. "Análisis de la política del sector agropecuario frente a la mujer productora de alimentos en la región andina: Perú. Documento síntesis." Preliminary report. IICA/BID Rural Women Project, December, Lima, Peru.

Castañeda S., Martha Patricia. 2000. "Identidad femenina y herencia: Aproximaciones a algunos cambios generacionales." Paper presented to the 22d International Congress of the Latin American Studies Association, March, Miami.

Castro, Fidel. 1981. "The Revolution within the Revolution." In Elizabeth Stone, ed., *Women and the Cuban Revolution.* New York: Pathfinder Press.

CDM (Centro de Derechos de Mujeres). n.d. "El régimen económico y el patrimonio familiar" (pamphlet). Tegucigalpa: Promotora Legal.

CEIMME (Centro de Estudios e Investigación sobre el Maltrato a la Mujer Ecuatoriana). 1995. *Encuentro latinoamericano, mujer indígena y participación política. Memoria, Foro alternativo de ONGs, Mar del Plata, Argentina, septiembre de 1994.* NGO alternative forum, Mar del Plata, Argentina, September 1994. Quito: CEIMME.

CEMUJER (Instituto de Estudios de la Mujer). 1994a. "Código de familia: Régimenes patrimoniales—Régimen de participación en las gananciales" (pamphlet). San Salvador: Ed. Malintzin.

———. 1994b. "Código de familia: Régimenes patrimoniales—separación de bienes" (pamphlet). San Salvador: Ed. Malintzin.

———. 1994c. "Código de familia: Régimenes patrimoniales—comunidad diferida" (pamphlet). San Salvador: Ed. Malintzin.

Centro de Derechos Constitucionales. 1996a. "Iguales en las leyes, desiguales en la vida" (pamphlet). Managua: Centro de Derechos Constitucionales-NORAD (Norwegian Agency for International Development).

———. 1996b. "Con ley o sin ley: Matrimonio, unión de hecho, disolución" (pamphlet) Managua: Centro de Derechos Constitucionales-NORAD (Norwegian Agency for International Development).

CEPAL (Comisión Económica para América Latina). 1993a. "Desarrollo y equidad de género: Una tarea pendiente" (pamphlet). Santiago: CEPAL, Unidad Mujer y Desarrollo.

———. 1993b. "La economía salvadoreña en el proceso de consolidación de la paz." Doc. LC/Mex/R.414. June. Santiago: CEPAL.

———. 1994a. "Mujeres desarraigadas y pobreza en Centro América: Una area de atención especial." Doc. LC/Mex/R.467. May. Santiago: CEPAL.

———. 1994b. "Programa de acción regional para las mujeres de América Latina y el Caribe, 1995–2001." Sixth regional conference on the Integración de la Mujer en el Desarrollo Económico y Social de América Latina y el Caribe, Mar del Plata, Argentina, Sept. 25–29, 1994. Conference document D6RI-ES.Gru. Santiago: CEPAL.

————. 1998a. "Unidad, mujer y desarrollo." In *Institucionalidad de la equidad en el estado: Un diagnóstico para América Latina*. LC/L 1150. Santiago: CEPAL.

————. 1998b. *Directorio de organismos nacionales a cargo de las políticas y programas para las mujeres de América Latina y el Caribe*. LC/L 1065, Rev. 1. Santiago: CEPAL.

CEPLAES (Centro de Planificación y Estudios Sociales), ed. 1998. *Mujeres contracorriente: Voces de líderes indígenas*. Quito: CEPLAES.

Cervone, Emma. 1998. "Prof. Abelina Morocho Pinguil: Entre cantares y cargos." In CEPLAES, ed., *Mujeres contracorriente: Voces de líderes indígenas*, pp. 163–207. Quito: CEPLAES.

Cevasco, Gaby. 1996. "Trabajadoras rurales en reunión continental." *Mujer Fempress* (Santiago) 181: 12.

CFEMEA (Centro Feminista de Estudos e Assessoria). 1996. *Guia dos direitos da mulher*. 2d ed. Rio de Janeiro: Rosa dos Tempos.

Chancoso, Blanca. N.d. "Las indígenas no sabían de esta reunión." In *Mujer Fempress, especial la mujer indígena* (Santiago).

Chaney, Elsa. 1979. *Supermadre: Women in Politics in Latin America*. Austin: University of Texas Press.

————. 1987. "Women's Components in Integrated Rural Development Projects." In Carmen Diana Deere and Magdalena León, eds., *Rural Women and State Policy: Feminist Perspectives on Latin American Agricultural Development*, pp. 191–211. Boulder: Westview.

Chant, Sylvia. 1997. *Women-Headed Households: Diversity and Dynamics in the Developing World*. London: Macmillan.

Chile, Ministry of Agriculture. 1967. *Law No. 16640, Agrarian Reform*. Santiago: Ministry of Agriculture. Translation by Land Tenure Center, University of Wisconsin, memo, n.d.

Chile, República de. 1961. *Código civil de Chile* (1855). Madrid: Instituto de Cultura.

————. 1992. *Censo general de población y vivienda, 1992*. Santiago: Instituto Nacional de Estadística.

————. 1995. *Informe nacional, IV conferencia mundial sobre la mujer*. Santiago: SERNAM.

Chinchilla, Norma Stoltz. 1998. *Nuestras utopias: Mujeres guatemaltecas del siglo XX*. Guatemala City: Agrupación de Mujeres Tierra Viva and Magda Terra Eds.

Chiriboga, Manuel, Rebeca Grynspan, and Laura Pérez, eds. 1996. *Mujeres de maíz: Programa de análisis de la política del sector agropecuario frente a la mujer productora de alimentos en Centroamérica y Panamá*. San José: IICA-BID.

CIDCA (Centro Internacional de Cooperación para el Desarrollo Agrícola), CESA (Central Ecuatoriana de Servicio Agrícola), SNV (Servicio Nelandes de Voluntarios), and CAMAREN. 1996. *El riego en la comunidad andina: Una construcción social*. Quito.

CIERA (Centro de Investigación y Estudio de la Reforma Agraria). 1984. *La mujer en las cooperativas agropecuarias en Nicaragua*. Managua: CIERA.

———. 1989. *La reforma agraria en Nicaragua, 1979–1989*, vols. 4, 7, 9. Managua: CIERA.

CIERA (Centro de Investigación y Estudio de la Reforma Agraria), ATC (Asociación de Trabajadores del Campo), and CETRA (Centro de Estudios del Trabajo). 1987. *Mujer y agroexportación en Nicaragua*. Managua: Instituto Nicaragüense de la Mujer.

CIT (Conferencia Internacional del Trabajo). 1988. "Revisión parcial del convenio sobre poblaciones indígenas y tribuales, 1957 (num. 107)." Report VI. Geneva: International Labour Office.

Claro Solar, Luis. 1978. *Explicaciones de derecho civil chileno y comparado, Vol. I, De las Personas*. Tomes 1 and 2. Santiago: Ed. Jurídica de Chile.

CMC (Central de Mujeres Campesinas). 1997. "Posiciones sobre la deuda agraria y bancaria de las organizaciones campesinas y demás sectores." Memo, CMC, San Salvador.

CMF (Centro Nacional para el Desarrollo de la Mujer y la Familia). 1994. *Ley de promoción de igualdad social de la mujer, no. 7142*. Colección Documentos no. 2. San José: CMF.

———. 1996. *Plan para la igualdad de oportunidades entre mujeres y hombres-PIOMH*. San José: CMF.

———. 1997. *Addendum de los sectores agropecuario y del ambiente al Plan para la Igualdad de Oportunidades entre Mujeres y Hombres-PIOMH*. San José: CMF.

———. 1998. *Compendio de indicadores de logro del addendum de los sectores agropecuarios y del ambiente al PIOMH*. San José: CMF.

CNC (Comisión Nacional Campesina) and Comisión Femenina. [1986.] "La demanda de la mujer rural: El derecho a la tierra." Folleto no. 11. Santiago: CNC.

Código Civil. 1996. *Código civil colombiano y legislación complementaria*. Envío no. 34R. Bogotá: Legis Editores.

CODIMCA (Consejo para el Desarrollo Integral de la Mujer Campesina) and Fundación Arias. 1997. *Encuentro nacional de mujeres rurales, 21, 22 y 23 de julio, Centro Notre Dame, El Progreso, Yoro, Honduras*. San José: Fundación Arias.

Collective. 1987. "Del amor a la necesidad." *Revista FEM* (Mexico City) 60: 15–17.

Collin, Ambrosio, and Henry Capitant. 1952. *Curso elemental de derecho civil.* 3d ed. Madrid: n.p.

Colombia, Departamento Nacional de Planeación and Misión Social. 1993. *Encuesta de caracterización socioeconómica* (CASEN) (data set). Bogotá: Departamento Nacional de Planeación.

Colombia, Departamento Nacional de Planeación (DNP). 1988. *Plan nacional de desarrollo, 1998–2002: Cambio para construir la paz.* Bogotá: Presidencia de la República and DNP.

Comisión de la Mujer. 1997. *La mujer peruana en la legislación del siglo XX.* Lima: Congreso de la República.

Comisión Mujer y Autodescubrimiento. 1990. "Conclusiones y resoluciónes." In *Memorias: Encuentro latinoamericano de organizaciones campesinas e indígenas: 500 años de resistencia indígena y popular,* pp. 18–31. Bogotá, October 7–12, 1989. Bogotá: ONIC (Organización Indígena de Colombia), ANUC (Asociación Nacional de Usuarios Campesinos), and FENSUAGRO-CUT (Federación Nacional Sindical Unitaria Agropecuaria).

CONADI (Corporación Nacional de Desarrollo Indígena). 1995. *Ley indígena.* Temuco: CONADI.

CONAIE (Confederación de Nacionalidades Indígenas del Ecuador). 1994. *Memorias de las jornadas del Foro de la mujer indígena del Ecuador.* Quito: CONAIE-UNFPA (UN Population Fund).

————, and CONAMIE/Comisión Nacional de Mujeres Indígenas del Ecuador. 1995. *Memorias: Encuentro de mujeres indígenas de las primeras naciones del continente, 31 de julio al 4 de agosto de 1995, Quito, Ecuador.* Quito: CONAIE.

Conferencia Episcopal Boliviana. 1999. "Madre fecunda para todos: Carta pastoral." Memo. May. La Paz.

CONTAG (Confederação Nacional dos Trabalhadores na Agricultura), FETAGS (Federações dos Trabalhadores na Agricultura), STRS (Sindicatos dos Trabalhadores Rurais). 1998. *Anais: Sétimo Congreso Nacional de Trabalhadores e Trabalhadoras Rurais.* Brasilia: CONTAG.

CONTAG, FETAGS, STRS, CUT (Central Única dos Trabalhadores), MMTR/NE (Movimento de Mulheres Trabalhadoras Rurais, Nordeste), Movimento Nacional de Quebradeiras de Côco, Conselho Nacional de Seringueiros, Movimento de Luta pela Terra, União Brasileira de Mulheres, SOF (Sempre Viva Organização Feminista), Associação Agroecológica Tijupá, FASE (Forma Avancada de Solidariedade e Educação), and ESPLAR. 2000. "Pauta de reivindicações da Marcha das Margaridas, mobilização das mulheres trabalhadoras rurais en adesão a Marcha Mundial de Mulheres 2000." August. Brasilia: CONTAG.

Coordinadora Nacional de Comunidades Campesinas, Grupo de Trabajo sobre Comunidades y Titulación. 1997. "Derechos individuales al interior de la comunidad." Paper presented to Primer Taller sobre Comunidades Campesinas y Titulación, June, Lima.

Corbo, Vittorio, and Stanley Fischer. 1995. "Structural Adjustment, Stabilization and Policy Reform: Domestic and International Finance." In Jere Behrman and T. N. Srinivasan, eds., *Handbook of Development Economics*, vol. 3B, chap 44. Amsterdam: Elsevier.

Córdova Plaza, Rosío. 1999. "Mandiles y machetes: El acceso femenino a la tierra en una comunidad ejidal de Veracruz, México." Paper presented at the workshop "Land in Latin America: New Context, New Claims, New Concepts," sponsored by CEDLA, CERES (Research School for Resource Studies for Development), and WAU (Wageningen Agricultural University). May. Royal Tropical Institute, Amsterdam.

Correia, Sonia. 1998. "Plataforma de Beijing." In ENLAC, ed., *Memorias del primer encuentro latino-americano y del Caribe de la mujer trabajadora rural, 15 de septiembre de 1996, Fortaleza, Ceará, Brazil*. Lima: Publicaciones S.R.L.

Costa Leonardo, Nuria, ed. 1995. *La mujer rural en México*. Mexico: Comité Nacional Coordinadora para la IV Conferencia Mundial sobre la Mujer.

Costa Rica, República de. 1887. *Código civil*. San José: Imprenta Nacional.

———. 1984. *Censo de población de 1984*. San José: Sección General de Estadísticas y Censos.

———. 1985. *Código civil y de familia*. San José: Ed. Porvenir.

Cuba Salerno, Amalia. 1993. "Participación de la mujer en la cadena agroalimentaria peruana." Memo. January. Lima: UNIFEM (United Nations Development Fund for Women).

Custred, Glynn. 1977. "Peasant Kinship, Subsistence and Economics in a High Altitude Andean Environment." In Rolf Bolton and Enrique Mayer, eds., *Andean Kinship and Marriage,* pp. 117–135. Washington, D.C.: American Anthropological Association.

CUT (Central Única dos Trabalhadores). 1991. *Mulheres trabalhadoras rurais: Participação e luta sindical*. São Paulo: Departamento Nacional dos Trabalhadores Rurais, Comissão Nacional da Questão da Mulher Trabalhadora.

Cuvi, María. 1992. "Políticas agrarias y papel de la mujer en el desarrollo del Ecuador." In CEPLAES-ACDI, ed., *Entre los límites y las rupturas: Las mujeres ecuatorianas en la década del 80*. Quito: Centro de Planificación y Estudios Sociales (CEPLAES) and Agencia Canadiense para el Desarrollo Internacional (ACDI).

Dahlerup, Drude. 1993. "De una pequeña a una gran minoría: Una teoría de la masa crítica aplicada al caso de las mujeres en la política escandinava." *Debate Feminista* (Mexico City) 4, no. 3: 165–206.

Daley, Caroline, and Melanie Nolan, eds. 1994. *Suffrage and Beyond: International Feminist Perspectives*. New York: New York University Press.

da Luz, Valdemar. 1996. *Curso de direito agrario: Contem o estatuto da terra*. 2d ed., Porto Alegre: Sagra-DC Luzzatto.

Dandler, Jorge. 1996. "Indigenous People and the Rule of Law in Latin America: Do They Have a Chance?" Paper prepared for the Academic Workshop on the Rule of Law and the Underprivileged in Latin America, November 9–16, Kellogg Institute for International Studies, University of Notre Dame, Notre Dame, Ind.

de Almeyda, Amézquita. 1977. "Condición de la mujer en el derecho de familia." In Magdalena León de Leal, ed., *La mujer y desarrollo en Colombia*, pp. 273–316. Bogotá: ACEP (Asociación Colombiana para el Estudio de la Población).

de Barbieri, Teresita. 1992. "Sobre la categoría género: Una introducción teórico-metodológica." *Revista Interamericana de Sociología* 2: 147–178.

———. 1996. "Certezas y malos entendidos sobre la categoría género." In Laura Guzmán and Gilda Pacheco, eds., *Estudios básicos de derechos humanos IV*, pp. 47–84. San José: IIDH (Instituto Inter-americano de Derechos Humanos).

Deere, Carmen Diana. 1976. "Rural Women's Subsistence Production in the Capitalist Periphery." *Review of Radical Political Economy* 8, no. 1: 9–17.

———. 1977. "Changing Social Relations of Production and Peruvian Peasant Women's Work." *Latin American Perspectives* 4, nos. 1 and 2: 48–69.

———. 1983. "Cooperative Development and Women's Participation in the Nicaraguan Agrarian Reform." *American Journal of Agricultural Economics* (December): 1043–1048.

———. 1985. "Rural Women and State Policy: The Latin American Agrarian Reform Experience." *World Development* 13, no. 9: 1036–1053.

———. 1986. "Rural Women and Agrarian Reform in Peru, Chile and Cuba." In June Nash and Helen Safa, eds., *Women and Change in Latin America*, pp. 189–207. South Hadley, Mass.: Bergin and Garvey.

———. 1987. "The Latin American Agrarian Reform Experience." In Carmen Diana Deere and Magdalena León, eds., *Rural Women and State Policy: Feminist Perspectives on Latin American Agricultural Development*, pp. 165–190. Boulder, Colo.: Westview.

———. 1990. *Household and Class Relations: Peasants and Landlords in Northern Peru*. Berkeley: University of California Press.

Deere, Carmen Diana, Peggy Antrobus, Lynn Bolles, Edwin Meléndez, Peter Phillips, Marcia Rivera, and Helen Safa. 1990. *In the Shadows of the Sun: Caribbean Development Alternatives and U.S. Policy*. Boulder, Colo.: Westview.

Deere, Carmen Diana, and Martin Diskin. 1984. "Rural Poverty in El Salvador: Dimensions, Trends and Causes." World Employment Programme Research Working Paper no. 64. Geneva: International Labour Office.

Deere, Carmen Diana, and Magdalena León. 1982. *Women in Andean Agriculture: Peasant Production and Rural Wage Employment in Colombia and Peru*. Geneva: International Labour Office.

————. 1987a. "Introduction." In Carmen Diana Deere and Magdalena León, eds., *Rural Women and State Policy: Feminist Perspectives on Agricultural Development in Latin America*, 1–17. Boulder, Colo.: Westview Press.

Deere, Carmen Diana, and Magdalena León, eds. 1987b. *Rural Women and State Policy: Feminist Perspectives on Agricultural Development in Latin America*. Boulder, Colo.: Westview Press.

————. 1997. "La mujer rural y la reforma agraria en Colombia." *Revista Cuadernos de Desarrollo Rural* (Bogotá) 38–39: 7–23.

————. 1998a. "Mujeres, derechos a la tierra y contrarreformas en América Latina." *Debate Agrario: Análisis y Alternativas* (Lima) 27: 129–154.

————. 1998b. "Gender, Land and Water: From Reform to Counter-reform in Latin America." *Journal of Agriculture and Human Values* 15, no. 4: 375–386.

————. 1998c. "Reforma agraria y contrarreforma en el Perú: Hacia un analisis de género." Serie de Estudios Mujer Rural y Desarrollo. Lima: Ediciones Flora Tristán.

————. 1998d. "Derechos de propiedad y acceso de la mujer a la tierra en El Salvador." *Boletín PRISMA* 32 (San Salvador): 1–15.

————. 1998e. "Mujeres sin tierra." *Tinkasos: Revista Boliviana de Ciencias Sociales* (La Paz) 1, no. 2: 47–66.

————. 1999a. "Género y derechos a la tierra en Ecuador." In C. D. Deere, M. León, Elizabeth García, and Julio César Trujillo, *Género y derechos de las mujeres a la tierra en Ecuador*. Quito: CONAMU and UNICEF.

————. 1999b. "Towards a Gendered Analysis of the Brazilian Agrarian Reform." Occasional Paper no. 16 of the New England Consortium of Latin American Studies. Storrs: University of Connecticut.

————. 1999c. *Mujer y tierra en Guatemala*. Serie Autores Invitados. Guatemala City: AVANCSO.

Deere, Carmen Diana, Magdalena León de Leal, and Jane Humphries. 1982. "Class and Historical Analysis for the Study of Women and Economic Change." In Richard Anker, Mayra Buvinic, and Nadia Youssef, eds., *Women's Roles and Population Trends in the Third World*, pp. 87–114. London: Croom Helm.

Deere, Carmen Diana, Niurka Pérez, Cary Torres, Miriam García, and Ernel Gonzalez. 1998. *Guines, Santo Domingo and Majibacoa: Sobre sus historias agrarias*. Havana: Ed. de Ciencias Sociales.

Deere, Carmen Diana, and Robert Wasserstrom. 1981. "Ingreso familiar y trabajo no agrícola entre los pequeños productores de América Latina y el Caribe." In André Novoa and Josh Posner, eds., *Seminario internacional sobre producción agropecuaria y forestal en zonas de ladera de América tropical*, pp. 151–167. Informe Técnico no. 11. Turrialba, Costa Rica: Centro Agronómico Tropical de Investigación y Enseñanza.

Deininger, K. 1999. "Making Negotiated Land Reform Work: Initial Experience from Colombia, Brazil and South Africa." *World Development* 27, no. 4: 651–672.

de Janvry, Alain, Gustavo Gordillo, and Elisabeth Sadoulet. 1997. *Mexico's Second Agrarian Reform: Household and Community Responses, 1990–1994.* San Diego: Center for U.S.-Mexican Studies, University of California, San Diego.

de Janvry, Alain, and Elisabeth Sadoulet. 1993. "Adjustment Policies, Agriculture and Rural Development in Latin America." In Ajit Singh and Hamid Tabatabai, eds., *Economic Crisis and Third World Agriculture,* pp. 118–146. Cambridge: Cambridge University Press.

de Janvry, Alain, Elisabeth Sadoulet, and Linda Wilcox Young. 1989. "Land and Labour in Latin American Agriculture from the 1950s to the 1980s." *Journal of Peasant Studies* 16, no. 3: 396–424.

de Jong, Sara. 1997. "Del diagnóstico al acceso a la titulación de tierra." In *Avance: Fortalecimiento institucional,* pp. 4–5. Cajamarca: Consorcio Interinstitucional para el Desarrollo Regional (CIPDER).

de la Cadena, Marisol. 1988. "Comuneros en Huancayo: Migración campesina a ciudades serranas." Documento de Trabajo no. 26. Lima: Instituto de Estudios Peruanos.

———. 1995. "'Women Are More Indian': Ethnicity and Gender in a Community Near Cuzco." In Brooke Larson and Olivia Harris, eds., *Ethnicity, Markets, and Migration in the Andes: At the Crossroads of History and Anthropology,* pp. 329–348. Durham, N.C.: Duke University Press.

de la Cruz, Rodrigo. [1995.] "Los derechos de los indígenas: Un tema milenario cobra nueva fuerza." In Ramón Torres Galarza, ed., *Derechos de los pueblos indígenas: Situación jurídica y políticas de estado,* pp. 7–15. Quito: CONAIE, CEPLAES, and ABYA-YALA.

de la Torre A., Ana. 1995. *Violencia contra la mujer rural en Cajamarca.* Cajamarca: APRISABAC (Atención Primaria y Saneamiento Básico) and Sub Región de Salud IV.

del Castillo, Laureano. 1996. "Impacto de la ley de tierras sobre las comunidades campesinas y nativas." *Vox Juris Revista de Derecho* (Lima) 6: 207–223.

———. 1997a. "Derechos de la mujer en el ámbito agrario." Paper prepared for the Seminario/Taller Ley de Tierras y Titulación en Cajamarca. April. Cajamarca: Red de la Mujer Rural "Flora Tristán" and REPRODEMUC.

———. 1997b. "Propiedad rural, titulación de tierras y propiedad comunal." *Debate Agrario* (Lima) 26: 59–79.

del Castillo, Laureano, Máximo Gallo, and Carlos Montes. 1995. *Ley 26505: La nueva ley de tierras: Análisis y comentarios.* Lima: CEPES, CIPCA (Centro de Investigación y Promoción del Campesinado), COINCIDE, SER, and SURCOS.

de los Reyes, Paulina. 1990. "The Rural Poor: Survival Strategies and Living Conditions among the Rural Population in the Seventh Region." In David E. Hojman, ed., *Neo-Liberal Agriculture in Rural Chile,* 146–167. New York: St. Martin's Press.

Demsetz, Harold. 1998. "Property Rights." In Peter Newman, ed., *The New Palgrave Dictionary of Economics and Law,* vol. 3, pp. 144–155. London: Routledge.

Departamento Nacional de Planeación, República de Colombia. 1998. *Macroeconomía, género y estado.* Bogotá: Tercer Mundo.

Desai, Sonalde, and Samia Ahmad. 1998. "Female-Headed Households." In Nelly Stromquist, ed., *Women in the Third World: An Encyclopedia of Contemporary Issues,* pp. 227–235. New York: Garland.

de Vries, Pieter. 1995. "The Local Redefinition of the Agrarian Question in Mexico: Transformations of Practices, Projects and Identities in the Age of Globalization." Paper presented at the conference "The Agrarian Question: The Politics of Farming in the Year 2000," May 22–24, University of Wageningen, The Netherlands.

DeWalt, Billie, and Martha Rees. 1994. *The End of the Agrarian Reform in Mexico: Past Lessons, Future Prospects.* San Diego: Center for U.S.-Mexican Studies.

DGPM (Dirección General de Promoción de la Mujer). 1998. "Conoce tus derechos como parcelera" (pamphlet). Santo Domingo: DGPM.

Díaz, Harry. 1990. "Proletarianisation and Marginality: The Modernisation of Chilean Agriculture." In David Hojman, ed., *Neo-Liberal Agriculture in Rural Chile,* pp. 127–145. New York: St. Martin's Press.

Dirección Nacional de Equidad para las Mujeres and Ministerio de Agricultura y Desarrollo Rural. 1998. *Mujeres rurales en cifras.* Bogotá: Dirección Nacional de Equidad and Ministerio de Agricultura y Desarrollo Rural.

Diskin, Martin. 1989. "El Salvador: Reform Prevents Change." In William Thiesenhusen, ed., *Searching for Agrarian Reform in Latin America,* pp. 429–450. Boston: Unwin Hyman.

Donnelly, Jack. 1984. "Cultural Relativism and Universal Human Rights." *Human Rights Quarterly* 6, no. 4: 400–419.

Dore, Elizabeth. 2000a. "One Step Forward, Two Steps Back: Gender and the State in the Long Nineteenth Century." In Elizabeth Dore and Maxine Molyneux, eds., *Hidden Histories of Gender and the State in Latin America,* pp. 3–32. Durham: Duke University Press.

———. 2000b. "Property, Household, and Public Regulation of Domestic Life: Diriomo, Nicaragua, 1840–1900." In Elizabeth Dore and Maxine Molyneux, eds., *Hidden Histories of Gender and the State in Latin America,* pp. 147–171. Durham: Duke University Press.

Dorner, Peter. 1992. *Latin American Land Reforms in Theory and Practice.* Madison: University of Wisconsin Press.

Dorner, Peter, and Don Kanel. 1971. "The Economic Case for Land Reform: Employment, Income Distribution and Productivity." In Peter Dorner, ed., *Land Reform in Latin America.* Land Economics Monograph No. 3. Madison: University of Wisconsin.

Dueñas Vargas, Guiomar. 1997. *Los hijos del pecado: Ilegitimidad y vida familiar en la Santa Fe de Bogotá colonial.* Bogotá: Editorial Universidad Nacional.

Durán Ariza, Alicia. 1991. "Informe final. Avances de la 'Política sobre el papel de la mujer campesina en el desarrollo agropecuario.'" Memo. Bogotá: Presidencia de la República, Consejería Presidencial para la Juventud, la Mujer y la Familia.

Echenique, Jorge. 1996. "Mercados de tierra en Chile." In Bastiaan Reydon and Pedro Ramos, eds., *Mercado y políticas de tierras (experiencias en América Latina),* pp. 73–108. Campinas: Instituto de Economía, Universidade Estadual de Campinas.

Echeverría, Rubén G. 1998. "Un creciente interés en lograr mercados de tierras rurales más efectivos." In Banco Interamericano de Desarrollo, ed., *Perspectivas sobre mercados de tierras rurales en América Latina,* pp. 1–13. Washington, D.C.: BID.

Ecuador, República de. 1994. *Ley de desarrollo agrario y reglamento,* Quito: Congreso Nacional.

———. 1998. *Constitución política de la República del Ecuador: Índice sistemático, comentario, concordancias.* 3d ed. Quito: Corporación de Estudios y Publicaciones.

Edwards, W. M. 1980. "Ten Issues in Carrying Out Land Reform in Colombia." *Inter-American Economic Affairs* 34, no. 3: 55–68.

El Salvador, República de. 1959. *Código Civil de El Salvador 1959 con estudio preliminar de Dr. Mauricio Guzmán.* Madrid: Instituto de Cultura Hispánica.

El Salvador. 1985. *Encuesta de hogares de propósitos múltiples.* San Salvador: Dirección General de Coordinación, Ministerio de Planificación.

———. 1992. *Censos nacionales, V de población, IV de vivienda.* Tomo general. San Salvador: Dirección General de Estadística y Censos.

Elson, Diane. 1991. "Male Bias in Macro-economics: The Case of Structural Adjustment." In Diane Elson, ed., *Male Bias in the Development Process,* chap. 7. Manchester: Manchester University Press.

Elson, Diane, María Angélica Fauné, Jasmine Gideon, Maribel Gutiérrez, Armida López de Mazier, and Eduardo Sacayón. 1997. *Crecer con la mujer: Oportunidades para el desarrollo económico centroamericano.* San José: Embajada Real de los Países Bajos.

Elu de Leñero, María del Carmen. 1975. *La mujer en América Latina*. Mexico City: Sepsetentas.

ENBRATER. 1986. *Primeiro Congresso Nacional de Mulheres Rurais, Brasilia, D.F., 25 al 28 de novembro de 1986, Conclusões*. Brasilia: Ministerio de Agricultura, Serviço de Extensão Rural.

Encuentros Nacionales de Promotoras Rurales. 1992. "Las reformas al artículo 27 constitucional, nueva ley reglamentaria." *Cuadernos Agrarios* (Mexico City), no. 5–6: 218–227.

Engels, Friedrich. [1884] 1972. *The Origin of the Family, Private Property, and the State*. New York: Pathfinder Press.

Engle, Patrice. 1995. "Father's Money, Mother's Money, and Parental Commitment: Guatemala and Nicaragua." In Rae L. Blumberg, Cathy Rakowski, Irene Tinker, and Michael Monteon, eds., *EnGENDERing Wealth and Well-Being: Empowerment for Global Change*, pp. 155–180. Boulder: Westview.

ENLAC (Encuentro Latino-Americano y del Caribe de la Mujer Trabajadora Rural). 1998. *Memorias del primer encuentro latino-americano y del Caribe de la mujer trabajadora rural, 15 de septiembre de 1996, Fortaleza, Ceará, Brasil*. Lima: Publicaciones S.R.L.

Enríquez, Laura. 1991. *Harvesting Change: Labor and Agrarian Reform in Nicaragua, 1979–1990*. Chapel Hill: University of North Carolina Press.

———. 1999. "Neoliberalism and Nicaraguan Farmers: Its Effects and Their Responses to It." Paper prepared for the Conferencia Científica 40 Aniversario de la Ley de Reforma Agraria Cubana, May 12–14, Havana.

Escobar, Arturo, and Sonia E. Alvarez, eds. 1992. *The Making of Social Movements in Latin America: Identity, Strategy and Democracy*. Boulder: Westview Press.

Escoto León, Claudio. 1965. *Leyes de reforma agraria en América Central*. Bogotá: IICA-CIRA.

Esparza Salinas, Rocío, Blanca Suárez, and Paloma Bonfil. 1996. *Las mujeres campesinas ante la reforma al Artículo 27 de la Constitución*. Serie Cuadernos de Trabajo. Mexico City: GIMTRAP.

"Estadísticas sobre el avance de Procede." 1998. *Estudios Agrarios* no. 10: n.p., in http://www.pa.gob.mx/publica/puo71011.htm, accessed 19 January 2000.

Eto Cruz, Gerardo. 1989. *Derecho de Familia en la Constitución y el Nuevo Código Civil*. Trujillo: Marsol Perú Editores.

Facio M., Alda. 1996. "El principio de igualdad ante la ley." In Movimento Manuela Ramos, ed., *Derechos humanos de las mujeres: Aproximaciones conceptuales*. Lima: Manuela Ramos.

Fajardo, Darío. 1983. *Haciendas, campesinos y políticas agrarias en Colombia, 1920–1980*. Bogotá: Editorial La Oveja Negra.

———. 1998. "La reforma agraria como ordenamiento territorial." Memo, September. Bogotá.

————. 1999. "La reforma agraria en las agendas para la búsqueda de soluciones al conflicto armado." Memo. Bogotá: FESCOL.

Fajardo, Darío, and Héctor Mondragón. 1997. *Colonización y estrategias de desarrollo.* Bogotá: IICA, Ministerio del Medio Ambiente and Instituto de Estudios Políticos y Relaciones Internacionales (IEPRI), Universidad Nacional de Colombia.

Fandiño, Mario. 1993. "Land Titling and Peasant Differentiation in Honduras." *Latin American Perspectives* 20, no. 2: 45–53.

FAO (Food and Agriculture Organization of the United Nations). 1979. *Report: Conference on Agrarian Reform and Rural Development, Rome, 12–20 July 1979.* Rome: FAO.

————. 1990. *Mesa redonda sobre los mecanismos jurídicos que posibilitan la participación de la mujer en el desarrollo rural.* Santiago: FAO, Oficina Regional.

————. 1992. *Situación jurídica de la mujer rural en diecinueve paises de América Latina.* Rome: FAO.

————. 1996. *Informe: Reunión regional sobre la mujer rural y la legislación agraria.* Santiago: FAO, Oficina Regional.

————. 1997. *Report of the World Food Summit, 13–17 November 1996.* Rome: FAO.

————. 1998. *Production Yearbook 1997.* Vol. 5. Rome: FAO.

FAO and INCRA. 1998. "Gênero e desenvolvimento rural e agrícola, material de apoio técnico." Document prepared for the FAO-INCRA workshop on Socio-Economic Analisis and Gender, May 14–15, Brasilia.

Fauné, M. Angélica. 1995. "Centroamérica: Mujeres y familias rurales." In Ximena Valdés, Ana María Arteaga, and Carolina Arteaga, eds., *Mujeres: Relaciones de género en la agricultura,* 125–208. Santiago: Centro de Estudios para el Desarrollo de la Mujer.

Feder, Gershon, and David Feeny. 1991. "Land Tenure and Property Rights: Theory and Implications for Development Policy." *World Bank Economic Review* 5, no. 1: 135–53.

Feijoo, María del Carmen. 1989a. *Una bibliografía anotada de los estudios sobre el status de las mujeres en América Latina.* Buenos Aires: CEDES (Centro de Estudios de Estado y Sociedad).

————. 1989b. "Estado actual de la investigación sobre mujer en América Latina." Memo. Montevideo: GRECMU (Grupo de Estudios sobre la Condición de la Mujer en el Uruguay).

Feldman, Shelley. 1998. "Conceptualizing Change and Equality in 'Third World' Contexts." In Nelly P. Stromquist, ed., *Women in the Third World: An Encyclopedia of Contemporary Issues,* pp. 24–37. New York: Garland.

Fempress. 1999. "Ecuador: El protagonismo de las indígenas." *Revista mujer/ fempress* no. 214 (September): n.p.

Fernandes, Bernardo Macano. 1996. MST: *Formação e territorialização.* São Paulo: Ed. Hucitec.

Fernández, Blanca. 1982. "Reforma agraria y condición socio-económica de la mujer: El caso de dos cooperativas agrarias de producción peruanas." In M. León and C. D. Deere, eds., *Las trabajadoras del agro,* 261–276. Bogotá: ACEP.

Fernández, Blanca, María Amelia Trigoso, Laureano del Castillo, William Becerra, Pedro Arias, Katherine Pozo, and Karla Aragón. 2000. *"Por una titulación de tierras con equidad": Una experiencia para compartir.* Lima: Ed. Flora Tristán.

Fernández-Kelley, Patricia. 1983. *For We Are Sold, I and My People: Women and Industry in Mexico's Frontier.* Albany: State University of New York Press.

FIDA (Fondo Internacional de Desarrollo Agrícola). 1989. *Informe de la Misión Especial de Programación a la República del Ecuador.* Rome: FIDA.

Figallo Adrianzan, Guillermo. 1990. "Derecho agrario y familia." In Fernando de Trazegnies Granda, et al., eds., *La familia en el derecho peruano,* pp. 412–425. Lima: Fondo Editorial, Pontificia Universidad Católica del Perú.

Figueras y González, Jesús. 1945. "Posición jurídica de la mujer." *Monografías jurídicas.* Vol. 49, pp. 58–105. Havana: Jesús Montero Ed.

Findley, Roger W. 1973. "Problems Faced by Colombia's Agrarian Reform Institute in Acquiring and Distributing Land." In Robert E. Scott, ed., *Latin American Modernization Problems: Case Studies in the Crises of Change,* 122–192. Urbana: University of Illinois Press.

Flexner, Eleanor, and Ellen Fitzpatrick. 1996. *Century of Struggle: The Woman's Rights Movement in the United States.* Cambridge: Belknap Press of Harvard University Press.

Flora, Cornelia. 1987. "Income Generation Projects for Rural Women." In C. D. Deere and Magdalena León, eds., *Rural Women and State Policy: Feminist Perspectives on Latin American Agricultural Development,* pp. 212–238. Boulder: Westview.

Flores, Andrea, Felipa Gutiérrez, and Arminda Velazco. N.d. "Nosotras las mujeres Aymaras." In *Mujer Fempress, Especial la mujer indígena.* Santiago: Mujer Fempress.

Flores, Margarita. 1994. "Tierra: Conflicto y paz en El Salvador." Paper presented to the 48th International Congress of Americanists, July, Stockholm.

FMC (Federación de Mujeres Cubanas). 1975. *Memories: Second Congress of Cuban Women's Federation.* Havana: Editorial Orbit.

Folbre, Nancy. 1986a. "Hearts and Spades, Paradigms of Household Economics." *World Development* 14, no. 2: 245–255.

———. 1986b. "Cleaning House: New Perspectives on Households and Economic Development." *Journal of Development Economics* 22, no. 1: 5–40.

Foley, Michael W., with George Vickers and Geoff Thale. 1997. "Land, Peace and Participation: The Development of Post-War Agricultural Policy in El Salvador and the Role of the World Bank." WOLA Occasional Paper Series. Washington, D.C.: Washington Office on Latin America.

Foro de Organizaciones No Gubernamentales. 1994. "Síntesis de las principales propuestas acordadas en el Foro de Organizaciones No Gubernamentales, Mar del Plata, 24 de septiembre de 1994." Memo. Lima: Centro de la Mujer Peruana "Flora Tristán."

Foucault, Michel. 1980. *Power/Knowledge: Selected Interviews and Other Writings, 1972–1977*. New York: Pantheon.

Fox, Jonathon. 1994. "Political Change in Mexico's New Peasant Economy." In María L. Cook, Kevin Middlebrook, and J. M. Horcasitas, eds., *The Politics of Economic Restructuring: State-Society Relations and Regime Change in Mexico*, pp. 243–276. San Diego: Center for U.S.-Mexican Studies, UCSO.

Fraser, Arvonne S. 1987. *The U.N. Decade for Women: Documents and Dialogue*. Boulder: Westview Press.

Fraser, Nancy. 1997. *Justice Interruptus: Critical Reflections on the "Postsocialist Condition."* New York and London: Routledge Press.

Freire, Paulo. 1973. *Pedagogy of the Oppressed*. New York: Seabury Press.

Fundación Arias. 1992. *El acceso de la mujer a la tierra en El Salvador*. San José: Fundación Arias.

———. 1997a. *Mujeres productoras de esperanza, Costa Rica*. San José: Fundación Arias.

———. 1997b. "Encuentro nacional: Forjando la organización de las mujeres rurales en Nicaragua, IPADE, 15–17 de octubre de 1997." Draft report, San José.

———. 1998a. "La legislación nacional relacionada con el acceso de las mujeres a la tierra y a la propiedad, El Salvador" (pamphlet). San José: Fundación Arias.

———. 1998b. "La legislación nacional relacionada con el acceso de las mujeres a la tierra y a la propiedad, Guatemala" (pamphlet). San José: Fundación Arias.

———. 1998c. "La legislación nacional relacionada con el acceso de las mujeres a la tierra y al propiedad, Honduras" (pamphlet). San José: Fundación Arias.

———. 1998d. "La legislación nacional relacionada con el acceso de las mujeres a la tierra y a la propiedad, Nicaragua" (pamphlet). San José: Fundación Arias.

———. 1998e. "La legislación nacional relacionada con el acceso de las mujeres a la tierra y a la propiedad, Costa Rica" (pamphlet). San José: Fundación Arias.

———. 1998f. "Diagnóstico sobre la organización de las mujeres rurales en Centroamérica" (pamphlet). San José: Fundación Arias.

Fundación Arias and CEASPA (Centro de Estudios y Acción Social Panameño). 1995. *El acceso de la mujer a la tierra en Panamá*. San José: Fundación Arias.

Fundación Arias and CIPRES (Centro para la Promoción, Investigación, y Desarrollo Rural y Social en Nicaragua). 1992. *El acceso de la mujer a la tierra en Nicaragua*. San José: Fundación Arias.

Fundación Arias and Tierra Viva. 1993. *La mujer y el acceso a la tierra en Guatemala*. San José: Fundación Arias.

FUNDE (Fundación Nacional para el Desarrollo). 1997. *Tierra, deuda agraria y políticas agrícolas, versión popular*. San Salvador: FUNDE.

FUNDESA (Fundación para el Desarrollo 16 de enero). 1997. "Proceso de participación de proindivisos en propiedades P.T.T. y elementos básicos para estrategia de desarrollo." Memo, San Salvador.

FUSADES (Fundación Salvadoreña para el Desarrollo Económico y Social). 1997. "Pobreza rural." *Boletín Económico y Social* (San Salvador) no. 138 (May).

Gabinete do Ministro Extraordinario da Politica Fundiaria and INCRA. 1998. "Cadastramento e seleção nacional." Memo. June. Brasilia.

Gaitán, Ángel Gabriel. 1996. *Las mujeres productoras de alimentos en Colombia: Diagnóstico y políticas*. San José: IICA-BID.

Galán, Beatriz. 1998. "Aspectos jurídicos en el acceso de la mujer rural a la tierra en Cuba, Honduras, Nicaragua y República Dominicana." Memo. Rome: FAO.

Garay, Amanda. 1996. "Women, Cultural Relativism, and International Human Rights: A Question of Mutual Exclusivity or Balance?" *International Insights* (Spring): 19–33.

García, Elizabeth. 1992. "La situación de la mujer en el sistema jurídico ecuatoriano." Doc. LC/R.1134. Santiago: CEPAL.

———. 1994. "Informe del seminario taller sobre procedimientos de trabajo de campo: Selección de áreas y equidad de género en la entrega de títulos de tierra." Report prepared for IICA, Quito.

———. 1999. "Resultados y conclusiones del estudio de validación del proceso de titulación del PRONADER." In C. D. Deere, M. León, E. García, and J. C. Trujillo, *Género y derechos de las mujeres a la tierra en Ecuador*, pp. 85–99. Quito: CONAMU.

García, Emilio. 1994. "Estrategia modernizante y el perfil del movimiento campesino contemporáneo." *Revista Mexicana de Sociología* 61, no. 2: 59–76.

García Laguardia, Jorge, ed. 1997. *Acuerdos de paz*. Guatemala City: Procurador de los Derechos Humanos.

Garrett, Patricia. 1982. "Women and Agrarian Reform: Chile 1964–1973." *Sociología Ruralis* 22, no. 1: 17–28.

GIA (Grupo de Investigación Agraria). 1986. "La demanda de la mujer rural." *Noticiero de la Realidad Agraria* (Santiago) 42: 1–10.

Girón, Bertila, and Silvia Halsband. 1995. *La mujer rural en El Salvador: Informe nacional CENTA-FAO*. San Salvador: CENTA-FAO.

Gobierno Nacional and FARC-EP. 1999. "Agenda común por el cambio hacia una nueva Colombia, La Machaca, mayo 6 de 1999." *Revista Cambio* no. 308.

Godinho Delgado, Maria Berenice. 1995. "A organização das mulheres na Central Única dos Trabalhadores: A comissão nacional sobre a mulher trabalhadora." Master's thesis, Pontificia Universidade Católica de São Paulo.

Golden, Penny. 1991. *The Hour of the Poor, the Hour of Women: Salvadoran Women Speak*. New York: Crossroad.

Gómez, Sergio, and Jorge Echenique. 1988. *La agricultura chilena: Las dos caras de la modernización*. Santiago: FLACSO and Consultorías Profesionales AGRARIA Ltda.

Gómez Cruz, Ricardo A. 1997. "Uso y tenencia de la tierra en El Salvador." Draft consultant's report, San Salvador.

Gómez-Restrepo, Ofelia. 1991. "Políticas para la mujer en el sector rural: Caso de Colombia." In IICA, ed., *Mujer y modernización agropecuaria: Balance, perspectivas y estrategias*, chap. 5. San José, Costa Rica: IICA.

González Cruz, María del Refugio, and Rosa Eugenia Durán Uribe. 1992. "Mujeres autoconstructoras: Estudio de caso de un programa estatal." In Alejandra Massolo, ed., *Mujeres y ciudades: Participación social, vivienda y vida cotidiana*, pp. 197–218. Mexico City: Colegio de México, PIEM.

González Montes, María de la Soledad. 1992. "Familias campesinas mexicanas en el Siglo XX." Ph.D. diss., Universidad Complutense de Madrid.

Graciarena, Jorge. 1975. "Notas sobre el problema de la desigualdad sexual en sociedades de clases." In CEPAL, ed., *Mujeres en América Latina: Aportes para una discusión*, pp. 26–45. Mexico City: Fondo de Cultura Económica.

Gramsci, Antonio. 1971. *Selections from the Prison Notebooks*. London: Laurence and Wishart.

Graubart, Karen. 2000. "'Con nuestro trabajo y sudor': Indigenous Women and the Construction of Colonial Society in Sixteenth- and Seventeenth-Century Peru." Ph.D. diss., University of Massachusetts, Amherst.

Green, Duncan. 1995. *Silent Revolution: The Rise of Market Economics in Latin America*. London: Latin American Books.

Guatemala, Congreso de la República. 1998. "Proyecto de decreto de Ley Fondo de Tierras." June. Memo. Guatemala City.

———. 1999. Ley del Fondo de Tierras. May. Memo. Guatemala City: Congreso de la República.

Guatemala, República de. 1981. *Censos nacionales de 1981, IX de población, cifras definitivas*. Guatemala City: Instituto Nacional de Estadísticas.

———. 1985. *Tercer censo agropecuario 1979*. Guatemala City: Dirección General de Estadística.

————. 1986. *Constitución política de la República de Guatemala y Código Civil*. Guatemala City: República de Guatemala.

————. 1996. *Censo nacional de población y V de habitación*. Guatemala City: Instituto Nacional de Estadística.

————. 1997. *Proyecto de Ley Orgánico del Instituto Nacional de la Mujer (INAM)*. Guatemala: INAM.

Guillén, Mariela, ed. 1996. *Un camino llamado Beijing: Informe de la gestión de la coordinación regional de ONGs de América Latina y el Caribe para la cuarta Conferencia Mundial sobre la Mujer, Beijing, septiembre 1995*. Lima: Flora Tristán.

Guzmán, Laura. 1991. "Políticas para la mujer rural: Caso de Costa Rica." In IICA, ed., *Mujer y modernización agropecuaria: Balance, perspectivas y estrategias,* chap. 4. San José, Costa Rica: IICA.

Guzmán, Virginia. 1996. "La equidad de género en una nueva generación de políticas." In Narda Enrique, ed., *Encrucijadas del saber: Los estudios de género en las ciencias sociales,* pp. 213–229. Lima: Programa de Estudios de Género, Pontificia Universidad Católica del Perú.

Hahner, June E. 1978. "The Nineteenth-Century Feminist Press and Women's Rights in Brazil." In Asunción Lavrin, ed., *Latin American Women: Historical Perspectives,* pp. 254–285. Westport, Conn.: Greenwood Press.

————, ed. 1980. *Women in Latin American History: Their Lives and Views*. Rev. ed. Latin American Studies Series. Los Angeles: Center for Latin American Studies, UCLA.

Hall, Anthony L. 1990. "Land Tenure and Land Reform in Brazil." In Roy Prosterman, Mary Temple, and Timothy Hanstad, eds., *Agrarian Reform and Grassroots Development: Ten Case Studies*. Boulder: Lynne Rienner.

Hamilton, Sarah. 1998. *The Two-Headed Household: Gender and Rural Development in the Ecuadorean Andes*. Pittsburgh: University of Pittsburgh Press.

————. 2000a. "Neoliberalism, Gender, and Property Rights in Rural Mexico." *Latin American Research Review*, forthcoming.

————. 2000b. "Blood, Sweat, and Tears: Gender and Entitlement to Land in Ecuador, Guatemala, and Mexico." Paper prepared for delivery at the 2000 meeting of the Latin American Studies Association, March 16–18, Miami.

Hammond, John L. 1999. "Law and Disorder: The Brazilian Landless Farmworkers' Movement." *Bulletin of Latin American Research* 18, no. 4: 468–489.

Haney, Emil B., and Wava G. Haney. 1989. "The Agrarian Transition in Highland Ecuador: From Precapitalism to Agrarian Capitalism in Chimborazo." In William Thiesenhusen, ed., *Searching for Agrarian Reform in Latin America,* pp. 70–91. Boston: Unwin Hyman.

Hartmann, Betsy. 1995. *Reproductive Rights and Wrongs*. New York: Harper and Row.

Hernández, Pedro, and Oscar Dada. 1997. *El programa de transferencia de tierras*. AVANCES no. 10. San Salvador: FUNDE.

Hernández, Teresita, and Clara Murguialday. 1993. *Mujeres indígenas ayer y hoy*. Managua: Puntos de Encuentro.

Hernández C., Rosalva A., and Héctor Ortiz E. 1996. Las demandas de la mujer indígena en Chiapas. *Nueva Antropología* (Mexico) 15, no. 49: 31–39.

Hipsher, Patricia. 1998. "Right and Left-wing Women in Post-Revolutionary El Salvador: Feminist Autonomy and Cross-Political Alliance-Building for Gender Equality." Paper prepared for presentation at the XXI International Congress of the Latin American Studies Association, September 24–26, Chicago.

Holston, James. 1991. "The Misrule of Law: Land and Usurpation in Brazil." *Comparative Studies in Society and History* 33, no. 4: 695–725.

Honduras, República de. 1975. "Decree No. 170, Agrarian Reform Law." Memo. English translation by the Land Tenure Center, University of Wisconsin.

———. 1976. *Censo de población y vivienda, 1974*. Tegucigalpa: Dirección General de Estadística y Censos.

———. 1977. *Censo nacional de población*. Vol. 2. Tegucigalpa: Dirección General de Estadística y Censos.

———. 1988. *Censo nacional de población y vivienda, 1988*. Vol. 2. Tegucigalpa: Dirección General de Estadística y Censos.

———. 1995. *Ley para la modernización y el desarrollo del sector agrícola (Decreto no. 3192)*. Tegucigalpa: Ed. Guaymuras.

———. 1997. *Código de familia*. Tegucigalpa: Ed. Guaymaras.

———. 2000. "Ley de Iqualdad de Oportunidades para la Mujer, Decreto No. 34-2000," *La Gaceta, Diario Oficial de Honduras*, no. 29, 22 May 2000, p. 177.

Howard, Rhoda E. 1993. "Cultural Absolutism and the Nostalgia for Community." *Human Rights Quarterly* 15: 315–338.

Hünefeldt, Christine. 1997. "Las cartas femeninas en las desaveniencias conyugales: Las mujeres limeñas a comienzos del siglo XIX." In Denise Arnold, ed., *Más allá del silencio: Las fronteras de género en los Andes,* pp. 387–406. Research Series no. 27. La Paz: IILCA/CIASE.

Hvalkof, Soren. 1998. "Beyond Indigenous Land Titling: Democratizing Civil Society in the Peruvian Amazon." Paper prepared for the Conference on Space, Place, and Nation in the Americas, University of Massachusetts, Amherst, November 1998.

IADB (Inter-American Development Bank). 1997. *Economic and Social Progress Report for Latin America 1997*. Washington, D.C.: IADB.

———. 1998. *Basic Socio-Economic Data: Statistics and Quantitative Analysis*. Washington, D.C.: IADB.

Ibarra, Hernán, and Pablo Espina. 1994. *Cambios agrarios y tenencia de la tierra en Cotopaxi*. Quito: Fondo Ecuatoriano Populorum Progresso (FEPP).

IICA (Instituto Interamericano de Cooperación para la Agricultura, Oficina en Guatemala). 1991. *Guatemala: Lineamientos para un programa sectorial agropecuario*. Guatemala: IICA.

IMU (Instituto de Investigación, Capacitación y Desarrollo de la Mujer). 1998. *Resumen ejecutivo del anteproyecto código agrario con perspectiva de género: Documento para consulta*. San Salvador: IMU.

————. 1999. *Anteproyecto código agrario con perspectiva de género*. San Salvador: IMU.

INCORA (Instituto Colombiano de Reforma Agraria). [1994.] *Ley 160 y sus normas reglamentarias*. Bogotá: Sistema Nacional de Reforma Agraria y Desarrollo Rural Campesino.

INCRA-CRUB-UNB. 1998. *Primeiro censo da reforma agraria do Brasil*. Brasilia: INCRA.

INDA (Instituto Nacional de Desarrollo Agrario). 1999. "Manual de procedimientos para la titulación de tierras del INDA." Quito: Dirección de Planificación, INDA.

INEI (Instituto Nacional de Estadística e Informática). 1995. *Tercer censo nacional agropecuario. Peru: Perfil agropecuario, avance de resultados*. Lima: Dirección Técnica de Censos y Encuestas.

Iñíguez de Salinas, Elizabeth, and Anselma Linares Pérez. 1997. *Guía jurídica para la mujer y la familia*. La Paz: Subsecretaría de Asuntos de Género, Ministerio de Desarrollo Humano.

INIM (Instituto Nicaragüense de la Mujer). 1993. "Situación de la mujer campesina y su acceso a la tenencia de la tierra." Paper presented to the Primer Encuentro Nacional Mujer y Tenencia de la Tierra, October, Managua.

————. 1995. *Informe del Gobierno de Nicaragua a la Cuarta Conferencia de la Mujer*. Managua: INIM.

————. 1996. "Intercambio de experiencias sobre el proceso de sensibilización de género con demandantes de títulos agrarias." Paper presented at the first Central American conference of the same name, December 9–10, Managua.

INRA (Instituto Nacional de Reforma Agraria) (Bolivia). 1997a. *INRA: Una herramienta para la tierra*. La Paz: INRA.

————. 1997b. *INRA: Una herramienta para la tierra: Ley del Servicio Nacional de Reforma Agraria, Reglamentos de la Ley del Servicio Nacional de Reforma Agraria*. La Paz: INRA.

INRA (Instituto Nacional de Reforma Agraria) (Cuba). 1960. *Leyes agrarias revolucionarias: Compendio de la legislación dictada durante el año 1959*. Havana: INRA.

INRA-INIM (Instituto Nicaragüense de Reforma Agraria, Instituto Nicaragüense de la Mujer). 1996. "Informe de Nicaragua." Paper presented at the First Central American Conference on Intercambio de Experiencias sobre el Proceso de Sensibilización de Género con Demandantes de Títulos Agrarios. December 9–10, Managua.

Instituto de la Mujer, ed. 1995. *Convención sobre la eliminación de todas las formas de discriminación contra las mujeres y recomendaciones*. Madrid: Instituto de la Mujer.

INTA (Instituto Nacional de Transformación Agraria). 1996. "Adjudicaciones a mujeres por departamento y sus municipios 1954–1996." Memo, December, Guatemala City.

Isbell, Billie Jean. 1978. *To Defend Ourselves: Ecology and Ritual in an Andean Village*. Latin American Monographs, no. 47. Institute of Latin American Studies, University of Texas, Austin.

ISDEMU (Instituto Salvadoreño para el Desarrollo de la Mujer). 1997. *Política nacional de la mujer*. San Salvador: ISDEMU.

ISIS Internacional. 1987. "Las mujeres aymaras se organizan." *ISIS Internacional: Edición de las Mujeres*, no. 6: 45.

Jackson, Cecile. 1993a. "Environmentalism and Gender Interest in the Third World." *Development and Change* 24: 649–677.

———. 1993b. "Women/Nature or Gender/History? A Critique of Ecofeminist 'Development.'" *Journal of Peasant Studies* 20, 3: 389–418.

Jacoby, Hanan. 1991. "Productivity of Men and Women and the Sexual Division of Labor in Peasant Agriculture of the Peruvian Sierra." *Journal of Development Economics* 37: 265–287.

Jansen, Kees, and Esther Roquas. 1998. "Modernizing Insecurity: The Land Titling Project in Honduras." *Development and Change* 29: 81–106.

Jaquette, Jane. 1982. "Women and Modernization Theory: A Decade of Feminist Criticism." *World Politics* 34: 267–283.

———, ed. 1994. *The Women's Movement in Latin America: Participation and Democracy*. Boulder: Westview Press.

Jaramillo, Carlos Felipe. 1998. "El mercado rural de tierras en América Latina: Hacia una nueva estrategia." In Banco Interamericano de Desarrollo, ed., *Perspectivas sobre mercados de tierras rurales en América Latina*, pp. 93–127. Washington, D.C.: BID.

Jarvis, Lovell. 1992. "The Unravelling of the Agrarian Reform." In Cristóbal Kay and Patricio Silva, eds., *Development and Social Change in the Chilean Countryside: From the Pre-Land Reform Period to the Democratic Transition*, pp. 189–214. Amsterdam: CEDLA.

Jiménez P., Angeles. 1995. "Igualdad." In Celia Amoros, ed., *Diez palabras clave sobre mujer*, pp. 119–149. Navarra: Ed. Verbo Divino.

Jordán, Rosa H. 1996. *Las mujeres productoras de alimentos en Ecuador: Diagnóstico y políticas*. San José: IICA-BID.

Kabeer, Naila. 1994. *Reversed Realities: Gender Hierarchies in Development Thought*. London: Verso.

———. 1997. "Empoderamiento desde abajo: ¿Qué podemos aprender de las organizaciones de base?" In Magdalena León, ed., *Poder y empoderamiento de las mujeres,* pp. 119–146. Bogotá: TM Editores and Universidad Nacional, Facultad de Ciencias Humanas.

Kabeer, Naila, and John Humphrey. 1994. "El neoliberalismo, los sexos y los límites del mercado." In Christopher Colclough and James Manor, eds., *Estados o mercados,* pp. 117–120. Mexico City: Fondo de Cultura Económica.

Kaimowitz, David. 1989. "The Role of Decentralization in the Recent Nicaraguan Agrarian Reform." In William Thiesenhusen, ed., *Searching for Agrarian Reform in Latin America,* pp. 384–407. Boston: Unwin and Hyman.

Kampwirth, Karen. 1998. "Women in the Armed Struggles in Nicaragua: Sandinistas and Contras Compared." Paper presented to the Latin American Studies Association International Congress, September 24–26, Chicago.

Katz, Elizabeth G. 1995. "Gender and Trade within the Household: Observations from Rural Guatemala." *World Development* 23, no. 2: 327–342.

———. 1999. "Gender and Ejido Reform." Memo. Draft report prepared for the World Bank Ejido Study, Barnard College, July.

———. 2000. "Does Gender Matter for the Nutritional Consequences of Agricultural Commercialization? Intrahousehold Transfer, Food Acquisition, and Export Cropping in Guatemala." In Anita Spring, ed., *Commercial Ventures and Women Farmers: Increasing Food Security in Developing Countries.* Boulder, Colo.: Lynne Rienner, forthcoming.

Kay, Cristóbal. 1995. "Rural Latin America: Exclusionary and Uneven Agricultural Development." In Sander Halebsky and Richard Harris, eds., *Capital, Power and Inequality in Latin America,* pp. 291–300. Boulder: Westview Press.

———. 1998. "The Complex Legacy of Latin America's Agrarian Reform." Working Papers Series, no. 268. Institute of Social Studies, The Hague, January.

Kay, Cristóbal, and Patricio Silva. 1992. "Rural Development, Social Change, and the Democratic Transition." In Cristóbal Kay and Patricio Silva, eds., *Development and Social Change in the Chilean Countryside,* chap. 17. Amsterdam: CEDLA.

Keck, Margaret, and Kathryn Sikkink. 1998. *Activists beyond Borders: Advocacy Networks in International Politics.* Ithaca, N.Y.: Cornell University Press.

Kirkwood, Julieta. 1990. *Ser política en Chile.* Santiago de Chile: Editorial Cuarto Propio.

Kiss, Elizabeth. 1998. "Justice." In Alison Jaggar and Iris Marion Young, eds., *A Companion to Feminist Philosophy,* pp. 487–499. Maiden, Mass.: Blackwell.

Kleysen, Brenda, ed. 1996. *Productoras agropecuarias en América del Sur.* San José: IICA-BID.

Kleysen, Brenda, and Fabiola Campillo. 1996. *Productoras de alimentos en 18 países de América Latina y el Caribe: Síntesis hemisférica/ Rural Women Food Producers in 18 Countries in Latin America and the Caribbean: Hemisphere Review.* San José: IICA-BID.

Krawczyk, Miriam. 1993. "Women in the Region: Major Changes." *CEPAL Review* 49: 7–19.

Ladin, Sharon. 1994. "Reporte de la XIII sesión del Comité para la Eliminación de la Discriminación contra las Mujeres (CEDAW), IWRAW (International Women's Rights Action Watch)." Memo, University of Minnesota.

Lafosse de Vega-Centeno, Violeta. 1969. "La Ley de Reforma Agraria y sus implicaciones en la estructura familiar." Serie Documentos de Trabajo, no. 3. Lima: Pontificia Universidad Católica del Perú.

Lago, María Soledad. 1987. "Rural Women and the Neo-Liberal Model in Chile." In C. D. Deere and M. León, eds., *Rural Women and State Policy,* 21–34. Boulder: Westview, 1987.

Lamas, Marta. 1986. "La antropología feminista y la categoría de género." *Revista Nuevo Antropología* 8, no. 30: 173–197.

———. 1996. "Usos, dificultades y posibilidades de la categoría género." In Marta Lamas, ed., *El género: La construcción cultural de la diferencia sexual.* Mexico City: Miguel Ángel Porrua grupo editorial, y PUEG.

———. 1998. "De la A a la Z: A Feminist Alliance Experience." In Victoria Rodríguez, ed., *Women's Participation in Mexican Political Life,* pp. 103–115. Boulder: Westview.

Lambert, Bernd. 1977. "Bilaterality in the Andes." In Rolf Bolton and Enrique Mayer, eds., *Andean Kinship and Marriage,* pp. 1–27. Washington, D.C.: American Anthropological Association.

Lara Flores, Sara María. 1994. "Las mujeres: ¿Nuevos actores sociales en el campo?" *Revista Mexicana de Sociología* 2: 77–88.

———, ed. 1995. *El rostro femenino del mercado de trabajo rural en América Latina.* Caracas: United Nations Research Institute for Social Development (UNRISD) and Ed. Nueva Sociedad.

Larguía, Isabel, and John Dumoulin. 1983. *Hacia una concepción científica de la emancipación de la mujer.* Havana: Ed. de Ciencias Sociales.

Larrea H., Juan. 1996. *Código civil con jurisprudencia: Selección elaborado por el Dr. Juan Larrea Holguín, actualizado a mayo 1996.* Quito: Corporación de Estudios y Publicaciones.

Las Dignas (Mujeres por la Dignidad y la Vida). 1993. "Discriminación hacia la mujer en el Programa de Transferencia de Tierras." Memo, San Salvador.

Lastarria-Cornhiel, Susana. 1988. "Female Farmers and Agricultural Production in El Salvador." *Development and Change* 19, no. 4: 855–616.

———. 1997. "Impact of Privatization on Gender and Property Rights in Africa." *World Development* 25, no. 8: 1317–1334.

Lastarria-Cornhiel, Susana, and María Teresa Delgado de Mejía. 1994. "El Salvador: Gender Strategy and Action Plan, Land Tenure and Titling." Report prepared for the World Bank, Washington, D.C., November.

Lavinas, Lena (Coordinator). 1987. *Anais do seminario mulher rural: Identidades na pesquisa e na luta politica*. Rio de Janeiro: Editora Universidade Federal do Rio de Janeiro.

———. 1991. "Productoras rurais: A novidade dos anos 90." *Reforma Agraria* (Campinas, São Paulo), May/June, pp. 4–9.

Lavrin, Asunción. 1978. "In Search of the Colonial Woman in Mexico: The Seventeenth and Eighteenth Centuries." In Asunción Lavrin, ed., *Latin American Women: Historical Perspectives*, pp. 23–59. Westport, Conn.: Greenwood Press.

———. 1994. "Suffrage in South America: Arguing a Difficult Cause." In Caroline Daley and Melanie Nolan, eds., *Suffrage and Beyond: International Feminist Perspectives*, pp. 184–209. New York: New York University Press.

———. 1995. *Women, Feminism, and Social Change in Argentina, Chile and Uruguay, 1890–1940*. Lincoln and London: University of Nebraska Press.

Lavrin, Asunción, and Edith Couturier. 1979. "Dowries and Wills: A View of Women's Socioeconomic Role in Colonial Guadalajara and Puebla, 1640–1790." *Hispanic American Historical Review* 59, no. 2: 280–304.

Leal Buitrago, Francisco. 1991. "Estructura y coyuntura de la crisis política." In Francisco Leal Buitrago and León Zamosc, eds., *Al filo del caos: Crisis política en la Colombia de los años 80*, pp. 27–56. Bogotá: Tercer Mundo Editores and IEPRI.

León, Magdalena. 1987. "Colombian Agricultural Policies and the Debate on Policies toward Rural Women." In Carmen Diana Deere and Magdalena León, eds., *Rural Women and State Policy: Feminist Perspectives on Agricultural Development in Latin America*, pp. 84–104. Boulder: Westview.

———. 1997a. "El empoderamiento en la teoría y práctica del feminismo." In Magdalena León, ed., *Poder y empoderamiento de las mujeres*, pp. 1–28. Bogotá: TM Editores and Universidad Nacional, Facultad de Ciencias Humanas.

———. 1997b. "¿Qué control tiene la mujer sobre la tierra? Análisis y seguimiento a los acuerdos establecidos en las conferencias mundiales." *Revista Profamilia* (Bogotá) 15, no. 30: 8–17.

———, ed. 1980. *Mujer y desarrollo en Colombia*. Bogotá: ACEP.

———, ed. 1982. *Debate sobre la mujer en América Latina y el Caribe: Discusión acerca de la unidad producción-reproducción*. Vol. 1, *La realidad colombiana*; vol. 2, *Las trabajadoras del agro*; vol. 3, *Sociedad, subordinación y feminismo*. Bogotá: ACEP and Editorial Pudencia.

———, ed. 1994. *Mujeres y participación política: Avances y desafíos en América Latina*. Bogotá: Tercer Mundo.

León, Magdalena, and Carmen Diana Deere. 1999. *Género y derechos de las mujeres a la tierra en Chile*. Santiago: CEDEM (Centro de Estudios para el Desarrollo de la Mujer).

León, Magdalena, Patricia Prieto, and María Cristina Salazar. 1987. "Acceso de la mujer a la tierra en América Latina: Panorama general y estudios de caso de Honduras y Colombia." In FAO, ed., *Mujeres campesinas en América Latina: Desarrollo rural, migración, tierra y legislación,* pp. 3–80. Santiago, Chile: FAO.

León, Rosario. 1990. "Bartolina: The Peasant Women's Organization in Bolivia." In Elizabeth Jelin, ed., *Women and Social Change in Latin America,* pp. 135–150. London: Zed and UNRISD.

Leret de Matheus, María Gabriela. 1975. *La mujer: Una incapaz como el demente y el niño (según las leyes latinoamericanas).* Mexico: Costa-Amic Ed.

Lewin, Linda. 1992. "Natural and Spurious Children in Brazilian Inheritance Law from Colony to Empire: A Methodological Essay." *The Americas* 48, no. 3: 351–396.

Lexadin. 1996. "Código civil para el Distrito Federal en materia común y para toda la república en materia federal—1928." Available from http://www.solon.org/-Statutes/Mexico/Spanish/ccm.html. Accessed 2 February 2000; last HTML revision 6 June 1996.

———. 1998. "Brasil. Código Civil, Lei no. 3071 de 1 de janeiro de 1916 (alterado pela MP 1675-40 em 29/07/98)." Available from http://www.lexadin.nl/wlg/-legis/nofr/oeur/lxwebra.htm. Accessed 22 February 2000.

Lipton, Michael. 1985. "Land Assets and Rural Poverty." World Bank Staff Working Paper no. 744. Washington, D.C.

Little, Cynthia J. 1978. "Education, Philanthropy, and Feminism: Components of Argentine Womanhood, 1860–1926." In Asunción Lavrin, ed., *Latin American Women: Historical Perspectives,* pp. 235–254. Westport, Conn.: Greenwood Press.

Llanos de Vargas, Carmen. 1996. *Las mujeres productoras de alimentos en Bolivia: Diagnóstico y políticas.* San José: IICA-BID.

Long, Norman, and Bryan R. Roberts. 1978. "Introduction." In Norman Long and Bryan Roberts, eds., *Peasant Cooperation and Capitalist Expansion in Central Peru,* pp. 3–44. Austin: University of Texas Press.

López P., Rosalia, and María Elena Jarquín S. 1996. "Organizaciones de mujeres: Entre la manipulación y la toma de conciencia (El caso de la Frailesca, Chiapas)." *Revista Mexicana de Ciencias Políticas y Sociales* 41, no. 164: 171–190.

Luciak, Ilja. 1999. "Gender Equality in the Salvadoran Transition." *Latin American Perspectives* 26, no. 2: 43–67.

———. 2000. "Gender Equality and Democratization in Central America: The Case of the Revolutionary Left." Prepared for delivery at the 2000 meeting of the Latin American Studies Association, March 16–18, Miami.

Lukes, Steven. 1974. *Power: A Radical View.* London: Macmillan.

Luna, Lola G. 1999. "La relación de las mujeres y el desarrollo en América Latina:

Apuntes históricos de dos décadas (1975–1995)." *Anuario Hojas de Warmi* (Barcelona), no. 10: 61–78.

Luna, Lola G., and Norma Villareal. 1994. *Movimientos de mujeres y participación política en Colombia, 1939–1991.* Barcelona: Universitat Barcelona and CICYT.

Luzuriaga C., Carlos. 1982. *Situación de la mujer en el Ecuador.* Quito: Maurilia Mendoza.

Lynch, Barbara Deutsch. 1991. "Women and Irrigation in Highland Peru." *Society and Natural Resources* 4: 37–52.

Macas, Luis. [1995.] "La ley agraria y el proceso de movilización por la vida." In Ramón Torres Galarza, ed., *Derechos de los pueblos indígenas: Situación jurídica y políticas de estado*, pp. 30–37. Quito: CONAIE-CEPLAES-ABYA YALA.

Macassi León, Ivonne. 1996a. "Informe sobre legislación y mujer rural: Situación de la mujer rural frente a la legislación en Peru." Working paper, March, Centro de la Mujer Peruana "Flora Tristán," Lima.

———. 1996b. "Mujeres rurales: A pesar de las leyes, persisten obstáculos que las discriminan." *La Chacarera* (Lima) 21: 36–39.

Macedo, Roberto. 1987. "Brazilian Children and the Economic Crisis: The Evidence from the State of São Paolo." In Andrea Cornia, Richard Jolly, and Francis Stewart, eds., *Adjustment with a Human Face: Protecting the Vulnerable and Promoting Growth*, pp. 28–56. Oxford: Clarendon.

Mack, Macarena, J. Medel, V. Oxman, L. Rebolledo, V. Riquelme, and X. Valdés. 1987. "La condición de la mujer rural en Chile." In Centro de Estudios de la Mujer, ed., *Mujeres campesinas, América Latina, algunas experiencias: Chile, Ecuador, Peru*, pp. 47–80. Santiago de Chile: Ediciones de Las Mujeres no. 6, ISIS Internacional.

Mackinlay, Horacio, and Juan de la Fuente. 1996. "La nueva legislación rural en México." *Debate Agrario* 25: 73–88.

MacPherson, C. B., ed. 1981. *Property: Mainstream and Critical Positions.* Toronto: University of Toronto Press.

Madden, Liddiethe. 1992. *El acceso de la mujer a la tierra en Costa Rica.* San José: Fundación Arias.

MAG (Ministry of Agriculture) and NORAD (Norwegian Authority for International Development). N.d. "A nombre de la pareja" (pamphlet). Managua: Ministry of Agriculture and NORAD, Programa de Capacitación Técnica a Productoras Agropecuarias.

Mama Maquín. 1998. "Presentation to the Inter-Regional Consultation on Women's Land and Property Rights under Situations of Conflict and Reconstruction." Memo, 16–18 February, Kigali, Rwanda.

Mannarelli, María Emma. 1991. "Las relaciones de género de la sociedad colonial peruana, ilegitimidad y jerarquías sociales." In María del Carmen Feijoo, ed., *Mujer y sociedad en América Latina*, pp. 63–107. Buenos Aires: CLACSO.

Manzanilla, V. 1977. *Reforma Agraria Mexicana*. Mexico City: Editorial Porrua.

Martínez, Luciano. 1992. "Mujer y empleo en el sector rural ecuatoriano." Memo. Quito: INEM-UNICEF.

Martínez, María Antonia, Sara Elisa Rosales, and Gilda Rivera. 1995. *El acceso de la mujer a la tierra en Honduras*. San José: Fundación Arias and Centro de Derechos de Mujeres.

Martínez, Ofelia, and Clyde Soto. 1996. "Políticas y planes de igualdad de oportunidades: Aspectos introductorios." In Grupo Igualdad, ed., *Igualdad: Derecho de todas las mujeres, obligación del Estado,* pp. 16–41. Asunción: CDE (Centro de Documentación y Estudios) and Fundación Friedrich Ebert.

Martins de Carvalho, Horacio. 1999. "Banco da Terra: O banco dos donos da terra." *Jornal Sem Terra* (March): 10.

Massolo, Alejandra, ed. 1992. *Mujeres y ciudades: Participación social, vivienda y vida cotidiana*. Mexico City: El Colegio de México.

Matear, Ann. 1997. "Gender and the State in Rural Chile." *Bulletin of Latin American Research* 16, no. 1: 97–106.

Mazeaud, Henri León, and Jean Mazeaud. 1976. *Lecciones de derecho civil: Parte persona*. Vol. 4. Buenos Aires: Ediciones Jurídicas Europa-América.

Medrano, Diana. 1996. "Recursos productivos y la participación: Aspectos jurídicos en el caso de la mujer rural en Colombia." Paper presented at the Regional Meeting on Agrarian Legislation, FAO, Lima, April.

Meertens, Donny. 1986. "Mujer y vivienda en un barrio de invasión." *Revista Foro* (Bogotá), no. 4: 38–46.

———. 1998. "Víctimas y sobrevivientes de la guerra: Tres miradas de género." *Revista Foro* (Bogotá), no. 34: 19–35.

Meinzen-Dick, R. S., L. R. Brown, H. Sims Feldstein, and A. R. Quisumbing. 1997. "Gender, Property Rights, and Natural Resources." *World Development* 25, no. 8: 1303–1316.

Melmed-Sanjak, Jolyne. 1998. "Mercados de tierras en América Central." In Banco Interamericano de Desarrollo, ed., *Perspectivas sobre mercados de tierras rurales en América Latina,* pp. 30–55. Washington, D.C.: BID.

Mendes de Almeida, Candido. 1870. *Código philippino ou ordenaçoes do Reino de Portugal*. 14th ed. Rio de Janeiro: Typ. do Instituto Philomáthico.

Méndez, María Julia. 1984a. "Sexo y reforma agraria." *Diario La República* (Lima), January 19: n.p.

———. 1984b. "Pena de muerte y reforma agraria." *Diario La República,* April 3: 11.

Mendoza Orantes, Ricardo. 1994. *Recopilación de leyes civiles, constitución, códigos: De familia, civil, procesal civil, leyes notariales*. San Salvador: Ed. Difusión.

———, ed. 1997. *Recopilación de leyes civiles actualizadas*. San Salvador: Dist. Difusión.

Menjivar, Rafael. 1969. *Reforma agraria: Guatemala, Bolivia, Cuba.* San Salvador: Ed. Universitaria.

México, Estados Unidos Mexicanos. 1992. *Resumen general del XI censo general de población y vivienda 1990.* Aguascalientes: Instituto Nacional de Estadística Geográfica e Informática.

Meyer, Carrie A. 1989. *Land Reform in Latin America: The Dominican Case.* New York: Praeger.

Mies, María, and Vandana Shiva. 1994. *Ecofeminism.* London: Zed Books.

Miller, Francesca. 1991. *Latin American Women and the Search for Social Justice.* Hanover, N.H.: University Press of New England.

Millones, José. 1996. "Ponencia." Paper prepared for the seminar on Mujeres cajamarquinas después de la conferencia mundial de Beijing, September, Ministry of Agriculture, Cajamarca.

Minnaar, Renee. 1998. "Género dentro de un discurso étnico: El ejemplo del hoy movimiento indígena en el Ecuador." In Guadalupe León, ed., *Ciudadanía y participación política,* pp. 69–80. Quito: Ed. ABYA-YALA.

MinAg (Ministerio de Agricultura). 1998. *Indicadores de género en el sector agropecuario del Perú (con base en los resultados del tercer CENAGRO).* Lima: Ministerio de Agricultura.

MinBienes (Ministerio de Bienes Nacionales). 1996. "Evaluación de la gestión y medición de impacto del Programa de Saneamiento y Regularización de la Pequeña Propiedad Rural." Memo, Santiago: Ministerio de Bienes Nacionales.

MinBienes (Ministerio de Bienes Nacionales) and Consultorías Profesionales AGRARIA Ltda. 1996. "Evaluación de la gestión y medición de impacto del Programa de Saneamiento y Regularización de la Pequeña Propiedad Rural." Vol. 1. Memo, November, Santiago.

Minc, Carlos. 1985. *A reconquista da terra: Estatuto da terra, lutas no campo e reforma agraria.* Rio de Janeiro: Jorge Zahar.

Mingo, Araceli. 1996. "El sinuoso camino de las organizaciones productivas campesinas." *Estudios Sociológicos* 14, no. 40: 75–95.

Ministerio de Agicultura, INCORA. 1989. *Informe de gerencia 1988.* Bogotá: INCORA.

Ministerio de Bienestar Social/SSDR/PRONADER/IICA. 1995. "Informe de resultados de la incorporación de estrategias en beneficio de las mujeres." Quito, March.

Ministerio de Justicia. 1993. *Código de Familia, Título IV.* San Salvador: Ed. Último Decenio.

MINUGUA (Misión de Naciones Unidas en Guatemala). 1995. "La problemática de la tierra en Guatemala." Memo, Unidad de Análisis y Documentación. Guatemala City, April.

Moghadam, Valentine M. 1998. "The United Nations Decade for Women and Beyond." In Nelly Stromquist, ed., *Women in the Third World: An Encyclopedia of Contemporary Issues,* pp. 477–485. New York: Garland.

Molano, Alfredo. 1997. "Abramos el Debate." *Semana* (Bogotá), no. 234: 26–27.

Molina, Giselle, Montserrat Sagot, and Ana Carcedo. 1992. "Análisis y diagnóstico de la ley de igualdad real de la mujer." Memo, CEFEMINA, San José.

Molyneux, Maxine. 1981. "Socialist Societies Old and New: Progress Towards Women's Emancipation." *Feminist Review* 8: 1–34.

———. 1985. "Mobilization without Emancipation? Women's Interests, The State and Revolution in Nicaragua." *Feminist Studies* 11, no. 2: 227–254.

———. 1986. "¿Movilización sin emancipación? Intereses de la mujer, el estado y la revolución: El caso de Nicaragua." In José Luis Corragio and Carmen Diana Deere, eds., *La autodeterminación en los pequeños países periféricos,* pp. 341–60. Mexico City: Siglo XXI.

Molyneux, Maxine, and Deborah Lynn Steinberg. 1995. "Mies and Shiva's Ecofeminism: A New Testament?" *Feminist Review* 49 (Spring): 86–107.

Monroy Cabra, Marco Gerardo. 1979. *Matrimonio civil y divorcio en Colombia.* Bogotá: Ed. TEMIS.

———. 1996. *Derecho de familia y de menores.* Bogotá: Librería Jurídica Wilches.

Montgomery, John D. 1984. "Land Reform as an International Issue." In John D. Montgomery, ed., *International Dimensions of Land Reform,* pp. 1–6. Boulder: Westview.

Montoya, Aquiles. [1993.] "El sector cooperativo: Elemento clave para una estrategia de desarrollo popular." *Revista Estudios Centroamericanos* 539: 855–876.

Morales Benítez, Otto. 1986. *Alianza para el Progreso y reforma agraria.* 2d ed. Bogotá: Publicaciones Universidad Central.

Mora Alfaro, Jorge. 1994. "Políticas agrícolas y apertura económica en los años noventa." In Hugo Noé Pino, Pedro Jiménez, and Andy Thorpe, eds., *¿Estado o mercado? Perspectivas para el desarrollo agrícola centroamericano hacia el año 2000.* Tegucigalpa: Posgrado Centroamericano en Economía y Planificación (POSCAE) and Universidad Nacional Autónoma de Honduras (UNAH).

Morineau Iduarte, Marta. 1975. "Condición jurídica de la mujer en el México del siglo XIX." In *La condición jurídica de la mujer en México.* Mexico City: Universidad Nacional Autónoma de México.

Morley, Samuel. 1995. "Structural Adjustment and the Determinants of Poverty in Latin America." In Nora Lustig, ed., *Coping with Austerity: Poverty and Inequality in Latin America,* chap. 2. Washington, D.C.: Brookings Institution.

Moser, Caroline. 1987. "What Hope for the Future?" In Caroline Moser and Linda Peake, eds., *Women, Human Settlements, and Housing,* pp. 185–203. London: Tavistock Publications.

————. 1989. "Gender Planning in the Third World: Meeting Practical and Strategic Gender Needs." *World Development* 17, no. 11: 1799–1826.

————. 1991. "La planificación de género en el Tercer Mundo: Enfrentando las necesidades prácticas y estrategias de género." In Virginia Guzmán, et al., eds., *Una nueva lectura: Género y desarrollo,* pp. 55–124. Lima: Centro Flora Tristán.

————. 1993. *Gender Planning and Development: Theory, Practice and Training.* London: Routledge.

Moya, Ruth. 1987. "Educación y mujer indígena en el Ecuador." Paper presented to the Regional Office for Education of UNESCO, Quito, March.

MST (Movimento dos Trabalhadores Sem Terra), Coletivo Nacional de Gênero. 2000. *Mulher sem terra.* São Paulo: Associação Nacional de Cooperação Agrícola and INCRA.

Muñoz, Jorge. 1999. *Los mercados de tierras rurales en Bolivia.* Serie Desarrollo Productivo no. 61. Santiago: CEPAL.

Muñoz, Jorge, and Isabel Lavadenz. 1997. "Reforming the Agrarian Reform in Bolivia." Development Discussion Paper no. 589. HIID, Harvard University, Cambridge, Mass., June.

Munzer, Stephen R. 1990. *A Theory of Property.* Cambridge: Cambridge University Press.

Naciones Unidas. 1976. *Informe de la Conferencia del Año Internacional de la Mujer, México, D.F., 19 de junio al 2 de julio de 1975.* New York: United Nations.

Nash, June, and Patricia Fernández-Kelley, eds. 1983. *Women, Men and the International Division of Labor.* Albany: State University of New York Press.

Nash, June, and Helen Icken Safa, eds. 1976. *Sex and Class in Latin America.* New York: Praeger Publishers.

Navarro, Marysa. 1979. "Research on Latin American Women." *Signs* 15, no. 1: 111–120.

Navarro, Wilson, Alonso Vallejo, and Xabier Villaverde. 1996. *Tierra para la vida.* Quito: Fondo Ecuatoriano Populorum Progresso.

Nazzari, Muriel. 1995. "Widows as Obstacles to Business: British Objections to Brazilian Marriage and Inheritance Laws." *Comparative Study of Society and History* 37, no. 4: 781–802.

Nicaragua, República de. 1997a. *Código Civil de la República de Nicaragua.* Vols. 1 and 2. 2d ed. Managua: Ed. Jurídica.

————. 1997b. *VII censos de población y III de vivienda 1995.* Managua: Instituto Nacional de Estadística y Censos.

Nicholas, Susan Cary, Alice M. Price, and Rachel Rubin. 1986. *Rights and Wrongs: Women's Struggle for Legal Equality.* 2d ed. New York: The Feminist Press.

Nitlapán, Equipo de. 1994. "Descolectivización: Reforma agraria desde abajo." *Envío* (Managua), November, pp. 17–34.

Nobre, Miriam. 1998. "Gênero e agricultura familiar a partir de muitas vozes." In Miriam Nobre, Emma Siliprandi, Sandra Quintela, and Renata Menasche, eds., *Gênero e agricultura familiar.* São Paulo: Sempreviva Organização Feminista (SOF).

Noé Pino, Hugo, Andrew Thorpe, and Rigoberto Sandoval. 1992. *El sector agrícola y la modernización de Honduras.* Tegucigalpa: Centro de Documentación de Honduras, Posgrado Centroamericano en Economía y Planificación del Desarrollo.

NPDC (National Population and Development Commission). [1999.] *Cairo + Report on Brazil.* Brasilia: Comisão Nacional de Poblação e Desenvolvimento.

Oakley, Annie. 1972. *Sex, Gender, and Society.* London: Temple Smith.

OAS (Organization of American States). 1961. *Official Documents Emanating from the Special Meeting of the Inter-American Economic and Social Counsel at the Ministerial Level Held in Punta del Este, Uruguay, from August 5–17, 1961.* Washington, D.C.: General Secretariat of the OAS.

———. 1997. *Report on the Situation of Human Rights in Brazil.* Washington, D.C.: OAS, Inter-American Commission on Human Rights.

Ocampo, José Antonio. 1998. "Políticas públicas y equidad de género." In Departamento Nacional de Planeación, *Macroeconomía, género y estado,* pp. 309–319. Bogotá: DNP, BME, GTZ, and Tercer Mundo Editores.

Ochoa, Silvia Nelly, and Fabiola Campillo. 1996. "La política del sector agropecuario frente a la mujer productora de alimentos en la región andina." In Brenda Kleysen, ed., *Productoras Agropecuarias en América del Sur,* pp. 115–304. San José: BID-IICA.

Ochoa Pérez, Verónica. 1998. "Sucesiones en materia agraria." *Estudios Agrarios* no. 9. Available from http://www.pa.gob.mx/publica/pao70901.htm. Accessed on 19 January 2000.

OIT (Oficina Internacional del Trabajo). 1987. *Informe VI (1): Revisión parcial del convenio sobre poblaciones indígenas y tribales, 1957 (num. 107).* Geneva: OIT.

OIT (Organización Internacional del Trabajo). 1996. *Pueblos indígenas y tribales: Guía para la aplicación del convenio num. 169 de la OIT.* Geneva: International Labor Office and International Center for Human Rights and Democratic Development.

Okin, Susan. 1989. *Justice, Gender and the Family.* New York: Basic Books.

Olavarria, José. 2000. "De la identidad a la política: Masculinidades y políticas públicas." In José Olavarria and Rodrigo Parrni, eds., *Masculinidad(es): Identidad, sexualidad, y familia,* pp. 11–28. Santiago: FLACSO-Chile, Red de Masculinidad, and Universidad de Academia de Humanismo Cristiano.

Olivera, Mercedes. 1995. "Práctica feminista en el Movimiento Zapatista de Liberación Nacional." In Rosa Rojas, ed., *Chiapas: ¿Y las mujeres qué?* Vol. 2, pp. 168–184. Mexico City: Ed. La Correa Feminista.

Oliveira Costa, Albertina, and Maria Cristina Bruschini, eds. 1992. *Uma questão de gênero.* Rio de Janeiro: Editora Rosa Dos Tempos and Fundação Carlos Chagas.

ONAM (Oficina Nacional de la Mujer). 1997a. *Anteproyecto de reforma al Código Civil, Decreto Ley 106.* Guatemala City: Ministerio de Trabajo y Previsión Social, ONAM, Proyecto Mujer y Reformas Jurídicas.

———. 1997b. *Las obligaciones legislativas a favor de las mujeres derivadas de los Acuerdos de Paz.* Guatemala City: ONAM, Adscrita al Ministerio de Trabajo y Previsión Social.

ONIC (Organización Nacional Indígena de Colombia). 1996. *Mujer, tierra y cultura: Ayer, hoy y mañana: Taller suramericano de mujeres indígenas, memorias, Santandercito, Cundinamarca, Colombia, 10 al 14 de julio de 1995.* Bogotá: ONIC and Dirección Nacional para la Equidad de la Mujer, Presidencia de la República.

Orellana, Nancy. 1996. *¿Quién por nosotras? Un estudio sobre las políticas estatales dirigidas a la mujer rural.* San Salvador: Instituto de Investigación, Capacitación y Desarrollo de la Mujer.

Ortner, Sherry B. 1974. "Is Female to Male as Nature Is to Culture?" In Michelle Zimbalist Rosaldo and Louise Lamphere, eds., *Woman, Culture and Society,* pp. 67–88. Stanford: Stanford University Press.

Osborne, Raquel. 1995. "Acción positiva." In Celia Amoros, ed., *Diez palabras clave sobre mujer,* pp. 297–329. Navarra: Ed. Verbo Divino.

Ospina R., Rosa Inés. 1998. *Para empoderar a las mujeres rurales.* Misión Rural, vol. 8. Bogotá: IICA and Tercer Mundo Editores.

Otero, Gerardo. 1989. "Agrarian Reform in Mexico: Capitalism and the State." In William Thiesenhusen, ed., *Searching for Agrarian Reform in Latin America,* pp. 276–304. Boston: Unwin Hyman.

Ots y Capdequi, José María. 1969. *Historia del derecho español en América y del derecho indiano.* Madrid: Ed. Aguilar.

Pacari, Nina. [1995.] "La mujer indígena, medio ambiente y biodiversidad." In Ramón Torres Galarza, ed., *Derechos de los pueblos indígenas: Situación jurídica y políticas de estado,* pp. 17–28. Quito: CONAIE-CEPLAES-ABYA-YALA.

———. 1998. "La mujer indígena: Reflexiones sobre su identidad de género." In Guadalupe León, ed., *Ciudadanía y participación política,* pp. 59–68. Quito: Ed. ABYA-YALA.

Pacay, Margarita. 1995. "Las mujeres retornadas también tienen derecho a la tierra." *Prensa Libre* (Guatemala City), December 14, 76–77.

Pacheco Balanza, Diego. 1999. "Tierra del padre o del marido, ¿da lo mismo?

Usos y costumbres y criterios de equidad." Draft report, Fundación Tierra, La Paz.

Padilla, Martha Luz, Clara Murguialday, and Ana Criquillón. 1987. "Impact of the Sandinista Agrarian Reform on Rural Women's Subordination." In C. D. Deere and M. León, eds., *Rural Women and State Policy*, pp. 121–141. Boulder: Westview Press.

Paraguay, República de. 1985. *Censo agropecuario 1981*. Asunción: Ministerio de Agricultura y Ganadería.

———. 1991. *Censo agropecuario 1991*. Asunción: Ministerio de Agricultura y Ganadería.

Pastor, Manuel. 1987. "The Effects of IMF Programs in the Third World: Debate and Evidence from Latin America." *World Development* 15, no. 2: 249–262.

Pateman, Carole. 1988. *The Sexual Contract*. Stanford: Stanford University Press.

Paulson, Susan. 1996. "Familias que no 'conyugan' e identidades que no conjugan: La vida en Mizque desafía nuestras categorías." In Silvia Rivera Cusicanqui, ed., *Ser mujer indígena, chola o birlocha en la Bolivia postcolonial de los años 90*, pp. 85–162. La Paz: Subsecretaría de Asuntos de Género, Ministerio de Desarrollo Humano.

Paulson, Susan, and Pamela Calla. 2000. "Ethnicity and Gender in Development Politics: Transformation or Paternalism?" *Latin American Journal of Anthropology*, forthcoming.

Paz Carcamo, Guillermo. 1997. *Guatemala: Reforma agraria*. Guatemala: FLACSO.

PCC (Partido Comunista de Cuba). 1976. *Sobre el pleno ejercicio de la igualdad de la mujer: Tesis y resolución*. Havana: Comité Central del Partido Comunista de Cuba.

Pedroni, Guillermo, and Alfonso Porres. 1991. *Políticas agrarias, programas de acceso a la tierra y estrategias de comercialización campesina*. Guatemala: Procurador de los Derechos Humanos.

Pérez Alemán, Paola. 1990. *Organización, identidad y cambio: Las campesinas en Nicaragua*. Managua: Centro de Investigación y Acción para los Derechos de la Mujer (CIAM).

Pérez Rojas, Niurka, and Dayma León Echevarría. 1998. "Género, reforma agraria y justicia social en Cuba (1959–1961): Primera aproximación." Paper presented to the XXI International Congress of the Latin American Studies Association, September, Chicago.

Perú, República de. 1975. *II censo nacional agropecuario 1972*. Lima: Oficina Nacional de Estadísticas y Censos.

———. 1984a. *Código civil, legislativo 295*. Lima: Ed. Cultural Cuzco, S.A.

———. 1984b. *Censos nacionales, VIII de población, III de vivienda, 12 de julio de 1981*. Lima: Instituto Nacional de Estadística.

———. 1987. "Ley general de comunidades campesinas, ley no. 24656 de 13/4/87." *Diario "El peruano"* (Lima).

————. 1994a. *Censos nacionales de 1993, IX de población, IV de vivienda: Resultados definitivos.* Lima: Instituto Nacional de Estadística e Informática.

————. 1994b. *Perú: Informe nacional sobre la mujer, la agricultura y el desarrollo rural.* Report prepared for the Fourth World Conference on Women in Beijing, China. April, Lima.

————. 1995. "Nueva ley de tierras, ley no. 26505" (pamphlet). Lima: Movimiento de Hermandades del Trabajo.

————. 1996. *Tercer censo nacional agropecuario. 1994. Resultados definitivos.* Lima: Instituto Nacional de Estadística e Informática.

Perrin, Michel, and Marie Perruchon. 1997. "Introduction." In M. Perrin and M. Perruchon, eds., *Complementariedad entre hombre y mujer: Relaciones de género desde la perspectiva amerindia,* pp. 7–22. Quito: Ed. ABYA-YALA.

Phillips, Lynne. 1987. "Women, Development, and the State in Rural Ecuador." In C. D. Deere and M. León, eds., *Rural Women and State Policy,* pp. 105–123. Boulder: Westview.

Placencia, María Mercedes, and Elvia Caro. 1998. "Institucionalidad para mujer y género en América Latina y el Caribe: Estudio regional." Report prepared for the Interamerican Development Bank, Quito.

Pollis, Adamantia. 1996. "Cultural Relativism Revisited: Through a State Prism." *Human Rights Quarterly* 18: 316–344.

Presidencia-DNP (Departamento Nacional de Planeación). [1998.] *Plan nacional de desarrollo, 1998–2002: Cambio para construir la paz.* Bogotá: Presidencia de la República and Departamento Nacional de Planeación.

Prieto, Mercedes. 1998. "El liderazgo en las mujeres indígenas: Tendiendo puentes entre género y etnia." In CEPLAES, ed., *Mujeres contracorriente: Voces de líderes indígenas,* pp. 15–37. Quito: CEPLAES.

Primer Encuentro. 1998. *Primer encuentro de mujeres campesinas e indígenas de América Latina y del Caribe, noviembre 28 a diciembre 2 de 1988, Bogotá, Colombia.* Bogotá: FENSUAGRO, ANUC, and ONIC (Organización Nacional Indígena de Colombia).

PRISMA (Programa Salvadoreño de Investigación sobre Desarrollo y Medio Ambiente). 1996. *La deuda del sector agropecuario: Implicaciones de la condonación parcial.* San Salvador: PRISMA.

PROCEDE (Programa de Certificación de Derechos Ejidales y Titulación de Solares). 1997. "Avances en la regulación de la tenencia de la tierra." *La Jornada* (Mexico City), January 8, 18.

PRO-EGEDAGRO. 1999. "Política para la equidad de género en el agro hondureño 1999–2015 y plan de equidad de género en el agro (1999–2002)." Draft proposal, February, Tegucigalpa.

PRONAM (Programa Nacional de la Mujer). 1999. "La mujer rural en México: Avance en la incorporación de la problemática de la mujer rural." Draft memo, PRONAM, Mexico City.

PROTIERRA (Comisión Institucional para el Desarrollo y Fortalecimiento de la Propiedad de la Tierra). 1997. "Estrategia y lineamientos de política para el tema tierras." Memo, April, Guatemala City.

Quiroga León, Anibal. 1990. "Matrimonio y divorcio en el Perú: Una aproximación histórica." In Fernando de Trazegnies Granda, et al., eds., *La familia en el derecho peruano*, pp. 82–99. Lima: Fondo Editorial, Pontificia Universidad Católica del Perú.

Quisumbing, Agnes R. 1998. "Women in Agricultural Systems." In Nelly Stromquist, ed., *Women in the Third World: An Encyclopedia of Contemporary Issues*, pp. 261–272. New York: Garland.

Quisumbing, Agnes R., Lynn Brown, Hillary S. Feldstein, Lawrence Haddad, and Christine Pena. 1995. *Women: The Key to Food Security*. Food Policy Report. Washington, D.C.: International Food Policy Research Institute.

Quisumbing, Agnes R., and John A. Maluccio. 1999. "Intrahousehold Allocation and Gender Relations: New Empirical Evidence." Policy Research Report on Gender and Development, Working Paper Series, no. 2. October. Washington, D.C.: International Food Policy Research Institute.

Radcliffe, Sarah. 1993. "People Have to Rise Up Like the Great Women Fighters: The State and Peasant Women in Peru." In Sarah Radcliffe and Sallie Westwood, eds., *"Viva": Women and Popular Protest in Latin America*, pp. 197–218. London: Routledge.

Ramos, Carmen. 1993. *Mujeres y revolución, 1900–1917*. Mexico City: Instituto Nacional de Estudios Históricos de la Revolución Mexicana.

Ramos, Josefina. 1990. "La situación jurídica de la mujer rural en Nicaragua." Paper presented to the workshop "Mecanismos Jurídicos que Posibilitan la Participación de la Mujer Rural en el Desarrollo Rural." September, FAO, Santiago.

Ranaboldo, Claudia. 1997. *Servicios de asistencia técnica privada en areas rurales: Las experiencias del FIDA en Bolivia*. La Paz: Centro de Información para el Desarrollo.

Rao, Mohan, and José María Caballero. 1990. "Agricultural Performance and Development Strategy: Retrospect and Prospect." *World Development* 18, no. 6: 899–913.

Rathgeber, Eva M. 1990. "WID, WAD, GAD: Trends in Research and Practice." *Journal of Developing Areas* 24: 489–502.

Razavi, Shahrashoub, and Carol Miller. 1995. "From WID to WAD: Conceptual Shifts in the Women and Development Discourse," pp. 1–14. Occasional Paper no. 1. Geneva: United Nations Research Institute for Social Development (UNRISD).

Rebolledo, Loreto. 1993. "Las campesinas y los procesos de transformación en el agro Chileno." In Soledad Gonzáles Montes, ed., *Mujeres y relaciones de género en la antropología latinoamericana*, pp. 87–104. Mexico City: El Colegio de México.

————. 1995. "Vivir y morir en familia en los albores del siglo." *Proposiciones* 26: 166–180.

Red de Educación Popular. 1992. *Protagonismo de la mujer en el levantamiento indígena*. Quito: Centro María Quilla y Red de Educación Popular entre Mujeres.

Reinhardt, Nola. 1988. *Our Daily Bread: The Peasant Question and Family Farming in the Colombian Andes*. Berkeley: University of California Press.

Renzi, María Rosa, and Sonia Agurto. 1994. *¿Qué hace la mujer nicaragüense ante la crísis economica?* Managua: Fundación Internacional para el Desarrollo Ecónomico Global (FIDEG).

————. 1998. *La esperanza tiene nombre de mujer*. Managua: Fundación Internacional para el Desarrollo Ecónomico Global (FIDEG).

República Dominicana. 1966. *Quinto censo nacional agropecuario, 1960*. Santo Domingo: Oficina Nacional de Estadística.

Revilla, Ana Teresa. 1990. "La familia campesina en la legislación agraria." In Fernando de Trazegnies Granda, et al., eds., *La familia en el derecho peruano*, pp. 428–447. Lima: Fondo Editorial, Pontificia Universidad Católica del Perú.

Reydon, Bastiaan, and Ludwig Ramos, eds. 1996. *Mercado y políticas de tierras (experiencias en América Latina)*. Campinas: Instituto de Economía, Universidade Estadual de Campinas.

Riger, Stephanie. 1997. "¿Qué está mal con el empoderamiento?" In Magdalena León, ed., *Poder y empoderamiento de las mujeres*, pp. 55–74. Bogotá: TM Editores and Universidad Nacional, Facultad de Ciencias Humanas.

Rivas A., Lucía, and Aurora Bautista. 1996. "Informe sobre la situación de la mujer y la tenencia de la tierra en Guatemala." Paper presented to the Primer Encuentro CentroAmericano, Intercambio de Experiencias sobre la Sensibilización de Género con Demandantes de Títulos Agrarios, December, Managua.

Robles B., Héctor, Gloria Artís, Julieta Salazar, and Laura Muñoz. 2000. *Y ando yo también en el campo! Presencia de la mujer en el agro mexicano*. Mexico City: Procuraduría Agraria.

Rocha Cassaya, Silvia. 1998. "Efectos comparativos de la titulación a la pareja y la titulación individual en las mujeres y los hombres del sector reformado." Consultancy report, Project IDF 28275, Unidad de la Mujer Campesina, Dirección General de Reforma Agraria, Ministerio de Agricultura, Ganadería y Forestal, December, Managua.

Rodríguez G., Arturo Nicolás. 1998. "Procede: Conceptos básicos y un perfil sobre sus avances." *Estudios Agrarios* (Mexico City), no. 10: n.p.

Rodríguez S., Eugenia. 2000. "Civilizing Domestic Life in the Central Valley of Costa Rica, 1750–1850." In Elizabeth Dore and Maxine Molyneaux, eds., *Hidden Histories of Gender and the State in Latin America*, pp. 85–107. Chapel Hill: Duke University Press.

Roeder, Marcia. 1994. "Género y riego." *Agua y Riego* (Lima) 3: 23–24.

———. 1996. "Género y riego: La mujer y su participación en los proyectos de riego." *Agua y Riego* (Lima) 8: 19–22.

Rojas, Rosa, ed. 1995. *Chiapas, ¿y las mujeres qué?* Mexico City: Ediciones del Taller Editorial La Correa Feminista.

Román, Isabel. 1994. *¿Conciliación o conflicto? Luchas campesinas y democracia en Costa Rica*. San José: Ed. Porvenir.

Roquas, Esther. 1995. "Gender, Agrarian Property, and the Politics of Inheritance in Honduras." Paper presented at the conference "Agrarian Questions: The Politics of Farming anno 2000," May 22–24, University of Wageningen, The Netherlands.

Rosales, Sara Elisa. 1994. "Informe final: El acceso, uso, tenencia y control de las mujeres a la tierra y a los servicios para la producción." Memo. Proyecto GCP/HON/017/NET/FAO, Tegucigalpa.

Rowlands, Jo. 1997. "Empoderamiento de las mujeres rurales en Honduras: Un modelo para el desarrollo." In Magdalena León, ed., *Poder y empoderamiento de las mujeres*, pp. 213–245. Bogotá: TM Editores and Universidad Nacional, Facultad de Ciencias Humanas.

Rubén, Raul, and Francisco Fúnez. 1993. *La compra-venta de tierras de la reforma agraria*. Tegucigalpa: Ed. Guaymuras.

Rubin, Gayle. 1975. "The Traffic in Women: Notes on the Political Economy of Sex." In Rayna Reiter, ed., *Toward an Anthropology of Women*, pp. 157–210. New York: Monthly Review Press.

Sacks, Karen. 1974. "Engels Revisited: Women, the Organization of Production and Private Property." In Michelle Zimbalist Rosaldo and Louise Lamphere, eds., *Woman, Culture and Society*, pp. 207–222. Stanford: Stanford University Press.

Safa, Helen. 1995. *The Myth of the Male Breadwinner: Women and Industrialization in the Caribbean*. Boulder: Westview Press.

Safilios-Rothschild, Constantina. 1983. "Women and the Agrarian Reform in Honduras." In *Land Reform: Land Settlement and Cooperatives*, pp. 15–24. Rome: FAO.

———. 1988. "The Impact of Agrarian Reform on Male and Female Incomes in Rural Honduras." In Daisy Dwyer and Judith Bruce, eds., *A Home Divided: Women and Income in the Third World*, pp. 216–228. Stanford: Stanford University Press.

Sagot, Montserrat. 1997. "The Struggle for Housing in Costa Rica: The Transformation of Women into Political Actors." In Ilse A. Leitinger, ed., *The Costa Rican Women's Movement: A Reader*, pp. 198–209. Pittsburgh: University of Pittsburgh Press.

SAIIC, South and Meso American Indian Rights Center. 1997. *Update on Guatemala*. Oakland, Calif.: SAIIC, April.

Salazar, Marcos. 1997. "La evolución del movimiento campesino en El Salvador." Paper presented to the seminar Uso y Tenencia de la Tierra, Guatemala City.

Salgado, Ramón (Coord.). 1994. *El mercado de tierras en Honduras*. Tegucigalpa: CEDOH (Centro de Documentación de Honduras).

———. 1996. "La tenencia de la tierra en Honduras." In Eduardo Baumeister, ed., *El agro hondureño y su futuro*, pp. 91–132. Tegucigalpa: CDR-ULA and Ed. Guaymuras.

Salguero, Elizabeth. 1995. *Primer encuentro de mujeres indígenas, campesinas, y originarias, Cochabamba, Bolivia, del 24 al 26 de 1995*. La Paz: Federación Nacional de Mujeres Campesinas de Bolivia "Bartolina Sisa," Coordinadora Nacional del Foro de ONG de Bolivia a la Cuarta Conferencia Mundial sobre la Mujer, Educación en Población-UNFPA.

———. 1996. "Informe, Reunión Nacional de Mujeres Rurales, La Paz, 21 y 22 de noviembre 1996: Socialización del primer Encuentro Latinoamericano y el Caribe de Mujeres Rurales." Memo, November, La Paz.

Sánchez, Enrique, ed. 1996. *Derechos de los pueblos indígenas en las constituciones de América Latina (Memorias del seminario internacional de expertos sobre régimen constitucional y pueblos indígenas en países de Latinoamérica. Villa de Leyva, Colombia, julio 17–22, 1996)*. Bogotá: COAMA.

Sánchez Gómez, Gonzalo. 1991. *Guerra y política en la sociedad colombiana*. Bogotá: El Ancora Editores.

Santa Cruz, Isabel. 1992. "Sobre el concepto de igualdad: Algunas observaciones." *ISEGORIA: Revista de Filosofía Moral y Política* (Madrid), no. 6: 145–152.

Santos, Boaventura de Sousa. 1997. "Hacia una concepción multicultural de los derechos humanas." *Análisis Político* (Bogotá) 31: 3–16.

Sapriza, Gabriela. 1985. *Obreras y sufragistas: ¿Un diálogo imposible?* Montevideo: Grupo de Estudios sobre la Condición de la Mujer en el Uruguay (GRECMU).

Schuler, Margaret. 1997. "Los derechos de las mujeres son derechos humanos: La agenda internacional del empoderamiento." In Magdalena León, ed., *Poder y empoderamiento de las mujeres*, pp. 29–54. Bogotá: TM Editores and Universidad Nacional, Facultad de Ciencias Humanas.

Schutte, Ofelia. 1998. "Latin America." In Alison Jaggar and Iris Young, eds., *A Companion to Feminist Philosophy*, pp. 87–95. Maiden, Mass.: Blackwell Publications.

Scott, Alison. 1991. "Informal Sector or Female Sector? Gender Bias in Urban Labour Market Models." In Diane Elson, ed., *Male Bias in the Development Process*, chap. 5. Manchester: Manchester University Press.

Scott, Cristopher. 1990. "Land Reform and Property Rights among Small Farmers in Chile, 1968–86." In David Hojman, ed., *Neo-Liberal Agriculture in Rural Chile*, pp. 64–90. New York: St. Martin's Press.

Scott, Joan W. 1988a. "Gender: A Useful Category of Historical Analysis." In Joan Wallach Scott, *Gender and the Politics of History,* pp. 28–50. New York: Columbia University Press.

———. 1988b. "Deconstructing Equality-Versus-Difference: Or, the Uses of Poststructuralist Theory for Feminism." *Feminist Studies* 14, no. 1: 33–50.

Sedo, Kattya. 1999. "Sobrevivirán las uniones de cooperativas" (interview with Sinforiano Cáceres, vice-president of FENACOOP, the National Association of Cooperatives). *El Observador Económico* (Managua), no. 89: 24–26.

Seiz, Janet. 1991. "The Bargaining Approach and Feminist Methodology." *Review of Radical Political Economics* 23, nos. 1–2: 22–29.

Seligson, Mitchell. 1980. "Thirty Years of Transformation in the Agrarian Structure of El Salvador, 1961–91." *Latin American Research Review* 30, no. 3: 43–74.

Seminario "Reformas al Artículo 4 constitutional." 1996. *Propuestas de las mujeres indígenas al Congreso Nacional Indígena.* Mexico City: Comisión de Seguimento de Mujeres de la ANIPA et al., and Benjamín Alvarez.

Sen, Amartya. 1980. "Economics and the Family." *Asian Development Review* 1: 14–26.

———. 1990. "Gender and Cooperative Conflicts." In Irene Tinker, ed., *Persistent Inequalities: Women and World Development,* chap. 8. New York: Oxford University Press.

Sen, Gita, and Caren Grown. 1985. *Development, Crises and Alternative Visions: Third World Women's Perspectives.* New York: Monthly Review Press.

SERNAM (Servicio Nacional de la Mujer). 1994. *Plan de igualdad de oportunidades para las mujeres, 1994–1999.* Santiago: Imprenta Andros Ltd.

———. 1997. *Propuestas de políticas de igualdad de oportunidades para las mujeres rurales.* Santiago: Imprenta Los Leones.

———. 2000. *Plan de igualdad de oportunidades entre mujeres y hombres: Lineamientos generales 2000–2010.* Santiago: SERNAM.

SERNAM/INDAP. 1997. *Mujer campesina y crédito en Chile.* Santiago: SERNAM/INDAP.

SERNAM/INDAP/CEDEM/FAO. 1994. "Seminario-taller: Bases para una propuesta de política de igualdad de oportunidades para la mujer rural." Memo, December, Santiago.

Serrano, Marcela. 1997. *El albergue de las mujeres tristes.* Santiago: Alfaguara.

Sevilla, Ampara. 1992. "Autoconstrucción y vida cotidiana." In Alejandra Massolo, ed., *Mujeres y ciudades: Participación social, vivienda y vida cotidiana,* pp. 219–237. Mexico City: Colegio de México, PIEM.

Sharrat, Sara. 1997. "The Suffragist Movement in Costa Rica, 1889–1949: Centennial of Democracy?" In Ilse A. Leitinger, ed., *The Costa Rican Women's Movement: A Reader,* pp. 61–83. Pittsburgh: University of Pittsburgh Press.

Shearer, Eric B., Susana Lastarría-Cornhiel, and Dina Mesbah. 1991. "The Reform of Rural Land Markets in Latin America and the Caribbean: Research, Theory, and Policy Implications." Land Tenure Center Paper no. 141. April, University of Wisconsin-Madison.

Shrage, Laurie. 1998. "Equal Opportunity." In Alison Jaggar and Iris Young, eds., *A Companion to Feminist Philosophy,* pp. 559–568. Maiden, Mass.: Blackwell.

Silva, Patricio. 1991. "The Military Regime and Restructuring of Land Tenure." *Latin American Perspectives* 18, no. 1: 15–32.

Silverblatt, Irene. 1980. "Andean Women under Spanish Rule." In Mona Etienne and Eleanor Leacock, eds., *Women and Colonization,* pp. 149–185. New York: Praeger.

————. 1991. "Interpreting Women in States: New Feminist Ethnohistories." In Micaela di Leonardo, ed., *Gender at the Crossroads of Knowledge: Feminist Anthropology in the Postmodern Era,* pp. 140–174. Berkeley: University of California Press.

Siqueira, Deis Elucy. 1991. "A organização das trabalhadoras rurais: O cruzamento de gênero e de classe social." In D. E. Siqueira, João G.L.C. Teixeira, and María Stela Grosso Porto, eds., *Tecnología agropecuaria e a organização dos trabalhadores rurais.* Brasilia: Universidade Nacional de Brasilia.

Sisto, María. 1996. "La política del sector agropecuario frente a la mujer productora de alimentos en el Cono Sur." In Brenda Kleysen, ed., *Productoras agropecuarias en America del Sur,* pp. 305–416. San José: BID-IICA.

Socolow, Susan. 1989. "Acceptable Partners: Marriage Choice in Colonial Argentina, 1778–1810." In Asunción Lavrin, ed., *Sexuality and Marriage in Colonial Latin America,* pp. 209–251. Lincoln: University of Nebraska Press.

Solario, Fortunata, Esther Revilla, Patricia Fuertes, and Gladys Navarro. 1996. *Intereses y garantías de las mujeres: Experiencias de crédito en Puno.* Lima: Servicio Nelandes de Voluntarios (SNV).

Sostres, María Fernanda, and Yara Carafa. 1992. "Propuestas de políticas agropecuarias para la mujer en la estrategia de desarrollo." In Coordinadora de la Mujer, ed., *Propuestas de políticas sectoriales para la participación de la mujer en la estrategia de desarrollo,* pp. 49–87. La Paz: Coordinadora de la Mujer.

Spedding, Alison L. 1997. "'Esa mujer no necesita hombre': En contra de la 'dualidad andina': Imágenes de género en los yungas de La Paz." In Denise Y. Arnold, ed., *Más allá del silencio: Las fronteras de género en los Andes,* pp. 325–343. La Paz: Instituto de Lengua y Cultura Aymara (ILCA) and Center for Indigenous American Studies and Exchange, Scotland (CIASE).

Spedding, Alison L., and David Llanos. 1998. "Derechos sobre la tierra: Lo que la ley INRA no dice." *Tinkazos: Revista Boliviana de Ciencias Sociales* (La Paz) 1: 14–25.

Spence, Jack, David Dye, Paula Worby, Carmen Rosa de León-Escribano, George Vickers, and Mike Lanchin. 1998. "Promise and Reality: Implementation of the Guatemalan Peace Accords" (pamphlet). Boston: Hemisphere Initiatives.

Stanfield, David. 1995. "Insecurity of Land Tenure in Nicaragua." LTC Research Paper no. 120. January. Land Tenure Center, University of Wisconsin, Madison.

Stanfield, David, Edgar Nesman, Mitchell Seligson, and Alexander Coles. 1990. "The Honduras Land Titling and Registration Experience." Memo. June. Land Tenure Center, University of Wisconsin, Madison.

Staudt, Kathleen. 1985. *Women, Foreign Assistance, and Advocacy Administration.* New York: Praeger.

Stephen, Lynn. 1993. "Restructuring the Rural Family: Ejidatario, Ejidataria, and Official Views of Ejido Reform." Occasional Paper no. 4. Latin American Studies Consortium of New England, University of Connecticut, Storrs.

——, ed. 1994. *Hear My Testimony: María Teresa Tula, Human Rights Activist of El Salvador.* Boston: South End Press.

——. 1996a. "Too Little, Too Late? The Impact of Article 27 on Women in Oaxaca." In L. Randall, ed., *Reforming Mexico's Agrarian Reform,* pp. 289–303. New York: M. E. Sharpe.

——. 1996b. "Interpreting Agrarian Reform in Two Oaxaca Ejidos: Differentiation, History, and Identities." In Wayne Cornelius and David Myhre, eds., *The Transformation of Rural Mexico: Reforming the Ejido Sector.* La Jolla, Calif.: Center for U.S. and Mexican Studies.

——. 1996c. "Relaçoes de gênero: Um estudo comparativo sobre organizaçoes de mulheres rurais no Mexico e no Brasil." In Zander Navarro, ed., *Politica, protesto e cidadania no campo,* pp. 29–61. Porto Alegre: Ed. da Universidade Federal do Rio Grande do Sul.

——. 1997. *Women and Social Movements in Latin America.* Austin: University of Texas Press.

——. 1998. "Gender and Grassroots Organizing: Lessons from Chiapas." In Victoria Rodríguez, ed., *Women's Participation in Mexican Political Life,* pp. 146–163. Boulder: Westview Press.

Sternbach, Nancy S., Marysa Navarro-Aranguren, Patricia Chuchryk, and Sonia Alvarez. 1995. "Feminisms in Latin America: From Bogotá to San Bernardo." In Barbara Laslett, Johanna Brenner, and Yesim Arat, eds., *Rethinking the Political: Gender, Resistance, and the State,* pp. 240–281. Chicago: University of Chicago Press.

Stetson McBride, Dorothy. 1987. *Women's Rights in France.* Westport, Conn.: Greenwood Press.

Stolen, Kristi Anne. 1987. *A media voz: Relaciones de género en la sierra ecuatoriana.* Quito: CEPLAES.

Stoner, K. Lynn. 1996. *From the House to the Streets: The Cuban Women's Movement for Legal Reform, 1898–1940*. Durham, N.C., and London: Duke University Press.

Stromquist, Nelly. 1997. "La búsqueda del empoderamiento: ¿En qué puede contribuir el campo de la educación?" In Magdalena León, ed., *Poder y empoderamiento de las mujeres,* pp. 75–98. Bogotá: TM Editores and Universidad Nacional, Facultad de Ciencias Humanas.

Stubbs, Jean, and Mavis Alvarez. 1987. "Women on the Agenda: The Cooperative Movement in Rural Cuba." In C. D. Deere and M. León, eds., *Rural Women and State Policy: Feminist Perspectives on Latin American Agricultural Development,* pp. 142–161. Boulder: Westview Press.

Suárez, Blanca. 1995. "Las manos más hábiles de los empaques: El aguacate y el mango en Michoacán." In Sara María Lara Flores, ed., *Jornaleras, temporeras y boias frias: El rostro del mercado de trabajo en América Latina,* pp. 103–122. Caracas: Ed. Nueva Sociedad and UNRISD.

Suárez, Mireya, and Marlene Libardoni. 1992. *Mulheres e desenvolvimento agrícola no Brasil: Uma perspectiva de gênero*. Brasilia: IICA, Escritorio no Brasil.

Subirats, Marina. 1998. "Cuando lo personal es político y es política: La Cuarta Conferencia de Naciones Unidas sobre la Mujer." *Icaria Antrazyt* (Barcelona) 116: 173–197.

Summerfield, Gale. 1998. "Allocation of Labor and Income in the Family." In Nelly Stromquist, ed., *Women in the Third World: An Encyclopedia of Contemporary Issues,* pp. 218–226. New York: Garland Publishing.

Tavares, Ricardo. 1995. "Land and Democracy: Reconsidering the Agrarian Question." *NACLA Report on the Americas* 28, no. 6: 23–29.

Téllez Kuenzler, Luis. 1994. *La modernización del sector agropecuario y forestal*. Mexico City: Fondo de Cultura Económica.

Thiesenhusen, William. 1989. "Introduction." In W. Thiesenhusen, ed., *Searching for Agrarian Reform in Latin America,* pp. 1–41. Boston: Unwin and Hyman.

———. 1995. *Broken Promises: Agrarian Reform and the Latin American Campesino*. Boulder: Westview Press.

Thomas, Duncan. 1990. "Intra-household Resource Allocation: An Inferential Approach." *Journal of Human Resources* 25, no. 4: 635–663.

Thomas, Florance. 1997. *Conversación con un hombre ausente*. Bogotá: Arango Editorial.

Thorpe, Andy. 1995. "Agricultural Modernisation and Its Consequences for Land Markets in Honduras." Paper presented to the Conference on Agrarian Questions, The Politics of Farming anno 2000, May, University of Wageningen, The Netherlands.

Tinker, Irene. 1990. "The Making of a Field: Advocates, Practitioners, and Scholars." In Irene Tinker, ed., *Persistent Inequalities: Women and World Development,* pp. 27–53. Oxford: Oxford University Press.

Tinker, Irene, and Jane Jaquette. 1987. "UN Decade for Women: Its Impact and Legacy." *World Development* 15, no. 3: 419–427.

Tinsman, Heidi E. 1996. "Unequal Uplift: The Sexual Politics of Gender, Work and Community in the Chilean Agrarian Reform, 1950–1973." Ph.D. diss., Yale University.

Tomasello Hart, Leslie. 1989. *Situación jurídica de la mujer casada: La reforma de la Ley 18.802 al Código Civil*. Valparaiso: Edeval.

Tomasevski, Katarina. 1993. *Women and Human Rights*. London: Zed Books.

Torres Galarza, Ramón, ed. [1995.] *Derechos de los pueblos indígenas: Situación jurídica y políticas de estado*. Quito: CONAIE, CEPLAES, and ABYA-YALA.

Torres Paredes, Rene. 1988. *Código de familia con modificaciones y concordancias*. La Paz: Ed. Los Amigos del Libro, Colección Jurídica "Guttentag."

Tribunales Agrarios. 1994. *Legislación agraria actualizada*. Mexico City: Tribunal Superior Agrario.

Trinchet, Oscar. 1984. *La cooperativización de la tierra en el agro cubano*. Havana: Ed. Política.

Udaeta, María Esther. 1993. "Mujeres rurales y políticas estatales en Bolivia: 1989–1993." *Revista de Desarrollo Rural Alternativo* (La Paz) 11/12: 103–130.

UNAG (Unión Nacional de Agricultores y Ganaderos). 1993. "Memoria del Cuarto Encuentro Nacional de Mujeres Campesinas." Memo, UNAG, Sección de la Mujer, Managua.

UNDP (United Nations Development Program). 1997. *Human Development Report 1997*. New York: UNDP.

UNESCO. 1966. *Statistical Yearbook/Annuaire Statistique 1965*. Paris: Imprimerie J. F. Mayenne.

United Nations. 1980. *Report of the World Conference of the United Nations Decade for Women: Equality, Development and Peace, Copenhagen, 14 to 30 July 1980*. Doc. A/CONF.94/35. New York: United Nations.

———. 1982. *Convention on the Elimination of All Forms of Discrimination against Women (1980)*. New York: United Nations; reprinted by the Human Rights Program, Department of Secretary of State, Minister of Supply and Services, Ottawa, Canada.

———. 1986. *Report of the World Conference to Review and Appraise the Achievements of the United Nations Decade for Women: Equality, Development and Peace, Nairobi, 15–26 July 1985*. Doc. A/CONF.116/28/Rev.1. New York: United Nations.

———. 1992. *General Assembly, Forty-seventh session, Item 79 of the preliminary list, A/47/50, Annex, "The Geneva Declaration for Rural Women."* Doc. A/47/308, E/1992/97. New York: United Nations.

———. 1993. *World Conference on Human Rights: The Vienna Declaration and*

Programme of Action, June 1993. Doc. DP7/1393-39399. New York: United Nations.

—————. 1995a. *Report of the International Conference on Population and Development, Cairo, 5–13 September 1994.* Doc. A/CONF.171/13/Rev.1. New York: United Nations.

—————. 1995b. *The Copenhagen Declaration and Programme of Action, World Summit for Social Development.* Doc. DPI/1707-9515294. New York: United Nations.

—————. 1996. *Report of the Fourth World Conference on Women, Beijing, 4–15 September 1995.* Doc. A/CONF.177/20/Rev. 1. New York: United Nations.

Urioste, Miguel. 1992. *Fortalecer las comunidades: Una utopía subversiva, democrática . . . y posible.* La Paz: AIPE (Asociación de Instituciones de Promoción y Educación), PROCOM, and TIERRA.

Urioste, Miguel, and Diego Pacheco. 1999. "Bolivia: Mercado de tierras en un nuevo contexto (Ley INRA)." Paper presented at the Workshop on Land in Latin America: New Context, New Claims, New Concepts." May 26–27. CEDLA, CERES, WAU, Amsterdam.

Valcarcel Carnero, Marcel. 1997. "Género y riego: Una mirada optimista." *Agua y Riego* (Lima), no. 9: 27–30.

Valdés, Teresa. 2000. "Estudios de género para el siglo XXI en América Latina: Algunas notas para el debate." Paper prepared for XXII International Congress of the Latin American Studies Association, March 16–18, Miami.

Valdés, Teresa, and Enrique Gomáriz, eds. 1995. *Mujeres latinoamericanas en cifras: Tomo comparativo.* Santiago de Chile: FLACSO and Instituto de la Mujer, España.

—————, eds. 1997. *Nicaragua: Mujeres latinoamericanas en cifras.* Santiago: Instituto de la Mujer, Ministerio de Asuntos Sociales de España, FLACSO.

Valdés, Ximena. 1994. "Chile: Mujeres rurales y su participación en el desarrollo: Bases preliminares para la implementación del Plan de Igualdad de Oportunidades en la agricultura y el sector rural." Consultancy report to INDAP/SERNAM, December, Santiago.

—————. 1995. "Cambios en la división sexual del trabajo y en las relaciones de género entre la hacienda y la empresa exportadora en Chile." In Sara María Lara Flores, ed., *El rostro femenino del mercado de trabajo rural en América Latina,* pp. 61–71. Caracas: Nueva Sociedad y UNRISD.

—————. 1999. "Presentación." In Magdalena León and Carmen Diana Deere, *Género y derechos de las mujeres a la tierra en Chile,* pp. 9–21. Santiago: CEDEM.

Valdés Paz, Juan. 1997. *Procesos agrarios en Cuba, 1959–1995.* Havana: Ed. Ciencias Sociales.

Valencia Zea, Arturo. 1978. *Derecho civil.* Vol. 5, *Derecho de familia.* 7th ed. Bogotá: Ed. TEMIS.

———. 1992. *Código Civil.* Vol. 6, *De sucesiones.* Bogotá: Ed. TEMIS.

Valencia Zea, Arturo, and Álvaro Ortiz Monsalve. 1995. *Derecho civil.* Vol. 2, *Derecho de familia.* 2d ed. Bogotá: Ed. Temis.

———. 1997. *Derecho civil.* Vol. 1, *Parte general y personas.* 18th ed. Bogotá: Ed. Temis.

Valenzuela, Alejandra, and Hector Robles Berlanga. 1996. "Presencia de la mujer en el campo mexicano," *Estudios agrarios: Revista de la Procuraduría Agraria* 5: 31–63.

Valenzuela, María Elena. 1997. "El programa nacional de apoyo a jefas de hogar de escasos recursos." In María Elena Valenzuela, Sylvia Venegas, and Carmen Andrade, eds., *De mujer sola a jefa de hogar: Género, pobreza y políticas públicas,* pp. 187–216. Santiago: SERNAM.

Valera Moreno, Guillermo. 1997. "Las comunidades en el Perú: Una aproximación estadística." *Aportes para el debate* (Lima) 6.

Van Cott, Donna Lee, ed. 1994. *Indigenous Peoples and Democracy in Latin America.* New York: St. Martin's Press.

———. 1999. "Latin American Constitutions and Indigenous Peoples." Memo, Department of Political Science, University of Tennessee.

Van Halsema, Ineke. 1991. *Housewives in the Field: Power, Culture and Gender in a South-Brazilian Village.* Amsterdam: CEDLA.

Vargas, Virginia. 1989. *El aporte de la rebeldía de las mujeres.* Lima: Centro de la Mujer Peruana "Flora Tristán."

———. 1992. *Como cambiar el mundo sin perdernos.* Lima: Centro de la Mujer Peruana "Flora Tristán."

———. 1998. "Modulo ciudadanía." In AGENDE, CFEMEA, and Centro de la Mujer Peruana "Flora Tristán," ed. *Mujeres al Timón,* pp. 87–117. Mexico City: AGENDE, CFEMEA, and Centro de la Mujer Peruana "Flora Tristán."

Vargas, Virginia, Saskia Wieringa, and Geertje Lyclama. 1996. "Introduction." In V. Vargas, S. Wieringa, and G. Lyclama, eds., *El triángulo del empoderamiento,* 1–53. Bogotá: Tercer Mundo.

Varley, Ann. 1994. "Housing the Household, Holding the House." In Gareth Jones and Peter M. Ward, ed., *Methodology for Land and Housing Market Analysis,* pp. 120–134. London: UCL Press

———. 1996. "From Private to Public: Gender, Illegality, and Legalization of Urban Land Tenure." Paper presented at the International Seminar Series on Informal Land and Housing Markets: The Role of Social Networks. November. Department of Urban Studies and Planning, MIT, with the Lincoln Institute of Land Policy, Cambridge, Mass.

Vázquez García, Verónica. 1996. "Donde manda el hombre, no manda la mujer: Género y la tenencia de la tierra en el México rural." *Cuadernos Agrarios,* no. 13: 63–83.

Velásquez Toro, Magdala. 1989. "Condición jurídica y social de la mujer." In *Nueva historia de Colombia,* vol. 4, pp. 9–60. Bogotá: Ed. Planeta.

———. 1995. "La república liberal y la lucha por los derechos civiles y políticos de las mujeres." In *Las mujeres en la historia de Colombia.* Vol. 1, *Mujeres en historia y política,* pp. 183–227. Bogotá: Presidencia de la República and Grupo Ed. Norma.

Venegas, Sylvia. 1995. "Las temporeras de la fruta en Chile." In Sara María Lara Flores, ed., *El rostro femenino del mercado de trabajo rural en América Latina,* pp. 213–246. Caracas: Nueva Sociedad and UNRISD.

Vermeer, Riné. 1989. "La política agraria de la administración Arias en el marco del ajuste estructural." In Reuben William, ed., *Los campesinos frente a la nueva década: Ajuste estructural y pequeña producción agropecuaria en Costa Rica.* San José: Ed. Porvenir, CECADE.

Villalobos, Lorena. 1993. *Mujeres en el desarrollo rural.* San José: Instituto de Desarrollo Agrario, Dirección de Planificación.

Villareal, Norma. 1995. *Fundamentos para la planificación con perspectiva de género: Resultado del diagnóstico en 13 municipios de la cuenca del río Risaralda.* Bogotá: Carder-Canada Project.

———. 1997. "Economía campesina, movimiento de mujeres y estado." *Revista Javeriana* (Bogotá), 65: 379–390.

———. 1998. "Sectores campesinos, mujeres rurales, y estado en Colombia." Informe preliminar de investigación (memo). Bogotá: Universidad Nacional, Facultad de Ciencias Humanas, Programa de Estudios de Género, Mujer y Desarrollo.

Villaroel, Buenaventura, and Guillermo Barrios Ávila. 1969. *Legislación agraria y jurisprudencia.* La Paz: n.p.

Víquez Astorga, Judith. 1996. "Situación de la mujer y la tenencia de la tierra en Costa Rica." Instituto de Desarrollo Agrario, Programa Mujer y Familia, San José, Costa Rica. Paper presented to the First Central American Conference on Intercambio de Experiencias sobre Sensibilización de Género con Demandantes de Titulación Agraria, December, Managua.

Vogelgesang, Frank. 1996. "Los derechos de propiedad y el mercado de la tierra rural en América Latina." *Revista de la CEPAL,* 58: 95–112.

Warman, Arturo. 1997. *La transformación agraria: Origen, evolución, retos.* Vol. 2. Mexico City: Secretaría de la Reforma Agraria.

WEDO (Women's Environment and Development Organization). 1998. *Mapping Progress: Assessing Implementation of the Beijing Platform 1998.* New York: WEDO.

Weeks, John. 1995. "Macroeconomic Adjustment and Latin American Agriculture since 1980." In John Weeks, ed., *Structural Adjustment and the Agricultural Sector in Latin America and the Caribbean,* pp. 61–91. New York: St. Martin's Press.

Wells, William C. 1925. "Women's Property Rights in Latin America." *Bulletin of the Pan American Union* 59, no. 3: 232–240.

Whittick, Arnold. 1979. *Woman into Citizen*. London: Athenaneum.

Wieringa, Saskia E. 1997. "Una reflexión sobre el poder y la medición del empoderamiento de género del PNUD." In Magdalena León, ed., *Poder y empoderamiento de las mujeres,* pp. 147–172. Bogotá: TM Editores and Universidad Nacional, Facultad de Ciencias Humanas.

Wilkie, James W., ed. 1993. *Statistical Abstract of Latin America*. Vol. 31. Los Angeles: UCLA Latin American Center Publications.

———, ed. 1998. *Statistical Abstract of Latin America*. Los Angeles: UCLA Latin American Center Publications.

Wood, Elisabeth. 1996. "The Peace Accords and Postwar Reconstruction." In James K. Boyce, ed., *Economic Policy for Building Peace: The Lessons of El Salvador,* pp. 73–106. Boulder: Lynne Rienner Publishers.

Woortmann, Ellen F. 1995. *Hedeiros, parentes e compadres*. São Paulo and Brasilia: Hucitec and Edunb.

Worby, Paula. 1999. "Guatemalan Refugee and Returnee Women Petition Their Rights: The Fight for Joint Ownership of Community Land." Manuscript, Program in Agrarian Studies, Yale University.

World Bank. 1996a. *El Salvador, Moving to a Gender Approach: Issues and Recommendations*. Report No. 14407-ES. Washington, D.C.: Sector Leadership Group.

———. 1996b. *Staff Appraisal Report, Honduras: Natural Resources Management and Land Administration Pilot Project*. Report No. 15917-110. Washington, D.C.: Sector Leadership Group.

Wyss, Brenda. 1995. "Gender and the Economic Support of Jamaican Households: Implications for Children's Living Standards." Ph.D. diss., University of Massachusetts, Amherst.

Ybarnegaray P., Roxana. 1997. "Tenencia y uso de la tierra en Bolivia." In Academia de Ciencias, ed., *Agricultura: Hoy y mañana*. La Paz: Academia de Ciencias.

Young, Iris Marion. 1990. *Justice and the Politics of Difference*. Princeton, N.J.: Princeton University Press.

Young, Kate. 1988. "Reflections on Meeting Women's Needs." In K. Young, ed., *Women and Economic Development: Local, Regional, and National Planning Strategies,* pp. 1–30. Oxford: Berg Publishers, and Paris: UNESCO.

———. 1991. "Reflexiones sobre cómo enfrentar las necesidades de las mujeres." In Virginia Guzmán et al., eds., *Una nueva lectura: Género en el desarrollo,* pp. 15–24. Lima: Centro de la Mujer Peruana "Flora Tristán."

———. 1993. *Planning Development with Women: Making a World of Difference*, London: Macmillan.

————. 1997. "El potencial transformador en las necesidades prácticas: Empoderamiento colectivo y el proceso de planificación." In Magdalena León, ed., *Poder y empoderamiento de las mujeres,* pp. 99–118. Bogotá: TM Editores and Universidad Nacional, Facultad de Ciencias Humanas.

Zamosc, León. 1994. "Agrarian Protest and the Indian Movement in the Ecuadorian Highlands." *Latin American Research Review* 29, no. 3: 37–69.

Zapata, Emma. 1995. "Neoliberalismo y mujeres rurales en México." In Ximena Valdés, Ana María Arteaga, and Carolina Arteaga, eds., *Mujeres: Relaciones de género en la agricultura,* pp. 377–406. Santiago: Centro de Estudios para el Desarrollo de la Mujer.

Zapata, Emma, Marta Mercado, and Blanca López. 1994. *Mujeres rurales ante el nuevo milenio.* Mexico City: Colegio de Postgraduados en Ciencias Agrícolas.

Zepeda L., Guillermo. 1998. "Cuatro años de PROCEDE: Avances y desafíos en la definición de derechos agrarios en México." *Estudios Agrarios,* no. 9. Available on http://www.pa.gob.mx/publica/pa070901.htm. Accessed 19 January 2000.

Zevallos, José Vicente. 1989. "Agrarian Reform and Structural Change: Ecuador since 1964." In William Thiesenhusen, ed., *Searching for Agrarian Reform in Latin America,* pp. 42–69. Boston: Unwin Hyman.

Zimmerman, Mary. 1954. "The Contractual Capacity of Married Women in the Americas: A Comparative Study." *Michigan State Bar Journal* 33, no. 7: 27–36.

Newspapers:

Correio do Povo (Pôrto Alegre, Rio Grande do Sul)

Diario de Centro América (Guatemala City)

Diario "El Peruano" (Lima)

Diario La República (Lima)

El Observador Económico (Managua)

El Periódico (Guatemala City)

El Peruano (Lima)

El Tiempo (Bogotá)

Jornal Sem Terra (São Paulo)

La Gaceta, Diario Oficial (Managua)

La Jornada (Mexico City)

La Prensa (Managua)

Prensa Libre (Guatemala City)

Revista Dinero (Bogotá)

Semana (Bogotá)

Index

ACNUR (Alto Comisionado de las Naciones Unidas para los Refugiados), 217, 219, 221–22
ADC (Alianza Democrática Campesina), 214–16, 358, 360
affirmative action, 8, 19–20, 22; and positive discrimination, 20, 194, 198, 200–1
Agarwal, Bina, 6 11, 15–17, 26–28, 31, 226, 289
agrarian reform, 61–106, 354–55; and civil war, 160, 164, 167, 174; and exclusion of women, 3, 63, 69–70, 81, 95, 99–105, 116, 349–50; and expropriation, 65–67, 354; and expropriation of women, 98; and form of land distribution, 67–68, 354; and household headship, 69, 76, 80, 85, 87–89, 91, 93, 102–4; and incorporation of gender equity, 106; and inheritance, 61, 105–6; legislation, 65, 102, 145, 332; scope of, 68–69, 88, 90, 93, 95, 98. *See also specific countries*
Agrarian reform beneficiaries: categories of, 67, 74, 76, 79, 80, 84–85, 87, 93; selection criteria, 71, 74, 80, 84–85, 89, 93, 103; by sex, 72, 75–76, 78, 80, 82, 84–87, 89–91, 93, 96, 98, 100–1
agriculture: census data, 2, 312–15; economically active population, 140, 362; exports, 140, 326, 362; productivity, and women, 16–17, 102; work, by women, *see* gender division of labor; labor market
Alliance for Progress: and agrarian reform, 62–64, 79–95
altruism, 14, 26, 339

AMNLAE (Asociación de Mujeres Sandinistas "Luisa Amanda Espinoza"), 204
AMTRS (Articulação de Mulheres Trabalhadoras Rurais do Sul), 130, 136, 360
ANAMURI (Asociación Nacional de Mujeres Rurales), 134, 360
ANAP (Asociación Nacional de Agricultores Pequeños), 76–77, 100
ANIPA (Asamblea Nacional Indígena por la Autonomía), 154, 257, 359
ANMTR (Articulação Nacional de Mulheres Trabalhadoras Rurais), 130, 191, 360
ANMUCIC (Asociación Nacional de Mujeres Campesina e Indígenas de Colombia), 86, 129, 172, 192–98, 336, 360
ANUC (Asociación Nacional de Usuarios Campesinos), 131, 193, 358, 360
Argentina: married women's property rights, 33–34, 49
Asociación de Mujeres de El Salvador, 132–33
Asociación de Mujeres Mexicanas Organizadas en Red, 132
Asociación de Mujeres Productoras Rurales de Costa Rica, 132, 202, 360
assets: distribution by gender, 2, 13, 23, 332. *See* land ownership
ATC (Asociación de Trabajadores del Campo), 96, 161, 359, 361

bargaining approach/framework, 26–28
bargaining power/strength/position: empirical evidence of, intra-family, 28–29, 119; of women in community, factors affecting, 8, 28; of women in family, factors affecting, 8, 27–30, 187, 225, 339–40. *See also* land ownership

Beijing conference. *See* United Nations conferences on women

bilateral inheritance. *See* inheritance

Bolivia: agrarian law of 1996, 171, 174–77, 243; —, and collective lands, 175–77; —, and gender, 176–78, 228, 245–246; —, and land redistribution, 177; agrarian reform, 68– 69, 73–76, 171; —, beneficiaries by sex, 75–76; —, and exclusion of women, 73–76; —, and expropriation, 65; indigenous movement, 239, 242–246; —, and gender issues, 244–45; —, and territorial rights, 243–44; inheritance and bargaining power, 29; inheritance practices, 271–73, 290; inheritance rights, 58, 60; inheritance by widows, 59–60, 281–82, 284; marital regimes, 51, 53–54; national women's office, 245; neoliberalism, 175; rural women's movement, 128–29, 244–45, 253

Boserup, Ester, 107–8

Brazil: agrarian reform, 66, 87–90, 171, 179, 191; —, beneficiaries by sex, 89–90; —, and peasant movement, 87–90, 171, 179–80; —, and women, 87–90, 104, 181; inheritance laws, 58–59, 277; inheritance practices, 277–80, 287; inheritance by widows, 60–61, 282, 287, 289; joint allocation and titling, 89, 188–92; land bank, 180–81; landless movement, 178, 180–81; land occupations, 178, 179; land ownership by sex, 313–14; land taxation, 188; marital regimes, 36, 51; married women's property rights, 43, 48; national women's office, 123, 188–89; women's land rights, 191–92; women's movement, 46, 188–92

CAP (Consejo Agrario Permanente), 153, 359

CBCS (Christian Base Communities), 128, 132, 178, 360

CEDAW (Committee to Eliminate All Forms of Discrimination Against Women), 122–23

CEFEMINA (Centro Feminista de Información y Acción), 199

Centro de la Mujer Peruana "Flora Tristán," 130, 304–5

Chapman Catt, Carrie, 45–46

child custody, 37, 39, 43–44, 48

Chile: agrarian reform, 64–65, 67–68, 92–95; —, beneficiaries by sex, 93; —, and expropriation, 66; —, and women, 93–96, 100, 104, 127; counter-reform, 141–44; —, and impact on women, 142–44; —,

and land market, 144, 324; family farming, 141, 144; income distribution, 144; indigenous land rights, 237–38; inheritance, evidence on, 315; inheritance practices, 275–77; inheritance rights, 56–58, 61; inheritance by widows, 56–57, 59–60, 282–83, 287, 289; land acquisition by sex, 315–16; land titling, 308–11; —, and female-headed households, 309–11; marital regimes, 49, 51–53; national women's office, 124, 126, 309; neoliberal policies, 141–43; Plan of Equality of Opportunities, 124–26; ; rural women's organizations, 134; women in the labor force, agricultural, 143–44

CIDOB (Confederación Indígena del Oriente, Chaco y Amazonia), 243, 357, 360

citizenship, women's, 38–39, 349

civil codes, 39–40; and civil marriage, 40; and consensual unions, 55–56, 61; and the dual-headed household, 43, 187; and gender equality, 187; and inheritance, 15, 56, 58–61; and marital regimes, 40–43, 50–55, 102–4; Napoleonic, 39; postmarital residency, 39, 42, 48; reforms in Latin America, 41–50

class: and ethnicity, 247–48, 261; and gender, 4, 9, 10, 18, 35, 247–48, 261, 274, 349–50

CMC (Central de Mujeres Campesinas), 133

CNC (Comisión Nacional Campesina), 134, 290

collective land: adjudication of, 67–68, 355; and indigenous identity, 248–49, 258; individualization of, and gender, 255–57; rights and gender, 229. *See* property rights, collective/indigenous

Colombia: access to credit, 195; agrarian law of 1988, 86–87, 192–95; agrarian law of 1994, 171–74; —, and women, 172, 194–95; agrarian reform, 66, 68, 85–87, 171, 173, 96; —, beneficiaries by sex, 86–87, 193, 196–97; —, and female-headed households, 87, 194–98; —, and inheritance rights, 85–86; —, and peasant movements, 85; —, and women, 85–87, 104; inheritance by widows, 59–60; land titling programs 299–300; —, joint adjudication, 172, 192–95, 299; —, women in, 299–300; marital regimes, 51, 55; married women's property rights, 43, 48; national women's office, 124; neoliberalism, 171; rural women's movement,

129, 172, 192; —, and relation with state, 131, 196; women's land rights, 192–95

communal land. *See* indigenous rights and land; property rights, collective/indigenous

complementarity thesis, 249–50, 252, 258

CONAIE (Confederación de Nacionalidades Indígenas del Ecuador), 158–59, 239, 240–42, 246–248, 252–54, 358

CONAVIGUA (Coordinadora Nacional de Viudas de Guatemala), 133, 361

Confederación Nacional Campesina, 131

CONFENIAE (Confederación de Nacionalidades Indígenas del Amazonia Ecuatoriana), 239, 358

CONMIE (Consejo Nacional de Mujeres Indígenas del Ecuador), 134, 253, 360

consensual unions, 33, 122; and agrarian reform, 92; and class and ethnicity, 33; incidence of, 33, 55, 306; and inheritance rights, 56, 61, 92; recognition of 55–56, 198, 312

constitution: and citizenship, 38–39; gender equality in, 121–22, 194; and indigenous rights, 237–38, 242, 244; women's land rights in, 188–89

CONTAG (Confederação Nacional dos Trabalhadores na Agricultura), 180, 188–90, 192, 357, 360

cooperatives: in agrarian reform, 67–68, 83–85, 96–97, 104; credit and service, 77; dissolution of, 142, 145, 161–63; exclusion of women in, 83, 220–21; production, 78–79, 355; women in, 85, 96–98, 100, 161–63, 341–42

Coordinadora de Mujeres Mapuches, 134

Coordinadora Nacional Plan Ayala 131

COPMAGUA (Coordinadora de Organizaciones del Pueblo Maya de Guatemala), 167

Costa Rica: agrarian reform, 65–66, 79–80, 95; —, beneficiaries by sex, 80, 200–1; —, and gender-progressive measures, 127, 198–200; —, and exclusion of women, 80, 104, 202; joint titling, 198, 200–1; Law to Promote the Social Equality of Women, 198–203; —, and positive discrimination, 198, 200–1; marital regimes, 38–39, 42–43, 51; national women's office, 126–27, 199, 337–38; Plan of Equality of Opportunities, 126–27, 203; rural women's organizations, 127, 132, 202–3; urban housing movement, 199

CPT (Comissão Pastoral da Terra), 178

credit, 326; for land purchases, 322–23, 327

CSUTCB (Confederación Sindical Unica de Trabajadores Campesinos de Bolivia), 129, 242–43, 357, 360

Cuba: agrarian reform, 63, 65–69, 76–79; —, and cooperatives, 100; —, and expropriation, 66; —, and women, 76–79;

cultural relativism, 230–32, 258–60

customary practices/rights/rules, 233–34, 258–59, 262; and discrimination against women, 229–30, 234–36

CUT (Central Unica dos Trabalhadores), 189, 357, 360

DAWN (Development Alternatives with Women in a New Era), 111

divorce, 33, 37; divorced women, property rights/claims, 55; initiated by women, 29–30; legislation on, 44, 50, 55; and remarriage, 30

domestic violence: women's bargaining power, 29

Dominican Republic: women's land rights, 333

dowry, 34; disappearance of, 57; women's control over, 34, 37

drug traffic and agrarian reform, 173–74

dual-headed household, 2, 8, 33, 49–50, 122, 332–33

ECLAC (Economic Commission for Latin America), 22

Ecuador: agrarian law of 1994, 158–59, 240–43; —, and gender, 159, 228, 241–42; —, and indigenous land rights, 158, 240–42; agrarian reform, 66, 68, 84–85; —, beneficiaries by sex, 84–85; —, and women, 84–85; common property, 36, 55; counter-reform, 158; indigenous movement, 239–41, 246; —, and gender issues, 247–54; —, and territories, 241–42; —, women's organization within the, 253–54; inheritance laws, 58; inheritance practices, 269–71; inheritance by widows, 59–60; inheritance and women's bargaining power, 29; land ownership by sex, 313–14, 322; land titling, 306–8; —, joint, 306–8; —, women in, 306–8; marital regimes, 54–55; married women's property rights, 48–49, 54–55; national women's office, 242, 245, 307

ECUARUNARI, 239, 247

efficiency argument for women's land rights, 16–17

El Salvador: agrarian code, 214–16; —, female-headed households in, 216; —,
joint titling, 214–15; —, women's participation in definition of, 215–16;
agrarian reform, 67–68, 97–99, 166,
216; —, beneficiaries by sex, 98, 212;
—, and inheritance rights, 99; —, and
women, 98–99, 211–13; agricultural
extension services, 328; counter reform, 163–64; —, impact on women,
164; individualization of land rights,
210–13, 216; inheritance of widows,
59–60, 281–82; land titling, 166; marital regimes, 42–43, 51, 54; national
women's office, 125, 166, 215; peace
accords, 164; —, and land distribution,
164–66, 214; —, and women's land
rights, 165, 211–14; rural women's organizations, 132–33, 211, 215
empowerment, women's, 10, 23–28; argument for women's land rights, 28–31;
definition of, 23; examples of, 29–30;
and participation in community structures, 72; processes of, 217–19; theories
of, 23–28
Encuentros Feministas, 24, 109, 134, 260
ENLAC (Encuentro Latino-Americano de la
Mujer Trabajadora Rural), 134–35, 261
equality, 2; argument for women's land
rights, 22–23, 330–31; versus difference, 16–18, 21; versus equity, 119–20;
formal versus real, 1, 17–20, 22–23,
330, 332; gains in formal gender,
331–33; to and between, 16–19
equality of opportunities, 19–20, 22; national
plans of, 22–23, 124–27, 298, 331–32
equity, 20–23; in inheritance rights, 119–20
EZLN (Ejército Zapatista de Liberación Nacional), 153–54, 257, 290

fall-back position, 27, 30; factors affecting,
in family, 27–29, 339–40; improvement
in, 77, 340
FAO (Food and Agriculture Organization),
115, 132
FARC (Fuerzas Armadas Revolucionarias de
Colombia), 174
Federación Nacional de Mujeres
Campesinas de Bolivia "Bartolina
Sisa," 129, 253, 360
Federación Nacional de Uniones de UAIMS,
132, 361
female-headed households, 8, 20; discrimination against, 81, 104–5; incidence of
rural, 72, 75, 80, 82, 87, 90, 96, 98, 205;
increase in, 144, 194, 312–13; poverty

of, 144; priority to, 20, 80, 87, 172,
185–86; recognition of land rights of,
73, 87, 104, 168, 340
feminist movement, 3–4, 258–60; See also
women's movement
feminist theory, 14, 110, 339
FEMUC (Federación de Mujeres Campesinas
de Honduras), 129, 361
FEMUPROCAN (Federación de Mujeres Productoras de Nicaragua), 135, 361
FEPP (Fondo Ecuatoriano Populorum Progresso), 322
FMC (Federación de Mujeres Cubanas), 77
FMLN (Frente Farabundo Martí para la Liberación Nacional), 133, 164–65, 211–14,
360
Folbre, Nancy, 14, 26
FONAPAZ (Fondo para la Paz), 168, 221
FONATIERRAS (Fondo de Tierras), 222, 223
food: intra-household allocation of, 14–15;
self-sufficiency and women's provision
of, 14–15
Fraser, Nancy, 9, 17–18, 21
FSLN (Frente Sandinista de Liberación Nacional), 204

GAD (Gender and Development), 111–13
gender: bias, 4, 22, 99; concept, 110–11; and
equality, 113, 184; identity, 9, 111; interests, 112
gender division of labor, 3, 11, 21–22; in
agriculture, 3, 83, 144, 289; and invisibility of women, 102, 340
gender progressive change, definition of, 6;
instituting, 224
gender relations, transformation of, 9, 21,
23, 25, 31, 331
Geneva Declaration for Rural Women, 117
Guatemala: agrarian reform, 63, 65–66, 68,
80–81, 95, 170; —, beneficiaries by sex,
81; —, and expropriation, 65–66; —,
and inheritance, 80–81; —, and women,
81, 171, 228; civil code, 220–21; —,
and women's rights, 49; heads of
household, 222; inheritance by widows,
59–60; joint allocation and titling, 171,
217–23; land bank, 169–70, 222–24;
land titling, 171; marital regimes, 49,
51, 55; married women's property
rights, 49, 55; national women's office,
217, 223; peace accords, 167–71,
216–17; —, and cooperatives, 220–21;
—, and displaced populations, 168,
216, 218–20, 223; —, and female-
headed households, 168, 216, 222–23;
—, and indigenous rights, 168; —, and

land rights, 167–69, 216, 219; —, women's participation in, 169, 216; —, and women's rights, 167–69, 223; repression of peasantry, 167; rural women's organizations, 133, 217–22

Honduras: agrarian law of 1992, 156–58, 295–96; —, gender in, 208–9; agrarian reform, 66, 68, 81–84, 95; —, beneficiaries by sex, 82; —, data on, 82; —, and women, 82–84, 209–10; counterreform, 156; —, and cooperatives, 156–57; —, and women's land rights, 156–58; example of property and bargaining power, 30; inheritance rights, 59–60, 82–84, 299; joint allocation and titling, 157–58, 208–10, 298, 333, 336; land titling program, 294–99; —, women in, 295–99; marital regimes, 42–43, 49, 51, 53, 298; national women's office, 210, 337; rural women's organizations, 129, 135, 209–10
household(s): assumptions regarding, 14, 339; inequities within, 11, 14–15
housewife/mother's clubs, 82, 94, 128, 165
housing movements, women in, 9, 199

IACW (Inter American Commission of Women), 46
illegitimacy. See consensual unions
ILO (International Labor Organization), 110, 232–34; Accord 107, 232–33; Accord 169, 231, 233–236
IMU (Instituto de Investigación, Capacitación y Desarrollo de la Mujer), 133, 215
income-generating projects, women's, 71, 86, 110, 123, 327
income pooling, 13–14
indigenous movement, 6, 228–30, 249–51, 258–59; and demands of, 229, 234–37; and Five Hundred Years of Resistance Campaign, 234, 239, 243–44, 261–62; and gender relations, 247–54, 259, 261; and relation to women's movement, 247, 254, 260–61. See Bolivia, Ecuador
indigenous population, 234–35
indigenous rights, 168, 232–36; and land, 168, 233–40, 251–52; and territories, 234, 237; and women's land rights, 234–36. See also specific countries
inheritance, 12–13, 264–66; in Andes, 266–272; and bargaining power of women, 37, 279, 289; and contestation by women, 274, 290–91; and control over land, 277, 280, 289–90; importance for women, 314–18; and legal

rights, 7, 35, 56–61, 117–18, 255, 290, 343; —, of widows, 56–61, 281–84, 343; practices, 264–65, 287–291, 334–36, 345; —, bilateral, 37, 264, 266–71, 274; —, parallel, 264, 266–68, 272; —, partible, 318; —, patrilineal, 265, 268, 270–78; regional variations in, 266, 271; and tendency toward gender equality, 268–69, 273–74, 279–80, 288–89, 344–45; and testamentary freedom, 56–60, 71, 99; by widows, 281–87, 343–44; —, and marital regimes 281–83. See also specific countries
Integrated Rural Development, 86, 110
Inter-American Development Bank, (IADB), 292, 302, 313
international agencies and gender advocacy, 171, 184–85, 216–17, 222–24
international women's conferences. See United Nations conferences on women

joint allocation and titling of land. See land rights; land titles; and also specific countries

labor force, agricultural, 362; women in, 45, 104, 143–44, 321–22
labor market, agricultural: feminization of, 5, 143, 155–56; wages from, 156
land: concentration of, 16; form of acquisition, by gender, 314–18; fragmentation of, 265; and poverty, 16; redistribution of, 349–50. See also land ownership
land banks, 139–40, 165, 180–81, 346–48
land colonization, 74, 84, 88–89
landholdings: average size by gender, 162, 164, 196, 301, 318–19, 321
landlessness, 350
land market(s), 293, 318–27; and depeasantization, 324–326; gender-biased, 314–29, 346; women as buyers, 144, 163, 275, 319–24, 346; women as sellers, 319–20, 324–27, 329. See also specific countries
land ownership: and bargaining power, 27–31, 187, 323–324, 329, 331, 338; and efficiency, 16–17; and gender inequality, 330; by sex, data on, 313–318
land reform. See agrarian reform
land rights, 3, 6–7; independent versus joint, 7–8, 187–88, 225–27, 338–40; meaning of, 3, 6–7; mechanisms of exclusion of women, 3, 102–5, 340–42; mechanisms of inclusion of women, 8–9, 126–27, 185–88, 210–11, 224–27, 294, 332–36, 349; for women, 3, 81, 107, 118,

land rights, for women *(cont.)*,
185–88, 228–29, 255, 332, 339–42;
women's need for, 255, 339–40
land titles: and credit access, 293; importance
of, 310–11; joint (with husband/
partner), 8, 84, 87, 185, 187–88, 224–26,
296, 299–300, 303–8, 313–14, 333–36;
obstacles to granting women, 225,
296–97, 302, 311–312; and women as
individual beneficiaries, 295–97, 299,
301, 309–10
land titling programs, 31, 139, 292–94,
311–12, 348–49. *See also specific
countries*
life expectancy, 15
literacy/illiteracy, 45, 118, 303, 328
Lutz, Bertha, 46

Madre Tierra, 133, 217, 361
Mama Maquín, 133, 217, 361
marital regimes, 12–13, 34, 37; and common
property 12–14, 34–35, 50, 53–54, 281,
311, 342; and default option, 40; and
family patrimony, 53; full common
property (comunidad absoluta), 12,
35–36, 50–51; and inheritance rights
and bargaining power, 32, 56–61, 283;
in nineteenth century, 32–36, 40–41;
participation in profits (gananciales),
31–35, 50–53, 281, 342; separation of
property, 35, 40–42, 50–53 , 342; in
twentieth century, 50–61; in UK and
US, 36–38. *See also* civil codes
marriage: incidence of compared to consensual union, 33
Mesa Permanente de Mujeres Rurales, 135,
361
Mexico: agrarian reform, 63, 67–73; —,
beneficiaries by sex, 72, 101; —, and
exclusion of women, 69–73; —, and
expropriation, 65; —, and inheritance
rights, 70–71; collective land rights, 69,
257–58; counter-reform, 150–56; —,
impact on women, 151–55; —, and
indigenous/collective land rights,
238–39, 341; —, and inheritance
rights, 152; —, and women's land
rights, 153–55, 228, 255, 257; inheritance practices, 273–74, 288, 317;
inheritance rights, 57–58, 255, 257,
282; inheritance by widows, evidence
on, 284–87; land acquisition by sex,
317–18; land market, 325–26; land titling program, 300–2; —, women in,
301–2 ; marital regimes, 40, 43–44,
51–52; national women's office, 123,

131–32, 357; rural women's organizations, 131–32, 153
MMTR (Movimento de Mulheres Trabalhadoras Rurais), 130, 360
MMTR-NE (Movimento de Mulheres Trabalhadoras Rurais do Noreste), 130, 136,
192, 360
movements, social. *See* indigenous movement; women's movement
Movimiento de Mujeres "Mélida Anaya
Montes," 132
MST (Movimento dos Trabalhadores Rurais
Sem Terra), 178, 180–81, 192, 347,
357–60
Mujeres por la Dignidad y la Vida "Las Dignas," 133, 211–12, 360–61

National Federation of Peasant Women of
Bolivia "Bartolina Sisa," 129, 253, 360
national women's offices, 5, 122–24, 327–28,
331. *See also specific countries*
neo-liberalism, 4–6, 137–41; and agrarian
legislation, 145, 171–72, 332–33; agricultural policies, 138, 161, 228, 326;
and counter-reform, 138–40, 145–49,
150–58, 160–64, 181–83, 228, 332; —,
and impact on women, 142, 145–47,
150–55, 162–64, 157–59, 182–83, 255;
—, and parcelization of cooperatives,
139–40,142, 157–58, 161–64, 182; —,
and parcelization of indigenous communities, 139, 142, 149–50, 158–59;
—, and privatization of state farms,
139–41, 160–61; and restitution of
lands, 139–41, 160; —, women's opposition to, 153–55, 157; stabilization
and structural adjustment programs, 4,
112, 137–38, 161; view of property and
land distribution, 139, 158, 292; and
women's land rights, 184–187, 255,
345–46. *See also specific countries,*
counter-reform
Nicaragua: agrarian reform, 64–68, 95–97; —,
beneficiaries by sex, 96, 160; —, and
cooperatives, 100; —, and expropriation, 66; —, and peasant organizations,
95–97, 133; —, and women, 95–97; —,
counter-reform, 160 –63; —, and cooperatives, 161–63, 324–25; —, and inheritance rights, 162; —, and land market,
163, 324–25; —, and land titling, 163,
205; —, and state farms, 160–61; —,
and impact on women, 161–163, 205;
female-headed households, 204–5; inheritance by widows, 59–60; joint allocation and titling, 204–8; —, data on,

206–8; land acquisition by sex, 316–17; marital regimes, 42–43, 49, 51; national women's office, 204, 357; resettlement of combatants, 160–61; rural women's movement, 133, 135, 204

nongovernmental organizations (NGOs), 4, 6, 109, 111–12, 132–34, 217, 224, 328–29; relationship with the State, 124–25; role in promoting women's land rights, 130, 217

Okin, Susan, 21
ownership of assets, 1–2, 12, 20, 22–23, 332

patriarchal ideologies, 3, 25, 102, 339
patrilineality, 263
peace accords, 165, 167, 214, 216; process leading to, 167; women in, 167–68, 211; women's land rights in, 165–67, 216. *See also* El Salvador, Guatemala
peasant organizations, 129–30; and discrimination against women, 105
Peru: agrarian legislation, 147–49; —, and inheritance, 148, 269, 290–91; agrarian reform, 64, 67–68, 90–92, 233; —, beneficiaries by sex, 90–91; —, and cooperatives, 91; —, and inheritance rights, 92, 148; —, and women's participation, 90–92, 104; counter-reform, 145–48; —, consequences of, 147–49; —, and cooperatives, 145–47; —, and indigenous/collective land rights, 145, 147–50, 239, 255–57; —, and land market, 320; —, and women, 145–46, 150, 255–57; inheritance and bargaining power, 29–30; inheritance and consensual unions, 92; inheritance practices, 266–267; inheritance rights, 60; inheritance by widows, 59–60, 281–82, 284; land market, women's participation in, 320–21; land titling, 147, 149, 302–6; —, joint adjudication and titling, 302–6; —, women in, 302–6; land ownership by sex, 312–15; marital regimes, 51, 54; national women's office, 357; peasant and indigenous communities, membership in, 148, 255–257
population, Latin America, 139, 362
post-marital residence practices, 7; patrilocal, 265–66, 274, 276, 278, 280; uxorilocal (uxorilocality), 29, 266–67, 272; virilocal (virilocality), 265–66, 272–274, 280, 287–88. *See also* civil codes
potestad marital, 32, 36, 39, 42–44, 54
poverty: reduction of rural, 144; and women, 16, 110, 118

PROCEDE (Programa de Certificación de Derechos Ejidales y Titulación de Solares Urbanos), 154–55, 238, 300
PRONADER (Programa Nacional de Desarrollo Rural), 306–8, 334
property rights: collective/indigenous, 158–59, 168, 229–31, 233–34, 236–39, 241, 244, 248–249, 258; —, and women, 229, 247–49, 257–58, 340; comparison with US and UK, 32–33; married women's 1, 9, 13, 20, 41–50 114–15, 118; —, and class position, 40, 45; in nineteenth century, 32–41, 42; single women's, 33–34; in Spanish colonial regime, 32–37; and twentieth century reforms, 41–50; in UK and US, 36–38. *See also* civil codes, inheritance and marital regimes
PTT (Programa de Transferencia de Tierras), 165, 167, 185, 211–14, 216, 225
public policy: and gender equity, 22; and women's land rights, 224

recognition versus redistribution, politics of, 9, 28, 350
Red Nacional de la Mujer Rural, 130, 361
Red Nacional de Mujeres Rurales e Indígenas, 134, 360
Red Nacional de Promotoras y Asesoras Rurales, 132
REDNAMURH (Red Nacional de Mujeres Rurales de Honduras), 135, 210, 361
refugees, 167–68, 194, 216, 218–20, 222–23
residence. *See* post-marital residence
Rowlands, Jo, 24
rural women's organizations. *See* women's movement, rural

social security benefits of rural women, 190–91
social security systems, 15, 343
suffrage, women's, 41, 47–48; and hemispheric conferences, 45–46

TIERRA (Taller de Iniciativa en Estudios Rurales y Reforma Agraria), 245

UAIM (Unidad Agrícola Industrial de Mujeres), 71, 123, 131, 152, 155, 359
UNAG (Unión Nacional de Agricultores y Ganaderos), 96, 133, 203–8, 359, 361
Unión Nacional Campesina, 129
Unión Nacional de Organizaciones Regionales Campesinas Autónomas, 131
United Nations conferences and women's land rights, 114–20

United Nations conferences on women, 4, 107, 113; Beijing (1995), 113–14, 118–20, 124–25, 217, 236, 261, 290; Nairobi (1985), 23, 110–111, 116, 121; Copenhagen (1980), 2, 107–8, 110, 115; Mexico City (1974), 107, 109, 112, 114, 121

United Nations Convention on the Elimination of All Forms of Discrimination Against Women, 1, 6, 49, 109, 114, 119–122, 168, 198, 208, 221, 234–36, 245, 331

United Nations Decade for Women, 4, 107

United Nations Working Group on Indigenous Populations, 233–34

universal human rights, 230–32, 259–60; feminist critique of, 231–32

urban housing movement, 9

URNG (Unión Revolucionaria Nacional Guatemalteca), 167, 216–17, 223

USAID (United States Agency for International Development), 108, 165, 166, 295, 322

WAD (Women and Development), 109–10

water rights: privatization of, 141; resistance to privatization, 158

well-being, women's: argument for women's land rights, 11–17

WID (Women in Development), 107–8

widows: and agrarian reform, 61, 69, 70, 98; and argument for land rights, 30; farm management by, 72, 289; and kin support, 30; and land, deprived of, 70, 88, 257; and land inheritance, 60–61, 281–83, 289, 343–44; and land titles, 301–2; and maintenance rights, 257; and property rights of, 281–84, 343–44; remarriage of, 256; vulnerability of, 15

women: abandonment of, 87, 200; contributions to family welfare by, 28–30; and control over land, 16–17, 289–90; difficulties faced by, 72; farm management by, 29–30, 302, 310, 327; leadership, in rural organizations, 77, 79, 251; and sharecropping by, 72, 302

women's access to: agricultural extension services, 72, 327–28; agricultural technology, 116, 118, 327–28; credit, 118, 322–23, 327–29; economic resources, 22, 114–20; information on laws, 28, 202, 254, 296, 306, 311, 342; irrigation, 327. See also land ownership

women's groups/organizations, 127–36; and access to land collectively, 342. See also women's movement, rural

women's movement, 3–6, 24, 121, 127–28, 135, 228, 234; and Beijing conference, 133–36; first wave of, 41, 44–47; international, 45–47, 107; and relation to feminist movement, 204, 224; and relation to the state, 4, 123–24, 204, 224, 336, 338; rural, 127–26, 184–85, 188–92, 202–4, 209–10, 226–27, 350; —, and demands for land rights, 72, 202–3, 209–10, 215, 219–22, 224, 226, 251–52, 257–58, 262–63, 290–91, 305; —, and women's land rights, 70–71, 184–86, 211–12, 215, 224–27, 350; and suffrage in Latin America, 46–47, 120

women's participation in decision making: on farm, 7, 29; in community, 72–73, 253–54, 262, 340–41

World Bank, 110, 166, 173, 180, 195–96, 205, 292, 309

World Conference on Population and Development, 113, 117–18